The Secret History of G ✔ KU-504-966

Dan Cruickshank is an architectural historian and television presenter. He is an Honorary Fellow of the Royal Institute of British Architects, a member of the Executive Committee of the Georgian Group, and on the Architectural Panel of the National Trust. His recent work includes the television programmes and accompanying books *Around the World in 80 Treasures* and *Dan Cruickshank's Adventures in Architecture*. He lives in Spitalfields, London.

Praise for The Secret History of Georgian London

'Funny, fantastical, full of impossible facts and scandalous stories. Scholarly, but also the ideal stocking (and suspender) filler'
Jeanette Winterson, Guardian

'Cruickshank removes the bland façade to expose one of London's biggest and lost lively industries – its trade in sex . . . The buildings are no longer there, but the records are, and Cruickshank excavates them to create a lively and scholarly panorama of Georgian London before the sex trade was chased underground by the Victorians and we all became prudish instead'
Daily Mail

'Fascinating . . . This is a colossal melting pot of a book: ambitious, rigorously researched, vigorously narrated and marvellously illustrated. All of life is here, but not as we know it'
Sunday Times

'Witty, elegantly written and memorable'
Architectural Review

'An original and engaging history of the capital . . . Cruickshank pieces together [the] evidence with meticulous care to create a compelling portrait'
Sunday Telegraph

'Monumental . . . This is a book of serious history, but Cruickshank is also a wonderful storyteller . . . a fascinating and deeply researched book, an invaluable guide to the rumbustious sex life of the Georgians and an investigation into the often curious desires enabled by the city's elegant façades. It is hard to imagine that it can be bettered'
Kate Williams, History Today

'Dan Cruickshank enters this world with relish. His huge book looks at the working practices of London prostitutes and bawds in great detail, offering many individual cases . . . the book's capaciousness and breadth is tremendous, providing much to fascinate, provoke and inform'

Country Life

'Engagingly and comprehensively assembled. Dan Cruickshank is a humane guide . . . His relish for the subject is clear but so too is his understanding of the harsh price often exacted'   *Literary Review*

'Dan Cruickshank's riveting tome is half highly referenced academic text, half bodice ripper, painting a pruriently evocative picture of the sexual mores and dichotomies of 18th century London society . . . Cruickshank charts a skilful course between macro and microcosm. His argument that the London of today was founded on the profligate scale of the sex industry is interleaved with touching and funny accounts, drawing on contemporary memoirs and records, that give a real sense of the people at the heart of the industry . . . These indelible details give the book a picaresque humanity, raising it from mere historical study, to arresting psychogeographical work'   *RIBA Journal*

'Richly informative . . . This is a monumental work which leaves no stone unturned in its quest to create a full and brutally honest picture of the lives of Georgian London's dispossessed . . . The result is a broad panorama and a compelling thesis which can be considered a commendable contribution to scholarship, as well as a gripping read'   *BBC History Magazine*

'[U]npacks a cornucopia of prostitutes, pimps and bawds . . . The stories are all well told, the material evidence and documents carefully deployed'

Independent

'The statistics Cruickshank assembles are fascinating . . . [he] offers well-researched evidence that the profits of the sex trade made possible the building of the elegant Georgian London we all admire and cherish. He has provided a rich social and architectural history'   *New Humanist*

'Despite the titillating title, this lively book is both well argued and sensible in its approach, as it chronicles how much of London life, from builders to artists and their models, fed off the capital's insatiable desire for sex'

The year's best history books round up, *Sunday Times*

The Secret History of Georgian London

How the Wages of Sin Shaped the Capital

DAN CRUICKSHANK

WINDMILL BOOKS

Published by Windmill Books 2010

8 10 9 7

Copyright © Dan Cruickshank 2009

Dan Cruickshank has asserted his right under the Copyright, Designs
and Patents Act, 1988, to be identified as the author of this work

First published in Great Britain in 2009 by
Random House Books
Random House, 20 Vauxhall Bridge Road,
London SW1V 2SA

www.randomhouse.co.uk

Addresses for companies within The Random House Group Limited can be found at:
www.randomhouse.co.uk/offices.htm

The Random House Group Limited Reg. No. 954009

A CIP catalogue record for this book
is available from the British Library

ISBN 9780099527961

The Random House Group Limited supports the Forest Stewardship
Council® (FSC®), the leading international forest-certification organisation.
Our books carrying the FSC label are printed on FSC®-certified paper.
FSC is the only forest-certification scheme supported by the leading
environmental organisations, including Greenpeace.
Our paper procurement policy can be found at:
www.randomhouse.co.uk/environment

Typeset by Palimpsest Book Production Limited
Falkirk, Stirlingshire
Printed and bound in Great Britain by
Clays Ltd, St Ives Plc

CONTENTS

ACT THREE
THE TASTE OF SIN

ACT FOUR
PUBLIC AND PRIVATE VIEWS

I started researching the relationship between the buildings of Georgian London and the city's sex industry in 1999 while working on a television programme that was finally broadcast on BBC2 as *Sex in the Georgian City*.

I had been fascinated by the architecture of Georgian London for many years before that – my first book on the subject, *London: the Art of Georgian Building*, was published in 1975. But back in 1999 the Georgian sex industry was a new area of research and I found myself drawn into a strange and exotic world with, to my amazement, a vast and varied number of connections not only to London's architecture and economy but also to the arts, sciences, commerce and, of course, the spheres of law, medicine, philanthropy, theology and social reform. The Georgian sex industry, mushrooming in size the more I studied it, seemed to entwine and make sense of so many apparently disparate aspects of the life and culture of Georgian London.

The sources from which I have extracted information while writing this book have been many and diverse. Mostly, I have used contemporary written accounts of every sort – but also paintings, prints, stage productions, and a whole range of tangible artefacts ranging from plaster panels and drinking glasses to archaeological finds, individual buildings and whole quarters of London. Although the fields of painting and the stage are dealt with in discrete sections of the book, literature is not. The reason for this is simple. Familiar and key works – such as *Moll Flanders*, *Fanny Hill*, *Pamela*, *The Adventures of Roderick Random* and *The Monk* – are used throughout as primary sources rather than being analysed in isolation.

In addition to the huge amount of well-documented period source material that existed when I began my research, the intervening years have produced an enormous number of new and important publications to scrutinise. Since I started my enquiries into Georgian London's sex industry, the subject has become a highly popular topic for scholarly study and many others have now ploughed what, back in 1999, was still largely a virgin field. I have in about equal measure benefited from and been horribly daunted by the array of very high-quality publications that have appeared since the late 1990s – mostly produced by very well-informed and perceptive American academics. Seminal works include Randolph Trumbach's *Sex and the Gender Revolution* and Arthur H. Cash's reconstruction and analysis of John Wilkes' contribution to *An Essay on Woman*. Both these books have been extraordinarily useful to me. I also want to give particular thanks to Hallie Rubenhold, whose book on Jack Harris and his *Covent Garden Ladies* has been invaluable, as has her advice and very generous help in suggesting other sources of information and topics for research, particularly London's bagnios.

Other authors whose books have proved especially useful include Jenny Uglow and Ronald Paulson (both for works on Hogarth, and Paulson in particular for insights into Henry Fielding), E. J. Bristow, E. J. Burford, Ivan Bloch, Robert A. Erickson, A. D. Harvey, Tony Henderson, Tim Hitchcock, Gerald Howson, Peter Linebaugh, Rictor Norton and Lydia Syson. My thanks to them all, and also to Martin Postle for his advice on Sir Joshua Reynolds and to Tim Carew for sharing his discoveries about a recently excavated bagnio on the Piazza in Covent Garden. Of invaluable assistance have been the many volumes of the *Survey of London*, the Proceedings of the Old Bailey, compiled by Clive Emsley, Tim Hitchcock and Robert Shoemaker and accessible online (www.oldbaileyonline.org), and the editorial team, headed by Alexander Pettit and Patrick Spedding, who compiled, edited and wrote the five volumes of *Eighteenth-century British Erotica*.

I also want to give my thanks to the editorial team at Random House, in particular Nigel Wilcockson, who responded to a huge and daunting text in a most cool and creative manner, to Emily Rhodes for all her able assistance – especially with picture research – and to Lynn Curtis for her speedy and nothing short of miraculous transformation of my text into a publishable proposition.

Lastly I would like to thank the BBC team that started this adventure with me back in 1999: Basil Comely, Sam Hobkinson, Sally Benton and Nicholas Barratt.

Dan Cruickshank, Spitalfields, August 2009

INTRODUCTION

Georgian London was the product of a potent mix of economic and social forces. The harmonious Georgian quarters of London such as Bloomsbury and Marylebone are, like the coherent classical city of Bath, corporate works of art and models of refined urban living, famed for their beauty and civilised virtues. But beauty was not the primary aim when these areas were constructed, nor was the creation of urban perfection.

Britain's inspirational and exemplary Georgian cities, towns and urban enclaves were largely and invariably created by ruthless speculating builders and ambitious landlords striving to make their fortunes or, at the very least, to escape the debtors' prison if the volatile economy of the age, as vulnerable as ours to unpredictable forces, should suddenly turn sour. Architectural beauty was only pursued in so far as it served to make the speculatively built houses easier to let or lease for the maximum amount of rent. Georgian cities were created by private financial adventurers with money to invest in the hope of making more money. By good fortune, indeed almost paradoxically, the pursuit of profit and short-term interest resulted in the creation of internationally admired works of timeless architectural beauty.

Since, therefore, the creation of Georgian cities was rarely the work of enlightened or altruistic artistic patrons or high-minded public benefactors but, rather, of private entrepreneurs embroiled in money-making exercises, it is fascinating to consider where the money for their schemes came from and who the investors actually were. The answer is complex in its fine detail but, broadly speaking, in times of economic confidence and flourishing trade following peace treaties – for example, after the Treaty of Utrecht of 1713 that terminated the War of the Spanish Succession, and the Peace of Paris in 1763 that put an end to the Seven Years' War – virtually anyone with money to spare chose to invest in speculative house building. When the economy was buoyant and stable and demand for houses high, the returns for speculators seemed generous and certain. Those already making money in London's most lucrative trades – for example, brewing, the river trades and port, the silk industry during the first half of the eighteenth century, and the construction industry itself – ploughed their profits into house building. And among these prime money-making ventures was the capital's sex industry, which was one of the most valuable commercial activities in eighteenth- and early-nineteenth-century London in terms of annual turnover.

This was not, of course, an industry that created wealth. It did not, as did the highly skilled silk industry for example, transform a humble raw material into a beautiful and financially valuable fabric. It was the service industry *par excellence* that distributed money into different strata of society and generated an estimated gross turnover of around £20 million per annum. In the late eighteenth century it vied in importance with brewing, construction, and the London docks, which in 1792 handled imports and exports worth around £27 million. Consequently, profits from the sex industry financed the development of whole sections of the city, so that – quite literally – much of Georgian London was built on the wages of sin.

It is extremely difficult to put the estimated annual turnover of London's sex industry into economic context because the financial records of London's prime eighteenth-century industries are now preserved only in a most fragmentary manner. But some idea of the financial magnitude of the industry, and the potential earning power of its workers, is revealed by the fact that a middling prostitute could, from the middle to late eighteenth century, expect to receive 2 guineas per assignation and so perhaps earn something over 400 guineas a year. In contrast, a labourer earned around £24 a year during the same period, and a journeyman tradesman – the city's ordinary semi-skilled working man – earned little more than £50 a year, while a highly skilled master craftsman, such as a cabinetmaker, could not hope to earn much more than £200. And a general housemaid – the trade from which many prostitutes emancipated themselves – earned only £5 a year during the first half of the eighteenth century, making it easy to understand why so many young women resorted to the sex industry.[1] 'In addition, a large and well-appointed 'Common' house cost in the mid-eighteenth century – according to Isaac Ware in his *Complete Body of Architecture* – around £600 to build, suggesting that speculative building was an activity in which most reasonably affluent members of the sex industry could afford to indulge.

The estimated annual value of London's sex industry can further be put into context if late-eighteenth-century tax revenues are considered. Until 1798, central government raised money from the population by taxing or charging duties on certain commodities or certain artefacts – for example, spirits, tea, hair-powder, watches and wall-paper – or by taxing property through the land and window taxes. But from 1798 there was an attempt to tax wealth more directly, and the idea of an income tax was launched: a graduated rate starting at two pence in the pound on incomes of between £60 and £200, and two shillings in the pound (or 10%) on annual incomes over £200. In the first year of this tax – 1799 – the government estimated revenue of £10 million but made less than £6 million.[2] So the entire national annual revenue from income tax was, arguably, less than half the estimated annual value of London's sex industry. The question, of course, is where the money came from, since it implies that by the end of the eighteenth century each of the sexually active male population of London and its environs was contributing, on average, £80 per annum to the sex industry. Given the generally low level of wages, this seems incredible, and either suggests that the £20 million per annum value of the sex industry is an overestimate or, more likely, reveals just how much the wealthier section of society was willing to pay for its pleasure.

But the sex trade did more than help fund the construction of the city. It created a rich new sub-division of society, made up of wealthy brothel-keepers, prosperous pimps and high-paid courtesans, who could afford to occupy fine houses, especially in fashionable, newly built areas such as Marylebone. Consistently from the mid-eighteenth century onward, social commentators calculated that one London woman in five was involved in some manner with the sex industry, with a former rake calculating in 1758 that there were as many as 62,500 prostitutes of various types in London and its environs. And even when this army of bawds, prostitutes or their 'bullies' did not lease entire houses, many were able to pay exceptionally high rents to landlords for part-occupation. In this way the profits from the sex industry were fed directly into, and bolstered, the wider economy of the city.

The sex industry played a significant role in the social life of Georgian London too. It was a sophisticated and well-organised enterprise that crossed class boundaries, overlapped with most aspects of daily life, and enjoyed a highly ambiguous relationship with the law. It also had a profound influence not only on the appearance of the city but on the fine arts generally. Indeed, much of London life was organised around the activities of the sex industry; thanks to the flesh trade, distinct and now long-forgotten purpose-designed building types such as hummums or bagnios appeared, and courtesans played the role of muse and model for painters such as William Hogarth and Sir Joshua Reynolds. London's sex industry – a world of riches, high glamour and artistic invention, yet equally of tragedy, brutal abuse and disease – offered a mirror to society and was perceived to carry a moral message for the age. It intrigued and inspired writers like Daniel Defoe, John Gay, Jonathan Swift, Henry Fielding and William Blake, many of whom saw London's underworld, which was deeply entwined with the illicit aspects of the sex industry, as a metaphor for, and reflection of, the equally corrupt and immoral worlds of politics and exploitative business. The only real difference was in the levels of accountability exerted in these parallel worlds. As John Gay observed in 1728, using one of the characters in his highly emblematic work *The Beggar's Opera* as a mouthpiece: 'the lower sort of people have their vices in a degree as well as the rich', but only the poor 'are punished for them'. Gay's opera was a very direct criticism of the materialistic and supposedly highly corrupt government of Sir Robert Walpole, which the principal opposition paper *The Craftsman* termed in 1729 the 'Robinocracy' that 'rules by Money, the root of all evils, and founds [its] iniquitous dominion in the corruption of the people'.[3] It is hardly surprising perhaps that money-making vice should flourish in an age when many believed that corruption and greed emanated from the top.

But the sex industry was not only a metaphor for the political corruption of the day, it was also one of the activities that oiled the machinery of often dubiously wielded political power. For instance, the members of Sir Francis Dashwood's Monks of the Order of St Francis of Medmenham – the most notorious of the eighteenth-century Hell Fire clubs – were rakes and sexual fantasists, but also mostly politicians and men of wealth, power and immense influence. Indeed Dashwood himself was, from 1762 to 1763, Chancellor of the Exchequer – perhaps one of the most unlikely the nation has ever known. Benjamin Franklin visited Dashwood during his visit to England in the early 1770s. He may have witnessed the antics of the club but clearly believed that Dashwood's country retreat at West Wycombe would be a good place to meet the luminaries of Britain's government in informal and relaxed circumstances. Franklin was right, for it was in this Hell Fire club – and others like it that were dedicated to sexual dalliance and drinking, and graced by cavorting harlots often dressed as masked nuns – that political decisions and alliances were made. It was a one-time member of Dashwood's club – the radical politician and journalist John Wilkes – who was eventually imprisoned in 1768 for libelling the King in his organ the *North Briton*, as well as the Bishop of Gloucester in a pornographic and blasphemous poem entitled *An Essay on Woman*. Here, indeed, was a heady and volatile mix of politics, art and sex, and the consequences of this bizarre brew were to help change the political complexion of Britain forever (see Postlude).

It is not until the revolutionary and radical attitudes of the age to sex are appreciated – inspired as they were after the 1750s by new discoveries about ancient and primitive societies – that the symbolism, meaning and message of much eighteenth-century art – painting, architecture and garden design – can be fully understood. The sex industry was deeply paradoxical; it undermined conventional notions of morality and health, and in many respects was anti-social, brutalising, abusive and illegal – but it was also a great and productive social catalyst. It created wealth and employment, funded the construction, maintenance and occupation of swathes of the capital's finest buildings, and was a crucial source of inspiration to a diverse body of artists.

The influence exerted by the Georgian sex industry also raises profound questions about the nature of the age and, most obviously, suggests the moral and spiritual uncertainty at its heart. Church-going decreased during the eighteenth century in comparison with peaks in attendance during the seventeenth and nineteenth centuries, and people in general were more inclined to live for the thrill of the moment with the fear of divine retribution for immoral actions becoming ever less persuasive. The reasons for this are complex but include the fact that organised religion was increasingly seen as hypocritical and irrelevant, and had been challenged by the liberating ideas of the Enlightenment which put greater emphasis on individual freedom of conscience. In addition, new scientific and anti-quarian discoveries offered a baffling array of beguiling intellectual novelties and accelerated the questioning of many traditional moral and theological certainties.

But this radical thinking had little, if any, influence on the most entrenched attitudes of the age, notably the social and legal inequality endured by women. Many were driven into the sex industry from sheer lack of opportunity in other walks of life or so as to gain economic independence in a male-dominated society, but if they fell foul of the law this endemic inequality meant that a blind eye was generally turned upon the prostitute's client while she could, in certain circumstances, be punished. As Jeremy Collier, theatre critic and theologian, observed in 1705, '[I]s not this a sign [that] Sex is crept into the Administration and that we live under a Masculine government?'⁴ As the detailed researches of Randolph Trumbach have revealed, in Westminster and Middlesex in 1720, 427 women were arrested for sexually related crimes while, during the entire decade after 1720, only 402 men were arrested.⁵ During the eighteenth century, life became ever-more materialistic, in a sense more superficial, and to a startling degree this was reflected in Georgian urban architecture where houses were built to look beautiful so that they would be let more easily and profitably, but were not necessarily soundly constructed and certainly not built to last, with their life expectancy being no more than the length of the average building lease of 60–99 years. In London's architecture, as with its sex trade, there was little of the spiritual or altruistic. Both were concerned with outward appearances, and primarily with profit.

In telling the story of the sex industry – a powerful but generally forgotten force behind the creation of Georgian London – this book gives voice to the long-forgotten ghosts of the city; it sees life in the metropolis through the eyes of those on the margins of society, from the perspective of the humble people who fall through the annals, almost unrecorded and unremembered. This history echoes the words and actions of the dispossessed, the 'picaresque proletarians', the outsiders and placeless poor who made up a large part of the population of Georgian London, who in many senses gave the city its distinct character, and who, through force of circumstances or perhaps from choice, formed the majority of the people involved in the capital's sex industry.

So, in many ways, the history of London's sex industry is the history of Georgian London's poor and outcast communities. It is also, to a degree, a history of crime in the capital because the sex industry was the common link between all aspects of London life: the familiar path to perdition in this world and the next; the portal between high living and fashion, and low life and crime. And this story reveals that Georgian London, although vigorous and visually beautiful, was also a very savage place at times, far removed from the imagined world of grace and elegance. It was a city where, from time to time, homosexuals were hunted down and hanged, infamous women were stoned to death while pinioned in the pillory, prematurely brutalised child prostitutes thronged the main thoroughfares, and where the mob could indulge in uncontrollable acts of violence and mutilation of the sort described by one mother who, as she cradled the terribly beaten body of her son which retained 'neither Eyes, nor Ears, nor Nose to be seen', felt 'his Brains [fall] into my Hand'.

It is the dramatic and paradoxical mix of different worlds, the counterpoints of beauty and of brutality, that characterise its life – and not least the exploitative yet inspirational role played by the sex industry – that make Georgian London a forever fascinating and incomparable city.

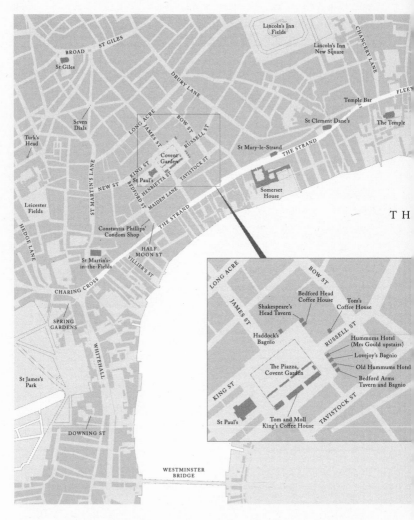

'The sexual highway': the heart of mid-eighteenth-century London, based on
John Rocque's map of 1746. Key locations of the city's sex industry are shown,
notably the bagnios, taverns and coffee houses in and around the Covent
Garden Piazza, and the great sexual highway running from the Royal
Exchange in the east, via the north side of St Paul's Cathedral, to Charing
Cross and St James's in the west. Along this highway, which was also the

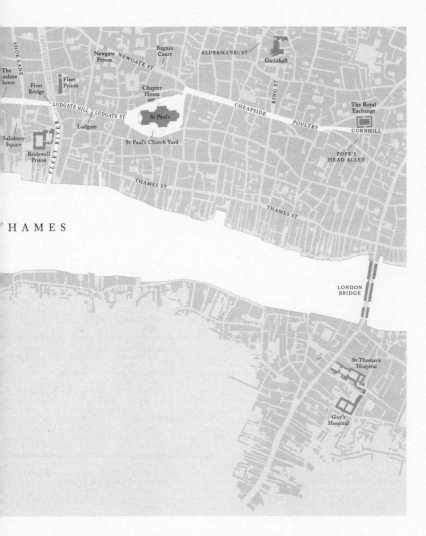

great thoroughfare of trade and commerce, harlots would patrol, pick up clients and have sex in the alleys and courts off Fleet Street, the Strand and in St James's Park. London's other great east–west highway – the promenade of death – led from Newgate Prison, via Holborn, St Giles and Oxford Street, to the scaffold at Tyburn.

AN ARTIST'S VIEW

William Hogarth and The Harlot's Progress

The most famous work of visual art to be provoked by London's early-eighteenth-century sex industry is William Hogarth's *The Harlot's Progress*. The images and the story they convey are well known from the sets of engravings that were soon produced and widely circulated after Hogarth completed the series of six paintings in late 1731. He told the tale of innocence corrupted and its doleful consequences with immense visual punch, and the series was an instant popular success because the moral message it carried struck a chord with the public: it confirmed popular notions about the sex industry, its victims, villains and methods of operation.

This success was due largely to the fact that Hogarth gave the work a sense of immediacy, relevance and authenticity by drawing heavily on contemporary incident and scandal, and by referring to well-known characters and stories that the public would have recognised instantly. So the series, immensely rich in detail and anecdote – mixing up-to-the-minute facts with timeless myth – offers a fascinating insight into London's sex industry of the era and forms an essential introduction to any study of the subject.

William Hogarth's series of six paintings depicting *The Harlot's Progress* were not all executed in 1731, for painting number three, showing a harlot in her humble dwelling in Drury Lane, was produced first, in 1730 – the development of a sketch showing a smiling harlot in a sordid garret preparing for her day's work – and provided him with inspiration and incentive for the series. As George Vertue explained, Hogarth . . .

> . . . began a small picture of a common harlot, supposed to dwell in
> drewry lane, just rising about noon out of bed, and at breakfast, a bunter

waiting on her. – this whore's deshabillé careless and a pretty
Countenance & air. – this thought pleased many, some advised him to
make another . . . which he did. Then other thoughts encreas'd, &
multiplied by his fruitful invention, til he made six.[1]

The original paintings are long since lost, destroyed in a house fire in
1755, but Hogarth issued sets of engravings in 1732, with pirated editions
appearing soon after, and it was due to the ready availability of prints
that the series had such a widespread impact and became Hogarth's first
great success with what he came to call his 'modern moral subjects'.[2] As
his biographer Jenny Uglow observes, 'Hogarth, so often an illustrator of
the news, had now, at thirty-four, become news himself.'[3]

The theme of the series, a harlot's progress through the stages of her
life, was not invented by Hogarth – it was ancient, emblematic and
universal. It's a morality tale in which the harlot symbolises the duality
of life, of human nature – she is deeply desirable yet also an image of
degeneration and disgust; she is a victim in the power of others yet can
also exercise – or threaten with – power; she can be evil incarnate or a
beautiful soul entombed within a once equally beautiful but gradually
diseased and decaying body. As Jenny Uglow observes, '[S]he was always
ambivalent, a creature of evil ambition or heart of gold.'[4] The harlot is a
timeless and fascinating subject and Hogarth's great triumph, when
depicting this myth, was skilfully to reinvigorate and reinforce the tale by
reference to the life stories of well-known contemporary characters. But
the greatest monster in his interpretation of this cautionary tale is not
any single character but, in a sense, the city that is their stage – London
– a vast, anonymous, hostile, soulless, wicked, all-devouring but also fatally
attractive place that makes and breaks, that tempts, inflames, satisfies, yet
corrupts and ultimately kills.

An innocent country girl – Moll Hackabout – is drawn to the city to
make her fortune. She is duped into the sex trade by a bawd who procures
her for the enjoyment of a notorious and amoral libertine. After her fall
Moll accepts her fate, begins to enjoy her sudden wealth and fashionable
status, and so, hardened and made cynical, she loses not only her virtue
but also, gradually, her heart, her soul and her health. Moll descends
through the stages of hell – becomes depraved, criminalised, poor, diseased
– and dies lonely and unloved, a victim, a sacrifice, to the wickedness of

the urban age. Contemporary convention suggested this was the penalty a harlot was expected to pay for having lived an immoral life even when – as Hogarth acknowledged – it was really through no fault of her own.

Some of Hogarth's stern and moralising contemporaries argued that prostitutes who suffered like Moll got no more than the fate they deserved; others – like Jonathan Swift – thought it droll to mock them. His spitefully ironic verse upon 'A Beautiful Young Nymph Going to Bed', written in 1734, robs a harlot of any dignity and makes her ghastly afflictions appear merely ridiculous:

> Corinna, pride of Drury Lane . . .
> Returning at the Midnight Hour;
> Four Stories climbing to her Bow'r;
> Then, seated on a three-legg'd Chair,
> Takes off her artificial Hair:
> Now, picking out a Crystal Eye,
> She wipes it clean, and lays it by.
> Her Eye-Brows from a Mouse's Hyde,
> Stuck on with Art on either Side,
> Pulls off with Care, and first displays 'em,
> Then in a Play-Book smoothly lays 'em.

Prominent by its absence from most contemporary observation is well-argued criticism of the villains responsible for the downfall of women like Moll and Corinna – the men to whose unprincipled lusts they fell victim and to whose wealth and power they were subject. An exception is Richard Steele. In 1712 he wrote a few short pieces in the *Spectator* that, although somewhat sentimental, offered a defence of prostitutes and an indictment of the selfish and lustful men who were the cause of their initial ruin (see page 37).[5]

Hogarth, in this series, offers only implicit criticism of sexually predatory males but he does display great sympathy towards the plight of prostitutes and makes a point of revealing Moll's redeeming characteristics. She was, he suggests, not only innocent at first but possessed an intensely romantic nature that made her particularly vulnerable. This point is made in the third image that shows Moll in her pauper's bedroom with her pin-ups. They show heroic characters – both fictional and real – who chose to challenge society and, in very different ways, stood for liberty.

It seems that Hogarth wants us – the viewer – to identity Moll with these anti-establishment victims rather than with degraded common harlots. There is 'Captain Macheath' – the devil-may-care highwayman hero of John Gay's *The Beggar's Opera* – and Dr Henry Sacheverell who in 1709 had delivered a series of sermons attacking the Whig Government, notably for its toleration of religious dissenters. For his audacity Sacheverell was charged with, and convicted of, seditious libel. His stance may seem at first glance an anti-libertarian one but in the 1730s, when England was in the grip of what many saw as Whig corruption and abuse of power, this ultra-Tory preacher, who had died in 1724, became something of a hero, especially among Jacobites who wanted rid of the Whig-supported Hanoverian kings and the return of the Stuarts. This series of paintings – like much of Hogarth's work – was not just a social or moral parable but also a powerful and direct commentary on contemporary politics.

The identities of several of the characters Hogarth incorporated into the six paintings – and which were indeed the medium of the moral message of the series – have long been disputed but, over the years, a consensus has emerged. One exception is the main character – Moll Hackabout – whose inspiration remains tantalisingly obscure. What seems clear is that she is a complex composite creation – inspired by both real and fictional characters – with clues to her true identity, or identities, hinted at by her name and her 'history' as depicted in the series. Moll was a common nickname for harlots or lawless women during the seventeenth and eighteenth centuries, in fiction and in fact – for example, Moll Cutpurse, Moll King, and, of course, Daniel Defoe's Moll Flanders, who is clearly one of Hogarth's inspirations from fiction. Another proto-type from fiction – at least for the young Moll Hackabout in her blooming innocence in picture one – must have been Polly Peachum from Gay's *Beggar's Opera*, which had enjoyed immense popularity only a few years before Hogarth started the series (see page 331).[6]

His use of the name Moll suggests that, from painting one, he wanted to make it clear that the innocent country girl arriving at the City inn was pre-destined to be a harlot. The surname Hackabout is more particu-lar and may in part have originated with a London whore called Kate Hackabout. She was the sister of a highwayman named Francis Hackabout who came to the public's attention when he was tried at the Old Bailey on 28 February 1730 for assaulting and robbing Aaron Durel and George

Bailey the month before. Hackabout, identified and taken while playing cards at the Anchor and Vine in Featherstone Street, Bunhill-fields, was only twenty-eight at the time, an ex-sailor and soldier and member of a notorious gang of thieves.[7] He was found guilty, sentenced to death and hanged on 17 April 1730.[8]

Kate was also arrested and tried in 1730. Her crime was less dramatic: she was found guilty of keeping a disorderly house by the Westminster magistrate Sir John Gonson, who appears in painting three of the series and was a leading figure in the Society for the Reformation of Manners, founded in East London in 1691 (see page 472). Kate was sentenced to hard labour and is then lost to history. It seems her fate and family circumstances made an impact on Hogarth, although it is also possible that he simply took a fancy to such an expressive name – hack being a popular euphemism for harlot since hackney carriages were available for hire to all.

Other contemporary figures also undoubtedly had an influence on the shaping of *The Harlot's Progress*. One was Colonel Francis Charteris, who appears in painting one. He was a notorious libertine, found guilty of rape in 1730 following a sensational trial (see page 311), sentenced to death but then reprieved owing to his connections and ability to offer large bribes to powerful men. Another possible influence was Ann Bond, the servant girl whom Charteris had raped and whose ordeal at the hands of her brutal and selfish master drew the public's attention to the vulnerability of humble country girls trying to make a living in London. Her case was also a reminder of the manner in which many young women – seduced, rejected and friendless – entered the sex industry. Both these themes were, of course, touched on by Hogarth in *The Harlot's Progress*. And then there was Sally Salisbury – the most famous London courtesan of the early decades of the eighteenth century – who achieved fame and fashion, if not exactly fortune, before being overtaken by disaster and dying in gaol in 1723/4 (see page 100). Sally was a phenomenon, famed for her high spirits and ready if earthy wit as well as her good looks, and her short and blazing life was certainly a morality tale in itself. She had been dead nearly ten years when Hogarth started work on the series, but it's hard not to believe that she played a part in influencing the work's narrative.[9]

Each of the six paintings in the series shows not only a different episode in the life, and fall, of Moll Hackabout but also distinctly different and characteristic parts of London. So the series sketches a brief outline of the areas of the capital where the sex industry operated, and – perhaps more to the point – implicates London itself in the fate that overtakes Moll, revealing it to be a city where sex and immorality are rife and ultimately destroy an innocent country girl. The moral punch, and message, of the series is massive.

Ronald Paulson has pointed out that the compositions of five of the six paintings appear to be inspired by Albrecht Dürer's early-sixteenth-century woodcuts illustrating the life of the Virgin Mary and of Christ, and so parallel the suffering and death of the innocent girl with that of the Saviour and His Mother. For example, the scene in painting one showing Mother Needham procuring Moll while Colonel Charteris looks on, bears very close affinities in its composition with Dürer's *The Visitation*, from his *Life of the Virgin* series, while painting three showing the scene in Drury Lane seems inspired by Dürer's *Annunciation*. In the Bridewell scene in painting four Moll's stance echoes Dürer's *Flagellation* of Christ, and the composition of the last painting – showing Moll in her coffin – looks broadly similar to Dürer's *Last Supper*.[10]

All this suggests most strongly that Moll Hackabout was not intended by Hogarth to represent a licentious harlot who merely gets her just desserts but that, on the contrary, she is an image of purity beset and destroyed by evil that is aided and abetted by a careless clergy, a venal aristocracy, quack doctors, ineffective laws and a brutal penal system. And all of this takes place within London – the Sodom of the modern age.

MOLL ARRIVES IN LONDON

The first image in the series shows Moll arriving from the country at the Bell Inn near Cheapside – the great commercial street in the heart of the City and the eastern end of a well-known sexual thoroughfare running west to St James's. So here, most appropriately, Moll starts her journey into London's sex industry – a journey that does indeed finally carry her west into the deeply sordid, sexual terrain of Drury Lane. The very name of the inn – a pun on belle or beautiful young girl – is mildly diverting but also sinister. This is a world where nothing is what it seems. The inn, reassuring in its everyday bustle, is nothing less than a gateway to perdition, a place that, through the black arts of seduction and lies, transforms belles into harlots.

PLATE 1 *of* The Harlot's Progress *by William Hogarth (1732).*
The innocent Moll Hackabout is procured by the bawd, supposedly Mother Needham, while the libertine Colonel Charteris looks on from the open door. A clergyman rides by, not noticing this scene of innocence being corrupted.

Moll, alone and vulnerable in the great bustling and heartless city, is easy prey for those with wicked intentions. Trusting and innocent, she is beguiled by an aged woman who looks respectable but is in fact a bawd. The woman smiles, not out of kindness but out of satisfaction, for she knows that this young girl is as good as hooked, ready to be served up to the middle-aged gentleman for whom she is procuring and who stands in a doorway nearby, casting an approving eye over Moll, perhaps even touching himself in his excitement. While the bawd extols Moll's beauty and seduces her into London's sex industry a clergyman, distracted by some scribbles on a piece of paper (a sermon . . . an amorous note?), turns his back on Moll and rides away. So much for the care of the Church!

The whole image is full of strange and curious clues to its underlying meaning and that of the entire series. A pile of pots teeters, foretelling the inevitable fall of Moll who at her breast wears a rose: ancient symbol of the Virgin Mary, the 'rose without a thorn' and epitome of purity. There is a goose bearing a label addressed to 'my lofing cosen in Tems stret in London' that sits in a basket besides Moll's initialled trunk – on which the letter M could well signify that her name was originally Mary. Thames Street, in which Billingsgate Market stood, was a great thoroughfare of trade running parallel to the river. It contained the houses and warehouses of honest and industrious merchants and 'citizens' of the city. It seems Moll has relations there and is planning to make her way to them with a goodly gift, perhaps intending to settle there with them in safety. But she is hijacked and her life changed.

There is much to ponder over in the painting but the identity of the three main supporting characters is generally agreed. The watching man is Colonel Charteris, the infamous libertine sentenced to death in 1730 for raping a servant girl named Ann Bond. The man dancing around Charteris, looking to him for instructions, is said to be his pimp John Gourlay. The bawd is a portrait of Mother Needham, a famed procuress and keeper of harlots, who had procured Ann Bond for Charteris and who, while pinioned in the stocks in April 1731, was so violently stoned by the mob that she died three days after her ordeal.

Such violence reveals that bawds – the women who ran whores and bawdy-houses – were generally loathed (see page 42). Yet the public response to prostitution was ambivalent. Social reformers and upright justices might see it as a moral deviation that condemned a tolerant society to divine vengeance, but most people accepted prostitution as a way of life and, in certain quarters of London, were distinctly protective towards the profession. But, perhaps paradoxically, the public's tolerance of working prostitutes was not extended to prostitutes turned bawds. Prostitution seems not to have been perceived as unequivocally evil, but recruiting for it was – no doubt because in popular opinion (as apparently in Hogarth's) bawds often had recourse to lies and trickery to ensnare girls and then used threats and violence to retain them. They were perceived as a plague from which no young woman was safe, with entrapment being one of the daily hazards of life in Georgian London.

A testimony laid before the writer and magistrate Henry Fielding in 1752 revealed a common trick used to detain girls. A sixteen-year-old hatter's daughter was decoyed into a bawdy-house and persuaded to take up the calling, being issued with flimsy clothing for which she signed an IOU for £5. The bawd then threatened that if the girl left the establishment before repaying the £5, she would have her imprisoned for debt. Saunders Welch, the high constable of High Holborn, claimed hundreds of girls were trapped in this way.[11]

MOLL THE HARLOT

Scene two shows Moll some time after her arrival in London. She has, presumably, been seduced by Charteris, accommodated in Mother Needham's bawdy-house in Park Place, St James's, and is now the 'kept' mistress of a wealthy Jewish merchant. What's immediately clear is that Moll has been corrupted – and she's been enjoying the process. The sweet, intoxicating yet fatal atmosphere of the more affluent portion of London's sex industry pervades this painting. The cosmetics that lie around suggest the artificial nature of Moll's life: she is dressed in an ostentatious and affected manner; a mask on a table reveals that she has recently been to a masquerade – an event that was usually no more than a forum for arousingly anonymous sexual encounters – and she appears to be behaving in a particularly petulant manner. She's kicking over a table, perhaps through high spirits or because she's drunk, but more likely to distract her 'keeper' – in the background a lover is being shown out of the room by Moll's discreet maid.

The pair of portraits hanging on the wall sets the tone of the scene. The merchant's room features paintings of Woolston and Clarke, both of whom were freethinkers and Deists, regarded as enemies of Christianity – even as infidels – because they ridiculed the stories of Christ's miracles and resurrection.[12] The Jew's room also contains two large canvases depicting stories from the Old Testament. One, entitled 'Jonah, why art thou angry?', shows the prophet raging against God because he has not destroyed

PLATE 2 *of* The Harlot's Progress. *Moll is being kept by a Jewish merchant, but – through drink and high living – is seriously starting to misbehave. She kicks over a table to distract her 'keeper' while a lover is ushered out.*

Nineveh and the Gentiles as promised, while the other shows David dancing with his harp while Uzzah steadies the Ark and is stabbed in the back for this sacrilegious act by God's priest. These actions are being echoed in the scene unfolding beneath the canvases where the Jew is engaged in balancing the toppling table. As Jenny Uglow explains, the paintings on the wall 'undermine the Jew, presenting him as vengeful and tainted, but both also criticise the harshness of Old Testament justice and the cruelty of religious zeal. The Jew (like Moll) is an outsider and a victim of prejudice.'[13]

The fact that Moll's startled keeper is a 'wealthy Israelite' suggests that the location of the scene is a house in or near Bevis Marks, or Duke's Place, around Houndsditch and Aldgate, on the north-eastern edge of the City, where the richer Jewish merchants had congregated since being allowed by Oliver Cromwell to return openly to England in 1656. London's small Jewish community played a significant role in London's sex industry, or at least it evolved attitudes towards it that attracted the attention of writers and painters. In contrast to the boisterous and often brutal and ignorant British and Christian habitués of bagnios and bawdy-houses, the Jewish visitors were both respectable and respectful of the feelings of the women. A pamphlet published in 1736 entitled *A Trip Through the Town* contains one of the earliest known reference to Jewish libertines. It talks of 'young Jews of the tribe of Mordecai' visiting Covent Garden's bawdy-houses 'three or four times a week, particularly on Sundays ... with Upright Gait, Morose Speech and pretty, smooth Countenance'.[14] Sunday was popular with these young Sephardic Jews because the Sabbath ended at sundown on Saturday and they could make use of the Christian Day of Rest for their entertainment.

Indeed, perhaps because of this Jewish preference, Sunday became a most popular day for sexual adventuring in London. The German visitor F. W. Schütz observed in 1792 that 'prostitutes parade the streets on Sundays, the same as on other days' while 'the tea-gardens are fuller of this class of women than on week-days', and Voltaire when in England from 1726–9 noted in his *Letters on England* that on Sundays in London 'no operas, no comedies and no concerts are allowed. Card playing is strictly forbidden. On these days people go to church, to the inns and to the prostitutes.'[15] Voltaire was in a good position to observe the sexual habits of Londoners because from 1727–8 he lodged in Maiden Lane, Covent Garden, only a few doors away from Bob Derry's notorious 'Cyder Cellar', frequented by such famous ladies of the town as Lucy Cooper (see page 237).

Why did Hogarth choose a Jewish keeper for Moll? Presumably because he wanted maximum contrast between the two of them. Jews were known for their sedate manner and considerate ways and taste, so set in this context, and with such a civilised and kind keeper, Moll's intemperate and coarse behaviour would appear doubly shocking. The civilised behaviour of Jewish clients within the sex industry was vouched for by many observers. *The Female Rake*, published in 1736, suggested that Jews were popular in bawdy-houses because they displayed not only consideration but care – compassion even – for the girls:

> Leave to young Levites that Praiseworthy Care
> Of saving Souls by Vigil and by Prayer.

By the 1760s and 70s, a bawd named Charlotte Hayes went out of her way to attract to her fashionable 'nunnery' in St James's 'rich Levites . . . from Bevis Marks', and included among her clients one of the richest members of London's Jewish community: Gideon Abudiente, better known as Sampson Gideon, a banker and one of the founders of the Stock Exchange. Charlotte particularly admired her Jewish clients' generosity to her 'nuns', who were treated 'with the greatest Civility, usually rewarding them with Golden Guineas'.[16]

THE HARLOT APPREHENDED

Scene three shows a ramshackle garret in a house that is apparently meant to be in Drury Lane, Covent Garden – a location notorious throughout the eighteenth century as the haunt of poorer prostitutes. A clue to the location is the name of a tavern in Drury Lane engraved on a pewter tankard that Moll has apparently appropriated and that appears in the bottom right-hand corner of the image. Her progress has been decidedly downhill since the previous vignette. She has clearly fallen from indulged kept woman to common prostitute, plying for trade in one of London's most dissolute districts. The imagery and symbolism in this scene is incredibly rich and far-reaching – really telling a story in itself and suggesting that this work was indeed initially conceived as a stand-alone painting.

There is still much speculation about the meaning of many details in it. Does the cat's posture, superficially harmless and characteristic, also carry a particular and crude message, implying a type of sexual congress that was a capital offence if proven in court but which greatly reduced the risk of an unwanted pregnancy? And what is the meaning of the pointed hat and birch or scourge of twigs that hang above Moll's bed? Is it a witch's hat and was she expected to role-play for her clients? Does she perhaps give and receive flagellation? Is this intended to reveal the increasing depth of her moral descent?

A clue is given by a small plaster of Paris panel, dating from 1740–50, which once embellished an upper-floor fireplace in the Cheshire Cheese Tavern off Fleet Street (see page 174). It shows a pair of prostitutes

PLATE 3 *of* The Harlot's Progress. *Moll has become a common prostitute in lodgings in Drury Lane. A birch hanging on the wall is indicative of depravity, while the pin-ups beside the bed reveal Moll's romantic and libertarian spirit.*

kneeling to either side of a man – who is naked from the waist down and tumescent – with one of them beating his exposed buttocks with a scourge of twigs identical to that depicted hanging in Moll's bedroom.[17]

Other details and scenes in the print tell more direct stories. The presence of the syphilitic maid – with her nose destroyed by the disease – is a clear warning of the fate that awaits Moll. Indeed, medicines littered around suggest that she is already in the early stages of infection. The men bursting into the room are led by Sir John Gonson, a Westminster magistrate notorious in the 1720s and 1730s for his campaign against prostitutes and the keepers of bawdy- and disorderly houses. He has clearly come with constables or bailiffs to arrest Moll for an offence connected with prostitution or debt, but his posture suggests he is surprised – or moved – by what he sees. Is it the scourge that for a moment stops him in his tracks or is it Moll's state of bewitching undress? And is

Hogarth making a critical point here about the real motives of self-appointed guardians of other's morals?

Knowing his sharp eye for irony and hypocrisy, the scene perhaps suggests that Gonson was obsessed with the suppression of the sex industry because he himself was sexually obsessed; a man who saw evil in all about him because he was consumed with guilt over his own evil thoughts. A man who was himself aroused by the very thing he sought to deny others. Hogarth seems to be suggesting that Gonson, a self-appointed moral crusader and leader of the 1720s and 30s witch-hunt against harlots and homosexuals, was not so much an authority figure as a ridiculous, almost comic one – had his actions not been so harmful to others.

The depiction of Moll herself is perplexing: at once sexually beguiling in her dishevelled attire, squalid, and almost painfully vulnerable. She is the fallen virgin on the abyss of oblivion (an analogy suggested by the presence of a small oval image of the Virgin near the bed), the victim of the immoral city, the sacrificial lamb awaiting slaughter. This association is suggested most firmly by Hogarth because hanging above the bed is a picture of Abraham about to sacrifice his son Isaac. Abraham's arm is being stayed by an angel. Will Moll similarly be spared by divine intervention? It seems hardly likely since the only use in her world for a 'Pastoral Letter' – presumably from the Rector of St Paul's, Covent Garden to his wayward parishioners – is as a wrapping for a morsel of food. As in the first painting in the series, Hogarth seems to be showing little faith in the words or actions of men of the Church.

Moll's action as she lies in bed is also significant. She is admiring a watch. This scene would have had a particular meaning to the early-eighteenth-century observer because a gold or silver watch was almost the badge of a harlot's office. All prostitutes aspired to own and display a good and ornamental watch. But Moll's toying with the watch here could carry additional or alternative meanings. It could perhaps be illustrating her fall by emphasising the link between common prostitution and common crime – Moll could either have stolen this watch from a client or it could be plunder given to her by the man whose labelled wig box is stored above her head. The name on the box opens a further window into Hogarth's mind, helps reveal his intentions when painting the original canvas and links this imagined scene to the real world. The wig box belongs to James Dalton.

Born in 1702, Dalton came from the criminal underworld. His father was hanged in 1721 for highway robbery, his mother and step-father transported, and in due course James himself became the 'captain' of a gang of footpads based in St Giles-in-the-Fields – in the early eighteenth century a notorious criminal underworld or 'rookery' – a serial offender with a string of convictions.[18] In May 1728 an advertisement appeared for a pamphlet that claimed to be 'a promiscuous mixture of iniquity, ingenuity and facetious drollery being a genuine narrative of all the street robberies committed by James Dalton and his accomplices'. Dalton was clearly on his way to becoming something of a public figure, although not quite in the heroic mould of Jack Sheppard who had soared to fame four years earlier with his series of spectacular gaol breaks.

The pamphlet, a copy of which survives in a volume of tracts in the British Library, is dated 1728 and includes 'some merry songs of Dalton's' that refer to his 'biting the Women of the Town', to his 'detecting and exposing the Mollies [homosexuals], and a Song which is sung at the Molly-Clubs'.[19] So Dalton seems to have amused himself by abusing prostitutes and persecuting and mocking homosexuals. The advertisement also promised information on Dalton's accomplices 'who were tried this session, and against whom Dalton (called their captain) and Neaves were admitted Evidences'. In an attempt to save himself Dalton had evidently turned King's Evidence – betraying his own gang.

It would seem that this pamphlet was intended to ridicule, expose and belittle Dalton – and may also have been intended to present him as conceited and foolish because the advertisement announces that this vainglorious and damaging document was not only 'taken from the mouth of James Dalton' but also 'to be had of James Dalton, in Wood Street Compter'.[20] Dalton, in short, appears to have been in possession of a satirically and ironically minded enemy, determined to mock him to death. Perhaps the author of the pamphlet wanted to use Dalton – the real and ignorant career criminal – as an antithesis for the romantic fictional criminal Captain Macheath. Quite why his name should feature in this glimpse of Moll Hackabout's reduced circumstances is rather puzzling, however.

What is certain is that on 16 January 1730 Dalton was sent to gaol yet again, this time for a 'Great Misdemeanour' in assaulting a Dr Mead with intent to rob him. Dalton was gaoled for three years and while inside was fingered for an earlier crime by a man named John Waller. Dalton was duly charged. At his trial, which took place on 8 April the same year, Waller claimed that while passing across a field between Tottenham Court and Bloomsbury, he was threatened with a pistol by Dalton and robbed.[21] The accused, while admitting to other crimes, denied this particular one and was adamant in his denunciation of Waller who, Dalton claimed, was a 'man of vile character, a common Affidavit man that was lately out of Newgate [and] as great a rogue as himself'. But since Waller had 'positively sworn the fact', the jury chose to believe him and Dalton was found guilty and duly hanged at Tyburn on 12 May 1730.

This was not, however, the end of the affair. Dalton had been correct when he accused Waller of being an 'Affidavit man' – that is, someone who denounced fellow criminals by means of a sworn statement in return for a favour or reward. In May 1732 Waller was found guilty of perjury and given a sentence that included being pilloried in Seven Dials – a punishment that had terrible and grisly consequences (see Appendix 1).

What did this story mean to Hogarth and why should he choose to refer to James Dalton in his painting? We will, of course, never know for sure, but this reference does suggest that Hogarth started this first painting after 12 May 1730 when Dalton was hanged. In that year the characters who were to feature in the subsequent series were cast before Hogarth in rapid succession and in the most dramatic and public of circumstances: Francis Charteris was condemned to death in February 1730 after a sensational trial in which he was found guilty of raping Ann Bond; Francis Hackabout was executed in March, James Dalton in May, and Elizabeth Needham was stoned to death by a mob in April 1731. Easy to see how an artist's imagination could be fired by such events. Tempting, too, to see Hogarth's reference to Dalton as implied criticism of an incompetent legal system that could allow a man to be executed on the testimony of a perjurer.

True, it was not until Waller was convicted in May 1732 that the strong possibility Dalton had been the victim of a miscarriage of justice was raised – and by then the six paintings of *The Harlot's Progress* had been completed. But the point is that the engravings had not yet been completed. These – executed by the artist himself – appeared later in the year. It is possible that Hogarth added the Dalton reference to the engraving of painting three at this stage, the series' commentary on society's ills continuing even after the paint had dried on the last canvas. Sadly, in the absence of the original paintings, it is now impossible to confirm the presence or absence of Dalton's name in 1731, which will remain one of the minor mysteries of Hogarth's art.

THE HARLOT IN PRISON

Scene four shows Moll confined in the Bridewell, the prison located on the Fleet River, just south of Fleet Street. Surrounded by low company, she beats hemp as part of her punishment. Hogarth emphasises the corruption of the place and the whole penal system by showing that those employed to supervise the imprisoned criminals are themselves no better. While the stern gaoler orders Moll to work harder, his ill-visaged wife has designs on the harlot's fine clothes and is clearly planning to rob her. In the background is a graffito image of a man hanging from a gallows. A name is scrawled near the image: Gonson. Evidently some of the prisoners, and Hogarth, blamed Gonson and the *agents provocateurs* of the Society for the Reformation of Manners for their plight.

A scene uncannily similar to that depicted here was described – and given documentary credence – by a French visitor to London, César de Saussure, who in the late 1720s visited the 'Bridewell or House of Correction . . . at Tottlefields, near Westminster'. Saussure describes in a letter to his family how he and a friend . . .

> . . . entered a big court, on one side of which was a low building containing about thirty or forty robbers, pickpockets etc, male and female, occupied in beating out flax . . . with a large and heavy wooden mallet. On one side of the room were the men and on the other women, and between these two lines walked the inspector, or Captain Whip 'em [who] held a long cane in his hand . . . and whenever one of the ladies was fatigued and ceased working he would rap them on the arms, and in no gentle fashion.

Among these female prisoners Saussure observed 'a fine, tall, handsome and well-dressed creature [who] wore a magnificent silk dress brocaded with flowers' and was the object of the Captain's particular attention . . .

PLATE 4 *of* The Harlot's Progress. *Moll is confined in the Bridewell and obliged to beat hemp. The gaoler looks on sternly, while his wife, with designs on Moll's fine dress, is clearly no more than a criminal herself.*

... he made her arms quite red with the little raps he gave her with his cane ... it was a most curious contrast, this handsome girl or woman in rich clothes, looking like a queen and having a mallet in her hand, with which she was forced to beat out hemp, and that in such a way that she was covered with large drops of perspiration. I confess that this sight made me quite unhappy.

Enquiring about her crime, he was informed that 'she had stolen a watch from her lover, and that it was not her first visit, for she always stole everything she could lay hands on'.

Passing along the room Saussure saw 'a young girl from fifteen to sixteen years of age, extremely beautiful, she seemed a mere child, and was touching to look at'. He asked her why she was imprisoned and she replied, 'Alas, because of my tender heart.' Her story was that she 'was a prisoner through having helped one of her comrades to steal some guineas from one of her lovers [and] had been seized and brought to Bridewell'. So the beautiful creature was a thieving child prostitute.

Her looks and plight deeply engaged Saussure's sympathy. He discovered that she was being detained indefinitely because she owed the establishment a crown for extra food, and unless this was paid 'she expected never to get out'. Saussure and his friend were captivated by the way the girl 'related all this sad story with tears and in such a touching way', and were so horrified by her harsh treatment that eventually they paid what she owed so that 'she could be liberated at once from this house of sorrows'. Before they parted Saussure exhorted the girl 'to lead a better life, and she vowed she would'. But she was, of course, a cunning young jade. A couple of months later, 'being at the play', Saussure 'saw this little creature in one of the principal boxes, dressed like a duchess and more beautiful than ever'.[22]

The memorable image of the hapless Moll beating hemp while so well attired provoked a number of contemporary speculations as to her real identity. As Jenny Uglow notes, the *Grub Street Journal* thought Moll was inspired by Mary Muffet, 'a well-known Drury Lane character committed to hard labour in Tothill Fields Bridewell in 1730 where she was reported as "now beating hemp in a gown very richly laced with silver"'.[23]

NEARING THE END

Scene five of *The Harlot's Progress* depicts Moll out of gaol, back in tumble-down lodgings and dying of syphilis. Her deformed maid is still with her, and now there is also a child who seems to be behaving in a distracted manner. Perhaps Hogarth is suggesting that the infant is congenitally deranged – a victim in the womb of his mother's disease. It's a gloomy scene. Two doctors squabble pointlessly over the best cure for Moll's terminal illness. One is Richard Rock, whose name is written on an advertisement – evidently used as wrapping paper – for his anti-venereal grand specific pills. The other is the famed quack Dr Jean Misaubin, and the dispute seems to be over whether the best treatment for Moll is the mercury pills, cupping or bleeding. All were, of course, useless, although Moll's bandaged jaw suggesting toothache seems to indicate that she's already been dosed with mercury, for the loosening of teeth and gum disease were among the side-effects of mercury treatment.[24] While this furious yet futile debate proceeds, a woman – Moll's landlady perhaps – ransacks her chest.

PLATE 5 *of* The Harlot's Progress. *Moll is dying in shabby lodgings while doctors quarrel over their competing cures for syphilis and the landlady, or bawd, rifles through Moll's possessions.*

The only slightly hopeful aspect to the scene is that the maid remains loyal and protective towards Moll and a perforated Passover biscuit – 'Jew's Bread' – hangs by the door as a fly-trap. This appears to suggest that Moll's former protector – the Jewish City merchant – still takes an interest in her, paying for her medical care and these modest lodgings.

MOLL'S DEATH

The final scene depicts Moll's end. She is dead – unloved and among mostly careless and false friends, gathered in a decaying room. It's a devastating image in which virtually no one is spared. Moll lies in a coffin that also serves as a bar counter, and carries a plate declaring that she died on 2 September 1731 at the age of just twenty-three. Around the coffin sit or stand a dismal collection of people – mostly, it would appear, fellow prostitutes. One – identified as the 'demi-mondaine' Elizabeth Adams, who was executed for theft in 1737[25] – appears to be enjoying the attentions of a clergyman who has his hand firmly inserted up her skirt and, in his excitement, spills his strategically placed flute of brandy in bawdily symbolic manner. Clearly such a cleric – intent on worldly pleasure – could offer no spiritual consolation or guidance. From the very start Moll has been let down by the Church; in scene one a parson fails to intervene as she is being procured, and here, in death, the officiating clergyman wants only to grope a hussy.

One of the supposedly mourning prostitutes attracts the attention of the undertaker while another complains of a wounded finger and, in the

PLATE 6 *of* The Harlot's Progress. *Moll lies dead in her coffin, surrounded by careless prostitute companions and a distracted clergyman. One mourner seems moved – a young whore who, looking at Moll, perceives her own likely fate.*

background, yet another of the company stares into the mirror, perhaps pondering a facial sore that is probably the result of venereal disease. In front of the coffin sits Moll's son, playing with a top, seemingly unaware of what is going on around him. But there are three people who appear genuinely affected: Moll's bawd – identified as Mother Bentley[26] – drowns her sorrow in brandy, if only for this lost source of income; Moll's loyal maid looks on aghast at the disrespectful behaviour of the clergyman; and, in the very centre of the composition, a young harlot stares spellbound at Moll in her coffin – literally coming face to face with her own future.

The challenge posed to the spectator by these details in the final painting is essentially a refinement of the challenge posed by the series as a whole: what will you do to help save this girl, all such girls, from the cruelty and corrupting immorality of London life?

SEX IN THE CITY

ONE

'SATAN'S HARVEST'

The Nature of the Sex Industry

During the eighteenth century London had more prostitutes plying their trade on the open streets, over a greater proportion of the city, than could be found anywhere else in Europe. Prostitution was rife in Paris and in Amsterdam, but there it was more discreet, controlled and contained. This startling difference, and especially the quantities of patrolling street prostitutes, earned London an evil reputation.

A book published in 1734 evokes a memorable image of London street life:

> When a person unacquainted with the Town passes at night thro' any of our Principal Streets, he is apt to wonder whence the vast body of *Courtezans*, which stand ready, on small Purchase, to obey the Laws of Nature, and gratify the Lust of every drunken Rake-hell, can take its Rise. *Where the Devil do all those B—ches come from?* being a common Fleet Street phrase ... when each revolving Evening sends them up from White-Chapel to Charing-Cross.

The publication is called *Pretty Doings in a Protestant Nation* and its author – apparently – a French Dominican named Father Poussin who is said to have 'resided six and thirty years in Great Wild-Street, near Drury Lane'. The book claims to offer 'a view of the Present State of Fornication, Whorecraft and Adulteration in Great Britain' and was 'inscribed to the Bona-Roba's ... of *Covent-Garden*; and to the Band of *Petticoat Pensioners*'. So popular was this publication that it was reissued, almost verbatim, fifteen years later under the title *Satan's Harvest Home*, with the contents being described as the collected 'memoirs' of an 'intimate Comrade' of 'the Hon. Jack S**n**r'.[1]

The title page of *Satan's Harvest Home* expands the lists of subjects

covered to include 'Procuring, Pimping' as well as 'Sodomy' – as homosexual activity was generally termed, and 'the Game of Flatts' – as sex
between women was specifically called and which John Cleland had
described so memorably the year before in the early pages of his novel
Fanny Hill, when the eponymous heroine comes under the hands of her
'wanton' tutoress Phoebe Ayres. Still innocent, Fanny recounts that
Phoebe 'turned to me, embraced and kiss'd me with great eagerness. This
was new, this was odd . . .'[2]

Pretty Doings goes out of its way to present London as the 'Sodom'
of the age, the epicentre of iniquity – but was its author accurate?[3] As
with most complex subjects there is, perhaps, no objective truth, no
absolute reality – most observers would have seen and felt things at least
slightly differently according to their sensibilities, position in society,
point of view and place of habitation within London. It is, however,
possible to put the lurid scenes evoked by *Pretty Doings* and *Satan's
Harvest Home* in context, to see what other contemporary observers wrote.
If Daniel Defoe is to be trusted as an observer, and most would agree
that he is, then this image of London's streets in the early eighteenth
century was probably no exaggeration. In 1728 Defoe had written, 'Go
all the world over and you'll see no such impudence as in the streets of
London, which makes many foreigners give in general our women a bad
character from the vile specimens they meet from one end of town to
the other.'[4]

It is interesting that Defoe evoked the opinions of 'foreigners' because,
to judge by contemporary accounts, many were indeed shocked by London's
streets. Their descriptions are particularly useful because they recorded
sights that most Londoners – with the exception of such astute observers
as Defoe – must have taken for granted and, as commonplaces, regarded
as hardly worth talking or writing about. Many accounts by visitors suggest
that *Pretty Doings* did not present an exaggerated or sensational view of
London's street life. For example, Baron Zacharias von Uffenbach, a
German who visited London in 1710, was struck 'by the great quantity
of Moors of both sexes . . . hawking their bottoms round the Strand and
Covent Garden',[5] while César de Saussure in the second half of the 1720s
observed of London that 'the corruption of morals is very great [and]
even shows itself in broad daylight [when] lords and other rich people
go in daylight to houses of debauchery without attempting to make a

secret of it. An Englishman, who knows his London very well, assured me there are more than 40,000 courtesans in the town.'[6]

Friedrich Wilhelm von Schütz, in his *Briefe über London* (Letters from London), published in Hamburg in 1792, was more than shocked by what he saw, he was overwhelmed:

> . . . so soon as the streets are lamp-lighted . . . they begin to swarm with street girls who, well got-up and well dressed, display their attractions. Certain it is that no place in the world can be compared with London for wantonness . . . the number of evening and night prowlers is so unbelievable.[7]

Defoe's opinion of the London sex trade was also shared by some of his compatriots. Jonas Hanway, the philanthropist, traveller and great reformer of morals, observed in 1758 that 'there is, I believe, no city in the world, where such rank enormities prevail, as in this great metropolis [where] vice is become so cheap . . . among many common people, that it is hard to say how far these acts of uncleanness may be carried'. As far as Hanway could see the ordinary 'inhabitants of London are more abandoned than their fore-fathers were, and among the higher classes, many refinements in vice, and various methods of carrying on the trade of lust, are introduced'.[8]

One London law officer who took prostitution very seriously indeed was Saunders Welch, a friend of the novelist, playwright and magistrate Henry Fielding and an acquaintance of William Hogarth. Welch, high constable of Holborn and from 1755 assistant to Henry Fielding's half-brother and successor Sir John Fielding at the Bow Street magistrates court, was the author of a most intriguing and informative plan for the reformation of London's sex industry. Entitled *A Proposal to Render Effectual a Plan to Remove the Nuisance of Common Prostitutes from the Streets of this Metropolis*, and published in 1758, the document launched its argument in a sensational manner that echoed the tone of *Pretty Doings*:

> Prostitutes swarm in the streets of this metropolis to such a degree, and bawdy-houses are kept in such an open and public manner, to the great scandal of our civil polity, that a stranger would think that such practices, instead of being prohibited, had the sanction of the legislature, and that the whole town was one general stew.[9]

London in 1720, just before expansion of the West End to the south of the 'Tyburn Road' (Oxford Street) and to the fields of Marylebone to the north.

The sex industry was city-wide, but with key locations in the east, north and west.

Welch calculated that if all the London women 'whose sole dependence is upon prostitution', then 3,000 would be a number that 'falls far short of the truth' (at a time when London's population was 675,000, this was a very modest total when compared with other eighteenth- and nineteenth-century estimates (see page 134)).[10] Like Defoe, Welch attempted to shame his fellow Londoners by asking them to imagine how their city of rampant vice must appear to outsiders:

> What idea must foreigners have of our policy, when in almost every street they see women publickly exposing themselves at the windows and doors of bawdy-houses, like beasts in a market for public sale, with language, dress, and gesture too offensive to mention; and find themselves tempted (it may be said assaulted) in the streets by a hundred women between Temple-Bar and Charing Cross, in terms shocking to the ear of modesty.[11]

The cause of the trouble was, according to Welch, 'a general depravity of morals, a constant supply of sharpers [cheats] and robbers to infest our streets, and a train of other evils [that flow] from minds depraved by lust and enervated by debauchery.' Gloomily, he concluded that since 1753 (when he had written on the related subject of robbery):

> . . . the evil has increased; prostitutes of a higher rank, and gayer turn, some from Bawdy-houses, others who have private lodgings of their own, publickly ply in the Strand and Fleet-Street at noon day; and except some parliamentary remedy be applied to stop this evil, it will not only be impossible for modest woman to walk the streets, as these harlots take every opportunity to affront and insult them, but an universal debauchery will also spread among our youth.[12]

Welch's campaigning had little effect, for when the young Newcastle-born engraver Thomas Bewick arrived in London in 1776, harlots still held dominion over many of the city's major streets. Bewick recorded that what 'constantly hurt my feelings, was the seeing of such a number of fine looking women engaged in the wretched business of *Street Walking*'.[13] The multitude of street-walkers in the centre of the city is confirmed by the *Gentleman's Magazine*. In April 1795 it observed:

... the public streets at the close of day ... are scarcely passable from the interruption occasioned by females, who, since first loss of virtue, and character, have gradually sunk into the grossest vices, and stand ready to draw in the inexperienced youth, or those of more advanced years whose reason has received a temporary shock from the intoxication of the bottle.[14]

Schütz made a close study of the way in which London's street prostitutes operated:

Many of them stroll the streets alone and it must be said to their credit that they are fairly discreet. Either they silently offer one their arm or make use of all sorts of formulas, such as, for instance, 'I should so much like to marry you', 'Your love would make me happy' ... a single repulsing word is enough to drive these street ladies away, or it suffices even to pass silently by; but one must be careful not to move the right arm, as this sign may be taken for consent. Many, however, are not content with soliciting, but try to force their affections on one. It is difficult to get rid of these, as sometimes four, five and more, in competition, attach themselves to one.[15]

Another German visitor – the historian and writer Johann Wilhelm Daniel von Archenholz – made an almost clinical study of London's street life and sex industry. In his *A Picture of England*, written in about 1780 although not published in England until 1789, Archenholz recorded that: 'So soon as it becomes dark these girls [professional prostitutes], well turned-out, in all seasons flood the principal streets and squares of the town.'[16] Displaying the enquiring mind of a social historian, he further investigated the workings of the trade:

Many go on the man-hunt in borrowed clothes which they hire by the day from the matrons, who for safety's sake pay another woman to follow the huntress continuously on foot in order to see that she does not run away with the clothes. If the girl makes no capture and comes home without money, she will be ill-treated and must go hungry. They therefore accost passers-by and take them either home or to taverns. They can be seen standing in groups. The best class of prostitutes, who live independently, are content to go on their own way 'til they are spoken to.[17]

Three commentators on London's sex industry. Thomas Bewick (left), shown here in reflective old age, was 'hurt' by the large number of prostitutes walking the city's streets when he arrived in London in 1776. Johann Wilhelm von Archenholz (centre) visited London in the early 1780s and made careful observations about the sex industry. Patrick Colquhoun (right), a police magistrate, calculated in 1795 that London contained 50,000 female prostitutes.

The boisterous but also beleaguered behaviour of London's street prostitutes was confirmed by an anonymous and evangelical author who in 1796 stated that 'it is generally allowed, that no persons are more miserable or mischievous than those unhappy women, who disgrace our streets, and subsist on the wages of iniquity'. This observer seems to have been particularly worried by the idea that these 'young women' were 'prepared for every enormity' and that 'having been seduced, deserted and banished from their friends, are frequently left without other resources than that of entering the recesses of debauchery, the general consequences of which are increasing wickedness, a ruined constitution, a premature death, and, as far as we can see, everlasting destruction'.[18]

Archenholz, while pondering London's prostitutes, added an extra – and rather intriguing – ingredient: 'Many married women even who live in distant parts of town, come to the Westminster district where they are unknown and carry on the profession, either from vice or need.'[19]

This loaded observation reflects much late-eighteenth-century discussion about the nature and meaning of prostitution. Archenholz is referring, in a most judgemental way, to a type of middle-class woman much spoken about at the time and termed a 'demi-rep' – meaning of doubtful morality and so 'demi' (i.e. half) respectable – who from time to time was alleged to escape the constraints of respectable married life

and enjoy intrigues of a sexual nature, in pursuit of pleasure, profit or –
on occasion – a delightful, dangerous and thrilling mix of the two.
Archenholz completes his account by painting a particularly lurid scene:
'At midnight the girls leave the streets and old beggar women of 60 and
more come out of their hiding places in order to serve drunken men
returning heated from their revels, who must satisfy their animal needs
blindly, as it were "at the gallop".'[20]

Individual observations about the large scale of London's sex industry
are supported by various overviews that were attempted during the
eighteenth and early nineteenth centuries. Indeed, by the end of the eighteenth century, despite all the attempts at reform and reduction through
legislation, London's sex trade was apparently conducted on a gigantic
scale. In 1795 Patrick Colquhoun, a police magistrate, calculated that there
were 50,000 prostitutes of various regular and irregular types in London
which then had a population of nearly one million.[21] Colquhoun was a
native of Glasgow, where he had worked as a merchant and magistrate.
After serving as Lord Provost, he moved to London in 1791. There in
1792 he was appointed a police magistrate, based first at the Worship
Street office and then at Queen Square until his retirement in 1818.

During his first three years of work in London Colquhoun was so amazed
and alarmed by what he saw that he felt compelled to extrapolate his
personal experiences into a citywide portrait of crime and debauchery.
In 1796 he published – initially anonymously – *A Treatise on the Police of
the Metropolis: Containing a Detail of the various Crimes and Misdemeanours
By which Public and Private Property and Security are, at present, injured
and endangered.* As with Welch nearly forty years earlier, having analysed
the problem and revealed its huge scale Colquhoun suggested *'remedies
for their Prevention'*.

Colquhoun's *Treatise* was a pioneering work (one historian has described
him as the 'first major writer on public order and the machinery of justice
to use "police" in a strict sense closely akin to modern usage'),[22] but it's
now difficult to verify his statistics and conclusions, confused as they are
by the moral opinions of the age. Nevertheless, he makes a useful distinction between the 20,000 full-time or professional prostitutes he reckoned
to have been former menial servants and factory workers, and the majority
whom he believed either to be casual and occasional prostitutes, resorting
to this extremity when times were tough, or else women who lived with

men to whom they were not married and so displayed a relaxed attitude to morals and conventions that, Colquhoun believed, could lead them easily into prostitution. His statistics remain open to debate (see page 138), but if roughly correct suggest that in about 1800 one-fifth of the female population of London of sexually active age was involved, in one way or other, in the capital's sex industry.

This now seems astonishing, but Colquhoun was not alone in setting so high an estimate. Many observers agreed that during the next couple of decades London's illicit sex life became even more garish and more active. At the time it was suggested that the moral life of London declined significantly after the French Revolution in 1789. Michael Ryan, in *Prostitution in London*, published in 1839, stated that it was an 'historical fact' that 'licentiousness spread through Europe' after 1789, and refers to William Wilberforce writing in his *Report of the Society for the Suppression of Vice* that 'the greatest obscenity had, in the year 1802, become more than commonly numerous'.[23]

It has even been suggested that the introduction of efficient gas street lighting after 1813 (Pall Mall had been gas-lit in January 1802, but only after Westminster Bridge was lit in December 1813 did gas street lighting spread rapidly) actually increased rather than reduced street prostitution. It might be supposed that improved lighting drove prostitutes off the main thoroughfares and into dark and obscure courts but, argued Ivan Bloch . . .

> . . . with the general lighting of the town an important change took place in the external manifestation of prostitution. Whilst the public prostitutes had hitherto had their headquarters in the City . . . and the West End, they now spread over all parts of the town, principally in the west . . . It was first observed in London not only how the night lighting of a big town encouraged the spread of prostitution to all its parts, but how greatly the nightly excesses in the higher grades of society also increased.[24]

To support his point Bloch quoted the *Midnight Spy* of 1766: 'Although it was already after 3 o'clock, the nymphs and shepherds still sacrificed on the altar of Bacchus, and the peak of lust was reached.'[25]

Despite the arrival of modern technology that brightened its streets, the establishment of an efficient police force and more coherent and stridently advocated codes of morality, London – that great centre of dark and ancient vice – showed no significant signs of reform during the first two decades of the nineteenth century. Changing attitudes to morality and a revolution in urban life merely meant that vice, rather than declining, gradually went underground. In the eighteenth century London's sex industry had been conducted openly as part of daily life, but by the mid-nineteenth century it existed covertly, a secret parallel world enjoyed in guilt and shame (street-walking was made an imprisonable offence in the 1820s). The myriad of lies that were the result of this still thriving but almost manically concealed sex industry were the most dramatic expression of the great social change that had overtaken Britain, with the result that, as Harold Perkin most astutely observed, 'between 1780 and 1850 the English ceased to be one of the most aggressive, brutal, rowdy, riotous and bloodthirsty nations in the world and became one of the most inhibited, polite, orderly, tender-minded, prudish and hypocritical'.[26]

TWO

'LADIES OF THE TOWN'

The Business of Prostitution

During the eighteenth and early nineteenth centuries women became prostitutes for many reasons. The principal cause was poverty, occasionally coupled with ambition for riches, fashion and fame that could not be gained through a life of toil as a domestic servant or honest drudge. As *Pretty Doings in a Protestant Nation* put it in 1734, there were among servant girls 'few young creatures now-a-days . . . endow'd with a Stock of Virtue sufficient to hold out against' temptation and seduction, especially since 'a poor Wench . . . who serves for four or five Pounds a Year wages, shall be liable to go through as much *Drudgery*, as a Livery-Horse'.[1]

Or entry into prostitution could be due to youthful indiscretion and subsequent loss of reputation, forcing the unfortunate girl, in her quest for survival, to seek refuge in the sex industry, as apparently happened to Ann Bell in the mid-eighteenth century (see page 413). Certainly this was Thomas Bewick's opinion when, on arriving in London in 1776, he was 'hurt' by the number of 'fine looking women' working as 'street walkers' and was informed that they 'were lost to themselves & to the world' because 'they had been seduced & then basely betrayed'.[2]

The key agent for entry into the trade was generally believed to be, as Hogarth illustrated in *The Harlot's Progress*, a conniving bawd who would charm, decoy or intimidate a vulnerable girl into prostitution. As late as 1835, despite many social changes, the machinations of an unscrupulous bawd and her bullies were still perceived to be the most usual means by which a female would enter into prostitution, and prompted the London Society for the Protection of Young Females to warn about those 'ever on the alert to entrap the innocent and the unwary [who] may be decoyed, seduced and ruined by one of those wretches in human form'.[3]

The essayist and playwright Richard Steele. In 1712 he wrote in a most compassionate way about prostitutes in his magazine the Spectator.

The other supposed major cause of female debauchery and fall into prostitution was male deceit. This had been identified very early in the eighteenth century by Richard Steele who, writing in the *Spectator*, blamed the immorality of the age not on whores but on those men who, given to the 'villainy of the practice of deluding women', entice 'little raw unthinking Girls, and leave them after Possession of them without any Mercy to Shame, Infamy, Poverty and Disease'.[4] In the edition of 4 January 1712 Steele continued this argument by pleading the 'poor and publick Whore's' case for forgiveness: 'No Vice or Wickedness, from which People fall into from Indulgence to Desires which are natural to all, ought to place them below the Compassion of the virtuous Part of the World.' To bolster his case, Steele attached a little story to his plea:

The other Evening passing along near Covent-Garden, I was jogged on the Elbow as I turned into the Piazza, on the right hand coming out of James-street, by a slim young Girl of about seventeen, who with a pert Air asked me if I was for a Pint of wine. [As] we stood under one of the Arches by Twilight . . . I could observe as exact Features as I had ever seen, the most agreeable Shape, the finest Neck and Bosom, in a

Word, the whole Person of a Woman exquisitely beautiful. She affected to allure me with forced Wantonness in her Look and Air; but I saw it checked with Hunger and Cold: Her Eyes were wan and eager, her Dress thin and tawdry, her Meen [sic] genteel and childish. This strange Figure gave me much Anguish of Heart. [I] could not forbear giving her a Crown. The poor thing sighed, curtsied, and with a Blessing, expressed with the utmost Vehemence, turned from me. This Creature is what they call *newly come upon the Town*, but who, I suppose, falling into cruel Hands, was left in the first Month from her Dishonour, and exposed to pass through the Hands and Discipline of one of those Hags of Hell whom we call Bawds.[5]

This is a curious tale, reflecting some of the emotional and moral complexities and dilemmas surrounding prostitution during the eighteenth century. Steele is compassionate in his attitude to the girl and sees her as a victim of the cruelty and selfishness of others, but he is patronising and almost self-congratulatory in the display of his enlightenment and charity. Also, it's not just Steele's sense of compassion that is aroused by the vulnerable young whore – he clearly finds her sexually alluring. As always the harlot induces both alarm and desire.

The author of *Pretty Doings in a Protestant Nation* offered a far cruder and more conventional explanation for the spread of prostitution, blaming it on poor economic planning coupled with the same predatory side of male behaviour attacked by Steele:

The Town being overstocke'd with *Harlots*, is entirely owing to those Numbers of *Women-Servants*, incessantly pouring into it from all Corners of the Universe, and those Debaucheries practis'd upon 'em in almost all the Families that entertain them . . . After they have been a little while in Town . . . and are out of Place, and having nothing to support them, they then prostitute their Bodies. Many of 'em . . . running . . . from Bawdy-House to Service, and from Service to Bawdy-House again . . . so that in effect, they neither make good Whores, good Wives or good Servants; and this is one of the chief Reasons our Streets swarm with Strumpets.[6]

These words echo – almost exactly – those written by Daniel Defoe a few years earlier. Prostitution, he argued, was simply a response to unemployment among servants and the 'amphibious life' it imposed: 'The reason why our streets are swarming with strumpets' was, argued Defoe, because a huge number of maidservants chased the few jobs available. Thus many of them 'rove from place to place, from bawdy-house to service, and from service to bawdy-house again . . . nothing being more common than to find these creatures one week in a good family and the next in a brothel'.[7]

Quite simply, before the Industrial Revolution of the late eighteenth century, many women from the poorer strata of society – which is to say the vast majority of the women in the land – were dependent upon casual and pauper work, notably 'needle' trades such as seamstress and mantua-maker, and were beset by economic uncertainty and privation since many such trades were seasonal or subject to sudden and dramatic slumps. For example, in 1807 around 30,000 women in London (perhaps one-sixth of the female workforce) were engaged in the seasonal trade of fruit and vegetable gardening. In these circumstances it is easy to see why so many working women actually chose lives of prostitution and crime.[8]

The intimate connections between prostitution and poverty – or at least economic insecurity and lack of education and prospects – has led the historian Tony Henderson to draw up a far from romantic profile of the typical eighteenth-century prostitute. Rather than deluded victim of male deceit or in other ways a fallen angel, she was instead an intensely pragmatic being:

> Born into poverty, more often than not outside London, frequently orphaned or deserted by their parents, trained (if at all) only for the most menial and ill-rewarded employment [such women were] forced by economic need . . . to enter prostitution on a full-time basis or to engage in acts of prostitution as circumstances demanded or allowed.

Henderson also observes that if prostitutes from such lowly back-grounds left the trade they 'seem to have experienced little difficulty in reintegrating into a part of society which the great majority of them had never really left'.[9]

Which of these routes to prostitution was the most common is open to debate, but perhaps the strangest path – and one that haunted the Georgian imagination – was abduction. This could be a subtle and insidious process, involving no more than the victim being picked up by a cunning bawd and ensnared into prostitution through false promises, deception and manufactured debts. There are many such tales in this book and William Hogarth, in his *Harlot's Progress*, reflects the debauching of Ann Bond in the first painting in the series (see page 312). Records of Henry Fielding's work as a Covent Garden-based magistrate also illustrate perfectly how seduction could lead, directly and dramatically, to virtual abduction and imprisonment within the sex industry.

In a report of 25 January 1752, published in the *Covent-Garden Journal*, there is a description of the inmates of a bawdy-house:

> [A]mong the women taken at this House, was one Mary Parkington, a very beautiful Girl of sixteen Years of age, who, in her examination said, that . . . her father dying, her mother married again [and] about three weeks ago she was seduced by a young Sea-Officer, who left her within a Day or two; that being afraid and ashamed to go home to her Mother, and having no Money, she was decoyed by a Woman to this Bawdy-House; where she was furnished with Clothes; for which she gave a Note for Five pounds; that she was there prostituted to several Men for Hire; and all the Money, except a few Shillings, she was obliged to pay over to the Mistress of the House [and she] was kept a Prisoner there, against her Will and Consent [and] threatened . . . if she offered to make her Escape, that [they] would arrest her on that Note of Five Pound.[10]

The anonymous author of *The Case of the Unfortunate Bosavern Penlez*, published in 1749, confirms the highly unpleasant nature of most bawdy-houses and bawdy-house keepers. Penlez was executed in 1749 for having been involved in an assault on, and theft from, a building in the Strand during a period of rioting caused by the mistreatment of sailors at a bawdy-house. Three sailors had been robbed of their watches and over £50 in cash and, when they demanded their possessions back, were ejected from the house by the bawd's gang of bullies. The enraged sailors went to Wapping, gathered a mob of their fellows, returned, raided and destroyed the bawdy-house, and also attacked another nearby.

This bold attack against private property, although provoked by outrageous behaviour, sent a chill through the London middle classes and even the generally enlightened Henry Fielding. In his capacity as magistrate he committed Penlez to Newgate for trial on the evidence of a bawdy-house keeper. The amiable and educated Penlez, who was not a sailor but a peruke-maker and just happened by ill chance to be in the wrong place at the wrong time, had to suffer the full rigour of the law and was executed.[11] The public didn't like the outcome of the affair and Fielding, who had been accused by some hostile journalists of being a paid protector of bawdy-houses, felt obliged to defend his role by rapidly publishing *A True State of the Case of Bosavern Penlez*, which appeared in 1749.[12]

What is interesting about Fielding's work is that, in the course of seeking to justify Penlez's highly unpopular execution, he lets slip that 'the nuisance which Bawdy-houses are to the public' is reflected by the fact that 'the Law clearly [also] considers them as a nuisance, and hath appointed a Remedy against them; and the Remedy it is in the Power of every man, who desires it, to apply'.[13] In other words, even Fielding, who was going out of his way to accuse Penlez, recognised the deeply unpleasant undercurrents to the case. Even as he wrote these words he must have known, too, that the law did not offer the public a satisfactory remedy against the 'nuisance' of bawdy-houses. Within three years Fielding himself was involved in developing and promoting a stronger piece of legislation – the Disorderly Houses Act of 1752 – which contained a specific clause to help with the suppression of bawdy-houses and brothels (see page 486).

The anonymous author of *The Case of the Unfortunate Bosavern Penlez* (possibly John Cleland, whose *Fanny Hill* was written the previous year) painted a grim picture of the life of the prostitutes working in bawdy-houses and under the control of heartless bawds and their male bullies. These 'fallen Angels', seduced, deserted and forced into prostitution by necessity and 'infinitely more deserving of Compassion than of Blame',[14] were terrorised and manipulated with threats of 'false Debt' by the bawdy-house owners:

> As soon as one of these obscene Foxes has, by any Means, decoyed one of those poor, young, tender Creatures, into their Bawdy-traps . . . [which] is effected commonly by indulging and humouring the giddy, wild, thoughtless Turn, natural to the Age, till . . . he fixes a good round Debt upon her, the imaginary terrors of which keep her in a state of slavery to him, scarse less cruel, and much more infamous, than that of a captive of *Barbary*. From thence forwards she is, Soul and Body, absolutely at his Command . . . Then, at his nod, must that tender

delicate person of hers ... be given up ... to the lust of every Ruffian who can afford the price he sets upon her, let his person be never so loathsome and infectious, to be touzed, and rumpled, like a bit of dirty paper.[15]

The ultimate fate of such a trapped, friendless and abused young prostitute – imprisoned by day and forced on to the streets at night to entice customers into the bawdy-house – was to be 'torn to pieces, in the flower of her age'[16] and finally cast into the street or into gaol.

Archenholz in the 1780s tells a similar tale:

The most wretched [prostitutes] live with *matrons*, who lodge, board, and clothe them. The dress worn by the very lowest of them is silk, according to the custom which luxury has generally introduced into England. Sometimes they escape from their prisons, with their little wardrobes under their arms, and trade on their *own bottoms*, when, if they are unfortunate, or happen not to be economical, they are soon dragged to gaol by their creditors.[17]

Dreadful as these stories are, the great fear of many Georgian Londoners was that abduction could be more literal, could in fact be kidnap coupled with imprisonment, isolation and intimidation to force the victim to become a sex slave. Public belief in the possibility of such a fate was widespread and reached its height in 1753 when a young maidservant, Elizabeth Canning (see page 140), claimed to have been abducted by gypsies and held captive for a month before she was able to escape. The truth or otherwise of her claims was hotly debated for years, ensuring that the spectre of abduction remained a popular obsession for decades to come.

'SHE CAPTAINS OF SATAN': THE BAWD

In popular imagination and perception as well as the words of the *Spectator*, bawds were the very 'Hags of Hell'.[18] This glib condemnation, however, ignores the complexities of the sex industry, a trade that was, among many things, a grim battle for survival in a hostile and fickle world. Once a whore had lost her looks through age, hard living or disease, what was to happen to her, what was she to do, if she had not secured useful

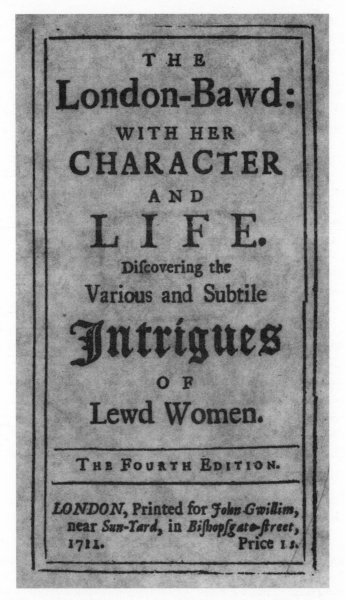

THE
London-Bawd:
WITH HER
CHARACTER
AND
LIFE.
Diſcovering the
Various and Subtile
𝕴𝖓𝖙𝖗𝖎𝖌𝖚𝖊𝖘
OF
Lewd Women.

THE FOURTH EDITION.

LONDON, Printed for *John Gwillim*,
near *Sun-Yard*, in *Biſhopſgate-ſtreet*,
1711.   Price 1 *s.*

The title page of The London-Bawd, *a satirical account of London's sex industry in the early eighteenth century.*

connections or managed to save enough money from her good years to
support her in her bad? A few whores managed their lives successfully
and there are examples of prostitutes achieving fame, social position and
riches (for example, Lavinia Fenton, see page 117), but these are very rare
exceptions. So the chief option open to most superannuated whores
was to cease to be the victim championed by such as Richard Steele and
become the bawd, attempting to profit from their years of experience at
the other end of the transaction: earning a living instead by running a
bawdy-house or brothel and making themselves indispensable to clients
seeking all and any manner of sexual dalliance. As Lord Rochester put
it in the 1670s, the bawd was 'the truest friend to lechers'.[19]

A publication of 1705, entitled *The London-Bawd*, offers a satirical,
sardonic and somewhat clichéd portrait of the bawd who, as described
there, is not far removed from the popular perception of a witch or of
that dark and ancient evocation of evil *Mother Midnight*, the bawd-cum-
midwife who wickedly contrived to have innocent girls new-born as
strumpets.[20]

First *The London-Bawd* makes the bawd's origin clear: she 'is the Refuse
of an Old Whore . . . one of Nature's Errata's and a true Daughter of
Eve, who having first undone herself, tempts others to the same
Destruction'. Then her aims and interests are revealed:

> She's a great preserver of Maiden-heads for though she exposes 'em to
> every new Comer, she takes care that they never shall be lost [and] a
> great Enemy to all Enclosures, for whatever she has, she makes it
> common. She hates Forty-one as much as an old Cavalier, for at that
> age she was forc'd to leave off Whoring and turn Bawd.

Next a physical description is offered:

> Her Teeth are all fallen out; at which her Nose and her Chin are so
> much concern'd, that they intend to meet about it in a little time, and
> make up the difference.

Finally her *modus operandi* and particular skills are explained:

> She is never without store of *Hackney Jades*, which she will let *any one
> Ride*, that will *pay for their Hire*. She is the very Magazine of Taciturnity;
> for whatever she sees, she says nothing; it being a standing Maxim with

her, *That they that cannot make Sport, shou'd Spoil none* . . . She has been formerly a Pretender to Musick, which makes her such a great Practitioner in *Prick-Song*, but she is most expert at a *Horn-Pipe* [and] she has an excellent Art in Transforming Persons and can easily turn a Sempstress into a Waiting-Gentlewoman.

The 'Hackney Jades' joke, as already mentioned, refers to hackney carriages, the eighteenth-century equivalent of taxis, which anyone could hire for immediate use, while 'horn-pipe' was a euphemism for sexual intercourse.[21]

A satirical image from 1773 of a London bawd, portrayed here as an 'Abbess' of the lowest type.

This physical description of the bawd is repeated by the perhaps soon-to-be whore Dorothea in *The Whore's Rhetorick* of 1683:

> . . . she had very near as many furrows in her face, as Hairs on her Head, her Eye-brows were thick and hoary . . . there was an uninterrupted communication between her Mouth and Nose . . . her breasts appeared

45

Elizabeth Creswell, a famed London bawd of the late seventeenth century, after a print by Marcellus Lauron. Gaunt, hooded and cloaked, she looks the very image of the mythic 'Mother Midnight'.

like a pair of Bladders, without the least particle of Air within and which
had hung some Ages in the smoke of a chimney; her Chin was acute and
leaning upwards as if it longed to kiss the under Lip; it was graced with
about a dozen hairs placed much after the same order they are in an old
Puss ... her Legs, a pair of Broomsticks covered with Parchment ... Her
nails were certainly visible ... so her tallons were laid open to every eye.[22]

The bawd described in *The Whore's Rhetorick* is named as Mother Creswel,
and is presumably the elderly cloaked and hooded woman – Elizabeth
Creswell – shown in a print by Marcellus Lauron the Elder, who lived
in London during the late seventeenth century until his death in 1702.[23]

Bawds were among the great and legendary figures of London's sex
industry: feared, hated, mocked and – very occasionally – respected or
even admired. Many perhaps secretly agreed with the amoral defence
offered by an 'Old Bawd' in *The London-Bawd:*

Nature that has given us Appetites, has also given us an inclination to
satisfie 'em; and 'tis no more than the Satisfying the Natural Desires and
Inclinations of Men and Women that I concern myself about ... my
business is to help a Gentleman that is in distress, to the Enjoyment of
a Gentlewoman; and a Gentlewoman that has the same like occasion,
to a gallant.[24]

These women by custom worked in conjunction with men who were
either their 'paramours' or 'bullies', and who would ensure the smooth
functioning and security of the bawdy-house. In addition there were pimps
and 'panders' who were business partners, described in *The London-Bawd*
as 'he-Bawds and procures of whores for other men'.

Not surprisingly, some bawds achieved quite a name for themselves in
their own lifetime. There was Mother Haywood, for example, who is
described in *Hell upon Earth* of 1729 as cursing and roaring 'at her maids
and drawers, to drown the cries and groans of departing Maidenheads'.
Mother Wisebourne (see page 104) and Mother Needham (see page 313)
also won widespread notoriety. In the mid-eighteenth century and the
decades afterwards there were such figures as Mrs Goadby (see page 207),
Charlotte Hayes (see page 211), Mrs Kelly (see page 53) and Mrs Gould.[25]
As for Mother – or Jenny – Douglas, she was, from the late 1740s until
her death in 1761, the most famed and notorious of all London bawds.

She is featured in William Hogarth's *The March to Finchley* of 1750; profiled in *The Humours of Fleet Street and the Strand, Being the Life and Adventures of the most noted Ladies of Pleasure*, written by 'an old sportsman' and published in 1749;[26] described in *The Modern Courtezan* of 1751 as a 'mighty Tut'res' who can teach her 'Fair-ones . . . every luring Art'; while in *Covent-Garden: a Satire* of 1756 Mother Douglas was hailed as 'Empress o'er all the bawds around'.[27]

The profits a bawd could make through her unholy endeavours were huge. The heroine of Cleland's *Fanny Hill* explains how she was enticed into a bawdy-house by one Mother Brown – who is supposed to have been modelled on Mother Douglas – and then introduced to an utterly objectionable libertine who agreed with the bawd to pay 'fifty guineas peremptory for the liberty of attempting me, and a hundred more at the complete gratification of his desires, in the triumph over my virginity'.[28] When it is considered that the London working man at the time would earn little more than £50 a year, this fee to the bawd of £150 was an enormous amount for so little outlay of time or money. As for Fanny's payment, it was 'to be left entirely at the discretion of his liking and generosity'. But was Cleland correct in the price he quoted for deflowering a virgin? Probably, since most of the more readily ascertainable facts in the book tend to be correct, and certainly the sum is supported by the story of the actress Lavinia Fenton whose own mother, in the 1720s, attempted to sell Lavinia's virginity for £200 cash and £200 per annum 'whilst she remained constant' (see page 118).

The story of the ensnaring, exploitative and greedy bawd is told time and again, in many permutations, throughout the course of this book. The wicked bawd becomes one of the monsters of the age and her story takes on the quality of a fairy tale; she's the cruel step-mother, abusing those whose trust she wins, while her already fallen harlots are the ugly sisters who goad and seek to degrade the newly trapped and still innocent novice. So agreeable was it to have the story of the wicked bawd confirmed by frequent repetition that virtually verbatim accounts of her occur in different books. For example in 1723 in *The Genuine History of . . . Sally Salisbury* (see page 106) there is a description of Mother Wisebourne's working methods. These are repeated virtually word for word in 1734 in *Pretty Doings in a Protestant Nation*, which tells the archetypal story of the wicked bawd:

There liv'd till about a Year ago, an elderly Woman, near King-street, Westminster who was every Day very needful in the World, yet every Day did a world of Mischief, who kept a House of free hospitality, but made Folks pay vastly dear for what they had. But her Customers paid the greatest Price with the greatest pleasure ... She had always a Bible in her Hand at Home, and always a to-be-ruined Damsel Abroad; each Morning she took her Rounds to all the Inns, to see what Youth and Beauty the Country had sent to *London* to make their Fortunes; and when she found a Rural pretty Lass step out of a Waggon, she drew her by smoothing Language to a private Box within [where] the antiquated *She-Captain of Satan's* Regiment would offer the poor innocent Creature an Apartment and all Accommodation in her House *gratis*, till she saw if she should like the Town.[29]

Thirty years later things were much the same. In 1758 Jonas Hanway, in his *Thoughts on the Plan for a Magdalen-House for Repentant Prostitutes*, condemned bawds as the 'ministers of Lucifer' who are 'supported in splendour' but whose ways led 'literally to the grave',[30] while in the 1780s Archenholz noted that ...

... these vile procuresses like to keep an eye on the country coaches which arrive daily in London ... and usually bring in country girls seeking service in the capital. Poor creatures of this kind are overjoyed when, on arrival in such a crowded place ... they find someone making them the friendliest advances ... Events now lead gradually to their fall.[31]

In *Pretty Doings* the 'house' is in many senses the key object. Accommodation in late-seventeenth- and eighteenth-century London was very expensive, with demand generally outstripping supply, and since the vast majority of houses were built speculatively by far from altruistic small-scale investors, rents were kept as high as possible. So only the reasonably wealthy could enjoy their own houses, with much of the population of Georgian London living as lodgers in terrace houses divided between several tenants or families. The speculative builder Nicholas Barbon calculated in 1685 that on average each London house was occupied by about ten or eleven people,[32] while the 1801 London census reveals that – typically – the small 1730s houses in Bentinck Street, Soho, off

Berwick Street, each contained four, five or six families.[33] So a bawd with a house of her own, or at least under her control, was a powerful person with a potentially most profitable asset. Exactly why is made crystal clear in *The Whore's Rhetorick*:

> The most convenient habitation for a Trading Lady [is] a small convenient House of her own, rather than ... Lodgings [whose] main inconveniency ... is that in them it will be difficult to contrive several small Chambers, or dark place of refuge, just large enough to contain a Bed, which may be easily had in her own House.[34]

The name by which a bawd's establishment was known and described was of no small importance to its proprietor, as *The London-Bawd* makes clear:

> [T]he House which I now keep, is a House of Convenience for Gentlemen and Ladies: And goes under several Denominations: Some call it *The School of Venus*; others a *Vaulting School*, others the *Assignation House*: and some that are my Enemies bestow upon it the Title of a Bawdy-house: but this title I never lay claim to, nor take pleasure in.[35]

Bawdy-houses existed on the edge of the law. If noisy and indiscreet, a house could be closed down as 'disorderly' and the bawd prosecuted. So name and perception were all-important, as was the ability of the bawd to disguise and transform her house and herself as and when required. The author of *The London-Bawd* states that: 'I have in my time run through Varieties of Changes', and as Robert A. Erickson makes clear in his seminal *Mother Midnight*, the bawd's chief disguise and means of protection was the veneer of respectability.[36] Typically, Mother Wisebourne made a point of clasping a Bible when she walked abroad and she placed one open in her hall, just in case some of her more suspicious but naïve neighbours might be fooled by so easy and obvious a ploy.

This seems to have been a time-honoured stratagem of the bawd, for Mother Creswel in *The Whore's Rhetorick*, when instructing Dorothea on the furnishing of her apartments, tells her that 'you must not be un-provided of the *Whole Duty of Man, Practice of Piety*, and such like helps to Devotion; as having been from the beginning a great pretender to Religion'.[37]

The house of Mother Brown – the bawd in *Fanny Hill* – was, to judge by appearances, the very model of chaste, affluent and tasteful respectability. Fanny, when she first entered, had a 'good opinion' of the place and was impressed and reassured by the 'very handsome back parlour . . . which seemed to me magnificently furnished [with] two gilt pierglasses, and a buffet, on which a few pieces of plates . . . dazzled, and altogether persuaded me that I must be got into a very reputable family'.[38]

The desirability of disguising a bawdy-house or brothel beneath a veneer of stylish respectability continued throughout the Georgian period and is one of the most striking aspects of the 1835 description of Madam Aubrey's notorious establishment in Seymour Place (see page 169).

The house was not just important as a place where prostitution could be pursued profitably and safely, a haven of unbridled fantasy. It was more than just a means of shelter. The house – or, in a sense, its architecture – became a favourite metaphor for the prostitute or at least for the prostitute's body and for female defences against debauchery.

Bernard Mandeville in *A Modest Defence of Publick Stews* of 1724 created a whole fortified city of the imagination, full of salacious sexual imagery and allusions. The restriction of prostitutes – which Mandeville thought a threat to good social order – he referred to as the 'stopping' of 'drains and Sluices' that had been intended to 'let out Lewdness', and which would result in the demolition of 'those Horn-works and Breast-works of Modesty' and expose 'those Ramparts and Ditches within which our Wives and Daughters lay so conveniently intrench'd'.[39] In similar vein, *Pretty Doings* refers to a 'Debauch'd Veteran ogling a fine Woman at Church, and taking a view of the Fortifications',[40] while in *Mother Midnight* Erickson offers 'the furthest extensions (and reductions) of a whore to a house' that his researches revealed.

In the *Covent Garden Magazine* of January 1773 a description of a 'nun', which is to say a prostitute, in Fenchurch Street in the City, states that she 'displays a pretty little tenement, and as delightful a woodland country round about as any one would wish to live in: the rent of which is just about as much as she can get',[41] while Ned Ward in 1699 wrote of a whore labouring under 'Sufferings and Sorrows' brought on by the 'Extasies of Joy' inspired by a bawd's conversation that 'struck up such an unextinguishable Fire in my most Pleasurable Apartment, that I fear its past the Power of Tunbridge Waters . . . or the Pick-a-dilly Engineer, to stop the Flames from consuming the whole miserable Tenement'.[42]

The humble and unpretentious London terrace house – the domain of the prosperous bawd – was truly sexual architecture. Its forms and rooms took on, in the minds of whores and writers, explicit sexual connotations. Throughout the eighteenth century this analogy between architecture, landscape and a prostitute's body is pursued with both vigour and invention. The pages of *Harris's List of Covent Garden Ladies* – the libertines' directory of London prostitutes circulated from the late 1740s (see page 180) – are a rich repository of examples. Typical is an entry in the 1788 edition which proclaims that:

> Miss Lister of 6 Union Street, Oxford Road [is] painted by the masterly hand of nature, shaded by tresses of the darkest brown [with] the neighbouring hills below full ripe for manual pressure, firm and elastic, and heave at every touch. The Elysian font, in the centre of a black bewitching grove, supported by two pyramids, white as alabaster, very delicate, and soft as turtle down. At the approach of their favourite lord unfold, and for three guineas is conducted to the harbour of never failing delight.[43]

CHILD PROSTITUTES

One of the most alarming and distressing sights on the streets of Georgian London was the number of children living rough and prostituting themselves. 'What a deplorable Sight is it,' recorded *Pretty Doings in a Protestant Nation* in 1734, 'to behold Numbers of the little Creatures pil'd up in Heaps upon one another, sleeping in the publick Streets, in the most rigorous Seasons, and some of them whose Heads will hardly reach above the Waistband of a Man's Breeches, found to be quick with Child'.[44] Foreign visitors, having been initially shocked by the high numbers of patrolling harlots, were shocked again when they noticed the youth of many of them. Archenholz, who was in London in the early 1780s, felt 'surprise, mingled with terror' to observe 'girls from eight to nine years old make a proffer of their charms; and such is the corruption of the human heart, that even they have their lovers'.[45]

A similar impression was made on F. W. Schütz who in 1792 was struck forcefully by the . . .

> . . . shamelessness of the children who, with the grown ups, roamed the streets and offered their services to passers by. Usually a crowd of female creatures stand in front of the theatres, amongst whom may be found children of nine or ten years, the best evidence of moral depravity in London. In general, the English nation oversteps all others in immorality, and the abuses which come to light through addiction to debauchery are unbelievable.[46]

There were allegedly brothels like the Temple of Aurora which supplied 'girls as young as eleven to the rich',[47] and even Mary Kelly's well-known West End brothel was found to include four minors among its resident prostitutes.[48] There was also an alarming tradition of child sex abuse among the poor and ignorant – with the resulting transmission of venereal disease – because of a received opinion among both males and females, that 'criminal communication with a healthy child' would be a cure for the disease.[49] Significantly, the report of the Lock Hospital for 1752 revealed that since its opening in 1749 more than fifty children had been admitted for treatment of venereal disease.[50]

In 1758 the magistrate Sir John Fielding came to some alarming conclusions about the child sex industry in London. He investigated the ages of twenty-five prostitutes arrested on 1 May and discovered that thirteen were eighteen or younger, with three being only fifteen. He noted the natural drift of vagrant girls into prostitution, and in another investigation, when forty prostitutes were arrested on a 'search night', Fielding stated that 'the major part of them have been . . . under the age of eighteen, many not more than twelve'. This was a particularly shocking statement at the time since in eighteenth-century Europe fourteen to fifteen was usually taken as the age of puberty in girls, so a large number of these street prostitutes were pre-pubescent.[51] Fielding was also aware of the brisk trade in children which, together with the plethora of abused child street prostitutes, led him to argue for 'an Asylum or House of Refuge for Orphans and Other Deserted Girls of the Poor in the Metropolis'.

The trade in children was often conducted under the guise of entering a child into apprenticeship, which typically involved the sale by poor and ignorant parents or grandparents of a daughter or granddaughter to a shady intermediary with contacts within the sex industry.[52] The *Newgate Calendar* describes one such case of attempted child-selling that took place in 1766. It is a peculiar tale because the transaction was conducted openly and in a most public space, albeit one that marked the eastern end of the great thoroughfare of the sex trade leading from St James's and Charing Cross in the west:

> On the 15th of January, 1766, an elderly man and woman were observed on the Royal Exchange, London, with a fine young girl, apparently fourteen years of age, but thinly and shabbily clothed, and consequently shivering with cold in that inclement season of the year. It was first conceived that they were asking charity, as the man had addressed two or three gentlemen, from whom he received a contemptuous denial. At length he accosted an honest captain of a ship, who instantly made known the base proposal which had been made to him, which was to purchase the unfortunate and innocent girl.

The man and woman were arrested by the beadles of the Exchange and carried before the magistrate sitting at the nearby Guildhall. The pair were examined and stated the girl was their own child. But to the magistrate '. . . it appeared so unnatural that parents in Britain should offer for sale their offspring that an inquiry . . . was set afoot'. Using the all-embracing vagrancy laws the couple were imprisoned while the case was investigated and the girl was sent to the London Workhouse 'to be taken care of'.

When the 'unnatural' couple appeared at the next Sessions the mystery had been solved. The man was named John Crouch, the woman was his wife and the girl their niece. They came from Bodmin, Cornwall, and having heard 'that young maidens were very scarce in London, and that they sold for a good price', Crouch took his niece out of the poorhouse in Bodmin and the three walked the 230 miles to London 'in order to mend their fortune by her sale'. The jury found the man guilty of 'an offence far short of his crime' – there simply wasn't a law dealing with the illicit sale of a relative into sexual slavery – and sentenced him to six months' imprisonment with a fine of one shilling. His wife was considered as acting under her husband's influence and was acquitted. The fate of the fourteen-year-old niece is not recorded but was probably grim indeed.[53]

The child-sex industry in London appears to have continued – indeed flourished – until the end of the Georgian period. In January 1816 the *Gentleman's Magazine* carried an impassioned article which proclaimed:

> The most public thoroughfares of this Metropolis exhibit, at noon-day, a train of infants already devoted to Infamy, and bearing the broad mark of Vice upon their countenances, which have not yet lost the traces of childhood! Let any man walk from the Exchange to Charing-cross, under the glare of the mid-day sun, and the slightest degree of observation will point out to him a multitude of victims to early disgrace who, in point of age, are hardly yet fit to be emancipated from the restraints of the nursery; and who, it is a melancholy truth, are no less distinguishable by their infantile appearance, than by the unblushing manner in which they force themselves upon the attention of the passenger.[54]

The author was worried and puzzled about the origin of these brazen children and could only conclude that 'they are, and from the very nature of the case must be, involuntary, passive, unresisting victims upon the altar of Moloch [an Old Testament god of sacrifice]! But whether over-awed through the operation of fear, or forced by open and undisguised violence, they are alike plunged into the abyss of destruction.'

The *Gentleman's Magazine* hoped that the '*Guardian Society* [formed] for providing an asylum for unfortunate females' would take action and 'that the claims of this most pitiable class of sufferers will not be permitted to pass unheeded by the philanthropic characters who conduct the affairs of this excellent Charity'.[55] But this worthy body of moral guardians had little effect, to judge by the claims made almost twenty years later by F. B. Talbot, the secretary of the London Society for the Protection of Young Females, who claimed there were over four hundred agents in London involved in abducting and tricking girls into the sex industry.[56]

THREE

MOTHER CLAP AND HER BOYS

Molly Houses and Others

Homosexual prostitution from the late seventeenth to the early nineteenth centuries was not treated in great depth or detail by contemporary literature and most information now comes from accounts of trials, newspapers and often idiosyncratic pamphlets. But when homosexual activity and prostitution did, at certain moments, come under intense scrutiny it is clear that they formed a significant if minority sector of London's sex industry. To understand legal and popular attitudes towards Molly Houses – as homosexual brothels were called – it is essential first to understand something of the legislation relating to all those sexual acts that were, during the Georgian period, generally regarded as 'unnatural'.

The law relating to homosexuality in Georgian London was, on the surface, very simple: sodomy was illegal and, in certain circumstances, punishable by death. The legal definition of sodomy was any sexual act deemed to be 'unnatural' which, as a rule of thumb, was any act that was undertaken for pleasure only and that could not lead to procreation – the sort of acts, indeed, that were believed to have taken place in Sodom and which, as the Old Testament makes clear, provoked God to violent fury.

It was to avoid a repetition of this divine retribution that during the eighteenth century various law makers, law enforcers and reformers took on the sex industry. The pursuit of unusual sexual acts in private and between consenting adults was not acceptable because God could see and He would not be amused. Sodomy was the term applied indiscriminately to many acts – including sex with animals and oral sex – all in theory illegal. What made the law confusing was that the sexual act which the legislation really had in its sights, and for which the statute making it a capital offence was instituted in 1533, was anal sex or buggery between men. Indeed at times eighteenth-century moral crusaders and magistrates seemed to have become fixated upon the 'evils' of homosexual sodomy, to the extent that in many contemporary accounts buggery is synonymous with sodomy and bestiality while other 'unnatural' acts go largely unmentioned, although the Old Bailey archives do record the fate of a woman who in 1677 was prosecuted and executed for 'Sodomy' because she was found guilty of the charge that 'she did commit Buggery with a certain Mungril Dog'.[1] As J. Weeks explains in *Sex, Politics and Society*:

> All acts of buggery were equally condemned as being 'against nature', whether between man and woman, man and beast or man and man. The penalty for the 'abominable vice of buggery' was death, and the death penalty continued on the statute books . . . until 1861.[2]

An obscure and partly satirical anonymous pamphlet, published in 1703 and entitled *The Shortest-Way with Whores and Rogues*, throws interesting light on the accepted definitions of these crimes. The pamphlet makes it clear that, to its author at least, 'sodomy' was synonymous with homosexuality while 'buggery' was the term for sex with animals. Sodomy, the author proclaims, is a 'Sin against nature . . . for God hath ordained that the Male and the Female should Couple together; and not Male and Male or Female and Female', while 'Buggery . . . is such an abominable act of Uncleanness that Moses tells us, *Whosoever lyeth with a Beast, shall surely be put to death*.' (Interestingly, as an example of buggery the author referred to the 1677 trial and execution of the woman for sex with a dog – a crime that the Old Bailey Trial proceedings had catalogued under sodomy.)

So there is much potential confusion in legal terms and definitions used in the seventeenth and eighteenth centuries. But unlike the above, most accounts suggest that buggery meant penetration of a body by a penis, so for buggery – under the name of sodomy – to be a capital crime it had to be proven (usually by evidence of ejaculation) that penetration had actually taken place. Both parties – the active and the passive – were considered equally guilty when the passive partner had 'submitted' willingly, so many sodomy trials were in fact the trial of a pair of people. However, one of the participants in the act could save themselves if they rapidly turned Queen's or King's Evidence against the other, although it would probably have been difficult for the active member of the duo to use this defence if hostile witnesses had noted their role.

Other sexual activities between men – such as embraces that resulted in emissions outside the body – were still punishable by law but were not capital crimes and were treated as assault. So, since penetration could be difficult to prove, a lenient and merciful jury had much leeway and could give the accused the benefit of the doubt, conclude that penetration had not taken place and find them not guilty or else impose punishment less draconian than execution. Often the accused claimed they had a right to do what they wished with their own body and, providing the congress was not violent or rape, it seems that most jurors agreed – or were unwilling to execute a man for a crime that had no very tangible consequence and no victim. Also, not all sodomy involved penetration between men. Since sodomy was the offence, it was possible to charge a male and female couple with this crime. The Old Bailey records, however, do not include instances of this.[3]

The popular view of illicit or 'unnatural' sex could be relentlessly unforgiving, and the personal and public consequences of ungoverned carnal pleasure were themes pursued in much eighteenth-century writing on sexual morals. *The Shortest-Way with Whores and Rogues* is an interesting case in point. Inspired by Daniel Defoe's pamphlet on *The Shortest-Way with Dissenters*, it contains a 'Dedication' by its anonymous author to 'Mr Daniel de Foe' that reveals the work to be a 'Satyr' upon vice.[4] Yet the pamphlet, although often almost ludicrously lurid in its imagery of the pain and punishment advocated for illicit sex, is also deadly serious in intent. As the author explains, if 'Whores and Rogues . . . should think my Saytr is too bitter; let Him use it as an Apothecaries Pill, that the more Bitter the more Purging'.

The pamphlet is a perplexing piece of prose, at once absurd, extreme and earnest. It is up to the reader to decide what is pure satire and what is serious polemic dressed in the garb of parody. 'Ladies of Pleasure' are warned that 'your practice will prove bitterness in the end, both to you and those concerned with you, for, if those impure flames be not quenched by the Blood of Jesus Christ, and the tears of sincere repentance, the reward of your whoredom with be unquenchable flames.' As for 'our London Night walker . . . the Scripture calls such Beastly Creatures as these by the Name of Dogs and Swine because of their likeness of temper and practice, and 'tis not doubted but those who are entrusted with the Government of this Great and Noble City, will take effectual Methods to cleanse our Streets from these Daughters of Sodom'.[5] The author then addresses the 'more Unnatural Acts of Uncleanliness'. Sodomy, which to this author meant 'an abuse of either sex against nature', was viewed as . . .

> . . . such a Filthiness as not to be found amongst the Beasts, for God hath ordained that the Male and the Female should couple together; and not the Female and Female, nor Male and Male. Sodomy (and Self Pollution, which is a sort of Murder) is a Sin so against Nature that Children (Nature's End) and Posterity are utterly lost by it.

This abhorrence of same-sex carnal relations is supported by reference to the Bible that, naturally, contains many moral lessons and punishments reforming writers could use to chill their readers. The anonymous author of *The Shortest-Way with Whores* . . . invoked Romans (1:18, 26–7) to argue that homosexuality was no more than an expression of God's 'wrath' against 'all ungodliness and unrighteousness of men' who, for their sins, 'God gave . . . up into vile afflictions: For even their women did change the natural use into that which is against nature. And likewise also the men, leaving the natural use of the women, burned in their lust one towards another, men with men working that which is unseemly.'

Josiah Woodward wrote in similar vein in *The Soldier's Monitor* of 1776 when issuing advice to those tempted by heterosexual depravity. Woodward pointed to the intriguing lines in Proverbs (22:14) that warn those tempted by vice that 'The Mouth of Strange Women is a deep pit' and he that sins 'is abhorred of the Lord [and] Shall fall therin'.[6]

When it came to the punishments recommended for women and men found guilty of 'Unnatural Acts', the author of the pamphlet displayed such a bloodthirsty (indeed perverse) imagination and absence of Christian sympathy that all here appears to be a parody of the strident attitudes of some of the contemporary societies for 'Reformation' of morals. 'Those who are found guilty of Incest' should suffer a punishment 'as remarkable' as their crime. The man should be executed and his 'carkass brought back to Prison and there the Female Sinner should have no other allowance to feed upon for 2 months but the dead body', and then have the word INCEST written in . . .

... indelible character upon her forehead, or if this e'nt sufficient, cut off her two Ears, her middle finger, and her right Leg. The Sodomite should be placed in a Tub, and have liquid and burning Brimstone poured down upon him till he expires ... or ... have his Genitils cut off and burnt by the common Hangman. He that's proved guilty of Buggery [here meaning bestiality], should be reprieved from execution, till he hath eaten up the Beast with which he has committed the Sin [and] be hang'd heels upwards, to denote that his Sin has been unnatural [or] let him be stoned to death, and when his Beastly carkass is Dead, let his Head be fastened to the Mare he has Bugger'd, and made a Spectacle to the World.[7]

The punishments envisaged for more conventional sinners were less grue-some although no less novel. 'Fornicators' were to be whipped from Guild Hall to Charing Cross and their estate confiscated and divided into three parts 'to carry on the War ... to the Person that makes the discovery ... and to the poor of the Parish ... the Gallant that's surprised with his Miss should have his estate confiscated to Maintain the hospitals', beat hemp for two years and then go into the army, while those guilty of 'self-pollution should advertise it in every News paper ... at their own cost'. The author concludes with the thought that 'were but these short methods of Penal Justice set on foot, debauchery wou'd lose ground, and the REFORMATION spread more'.[8]

An incident that took place in Covent Garden in the seventeenth century reveals exactly why such puritanical, vengeful and God-fearing Christians, of the type that were (perhaps) being parodied in *The Shortest-Way with Whores*, were horrified by the potential consequences of licen-tious behaviour. Samuel Pepys recorded a dinner conversation he had on the 1st July 1663 about Sir Charles Sedley, who had exposed himself on the balcony of the aptly named Cock Tavern in Bow Street where he came ...

... in open day into the Balcone [sic] and ... showed his nakedness, acting all the postures of lust and buggery that could be imagined and abusing of scripture ... saying that there he had to sell such a powder as should make all the cunts in town run after him ... and that being done, he took a glass of wine and washed his prick in it and then drank it off; and then took another and drank the King's health.

Sedley was arrested and during his trial the public's indignation – fear almost – was very evident. As Pepys explained, 'The Judges did all of them round give him a most high reproof; My Lord Chief Justice saying: That it was for him, and such wicked wretches as he was, that God's anger and judgments hung over us' (see page 469).[9]

Quite simply, for conventional God-fearing Christians 'vices were sins and insurrections against God [inviting] Divine retribution'.[10] King William III's 1698 'Royal Proclamation for Preventing and Punishing Immorality and Profaneness' is very exact and explicit. The nation must improve its morals lest 'the open and avowed Practice of Vice . . . provoke God to withdraw his Mercy and Blessings from Us, and instead thereof to inflict heavy and severe Judgements'.[11] The crime and the punishment were clear – if London was to become the new Sodom, remember Sodom's fate. And if you enter the 'deep pit' that is 'the Mouth of Strange Women', remember that you only do so because you have sinned and are cast aside, damned and 'abhorred' by the Lord.

This crusading and moralising spirit resurfaced in the mid-eighteenth century. One particular aim of Saunders Welch's 1758 *Proposal to Render Effectual a Plan to Remove the Nuisance of Common Prostitutes from the Streets of this Metropolis* was to bring about a moral regeneration of London. Prostitution was to be checked, so that young men could be saved from the corrupting influence of lust and illicit sex that, Welch believed, destroyed not only their bodily health but their enterprising spirit:

> The effect which such open prostitution has upon unwary youth is but too well known. Thousands have been tempted and seduced, to their utter ruin, in their passage thro' the streets where these infamous houses abound; into whose minds lewdness would not have found its way, had not the temptation been placed in this barefaced manner before their eyes.[12]

Welch, like earlier moral campaigners, wanted to save people from themselves. He wanted not only to prevent the public expressions of the sex industry – masses of patrolling harlots and lewd acts in public – but also to stop or reduce sex in private between consenting prostitute and client. No matter how discreet the offending couple might be, God could see, and he, Welch believed, would not be forgiving.

THE MOTHER CLAP TRIALS

The Old Bailey records suggest that attitudes to homosexuality changed during the first quarter of the eighteenth century. In the early years of the century sodomy trials were rare and few of the accused were ever found guilty – roughly one trial every three years between 1699 and 1721, with all the accused found not guilty. But in 1726 there was a dramatic reversal. There were ten sodomy trials in two years, the majority of the accused were found guilty and four were actually executed. During the same period there were five trials of the lesser crime of 'Assault with Sodomitical intent'.

This dramatic statistical change reflects the fact that concerted action had been organised by one of the vigilante reforming societies dedicated to the promotion of public 'manners' or morals. By using informers and *agents provocateurs* and collecting evidence in a thoroughly documented manner, such societies as that for the Reformation of Manners presented prosecutions that juries were compelled to find convincing. The focus of this particular action were Molly Houses – as taverns or brothels used by homosexuals were called – in the well-known homosexual haunts of Moorfields, with its 'Sodomite's Walk', Saffron Hill, and the area around St Paul's Cathedral in the City, with a particular target being Mother Clap's Molly House in Field Lane in Holborn.[13]

The story of the 1726 homosexual witch-hunt can be told best and most directly through the texts of Old Bailey proceedings. These outline the sphere of operations, imply the nature of early-eighteenth-century homosexual life in London, reveal the agencies that entrapped people and their methods, and, of course, make clear how evidence was used and assessed, cases conducted and prosecutions secured. These records still make chilling reading and, being largely verbatim reports of the trials, possess an authenticity and directness that give these dreadful tribunals – in which people were tried for their lives for no other reason than preferring to live outside the moral conventions of society – a compelling immediacy.

The trials of men associated with Mother Clap's establishment and accused of the capital crime of sodomy were held at the Old Bailey on

The north side of St Paul's Cathedral was a popular meeting place for homosexuals in early and mid-Georgian London.

20 April 1726 before Sir Francis Forbes, Lord Mayor of the City of London; Lord Chief Justice Raymond; Mr Baron Price; Sir William Thomson, Recorder; and John Raby, Serjeant at Law. There were two juries, each consisting of twelve men, one of London and one of Middlesex.[14] The first accused to come to trial for his life was Thomas Wright on a charge of 'Sodomy'.[15] He was indicted for 'committing Buggery with Thomas Newton on January 10th 1724/5' and the case against Wright was based on evidence sworn by Newton, who seems to have turned King's Evidence to save his own life. A more sinister possibility is that, as a known homosexual prostitute, he had been blackmailed by vigilante moral reformers into ensnaring and informing upon homosexuals, and thus forced to bring about the death of his former friends and lovers. The precise role of these seemingly relentless moral crusaders remains a matter for speculation because no vigilante 'Reformation' society is named in these proceedings, although some of those who offered evidence appear to have been in the employment of one or several of the existing societies.

In his evidence Newton stated that 'last January 12 month the Prisoner had the Carnal Use of my body at his own house, in Christopher's Alley in Moor-fields'. Wright was a wool-comber by trade but, according to Newton, 'sold a dram among such company as came to his house [and] afterwards remov'd to Beech Lane, and there kept rooms for the entertainment of Sodomites'. Newton then revealed his own background as a male prostitute. Wright had, stated Newton, 'often fetch'd me to oblige Company in that way, and especially to one Gregory Turner'. The court now heard something about conduct in Wright's Christopher Alley lodging when he received company. The information was offered by William Davison and Joseph Sellers, who appear to have been undercover investigators and *agents provocateurs* working for the 'Reformation' societies. They told the court the . . .

. . . discovering of the Molly Houses, was chiefly owing to a quarrel betwixt Mark Partridge and [someone called] Harrington: For upon this Quarrel Partridge to be revenged on Harrington, had blab'd something of the Secret, and afterwards gave a large Information of a great many others [and] by his means we were introduced to the Company.

When the agents infiltrated Wright's lodging they found 'there were about 8 or 9 [men] in a large room, one was playing upon a fiddle, and others were . . . dancing in obscene Postures . . . Singing baudy songs and talking leudly and acting a great many Indecencies'. Despite an altercation, during which several of the party called Partridge a 'treacherous . . . blowing-up Mollying Bitch', Wright seems to have enjoyed the evening and, according to the agents, 'was very fond of us all and kist us all at parting in a most indecent manner'.

Wright produced one witness to offer a character reference who told the court that the defendant was 'esteem'd an honest man' – a statement that was not particularly relevant to the charge since it was not his honesty that was in dispute but his morals. With no more evidence sought or delivered, the jury found Wright guilty and the judges delivered the sentence of death.

Now Gabriel Lawrence was brought before the court, also on a charge of sodomy, and was indicted for 'feloniously committing with Thomas Newton, aged 30 years, the heinous and detestable Sin of Sodomy'.[16] Again the most serious evidence against the accused came mainly from

Newton: 'At the end of last June [1725], one Peter Bavidge (who is not yet taken) and Eccleston (who dy'd last week in Newgate) carry'd me to the House of Margaret Clap (who is now in the Compter [a small local prison under the control of the parish watch]) and there I first became acquainted with the Prisoner.'

Newton now pinpointed the location of Mother Clap's Molly House as being next to the Bunch of Grapes Inn or Tavern on Field Lane, Holborn. He also offered a brief description of the establishment: 'It bore the publick Character of a Place of Entertainment for Sodomites, and for the better Conveniency of her Customers, she had provided Beds in every Room in her House. She usually had 30 or 40 of such Persons there every Night, but more especially on a Sunday.'

This is a fascinating account – Mother Clap's Molly House seems similar in arrangement and scale to heterosexual brothels and bagnios such as Haddock's in Covent Garden (see page 227), and the homosexual side of the sex industry, like the heterosexual side, favoured Sunday as their busiest night.

Newton then described how Lawrence committed the crime for which he was on trial: 'I was conducted up one pair of Stairs, and by the Perswasions of Bavidge (who was present all the Time) I suffer'd the Prisoner to commit the said Crime.' So Newton admitted that he was not raped or forced to participate in the act of buggery but 'suffer'd', or allowed, the act to take place, albeit under the persuasion of two men. This admission made him liable to the same capital charge as was laid against Lawrence. This knowledge must have worried him when Margaret Clap was arrested in February and her clients were being traced, arrested and charged. The idea might well have crossed his mind then that if he didn't turn King's Evidence quickly and offer testimony in exchange for his life, someone else would provide the proof being sought by the prosecution and he would then be next in line for sentencing to death. This thought process is certainly hinted at in Newton's evidence: 'When Mrs Clap was taken up, in February last, I went to put in Bail for her; at which Time, Mr Williams, and Mr Willis told me, they believ'd I could give Information, which I promis'd to do, and I went next Day, and gave Information accordingly.'

Williams and Willis are somewhat mysterious characters but Old Bailey trial evidence of 1726 suggests that Willis was a constable patrolling the area around Sodomite's Walk in Moorfields and no doubt in the pay of the 'Reformation' society that was in pursuit of Mother Clap and her clients.[17] Perhaps the pair simply told Newton of their 'belief' that he was in a position to give 'information' or perhaps they threatened him with the fateful consequences of failing instantly to turn informer. Whoever they were and whatever their methods, Newton decided to act on their 'advice', to save himself through condemning others, and in the process give the prosecution the vital sworn – rather than circumstantial – evidence it needed if it were to press for extreme sentences. But to remain safe he had to tell all he knew, provide evidence against others before they could lay evidence against him – so he cast his mind back to liaisons more than a year old, such as that with Thomas Wright.

As Lawrence's trial proceeded, the prosecution brought forward a witness whose evidence was not specifically directed against Lawrence but London's homosexual culture as a whole and Mother Clap's establishment in particular. The aim seems to have been not only to damage Lawrence in the jury's eyes by associating him with Mother Clap's but also to make it clear that the reformers would not rest until the evil place and others of its kind had been eradicated. The witness, named Samuel Stephens, appears to have been another undercover investigator, or plain-clothes constable, in the employment of the 'Reformation' societies. Stephens deposed that:

> Mrs Clap's House was notorious for being a Molly-House [and] in
> order to detect some that frequented it, I have been there several Times,
> and seen 20 or 30 of 'em together, making Love, as they call'd it, in a
> very indecent Manner. Then they used to go out by Pairs, into another
> Room, and at their return, they would tell what they had been doing
> together, which they call'd marrying.

Lawrence was obliged to admit that he had 'been several Times at Clap's House' but attempted, against all the evidence, to maintain that he 'never knew that it was a Rendezvous for such Persons'.

His character witnesses offered a better defence. One was a cow-keeper who for eighteen years had supplied Lawrence – a milkman – with milk and had never in all that time seen him misbehave. He referred in particular to an 'Oxfordshire Feast [where] we have both got drunk, and come Home together in a Coach, and yet he never offer'd any such thing to me'. Another witness revealed that he was Lawrence's father-in-law and that, although a widower for seven years, Lawrence had a thirteen-year-old daughter. But it did no good. Lawrence was found guilty and sentenced to death.

The last of the Mother Clap defendants – William Griffin – was now indicted for committing sodomy on 10 May 1725 with Thomas Newton, who again gave evidence for the prosecution.[18] He deposed that 'the prisoner and Thomas Phillips (who has since absconded) were lodgers for near two years at Clap's house [and] I went up stairs, while the prisoner was a bed, and there he committed the Act with me'. Samuel Stephens (but now spelled Stevens) again gave evidence, this time to inform the court that he had seen 'the Prisoner and his gang at Clap's house'. Like his two fellow prisoners, Griffin was found guilty and sentenced to death.

During this same session two other men, unrelated to Margaret Clap's Molly House, were also tried for sodomy. One, George Kedear, was found guilty and sentenced to death,[19] while the other, George Whytle, was found not guilty.[20] They had been convicted on evidence from an eighteen-year-old called Edward Courtney who in both cases was the man said to have been buggered. So, as with the Mother Clap trials, it seems that one of the men facing criminal charges escaped prosecution by turning informer, probably under pressure from a 'Reformation' society.

During his trial Kedear sought to save his life by stating that Courtney had 'ask'd me to do it; but I told him I could not ... What, says he, I suppose I am not handsome enough for you, but if you don't like me, I have got a pretty younger Brother, and I'll fetch him for you.' Kedear further stated that on another occasion Courtney 'again solicited me to do it, and beg'd me to go into the Privy ... he told me that he had nothing to subsist upon but what he got by doing such things – I advis'd him to leave off that course of Life; but he said he wanted Money, and must have it, and if I would not help him to some, he'd swear my Life away.'

Despite this defence the jury decided to accept Courtney's evidence because he had turned informant and sworn his evidence first. Courts were well aware that if an informant's evidence were overturned in favour of arguments offered by the accused then one of the main incentives to inform – the knowledge that not only were you protected from prosecution but the court was prejudiced in your favour – would be seriously undermined. And without a plentiful supply of informants swearing evidence, the courts would find it very hard to implement the letter of the law. But courts had a serious problem when the main witness for the prosecution was a wayward and bad character such as Courtney – and in the following case against Whytle, Courtney's evidence was indeed rejected by the jury in favour of that offered by the defendant and his array of character witnesses.

During this case it was revealed that not only did Courtney make a habit of threatening to swear away the lives of people who did not do his bidding but he was a 'scandalous fellow' who had been in Bridewell Prison three times. Courtney admitted the fact with an air of defiant good humour, saying he was gaoled 'for no harm', and then told the court about his life in a Molly House, being 'saucy' to a constable and 'raising disturbance about a Mollying Cull in Covent-Garden'. The jury duly found Whytle not guilty and, presumably, felt at least a little uncomfortable about earlier condemning Kedear to death on the evidence of such a wretched fellow. A perjury case could have been pursued – as was to happen a few years later with John Waller (see page 536) – but there is no evidence that Courtney was prosecuted; probably no one thought this useless teenager worth the trouble.

On Monday 9 May 1726, just over two weeks after their trials, the three convicted Mother Clap 'sodomites' – Thomas Wright, Gabriel Lawrence and William Griffin – were executed together at Tyburn, all strung up from the triangular scaffold.[21] But these three hapless men, executed for nothing other than following their nature with a consenting fellow, did not form the only spectacle at Tyburn that day. At the same time as the three men hung from 'the tree', Catherine Hayes was being burned alive for the crime of 'petit treason' – the murder of her husband.[22] Such was the Devilish Year of 1726, but it was not yet over. There was still much mischief in store.

Two months after these executions Margaret Clap, the woman whose establishment the hanged men had frequented, came to trial. On 11 July 1726 she entered the dock at the Old Bailey, charged with keeping a brothel 'in which she procur'd and encourag'd Persons to commit Sodomy'.[23] Margaret Clap, unlike her late customers, was not on trial for her life. Running a homosexual bawdy-house was not a capital crime, but if found guilty her punishment could be savage enough. She was liable to be fined, imprisoned for a significant time, and – most dangerous of all – made to stand in the pillory exposed to the violent retribution of the public.

Also to be tried at the same Old Bailey Session was a collection of her former customers. But, as with their former hostess, these men were not being tried for their lives. They were charged with 'sodomitical intent', a homosexual act in which buggery did not take place. Classed as an assault, conviction resulted in a fine, imprisonment and the pillory.

First to be tried was Martin Mackintosh, who was 'indicted for Misdemeanour in assaulting Joseph Sellers with an Intent to commit with him the detestable Sin of Sodomy on November 12'.[24] Unfortunately for Mackintosh, Sellers was an *agent provocateur* in the pay of the societies. In court he revealed his subtle working methods. Mark Partridge, whose fellow homosexuals had attacked him at Thomas Wright's house, was indeed exactly what they accused him of being: a 'treacherous . . . blowing-up Mollying Bitch'. Partridge was Sellers' creature, presumably because the other man had enough compromising evidence about his activities to hang him. As Sellers explained:

> Mark Partridge carried me and others to several Sodomitical Houses in order to detect some Persons that frequented them, among the rest he carried us to Mr Jone's a Tallow-Chandler at the Tobacco Roll and Crown or the Three Tobacco-Rolls in Drury-Lane. As soon as we came in, Gabriel Lawrence (since hang'd for Sodomy) began to scold at Mark Partridge, calling him vile Dog, a blowing-up Bitch and other ill Names because Partridge had blab'd out something about one Harrington's being concern'd with him in such Practice. Partridge excus'd himself by telling the Company, that Harrington first divulged the Secret and that what he said was only to be even with him.

This explanation calmed the company, allowing Sellers to get on with his work of entrapment. As he explained to the court, his cover and protection was to play the role of Partridge's 'Husband' – a guise that allowed him to fit into the milieu and prevented 'my being attacked by any of the Company'. Sellers cast around and probably selected Mackintosh as a target for enticement because he appeared the most outrageous and incautious member of the company. As Sellers put it, '[T]he Prisoner sold Oranges and for that reason he went by the Maiden Name as they call'd

Orange Deb' and he and Lawrence 'appear'd very fond [of one] another, they hug'd and kissed and employ'd their [hands?] in a very vile Manner'. A little more light is, perhaps, thrown on this 'company' of homosexuals during a trial for sodomitical assault that took place in 1728 and which might well refer to the same club. The court was told that 'when any Member enter'd into their Society, he was christened by a female Name, and had a Quartern of Geneva thrown in his Face; one was call'd Orange Deb, another Nel Guin, and a third Flying Horse Moll'.[25]

It's easy to imagine the shrewd and calculating Sellers posing as a 'Husband' among such a collection of fine and exotic 'ladies', waiting to pounce on the first who went too far. Eventually 'Orange Deb' presented Sellers with his opportunity. As he told the court, '[T]he Prisoner came to me, put his Hands in my Breeches, thrust his Tongue into my mouth, swore that he'd go 40 Mile to enjoy me and beg'd of me to go backward, and let him – but I refusing he offer'd to sit bare in my Lap upon which Partridge snatch'd a red hot pocker out the Fire and ran it into his arse.'[26]

This most dramatic termination to the affair, and to Mackintosh's ardour, was witnessed and confirmed by Samuel Stevens, another of the regular 'Molly hunting' agents who was present at the scene (evidently also in disguise) and later in court. All Mackintosh could offer in his defence were some men who had been his 'Bed-fellows' and who 'depos'd that he never offer'd any such thing to them', and the fact that he had a wife and child and 'took care of his Family'. Seeing the court was unworried by the way in which the agents entrapped Mackintosh, the jury duly found him guilty and he was sentenced to the pillory, a fine and imprisonment.

As Mackintosh was sent down William Brown was brought up into the dock. The charge against him would have had a familiar ring to any who had been in court on 20 April when the three customers of Mother Clap were tried for their lives and found guilty. Here, in Brown's case, the same enticer and informer was at work.[27] Brown was 'indicted for a Misdemeanour, in assaulting Thomas Newton, with an Intent to commit Sodomy with him'. The infamous Newton, to a major degree responsible for the death of Wright, Lawrence and Griffin because of the evidence he had given in the courtroom in April, once again entered the arena of his perfidy. What on earth could he have felt? If it was guilt, no one would have known from the evidence he now offered. It was the same old story.

The familiar figures of Willis and Stevens (now named Stevenson) were evoked, and at last described as 'the Constables having a Warrant to apprehend Sodomites'. Seemingly without remorse or shame, Newton told the court how he acted as a decoy to entrap a fellow homosexual: 'I went with them to an Ale house in Moorfields, where we agreed that I should go out, and pick one up, and they'd wait at a proper Distance.' The words Newton used and the detailed knowledge of which he boasted suggests that he had developed something of a professional pride in his mastery of the act of betrayal:

> There's a Walk in the upper Moorfields, by the Side of the Wall that
> joins to the Watch-house and parts the upper Field from the middle.
> I knew this to be a Place that Sodomites frequented, and was well
> acquainted with the Methods they took in picking one another up. So
> I takes a Turn that Way, and leaning over the Wall, the prisoner passes
> by, and looks at me and at a little Distance from me, he stands up
> against the Wall as if he was making Water, then he moves higher and
> higher to where I stood till he came close to me. – 'Tis a fine Night
> says he, Aye, says I, so it is. Then he takes me by the Hand, and (I
> shewing no dislike) he guides it to his Breeches, and puts his Privities
> into it. I held him fast, and call'd out to my Companions, who coming
> up we carry'd him to the Watch-house.

The cunning Newton, worried that some members of the jury might be shocked by this blatant act of entrapment, hastened to reassure them that the prisoner was no random passer-by but someone he had seen 'before at the house of Thomas Wright, who was hang'd for Sodomy'. Willis and Stevenson told the court that the prisoner, when asked why he had made such an offer to Newton, 'stated that he thought it no crime in making what use I please of my own body'. This was a brave answer with which most sentient people in London during the 1720s must surely have agreed, in private at least. But by the time of his trial Brown had decide to take a position that was more cautious and did not challenge the Christian orthodoxy that homosexuality – like other illicit sexual behaviour – was a sin calculated to excite the wrath of God against His people.

Instead of again asserting his right to the free use of his own body, Brown merely told the court that while 'going across the Fields he stood up only to make Water, at which Time, Newton came and seiz'd him'. Brown also called a number of 'Men and Women to his Reputation who depos'd that he had been married 12 or 13 Years, had the Character of an honest Man, [and] a kind Husband'. But the jury, rather than displaying a hearty contempt for Newton and rejecting his seemingly manufactured and clearly unsafe evidence, took his word against Brown and found the defendant guilty.

Next up was Margaret Clap, and her trial opened with evidence from the ubiquitous undercover agent and constable Samuel Stevens, who had given damning evidence at the April trials of Gabriel Lawrence and William Griffin and earlier in the current Sessions against Mackintosh and Brown. From the start it was clear that this was to be the show trial for the 'Reformation' societies, who at last had the great 'She-Devil' in their hands and at their mercy. Stevens told the court that on the night of Sunday 14 November:

> I went to the Prisoners House in Field-Lane, Holbourn [and] found near Fifty Men there, making Love to one another as they call'd it. Sometimes they'd sit in one anothers Laps, use their Hands indecently, Dance and make Curtsies and mimick the Language of Women – O Sir! – Pray Sir! – Dear Sir! Lord how can ye serve me so! Ah ye little dear Toad! Then they'd go by Couples, into a Room on the same Floor to be marry'd as they call'd it. The Door at that Room was kept by Ecclestone to prevent any body from balking their Diversions. When they came out, they used to brag in plain Terms, of what they had been doing, and the Prisoner was present all the Time, except when she went out to fetch Liquors. There was Griffin among them, who was since hang'd for Sodomy.

Having created this powerful, almost theatrical, image of depravity and criminality, Stevens – in this case the main rather than a supporting witness – now set out to implicate Margaret Clap more fully in proceedings taking place within her establishment. Stevens wanted to establish that she didn't just witness the crimes of her customers but actively participated in them. In an attempt to do this he referred to a conversation that he claimed to have overheard in which Margaret Clap boasted that she had helped one of her customers, a man named Darwin, baffle a magistrate and get off a charge of 'Sodomitical Practices with a link boy'. As evidence against Clap this unsubstantiated accusation of perjury was small beer indeed, little more than hearsay. But that was all Stevens had to say about her direct involvement in the criminal acts that allegedly took place in her Molly House. Instead of providing more detail he returned to generalities: 'I went thither two or three Sundays following, and found much the same Practices as before. They talk'd all manner of the most vile Obscenity in her Presence, and she appear'd wonderfully pleas'd with it.'

Stevens' very general and emotive 'evidence' was supported by ace *agent provocateur* Joseph Sellers, who had also entered Clap's establishment in the guise of a client, for he 'depos'd to the same Purpose and added he believ'd there were above 40 Sodomies committed that Night'. Quite how he made this calculation Sellers did not reveal.

One of the most striking things in all the Mother Clap trials of 1726 is that none of the defendants had a lawyer to represent them in court or, presumably, to advise them on their defence, to cross-question prosecution witnesses or to challenge the validity of prosecution cases that were often based largely on an *agent provocateur*'s ability to trap their prey into incriminating themselves. No one made the basic point: if the *agent provocateur* had not been present then, in several cases, no crime would have been committed. The defence seems to have been left entirely to the defendants themselves, who, frightened and ignorant of the law, fell back on the simple tactics of denial, of counter-accusing their accusers and offering character witnesses.

Left to her own wit and devices Margaret Clap made but a poor advocate for her cause. In her defence she told the court that the Darwin conversation 'was taken up only for a Quarrel' – that it was a bit of fun and banter and not to be taken too seriously – and that the court should 'consider' that as a woman 'it could not be thought that she would ever be concern'd in such abominable Practices' as buggery. Margaret Clap's defence may not have been skilful but it still seems extraordinary that the jury found Stevens' highly charged and emotive evidence, in which opinion was mixed with apparent facts, 'full and positive' and decided that Margaret Clap was guilty as charged.

She was duly fined 20 marks (a mark was an ancient term for two-thirds of a pound, or 13 shillings and 4 pence), sentenced to a term of two years' imprisonment and ordered to undergo the ordeal of the pillory.[28] She was to be exposed in Smithfield, a location near her Field Lane home, and so was condemned to be humiliated in the eyes of her neighbours and probably injured, possibly mutilated or even killed, at the hands of the mob. Martin Mackintosh and William Brown were each fined 10 marks, imprisoned for a year and ordered to stand in the pillory – Mackintosh near Bloomsbury Square and Brown in Moorfields.

The three prisoners must have been terrified of what lay in store, but it seems that the public did not share the moral outrage of organisations such as the Society for the Reformation of Manners which had orchestrated Margaret Clap's downfall. There is no evidence that Margaret Clap, Mackintosh or Brown were harmed in any significant way by the mob – no doubt a reflection of public attitude at the time both to the crimes these people were found guilty of and the manner in which they were arrested and tried. It would appear that Londoners had by now realised there was a witch-hunt underway – with prosecutions being achieved through the use of wretched informers and cunning undercover agents – and they made it clear that they didn't approve.

The judicial mood duly changed. The persecution and killing of the first half of 1726 was not repeated. There were only two further trials of homosexuals at the Old Bailey that year and no more executions, and during all of 1727 only three sodomy-related trials took place there and no executions, even though one trial ended with two men being found guilty of committing sodomy in the porch of Stepney parish church.[29] Rather than suffering execution, the convicted men were imprisoned and exposed in the pillory. In 1728 there was only one sodomy trial, which did end in execution, and in 1729 two trials which both ended in not guilty verdicts.

The legal records of these last years of the 1720s are typical of the decades that followed. No doubt the trials of April 1726, with their revelations about the deadly roles of informers and *agents provocateurs*, sent a chill through London's homosexual community, drove it underground and made it far more cautious. That could explain why prosecutions declined dramatically during the second half of the 1720s. But convictions also declined, as did the activities of informers and undercover agents. It seems that the persecution, pursuit and savage execution of homosexuals was suddenly off the agenda. The 'Reformation' societies were seen to have gone too far; their unprincipled actions provoked public revulsion and they lost not just the respect of Londoners but also official support. As we have seen, this attitude is reflected in Hogarth's *Harlot's Progress* where, among the many people and institutions singled out for rebuke, is the magistrate Sir John Gonson, a leading member of the Society for the Reformation of Manners, presented by Hogarth as an absurd if sinister hypocrite.

The more tolerant attitude to homosexuals that was seemingly provoked by, and prevailed after, the bloody excesses of 1726, is hinted at in an Old Bailey trial that took place on 4 December 1730.[30] Two men were indicted: William Hollywell for 'an assault with an intent to commit the detestable crime of buggery' and William Huggins 'for consenting and submitting to the same'. The circumstances surrounding the charge and the trial are remarkable and revealing. A man called John Rowden gave evidence. He stated that it had long been his business 'to show the upper part of the Cathedral of St Paul' and that 'betwixt 12 and 1 O'Clock' when he was going to dinner he . . .

> . . . heard some persons that seem'd to be coming up softly, he hearken'd, but heard no Voices, that suspecting something more than usual, he look'd through the Light of the Newel Stairs, he being about 30 or 40 Steps from the Prisoners, and did discover the Prisoners in very indecent Postures, whereupon he made haste to them, and surpriz'd them in the following Posture; Huggins's Breeches were down, he stooping very low, so that he could not see his Head, his Shirt was turn'd up on his Back, and his Back-side was bare; Hollywell was standing close by, with his fore Parts to the other's Posteriors, and his Body in Motion, but his fore Parts he could not then see, his Back being towards him.

No sooner had Rowden discovered the pair of horribly compromised men than they discovered him. This, naturally, caused immediate and utter confusion. As Rowden deposed: 'Huggins was busy'd in putting up his Breeches, and Hollywell struggled with him to have got from him, and to have gone off, and tore his Turnover, but he having disengag'd himself, Hollywell got to the Church Door, but could not get out, it being Lock'd.' Rowden retreated from the scene and, after locking the pair in the side-aisle, rushed to tell the Clerk of Works and the Dean about his discovery. When the party returned to the scene Hollywell was not to be found. He had tried to escape, seemingly confirming that a crime had taken place with Hollywell in the more dangerous position, since he had apparently been caught in the act of penetrating Huggins. In contrast the other man, it would appear, awaited the arrival of the Cathedral officials. Presumably, as the passive partner in the affair, he felt relatively safe. In this he was mistaken.

He was arrested and a search launched for Holywell, who after 'a considerable time . . . was found hidden in a gallery adjoining to the Organ-loft'. Both men were carried to the Justice where 'Hollywell's shirt was examin'd' and what 'appear'd plain Tokens of Emission' were discovered. This piece of evidence, humiliating as its detection may have been, was to help save his life. When the trial opened Huggins called many character witnesses who confirmed he was a 'loving husband' with children and a regular church-goer, while Hollywell called not 'one single evidence to his character'. Both were found guilty but neither was executed.

Despite Rowden's explicit description of the men locked together with Huggins bent over and naked from the waist down, the court in its tolerance and wisdom gave the prisoners the benefit of the doubt and decided that they had not committed sodomy. It chose to take the 'Tokens of Emission' found on Hollywell's shirt as evidence that he had ejaculated outside Huggins' body. Penetration had not therefore taken place, so technically the crime was the misdemeanour of assault rather than the capital felony of sodomy. This meant that rather than being executed each man was fined, imprisoned and placed in the pillory. A tough enough punishment but, with luck, bearable.

If the court in April 1726 had shown such common sense and inclination towards mercy then the executions of Wright, Lawrence, Griffin and Kedear would not have taken place. But then again, it was probably public reaction to the unethical nature of their trials and brutal deaths that led courts subsequently to display more tolerance and mercy in such cases. The very public sacrifice of three lives may well, during the following decades, have saved the lives of many men who had the misfortune to find their sexual inclinations fatally at odds with the wayward and hypocritical morality of the age.

But the spectre of homosexual persecution, if assuaged by this case, was not obliterated. During the Napoleonic Wars there appears to have been a crisis of confidence in the virility and war-like capacities of the current generation of Britons. It is referred to, obliquely and wittily, by Jane Austen in 1814 in *Mansfield Park* where a character talks about the ranks of admirals in the Royal Navy and observes, 'of Rears, and Vices, I saw enough'.[31] Jane Austen knew all about sodomy because her brother Frank had served on a Royal Navy ship that became embroiled in a homosexual scandal which ended with a court martial.[32]

Public concern about creeping effeminacy in the armed forces came to a head in July 1810 with the scandal of the 'Vere Street coterie' when, in a Bow Street Runners raid on a Molly House called the White Swan, twenty-seven men were arrested for sodomy and attempted sodomy. Eventually eight of the accused were convicted, six for attempted sodomy which resulted in them being exposed and savagely assaulted in the pillory, and two for sodomy which led to their execution in March 1811. One of the victims, Thomas White, was a sixteen-year-old drummer boy who had not even been present in the Molly House during the raid.[33]

FOUR

FACTS AND FANTASIES

Moll King and Betsy Careless

Moll King and Betsy Careless were two of the most extraordinary and compelling female figures of the London sex trade during the first half of the eighteenth century. They were both criminals at times and both businesswomen; they both enjoyed the high life and low company, and united the world of prostitution with that of the arts. The life of Moll King in particular demonstrated the way that wealth acquired through crime and sex fuelled the construction of Georgian London. Both women knew and were known – or at least mentioned – by a wide circle of prominent Londoners including Daniel Defoe, William Hogarth, Henry Fielding and Tobias Smollett. And both of them occupied a place somewhere between fact and fantasy in the popular imagination, with Moll King in particular achieving almost legendary status, with a fantastic story that almost defines the age.

Although a famous character in the history of Georgian London, the facts of Moll King's life remain shadowy. She seems at times to be almost a composite or partly apocryphal figure, one who reflected the lives of many others through the power of story-telling and urban gossip. According to Gerald Howson in his 1970 book about Jonathan Wild, *Thief-Taker General*, there were at least two well-known Moll Kings operating within early-eighteenth-century London's low-life, both of whom confused matters further by using aliases. There was the Moll King married to or living with Tom King, who ran a famed Covent Garden coffee house (see page 8), and the Moll King who was an associate of Jonathan Wild and a notorious pick-pocket, and arguably the model for Daniel Defoe's *Moll Flanders*, published in early 1723.

Taken from Life in Newgate

The famous Moll Flanders, *of beauty the toast,*
Belov'd and distinguish'd, long flourish'd the toast;
But beauty is frail and soon comes to decay,
When shift and contrivance must enter in play;
Her arts of intrigue, as this book shall unfold,
Will keep you awake while her story is told.

The claim made of this engraving of Moll Flanders (1722) is that it is a portrait of Moll when she was in Newgate Prison, the idea being to persuade readers of Defoe's book that she was a real person. Though, of course, fictional, she seems to have been inspired in part by the true-life adventures of Moll King.

Howson may be right or he may be wrong. His conclusion is based on sound research and probability – notably the number of times pickpocket Moll was sentenced to transportation to America during the 1720s, making it hard to imagine how she could also have managed a coffee house. But she may not actually have made all the trips that records suggest and, of course, Moll or more properly Mary King was a common name in late-seventeenth- and eighteenth-century London. It is now impossible to be sure how many individual women each named Mary or Moll King may or may not have shuttled between London and America during the 1720s. (To add to the confusion there is even current speculation that one Moll was actually born Elizabeth Adkins.) To confirm his point Howson observes that 'between 1697 and 1713 eleven women called Mary King were indicted of various offences at Middlesex Sessions alone'.[1]

In the end, the case for there being two infamous Moll Kings is no more than informed speculation. Certainly there are no contemporary references to there being two equally notorious Moll Kings living at the same time, in the same sphere of society, and a number that imply there was only one. Indeed, Howson himself refers to a documented court case of 1691 that mentions a Moll King being indicted for theft, along with Tom King, but acquitted.[2] So here, it seems, are united Moll the thief and Moll the partner of Tom King, coffee-house proprietor. Confusingly, though, the date here is far earlier than other references. In the end there is just not enough incontrovertible evidence to prove the point conclusively. But, the transportation issue aside, the information available can be ordered to make the life history of one extraordinary woman who started as a street trader, prostitute and thief, became the owner of a popular and money-making coffee house, and ended her days as a well-to-do house builder and property owner, living comfortably on Haverstock Hill in Hampstead.

Some background information appears in an anonymously written pamphlet of dubious authenticity. Entitled *The Life and Character of Moll King, late Mistress of King's Coffee House in Covent Garden*,[3] it appears to have been published soon after her death in 1747.[4] *The Life and Character* states that Moll was born in 1696, 'in a Garret in Vine Street', in the impoverished area of St Giles-in-the-Fields, although of course Howson's 1691 court reference suggests that Moll King must have been born at least twenty years earlier. She was the daughter of a shoemaker and a mother who 'sold Fruit, Fish and Greens about Streets', and the pamphlet states that Moll went into service but 'being tolerably handsome and very sprightly' could 'not brook Confinement within Doors'.[5] So Moll returned to the streets – initially to sell fruit rather than herself – but like many of her more spirited fellow servants and street-vendors who wanted money and some excitement, she soon entered the sex industry.

According to *The Life and Character* Moll had 'several Sweethearts before she was 14 Years old' when she married a fallen gentleman named Thomas King, known as 'Smooth'd-Fac'd-Tom', but this romance came to an end after 'some years together' when Moll was seduced by a man called Murray, 'who is now in a very high station in one of the Publick Offices'. This relationship also faltered and Moll 'shar'd her Favours' and so became one of 'the gayest Ladies of the Town' and friend of the then great courtesan and 'Toast of the Town' Sally Salisbury (see page 100).

Unlike many of her prostitute colleagues, Moll displayed 'very good natural sense . . . and [was] remarkably sober . . . and whilst she saw the Town Ladies get dead drunk with their Sparks, she took care to keep herself cool, that she might make her Property of both the Gentlemen and their Misses'.[6] If this chronology and biography is broadly correct then it must have been at about this period, between 1715 and 1720, that cool-headed and calculating Moll became associated with the notorious racketeer, gangster and 'thief-taker' Jonathan Wild, although *The Life and Character* makes a point of stating that Moll 'was never a common or reputed Pick-pocket'. This bold statement seems to be contradicted by the description of her acquiring the 'Property' of drunken 'Gentlemen and their Misses'. Perhaps the point being made is that Moll was an uncommon pick-pocket.

It may also have been at this period that she started to use various aliases – notably Mary or Maria Godson – and when she returned to Tom, then 'a waiter at a bawdy-house in Covent Garden', the pair started a stall in Covent Garden selling nuts.[7] It proved a financial success, some money was saved, and soon the couple took 'a little House, or rather Hovel, in Covent-Garden Market to sell . . . Coffee at a Penny a Dish . . . and Tea and Chocolate in Proportion . . . for the Market People'.[8] Business prospered so they also rented the two houses adjoining but even then 'had scarcely Room to accommodate their Customers'.[9]

To serve the market workers Moll and Tom were obliged to open at one or two in the morning, 'and as that part of the Town is remarkable for the Rendezvous of young Rakes and their pretty Misses' the coffee house became 'a very proper Office to meet at, to consult of their nocturnal Intrigues' and soon 'became so very famous for nightly Revels . . . that it got the Name of a College and it was frequent amongst the Players and witty Beaux to accost each other, with, *Are you for* King's College *to Night, to have a Dish of Flash with Moll?*'[10] The poet Edward Thompson states that 'noblemen and the first beaux of the Court would go to [Moll's] place in full dress with swords and bags and in rich brocaded coats, and walked and conversed with persons of every description'.[11]

The fact that the coffee house was named after Tom might be significant and suggest that, at this early stage, Moll not only worked there but also pursued a profitable parallel life and trade as Moll King the pick-pocket and, in the manner of her associate Jonathan Wild, Moll King the loan shark. *The Life and Character* hints as much. It explains that Moll 'had a great many of the poor Females under her Thumb ... because she lent them Money at a high Interest'. But she seems to have played a parody of Robin Hood, taking maximum profit only from those who could afford to pay up. To 'the poor sort of Market People in the Neighbourhood' Moll lent money at a lower rate than to the 'Town Misses' who were 'obliged to pay dearer' because Moll 'made a great Distinction between Industry and Vice'.[12]

Moll King appeared on the public scene in 1723 in a sensational little publication entitled *The Life of Captain John Stanley*,[13] which, according to Howson, was probably written by the Ordinary or Chaplain of Newgate Gaol, Reverend Putney.[14] Stanley was hanged in 1723 for murdering his mistress but about five years earlier had been, according to this biography, intimate with Moll.

Stanley was born in 1701. By 1718 he was a handsome young man who sought to make his way in the world by using his charm and looks to live off rich women. Like many swaggering young fellows of the time who survived by their wits and were ready to settle debts and insults with a duel, he termed himself 'Captain'. One of his haunts was St Anne's Church, Soho, built in noble style during the 1680s to the designs of Sir Christopher Wren and William Talman. In the early eighteenth century it was a popular gathering place for the rich and fashionable, including some young 'Madams [who] pray in their Paint, and see their Heaven in Man'.[15]

Captain Stanley went to St Anne's to prey on these flighty and distracted young women – and so did Moll. Stanley had designs on their fortunes and persons; Moll merely wanted their gold watches. As the *Life of Captain John Stanley* relates, Moll, married at the time and 'well known for her Dexterity in borrowing Gold Watches or Snuff Boxes from Ladies', would sit in a pew next to her victim and skilfully rob them 'by means of false Hands which lay demurely before her, while her true were busy elsewhere'.[16] The use of false hands, presumably gloved, as a decoy seems to have been a recognised ploy among more skilled and nerveless pick-pockets and was made famous a couple of years later by the notorious female criminal Jenny Diver (see page 332).

The *Life* tells a picaresque tale about the way in which Moll and Stanley met. She spied him in St Anne's, took a fancy to his looks, and decided to use her skills to strike up an acquaintance. She stole his watch, replaced it with a gold box of twice its value, and then told him she knew the woman who'd taken his watch and where she could be found. The pair then went to a tavern and, while there, Moll accused Stanley publicly of stealing her gold box. She described it to the interested onlookers, who then searched him and found it. He was at her mercy. If she chose to prosecute, he would probably hang. But instead Moll desired that all should withdraw and then 'threw herself about his Kneck and embracing him, declared how long how much she lov'd; and instead of his being made a Prisoner, own'd herself a Captive to his Beauty'.[17]

For a while they were inseparable and 'she was a perfect Venus, and he as Adequate an Adonis [as] Love darted from her Eyes to snatch the Beauty that dwelt in his'. This might all seem a little irregular since Stanley was less than eighteen and Moll, by one calculation, would have been nearly fifty. But if this was indeed her age then young Stanley, clearly a canny chap, realised he could learn a lot from Moll. In addition he may have shared the civilised view, expressed later by Lord Chesterfield and Benjamin Franklin, of the advantages to a young man of having intercourse with older women. As Franklin put it:

> . . . they have more knowledge of the world and their minds are better
> stored with observation [while] covering all above with a basket, and
> regarding only what is below the girdle, it is impossible of two women
> to know an old from a young one . . . and lastly, they are so grateful.[18]

The affair between this ill-matched couple seems to have ended quickly and abruptly when Moll was 'apprehended', convicted at the Old Bailey and 'afterwards Transported'.[19]

Tom King remains an even more mysterious figure than his wife. By repute he was born in 1694, either at Thurlow, Essex or West Ashton, Wiltshire,[20] came from a good family and had been well educated at Eton and King's College, Cambridge.[21] In Moll's *Life* Tom is referred to as a 'fallen gentleman'. How or when he fell is not revealed; presumably he was a dissolute character who slipped down the social ladder. Tom and

Moll perhaps married in 1710 – although more likely after he left Cambridge in 1713, as her *Life* states. She certainly took his name but it was common practice for a whore to adopt the surname of her current protector. When she and Tom parted, the 'Murray' mentioned in her *Life*, whose mistress she became, is alleged to have been William Murray, who later became the Earl of Mansfield and Lord Chief Justice, but he would have been only thirteen years old in 1718 so this seems fairly unlikely. When her relationship ended with Murray – whoever he may have been – Moll perhaps continued her career as pick-pocket, and became a pawn in the complex criminal games being played by Jonathan Wild, but seems at about this time to have become reconciled with her husband.

The argument that Moll King was the inspiration for Moll Flanders is supported by the fact that Defoe knew her – at least by reputation – and wrote about her. Moll appears as herself in one of Defoe's more factual works in which he reveals how she fell foul of the 'thief-taker' Jonathan Wild. In his *True and Genuine Account of the Life and Actions of the Late Jonathan Wild*, published in 1725, Moll features as a common pick-pocket. Defoe's account reveals Wild's cunning working methods.

By this date, round about 1720, Wild had acquired a public reputation as a man who could trace stolen goods. For a sum paid to an anonymous messenger, and no questions asked, the property could be regained. The deception that Wild practised was that, through his activities as a 'thief-taker', he had gained a deep knowledge of the criminal underworld, could probably identify the thief and, using threats, get them to return the stolen items for a price. The reality was very different. Wild was, in the end, commissioning the crimes, running the thieves, receiving the stolen property, and then, rather than taking the risk of selling it to a fence, would sell it back to the victim (under the pretence of doing them a service) while also accepting a finder's commission. The proceeds he would split with the thieves who, if they didn't like their cut, Wild would threaten with, and on occasion deliver to, the law and thus execution.

In Defoe's account, a woman who has been robbed goes to see Wild and asks him to help her regain a watch and other 'trinkets' stolen at 'St Ann's Church, Westminster' [presumably Soho]. On hearing this, Defoe recounts that 'Wild asked a servant, "Where was M-ll K--g last Sunday?" "About Westminster," says the man, "but the bi--h would not tell where." Wild then told the lady, "Madam, I fancy I shall be able to serve you . . . If it be M-ll K--g , that woman I have in my thoughts, as I believe 'tis, for she is a dexterous jade at her work. I'll have her safe before morning."' The lady, who had said she would pay up to £30 for the return of her stolen goods, was alarmed by Wild's threatening tone and cried, "'O sir! Don't take her up. I assure you I won't prosecute. I'll rather lose my watch than have any poor wretch hanged for it." "Why, madam," says Mr Wild, "we can't talk with her but by threatening. We must not make a bargain with her, that would be to compound a felony."' The stolen goods were duly returned to the lady, via a porter who stopped her in the street, and she paid 18 guineas for them and then a 'gift' of another 15 guineas to Wild for his trouble and services. And as Defoe observed, '. . . 'twas very likely (he) had part of the 18 guineas too from M-ll K--g , who he frighted out of the watch with threatening to have her put into Newgate for stealing of it'.

Defoe's story appears to be based on fact even if not entirely accurate in its details. As Howson explains, Moll King was caught on 18 October 1718 stealing two gold watches in St Anne's Church, Soho, and in December was tried under the name of Mary Goldstone and sentenced to death.[22] She 'pleaded her belly', was confirmed as pregnant by a panel of matrons, and her sentence commuted to fourteen years' transportation. She remained in Newgate until early 1720 and then, after giving birth, was transported to America. What happened to her next is hazy and open to interpretation. Howson's researches suggest she was transported to Annapolis on 23 April 1720 under the name of Mary Gilstone[23] but immediately returned illegally, which was a capital crime. The *Weekly Journal or Saturday's Post* (of which Defoe was part-editor under Nathaniel Mist) reported on 2 July: 'One Mrs King, an old Pick-Pocket and Shop-lifter, who about a twelve month ago was transported to the English Plantations in America, for Seven Years, has found means to come back again, after whom diligent Search is made by them that prosecuted her, that she may be apprehended and brought to Justice.'[24]

Moll was soon caught and sentenced to death, again, yet for some unknown reason was a second time reprieved and instead incarcerated in Newgate. It is likely that Wild saved her, but at a price. Moll was in his debt, once again within his power, and she had to work for him – not just as a thief but 'peaching' those of his troublesome or rebellious gang members he wanted rid of.

When released she seems to have thieved under Wild's 'protection' and for his benefit until caught on 14 June 1721 robbing a house in Little Russell Street, Covent Garden. She was committed to Newgate and the event was reported in the *Daily Journal* of 17 June 1721 (to which Defoe was also connected): 'On Friday, Moll King, one of the most notorious Pickpockets of the Town, and eminently famous for assisting in Stealing Watches at Ladies' sides at Church, was again committed to her old Mansion House, Newgate.'[25] On her indictment Moll was called Mary Godson, alias Bird, alias King. At the same time she was pursued for returning from transportation. For this and the robbery Moll was, in July 1721, once again sentenced to penal servitude in Newgate with a 'reward' for her arrest going to Wild.[26] So it seems Wild turned her in for money. Or perhaps he did more. It's likely he arranged her acquittal for the robbery and, again, her capital conviction for returning from transportation was commuted to a period in Newgate where she was to stay at the 'pleasure' of the authorities. All this was probably done by him to punish and frighten Moll, to keep her and his troublesome gang members under control by demonstrating his influence within the processes of the law.

It was probably during this time that Daniel Defoe met Moll in Newgate while visiting his friend Nathaniel Mist, who was held there from 19 June 1721 until the following September. If inspired then by Moll's history, Defoe transformed it into a moral tale very quickly for *Moll Flanders* was published in January 1722. At the end of the same month the real Moll was transported to Annapolis but seems, once again, speedily to have absconded back to London where she was as rapidly rearrested.[27] This was reported in the *Daily Journal* of 20 September 1722 and *Saturday's Post* of 22 September: 'Moll King, a most notorious offender, famous for stealing Gold watches from Ladies' Sides in the Churches, for which she has been several Times convicted, being lately returned from Transportation, has been taken and is committed to Newgate'.[28] Moll was held for many months at Newgate while the transportation agent responsible for prosecuting her repeatedly failed to appear. Again this was probably Wild's doing but she appears to have been sent back to Annapolis where she arrived in 1723 and then finally disappears.

Perhaps she managed to return to London once more and this time succeeded in melting into the teeming life of the metropolis, helped by the anonymity of her common name and the fact that she was known by so many aliases – at least a dozen according to Howson, including Godm.. Golston, Golstone, Gilstone, Goulston, Gouldstone, Gouldston, Godfrey, Godson and Bird. If these names do truly represent one woman and all the sentences for transportation were in fact carried out, then Howson calculates Moll crossed the Atlantic an incredible eleven times after 1720.[29] The unlikelihood of this being the case confirms that the sparse, incomplete and inconclusive evidence that may or may not relate to Moll's life has to be interpreted with extreme caution.

If Moll did indeed return to London in late 1723 or 1724 and evade recapture she might well have been assisted by the fact that Wild by then had serious troubles of his own and was not in a position to threaten, bully or turn her in for reward money. If this was the case then Wild's arrest for theft, followed by the dramatic exposure of his many crimes by his long-suffering gang members and his execution in May 1725, would have come as a great liberation for Moll. She would finally have been free from a very dangerous adversary and able to concentrate on the Covent Garden coffee shop that is first documented in 1732.[30] As the establishment became well known and Moll's name familiar she must, if she had returned illegally from transportation, have feared arrest. Having the shop in the name of Tom King and her own string of aliases would, of course, have helped cover her tracks, but it's also possible that it was at this time Moll herself laid the seeds of the later confusion about her identity by creating a false life history that suggested there were several contemporary Moll Kings.

Things must have become particularly difficult for her when the riotous behaviour of customers – mostly rakes, prostitutes and their bullies or culls – became so notorious that it attracted the attention of the reforming magistrate Sir John Gonson and the Society for the Reformation of Manners. They wanted to suppress the establishment and so sent in under-cover agents in an attempt to collect evidence to have the place closed and Moll arrested for keeping a disorderly house. To minimise the amount of legally useful evidence these spies could collect Moll developed an argot – 'talking flash' – so that she, her staff and initiated customers could not be understood by strangers.

The Life and Character describes the coffee house at the peak of its fame – or infamy: it was a place of 'nightly Revels, and for Company of all Sorts' where 'Every Swain, even from the Star and Garter (grandees) to the Coffee-House boy, might be sure of finding a Nymph in waiting

[and] here you might see Ladies of pleasure, who appear'd apparelled like Persons of Quality . . . attended by Fellows habited like Footmen, who were their Bullies, and wore their Disguise, the more easily to deceive the unwary Youths, who were so unhappy as to Cast their Eyes upon these *deceitful water-Wag-Tails*.'[31]

George Alexander Stevens also described the Long Room at about the same time: '[Y]ou might see grave-looking Men, half mizzy-ey'd, eyeing askance a poor supperless Strumpet asleep on a Bench, her ragg'd Handkerchief fallen exposing her bare bosom on which the old Lechers were doating.'[32]

The Life and Character contains an example of Moll's 'flash dialogue' and a 'key' to its meaning which makes it clear that she pioneered early-nineteenth-century East London underworld slang, incorporating words and phrases that were to become common street language. For example, one of her customers tells her to 'tip the Meg [a half-penny] to the Kinchin [little child]' which sounds like a line straight out of *Oliver Twist*. Other words and phrases are familiar too. The customer asks Moll, 'Does Jack doss in your Pad now?' which, using Jack as a generic term for man – as in John Doe – means, is a man of Moll's acquaintance sleeping in her bed? Other familiar words are 'Ken' meaning house, 'Buttock' meaning whore, 'Rum' meaning good-natured, 'Old Codger' meaning an old man, and 'Day-Lights' meaning eyes.[33]

Tom King died in or soon before 1739, and on 24 May the same year Moll was charged with keeping a disorderly house following a riot in and around her premises.[34] Lillywhite states that 'Moll King, Mistress of Tom's Coffee House Covent Garden was brought to the King's bench to receive judgement, when the Court committed her to the King's Bench Prison, Southwark, till they took time to consider of a punishment adequate to the offence of keeping a disorderly house.'

The Life and Character describes, in part, the legal battles in which Moll appears to have become embroiled in her latter years. It mentions her being found guilty of attacking a customer and that she was sentenced to pay 'a fine of Two Hundred Pounds . . . and to be committed to the Prison of the King's-Bench until the said Fine was paid', but that she refused to pay, arguing that if she was obliged 'to pay Two Hundred Pounds to all the insolent Boys she had thrash'd for their Impudence, the Bank of England would be unable to furnish her with cash'.[35]

The Life and Character also mentions her continued persecution by Sir John Gonson, who was 'indefatigable in paying her nocturnal Visits' but whom 'she generally found out some way or other to pacify'. Some sources say Moll was confined in the King's Bench for three months, but Howson notes a record he discovered stating that 'Mary King, Wife of Tom King' was transported in 1734. Was she really sentenced to transportation again, perhaps aged sixty-four? Was it even the same Moll? Or was she in fact aged only thirty-eight then and not actually transported at all?[36]

In 1738 or 1739 Tom or Moll purchased land – 'an estate' according to *The Life and Character* – on Haverstock Hill, along the east side of the road to Hampstead, at the junction with what is now Steele's Road. Here they or she built three or four terrace houses and perhaps a small detached house – 'a very genteel Country-House' as *The Life and Character* would have it,[37] while *Nocturnal Revels* merely states that 'she built a row of houses on the road near Hampstead'.[38]

This was a typical example of the way in which the sex industry contributed to the expansion of Georgian London and ploughed its profits back into the wider economy. These houses were speculations, built to let, except for one, said to have been a 'villa', that was occupied by Moll in around 1745.[39] The houses were known until 1888 as 'Moll King's Row' and are apparently shown on Rocque's London map of 1746, among a cluster of buildings near Chalk Farm, isolated on a then still rural road.

Intriguingly, the same row is shown in the far distance in Hogarth's *March to Finchley*, painted in 1750. Was the artist making a covert point about the mores of the age? On the right of the painting he shows Mother Douglas' brothel, with poetic licence transported from the Covent Garden Piazza to Tottenham Court Road, with its delightful young women disporting themselves in front of the troops; in the crowd prostitutes mix with soldiers lumbering off to meet the threat from the north; and in the distance, on their line of march, lurks the residence of the woman many considered to have done much to undermine the morals of London.

Moll's houses still survive, although now utterly disregarded and much rebuilt during the nineteenth century. But in their heyday this little cluster of buildings housed a fascinating microcosm of characters interested, in varied ways, in London's sex industry. There was Moll herself – then living with her second husband, 'Mr Hoff', in the villa. Opposite was the

The March to Finchley *by Hogarth (1750). For the purposes
of the picture, the house on the right, showing the occupants of
Mother Douglas' brothel, has been transported from Covent*

cottage in which Richard Steele, the *Spectator* essayist and apologist for the
whore, had lived until 1719 when he moved to Wales. Next door to Moll,
in one of the houses she had built, resided the one-time prostitute Nancy
Dawson, who became famous thanks to the lascivious horn-pipe she
danced in *The Beggar's Opera* (see page 331).[40] It was in this house on
Haverstock Hill that Moll died in 1747, aged either fifty-one or seventy-

Garden to Tottenham Court Road. In the far distance is 'Moll King's Row' on Haverstock Hill, leading to Hampstead.

seven. The event is commemorated in the long title of *The Life and Character of Moll King*, which states that she 'departed this life at her Country-House at Hampstead on Thursday the 17th September 1747'.

Years later, in 1779, she was offered an obituary of sorts in the anonymously written *Nocturnal Revels*, which states that she made a huge fortune from the 'follies, vices and profligacy of the age',[41] and that 'before the modern institution of Nunneries [well-managed brothels], the chief scene of action for promiscuous amours lay in the vicinity of Covent-Garden' with 'Moll King's in the centre of Covent-Garden' being notable for 'nocturnal revels' and as a 'rendezvous' and 'a great receptacle for Rakes and Prostitutes of every rank'.[42]

As late as 1828, when J. T. Smith published his rambling memoirs of life in late-Georgian London, Moll King was still remembered as one of the characters who had made Covent Garden 'the hot-bed' of the 'principal ... vices'.[43] Until the end of her life, and indeed long after, Moll remained a legendary and chimerical figure. Like Macheath in *The Beggar's Opera*, she is the quintessential outlaw, embodying those characteristics – audacity, independence, resilience and sexual power – that her own age simultaneously feared, admired and expected to find in its anti-heroes, living in a world free from the shackles of convention.[44]

BETSY CARELESS

Betsy Careless flamed bright in early-Georgian Covent Garden for a brief period but left an indelible impression, becoming part of the folk culture of the capital, commemorated in its verse, prose and painting. She was at once Beauty and the Beast, the epitome of glorious and reckless freedom – an independent but doomed whirlwind of energy.

Decades after her death Betsy still haunted the imagination of the essayist William Hazlitt, a man who lodged near Covent Garden during the 1820s where he became unpleasantly intimate with the social consequences of unconventional sexual obsession that he revealed in his *Liber Amoris* of 1823, in which he candidly confessed to his infatuation with his landlord's young daughter.

In his essay on *Art and Literature*, Hazlitt referred to William Hogarth's *Rake's Progress* and, in particular, to the brothel or bagnio scene – supposedly set in the licentious Rose Tavern in Russell Street. He observed, '[W]itness the girl picking the Rake's pocket in the bagnio scene, whom we might suppose to be "the charming Betsy Careless", the poet's wife, handsomer than falls to the lot of most poets.'[45] Hogarth painted the *Rake's Progress* series in 1732–3 when Betsy was in her prime, so the image of the pick-pocket whore could well be her portrait. Certainly the young woman's attractive looks match written descriptions of Betsy, who seems to have possessed an angelic beauty.

The bagnio scene from A Rake's Progress *by Hogarth (1735). The girl with her hand in the rake's shirt is reputed to be a portrait of Betsy Careless. The young woman undressing on the right is a 'Posture Moll', who is about to perform, naked, on the pewter plate being brought into the room.*

The best of these was that written by Henry Fielding in the late 1740s in his novel *Amelia*, published in 1751.[46] Remembering Betsy or 'Betty' Careless in her youth in the early 1730s, when she was deceptively innocent in appearance, he wrote:

I happened in my youth to sit behind two ladies in a side-box at a
play, where, in the balcony on the opposite side was placed the inimitable
B—y C—s in company with a young fellow of no very formal or indeed
sober appearance. One of the ladies, I remember, said to the other,

93

'Did you ever see anything look so modest and so innocent as that girl over the way? What pity it is such a creature should be in the way of ruin, as I'm afraid she is by being alone with that young fellow!' Now this lady was no bad physiognomist, for it was impossible to conceive a greater Appearance of Modesty, Innocence and Simplicity, than what Nature had displayed in the Countenance of that Girl; and yet, all appearances notwithstanding, I myself (remember, Critic, it was in my youth) had a few Mornings before seen that very identical Picture of all those ingaging Qualities in Bed with a rake at a Bagnio, smoking Tobacco, drinking Punch, talking Obscenity, and swearing and cursing with all the Impudence and impiety of the lowest and most abandoned Trull of a soldier.[47]

Fielding was to have a professional relationship with Betsy, or at least with some of her more intimate companions, after he became a magistrate in 1748. By chance most of the frequent and key offenders familiar to him then are portrayed in L. P. Boitard's painting of 1739 entitled *The Covent Garden Morning Frolick*. It shows Betsy in a sedan chair that is ridden by Captain 'Mad Jack' Montagu and led by her servant and link-boy Laurence Casey. Fielding regarded Montagu, his companion Captain Laroun and Casey as 'the three most troublesome and difficult to manage of all my Bow Street visitors'.[48] Captain Laroun may have been the Dutch-born painter, former soldier, amateur actor and musician Marcellus Lauron the Younger, who documented London's low-life and ludicrous characters.

Casey was a compelling character in his own right, seemingly as wild as his mistress, and eventually sentenced to transportation to the colonies in America. His job as Betsy's link-boy was most suggestive. Link-boys were usually street urchins who, for a small sum, would escort travellers through the dark streets, lighting their way by means of a torch or link. So usual was this activity that many houses had link extinguishers – in the form of iron cones – located near their front doors. Presumably Betsy employed her own link-boy because her nocturnal excursions were so regular – and some potentially hazardous – that she required a ready, reliable and spirited companion.

By the early eighteenth century link-boys had long been part of London's criminal and sexual mythology. They were popularly supposed to work

A 1747 print of Louis Philippe Boitard's painting of 1739, The Covent
Garden Morning Frolick. *It shows Betsy Careless, after a hard night's
work, being taken home asleep in a sedan chair, on top of which sits 'Mad
Jack' Montagu. Betsy's link-boy 'Little Cazey' leads the procession.*

in cahoots with footpads and highwaymen. Ostensibly lighting a traveller
safely home, those who were criminally inclined instead led them into an
ambush, and so link-boys were simultaneously viewed as street guardians
and unholy street terrors. William Hogarth in his *Four Stages of Cruelty*
of 1751 represents this darker aspect of the link-boy when one is shown
putting out the eyes of a bird with needles heated on his link.

But thievery and cruelty were not the only evils with which link-boys
were commonly associated – they were also assumed to be readily available as child prostitutes. This is revealed in a most direct manner by the
Restoration libertine, courtier and poet Lord Rochester, who, in one of
his late-seventeenth-century works, 'The Disabled Debauchee', vies with
his mistress for the attentions of their link-boy:

> Nor shall our love-fits, Chloris, be forgot,
> When each the well-looked linkboy strove t' enjoy,
> And the best kiss was the deciding lot
> Whether the boy fucked you, or I the boy.

A link-boy, seemingly inspired by Boitard's 1739 image of 'Little Cazey' in The Covent Garden Morning Frolick.

Perhaps this association between link-boys and illicit sex was due to the obvious phallic imagery of the boy's occupation: at the climax of his journey he was obliged to quench his long, rod-like torch in an iron cone or orifice. Or perhaps it was the youth and sexual availability – for a price – of the boys engaged in this pursuit, or the frisson of danger in associating with youths who were almost invariably part of the vast and dark criminal underworld. The erotic tradition of the link-boy helps to explain the meaning of one of Sir Joshua Reynolds' 'fancy pictures' showing Cupid in the guise of a link-boy, holding a large smoking torch – a huge phallus – seemingly emerging from his groin. On his back are demonic bat-wings (see page 97).[49]

Casey preceding Betsy through the dark streets of Covent Garden with a huge flaming link could have been doing more than just lighting her way. Onlookers may have seen their progress as a ritual procession, a symbolic declaration that Betsy – the inflamer of ardent passion – was on the move. There are no contemporary accounts that cast her precisely in the role of goddess of love – or at least of sex – nor goddess of death, by afflicting her partners with fatal diseases. But she does seem to have been held responsible for depriving men of their reason – of driving them mad with desire and further demented through syphilis.

In the last scene of Hogarth's *A Rake's Progress* the hapless anti-hero is shown incarcerated among his fellow lunatics. Some inmates rave, others are melancholic – all are the object of amusement or distraction for paying

Cupid as a Link-Boy, *painted by Sir Joshua Reynolds in 1774. The boy grips a mighty flame-belching phallus and has devilish bat-wings on his back.*

visitors. On the staircase is carved 'charming Betsy Careless' – inscribed, presumably, by William Ellis, shown sitting on the staircase and described as a 'maniac' who 'lost his reason through love for his Betty'.[50] The carved inscription is clear in engravings, but now impossible to discern on the painting.

Little of Betsy's working method – or indeed of her early life – is known. It is thought she was born in about 1704 of humble parents, entered early into the sex industry, and as a young girl was 'protected' by a notoriously libertine barrister named Robert Henley. He seems to have deserted her when her behaviour became too consistently drunken and riotous. After this Betsy was never again a 'kept woman' and nor did she work with a bawd. Instead, free of spirit, she operated out of various bagnios and taverns of her own choosing, and from 1729 from a small bagnio of her own in Tavistock Row, Covent Garden. This independent method of working is implied by both Hogarth and Fielding and by one enigmatic reference in the personal papers of John Appy, who eventually became secretary and judge advocate to His Majesty's forces in North America.[51]

In his papers Appy recorded that in the 1730s he had supper at the Turk's Head – for 1/1d, was 'at Skelton's Bagnio' with Nancy Beaver for 3/-, and 'at' Betsy Careless's for 3/6d. This reference presumably referred to the cost of dining and drinking at Betsy's bagnio and was not the charge for a night with her. Or if it was then Betsy came very cheap – certainly by the 1740s the standard nightly fee for a harlot of even small renown was around two guineas. At this time Betsy's favoured companion was Sir Charles Wyndham, who, because of his rakish ways, had been ejected from the family home by his wife. But this feckless fellow, rather than keeping Betsy, was kept by her.

The last scene of A Rake's Progress *by Hogarth (1735). The rake, now insane, has been sent to Bedlam. On the staircase sits William Ellis, driven to madness by his hopeless love for 'Betty Careless' whose name he has carved on the hand-rail.*

In 1733, in an attempt to amass some money before she lost her looks and energy, Betsy took a house in the Little Piazza, Covent Garden and turned her hand to being a bawd. But this enterprise failed and in 1734 she was obliged to leave the familiar pleasure ground of Covent Garden for cheaper and less fashionable accommodation in the City. In early 1735 an advertisement appeared in the *London Journal* announcing, 'Mrs Betsy Careless from the Piazza in Covent Garden . . . in Prujean's Court in the Old Bailey where she hopes that all her friends will favour her with their company'. But the ill-situated Old Bailey was not the equal of lively Covent Garden and, it must be supposed, Betsy Careless was not the woman she had once been either. The new business foundered and Betsy, at a little over thirty years of age, paid the price for her high-spirited independence. She descended into poverty and ill-health and then disappears from history. Many books state that her death was announced in the October 1739 *Gentleman's Magazine*:

> . . . buried from the Poor-house of St Paul's, Covent Garden, the famed Betty Careless who helped gay gentlemen of this country to squander £50,000.[52]

However, I can find no such entry in the bound volumes of the *Gentleman's Magazine* in the British Library, and, in fact, there is an alternative account. The 1811 edition of the *Anecdotes of the Celebrated William Hogarth* states that in the third plate of *Marriage-à-la-Mode* the woman shown 'is said to have been designed for the celebrated Betty Careless [because] of the initials B.C. on her bosom' and then states that she 'was buried from the poor-house of St Paul's, Covent Garden on April 22, 1752'.[53] This view is supported by E. Beresford Chancellor in her *Annals of Covent Garden* of 1930, who cites as evidence the burial records of St Paul's Church.[54]

FIVE

WINNERS AND LOSERS

Sally Salisbury and Lavinia Fenton

The stories of individual prostitutes can offer penetrating insights into different aspects of Georgian London's sex industry. The life of Sally Salisbury – who became a byword for audacity and freedom of spirit, and whose life history was almost certainly one of the key inspirations for Hogarth's *Harlot's Progress* – illustrates the heavy price most women in the sex industry ultimately had to pay. At the other extreme, Lavinia Fenton's story is one of almost fantastic escape from the dire fate of abuse, disease and poverty that her upbringing as a child prostitute had seemingly preordained for her.

SALLY SALISBURY

The lives of many of the London-based real-life characters referred to by Hogarth in *The Harlot's Progress* are morality stories in their own right. None more so than that of Sally Salisbury, who, by her extravagant conduct, set the pattern for the high-spirited, high-living, quick-witted and quick-tempered eighteenth-century London courtesan. Sally's life was a dramatic series of studies in light and shade, triumph and tragedy. Of humble origin, from the street she found her way into the brothels of Covent Garden, achieved financial and social success, had a string of rich and powerful protectors then fell victim to her own uncontrolled temper, was gaoled in Newgate and died in 1724, in all likelihood of venereal disease. She was a little over thirty years old.

During her lifetime Sally was a celebrity and a London legend; after her death a warning and cautionary tale. She was in her prime in the early 1720s, the toast of the town, and for some her freedom from convention and restraint was an inspiration, a welcome challenge to authority and to the rule of hypocrisy. No doubt the young William Hogarth knew all about Sally – she was a famed London character and the first great courtesan of the new century – and admired her defiance.

Such was Sally's notoriety that biographies appeared in 1723 and 1724, when she was barely thirty. The first, entitled *The Genuine History of Mrs Sarah Prydden usually called Sally Salisbury*, included information – calculated to appeal to the salacious curiosity of the public – about a number of Sally's more famous 'Gallants', including a letter from one named Antony Bole.[1] The authorship of *The Genuine History* was anonymous, but, although written in the third person, may perhaps have in part been Sally's own work. The second biography, called *The Authentick Memoirs of the Life, Intrigues and Adventures of the Celebrated Sally Salisbury*, was credited to a man called Charles Walker and seems to have been written by the beginning of March 1724.[2] What is very clear from even a cursory glance at the two books is that one feeds off the other, suggesting one is no more than a pirated, somewhat rewritten and expanded version of the original. But which is the more 'Authentick' of the two is now hard to say and hardly matters much since both agree on the main points of the story.

Sally was born in Shrewsbury in 1692, had a father with the 'character of a very honest man' although 'continually in troubles, and the bailiffs were his well known enemies', which led the family to move to London when Sally was only four years old. The place chosen for the new family home was Parker's Lane in the Parish of St Giles – an unfortunate choice of location because St Giles had by then the reputation of a slum area and was to decline further during the first half of the eighteenth century. But presumably the Prydden family, impoverished and being pursued for debt, had little choice but to find cheap and anonymous lodgings among other poor and harassed families.

Sally's father was a bricklayer and in the 1690s the need to rebuild the City after the Great Fire of 1666 had led to a speculative building boom in which great fortunes were made. There was a huge demand for all manner of buildings – shops, churches, warehouses, manufactories and,

The Celebrated Mrs Sally Salisbury
(MRS PRIDDEN)

The extravagant courtesan Sally Salisbury, engraved here by John Smith,
was a celebrity in her day, but her early death, most likely from venereal
disease, turned her life into a cautionary moral tale.

in particular, dwelling houses – and good money to be made by those who could supply the right service at the right price and speed.

There is, however, no evidence that Sally's father benefited greatly from this boom. All we know from the biography is that the family stayed in St Giles and Sally, aged about nine, was apprenticed to a milliner in Duke's-place, Aldgate. The choice of trade and location says a lot. Duke's-place was not a fashionable street but it was a reasonably wealthy one for it was largely populated by rich Jewish City merchants of the type illustrated in painting two of Hogarth's *The Harlot's Progress*.

Milliners' and mantua-makers' shops had a poor reputation at the time. They were associated with vice, considered almost synonymous with brothels, and women working as prostitutes were regularly recorded as being mantua-makers by trade. As Alexander Pettit explains in *Eighteenth-Century British Erotica*: 'Most prostitutes who were not on the game worked as milliners, and most milliners were prostitutes, to the extent that this occupation was widely regarded as just a cover for prostitution'.[3] *Pretty Doings in a Protestant Nation* offers an 'Opinion' of 'the late Colonel Chart—s' – that is, the infamous rapist glimpsed in *The Harlot's Progress* – 'that when we caught a fine *Sempstress* or *Mantua-Maker* on the publick Streets after Nine at Night . . . it might . . . be lawful to charge her in Custody of the first Hackney Coach, and convey her to the next Bagnio as a proper and rightful Chattel of the Publick's'.[4]

While working in the Duke's-place milliner's shop the young Sally was probably introduced to the practice and potential of the sex industry but, if so, the training didn't last long because when a 'parcel of lace miscarried' Sally was accused of stealing or stupidly losing it and was whipped. She was outraged by this treatment and fled the establishment. Captain Walker picks up the story when Sally is about sixteen:

> . . . being unable to exist a single hour out of the bustle of people . . .
> she got hold of a budget full of plays, Pamphlets and other papers, and
> stood to dispose of them, or her self, at the Corner of Pope's-head
> Alley in Cornhill, and at the corner of another Alley opposite to the
> Royal-Exchange; She had not long been scituated on that advantageous
> Ground, before she became the Talk of the Apprentices and young Lads
> of those parts; but seeming like a very girl, and being but in mean
> apparel, she escaped the Notice of Gentlemen. I remember still, as I

went to school, I was told there was a beautiful Wench, who sold Papers about Cornhill, that ever appear'd on a sunny day; and that several boys had given her half a Crown, for an hour of her Love; that being her usual price.

But soon Sally did come to the notice of bigger game, a wealthy Dutch merchant '. . . who took her and wholly new rig'd her, promising to make her his wife, if she could love him and no other'. Sally quickly acquired the management of a good part of his gold: 'about 20 pounds of which she made over to her self and carried it to a Place of Security'. But this position did not last long.

One day, as he kiss'd her unseasonably, and ask'd her a hundred Times if she could love him, and him alone, she unluckily cry'd. *D— you, and your broken tongue, can I love rotten teeth and stinking Fifty?* And so flew off his knee . . . but . . . the jilting Beauty, after this broadside, got away safe, with all her rigging and new tackling, and enough of wealth about her.

Sally was then, in around 1709, kept by someone the biographies describe as the 'Colonel', who was in fact the notorious libertine Colonel Francis Charteris (see page 311). This liaison did not last long and ended with Sally being abandoned by the villainous Charteris. This was a moment of crisis for the girl. Suddenly unprotected, she could quickly have become a desperate and impoverished street-walker. But Sally was resilient and – perhaps more to the point – witty, vivacious and attractive. She moved to a distiller's in New-street, by St Martin's Lane (now New Row, Covent Garden), and 'there made herself extremely common' – presumably, popular and much sought after – and changed her name to Salisbury when 'told she looked like the Countess of Salisbury'. Now aged nineteen, Sally met the notorious bawd Elizabeth Wisebourne and was transformed from a freelance petty whore and sometime kept woman into a groomed and polished woman of the town, dressed, presented and housed in style by Wisebourne, who, as the biography puts it, gave Sally 'the finishing stroak to her fame and reputation'.

Elizabeth Wisebourne (also spelled Whyburn and Wiborne) was one of the more curious and disturbing characters of Queen Anne's London and highly influential in shaping the capital's sex trade. She presided over its transformation from a wayward, romantic, exuberant – in many ways anarchic – part of Restoration London into an almost industrial process. She was born in 1653, the daughter of a Puritan divine named Canon Percival Wiborne, and when young lived in Italy.[5] Here she observed the elegant, controlled and relatively hygienic workings of seraglios and realised there was a chance to make a fortune in London by introducing such useful establishments. She evolved a business plan, learned something of medicine, particularly anti-venereal treatments, and on her return to London in the 1670s made a point of meeting most of the high courtesans and their courtier customers.

By 1679 Wisebourne was running a discreet business in Drury Lane, an area that had already become London's primary theatre district following the opening in 1663, with letters patent granted by Charles II, of the Theatre Royal Drury Lane (the area's theatrical credentials were reinforced when John Rich opened his Covent Garden Theatre in Bow Street in 1732), and so was much frequented by actresses, prostitutes and their pimps, bullies and their customers. But although her house was conveniently located in the heart of London's sex district, Wisebourne made it a policy to maintain a façade of respectability and religion. Hypocrisy and deceit became important tools of her trade, pioneering one of the eighteenth-century bawd's basic business methods. The only way for such a woman to thrive and survive in a potentially hostile world was to perfect the art of lying – helped, perhaps, by a touch of intimidation and blackmail. So there was always a Bible open in Wisebourne's entrance hall, to confuse any stranger or magistrate who happened to gain entry, and to fool the world at large she made a point of carrying one on her rounds through the town as well as attending church every Sunday. This display of piety worked well for her and, presumably, for her clients who in the early years of the eighteenth century increasingly preferred discretion to the openly rakish ways of the Restoration.

By 1708 Wisebourne was the close friend of John Jacob Heidegger, the son of a Swiss clergyman, who became famous for productions of Italian opera at the Haymarket Theatre in collaboration with Handel and for his ostentatious – indeed, pornographic – masquerades, for which no doubt Wisebourne supplied performers. Heidegger may well have been Wisebourne's lover, and his patron, the Duke of Wharton, who founded the Hell Fire Club in 1719 (see page 390), probably helped to keep her out of the reach of the law. Also by this time the business-minded Wisebourne was working with Moll Davis, who not only cured young harlots of the pox but repeatedly restored them to a financially rewarding state of virginity.

The Genuine History of . . . Sally Salisbury contains a description of Wisebourne's recruitment methods, which involved picking up innocent country girls newly arrived at London inns where she would tell them, ''Twas pity such well shap'd limbs should twirl a Mop; such red and white cheeks should be sullied by cinders and charcoal, such a ready Wit be subjected to the unreasonable clamours of a bawling mistress', and offer them free lodging 'till she saw if she should like the Town, for 'twas but a sad wicked place full of temptations for young girls, but the Almighty would deliver his good Children'. At other times Wisebourne – the 'Devil's She-Captain' – would go to 'Hospitals and Bridewells, and pick out all the well-lim'd Creatures, beautiful and young . . . These she'd trick out with patch and paint, and let out at extravagant prices; always calling them young Milliners, or Parson's Daughters.'[6] She would also, according to some sources, purchase children from the 'apprentice' market next to St Martin's Church.[7]

One contemporary observer – *Spectator* journalist Richard Steele – was visiting an inn one day around Christmas 1712 and heard her at work: 'The last Week I went to an Inn in the City . . . and as I waited by one of the Boxes [a compartment partitioned off in the public room of the inn] . . . I heard an old and young Voice . . . I thought it no Breach of good manners to peep at a Crevice . . . but who should I see but the most artful Procuress in the Town, examining a most beautiful Country-girl, who had come up in the . . . wagon . . . Her innocent *forsoothe's, Yes's and't please you's* . . . moved the good old lady to take her out of the Hands of a Country Bumpkin her Brother', who believed the respectable-looking procuress when she told him she was hiring his sister as a maid.[8]

The Genuine History of . . . Sally Salisbury offers Sally's own description of her time at Wisebourne's and an insider's view of her establishment:

> Mrs Salisbury has often, with laughter, said herself, That the old Maid-Merchant caused her to pluck off all her clothes, felt every Limb one by one, touch'd her to see if she was sound . . . soon after, new cloath'd her from top to toe, silently admiring her beauty and features. Certain females,

who say they were at that time, of Mother Wisebourn's Pupils, affirm that the venerable old Vice-aider did something to Mrs Sally's Body, which was a secret to them, and then sold her Virginity to a person of quality.

Sally's fame grew rapidly, as did her reputation for beauty, wit and audacity. Her life was full of risks but also seemed free and, in many ways, independent. She had a strange power to attract, and appeared to be in control – a thing very few women could claim in early-eighteenth-century Britain. Her clients are said to have included peers such as Lord Bolingbroke and the Duke of Richmond, and even the future George II.

Sally became a reference point. The *Spectator* of 8 October 1711 published a 'letter' that was part of Richard Steele's intermittent campaign to defend prostitutes from canting hypocrites. It purported to come from 'a poor strolling Girl about Town' whose story was archetypal and in part mirrored that of Sally. The 'strolling Girl' had been abandoned by a false lover, 'left in a brothel' where the 'Matron . . . expected I would see company' and so was 'exposed to the next bidder who could purchase me of my patroness'. The letter made the point that the prostitute was the victim both of false and lustful men and of poverty, and was consequently forced to inhabit a world that was 'so much the work of Hell' that the last shreds of her virtue and restraint were the things most prized by her tormentors, whose 'pleasure in the possession of us wenches, abates in proportion to the degrees we go beyond the bounds of innocence; and no man is gratified, if there is nothing left to debauch'. But the letter, signed Rebecca Nettletop, ends on a strange note: 'I now live with Sal [who] is more shrewd than any body thinks.'[9] Quite how 'shrewd' Sally really was, given the fact that she was in Wisebourne's hellish brothel, is a moot point, but the letter does at least imply that she was mistress of her own circumstances.

Certainly many of the myths that surrounded Sally at this time seem to bear this out: she and a companion were taken to Newmarket by a peer and, as *The Genuine History* explains, foreseeing 'a gloomy prospect' in sleeping with him, instead 'tied him in his Bed . . . and ran away with all his best Cloaths, Gold Watch, Rings &c', after 'spreading the Trick, that was serv'd him, all about, before they went'.[10] Luckily for Sally, the peer laughed it all off rather than having her hanged as a thief. She had clearly calculated nicely – in this instance, at least – what level of cheek was acceptable.

Once, when complimented on her gaming skills by a grandee who was an illegitimate son of Charles II – probably Nell Gwynne's son, the Duke of St Albans – Sally got away with the retort, 'Aye, My Lord, Whores and Bastards are always lucky.' She even played the role of artist's muse. The poet and diplomat Matthew Prior was inspired by her company and tolerated her little tricks, such as the time she made him an object of public ridicule by secretly snipping away parts of his periwig while they were out walking in Spring Gardens.[11]

But ultimately Sally was not shrewd, nor wise, nor particularly lucky. Despite the well-regulated nature of Wisebourne's bawdy-house, Sally, presumably through lack of caution as much as ill luck, become pregnant and then diseased. In response to the first condition Wisebourne induced an abortion – '. . . what the young lady swallow'd at top, and what she evacuated at bottom, is matter of conception' – and to the second a doctor was summoned and, 'Our young Lady-errant was, in five weeks time, well enough after her confinement to remove to Kensington, with Mrs Lydia B—t, a Mantua-maker.'

When cured Sally took up with 'someone of quality' who lodged her in 'Villiars-street in York Buildings', but this adventure was short-lived and Sally 'in about three months, return'd . . . to Mrs Elizabeth Wisebourne's, as bright in apparel as looks'.

Soon after this, in 1713, she caused a riot in Wisebourne's house, attracting the type of attention that for years the bawd had managed successfully to avoid. Constables were called and Sally was arrested for disorderly conduct; no doubt she was horribly drunk – a vice her biographies hint at for they reveal that she was very fond of 'Usquebaugh Tea', that is to say tea with a slug of whisky, and Ratafia, which was a strong liqueur flavoured with peach or cherry kernels and bitter almonds.[12] Ratafia appears to have been widely popular among whores and in bagnios – or bath houses (see page 215) – and could literally be a killer if consumed in large and regular amounts because peach and cherry kernels and almonds produce hydrogen cyanide. Sally was committed to Newgate but soon released by a judge named Blagney who was infatuated with her.

She next moved into a house 'taken' for her by one of her gallants 'in the New-Buildings . . . near "the Temple" . . . [that was] beautiful and well furnished . . . with a small, but pretty garden behind it, looking over into Shepherd's Fields'. This is a perplexing description. At that time the

New Buildings was the term generally used to describe the new developments north of Oxford Street and running west from Tottenham Court Road through Marylebone to the Edgware Road. The area gradually became a favoured place of work and residence for high-class courtesans, but in 1714 or so when Sally moved into her new home very little had been built, with the first major development – on the Cavendish Harley Estate around Cavendish Square – not getting underway until about 1717. Sally may have been as pioneering in her occupation of a house in the New Buildings as she was in other things, or else her New Buildings may have been no more than just some other new buildings, perhaps near present-day Shepherd Market in Mayfair, although this area was generally not built upon until the mid-1730s. The Temple mentioned might well refer to a long-forgotten ornamental building or perhaps suggests that the location of Sally's new residence overlooked a garden in the Temple, one of the Inns of Court lying south of Fleet Street which was then a favoured hunting ground of harlots.

Wherever their location, her move to the New Buildings didn't last long. When Elizabeth Wisebourne died in 1719 Sally seems to have been back in residence at her house. With the old bawd's death her establishment closed and Sally was back on the town. But she was a star attraction and was soon picked up by Wisebourne's younger friend and rival bawd, Elizabeth Needham. So Sally moved from Drury Lane to the far more fashionable Park Place in St James's.

At first Sally flourished, but through either excess of drink or flattery or perhaps illness she gradually lost touch with reality and – far more seriously – lost all self-control. Events came to a head just before Christmas 1722. In a moment of drug-induced or liquor-fuelled madness she brought catastrophe upon herself. 'For being now at the Summit of all her glory', *The Genuine History* explains, she requested a 'noble young person to meet her at a Grape-House in Chan-Street'.[13] The meeting took place but 'this Virago-Lady finding that the youth whom she most admired, had given a piece of paper [an opera ticket], out of his hand, to another of her own sex, Her own sister', she stabbed him 'unawares with a large keen Scimeter; and then made an Attempt upon her fancied rival's arm, covering her with blood, but not dangerously wounding her'.

This appalling scene needs some further explanation. A copy of *The Genuine History* in the British Library, inscribed as belonging to

'W. Musgrave', bears brief annotations in an eighteenth-century hand. These make it clear that the 'noble young person' was 'The Honble. John Finch, son of the Duchess of Winchelsea', and that the location and exact date of the attack was, 'The Three Tuns Tavern, Chandos Street, Covent Garden, on the 22nd December 1722'.[14]

The *Newgate Calendar*'s account of the affair gives a few more details that suggest Sally's state of mind at the time of the attack and her level of intoxication.[15] She apparently arrived at the tavern soon after midnight to join Finch in bed. At two in the morning the tavern 'drawer' was summoned to the room and ordered to 'draw a pint of Frontiniac for Mrs Salisbury' and serve her with a 'French role and a knife'. After delivering the sweet muscadine Frontignac wine and bread, the 'drawer' heard the row break out.

Sally's attack on Finch can perhaps best be explained as a crime of passion resulting from her complex and confused emotional life. Despite all she had gone through she still had a heart. Finch was a client yet Sally evidently loved him in her way, even if that love was expressed in jealousy and possessiveness. Far more alarming is the fact that she also turned the knife on her sister, suggesting that there was something very seriously wrong with her that night. Sally bore a deep love for her sister Jenny, who had been blinded by smallpox and lived under her protection. This frenzied attack on two of the people she loved best suggests that at the time Sally was seriously mentally disturbed, presumably as a result of alcohol or even drugs.

Marijuana was known to be in use in early-eighteenth-century London among aristocratic gangs known as Mohocks, named after the tribes encountered on the border of Canada and New England. The British tended to refer to these American peoples as 'savages' but they were models of civilised and rational behaviour in comparison with their aristocratic London namesakes. The marijuana available to them in eighteenth-century London had several possible sources. It could have been ganja or bhang brought back from India, hashish from the Middle East, or else a by-product of England's hemp industry.

Hemp was at the time grown in prodigious quantity – indeed, hemp farming was encouraged by Elizabethan statute – to supply netting and ropes for England's fishing and maritime industries. It was also used for its medical properties and as a recreational drug. *Gerarde's Herbal, or General Historie of Plants* of 1633 lists and describes several varieties of native hemp and refers to its medicinal qualities; for example, its 'liquor' was thought a cure for 'Yellow Jaundice' while the 'inyce [of Water Hemp] droped into ears, assuageth the paine thereof'. Hemp is the catch-all English word for plants of the cannabis family. Although not all hemp is psychoactive much of it is, in various potencies. Marijuana alters consciousness, perception, and modifies behaviour. It can induce a sense of peace, of calm and meditative reflection, or in stronger dosage provoke paranoia, schizophrenia and violence. The fearless assassins of the Middle East who, during the Crusades, used swift and stealthy murder as a weapon of terror were named after the marijuana or hashish their murder squads consumed before attacks, while the same drug was used by the Hindu Thugees of India in their fanatical assaults on their enemies.

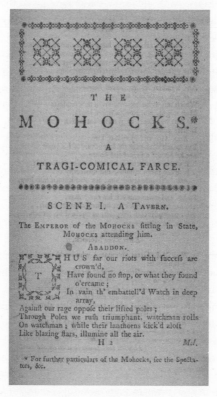

The opening page of John Gay's 1712 play The Mohocks. *Aristocratic street-gangs of Mohocks were a constant threat in early-eighteenth-century London.*

Whichever drug drove the Mohocks – alcohol, marijuana or even opium from the once-bountiful opium poppy fields of Merton, South London – from around 1710 they started to commit acts of extreme and seemingly random violence on the streets of London. Men and women were suddenly the targets of arbitrary and unprovoked attack. There were terrible acts of mutilation, with noses, ears or hands being lopped off. Lady Wentworth informed a friend that the Mohocks 'put an old woman into a hogshead and rolled her down a hill, they cut off some nosis, others' hands, and several barbarous tricks, without any provocation'. She observed that they 'are said to be young gentlemen [and] never take any money from any'.[16]

John Gay, the future author of *The Beggar's Opera*, which ennobled the underclass of whores and highwaymen, had no time for these upper-class hooligans who in their excesses outdid the worst criminal cutthroats. It was the social order turned upside down. Gay asked, 'Who has not trembled at the Mohocks's name?' and in 1712 wrote a play entitled *The Mohocks*, though it was not performed at the time for fear of retribution. It includes a song which suggests the motives and motivation of the Mohocks – anarchy and alcohol – as perceived by those they terrorised:

> Come fill up the Glass,
> Round, round let it pass,
> Till our Reason be lost in our Wine:
> Leave Conscience's Rules
> To Women and Fools,
> This only can make us divine.
>
> *(Chorus). Then a Mohock, a Mohock I'll be,*
> *No Laws shall restrain*
> *Our Libertine Reign,*
> *We'll riot, drink on, and be free.*

In the same year that Gay wrote his play, Jonathan Swift wrote in a letter: '[O]ur Mohocks go on still, and cut people's faces every night: faith they shan't cut mine. I like it better as it is.' Swift, though, saw this bizarre conduct as not entirely mindless and arbitrary. He thought it part of a deep and dark Whig conspiracy to cause chaos and make violence so common an event that the Tory leader, Lord Oxford, could with ease and impunity be assassinated.

Coordinated action was finally taken against the young thugs, and perhaps would-be political assassins, when in 1712 a bounty of £100 was offered for the capture of a gang member. Gradually the Mohock violence subsided, although the name took on a generic meaning and was applied to any drunken and riotous middle- or upper-class young men. William Hickey in his *Memoirs* refers to the 'outrages' and arrest in 1774 of a 'Mohawk quartet'.[17]

The Genuine History speculates that Sally 'learn'd her bullying way, by going o-Nights among the mohocks, drest like a beautiful Youth: And this is most certain, because she was once taken by two constables, and would have been punished, had they not rifled her breeches and discover'd her Sex.' She was also present when her Mohock companions 'had barbarously roll'd an old Woman down Snow-Hill in a Tub' and 'still laughs' when she remembers discovering that the old lady, 'taken out bruis'd and groaning, and half-dead . . . 'twas a near Relation of hers, who had been her best Friend . . .'[18] The *Authentick Memoirs* also mentions the pleasure she took 'in Nocturnal Rambles, as turning Mohock and Rake . . . breaking windows with whole handfuls of Half-pence . . . alleviating the crime by her leaving money behind to pay for them'.[19]

This association with the Mohocks could have introduced Sally to drugs. The general consensus on her behaviour at the time, recorded in several accounts, is that it was irrational and emotionally extreme. *The Genuine History* records that 'she did not show fear or concern, but would have wrapt up the action in a scene of gaiety and laughter', while people who were in the tavern at the time of the attack, and later gave evidence at her trial, made it clear that her passion changed instantly from fury to sorrow, regret and concern. Having stabbed her lover, she appears instantly to have sobered up and sent for a surgeon. He, according to the Ordinary's Account, thought it necessary to 'extend the wound' to avoid internal bleeding upon which Sally screamed, 'O Lord! What are you doing?' and fainted away. But she soon recovered and asked her victim how he was doing. 'Very bad, and worse than you imagine,' was the reply, which prompted her to attempt to console Finch and reassure him that the wound was not so bad. And so they parted, each in a separate sedan chair, but not until 'the wounded gentleman had . . . saluted her as a token of forgiveness'.

Finch, although stabbed in the chest – with a bread knife rather than a scimitar – hung on to life, but his final recovery was far from certain. So Sally, who was arrested and carried to Newgate to await trial, must have been in emotional agony – worry for him combined with fear for her own perilous position. *The Genuine History* merely states that she expressed her 'great love' for Finch and affirmed 'that if he died, she should ne'er want to live'.[20] Indeed, if he died there was very little chance that she would. But before the trial Sally had to endure prolonged confinement in gaol and public character assassination by the press and all manner of observers and gossips, as was only to be expected. She was a celebrity, long of intense interest to the public, and the attack in the Three Tuns Tavern was the sensation of the year, the talk of the town during Christmas 1722.

A typical reaction is the letter written on Christmas Day to the Countess of Mar in Paris by Lady Mary Wortley Montagu, who would have known many of Sally's aristocratic clients well, and probably even Sally herself:

> The freshest news in town is the fatal accident that happened three nights ago to a very pretty young fellow, brother to Lord Finch, who was drinking with a dearly beloved drab [prostitute], whom you may have heard of by the name of Sally Salisbury. In a jealous pique she stabbed him to the heart with a knife. He fell down dead immediately, but a surgeon being called for, and the knife drawn out of his body, he opened his eyes, and his first words were to beg her to be friends with him, and kissed her. She has since stayed by his bedside till last night, when he begged her to fly, for he thought he could not live; she has taken his advice and perhaps will honour you with her residence in Paris.[21]

The letter captures accurately the mood of the moment, in particular the popular belief that the lovers retained their passion for one another, even if it is wrong in many of its key facts: Finch did not 'die' and then recover; Sally did not lay siege to his bed nor did she attempt to fly to Paris. She could do neither since she was incarcerated in Newgate.

Few viewed Sally as wicked or even as a criminal. It was generally accepted that she had acted out of love not hate, that this was a crime of passion and not committed for any material gain. The fact that Finch recovered and remained forgiving, loyal and publicly supportive helped her case tremendously – as did visits to her in prison from powerful friends and the gifts that allowed her to present a respectable figure in court.

Lady Mary Wortley Montagu, who wrote a letter to the Countess of Mar in Paris on Christmas Day 1722 describing Sally Salisbury's attack on John Finch.

The trial opened at the Old Bailey on 24 April 1723 when Sally was charged with violent assault and intent to commit murder because it was the prosecution's contention that the attack was premeditated, unprovoked, and the accused 'showed no concern afterwards'.[22] They chose to argue their case by portraying Sally as a calculating villain who only pretended remorse in order to avoid the full consequences of her actions.

After enjoying months of popular support, the prosecution's hard-line tactics must have surprised and shocked Sally and her friends, and, of course, if proven would lead inexorably to her execution. Sally was now on trial for her life and it was a bitter battle. The prosecution sought to destroy what shreds of good character she had left in order to discredit her version of events. When Sally's counsel argued that her attack on Finch was not premeditated but the rash response of a moment when she believed he wanted to take Jenny to the opera so that he could 'debauch' her, the prosecution ridiculed the very idea that a woman of

Sally's character could 'be supposed to have any very tender regard for her sister's reputation'.[23]

The defence pinned their hopes on the victim's response to the attack working to Sally's advantage. *The Genuine History* records that Finch, when stabbed, said 'that he forgave her, and should die with pleasure'.[24] But the prosecution dismissed this as only showing Finch's 'sweetness of Temper' and offering no legal grounds for mitigation.

The prosecution found it harder to sustain its claim that Sally's remorse stemmed purely from self-interest and the fact that she had immediately called a surgeon showed only concern for herself, for she well 'knew the consequence of killing a man'.[25] The defence brought forward witnesses who claimed that Sally 'did not appear glad, but concern'd' by her own actions. *The Genuine History* records that one of the witnesses described how Sally consoled Finch, after the surgeon had got the mass of blood out of his body, by telling him, 'Jacky, you are not so bad as you believe,' and how she told the surgeon that 'she had done the injury', desiring 'him, for God's sake, to do his utmost', and that she then went home with Finch 'and sate by his Bed till three o-Clock the following afternoon'.[26]

The trial ended with Sally's life balanced on a knife edge. The court-room was packed with her fashionable friends and supporters as the Lord Chief Justice summed up the evidence. *The Genuine History* explains that he 'seem'd of opinion that there was Malice propence' and that Sally had indeed 'an intent to Murder the Gentleman'.[27] But the jury was not persuaded. It found her guilty of assaulting and wounding Finch but acquitted her of 'intent to kill and murther'. Sally was not to be hanged. She was instead fined £100, imprisoned for a year, and obliged to give security for good behaviour for two years.

All should have been well. The trial had made her more famous then ever – indeed had prompted the publication of her two biographies – and friends maintained her in comfort in gaol. At the age of only thirty-one or so she had become something of a heroine, the epitome of the free-spirited and rebellious 'roaring girl'. But her luck had run out. As Sally's sentence drew to an end she sickened and then, with only three months to go, died in early 1724. Afterwards no one could agree what had killed her. Some said she'd died of 'Gaol Fever', a familiar ailment brought about by the filthy and fetid conditions of confinement; others claimed it was a 'brain fever brought on by debauch' – a euphemism for syphilis.

Sally's story, plight and sorry end captured the imagination and sympathy of many, and burnished her legend by bringing her posthumous fame. The French visitor to London, César de Saussure, wrote home to his family about her over a year after her death:

> Sometime ago a courtesan by the name of Sally Salisbury, famed for her rare beauty as well as her wit and vivacity, became the fashion of London . . . one night, at a wine supper, one of her admirers displeased her . . . whereupon she seized a knife and plunged it into his breast . . . You will expect no doubt that her lovers abandoned her in her distress; in fact they did no such thing, but rather crowded into the prison, presenting her with every comfort and luxury possible [with] the wounded man [asking] for her discharge . . . but Sally died of brain fever, brought on by debauch.[28]

Such, in essence, was the legend of Sally Salisbury as passed down through generations of Londoners – a rare and spirited beauty, a wit, a force of nature, who met a sad and early end.[29] She was buried in the churchyard of St Andrew's, Holborn, that had recently been rebuilt in grand manner to the designs of Sir Christopher Wren. The church was gutted in the blitz of 1940 and her grave has been lost and forgotten. As with virtually all the other whores of eighteenth-century London, the bones of the once fêted Sally Salisbury lie in deep and eternal obscurity.

LAVINIA FENTON

I met Lavinia Fenton in Yorkshire in 1999. She was no shade but full of life and, if not a duchess like her eighteenth-century namesake, was styled Lady Bolton, lived at Bolton Hall, and was married to Lord Bolton, a descendant of the duke who married 'Polly Peachum' – or rather the first Lavinia Fenton who rose to fame and fortune by portraying Polly Peachum in *The Beggar's Opera*.

This extraordinary meeting was the culmination of an investigation for a television programme into the confused and mysterious history of the eighteenth-century Lavinia. All that was really clear about her, despite the existence of her *Life* published in 1728, was that she and her history embodied one of the most unlikely achievements of social-climbing in Georgian Britain.

She was born into humble circumstances, became embroiled in London's morally compromised low-life, possibly even working as a child prostitute – and not only survived but scaled the ramparts of the aristocracy. Those prostitutes who flew so high that they escaped the sex industry altogether can be numbered on one hand. Lavinia Fenton was the first of them in the eighteenth century, and in many ways the most fascinating.

Later members of this exclusive club of high-flying harlots and actresses included the (afterwards) admirably virtuous Elizabeth Farren, who in 1797 became the Countess of Derby, and Elizabeth Armistead, a former St James's courtesan and one-time mistress of the Prince of Wales, who became the companion and in 1795 the wife of the powerful Whig politician Charles James Fox.

My meeting in Yorkshire with Lavinia's namesake was a vivid reminder of the enduring magic of *The Beggar's Opera*, its memorable cast of characters and famous players. The twentieth-century Lavinia had been intrigued and inspired by the original to such an extent that she attempted to emulate her life story, finding and eventually marrying a descendant of the same ducal family who had ennobled the eighteenth-century 'actress'. A strange echo indeed.

Lavinia Fenton's life could, indeed quite logically should, have been brutal and short. *The Life of Lavinia Beswick, alias Fenton, alias Polly Peachum,*[30] published in 1728 to exploit her new-found celebrity, puts something of a gloss on her early years but essentially reveals that they were grim and troubled. Lavinia's mother was, it seems, deceived by her father, a Lieutenant Beswick of the Royal Navy. The account given in the *Life* is the stuff of eighteenth-century melodrama. Beswick proposed marriage to Lavinia's mother but betrayed her and absconded to sea. With her character in ruins and a bastard on her hands, the unmarried mother trod the usual path and in 1708 took her newborn baby to the anonymous melting pot of London in search of employment, a new life . . . in short, a remedy for all the problems caused by her misplaced trust in a man.

The solution was found in her marriage to a Mr Fenton who kept a coffee house in Charing Cross. This trade, closely associated with prostitution, and the location of this house in particular, in one of the

This nineteenth-century print, after Hogarth's mid-eighteenth-century portrait, in all probability shows a middle-aged Lavinia Fenton once she had become the Duchess of Bolton.

heartlands of London's early-eighteenth-century sex industry, suggest most strongly that Mr Fenton may have been of somewhat dubious character. Indeed the *Life* rather confirms this was the case since apparently Lavinia, at a very young age, was made an object of diversion for Fenton's customers: 'being a Child of a vivacious lively Spirit, and a promising Beauty [Lavinia] was a Play-thing for the Fops, and she never fail'd to afford them an Agreeable Diversion; and tho' at this time she was but 7 or 8 years of age, she had some singular turns of wit'. One of the customers, a 'comedian', undertook to teach her music.

To get the child away from this worrying environment, Lavinia was sent by her mother to a 'boarding school', which she left after a passion she conceived for a young lawyer foundered thanks to her lowly social status. She returned to her mother at around the age of thirteen. Her home now seems to have been in the Old Bailey where 'dress and company soon made her vain' and 'it needed no further allurements' to incite her into a world of amorous intrigues. But, the author of the *Life* argued, 'it cannot be said by her greatest enemies, that she was ever a common prostitute, as some would insinuate'.[31] A curious defence. If not Lavinia's 'greatest enemies', then who exactly was insinuating that she was a former prostitute? Presumably none other than the anonymous author of the book, who realised that such an allegation, couched innocently in the form of a denial, made good copy.

Having raised and then dismissed the charge of prostitution, the author of the *Life* goes on to suggest something even worse: that the teenage Lavinia was being pimped – in a most shrewd and businesslike manner – by her own mother. It was in 1725, reveals the *Life* – when Lavinia would have been about sixteen or seventeen – that she 'fell first a Sacrifice to Priapus'. At this time Lavinia's mother 'had an intrigue upon her hands, which began at the Play-house, and ended in the Bed-chamber'. The mother's lover desired Lavinia as well, which, as is easy to imagine, provoked something of a crisis in the relationship between mother and daughter. But the issue, it seems, was not the ethics or morals of mother and daughter sharing the same man, but – from the mother's point of view, at least – that such an arrangement would greatly reduce Lavinia's value as a maiden property. She must, argued her mother, reserve herself for 'a great man', and always remember that 'the first Market a Woman made was always the best; and second-hand Goods would fetch but a second-hand price'.

Lavinia's mother seems to have recognised there was some urgency in the case and, lest Lavinia 'should fling away her Charms on some one who could not purchase them at a price more exorbitant than Lais demanded of Demosthenes', made overtures 'to a certain ludicrous knight, known by the name of the Feather'd Gull'. The deal struck by the mother, and outlined in the *Life*, was that upon 'first surrender' Lavinia should be paid £200 cash and 'be deck'd in all the Mundus Mulieris [women's things] at the Knight's Expence, that she should have 200 l. per annum whilst she remained constant'. But while this transaction was being hammered out between her mother and the knight, Lavinia herself 'was no less active in providing for herself; and a Portugueze Nobleman, being her only Favourite, she consented, unknown to her Mother, to give him the prize, which he generously rewarded'.

The *Life* describes Lavinia's deflowering in most elegant manner. The 'Nobleman' sent his coach for her on Friday and 'kept her till Monday'. This love match was not rewarded in quite the manner it deserved for the gentleman, noble or not, promptly ran out of funds and was soon imprisoned in the Fleet as a debtor. This was a stern test of Lavinia's character and, according to the *Life*, she rose triumphantly to the challenge. She decided to get a job, earn money, and buy her lover out of gaol.

In 1725 Lavinia 'began to think of treading the stage', and to win herself attention and a job composed a witty poem about a 'vain fop' and gave it to a 'nobleman' – presumably a well-intentioned and besotted client – who used this 'evidence of her wit' to get Lavinia taken up by a company run by Mr Huddy. Under his guidance Lavinia first appeared on stage in 1726, proved her worth, and then reappeared as the saucy Cherry Boniface in George Farquhar's 1707 comedy *The Beaux' Stratagem*. Soon afterwards she was introduced to the theatre manager John Rich and taken on at his playhouse in Lincoln's Inn Fields as a 'slated actress at the wage of 15 shilling a week'. The stage was now set for Lavinia's greatest theatrical triumph – the one that would transform her life. John Gay's *The Beggar's Opera* came to Rich's theatre, the parts were cast, and Lavinia, although only nineteen or twenty years of age and inexperienced, was given the part of Polly Peachum when it was discovered that she could sing sweetly.

The Beggar's Opera opened to a house packed with 1,341 people, including 98 on stage. By the time the curtain fell on the first night it was clear that something extraordinary had happened. The age had its defining theatrical work. The opera enjoyed an unprecedented run of 62 consecutive performances and, as 'waggs' said at the time, 'made Rich very gay, and . . . Gay very rich'.[32] The opera also, within days of its première, made Lavinia 'the most celebrated Toast in Town' and, naturally, 'Persons of the highest Rank and Quality made love to her'.

The *Life* is intriguingly discreet when developing this theme for it states merely that 'the first lover that courted her favours since she has charm'd the Town with her fine Warbling in *The Beggar's Opera*, was a noble Knight of the Bath; a person of too noble a mind to participate of the pleasure with her, without some valuable Consideration'. This 'noble knight of the Bath' was the Duke of Bolton, who attended the first and many successive nights and sat in his box ogling Lavinia. He was a married man and, of course, Lavinia's social superior to a marked degree, so this public display of sudden and deep devotion caused quite a stir. Indeed, it became one of the most famous and memorable features of the opera's first season.

It is now impossible to know how Lavinia responded initially to the duke's conduct. The *Life*, written within weeks of the opera's première, was published before the relationship developed further. The biography simply implies that Lavinia, like any good harlot, sold herself to the duke for a 'valuable Consideration'. But there was to be far more to this particular intrigue. The relationship may have had a slow and strange start but soon Lavinia had decided that the duke was a sound investment of her time and talents.

This is revealed most clearly by Hogarth's painting of the last scene of the opera, in which Macheath – in the classic pose of Hercules – is making his choice between the two women who love him, Lucy Lockit and Polly Peachum, both of whom are pleading for his life to their respective fathers. Macheath had, like Hercules, to choose between sensual pleasure and virtue. He loved both women in their different ways, but while one – the gaoler's daughter – could save his body from execution, the other – Polly – could perhaps save his soul as well. Hogarth's painting is powerful and complex in its subtle gradations of meaning.

As is true of the opera it portrays, Hogarth's image dissolved the boundaries between good and bad, fact and fiction, life and art. It shows Lavinia, in the persona of Polly, appealing for Macheath's love and life. But she is looking not at her fellow actor to whom she ostensibly pleads but into the eyes of one of the members of the audience, sitting close by on the stage – the highly affected figure of the Duke of Bolton. Hogarth sets reality within a play that reflects reality, with the actors playing both their parts in the play and their parts in life. As well as showing the connections between art and life, the painting also makes clear that, by the time it was completed in 1731, the relationship between Lavinia and the duke was well known.

The painting also holds another clue. Hogarth produced a number of versions of this work and, as Lisa Hilton points out in her biography of Lavinia, these contain significant differences that appear to track the course, or at least the notoriety, of the relationship between the actress and the aristocrat.[33] In the version now in the Mellon Collection in Washington DC, the scene is more cramped and the Duke of Bolton does not appear. This version is dated to 1728–9. In the 1731 version in

Tate Britain the duke is present and Lavinia looks directly – seemingly longingly – at him, and is thus in character both as Polly and as herself, a shrewdly calculating young harlot-cum-actress. Perhaps this reflects the popular belief, and in fact the reality, that in its early stages the relationship was an on-off affair.

This is hardly surprising since in 1728 the duke was forty-three years old – over twice Lavinia's age – and had been a Whig MP and a husband for fifteen years. He might also have been a trifle alarmed by what the spotlight of sudden and intense celebrity revealed about the object of his desire. Her past was exposed and discussed, in turn found amusing, titillating or offensive. Some mocked or ridiculed her for it, others perhaps admired her fortitude. For the poet, playwright and clergyman Edward Young, Lavinia, or 'Polly' as most of her contemporaries now called her, was no more than a greedy and grasping harlot:

> Polly, a wench that acts in 'The Beggar's Opera', is the *publica cura* of our noble youth. She plays her Newgate part well, and shows the greatest advantage of being born and bred in the Mint . . . She, 'tis said, has raised her price from one guinea to one hundred, tho' she cannot be a greater whore than she was before, nor, I suppose, a younger.[34]

The erudite Latin quote used by Young was inspired by a line in one of Horace's *Odes* in which, when referring to the great *hetaera* – or courtesan – Barine, he described her as the great 'public cure' and 'love object of the young'.[35] Classically educated and bookish eighteenth-century clergymen did little to prevent young women from falling into the snare of prostitution – as is suggested by Hogarth's *Harlot's Progress* – while others such as the self-seeking Young thought it appropriate to belittle, admittedly in a most stylish manner, the efforts of a young prostitute attempting to rise out of the trade.

Even the *Life*, which the duke must have devoured, having focused on Lavinia's unfortunate relationship with her loose-moralled and pimping mother, proclaimed that Lavinia's 'amours are not inferior to those of the celebrated Sally Salisbury, nor have her Gallants been less generous to her than they were to that once famous beauty'. This was a comparison that the duke could hardly have found agreeable or reassuring.

The *Life*, published opportunistically – and, as it turned out, prematurely – offered its own fanciful and utterly wrong prediction about the likely ending to Lavinia's career. It observed meanly that John Rich's generosity to Polly 'gives occasion for people to make their observations, and most are of opinion, that the nimble Harlequin has a private understanding with her'. Rich was referred to as the 'nimble Harlequin' because he had, under the name John Lun, made his reputation and fortune performing the role of Harlequin, and the hard evidence offered for the alleged sexual 'understanding' between Rich and Lavinia was the fact that 'since she has been so famous for acting her part in *The Beggar's Opera* she has been advanced to thirty shillings per week, and if she merits the same praise in other performances, as she does in this, it is not doubted but it will be raised to something more considerable'.

Having cast Lavinia's triumph in this somewhat lurid light, the author of the *Life* made some amends by praising her taste in poetry and painting, her knowledge of the classical authors, her wit, modesty, good sense and charitable actions. As a back-handed compliment, it pointed out that, although her life bore comparison with that of the notorious harlot Sally Salisbury, Lavinia's conversation 'has a penetrating Genius, whereas the other had only some low flights of wit to recommend her, and by being twice in her company, her conversation became insipid, dull and nauseous', whereas Lavinia 'has so many smart, as well as polite Repartee's, such a grace in delivery, and withal so little affectation . . . that the oftener any one hears her converse, the oftener he will desire it'.

The *Life* then offered the highest compliment that could by tradition be bestowed upon a socially ambitious and intelligent harlot – 'her beauty has not gained her so many admirers as her sense' – and came to an abrupt end. It stated that Lavinia 'relieves' the 'Portugueze gentleman' with a gift of £300 '. . . and now they live together in one house, enjoying the utmost felicity, and their tempers exactly suiting each other, makes up a complete harmony. FINIS'.

In fact, Lavinia soon threw in her lot with the Duke of Bolton, gave up the stage, and during the next twenty years lived with him and bore him three sons. The duke, in turn, proved as loyal, faithful and devoted to her as did the mysterious 'Portugueze gentleman' mentioned in the *Life*. He purchased the theatre box from which he had watched Lavinia perform and installed it in his local church to serve as the family pew. What his wife thought of this extravagant action is not recorded.

He also, in 1739, became one of the founding Governors of London's

Foundling Hospital, an institution that, by taking responsibility for some of the city's unwanted offspring, did something to tackle one of the grimmer consequences of the sex industry (see page 246). It must surely have been Lavinia, who knew all about harlots' children being abandoned, fatally neglected in parish workhouses or sold into the sex trade, who persuaded him to his patronage. In 1751, when the duke's long-estranged wife died, he married Lavinia but, three years later, was himself dead.

In London's Tate Britain hangs the portrait, painted by William Hogarth at some time during the decade beginning 1745, of a handsome and somewhat matronly woman. It is thought to portray Lavinia Fenton, perhaps soon after she became the Duchess of Bolton. She looks peaceful, respectable and, perhaps more important, respected. At about this time Lady Mary Wortley Montagu observed that 'Polly, bred in an alehouse, and produced on the stage, has obtained wealth and title. And found the way to be esteemed. So useful is early experience.' A pithy but reasonable epithet for a woman who lived by her wits and her looks and managed to survive – indeed thrive – in a potentially hostile world.[36]

SIX

 'MEASURING THE
MAYPOLE'

The Value of the Sex Industry

According to contemporary observers the prostitutes of Georgian London
fell into a number of distinct categories. First, there were the poor street
girls or 'Hackneyed Prostitutes', according to the *Doings of London*[1] of
1830, who haunted street corners, slept rough, were infected with venereal
disease and were part of the criminal underclass. Second were prostitutes,
many little better than street girls, who operated from rented rooms in
the houses of a whoremaster or 'Mother' and who would probably have
to solicit for clients in the street, in taverns, or be taken to meaner bagnios
on demand.[2] It was the upper echelon of these girls who advertised themselves in *Harris's List* (see page 180). Third were the women who, after
c.1750 (when Parisian-style brothels were introduced into London by Mrs
Goadby, see page 207), were under the protection of madams in fashionable seraglios, 'nunneries' or brothels. Many of this class of prostitutes
had male protectors who provided them with comfortable rooms – or
even entire houses – of their own, but they were still generally obliged
to take extra clients or to visit grand bagnios.

Fourth were the high courtesans or 'fashionable' prostitutes – the kept
mistresses of rich and powerful men. These were women of great style,
wealth and influence, who could even prove to be a power in the land.
I. M. Davis in *The Harlot and the Statesman* refers to a report of 1782
which reckoned that the eight leading London courtesans of the time
were each spending the colossal sum of around £3,000 a year on their
ordinary expenses.[3]

More simply, Michael Ryan, in his *Prostitution in London* of 1839,
divided prostitutes into those who had their own dwelling and those who
lived under the control or protection of others.[4]

An anonymously written pamphlet of 1758, *A Congratulatory Epistle from a Reformed Rake* – part satire, part campaigning text – grades London prostitutes into ten types. There were 'Women of Fashion who Intrigue', 'Demi-reps', 'Good-natured Girls' and 'Kept Mistresses' – all of whom the author classed as either amateur or non-predatory prostitutes and thus arguably not 'pests to society'. Then there were the types of professional whores, found in 'Genteel' and in 'low infamous Bawdy Houses', working down in status from 'Ladies of Pleasure', 'Whores', 'Park-walkers', 'Street-walkers', 'Bunters' and ending with – at the bottom of the heap – 'Bulk-mongers'. The anonymous author was not kind when describing the subjects of his study:

> *Bunters* are seldom used as *Women* . . . If *Street-walkers* and *Bulk-mongers* sometimes take a Youth's own Handkerchief instead of Three-half-pence . . . for a *Manual-abortion*; Do not *Ladies of Pleasure* frequently excite their *Culls*, when Finances fail, to take an airing (solus) upon *Hounslow-Heath* [which is to say, turn highwayman].[5]

The anonymous author of *Nocturnal Revels*, of 1779, also touched on the different classes of prostitutes and on the London locations where they operated:

> From kept-mistresses we shall descend a line lower to those Fair ones who are to be obtained on a minutes warning, for a stipulated sum. Before the modern institution of Nunneries, the chief scene of action for promiscuous amours lay in the vicinity of Covent-Garden . . . the nocturnal revels at Moll King's in the centre of Covent-Garden market. This rendezvous was a general receptacle for Rakes and Prostitutes of every rank.[6]

By 1750 prostitution in London was more organised and, at the upper end, more discreet and elegant. This was due largely to the introduction of the Parisian-style brothel or seraglio. Thanks, as *Nocturnal Revels* explains, to:

> The period when these *Nocturnal Revels* were put upon a more eligible and polite footing than they had hitherto been, which was by the institution of the Nunneries at the West End of town . . . first planned . . . by Mrs Goadby . . . at her house in Berwick Street, Soho.[7]

Each class of prostitute would charge a different amount of money, and the charges within each class would also vary greatly. Another complicating factor was that prostitutes used various different methods to determine charges. Some charged by the hour, some by the act, and some, it would seem, by the size of the client's member. Much information can be gleaned from *Harris's List of Covent Garden Ladies*, a user's guide to London prostitutes, which not only gives the name, physical description, sexual skills and addresses of the ladies but also their charges, which seem generally to be calculated by the night. Indeed, several entries make this clear.

For example, in one instance a charge is quoted directly as 'three Guineas for one night'; Mrs Dodd of 6 Hind Court, Fleet Street, 'after giving you a whole night's entertainment is perfectly satisfied, and will give you a comfortable cup of tea in the morning, for one guinea'; Mrs Lewes 'expects 3 guineas for a whole night'; while Miss Nancy Davies charged on the basis of five shillings per hour. More exotic was the manner in which Miss Corbet calculated her charges. As the 1788 edition of the *List* explains, she had 'one fixed rule' in regard to price: 'She always measures a gentleman's *maypole* by a standard of nine inches and expects a guinea for every inch it is short of full measure'.

The sum charged per night presumably reflects the minimum sum a prostitute might expect to make per 'day's' work. To make more than this sum in a twenty-four-hour period she would have to take on clients in the day as well as at night. Quite possible, but in my following calculation of the value of the sex industry in the late eighteenth century I err on the conservative side and work on the basis that the per night charge is the full amount a girl made in a twenty-four-hour period.

Evidence for the scale of charges is a little difficult to fathom, mostly because contemporary sources that claim to offer information do not appear to draw a clear line between fact and satire. For example, *Nocturnal Revels* purports to be a factual account of notable London harlots, bagnios and seraglios from the 1720s to the 1770s. When dealing with the high-class seraglio in King's Place, St James's, presided over by Charlotte Hayes, the book offers a list of services along with charges and these are usually taken as accurate. The names of the clients are intended to be humorous but most, it seems, were familiar nicknames so the people mentioned were identifiable. Eight clients, acts and charges are noted, along with the names and attributes of various prostitutes.

We learn that on Sunday 9 January 1769 'Alderman Drybones' paid a pretended virgin called Nell Blossom, aged nineteen, 20 guineas for the pleasure of deflowering her. Sir Harry Flagellum paid 10 guineas for services that, to judge by his nickname and that of the proposed girls – 'Nell Handy from Bow-Street' or 'Bet Flourish from Berners Street, or Miss Birch herself from Chapel Street' – involved flagellation. Lord Spasm paid 5 guineas for 'A Bona Roba' from 'St Clement's or Black Moll, from Hedge-Lane ... or barge-a—se Wilson, from Rupert Street'. Colonel Tearall paid 10 guineas for a 'modest woman' whom he could happily abuse. A clergyman, Dr Frettext, paid 2 guineas for a girl with 'very white, soft hands', and the names of the two girls proposed – Polly Nimblewrist and Jenny Speedyhand – leave little doubt about the sexual favour the good doctor was buying. Lady Loveit paid the very large sum of 50 guineas to be 'well mounted' by a Captain O'Thunder or Sawney Rowbone. Count Alto paid 10 guineas for an hour with a 'woman of fashion', while Lord Pyebald paid 5 guineas for the company of a young lady with whom he did not propose to come to 'any extremity'.[8]

Charlotte Hayes' 'cloister' or 'nunnery' in King's Place was at the upper end of the sex trade – seemingly in the penultimate class. If the charges – which the text implies are sometimes for the night, sometimes for one hour or one act – are accurate, then they are most informative. Of the clients, one is charged 2 guineas, two are charged 5 guineas, three are charged 10 guineas, one is charged 20 guineas and one is charged 50 guineas. This makes the average charge just over 14 guineas. Charlotte's competition, Mrs Goady, is said in a 1773 edition of the *Covent Garden Magazine* to have charged 50 guineas for a 'virgin' while, as was the case in most other establishments, the common charge was 5 guineas.[9]

These are huge amounts of money when set against the wages earned at the time. A skilled London tradesman or journeyman earned in the 1770s around 3 shillings a day, which, working a six-day week, meant a weekly salary of 18 shillings to £1, while a curate's median annual stipend or a minor government clerk's annual wage was £50 or 50 guineas. So a reasonably high-class harlot could earn – in one night – what a working man would take between three and four months to earn, and a 'virgin' could earn in one night – or rather earn for her bawd – what a junior cleric or civil servant earned in a year. It's important to remember, though, when pondering these high sums that the majority of the middle range of

A strange scene from a seraglio of c.1770, perhaps Charlotte Hayes' King's Place Nunnery. Note the large mirror behind the couch in an alcove.

prostitutes – those not working the streets and not kept women or high courtesans – worked within the context of bawdy-houses or brothels, and that most of their earnings went to the bawd or 'abbess' who funded, housed and protected them.

The earning power of high-class harlots is revealed in numerous contemporary publications. James Boswell, in his *London Journal* of 1762–3, observed that London was full of 'free-hearted ladies of all kinds' with a 'splendid madam' costing 'fifty guineas a night',[10] while *Nocturnal Revels* revealed that Miss Emily C-l-h-st 'can command almost any price' and 'has more than once refused a £20 Bank Note because she did not like the presenter'.[11]

Archenholz recorded in the 1780s that the famed and high-class actress/courtesan Kitty Fisher 'knew her own merit' and 'demanded a hundred guineas for a night'.[12] He also hinted at the incredible wealth of high-class courtesans when he wrote:

> The uncertainty of payment leads all landlords who let rooms to such girls to double their rent. The extortionate sums generally obtained, and which are usually paid regularly for safeties sake, induce people in reasonably good circumstances to open their houses to these unfortunate girls. They are given the best rooms and the best furniture, for a weekly rent which far exceeds the yearly house rent with all taxes.[13]

The general financial benefit to London of the sex industry was implied by Archenholz when he observes that 'without these girls many thousand houses in the West End of London would stand empty'.

Speculative house building had – since the Great Fire of 1666 – been one of London's main economic activities. It involved landlords, the building trades, merchants who lent and made money on building projects, and occupants who purchased building leases and undertook to pay ground rent and local and national rates and taxes. If the cycle of demand and supply were broken, if there were not enough people willing and able to occupy new housing and provide reasonable profits for the speculators, then London's economy would slump. The vast number of people employed in the building trades would suffer, as would landowners, landlords and financiers. And, according to Archenholz, bulwarks against a possible slump, among the most reliable tenants for newly built houses, were richer members of the sex trade.

It would seem, in fact, that their industry underpinned the entire expansion of Georgian London – a period now seen as an exemplar of artistic achievement, architectural endeavour and creative urban planning. Georgian London was a corporate work of art, a place of beauty forged out of the quest for profit – and key partners in this collaboration were the rich West End courtesans and the owners of profitable bagnios and brothels – people like Moll King, as we have seen, with her terrace of houses on Haverstock Hill (see page 89). Property was considered a safe way to invest money: Moll would have gained a good annual income from her rents, and a valuable asset against which money could be borrowed for other business ventures.

The high charges demanded, and achieved, by the upper echelon of harlots were of course counterbalanced by the far meaner sums made by the numerous classes of lower-earning whores. Some idea of their charges is given by the editions of *Harris's List* from which an average sum can be deduced. The British Library possesses five copies of the *List* – two for 1788, and one each for 1789, 1790 and 1793. The last one contains 81 entries and the first 75. The average sum requested by the 45 ladies whose charges are given is a little over 2 guineas.

The charges made for courtesan Fanny Murray, who appeared in the early 'parchment' version of the list – presumably in the 1740s, where she was listed as aged nineteen – bear this out. Her *Memoirs*, published in 1759, state that Fanny, 'after being thus initiated in the Arcanum of Mr H—r—s's system of fornication . . . plied regularly in the flesh-market . . . by which means she increased the price of her favours, never now receiving under two guineas'.[14] It's also stated in Fanny Murray's *Memoirs* that the girls entered on *Harris's List* paid him 'poundage' – a fee – for the good publicity they received. It has been stated that this was as high as 25 per cent of their earnings, but it seems highly unlikely. It is possible that the girls in the *List* charged their customers a 'surcharge' to compensate for Harris's 'poundage', but such an action would have been commercially unwise since by doing so they would have priced themselves out of the market. All things considered, it is far more probable than not that the charges quoted in the *List* reflect the true average.

The girls listed by Harris represent the large majority of middle-market London prostitutes – above the street girls yet well below the high-class courtesans. The fact that their average of 2 guineas a night reflects the lower end of the middle range is supported by some evidence offered by Casanova. During a London jaunt he enjoyed the fare offered at a bagnio and was charged 6 guineas, which he thought good value.

The lower classes of prostitute charged far less than 2 guineas per session or night. Their probable and usual charges were suggested in many contemporary accounts. Some street prostitutes would demand only the price of a glass of gin for their services or would participate in a 'three-penny upright'. The *Covent Garden Magazine* states that 'for a flying leap is half a crown, for a nights lodging 5 shillings; likewise a bottle of wine is expected. Streetwalkers who would satisfy your wishes for 3d and a dram and give more than you desire [i.e. the pox]'. There were also

'Two-penny Bunters', and James Boswell in his *London Journal*, written in 1762–3, records that a 'civil nymph with white-thread stockings who tramps along the Strand' will 'resign her engaging person to your honour for a pint of wine and a shilling'.[15] On another occasion Boswell again paid a shilling to 'toy' with a girl in a court off the Strand, but several times was charged no more than sixpence by street prostitutes. However, no doubt correctly, A. D. Harvey in *Sex in Georgian London* observes that a shilling seems to have been the going rate for sex with a street-walker – which was actually a pretty large sum, equal to the weekly rent for a garret or basement room in a poorer part of London.

The archives of the Old Bailey offer insights into levels of payment – as well as practices – at the lower and overtly criminal end of the sex industry. For example, in December 1750 John Omitt was tried for house-breaking, and in his defence – which was successful – undermined the credibility of a prosecution witness by claiming that she was 'a very disorderly woman' and that 'last Saturday night . . . I was coming down Shoe-lane, she ask'd me to give her a dram; she took me with her to this house . . . there I gave her eighteen pence to go upstairs, to lie with her'.[16] The woman was called Mary Maxwell and Omitt's assessment of her poor character was supported some time later when in April 1754 she was transported after being found guilty of 'Grand Larceny'.[17] Anne Jones similarly, transported as a pick-pocket after her trial in February 1751, had picked up a man in James Street, Covent Garden at 9 o'clock at night, taken him for a 'dram' in a house in Rose Street 'that was not an alehouse', and then accepted 2 shillings because, as the man explained to the court, 'we was likely to be concerned together'. Instead she attempted to steal a guinea that she secreted in her mouth. Anne Jones' defence, 'he gave me the guinea to stay with him all night', was not accepted by the jury – presumably because such a high payment for the services of such a low woman was not credible.[18]

In the absence of fuller evidence, it is perhaps a reasonable basis for calculation to argue that the very large sums made by the small number of top-earning prostitutes balance out the very low earnings of the large number of common prostitutes, and therefore that the average earnings of the majority of middling prostitutes should be taken as the average for the profession as a whole: that is, 2 guineas per prostitute per night.

Given the amount of documentary evidence – albeit often anecdotal

– it is possible to ask and partially to answer two key questions: how many prostitutes were there in London during the late eighteenth century and how many nights on average did each work per week?

The first question can be answered by reference to contemporary documents, while the second can probably never be answered satisfactorily, although prostitution seems to have been a seven-day-a-week business since we know Sunday was the favoured time for clients to visit bagnios or brothels. In *Nocturnal Revels*, when a list of clients and prostitutes is drawn up, it is made clear that the proposed liaisons will take place on a Sunday. So, if a prostitute worked seven days a week, at the average fee of 2 guineas a night, she earned a maximum of 730 guineas per annum, but if she worked the more likely average of four nights a week then her average annual income was 416 guineas.

The numbers of prostitutes operating in eighteenth-century London are estimated in several publications. In the second half of the 1720s a French visitor to London recorded that 'An Englishman, who knows London very well' put the number of 'courtesans in the town' as already 'more than 40,000'.[19] *A Congratulatory Epistle from a Reformed Rake to John F—g, Esq upon the new Scheme of Reclaiming Prostitutes* of 1758 (printed by G. Burnet) suggested that, 'according to ... calculation ... there are Sixty-two Thousand, Five Hundred Whores, including, *Women of Fashion who Intrigue, Demi-reps, Good-natured-Girls, and Kept Mistresses*, who become common by Rotation',[20] and in the 1780s Archenholz stated that 'London is said to contain fifty thousand prostitutes, without reckoning kept mistresses', which is to say 50,000 full-time prostitutes.[21]

These estimates are high and evidently not based on carefully collated evidence. They should be considered against a number of far lower estimates. For example, in 1758 the reforming magistrate Saunders Welch calculated that there were at least 3,000 prostitutes working in London,[22] and in 1760 Jonas Hanway, one of the two founders of the Magdalen House (see page 280), supported Welch's estimate, and agreed that in the cities of London and Westminster 'it is generally computed that there are 3,000 common prostitutes'.[23] The number of high courtesans, kept women and occasional prostitutes are evidently not included in this total.

Recently Randolph Trumbach has investigated this subject and gathered some most revealing information. Welch and Hanway must, he observes, 'have based their estimates on the number of women they saw on the streets and the number who were arrested. We cannot see the women, but we can look at the arrests.'[24]

The Society for the Reformation of Manners kept lists of the prosecutions they instigated and these show that in 1700, 1701, 1702, 1704 and 1707, 3,957 prostitutes were arrested. The Session Rolls for Middlesex and Westminster for 1720 and 1721 reveal that 632 women were committed as prostitutes, and Trumbach calculates that these represent about 55 per cent of the women arrested. These figures, coupled with the numbers of prostitutes cared for in the Lock Hospitals and Magdalen House (see page 245), lead him to conclude that Welch's estimate of 3,000 active prostitutes in 1758 'seems very likely'.[25]

How then do we explain the far higher contemporary estimates? What is clear is that, even if not scientifically deduced, these cannot simply be ignored, especially since they are supported by the more methodically calculated estimate offered by the police magistrate Patrick Colquhoun, who in 1795 calculated that there were 50,000 prostitutes working in the capital, although not all full-time.[26] In 1801, according to the census of that year, London was estimated to have had a population of 730,000 living in 110,000 houses. By 1819 the population had increased to well over one million.[27] If Colquhoun's figure is correct, and if it is assumed that a third of the total population of 730,000 were women of sexually active age – say 250,000 – then a staggering one London woman in five was involved in one way or other with the sex industry in the mid- to late eighteenth century.

This estimate is apparently supported by the anonymous author of *A Congratulatory Epistle from a Reformed Rake* of 1758, who states that:

> . . . if I were to judge, by my own Experience, and that of my
> Acquaintance, I might venture to pronounce, that amongst every five
> Women there is (at least) one Whore; as I can with the greatest Veracity
> assert, that among all my Female Acquaintance, I could never think of
> any five, but what I either had, or could have, lain with one of them.

And this, the author claims, was the same for 'every Man who has a general unlimited Acquaintance with the Sex'.[28] This assumption formed the basis of the author's very high estimate of 62,500 prostitutes in London. He reckoned that the population of the 'Metropolis, it's Suburbs and Adjacencies' was near 'a Million inhabitants' with half being women, of which 'five-eights . . . are at the Age of Womanhood, or debouchable'. Dividing this population by five gives the figure of 62,500 prostitutes in London, and 450,000 in England, although his definition of a whore evidently includes promiscuous women who had sexual 'intrigues' for pleasure and not primarily for financial profit.[29]

If Colquhoun's figure of 50,000 prostitutes still seems high as a basis for calculating the value of London's late-eighteenth-century sex industry it is worth remembering that he was referring solely to female prostitutes. If male prostitutes also were counted, along with the many shady figures running the bagnios and brothels, then the total number of people involved in the London sex industry in 1790 would be far higher than 50,000. To put these figures in context, and by way of comparison, the *Universal Daily Register* of 1 August 1786 estimated that one-sixth of the population of London were either 'Rakes or Whores', which suggests around 120,000 people were involved in the sex industry – as either users or suppliers.

Colquhoun offered a breakdown of his estimate of the number of prostitutes. He calculated that 2,000 were well-educated women, 3,000 were persons above the rank of menial servant, 20,000 were menial servants seduced early in life and who lived solely by prostitution, and that 25,000 were from different ranks of society who lived partly by prostitution, including 'low females who co-habit with labourers and others without matrimony'. This key observation reflects a very unscientific moral prejudice on Colquhoun's part. Half the prostitutes listed by him were in fact, and at worst, only casual prostitutes and perhaps not really prostitutes at all, but women living with men on a regular basis while not legally married. But to Colquhoun, such women were not only technically and morally prostitutes but also – because of their 'low' class and apparently unprincipled behaviour – capable of acting as regular prostitutes as and when it suited them. He was demonstrably a far from objective and sympathetic observer of the tragic fate that poverty and discrimination could impose on London's working-class women.

Of the 20,000 regular prostitutes, Colquhoun observed that a number were factory workers – a new class of working women in London. He assumed that this particular type of employment had a corrupting influence because it attracted many vulnerable country girls to London and mixed male and female workers in a most promiscuous manner.

A late-eighteenth-century engraving of a London prostitute.

But the very fact that Colquhoun went to such lengths to establish accurate figures – and the fact that other contemporary observers such as Archenholz tend to confirm them – does suggest that London really was the sex capital not just of England but of the world.[30] Colquhoun's figures also give an indication of the extraordinary value of prostitution to the eighteenth-century economy. If we can assume, as I have suggested earlier, that the average prostitute earned 2 guineas per night, and if we can assume, too, that each prostitute worked no more than four nights a week, then the annual gross value of the sex industry in London in the last quarter of the eighteenth century was a colossal 20.8 million guineas or £21,840,000 – and this figure ignores income from male prostitutes and aspects of the industry unrelated to direct sexual encounters. In other words, whatever the precise annual figure may have been, it is clear that the sex industry – even if it created little wealth – was one of the most valuable industries in late-eighteenth-century London.[31]

Nearly half a century later, in 1839, Michael Ryan, MD published a detailed social and medical analysis of the capital entitled *Prostitution in*

London. In this work Ryan pulled together recent and contemporary reports on the subject, and offered his own views and opinions. Naturally he mentioned 'the late Mr Colquhoun, a magistrate of police' who in 'about the year 1793 . . . concluded, after tedious [i.e. lengthy] investigations, that there were 50,000 prostitutes in this metropolis'. 'At that period,' he went on, 'the population was one million, and as it is now doubled, the number of abandoned women might perhaps be supposed to have doubled.' In other words, if the basis of Colquhoun's findings were to be believed, there ought to have been around 100,000 prostitutes in the London of the mid-1830s.

In fact, Ryan was sceptical about Colquhoun's estimate. 'One of the present commissioners of the metropolitan police,' he wrote, 'has assured me no reliance could be placed on the accuracy of Mr Colquhoun's figures, and that even now, when the new police is much better organized, no certain results can be arrived at.'[32] The commissioner to whom Ryan refers may have been Edwin Chadwick, who was closely involved in 1839 with the *First Report of the Commissioners appointed to inquire into the best means of establishing an efficient constabulary.* This report cast a similarly critical eye over Colquhoun's figures and points out that the male population of London in his time was 400,000 (based on the 1801 census), so that, after deducting young and aged, there was a population of only 250,000 adult males to 'support' prostitution. Even allowing that all these men were 'licentious in their habits', Colquhoun's calculation suggested the unlikely statistic that London possessed one prostitute for every four adult males and 'that every third or fourth female was a prostitute'.[33]

Significantly, though, the Commissioner's report does not say that Colquhoun's figures were wholly wrong, it simply uses more solid statistics to question his estimates. And although Ryan casts doubts on Colquhoun's calculations, he also quotes a *Report of the London Society for the Protection of Young Females and the Prevention of Juvenile Prostitution,* produced in 1835 by J. B. Talbot, which stated that 'not less than 80,000 prostitutes exist in London, – a great proportion of whom are of tender age'. Talbot went on to say: 'It is computed that 8,000 die every year, and yet the number so far from being reduced is on the increase – the market . . . being constantly supplied by those who are ever on the alert to entrap the innocent and the unwary.'[34] He then computed that in London there were 5,000 brothels with '400,000 persons . . . directly and indirectly connected with prostitution, and that £8,000,000 is expanded annually in London on this vice alone'. Talbot 'proved' this with the following calculation:

> ... some girls obtain from twenty to thirty pounds a week, others more; while most of those who frequent theatres &c receive from ten to twelve pounds. Those of a still lower grade obtain about four or five pounds, some less than one pound, and many not ten shillings ... If we take the average earnings of each prostitute at £100 per annum, which is under the amount, it gives the yearly income of £8,000,000.

This average income per prostitute per annum is very small – Talbot himself admits it is 'under the amount' – and certainly much less than we know prostitutes were earning in Colquhoun's time. But Talbot then goes on to include another intriguing analytical calculation:

> ... suppose the average expense [wages and cost of support] of 80,000 [prostitutes] amounts to £20 each, which is over the mark, £1,600,000 is the result. This sum deducted from the earnings, leaves £6,400,000 as the income of keepers of prostitutes; or, supposing 5,000 to be the number, above £1,000 per annum each, an income much larger than that of many professional men, military and naval officers, or responsible tradesmen. There is no exaggeration in this calculation.[35]

Prostitution, in other words, remained a major economic force in Talbot's time. In earlier decades there can be no doubt that it was one of the industries that created London's wealth and forged its expansion.

ELIZABETH CANNING

Abduction into Prostitution

On the night of 29 January 1753, eighteen-year-old Elizabeth Canning appeared at the door of her mother's house near St Mary Alderman-bury Church in the City of London. She was dressed in rags and appeared emaciated, exhausted and disorientated. She had been missing for four weeks and, when questioned, had a sensational story to tell.

As family and neighbours gathered around, Elizabeth explained what had happened to her on the night of 1 January as she walked across the western end of Moorfields, to the north-east of her home. Her account of events was later recounted in the *Newgate Calendar*.

She had visited her aunt and uncle, Thomas and Mrs Colley, near Saltpetre-bank (now Dock Street, just off the Ratcliffe Highway near the Tower), and stayed with them until about nine at night when they escorted her home as far as the junction of Aldgate and Houndsditch. Then, while walking alone across Moorfields, near the wall of the Bethlem Hospital, she claimed she was assaulted by two men . . .

> . . . who robbed her of half a guinea . . . and three shillings, [one]
> took her gown, apron, and hat . . . on which she screamed out; but he
> bound a handkerchief round her mouth, and tied her hands behind
> her, after which, she received a violent blow on the head, which,
> added to her former terror.

Elizabeth later claimed that the 'two lusty men' shouted 'd—n you, you b—h, we'll do for you by and by' which induced a fit [she had a history of sudden lapses into unconsciousness] and claimed that 'the first thing I remember after this was, I found myself by a large road, where was water, with the two men that robbed me'.[1]

In Elizabeth's version of events, she realised she was being abducted but, it seems, despite the horror of the situation, kept her wits about her and tried to determine how long she had been carried, to identify where she was and where she was being taken. It was, she calculated, about four in the morning and about half an hour after recovering from her fit when she arrived at a house. Upon entering this remote dwelling, according to Elizabeth's account of her ordeal, she saw three gypsies – a woman and two girls. The *Newgate Calendar* explains what is said to have happened next:

> . . . the woman took Canning by the hand, asked her if she chose to go their way, and, if she would, she should have fine cloaths. Canning, understanding that her meaning was to commence prostitute, replied in the negative; on which [the woman] took a knife from a drawer, cut the lace from her stays, and took them from her, then . . . pushed her up a few stairs out of the kitchen, to a place called the Hayloft, and shut the door on her.

Eighteen-year-old Elizabeth Canning, who claimed to have been abducted by gypsies planning to force her into prostitution.

Elizabeth recalled that dawn broke 'three hours or better' after she arrived at the house, and stated that she found there was only hay for her to sleep on and bread and water to sustain her. This, she claimed, was what she lived on for twenty-eight days, without even the means for the decent 'evacuation of nature', and all the time alone and terrorised by the gypsy woman's threat that any attempt to leave the room would result in her throat being cut.

The purpose of this regime of torture and terror seemed obvious to all who heard Elizabeth's tale. The woman who had cut and stolen her stays and another older woman who appeared to be the mistress of the house were intent on breaking Elizabeth's bodily strength and will – of starving her into submission – so that she would do their bidding and consent to work for them as a prostitute. So, it appeared, the ghastly truth was that Elizabeth's abductors and gaolers were gypsies, bawds and prostitutes, that her gaol was a brothel and she was intended to become their profitable sex-slave.

This shocking story preyed upon the worst and deepest fears that had lurked for four weeks in the breasts of Elizabeth's family and friends. Here was their nightmare become ghastly reality. Most who heard the girl's account of her terrible ordeal believed such things could and did happen, and here – in terrifying detail – was an actual example that confirmed popular prejudices and assumptions.

Such readiness to believe Elizabeth's story also suggests the deep disquiet with which many Londoners regarded the powerful and all-pervasive sex industry. It was, in popular perception, a dark and ubiquitous presence that could at any moment engulf and transform the life of even the most innocent. The superficial facts of the tale all helped to confirm its apparent truth. Moorfields, then a large and perilous open area, was notorious as a night-time prowling ground for foot-pads and licentious homosexuals, and so was a predictable location for such an assault to take place. It was also predictable that gypsies should be involved, a strange, suspect and feared people who lived largely outside the laws and conventions of society.

But the girl's abductors were not apparently to have their way. Having suffered this extraordinary and brutal kidnap, Elizabeth, after a month's imprisonment according to her own account, achieved an equally extraordinary escape. As the *Newgate Calendar* explained, at 'about four in the afternoon of Monday the 29th of January', she . . .

... pulled down a board that was nailed on the inside of the window, and getting her head first out, she kept fast hold by the wall, and then dropped into a narrow place by a lane, behind which was a field. Having got into the highway, she enquired her way to London, but did not stop. When she came into Moorfields the clock struck ten; and she thence proceeded to her mother's near Aldermanbury.

Among the people who heard Elizabeth's initial account of her sufferings were 'two gentlemen with whom she had lived as a servant' – John Wintlebury and Edward Lion – and this turned out to be most significant. Perhaps inspired by the presence of one of these gentlemen, she claimed that the place of her confinement was 'near the Hertfordshire road', because during her confinement she saw Mrs Wintlebury's 'coachman go by, which she used to go into the country into Hertfordshire'. Elizabeth seems to have been referring to the Hertford stagecoach that she used to 'carry things to' for Mrs Wintlebury. So, by strange chance, the activities of the wife of one of these gentlemen who happened to be present became the prime means by which Elizabeth identified the location of her gaol.

The increasingly enraged and indignant people who heard Elizabeth's initial account overlooked this bizarre coincidence. What maddened them was that a girl had disappeared for a month, that neither her mother, friends nor employers had any idea where she had been, and that she had returned in a shocking state. Therefore, improbable as it may seem, opinion held that her story must be true – not least because of a deep-rooted if horribly prejudiced general belief that gypsies did do such things. So the information that Elizabeth provided – the Hertfordshire road, the distance from Moorfields, the gypsy woman and girls and the older woman who was probably a bawd, the water near the house – was pondered over and discussed, mostly in the tavern near Elizabeth's home where she had once worked as a servant and which was run by Wintlebury.

During the next thirty-six hours the amazing story took further shape, with much of its detail provided not by Elizabeth directly but by other people – such as Wintlebury – who by chance were present when she told her tale, who perhaps heard only parts of it and that imperfectly, and who had in many cases derived the information and answers they wanted and expected by putting leading questions to the simple and exhausted girl. Certainly, as later events were to prove, several people present at Elizabeth's return home remembered hearing significantly different versions of what she was supposed to have said.

On 31 January Elizabeth was taken before Alderman Chitty to give an official and definitive version of events. This was a good idea but didn't quite work because – as was later revealed – Chitty failed to take, or to keep, full notes of what she said and so the accuracy of his later account was itself open to doubt. But apparently during this interview Elizabeth gave a number of additional details about her abduction and the room in which she was confined.

Her abductors 'forced her along through Bishopsgate-street, each holding her up under the arms, but she did not remember any thing more that passed'; the room was 'little, square, dark or darkish' with 'an old stool or two, an old table, and an old picture over the chimney – two windows . . . one fastened up with board' and below one 'a small shed of boards or pent-house'.[2] Already inconsistencies and peculiarities were emerging. How could an unconscious young woman be carried along busy Bishopsgate-street at about ten at night with no one apparently noticing or intervening? But for the moment these problems with Elizabeth's story didn't seem to matter. The necessity of finding her abductors and gaolers was paramount.

Soon after the interview with Chitty, Elizabeth's friends, after much amateur sleuthing, had, as the *Newgate Calendar* explained, 'reason to suspect that the house in which she had been confined was that of Susannah Wells'. Acting upon nothing more than inconsistent evidence, rumour and prejudice, a mob was formed, near-vigilante in character, a warrant obtained from the Lord Mayor of the City to apprehend Wells and all in the house, and Elizabeth's avengers made their way to Enfield Wash, about ten miles distant, where their quarry was said to reside.

But who exactly was the young woman who had disappeared and then reappeared in such dramatic circumstances, causing so much fury and frantic activity? Not surprisingly very little was – or is – known about Elizabeth Canning. She was said to have worked as a servant for two or three years before her abduction. After working for Wintlebury she was employed in the family of Edward Lion, who appears to have been an affluent City-based carpenter or perhaps builder. When the case – and Elizabeth – became notorious, many explored her history and character but none found that she had any secrets to hide. The novelist Tobias Smollett, who like many became fascinated by her story, described her simply as an 'obscure damsel of low degree'[3] and found nothing against her. All seemed to agree she was humble, unexceptional, apparently chaste and a conscientious worker. So, with this character, it is easy to understand why so many believed Elizabeth's story and were prepared to act.

Edward Lion, Wintlebury and a representative of the Lord Mayor led the party intent on obtaining justice and revenge. Elizabeth too was present so she could identify locations and people. When they arrived at Susannah Wells' house, Elizabeth was taken from room to room and attempted to match her story to the physical evidence. There were several inconsistencies that were noted at the time. For example, the room in which she said she had been confined was not little, square and dark, but measured nearly 36 feet by 5 and was light and open to the roof tiles, nor did it have the furnishings and details she had described, and there wasn't a 'pent-house' outside the window that might have helped her descend to the ground.

Nothing quite rang true, but what really mattered at the moment was that, despite all these discrepancies in detail, Elizabeth confirmed the gypsy bawdy-house as the place of her confinement. That was all the vigilantes wanted to hear. Elizabeth indeed went further. In the account sworn to Chitty she had claimed that her stays had been stolen by a 'tall, elderly, swarthy woman', and in the house was a person who fitted this very broad description. With little hesitation Elizabeth identified this woman – a gypsy named Mary Squires – as her assailant, and also claimed that another woman present was one of the gypsies who had 'stood by' while the stays were cut off. This woman's name was Virtue Hall, by her own admission a prostitute working at 'Mother Wells' bawdy-house.

This was enough for the mob. These two women, along with Susannah Wells, were carried before the local magistrate, Mr Merry Tyshmaker of Edmonton, who summarily and, on Canning's confused evidence alone, committed Squires and Hall to gaol to await trial – Squires for robbery, Wells for aiding and abetting – while Hall was discharged since even in these clearly heated and prejudicial circumstances there seemed no grounds on which to hold her.[4]

After the frantic and chaotic detection process and the detention of the suspects there should have been a cooling-off period, time for an

A nineteenth-century print based on Hogarth's mid-eighteenth-century portrait of Henry Fielding, who became closely involved in Elizabeth Canning's case.

objective examination of the case and the inconsistencies that had arisen between Canning's description of her place of confinement and the layout of Wells' house. But this did not happen – largely due to the role now played by Henry Fielding.

In early 1753 Fielding was a very ill man. He was in virtually constant pain from gout and 'dropsy' and could only move with the use of crutches. He had been a Westminster magistrate since 1748 and Justice of the Peace for Middlesex since 1749. In May 1754 he would be obliged finally to retire as a Justice, due to his ailments, dying five months later.[5] But despite his increasing indisposition Fielding was, in early February 1753, still exercising legal power, though he probably realised only too well that his illness was terminal. This atmosphere of impending mortality may explain what happened next.

Fielding had fought long – and generally humanely – to control the excesses and growth of the sex industry and to save vulnerable young women from becoming ensnared in it. Now, with his own campaigning days rapidly drawing to a close, came this extraordinary case. Fielding, like many after him, became obsessed by it.

Here was a story that seemed emblematic of the whole troubled age, and particularly of life in the great, voracious city of London that Fielding's colleague Saunders Welch dismissed as a 'great scandal' and 'one general stew'.[6] Elizabeth, seemingly the very image of simplicity and innocence, had been set upon by people who appeared the embodiment of lawless corruption and whose only aim was to exploit her and in the process drag her down into their pit of depravity, disease and despond. This was devilish work indeed.

Elizabeth's lawyer asked Fielding for his 'opinion' upon the case and on 7 February the victim swore her evidence before the ailing and prematurely aged magistrate. Fielding scrutinised Elizabeth, listened to her closely and decided to accept this strange story at face value. He then issued a warrant for the apprehension of Virtue Hall. Clearly he was not convinced by her initial statement that she knew nothing about Canning, the theft of her stays or her imprisonment.

Hall was picked up, and on 13 February questioned by Canning's counsel and by Fielding. Her interrogation lasted for six hours, but she stuck steadily to her story and maintained her innocence. It did her no good. Then something critical happened – accounts of what exactly vary tremendously. Some say Fielding was 'kindness itself' to Virtue and 'coaxed' her story out of her.[7] Others state that he and the counsel were threatening, with Fielding finally declaring to Virtue that she would be committed to gaol for trial as a felon and so stand or fall by the evidence that should be produced against her. Upon this threat, some accounts state, an exhausted and intimidated Hall agreed to tell her inquisitors what they wanted to hear, in an attempt to save herself. Others simply say that Virtue now decided to tell 'the truth'. Yes, she said, Elizabeth Canning had been at Susannah Wells' house, and she had been robbed in the way she described. This statement, rapidly written up by Canning's lawyer, became the main evidence against Squires and Wells.

The trial opened at the Old Bailey on 21 February 1753, less than a month after Canning's reappearance. The court was packed and – towards the defendants – the atmosphere hostile. The public had already made up its mind: the gypsies were guilty. A mob gathered outside the court set upon intimidating character witnesses arriving to offer evidence for Squires and Wells. But three brave men got through and corroborated Mary Squires' simple defence, upon which her life now rested. During the time of Canning's alleged incarceration Squires claimed she had been travelling in Dorset, and these three men all swore they had seen her there during January.

Canning then told the court her story as did several of the people who had heard her tell it on 29 January and who had formed part of the expedition to Enfield Wash. During these accounts some of the differences between Canning's description of Wells' house and the reality were noted, as were those details that were consistent. The balance of opinion seemed to be in Canning's favour, but any discrepancies were, of course, legitimate grounds for suspicion about the veracity of her tale as a whole. An apothecary, Sutherton Bakler, gave evidence about Elizabeth's physical condition when she returned home and confirmed that she certainly was not faking ill health. She was, stated Bakler, 'extremely low and weak [with her] pulse scarcely to be felt'.

Virtue Hall's evidence given now against Squires and Wells was particularly damning. Not only did she confirm Canning's story, she added several incriminating and provocative details. One of the 'gypsey men' who abducted Canning was, she claimed, John Squires, Mary's son, and she confirmed that when Squires asked Canning to 'go her way' she 'meant for her to turn whore'. Hall also explained her own presence in the house. 'I went there as a lodger, but I was forced to do as they would have me.'[8] So Hall – a girl forced into prostitution by Squires and Wells – appeared to be living proof of what had been intended for Canning.

Perhaps unsurprisingly, Squires and her witnesses were not believed and both defendants were found guilty. Wells was sentenced to six months in gaol and branding on the thumb and Squires to be hanged for stealing the stays. But this wasn't the end of the trial. When found guilty Squires, in her desperation and ignorance of legal procedures, suddenly offered another alibi that she hoped might be more acceptable and convincing. This was a ghastly mistake for immediately the three men who had appeared in her defence – John Gibbon, William Clarke and Thomas Greville – appeared to have been lying to the court. They, for their trouble and courage, were now charged with perjury.

The public was satisfied, the frightful and corrupting gypsy was to hang and, presumably, Fielding was happy with this last successful attack on one of the more dangerous denizens of the great city of vice. But, much to his credit, the Lord Mayor of London – Sir Crisp Gascoyne – who had sat among the judges during the trial, was not satisfied with the verdict. Indeed, he was deeply concerned by what he saw as a witch-hunt characterised by prejudice, hatred and threats of violence. And, more to the point, he was worried by the inconsistencies in Canning's evidence. Being the City's chief magistrate, the Lord Mayor was able to act speedily in a desperate bid to prevent what he believed to be a terrible miscarriage of justice. First he launched his own inquiry, found more witnesses (no doubt those who had been intimidated before the court and turned away by the mob) who confirmed that Squires was indeed in Dorset at the time of the imprisonment, and himself questioned Hall, who abruptly 'recanted'. This cast Fielding – who had acquired Hall's evidence – in a very unfortunate light and led to serious criticism of him, for example from Sir John Hill whose pamphlet, entitled *The Story of Elizabeth Canning Considered*, accused him of bullying the witnesses into giving false evidence.[9]

In addition to the collapse of Canning's only supporting witness, the case against the three men charged with perjury was making no headway because no evidence could be found to use against them. It appeared they had after all been telling the truth. This was enough for Sir Crisp. He persuaded the King to grant a stay of execution, although he was too late to save Wells, who had already been branded as ordered.

These actions did not serve to make the Lord Mayor popular with the London mob who wanted gypsy blood. As the *Newgate Calendar* explained, 'he was abused with a degree of virulence that reflected the highest infamy on his calumniators', and simply because he wanted to discover the truth. But inexorably the weight of evidence gathered by Sir Crisp moved informed opinion in Squires' favour and it became increasingly obvious that her conviction was unsafe.

Feeling an obligation to defend and explain his actions, Fielding published in March 1753 *A Clear Statement of the Case of Elizabeth Canning*. In this pamphlet he admitted that Canning's 'extraordinary narrative ... consisting of many strange particulars' resembled 'rather a Wild dream than a real fact', but defended his actions and Elizabeth's testimony because 'there is something within myself which rouses me to the protection of injured innocence'. But Fielding realised that now he, as well as Elizabeth, was on trial. 'As to my own conduct in this affair', he wrote:

> I know it to be highly justifiable before God and before Man [and] I
> frankly own, I thought it entitled me to the very reverse of censure
> [being] principally urged [by] a desire to protect innocence and to detect

guilt . . . If Elizabeth Canning be guilty of a false accusation, I own she hath been capable of imposing on me; but I have the comfort to think the same imposition hath passed not only on two juries, but likewise on one of the best judges that ever sat on the Bench of Justice . . . In this case . . . one of the most simple Girls I ever saw, if she be a wicked one, hath been too hard for me.

But Fielding clearly believed he had not been duped for he proclaimed:

I am at this very time, on the 15th day of March, 1753, as firmly persuaded as I am of any fact in this world . . . that Mary Squires the Gipsy-woman, IS GUILTY of the robbery and cruelty of which she stands convicted . . . and that Elizabeth Canning is a poor, honest, innocent simple girl, and the most unhappy and most injured of all human beings.[10]

It was of course only natural that Fielding should continue to support Elizabeth – despite shifting public opinion – because he had, to a degree, staked his reputation on the truth of her account. His role in pressing the case against Mary Squires and in getting Virtue Hall to give evidence that she subsequently recanted was far from admirable. If Canning was lying, then Fielding was humiliated before the public for it did indeed mean that a teenage servant girl with a most improbable story to tell had deluded an experienced magistrate, gifted author and social campaigner with a deep and sagacious understanding of human nature.

His most perceptive biographer – Ronald Paulson – points out that Fielding was particularly susceptible to certain types – 'figures of pathos' – like the sixteen-year-old prostitute he found in a bawdy-house in Covent Garden (see page 493) and the pretty young thief in Shoreditch (see page 497). He had spent his fiction-writing career outlining circumstances that now seemed to confront him in real life in the story told by Elizabeth Canning: '[H]ere is the plot of *Tom Jones* and, with the disbelieved hero feminised, of *Amelia*.'[11] For Fielding, Canning's account *had* to be true; it was art becoming reality, the moral message of his fiction vindicated.

Nevertheless the mounting public hostility to his role in the case seems to have worried Fielding deeply, and in his determination to justify his own conduct and explain why Squires' sentence was being questioned he even concocted his own conspiracy theory. The Lord Mayor, Sir Crisp

Gascoyne, was – argued Fielding – the real target. His enemies had set up a plan to secure his public humiliation by enticing him to defend Mary Squires. As Fielding explained in a letter of 27 April 1753 to the Duke of Newcastle, the people now gathering affidavits to use against Canning were in his view:

> . . . a set of the most obstinate fools I ever saw, and who seem to me rather to act from a Spleen against my Lord Mayor, than from any motive of Protecting innocence, tho' that was certainly their motive at first. In Truth, if I am not deceived, I suspect that they desire that the Gipsey should be pardoned, and then to convince the World that she was guilty in order to cast the greater Reflection on him who was principally instrumental in obtaining such Pardon.[12]

But Fielding's explanation didn't wash with many. Allan Ramsay, in *A Letter to the Right Honourable Earl of — Concerning the Affair of Elizabeth Canning*[13] in 1753, admired the 'stile and composition' of Fielding's pamphlet, observing that he knew none of his 'performances that more discover the ingenuity of the man of wit, the distinctness of the lawyer, or the politeness and candour of the gentleman',[14] but then methodically, almost apologetically, tore Fielding's case apart:

> I could not help being surprised to find upon what slight grounds [Fielding] and many other sensible men, had founded their belief of [Canning's] veracity, and that they should be satisfied with evidence that seems to be in no manner adequate to the nature of the facts meant to be proved by it, especially when a life is concerned.[15]

More brutal was the response of Sir John Hill who in 1753 published *The Story of Elizabeth Canning* which was largely a critique of Fielding's conduct and publication, and concluded with the statement that 'for you, *Mr Fielding* . . . your private Treatment of this Subject, both before and in your Pamphlet, merits the strongest Censure'.[16]

Possible conspiracies in motion against him, popular anger – including death threats – and a public dispute with Fielding were things the Lord Mayor could – and did – withstand. What he and the courts could not ignore was a simple and startling proposition. If Squires and her witnesses had been telling the truth, then Canning had been committing deepest perjury – to a degree that would have led to a woman's execution. Was

Canning, so young and seemingly so innocent and simple, in fact insane? Was she perhaps evil instead? Or did she have something appalling to hide?

Despite Fielding's continuing and impassioned support for Canning there was mounting public pressure to test the truth of her fantastic and seemingly flawed tale in a court of law. The procedure, however, was slow. In May 1753 Mary Squires was formally pardoned. In September the trial for perjury of her three witnesses opened and was immediately dismissed because the prosecution could offer no evidence, which, of course, was a further blow for Canning's cause.[17] Public interest in the case remained intense with opinion divided, emotionally rather than rationally and in quasi-biblical manner, between the pro-Elizabeth 'Canningites' or Canaanites and the pro-gypsy 'Egyptians'.

But, divided as it was, the weight of public opinion started to shift against Canning and the truth of her account, as is suggested by a feature that appeared in the July 1753 edition of the *Gentleman's Magazine*. It shows a 'Ground Plot or Plan of Mother Wells's House, Barn and Garden'[18] and a perspective of her kitchen. The drawings are based on an actual survey, not on Canning's description, and the discrepancies between the two are obvious. The key to the illustrations is telling. It shows the room where Canning 'says' she was confined, and reveals a small opening between the kitchen and hayloft – which, significantly, Canning failed to mention – 'so that Canning if confined there might see into the kitchen'. Obviously the *Gentleman's Magazine* was, like Sir Crisp, doubtful about Canning's evidence.

Most telling of all, perhaps, is that Canning's 'friends' – whose reputations were now linked with hers – did what they could to delay a new legal examination of her case. But ultimately to no avail. Finally, on 29 April 1754 – over fifteen months after her mysterious disappearance – Canning was put on trial at the Old Bailey, charged with 'wilful and corrupt perjury' for swearing that Mary Squires had robbed and threatened her.

The furore surrounding this case was even more explosive than that provoked by the earlier trial, with the Lord Mayor again becoming a particular target for displays of violence, including an attack upon him while he was travelling in his coach. The entire capital, indeed nation, once again took sides. The point at issue was still presumed innocence versus presumed diabolical and deep-rooted evil, but now it was not quite so obvious who the real monster was – the City-bred teenager or the 'swarthy' gypsy? Could it be that this simple little servant girl really contained a more malevolent and corrupt spirit than the bawdy-house-dwelling Romany prostitute?

Speculation rose to dizzy heights. If Canning had not been abducted, what on earth had she been doing during the month of her disappearance? The obvious answer to many was that she was not innocent at all but had secretly been pregnant when she disappeared and had gone off to give birth or even have an abortion. There was absolutely no evidence to support these theories and no investigations into them were ever formally undertaken but, if Canning had gone away to hide a guilty secret – or perhaps to indulge in an illicit romance – then at least her bizarre actions could be understood if not forgiven. When she returned home she had to offer an explanation, so she invented the story of abduction by gypsies – the bogeymen of the age – and provided a vague location and description of her place of confinement which – no doubt to her horror – was given a precise identity by her eager supporters. Then, as tends to happen, one lie perhaps led to another, to conceal one deceit she had to create others, until they all spiralled out of control and a woman's life was in jeopardy. If this had been the case Canning was certainly not very bright or very brave but neither was she insane nor evil. Indeed, she was no more than she had appeared – a simple, teenage servant girl, desperately frightened because she had become embroiled in a secret and dangerous affair that was way beyond her power to control.

The trial itself offered no clue as to any possible motive. Canning made no attempt to explain, justify, expand or retract her original account of events. She merely doggedly stuck to her tale. Counsel for the Crown offered a bland interpretation of Canning's actions. She had, he argued, absconded 'to preserve her character', and her outlandish story was concocted to obtain sympathy and money 'although she must wade through blood to attain it'. Since there was now no one else able or willing to support Canning's story (Virtue Hall having recanted and withdrawn her evidence), the trial was no more than a battle between Canning's witnesses, who vouched for her character, and Squires', who corroborated her claim to have been near Abbotsbury in Dorset at the time of Canning's alleged imprisonment. During the course of the trial much was made of the many inconsistencies in Canning's various accounts and the discrepancies between her description of Wells' house and its actual appearance. But since the record of what Canning had actually said was so poor, inconsistencies and discrepancies were not in themselves conclusive evidence of guilt.

A satirical print of 1753, entitled 'Elizabeth Canning vindicated', showing how the accused gypsy Mary Squires could be in two different places at virtually the same time. Clearly, to the popular mid-eighteenth-century mind, gypsies – in behaviour and dress – were synonymous with witches.

More curious is the fact that witnesses appeared at this trial who should have given evidence at the earlier one. These included, for example, a gypsy couple called Fortune and Judith Natus who swore they were living in the alleged room of confinement in Wells' house when Canning claimed to have been there.

During the trial detailed plans of Susannah Wells' house, along with a perspective of the loft, were produced and scrutinised, and seemingly undermined Canning's account of her ordeal. There is one curious fact about these drawings.[19] 'The truth and Exactness of them' was attested by the man who surveyed the house and drew them. His name was John

Donowell and he happened to be the architect employed at the time by
Sir Francis Dashwood – one of the founders of the Medmenhamite Hell
Fire Club (see page 390) – to create buildings at West Wycombe, including,
in 1748, the sexually explicit Parlour and Temple of Venus (see page 397).
Is this strange coincidence a possible clue to an eventual unravelling of
the mystery or just one more confusing diversion from the truth?

There were seven full days of evidence-giving. When it had all been
offered and the summing-up concluded, the jury was left completely
baffled. Like the rest of the population it was divided, with jurors' opinions
based not so much on evidence or proof as on gut feelings and assumptions. There was no clear consensus. This, of course, was a serious problem.
For the peace of mind of the capital – the country even – a verdict must
be reached so that the case could be decently laid to rest and forgotten.
For many it was just too disturbing. It revealed not just base prejudice in
operation but also that the law was useless if people – seemingly innocent and of impeccable character – ignored the sacred importance of the
judicial oath and simply lied in court. Criminals might be expected to
attempt this but not young servant girls of apparent good character.
Criminals might equally be expected to lie in order to escape punishment
or execution, but the innocent-looking Elizabeth Canning had perhaps
done something far worse. She had not, it seemed, lied to save herself
but so as to take the life of another person whom she had in all probability never even met before. This startling case was, in a sense, the world
turned upside down, with moral certainties questioned and nothing what
it seemed. As the jury sweated to reach a decision so, it would seem, did
the authorities and the legal fraternity. They probably concluded that the
best solution now was for Canning to be found guilty and so transformed
from a perplexing and innocent teenage servant into just one more lying
criminal wretch.

And this was what happened. The jury sought a compromise. They
wanted to find Canning guilty of perjury but not of 'wilful and corrupt
perjury', which meant that, although she had committed perjury, it was
done by mistake or out of confusion. Such a verdict would have been
tantamount to an acquittal, but the court would not allow it. So, reluctantly, the jury found Canning guilty as charged, but added to their verdict
an 'earnest recommendation for mercy'. Her sentence was one month's
imprisonment and seven years' transportation.

This verdict satisfied the law but it did not satisfy Canning's supporters or much of the public. Sir Crisp felt compelled to justify his conduct and in July 1754 published *An Address to the Liverymen of the City of London from Sir Crisp Gascoyne . . . relative to his conduct in the cases of Elizabeth Canning and Mary Squires*.[20] In this pamphlet Sir Crisp observed that Squires, 'an infirm old woman . . . one of the people called Gypsies . . . was convicted . . . in the minds of men, before she was tried',[21] but that after the conclusion of her trial he was 'dissatisfied with the verdict'. The reasons he cites are 'the improbability of the story . . . the antecedent prejudice in men's minds. The outrages of the mob preventing the solemn and sacred freedom which should attend upon all trials, and the contradictory evidence given upon this.' Sir Crisp also described his extraordinary interview with Virtue Hall, who 'instantly burst into a flood of tears, and confessed that all she had sworn was false'. He asked Virtue 'how she came to forswear herself' and she answered that 'when she was at Mr Fielding's she first spoke the truth, but that she was told that was not the truth, and was terrified and threatened to be sent to Newgate and prosecuted as a felon, unless she would speak the truth – and therefore she swore what was false to save her own life'.[22]

Fielding is clearly a target for Sir Crisp, who points out that the magistrate examined not only Virtue Hall but, at the same time, Judith Natus, who told him the story she later told at Canning's trial – that she and her husband were living in the room at Wells' house during the period Canning claimed to have been imprisoned in it. Sir Crisp then dryly states, 'What reason there was to prefer the account of Canning, improbable and unconfirmed as it was, to the probable account first offered by Virtue Hall, and confirmed by Judith Natus, I cannot comprehend.'[23]

In fact this point is addressed by Fielding in his *Clear State of the Case*. He explained that he did not like Squires' 'Alibi Defence' because it was open to 'falsehood very easy to be practiced on all occasions, where there are gangs of people, as Gypsies &c'.[24] So Fielding believed Hall and the Natus were simply lying under oath because they were part of a gang of gypsies whose first duty it was to protect each other. Gypsies – like criminals – were people whose oath was not to be trusted. Was this Fielding being realistic or just horribly prejudiced? As Sir Crisp put it, 'If Virtue Hall's examination had been taken, as she would have freely given it; if no threats had been used to frighten her ... the troubles, which ensued, could not have happened.'[25] Sir Crisp also mentioned 'certificates from more than sixty persons' confirming that Mary Squires had been near Abbotsbury in January 1753 'which were transmitted to Mr Fielding', who 'I wish [having] published so much on this subject, had now obliged the world with the publication of these'.[26] Finally Sir Crisp demolished Canning's story, picking apart its many inconsistencies, contradictions, absurdities and errors of detail, and asking, for example, 'if Canning was in a fit, how could she swear that she was carried through Bishopsgate-street? And if she was carried through that street, how could she swear she was in a fit?'[27] The alleged gaol at Wells' house he found the 'most insecure prison in the world', which 'of itself bears strong testimony against Canning'.[28]

But rather than bringing debate over the case to a close, Sir Crisp's pamphlet merely provoked a violent response from Canning's friends and was met by a flurry of publications refuting its points of fact and conclusion. One, *A Refutation of Sir Crisp Gascoyne's Address ... in a narrative of facts* of 1754, is an immensely long and detailed affair that is as much concerned with saving the reputation of Canning's friends as with saving the reputation and freedom of the girl herself.[29] It also offered much lurid, but legally irrelevant, information about Wells and her home:

> She was, when young, a common-prostitute, and when she grew old
> became a bawd; her husband was hanged for sheep-stealing, and both
> had been convicted of perjury ... Her house was a receptacle not of
> whores only but thieves.[30]

It also dismissed the evidence of Fortune Natus because 'he was an inmate of Mother Wells's brothel' and an 'honest man ... would never have chosen for himself, and especially his wife, such a lodging'.[31] Probably Fielding knew all this before, or soon after, he became involved with Canning's case and allowed this background information to sway his legal opinion of the facts laid before him. *A Refutation* also claims that there was no proof that Virtue Hall retracted her evidence 'Publically' or 'Voluntarily', as Sir Crisp claimed, because 'some difficulties were got over privately'. And – more seriously – it contains a pair of very sinister assertions. First, that an appeal against Canning's sentence was 'vigorously opposed', lending strength to the argument that it was ultimately more convenient for the authorities to have her discredited as a felon. Second, that 'all possible arts were used to send her abroad among the refuse of the gaol, and in the power of wretches, who had determined to commit the last outrage on her person'.[32] If this charge is to be believed, the authorities wanted her silenced forever.

Fielding did nothing after Canning was convicted. He was ill, of course, and in June left London for good on his way to Portugal where he died four months later. But Elizabeth Canning still had many friends and supporters who came to her relief. Elizabeth Cooke, wife of a former Governor of the Bank of England, raised £100 to be put in trust for her use, and sympathetic East India Company directors arranged for her journey of exile to New England to be taken in comfort rather than aboard a convict ship where her life could well have been threatened. She sailed for Wethersfield, Connecticut in August 1754, to serve the Reverend Elisha Williams, one-time Rector to Yale University. Elizabeth's simple character evidently impressed her new neighbours and her status as felon does not seem to have hampered her greatly. She continued to be something of a celebrity with her case remaining in the public eye. For example, in 1762 Voltaire published his own *Histoire d'Elisabeth Canning*, using the story as a vehicle to mount an attack on tyrannical France where such an outcast as a gypsy prostitute could never have expected the compassion and objective justice displayed in England.

Elizabeth Canning did not return to a humble servant's life in London. Instead, in November 1756 she married John Treat, a great-nephew of the Governor of Connecticut, had five children and died in New England in June 1773. As far as anyone knows she never wavered from her original account of what happened during her 'missing month' of January 1753 and so the mystery remained unresolved. The *Gentleman's Magazine*, in August 1773, was greatly disappointed that Canning had not made the expected deathbed confession: 'Notwithstanding the many strange circumstances of her story, none is so strange, as that it should not be discovered ... where she had concealed herself during the time she had invariably declared she was at the house of Mother Wells.' But, just perhaps, Elizabeth had no deathbed confession to make. The *Newgate Calendar*, looking back on the events of 1753–4, was amazed by the fact that, no matter who was right or wrong, it was clear that on one side or the other a large number of people must have been involved in a complex conspiracy of lies:

If Canning was guilty, her crime was of the most enormous magnitude, that of endeavouring to swear away a life, in order to cover, perhaps, her own disgrace [if] debauched in her absence, and that the whole was a concerted scheme to conceal the truth. If she was innocent, what a variety of perjuries must have been committed by the opposite parties!

The authors of the *Newgate Calendar* were right to be astonished. Elizabeth's account of what befell her, true or false, provoked a number of people to tell stories which, mutually incompatible, meant many lies were sworn under oath – either to defend Elizabeth or to save Mary Squires. Such concerted deceit by so many individuals left the legal system, founded on the fact that juries were dependent on the believability of sworn evidence, in serious disarray. As Fielding wrote in his *Clear Statement of the Case of Elizabeth Canning*: '[B]y the law of England ... no man can be committed to prison, without a charge on oath before a lawful magistrate [and] this charge must be again proved on oath, to the satisfaction of [a jury] ... before the accused can be required to answer to it.'[33] Trust in the evidence offered by people under oath was the cornerstone of the law. This case had knocked that cornerstone askew.

After nearly 260 years Elizabeth's case remains utterly perplexing and debate over the veracity of her tale continues. If she was lying – which seems far more likely than not – then given the impeccable character she displayed before and after her trial, it can only be assumed that the perilous course she chose to follow was less frightening and threatening than telling the truth about what really happened to her in January 1753. If so, what worse horror could have befallen her then? And if Elizabeth's story was essentially a lie, how could her description of Susannah Wells' house, although wrong in most details, be uncannily correct in broad terms? There was a house of the right scale, reputation and location on the Hertford road, and it did possess a kitchen and a hayloft of sorts as Elizabeth described. Just a lucky guess or had she been there fleetingly in circumstances never truly revealed?

Lillian de la Torre in *Elizabeth is Missing* (1947) concludes that Canning was an hysteric who suffered amnesia for a month, simply couldn't remember where she'd been or what she had done (although seemingly had spent some time in Enfield Wash), became fearful and ashamed and so told a mix of truth and naïve lies to conceal what had happened. John

Treherne, in *The Canning Enigma* of 1989, dismisses Elizabeth's account of events as 'scullery-maid's rigamarole',[34] and wonders not whether she lied but why; while Judith Moore in *The Appearance of Truth*, a very clinical and academic study of the case, published in 1994, states, 'I do not believe that a solution to the Canning case is possible,' then offers her opinion that 'Elizabeth Canning's whole story was true' and that she described it 'as accurately as she was able to'.[35] And so this extraordinary story continues to divide opinion and the mystery remains. As the *Newgate Calendar* rightly concluded:

> This story is enveloped in mystery; and the truth of it must be left to the discoveries of that important day, when all mists shall be wiped from our eyes, and the most hidden things shall be made plain.

THE ARCHITECTURE
OF SIN

SEVEN

BUILDING ON VICE

The Sex Industry and the Creation of Georgian London

The built fabric of London, and the life lived within its buildings and streets, echoed to the motion and machination of the city's sex trade. Virtually every part of the vast and sprawling organism of Georgian London had a role to play in what was now one of its most lucrative activities and many of its buildings were constructed, or leased, using money generated by the sex industry. The roles played by various locations evolved during the 150 years after 1680 as London grew and functions shifted, but the sex industry nevertheless remained citywide.

By 1700 the reconstruction of the City after the Great Fire of 1666 was mostly complete, and large industrial and maritime suburbs had spread to its north, east, and across the river in Southwark. The City was linked to Westminster by the important thoroughfare of trade and commerce running from the Royal Exchange, the Guildhall and Cheapside in the east, via Ludgate Hill, Fleet Street, Temple Bar and the Strand, to Charing Cross and St James's Park in the west. During the seventeenth century much development had taken place to either side of this thoroughfare, especially around the Strand, and to the north of which Covent Garden and Seven Dials had taken form after 1630. This major east-west route was parallelled farther north by the similarly orientated but more meandering Great Ormond Street, Queen Square, Bloomsbury Square, Great Russell Street-axis that marked the northern extent of West London and which, in the late seventeenth century, had become a favoured location for new high-class developments.

By 1750 the balance of London had changed: the West End, in particular, had been developed prodigiously, shifting the heart of fashion further to the west and making Soho – where coherent development had started in the 1680s – a central rather than peripheral area, while to its north and east the City had greatly expanded with the development of extensive mercantile, manufacturing and industrial enclaves, such as the silk-trade area of Spitalfields and Shoreditch and the quays in Wapping and Limehouse.

The sex trade operated everywhere, with only the tone and type of its activities varying from location to location. Cheap bawdy-houses and tainted whores, for instance, tended to be found in poor areas such as Drury Lane, Seven Dials, St Giles and Whitechapel, while exclusive seraglios and 'convents' were located near the court in St James's – for example, Elizabeth Needham's establishment of the 1720s in Park Place, running between St James's Street and Green Park, and four decades later Charlotte Hayes' 'nunnery' in King's Place, off Pall Mall.

Randolph Trumbach, in his seminal 1998 publication *Sex and the Gender Revolution*, offers a sexual geography of London which points out that although the trade remained ubiquitous, at different times various locations within the city played particularly prominent roles. Throughout the eighteenth century, for instance, the great business thoroughfare running west from the Royal Exchange and Cheapside via Ludgate Hill and Fleet Street to St James's Park, thus linking the financial and trading centre of the City with the political power base of aristocratic West London, also became 'the principal place for prostitutes to ply for customers'.[1] It was perhaps predictable that this bustling route of commercial and political power also served as the main artery of London's sex industry and the favoured domain of its legion of street-walkers.

Negotiating this thoroughfare then was a memorable experience, as Defoe explained in the 1720s:

> With what impatience and Indignation have I walked from Charing-Cross to Ludgate, when being in full Speed upon important Business, I have every now and then been put to the Halt; sometimes by the full Encounter of an audacious Harlot, whose impudent Leer shewd she only stopp'd my Passage in order to draw my Observations to her; at other times by Twitches on the Sleeve. Lewd and ogling Salutations; and not infrequently by the more profligate Impudence of some Jades, who boldly dare to seize a Man by the Elbow, and make insolent Demands of Wine and Treats before they let him go.[2]

A scene described in the *Grub Street Journal* of 6 August 1730 may not have been entirely untypical of life encountered at certain hours along the thoroughfare: a group of women was 'taken at 12 or 1 o'clock, exposing their nakedness in the open street to all passengers and using most abominable filthy expressions'.[3] The group included Kate Hackabout, whose name, and perhaps manners, captured the interest of William Hogarth (see page 4). A report in *The Times* confirms that by the late-eighteenth century little had changed in the Strand: '[T]he indecencies practiced by the crowds of prostitutes before Somerset-House every night, not only put modesty to the blush, but absolutely render it dangerous to pass.'[4]

Indictments against the proprietors of 'disorderly houses' in Westminster and Middlesex from 1720–9 help create an intriguing profile of London's illicit sex life. Disorderly houses were not necessarily bawdy-houses, but most probably were, and these statistics show that this activity was focused in three distinct areas. Trumbach's analysis of records reveals that Covent Garden and its immediate environs were the location of 71.1 per cent of the indictments (with 193 disorderly houses located in St Giles-in-the-Fields but only 1 in the parish of St Anne, Soho); the area around the periphery of the City contained 14.7 per cent of the houses mentioned in the indictments (with 39 in Cripplegate and Clerkenwell and 15 in Shoreditch), while the remaining 14.2 per cent of the indictments referred to houses in Whitechapel and Wapping (with 36 in the large parish of Stepney and 10 in St Mary, Whitechapel).[5] This concentration of the trade is generally confirmed by recent research undertaken by Tony Henderson. He has traced the location of bawdy-houses prosecuted in City wards in three periods: 1710–49, 1750–89 and 1790–1829, and discovered that in Aldgate – representing a portion of what was Whitechapel – there was 1 bawdy-house in the first period, 12 in 1750–89 and 26 in 1790–1829. In Farringdon Without, including part of Clerkenwell, there were 70 in 1710–49, 44 in 1750–89 and 48 in 1790–1829.[6]

This disposition of bawdy- or disorderly houses, suggesting the locations of London's busiest sex-trade areas, is slightly enlarged upon by evidence offered in 1770 by Sir John Fielding to a parliamentary committee pondering the policing of the capital. Fielding pointed out that 'the great number of brothels and irregular taverns ... kept by most abandoned characters such as bawds, thieves [and] receivers of stolen goods ... and carried on without licence from the Magistrate are another great cause of robberies, burglaries and other disorders'. He then went on to locate the offending buildings and their quantity:

The principal of these houses are situate in Covent-garden, about thirty in St Mary-le-Strand, about twelve in St Martin's in the vicinity of Covent-garden, about twelve in St Clements, five or six at Charing Cross, and in Hedge Lane about twenty; there are many more dispersed in different parts of Westminster, in Goodman's-fields, and Whitechapel, many of which are remarkably infamous, and are the cause of disorders of every kind, shelters for bullies to protect prostitutes, and for thieves.[7]

This evidence confirms that the sex industry's heart was Covent Garden and its neighbouring areas (Hedge Lane was just east of Leicester Square), where prostitution flourished alongside taverns, bagnios, theatres, coffee houses and jelly houses (popular gathering places for prostitutes, who would consume exotic jellies out of special jelly glasses). But from the mid-eighteenth century Soho and Marylebone (which hardly make an appearance in Trumbach's 1720s statistics) increasingly became the favoured locations for hotel-like brothels and the homes of actresses, middling and superior prostitutes, and 'kept' women, with, most significantly, many of the prostitutes mentioned in the 1788 and 1793 editions of *Harris's List* having Soho addresses.

Legal records and popular publications must be treated with extreme caution when used to draw up a profile of the sex trade in Georgian London because the grander of these establishments were so discreet they managed virtually to remain invisible and essentially above the law, so generally do not appear in legal documents. However, they were from time to time noted by curious foreign visitors. For example, in the early 1780s Archenholz observed that there were many . . .

. . . houses, situated in the neighbourhood of St James's, where a great number [of courtesans] are kept for people of fashion [with] admission into these temples . . . so exorbitant . . . that the mob are entirely excluded. A little street called King's Place is inhabited by nuns of this order alone, who live under the direction of several rich abbesses. You may see them superbly clothed at public places; and even those of the most expensive kind. Each of these convents has a carriage and servants

in livery; for the ladies never deign to walk any where, but in the park
[and] I have seen many people of rank walk with them in public, and
allow them to take hold of their arms, in the most familiar manner.[8]

The Congratulatory Epistle from a Reformed Rake of 1758 offers its own
view of the favoured haunts of London's sex trade and indicates the
moment when the industry started to embed itself in the relatively recently
developed streets around Soho Square. The anonymous author states that
it is now wrong to assume that a 'search' for prostitutes should be 'limited'
to the familiar areas of Drury Lane, Bow Street, St Giles and Hedge
Lane where 'such Houses as Mrs Doug—s's, Mrs Sh—ter's, Mrs
G—ld's &c.&c.&c.' could be found 'when I indulged myself in the Follies
and Vices of the Town'. These days, observed the author, 'I apprehend
these Houses are no longer kept open in the Purlieus of Covent-Garden
for the Convenience of incontinent Passengers.'[9] Where then had such
establishments gone? Mostly to Soho – such as that of Mrs Goadby, who
in about 1750 opened her pioneering Parisian-style seraglio in Berwick
Street (see page 207).

Interestingly, the difference between the manner in which the sex
industry operated in Covent Garden and in Soho is still reflected in the
surviving historical fabric. The long-time commercial and industrial nature
of Covent Garden – moving from entertainment uses in the eighteenth
century to those relating to the wholesale fruit, vegetable and flower
markets as well as publishing – means that hardly any Georgian domestic
buildings there retain their original ground floors or ornate doorcases.
Most were long ago removed to accommodate shopfronts, tavern frontages
or warehouse doors. On the other hand, the late-seventeenth-, eighteenth-
and early-nineteenth-century houses of Soho – an area of discreet brothels
that also retained a significant residential, if not wealthy, population –
still contain many original ground-floor details.

A perhaps typical Soho-based prostitute was the literary-minded
Bet Flint, who lived in Meard Street, Soho. The house in which she
lodged during the 1760s in furnished rooms was constructed in 1732 by
the speculative builder John Meard and still survives. It is now numbered
9 and is, as it happens, one of the few original houses in this largely intact
early-Georgian street to have had a later shopfront inserted in its ground
floor. Elizabeth Flint was a curious and now, sadly, obscure character.

She was, according to Dr Johnson, 'generally a slut and drunkard; occasionally whore and thief' but also 'a fine character', and he observed in reference to this Meard Street house that 'Bet . . . had, however, genteel lodgings, a spinet on which she played, and a boy that walked before her chair'.[10] Johnson had 'literary' dealings with Bet. As he explained to Mrs Piozzi, his friend and herself an able diarist:

Bet Flint wrote her own life, and called herself *Cassandra*, and it was in verse; it began:

> When nature first ordained my birth
> A diminutive I was born on earth.
> And then I came from a dark abode,
> Into a gay and gaudy world.

So Bet brought her verses to me to correct; but I gave her half-a-crown, and she liked it as well. Bet had a fine spirit.

Soho Square (looking north), built from the 1680s onwards, was well occupied throughout the eighteenth century and was an important centre for prostitution. Mrs Cornelys' Carlisle House, the site of risqué masquerades, was on the east side of the square.

Sadly Bet's verse autobiography was not completed, perhaps because she contrived to get herself arrested on the charge of stealing a counterpane from her landlord. This led to a sequence of events that delighted Johnson. Bet had, he said, 'a spirit that could not be subdued', so when she was obliged to go to gaol to await her trial 'she ordered a sedan chair, and bid her footboy walk before her. However, the footboy proved refractory, for he was ashamed, though his mistress was not'. Bet was acquitted and Johnson recalled her saying, "'[S]o now the counterpane is my own, and now I'll make a petticoat of it." Oh! I loved Bet Flint.'[11]

Much of the Oxford Road (now Street) running east-west along the northern edge of Soho was appropriated by the sex trade as it became gradually built along and around during the eighteenth century. Humble developments such as Oxford Market and modest streets such as South Molton Street rapidly became the haunts of cheaper prostitutes. After 1750, as various estates developed the land to the north of the west half of Oxford Street, a whole new theatre for sex was created. The 'New Buildings', as the smart and discreet streets in Marylebone were known, soon became a favoured location, not for common street-walkers but for exclusive brothels, and the place of operations and residence of high-class courtesans.

In the 1780s Archenholz calculated that 30,000 prostitutes lived in Marylebone (perhaps a misprint in the 1789 edition for 13,000), of whom 1,700 inhabited whole houses; while the *Gentleman's Magazine* observed in April 1795 that, 'the affect of prostitution' was not 'confined to the more public streets in the metropolis' but could be seen in one of its 'most extensive parishes . . . Mary-la-bone whose increase has taken place within these few years' owes 'a very considerable part of [its] inhabitants to persons of this description'.[12]

A startling portrait of a brothel in Marylebone is included in Michael Ryan's *Prostitution in London* of 1839. Marie Aubrey, a Frenchwoman, and her 'paramour' John Williams 'kept' a house in Seymour Place, Bryanston Square in the mid-1830s in which lived 'about twelve or fourteen young females . . . mostly from France or Italy' who had been enticed to London, under false pretences of respectable employment, and were held dependent and more or less as prisoners. The house was . . .

... an establishment of great notoriety, visited by some of the most
distinguished foreigners and others, and carried on in a style little short
of that observed in the richest and noblest families. The house consisted
of twelve or fourteen rooms, besides those appropriate to domestic uses,
each of which was genteelly and fashionably furnished. The saloon, a
very large room, was elegantly fitted up; – profusion of valuable and
splendid paintings decorated its walls, and its furniture was of a costly
description. As a necessary appendage, there was a small room on the
ground floor appropriated as a counting house; a service of solid silver
plate was ordinarily in use when the visitors required it, which was the
property of Marie Aubrey.[13]

The 1788 edition of *Harris's List of Covent Garden Ladies* recognised
the new role of Marylebone while also confirming the lasting importance
of more traditional locations: 'Marybone ... now the grand paradise of
Love' was placed alongside 'Covent Garden, her elder sister', while 'antient
Drury ... Bagnigge, St George's Spa ... deal out each night their choicest
gifts of love'. The *List* also recommended to the 'sons of pleasure ... the
purlieus of White Chapel, The Royalty ... Wapping and Shadwell'.

The part of town south and west of Covent Garden was a place of
ancient and notorious repute – the Strand and the area around Charing
Cross and St Martin's-in-the-Fields were favoured pick-up spots for
common street prostitutes who would take their clients into the system
of alleys off the Strand or else the shady bowers of nearby St James's Park.
James Boswell, as he recounted in his *London Journal* of 1762–3, made use
of both locations, and in his descriptions reveals much about the al fresco
nature of the lower levels of the mid-eighteenth-century sex industry:

> I picked up a girl in the Strand; went into a court with intention to
> enjoy her in armour [a condom made of sheep's gut]. But she had none.
> I toyed with her. She wondered at my size, and said if I ever took a
> girl's maidenhood, I would make her squeak. I gave her a shilling,
> and had command enough of myself to go without touching her.
> I afterwards trembled at the danger I had escaped.[14]

Charged with the sexual thrill of the rough and tumble of public sex
among the lower orders, Boswell on another occasion went to St James's
Park and:

. . . picked up a low brimstone [i.e. a tough whore], called myself a barber and agreed with her for sixpence, went to the bottom of the Park arm in arm, and dipped my machine in the Canal and performed most manfully . . . In the Strand I picked up a little profligate wretch and gave her sixpence. She allowed me entrance. But the miscreant refused me performance. I was much stronger than her, and volens nolens [whether she wanted to or not], pushed her up against the wall. She, however, gave a sudden spring from me; and screaming out, a parcel of more whores and soldiers came to her relief. 'Brother soldiers,' said I, 'should not a half-pay officer roger for sixpence? And here has she used me so.' I got them on my side, and I abused her in blackguard style, and then left them.[15]

Charing Cross, looking towards the Strand, in c. 1730–40, as shown in a nineteenth-century engraving. This was one of the most important street junctions in London, until finally swept away in the nineteenth century for the creation of Trafalgar Square. It marked the end of the great commercial thoroughfare which led west from the City and was a pivotal point of the sex industry.

Francis Place, a radical and an acute social observer who ran a tailor's shop in the Strand, described his immediate surroundings and nearby Charing Cross in the first decade of the nineteenth century and paints a clear picture of life in one of central London's poorer and least-regulated sex districts:

> On the eastern side [of Charing Cross] was Johnson's Court
> [containing] 13 houses . . . all in a state of great dilapidation, in every
> room in every house excepting one only lived one or more common
> prostitutes of the most wretched description . . . the place could
> not be outdone in infamy and indecency by any place in London.
> The manner in which many of the drunken filthy young
> prostitutes behaved is not describable nor would it be believed were
> it described.

Place then goes on to describe the 'low brothels' with which his shop was surrounded, the 'dirty Gin Shop . . . frequented by prostitutes and soldiers', and – most startling of all – an old wall at nearby Privy Gardens which each night was patrolled by a 'horribly ragged, dirty and disgusting . . . set of prostitutes' who 'used to take any customer who would pay twopence, behind the wall'.[16]

The streets and courts north of Charing Cross, around the church of St Martin-in-the-Fields, seem to have been a favourite location for the trade in children. They would be offered as 'apprentices' to 'masters' in exchange for ready cash with no questions asked. The sex industry that flourished along the Strand continued east along Fleet Street, a location famed for its multiplicity of patrolling harlots as was made clear in the opening pages of *Pretty Doings in a Protestant Nation* of 1734 in which the author claims that 'Where the Devil do all those B—ches come from?' was a common Fleet Street phrase.[17] And as early as 1699 Ned Ward in the *London Spy* described Salisbury Court – also referred to as 'Sodom' – off Fleet Street as 'a Corporation of Whores, Coiners, Highway-men, Pickpockets and House-Breakers'.[18]

But Francis Place, when describing something of the character of the Fleet Street sex trade in the late 1780s, implies that the harlots here were not as poor, lurid or alarming as those stationed along the Strand and around Charing Cross. While an apprentice to a maker of leather breeches, Price, with his fellow apprentices, spent much time with 'the prostitutes who walked Fleet Street' and found them honest and even generous:

> It may seem strange but it is true, that on no occasion did I ever hear one of these women urge any one of these youths to bring her more money than he seemed willing to part from . . . the women were generally as willing as the lads to spend money when they were flush. With these youths and these women I sometimes spent the evening eating and drinking at a public house . . . and never had any serious quarrel with any one of my companions.[19]

Fleet Street and Shoe Lane, with their network of dark and narrow alleys even more labyrinthine than those off the Strand, were the perfect terrain for those operating on the cheaper, potentially criminal side of London's sex industry, as the Blewit/Hartrey case makes clear (see page 476). It was to lodgings and bawdy-houses secreted in these alleys that the harlots took their clients and, incredibly, some highly ephemeral artefacts survive that identify an existing building as once part of Georgian London's sex industry and suggest the manner in which a bawdy-house may have been furnished.

In Wine Office Court, north of Fleet Street, stands the Cheshire Cheese Tavern. Its architecture and details suggest it was purpose-built in the second half of the seventeenth century although much altered in c.1755. Its ground-floor fireplaces are unusual and especially indicative – their chimney breasts are supported on massive stone corbels which allow heat from the hearth to radiate in a 180-degree arc, something highly desirable in a public room with many people gathered around the fire and a detail found only in late-seventeenth- and early-eighteenth-century taverns (for example the Owl and Pussycat in Redchurch Street, Shoreditch).

In 1962 the Museum of London was presented with eight plaster of Paris bas-relief panels taken from the Cheshire Cheese, some intact, others only fragmentary, each originally measuring around 200 x 160 mm, which show men and women involved in a variety of sexual activities. Costume detail suggests a date of 1740–50, as do the French Rococo-style chairs and stools on which some of the figures sit, which might also be evidence that the panels were cast from moulds made in France.

A fragment of a plaster panel of c.1740–50 from the Cheshire Cheese Tavern, Fleet Street, showing a pair of prostitutes. One is giving pleasure to a client with a birch.

Those which are intact or easy to read show, for instance, a woman sitting on a stool – naked apart from stockings and a disarranged shift revealing her bare breasts – being penetrated by a man whose breeches are around his knees. Another intact panel shows a similar scene but with the man sitting on a chair, while yet another depicts a woman bending over and being penetrated from behind, although presumably not anally. Of this panel the Museum of London observes, the 'blunt-toed shoes imply the scene is after 1740'.

These are very orthodox sexual activities. Slightly more imaginative is the fragment showing a threesome with a standing man, naked from the waist down, being flagellated and masturbated by two kneeling women, and a partially destroyed panel showing a figure reclining on the ground while pulling on a basket in which sits another figure – whose sex is unclear – being penetrated by the reclining figure which is smiling with pleasure in a slightly unsettling manner. Intriguingly, one pair of expert observers have described this scene as a woman lying prostrate, wearing a bonnet and a dildo, and that it is a man being lowered in the basket.[20]

Two further plaster panels from the Cheshire Cheese Tavern.

The unlikely and athletic nature of this scene is reminiscent of the notorious and highly influential 'sixteen postures' drawn by Giulio Romano in Italy in the early sixteenth century that were each accompanied by a sonnet penned by Pietro Aretino. Other fragments are hard to make out, but one shows the top half of a man's body – wearing a tie wig and a blissful expression – framed by the naked legs of a woman. Some of the panels are soot-stained and the Museum of London records that they came from a second-floor room on the south side. The Cheshire Cheese remains in business but this room is not open to the public.

With some imagination it is possible to reconstruct the scene. The panels are much too erotic ever to have decorated a conventional domestic interior so they must have been from a room used by prostitutes or that was in some way involved in the sex industry. The Cheshire Cheese is first recorded in the 1760s and before that the White Horse Inn occupied part of the site but the simplest explanation is that the taverns didn't run a bawdy-house on their upper floor but let the rooms to someone who did, or perhaps the room was used by a gentleman's dining club of a particularly libidinous type. Intriguingly, an article in the *Gazetteer* of

18 October 1760, covering the suspicious death of the young prostitute
Ann Bell, mentions the fact that she lodged with Mrs Jane Mead in
Wine-Office Court, Fleet Street (see page 417). Was Jane Mead a bawd,
and were the upper floors of the Cheshire Cheese her bawdy-house?
If so, then the tiles must have lined the inner cheeks of a fire-opening,
with the scenes they depicted flickering and dancing by the light of
flames in a very lifelike manner. The purpose of the panels was probably
no more than is obvious and very similar to the numerous erotic images
found in bath houses, private houses and a brothel in Pompeii – to titillate, inflame and inspire the imagination of customers and get them into
an excited frame of mind when they'd be willing to pay good money for
satisfaction.

But what is perhaps most extraordinary about these panels is that
they were not made to last nor would they have been expensive to
purchase. They are mass-produced ephemera that could have been
fixed within the fire-opening in a few hours and, accompanied by
a few well-chosen prints and erotic porcelain or earthenware (the
Museum of London also has a Delft-made phallus in its collection),
show how an ordinary room could have been transformed into a bawdy-

St Clement Dane's Church at the junction of the Strand and Fleet Street –
a major landmark on the city's sexual highway from the Royal Exchange in
the east to St James's Park and Charing Cross in the west.

house interior quickly and cheaply. The fact that such fragile items have survived for around 250 years to tell their tale is nothing short of phenomenal.[21]

The junction of the two ancient thoroughfares of the Strand and Fleet Street – the area around St Clement Dane's Church – was for much of the Georgian period a notorious homosexual pick-up point. Indeed homosexual liaison seems, in the first part of the eighteenth century, to have been something of a City speciality, although a 1726 edition of the *British Gazetteer* suggested further locations when it reported that in addition to twenty Molly Houses – as homosexual taverns were called – being broken up, a stop had also been put to 'nocturnal assemblies in the Royal Exchange, Moorfields, Lincoln's Inn, the south side of St James's Park and Covent Garden Piazza'.[22]

The Royal Exchange in the heart of the City, with its shady arcades and throng of waterside labourers – called 'water rats' – offering themselves for hire, was a particularly attractive gathering place for homosexuals in the early eighteenth century. In 1699 the *London Spy* described a City outing: '[W]e … went on the *'Change*, turn'd to the Right, and Jostled in amongst a parcel of Swarthy Buggerantoes, Preternatural Fornicators, as my Friend call'd them, who would Ogle a Handsome Young Man with as much Lust, as a True-bred English Whoremaster would gaze upon a Beautiful Virgin.'[23]

The Barbican and the central portion of Cheapside were also particularly popular cruising grounds for homosexuals,[24] while St Paul's Cathedral and the courts and alleys immediately around it were favoured locations not just for meeting and homosexual intrigue but also, it seems, for extramural sex. A notorious location seems to have been the alley to the north of the cathedral's still surviving Chapter House, perhaps because it was both screened and easy to escape from.

Another well-known pick-up place was called 'Sodomite's Walk', which, according to Old Bailey trial proceedings for July 1726, was located 'on Upper Moorfield by the side of the Wall that joins to the Watch-house and part of the upper Field' (see page 62).[25] Before development encroached on the area in the late eighteenth century and Finsbury Square was created from 1779–90, Moorfields was large in extent – comprising Moor Fields, to its north Middle Moor Fields, and then north again Upper Moor Fields, the northern boundary of which was the thoroughfare now known as Worship Street. According to John Rocque's London map of 1746, Middle and Upper Moor Fields were divided by a wall with a watch house at its east end. This wall, now commemorated by the southern edge of Finsbury Square, was presumably the location of 'Sodomite's Walk'. The same Old Bailey trial report confirms the notoriety of the Walk and suggests that the use of *agents provocateurs* was accepted practice for ensnaring homosexuals here.

Molly Houses flourished around Field Lane and Saffron Hill in Holborn, just to the west of Smithfield, which, with neighbouring Cowcross Street, had been one of the centres of London's medieval and Tudor sex industry – the illicit corollary to the ancient and from the mid-twelfth to mid-sixteenth centuries legally sanctioned sex quarter just south of the Thames around Borough and Bankside. The Thames, or at least the seafaring neighbourhoods along its banks, was long associated with London's sex trade. The maritime areas of Wapping and Rotherhithe were notorious for their cheap prostitutes serving seamen, while the Ratcliffe Highway, running parallel with the Thames and east from the Tower and East Smithfield towards Shadwell and Limehouse, was well stocked with taverns and bawdy-houses, providing the East End's equivalent to Covent Garden and the Strand, supplemented by what in 1787 Sir John Hawkins called the 'halo of brothels' that surrounded the theatre district of Goodman's Fields at Aldgate and Whitechapel.[26]

The flavour of this maritime prostitution is well evoked by Francis Place. In the late 1780s he and his friends 'spent many evenings at the dirty public houses' frequented by the poor prostitutes who worked in and around St Catherine's Lane, just east of the Tower. Place, who knew London well, was so astonished by what he saw here that he described the women as if they came not from his own city but from another and alien world:

> . . . they wore long quartered shoes and large buckles, most of them had
> clean stockings and shoes, because it was for them the fashion to be
> flashy about the heels, but many had ragged dirty shoes and stockings
> and some no stockings at all . . . many of that time wore no stays, their
> gowns were low round the neck and open in front, those who wore
> handkerchiefs had them always open in front to expose their breasts . . .
> but numbers wore no handkerchiefs at all . . . and the breasts of many

hung down in a most disgusting manner, their hair among the generality
was straight and 'hung in rat tails' over their eyes and was filled with lice.

And the wary Place noted that 'drunkenness was common to them all
and at all times' as was fighting 'among themselves as well as with the
men', so that 'black eyes might be seen on a great many'.[27]

Female violence was indeed a standard component of low-life prostitution in London's more dark and dangerous areas. Hockley-in-the-Hole
in Clerkenwell was the location of a variety of exotic, savage and exciting
activities that were peripherally part of the sex industry and certainly
attractions for prostitutes plying their trade. These events included bear
and bull baiting, wrestling, boxing, and all manner of martial arts including
sword-fighting contests – a broadsword contest between an Englishman
and a Moor in 1710 is described by Baron von Uffenbach.[28] Also, from
time to time, bloody contests would be staged between bare-chested female
pugilists. In the *London Journal* of June 1722, John Trenchard, when
discussing boxing matches in London, reported that 'two of the feminine
gender appeared for the first time on the theatre of war at Hockley-in-
the-Hole, and maintained the battle with great valour for a long time,
to the no small satisfaction of the spectators'. The main protagonist was
Elizabeth Wilkinson of Clerkenwell who 'challenged and invited' Hannah
Hyfield to meet her on the stage for 3 guineas. The fighters were to hold
half-a-crown in each hand and the first to drop a coin – which must also
have helped to make each punch harder – would lose the contest. Wilkinson
won, and seems to have been a regular pugilist for soon afterward she
beat a woman from Billingsgate.

More conventional displays of the martial arts – with small broad-
swords, rapier, quarterstaff, cudgel and fists – were organised by James
Figg, who from 1720 presided over the 'Boarded House' in the Bear Garden,
Marylebone Fields. Figg was England's first recognised boxing champion
and impresario, and such was his fame that Hogarth painted his portrait
and designed his business card. James Figg and his fellow masters of the
arts of defence were much admired in early-Georgian London. They
were seen as tough and brave men of honour. As Mrs Peachum told
Filch in *The Beggar's Opera*, '[Y]ou must go to Hockley-in-the-Hole and
Marybone, child, to learn valour.'

COVENT GARDEN AND JACK HARRIS'S
LIST OF COVENT GARDEN LADIES

However many new and different areas of London came to prominence during the eighteenth century as centres of the sex trade, Covent Garden retained its reputation as a flesh-market. This fact is constantly confirmed by contemporary eyewitness accounts and also by one of the most remarkable publications of the age, *Harris's List of Covent Garden Ladies*. This directory of London prostitutes seems to have been started in the late 1740s by Jack Harris (a.k.a. John Harrison), a pimp and 'head-waiter' at the Shakespeare's Head Tavern in Covent Garden, and by the hack writer Sam Derrick, who was in 1761, improbably, to replace 'Beau' Nash as Master or Ceremonies in the ultimate pleasure ground of Bath.

The frontispiece for the 1773 edition of Harris's List of Covent Garden Ladies. *It shows a harlot, in Covent Garden, displaying a handsome pair of ankles and accepting money from a client.*

The first editions were no more than handwritten manuscripts kept by Harris for easy reference, but printed editions for sale, with pithy and often witty and ribald texts, appeared from the late 1750s and were regularly updated.[29] The anonymously written *A Congratulatory Epistle from a Reformed Rake* of 1758 offers an account of these early *Lists* and something of a 'user's' appreciation:

> Passing an evening, a few weeks ago, at a certain Tavern near Covent-Garden [we] rung for the Gentleman-porter and actually asked him if he could get ... some girls; to my great surprise he pulled out a List, containing the Names of near four Hundred, alphabetically ranged, with an account of their Persons, Age, qualifications, and Places of Abode ... Believe it who will (for it is scarce credible) among these four Hundred Whores, near a Hundred were marked in the Margin as living in Bow-street, and the Courts adjacent, and upwards of half the rest, in about Covent-Garden. A Blood in Company began to question Bob, concerning his Catalogue, 'What new faces have you got Bob?' – 'Please your Honour, I've nothing very new, withal 'tis Nancy Wilson – but she has just got hold of an Oxford Scholar worth sixteen thousand ...' 'What else have you got worth looking at?' – 'Why an' please you – there is Jenny Belse, and Polly Martin, – fresh out of keeping in Bow-street ...'

And a list of girls are named, with Bob promising to have ...

> ... next week two of the finest Girls in England, that have not been debouched above a Fortnight – Mrs D—g—s expects 'em in Town every day from Salisbury.... Thus ... did this audacious Pimp harangue, and talk of Covent-Garden and Bow-street, as if those Places were entirely over-run with Bawds and Whores ...[30]

The early editions of the *List* include the names of women who were to become the leading courtesans of late-eighteenth-century London, including in the 1761 edition Lucy Cooper (see page 237) and Kitty Fisher (see page 351). But perhaps the most intriguing of all the future high courtesans that Harris listed was Fanny Murray. So famous a character did she become that various memoirs and accounts of her life were published, from which we not only learn of her first encounter with Harris but also receive an insight into his working methods and relationship with the prostitutes he promoted.

According to the *Memoirs of the Celebrated Miss Fanny Murray* of 1759 she was born in Bath in 1729, orphaned by the age of twelve when she commenced working as a 'retail merchant of nose-gays and bath rings at the rooms', was soon seduced 'by the celebrated Jack (Spencer) of libertine memory' (the son of the 3rd Earl of Sunderland and grandson of the Duke of Marlborough, eventually the father of the 1st Earl Spencer and one of the supporters in 1739 of the foundation of the Foundling Hospital), and then at the age of about thirteen taken up by the nearly seventy-year-old Richard 'Beau' Nash – the City's famed Master of Ceremonies. At this time, roughly 1742, the *Memoirs* note that Fanny's personality was 'gay [and] volatile' and her . . .

> . . . person . . . extremely beautiful; her face a perfect oval, with eyes that
> conversed love, and every other feature in agreeable symmetry. Her
> dimpled cheek alone might have captivated, if a smile that gave it exis-
> tence, did not display such other charms as shared the conquest. Her
> teeth regular, small, and perfectly white, coral lips and chestnut hair.

Bath soon became too small a place for such a precociously experienced beauty and Fanny moved to London, away from her elderly protector and into the potentially dangerous and dark world of freebooting whoredom. Presumably she was in search of thrills, freedom and riches. It was a huge gamble. Naturally she gravitated to Covent Garden and seems rapidly to have ingratiated herself with the 'Pimpmaster General', Jack Harris. The *Memoirs* make clear what happened next.

> Notwithstanding Fanny's extensive commerce, Mr H—s, the celebrated
> negociator in women, applied to get her enrolled upon his parchment
> list, as a *new face*; though, properly speaking, she had now been upon
> the town [that is, working as a whore in Bath] near four years. However,
> the ceremony was performed with all the punctilios attending that great
> institution; a surgeon being present for a complete examination of her
> person, and to report her well or ill, and a lawyer to ingross her name,
> &c. after having signed a written agreement, to forfeit twenty pounds, if
> she gave the negociator a wrong information concerning the state of her
> health in every particular. Then her name as ingrossed upon a whole
> skin of parchment.[31]

At this date, roughly 1747/8, *Harris's List* was still issued in manuscript form and no early copies are known to survive, but the *Memoirs* contain the text of the supposed entry describing Fanny and offering her on the market:

Condition: perfectly sound wind and limb. Description: A fine brown girl, rising 19 years next season. A good side-box piece – and will shew well in the flesh market – wear well – may be put off for a virgin any time these 12 months – never common this side of Temple-Bar, but for six months. Fit for high keeping with a Jew merchant – N.B. a good praemium from ditto – Then the run of the house – and if she keeps out of the Lock, may make her fortune, and ruin half the town. Place of abode: the first floor at Mrs —'s, a milliner at Charing Cross.

Hallie Rubenhold has made a good job of decoding this entry.[32] For example, 'side-box piece' refers to the type of ornamental prostitute found sitting in the side boxes at the theatre, and the reference to Temple Bar – the traditional boundary between the City and the West End – meant that Fanny was a new face in Covent Garden. The 'good praemium' refers to the high sum that a rich 'Jew merchant' (sought after as generous, kind and reliable clients – see page 10) might be persuaded to pay above the odds for the pleasure of relieving Fanny of her 'virginity' – which would have been 'restored' many times during her first twelve months in town.

Appearing on *Harris's List* and enjoying his patronage seemed to work for Fanny because, as the *Memoirs* explain, '[A]fter being thus initiated in the arcanum of Mr H—r—s's system of fornication, she plied regularly in the flesh-market at the houses during the season by which means she increased the price of her favours, never now receiving under two guineas.'[33]

The ladies on *Harris's List* had to pay for the business it brought them and the *Memoirs* contain a passage explaining the deal they struck with him. The arrangement described is picturesque and titillating and clearly calculated to amuse and arouse – the *Memoirs* were, after all, intended to be a softly erotic read. Of course they can't be taken as absolute fact but there is, in all probability, more than a grain of truth in the system and practices described.

Fanny, we are told, was soon introduced to the 'Whores Club which assembled every Sunday evening near Covent-garden, to talk over their various successes, compare notes, and canvass the most probable means of improving them the week following'. The 'Whores Club' had a long list of rules and, in describing these, the anonymous author of the *Memoirs* gives full rein to sexual fantasy. Every member of the club must, we are told, 'have been debauched before she was 15' and must be on *Harris's List*, while any member 'who may become with child' was to be struck off for 'no longer coming under denomination of a whore'. Each member was to pay half-a-crown for the support of fellow members in distress, and no man was to be admitted to the ladies' club-room but 'our negociator . . . who has the privilege of chusing what member he pleases for his bedfellow that night, she not being pre-arranged'.

The *Memoirs* also state that the club had about a hundred members, some of 'noble families, and most of them of creditable and honest parents'. One of the main purposes of club gatherings was to allow the whores to clear 'their arrears with their factor Mr H—s, who had five shillings in the pound freight for conveying them to the arms of their enamorato's'. So for the good publicity that went with their 'listing', the harlots were obliged to pay Harris a 'poundage' of 25 per cent of their earnings. (This seems highly unlikely unless the charge applied only to the girls living and working under his immediate protection, and so also covered accommodation, food and various services.)

A humorous anecdote included in the *Memoirs* throws a little light on how Harris' money-spinning 'system of fornication' worked. We are told a certain 'Doctor Wagtail' lit upon Fanny one night in Drury Lane and carried her to the Shakespeare's Head Tavern. They entered a private room and Fanny desired him '. . . as he was an entire stranger, to make her a present before-hand'. He agreed, but had only five shillings and sixpence on him. Fanny 'flew into a passion, telling him he was some garreteer scribbler. Some poor hackney poet'. This commotion attracted Harris, 'the negociator, who under pretence of snuffing the candles, had a mind to gain some intelligence concerning the cause of this tumult'. The doctor put his case, revealing both his ardor and his lack of ready money. Harris told the doctor that the young woman was 'the celebrated Miss Fanny M— . . . who never went under two guineas'. The doctor, who could restrain himself no longer, handed Harris his silver-hilted sword 'and asked him to have as much upon it as would satisfy the lady'. Harris, realising he could push the frustrated and lustful man further, stated that the sword would not pawn for above a guinea and a half, and demanded the fellow's periwig as well. The doctor handed it over and the satisfied Harris then retired with his pledges, leaving his victim to come to more intimate terms with the 'celebrated' Fanny.

With their *List* Harris and Derrick had found a solid source of revenue and, it would seem, of pleasure. But the money – as well as the pleasure – came not just from the prostitutes, but also eventually their clients. Information was essential for the profitable functioning of the sex industry: clients had to know where to find prostitutes who, in turn, needed to make themselves and their whereabouts known to potential clients. At a stroke *Harris's List* made life easier for all concerned. The initial plan seems to have been that clients would consult Harris for information in person – no doubt tipping him handsomely – but it was only a matter of time before the information was circulated in published form, with people paying to possess it at the rate of two shillings and sixpence per copy.[34] Publication instantly made the *List* more readily available to many more people and thus, by making contacts between prostitutes and clients far easier, significantly increased the amount of money flowing into London's sex industry, and ultimately into the pockets of men like Harris and Derrick.

The moment that *Harris's List* went on public sale is suggested by a satirical little article that appeared in the *Centinel* on 2 June 1757. Describing prostitutes in the style of an advertisement for an auction of ships and their cargoes, the article implies that Harris's 'Pimp's-list' was available for purchase at three Covent Garden locations:

> For Sale by the Candle At the Shakespeare's Head Tavern Covent Garden: The Tartar and the Shark Privateers with their Cargo from Haddock's, Harris, Master; Square stern'd Dutch Built, with new sails and rigging. They have been lately docked And refitted, and are reckoned prime sailors. Catalogues with An account of their Cargo may be had at Mrs D[ouglas]'s in The Piazza, or at the Place of Sale. To begin at twelve at night.[35]

The Shakespeare's Head Tavern was a very near neighbour of the famed Haddock's Bagnio (see page 227), while Mother Douglas' establishment was squeezed between them in a building on the north-east side of the Piazza.

By the 1770s *Harris's List* had evolved into a regularly issued and updated publication on sale in a number of London establishments, and in the early 1780s was noted by Archenholz as one of the peculiarities of London:

> A tavern keeper . . . prints every year an account of the women of the town, entitled, *Harris's List of Covent-Garden Ladies*. In it, the most exact description is given of their names, their lodgings, their faces, their manners, their talents, and even their tricks . . . eight thousand copies are sold annually.[36]

In fact the *List* was not unique to London but spawned provincial imitations, notably *Ranger's Impartial List of the Ladies of Pleasure in Edinburgh*. The Preface to the 1775 edition of the Edinburgh *List* offers a time-honoured and spirited apology for prostitution that attempted to raise its exponents to the status of national ornaments and muses:

> Do they not sacrifice their health, their lives, nay their reputations, at the altars of love and benevolence . . . what villainies do they not prevent? What plots, what combinations do they not dissolve? Clasped in the delicious arms of beauty, the factious malcontent forgets the black workings of his soul . . . Though custom has loaded them with the infamous and ungenerous appellation of prostitutes, do we not owe to them, the peace of families, of cities, nay of kingdoms . . . were they hindered . . . think how terrible might the consequences be . . . wild frenzy breaking all restraint will bear down decency, relation, kindred and religion – What . . . litigation, bloodshed, incest!

The Edinburgh *List* gives little insight into Edinburgh's centres of prostitution other than suggesting that the women of the town tended to be lodged in the tight closes off the High Street and Cannongate.

On the other hand, the editions of *Harris's List* that Archenholz would have perused offer a fascinating vignette of London areas where the trade was conducted and reveal with extraordinary accuracy the disposition of the majority of the city's middle-ranking prostitutes towards the end of the eighteenth century. The introduction to *Harris's List of Covent Garden Ladies: or Man of Pleasures Kalender for the Year 1788*,[37] makes it clear that Marylebone was 'now the grand Paradise of Love' alongside 'Covent Garden, her elder sister', and the addresses listed do indeed suggest that, at the time, the majority of prostitutes of the middle rank worked and lived in the more modest streets north of Oxford Street and west of Tottenham Court Road (essentially the Marylebone of the 1780s), and in Soho. For example, Miss Lister, 6 Union Street, Oxford Road; Miss Johnson, 17 Goodge Street, who the *List* noted had 'such elasticity in her loins, that she can cast her lover to a pleasing height and receive him again with utmost dexterity', and Miss Dunford 'at a Sadlers, Charles Street, Soho', who was . . .

> . . . fond of music, plays with the greatest dexterity . . . full skilled in pricking, altho' the principal part of her music is played in duets . . . she has not the smallest objection to two flats . . . she generally chooses the lowest part (and) sometimes plays the same tune over twice.

This mini-masterpiece of smutty innuendo duly advertised Miss Dunford as a bisexual available for lesbian ('flats') intrigues, among other things.

SEX AND THE LONDON HOUSE

The houses occupied by the young women mentioned in *Harris's List* were not, of course, purpose-designed for the sex industry, but were standard examples of speculatively built London domestic architecture. It had become standard practice for builders to acquire building leases from ground landlords, run up the shells of houses as quickly and cheaply as possible, and sell on the remainder of the lease and shell to the first occupant, who would then finish the interior of the house to suit their own taste and pocket. The advantages of the speculative system were that builders could make a fast profit by selling on the lease and shell for substantially more money then they had spent on the materials and labour of construction; the landlord got his ground developed for no expenditure and, although only receiving a small ground rent, his estate would, when the lease expired after 60, 80 or 99 years, gain possession of the houses; meanwhile the occupant was housed at a reasonable price. The potential disadvantages of the system were that corners were cut for the sake of profit and consequently vast areas of London were covered with tawdry and unsound constructions.

A series of Building Acts were passed after 1667, and throughout the eighteenth century in an attempt to ensure sound- and fire-resistant construction, and some estates attempted to apply building controls, but these generally had only minimal effects so that, by the mid-eighteenth century, many observers started to despair of the quality and solidity of London's rapidly growing, speculatively built housing stock.

Isaac Ware, in his *Complete Body of Architecture* of 1756, fretted that:

> The nature of tenures in London has introduced the art of building slightly [weakly]. The ground landlord is to come into possession at the end of a short term, and the builder, unless his Grace tye him down to articles, does not chuse to employ his money to [the landlord's] advantage. It is for this reason we see houses built for sixty, seventy or the stoutest of this kind for ninety-nine years. They care they shall not stand longer than their time occasions, many to fall before it is expired; nay, some have carried the art of slight building so far, that their houses have fallen in before they were tenanted.[38]

The London art of 'slight building' became notorious. Jean-Pierre Grosely in his *Tour of London* of 1772 confirmed that 'the solidity of the building is measured by the duration of the lease' and that 'the outside [of the houses] appears to be built of brick, but the walls consist only of a single row of bricks . . . made of the first earth that comes to hand, and only just warmed by the fire'; while James Peller Malcolm wrote in 1808 of 'the horrid effect produced by the fall of frail houses' and calculated 'there are at this moment at least 3,000 houses in a dangerous state of ruin within London and Westminster'.[39] But, if not notably sound in construction, the average London house was often beautifully and elegantly detailed and proportioned, and – of immense importance for a whole range of occupants, including those from the sex industry – it possessed a plan and form that was highly flexible and convenient, with staircase and landings serving as circulation space, allowing a large number of rooms to be accessed independently.

If not purpose-designed, many of the houses serving the sex industry would have been purpose-built, for large numbers were no doubt constructed as investments by bawds, pimps or successful prostitutes, using profits made from the sex industry, as was the case with Moll King (see page 89). In addition, large numbers of houses would have been constructed by speculative builders who had sex-industry workers in mind as potential lessees, and many more would have been rented to prostitutes.

Archenholz observed the connection between London property and sex industries:

> The uncertainty of receiving payments makes the house-keepers charge
> [prostitutes] double the common price for their lodgings. They hire by
> the week a first floor, and pay for it more than the owner gives for the
> whole premises, taxes included. Without these, thousands of houses
> would be empty, in the western parts of the town. In the parish of
> Mary-le-bone only, which is the largest and best peopled in the capital,
> thirty thousand ladies of pleasure reside [probably a misprint for 'thirteen
> thousand', see page 169] of whom seventeen hundred are reckoned to be
> house-keepers. These live very well, and without ever being disturbed by
> the magistrates. They are indeed so much their own mistresses, that if a
> justice of the peace attempted to trouble them in their apartments, they
> might turn him out of doors; for they pay the same taxes as the other
> parishioners, they are consequently entitled to the same privileges.[40]

So in the late eighteenth century even superior prostitutes were notorious for the 'uncertainty' of their income and thus were insecure in their homes. They could be wealthy 'kept' women one moment, enjoying the income and lifestyle of their affluent and perhaps aristocratic protector, and then suddenly out of favour and, with no secure income, soon out of the house. This was, at best and even for high-class whores, a very insecure profession – which explains why a harlot's dream was, as Archenholz explained, to secure 'annuities paid them by their seducers' or, more desperately, to obtain 'other settlements into which they have surprised their lovers in the moment of intoxication'.[41]

Ivan Bloch, in his less-edited version of Archenholz's text, gives more of the German visitor's thoughts on this subject:

> These annuities certainly secure them from need, but they are usually
> not sufficient to enable them to live sumptuously in the capital and to
> enjoy expensive pleasures; they therefore permit lovers' visits, but only
> those whom they like – the others are sent away.[42]

The ability and willingness of certain prostitutes and their protectors to pay over the odds made them most attractive and valuable tenants. In *Fanny Hill* John Cleland describes how the heroine was set up by her lover Charles in a lodging in fashionable St James's where 'he paid half a guinea a week for two rooms and a closet on the second floor'. Cleland makes the point that this was a high rent. The landlord, observes Fanny, 'had no reason to complain' because Charles was 'too liberal not to make him regret our loss', and she thought the lodgings 'ordinary enough, even at that price'.[43] By comparison, the occasional harlot Bet Flint in the 1760s paid five shillings a week for her humble Soho furnished apartment, but even this rent was relatively expensive at a time when the average skilled London tradesman was earning between two shillings and sixpence and three shillings a day, and the going rate for a garret at the time was around one shilling a week.

Even if not particularly welcome tenants to some, prostitutes might be

An erotic scene from a late-eighteenth-century edition of John Cleland's Fanny Hill.

the only rent-payers a landlord could get. *Pretty Doings in a Protestant Nation* tells of 'a fine young Creature, genteely dres'd, attended by a Woman four times her age' who called at a house near Red-Lyon-Square looking for lodgings. The pair quibbled over details, including 'the want of a Back-Door', and an opposite row of houses were seen as a possibly 'intolerable Inconvenience' because the girl proclaimed that it was 'Death to her to be overlook'd', but she finally agreed to take an apartment. The landlady, who knew the business of her new tenant, was delighted to have 'lett her first Floor to a Male and Female, to do the Work of Creation in without a Licence from the Clergy', and added, '[H]ow should people be able to pay their Rent and Taxes if they were to be over-scrupulous in such Matters; especially, when half the Lodgings within the Bill of Mortality are fill'd with *Coiners of false Love?*'[44]

Discretion, gravity and a judicious level of display seem to have been the hallmarks and safeguards of a successful and independent prostitute working from her own lodgings. As Archenholz observed of well-to-do Marylebone-based prostitutes:

> ... their apartments are elegantly, and sometimes magnificently
> furnished; they keep several servants, and some have their own carriages
> ... The testimony of these women, even of the lowest of them, is
> always received as evidence in the courts of justice [which, taken all
> together] gives them a certain dignity of conduct, which can scarcely be
> reconciled with their profession.[45]

Not all Marylebone sex establishments were discreet all the time; some, on occasion, made use of the most sexually charged detail of the common London house – the window. Throughout the eighteenth century it was usual for prostitutes to solicit from the windows of the houses from which they operated, and sometimes their displays could be most startling. Michael Ryan, in his *Prostitution in London* of 1839, felt obliged to resort to Latin to describe what some prostitutes got up to. Quoting J. B. Talbot of the London Society for the Protection of Young Females, Ryan explained that prostitutes 'often exhibit themselves at the windows in the day time, in alluring positions; and in the evening or approach of dusk, in the more retired streets, variis modis corporibus nudis, saltant, ludant, et contant', or as the historian Ivan Bloch translates it, 'often stand naked at the window and execute all manner of indecent movements and postures'.[46]

This, stated Talbot, 'was the custom at Madame Aubrey's [in Seymour Place, Marylebone] and was complained of by the neighbours'.[47] This tradition of sexual display made the house window a tender subject in Georgian London, to the extent that Archenholz observed in the 1780s that 'to show oneself at the window is considered very improper. Nothing less than some street incident which may arouse curiosity can excuse an honourable woman from opening a window.'[48] Quite simply, to peer through a window was, in many parts of town, tantamount to offering oneself to passers-by, for, as Bloch explained, 'sitting at a window counted for a long time in England as a sign of prostitution'.[49]

EIGHT

AT HOME WITH
MRS CORNELYS

The World of the Masquerade

As well as the squares, streets, private establishments and public buildings such as the Royal Exchange that had been appropriated by the sex trade, London also possessed places of pleasure that were natural attractions for prostitutes and their clients. From 1660 Vauxhall Gardens – south of the Thames – had played a key role in the capital's sexual intrigues, as had Ranelagh Gardens in Chelsea from 1742 and the Pantheon on Oxford Street from 1772. In addition to these great pleasure resorts there were numerous smaller 'wells' or spas on the periphery of the city where Londoners went to relax in pleasant gardens and, if possible, drink from local springs offering water that, if not always medicinal, was at least relatively unpolluted.

Vauxhall Gardens, South London, opened in the 1660s and was a scene of amorous delight in Georgian times.

Good examples were Marylebone Gardens, which, like Hockley-in-the-Hole, featured animal-baiting and displays of fencing and the 'art of defence'; Bagnigge Wells in King's Cross with its iron-rich and purgative waters, and Hampstead Wells – near what is now Well Walk – which even had a Pump room but which closed in 1733 because it had become too popular with the city's low-life.

There were also specific business initiatives and haunts of pleasure launched to further the interests of, and work profitably with, the sex industry. London's theatres can be included in this category, when certain impresarios were in charge and when consciously lascivious productions or events such as masquerades were in hand. There were also public gathering places – such as Mrs Cornelys' assembly rooms in Soho Square, which became famed for their risqué masquerades – that were honey-pots for prostitutes, pimps and their clients.

Masquerades were one of the many cultural innovations encouraged by the experiences of the Grand Tour. Returning travellers wished to continue enjoying some of the pleasures they had experienced in Italy. One of the first people to promote masquerades in London was John Jacob Heidegger, who was also partly responsible for the popularisation of another Italian cultural phenomenon: opera.

Heidegger, the son of a Swiss clergyman, arrived in London in 1708, seems soon to have become a close companion and business partner of the notorious bawd Mother Wisebourne (see page 104), and in 1709 solved his financial difficulties by staging a rudimentary opera called *Tomyris, Queen of Scythia*. This had been written in 1707 by the Huguenot journalist Peter Anthony Mote, who, a few years later, died in mysterious circumstances in a bawdy-house, probably a victim of autoerotic asphyxiation. This musical production seems not to have been as profitable as Heidegger would have liked, but the following year – 1710 – he held a series of masquerade or carnival balls at the Haymarket Theatre that 'attracted the First Quality because of their gaiety and lewdness'.[1]

These carnivals became immensely popular because of their risqué quality, with masked prostitutes mingling with the rich and fashionable. They were preached against by moralists as scenes 'of Outrageous and flaming Debauchery, where temptation is passionately courted', and where, as one pamphlet of 1721 would have it, 'a whore [is known] by a Vizor-Mask; and a Fool by talking to her'.[2] By 1721 Heidegger's entertainments

John James Heidegger, Handel's partner and the man who brought masquerades to London.

had become so outrageous that action was taken to suppress them and he himself so notorious that the young William Hogarth felt compelled to mock him, and the taste of the times, in a satirical print entitled *Masquerades and Operas*, published in 1724.

Seeking new sources of revenue, Heidegger teamed up with George Frederick Handel in 1729, hiring the King's Theatre to stage the composer's operas. By this time, however, Handel's formal Italian-style operas were falling from public favour, particularly in the wake of the phenomenal triumph of *The Beggar's Opera*. Following the success of the *Messiah* in 1741 Handel finally abandoned the opera form, by which time he had also parted from Heidegger.

Ultimately, Heidegger left little lasting evidence of his presence in the capital he had scandalised in the early years of the eighteenth century – except for one most evocative fragment. For a time during the 1740s he lived in the elegant Maids of Honour Row on Richmond Green, built in 1724 and adjoining the site of the Tudor royal palace. In the entrance hall of his former house, now number 4, still prance near life-size painted figures, set in exotic Swiss and Chinese landscapes, created between 1744 and 1748 for Heidegger by the skilful scene-painter Antonio Joli. Walking through this interior – mingling with the shades of a murky, decadent and distant past – can still be a slightly unnerving experience.

Heidegger died in 1749 when his outlandish masquerades – which had fallen from fashion for a while – were just about to enjoy a dramatic revival. Masquerades must have lingered on because Hogarth shows masquerade masks in *The Harlot's Progress* of 1732 and in the bagnio scene of *Marriage à la Mode* of 1743, but the *Gentleman's Magazine* for December 1754 writes of masquerades as novelties and – in the process – suggests that this new breed was as risqué as in Heidegger's day. It explains very succinctly why masquerades were viewed as a threat to public morals and an aid to prostitution:

> Among the numerous modes which the wantonness of luxury has of late introduced into the kingdom, for the destroying of time, I know of none more fatal to the virtue and reputation of the female sex, than masquerades – the masquerade houses may . . . be called shops, where opportunities for immorality, prophaneness, obscenity, and almost every kind of vice are retailed to any one who will become a customer, and at the low rate of seven and twenty shillings, the most abandon'd courtezan, the most profligate rake, or common sharper purchases the privilege of mingling with the first peers and peeresses of the realm; and not seldom affronts both modesty and greatness with impunity.[3]

The London masquerades of the mid-eighteenth century are indelibly associated with Mrs Cornelys, who made them a popular – and notorious – adjunct of the sex industry. She had been born Theresa Imer in Vienna, worked as an opera singer partly in London in the mid-1740s and also as an actress, dancer and prostitute when she became one of Casanova's lovers. By the late 1750s she was living in Rotterdam as the mistress of Cornelius de Rigerboos whose Christian name she took when she decamped to England in October 1759 with a cello player named John Freeman who'd convinced her he was really a clergyman with a living in England. The pair started by giving a series of concerts and then hit upon the idea of offering concerts for an assembly of subscribers in an elegant apartment.

Theresa Cornelys, the creator of mid-Georgian London's 'fairy palace' in Soho Square.

Mrs Cornelys gained support for the project from a number of well-connected London characters – including the infamous beauty Elizabeth Chudleigh, later to become the bigamous wife of the Duke of Kingston – and in 1760 leased the late-seventeenth-century Carlisle House in Soho Square. At first the assemblies, funded by tickets sold to a 'Society' of subscribers, consisted of dancing and card-playing but soon began to include concerts and exotic masquerades. As the venture promised success, Mrs Cornelys spent large sums adapting, enlarging and furnishing Carlisle House so that it was soon able to hold 500 in high style. The additions included a splendid assembly room with a column-framed apse at one end for musicians, mirror-clad walls, chandeliers and Rococo plaster decoration. For two decades Mrs Cornelys had one of the most sexually charged reputations in London, and Carlisle House was one of the city's wonders and an acknowledged centre of intrigue. All were attracted and accommodated, confirming the masquerade as the great social leveller – as the alarmed author of the article in the *Gentleman's Magazine* had observed – where Londoners of high and low degree could mingle in liberated and anonymous intercourse.[4]

Carlisle House was open once or twice a month for balls and concerts, and throughout the 1760s Mrs Cornelys continued to add attractions – including rooms decorated in the Chinese taste, and a 'Chinese' bridge perhaps designed by Thomas Chippendale – to ensure that 'subscriptions' rolled in.[5] By 1770 she had created one of the most extraordinary interiors dedicated to pleasure and amusement that London has ever known. When Fanny Burney visited Carlisle House in 1770 she was utterly overwhelmed – both by the architecture and by the press of perspiring revellers:

> The magnificence of the rooms, splendor of the illuminations and
> embellishments, and the brilliant appearance of the company exceeded
> anything I ever before saw. The apartments were so crowded we had
> scarce room to move, which was quite disagreeable, nevertheless, the
> flight of apartments both upstairs and on the ground floor seemed
> endless . . . The Rooms were so full and so hot that nobody attempted
> to dance.[6]

Tobias Smollett, in *The Expedition of Humphry Clinker*, published in 1771, gave it as his opinion that 'Mrs Cornelys' assembly, which for the rooms, the company, the dresses, and decorations, surpasses all description',[7] while also in 1771 Horace Walpole, that waspish observer of the follies of others, revealed a fascination with Mrs Cornelys' extravagant entertainments. In a letter to Sir Horace Mann he described Carlisle House and explained that she had . . .

> . . . enlarged it, and established assemblies and balls by subscription. At first they scandalised, but soon drew in both righteous and ungodly. She went on building, and made her house a fairy palace, for balls, concerts, and masquerades. Her Opera, which she called *Harmonic Meetings*, was splendid and charming.[8]

Branching out to include operas in her repertoire was to be one of the causes of the collapse of Mrs Cornelys' fortunes. Public and money-making opera performance in London required a licence but, unfortunately, Mrs Cornelys didn't have one, and calling such events 'Harmonic Meetings' did not solve the problem. She was pursued by jealous rivals and opera impresarios, sued, embroiled in well-publicised legal actions and ultimately fined. General suspicion surrounding the morality of her business activities probably didn't help her cause. A print published in about 1770 entitled 'Wantonness Mask'd' (a title seemingly inspired by Act V of Shakespeare's *Love's Labour's Lost*) suggests the prevailing attitude towards Mrs Cornelys, her entertainments and her discomfiture. It shows a scene at a masquerade – no doubt in Carlisle House – where a 'Buck' unmasks but the harlot he clutches does not, instead staring out of the scene, straight at the viewer, in a most challenging, uncontrite and provocative manner.[9]

This popular disapproval of Mrs Cornelys' attempt to disguise her establishment – which was essentially a place of sophisticated sexual assignation and prostitution – as a temple of the arts seems to have been accompanied by official action against her. In 1771 she was, according to the *Universal Magazine*, indicted for keeping a 'disorderly house' by suffering . . .

> . . . divers loose, idle, and disorderly persons, as well men as women, to be, and remain, during the whole night, rioting, and otherwise misbehaving themselves . . . That she did keep and maintain a public masquerade, without any license . . . and did receive and harbour loose and disorderly persons in masks.[10]

To these woes were added the expense of building works, the mass of unpaid bills to tradesmen and, from January 1772, the very stiff competition from the large, glamorous and ultra-fashionable assembly rooms of the Pantheon that opened nearby on Oxford Street. The consequence of all these troubles was bankruptcy, and in October 1772 confinement in the King's Bench debtor's gaol.

But this was not the end for Carlisle House as a place of entertainment or for Mrs Cornelys. Her creditors got hold of the lease for Carlisle House and its contents, tried to convert both into a large sum of cash and, when this proved difficult, re-opened it for concerts and masquerades. By 1776 Mrs Cornelys was back in charge.

William Hickey in his *Memoirs* describes going to Carlisle House some time after Mrs Cornelys' return – seemingly in late summer 1780 – with Emily Warren, a famed high courtesan, mistress of his absent friend Bob Pott and model for Sir Joshua Reynolds (see page 362):

> The night I came to town there was to be a masquerade at Mrs
> Cornelys's rooms in Soho Square, and Emily said I must go with her to
> it. I therefore sent for a domino [a type of mask that covered the eyes
> only], etc, and at ten o'clock she and I drove there. She was in a man's
> domino, with a smart hat and feather, and looked charmingly, her fine
> figure and graceful air attracting attention wherever she appeared.

Emily had told Hickey she would not unmask during the evening – an action that, given her beauty and notoriety, would only encourage additional attention from prowling males – but . . .

> . . . vanity, however, prevailed . . . for finding herself followed and
> admired in every direction, she could not resist the taking off her mask
> to let the delighted beholders see that the face corresponded with the
> figure they had been pursuing from room to room.[11]

What Hickey does not reveal is that, at this time, Mrs Cornelys was once more struggling to survive. Her rooms were no longer the height of fashion and attendances were down so she diversified by opening an 'Academy of Belles Lettres' in Carlisle House, which included language classes and a library of new books 'for ladies and gentlemen'. She also launched a Sunday night 'Promenade' reception that prospered for a while since most other assembly rooms were closed then. William Hickey was enthusiastic:

In the early part of the winter, a new species of evening's amusement became quite the rage under the name of 'The Promenade'. Mrs Cornelys's truly magnificent suite of apartments ... were opened every Sunday night at seven o'clock for the reception of company. So much did it take that the first people of the kingdom attended it, as did also the whole beauty of the metropolis, from the Duchess of Devonshire down to the little milliner's apprentice from Cranbourne Alley.[12]

A fascinating and very detailed description of a 'Promenade', of Carlisle House and the atmosphere within it was recorded by Samuel Curwen, an American loyalist taking refuge in London. In his journal for 12 November 1780 he noted that after tea he went ...

... to Carlisle House ... wherein the well-known Mrs Cornelys used to accommodate the nobility, etc., with masquerades and coteries [for] a Sunday evening entertainment, called the promenade, instituted in lieu of public amusement ... The employment of the company is simply walking through the rooms; being allowed tea, coffee, chocolate, lemonade, orgeat [a flavoured syrup], negus [a type of wine punch], milk, etc.; admission by ticket, cost, three shillings; dress, decent, full not required; some in boots ... The ladies were rigged out in gaudy attire, attended by bucks, bloods, and maccaronies [dandies], though it is also resorted to by persons of irreproachable character ... The arrangement of the house is as follows:—From the vestibule where the tickets are received, the entrance is through a short passage into the first room, of a moderate size, covered with carpets, and furnished with wooden chairs and seats in Chinese taste; through this the company passes to another of a larger size, furnished and accommodated as the former; passing this, you enter the long-room, about eighty feet by forty; this is the largest, and lighted with glass chandeliers and branches fixed to side walls, against which stand sofas covered with silk,—floors carpeted. Hence tending to the left, you cross the hall, and enter the wilderness or grotto, having natural evergreens planted round the walls ... The company usually resorting there about seven hundred ... this evening the house was thronged ... it was full two hours before I could procure a dish of tea ... and when served, it was in a slovenly manner on a dirty tea-stand. I never saw a place of public resort where the company was treated with so little respect by servants.[13]

The creation of the Sunday Promenade was the last adventure for Mrs Cornelys and Carlisle House. In 1783 the house and its contents were advertised to be let, in March 1784 the ratebooks record it as empty, and in 1791 this house of fantasy – this Georgian 'fairy palace' – was demolished. As for Mrs Cornelys, her last recorded business venture was as a 'Vendor of Asses' Milk' – a somewhat enigmatic-sounding trade – from a house in semi-rural Knightsbridge, but this activity was evidently not a success either for soon she was in the Fleet debtors' gaol, where she died in August 1797 at the age of seventy-four.[14]

NINE

THE RAKE'S
REPOSE

Coffee Houses and Brothels

COFFEE HOUSES

During the first half of the eighteenth century London prostitutes habitually took shelter in, or made use of, taverns, bawdy-houses, brothels and coffee houses. Of these institutions the one that had the most distinct architectural form at the time was perhaps the coffee house, which many accounts make clear was among the key places where prostitutes could display themselves – particularly in Covent Garden over a 'capuchin' as milky white coffee, the forerunner of the cappuccino, was called – and where they would keep assignations and pick up clients. London coffee houses were of seventeenth-century origin[1] and usually included a common or long room furnished with benches, long communal tables and a large open fireplace where pots of coffee could be kept warm.

The most famous Covent Garden coffee house – indeed something of an institution in early-Georgian London – was that presided over by Tom and Moll King (see page 81). It was located in a row of three timber-built huts on the south side of the Covent Garden Piazza, set among ad hoc stalls serving the area's gradually expanding fruit, vegetable and flower markets. Intended initially to serve the market workers, much of whose trade was nocturnal, Tom King's Coffee House opened at about midnight. This soon made it popular with Covent Garden's other night workers, notably the whores who patrolled its streets, and during the 1730s the establishment's 'Long Room' became the focus of much of the area's rowdy, late-night low-life.

Tom King's Coffee House gets its first public mention in the Prologue of Henry Fielding's *The Covent Garden Tragedy* of 1732, in which he asks,

'The great square of Venus': the Covent Garden Piazza, looking east down Russell Street, before the fire of 1769 that destroyed the arcaded 1630s terrace of houses on the south-east corner. These contained the old Hummums Hotel, Lovejoy's Bagnio and the Bedford Arms Tavern. The arcaded houses to the north of Russell Street contained the Bedford Head Coffee House, the Shakespeare's Head Tavern in the north-east corner and, on the north side of the Piazza, Mother Douglas' brothel and to its west Haddock's Bagnio. Tom King's Coffee House was in the sheds on the right.

'What rake is ignorant of King's coffee house?' (Fielding describes it in a footnote, clearly for the benefit of those who were not rakes, as 'a place in Covent Garden well known to Gentlemen to whom Beds are unknown'.) But the Kings' establishment was no brothel or bawdy-house, for it contained no beds for the use of whores or their clients, and it made no pretence of being a bagnio. This was a canny move by the Kings, intended to protect them from being prosecuted for running a disorderly house of ill repute.

But although it offered no bedding arrangements there was no secret about the real purpose of the Kings' coffee house or the intentions of the majority of its customers. After midnight it was the resort of 'all the Bucks, Bloods, Demireps and Choice Spirits in London', where every evening could be seen 'Women of the Town, the most celebrated, and dressed as elegant as if to sit in the stage box at an opera', and all ready for hire at a moment's notice.[2] It was presided over by a famed coffee-girl named Black Betty, who appears to be commemorated by the Black-a-moor trade sign that hangs over the coffee house in a print forming the frontispiece to a 1738 edition of the poem *The Humours of Covent Garden*. But the greatest character of the establishment – indeed one of the great characters of London's early-eighteenth-century sex industry – was of course Moll King herself,[3] described in *The Humours of Covent Garden*:

> High in the midst is the fat Priestess seen,
> Known by her comely face, and portly mean,
> And voice Sonorous, who to urge invites
> The Votaries to Bacchanalian Rites
> Her Rosey Visage with rich Rubies Shines,
> Painted with the best Blood of generous Wines.

The Kings' coffee house seems to have continued into the mid-1740s; certainly three sheds in the correct location appear on John Rocque's London map of 1746, although perhaps these had been rebuilt, for some reports suggest that the original sheds were removed during the mid- or late 1730s when Moll was either committed to the King's Bench or had been transported to America.

The fact that Hogarth shows Tom King's Coffee House in his *Morning*, painted in 1738 as part of *The Four Times of the Day* series, doesn't mean it then still survived. This is not a documentary painting, as is revealed by Hogarth's decision to relocate the coffee house for artistic reasons to in front of St Paul's Church. It's a moral study and an essay in contrasts: the pious, aged woman going to church is contrasted with the pretty young prostitute being kissed outside the coffee house; the faces of two figures in the painting seem to be based on Caius Gabriel Cibber's sculpture depicting the difference between *Melancholy* and *Raving Madness*; while the 'Primitive Hut' occupied by the coffee house, full of life and passion, is contrasted with the chaste and stately beauty of the temple-like front of St Paul's.

The coffee house itself is a thing of contrasts. Its rustic, hut-like form suggests the virtues of the simple innocence of rural life or of the 'noble savage', yet inside a brawl is underway, revealing this to be the den of ignoble savages and no bucolic dream.

There could be yet another level of contrast in the painting. The

Hogarth's Morning *(1738), showing Tom King's Coffee House, relocated, for artistic reasons, to in front of the portico of St Paul's Church. The plate, engraved from a painting, shows the scene in a mirror-image of reality.*

apparently pious lady is, some argue, intended as a portrait of the ageing Betsy Careless with her link-boy Little Casey or Cazey (see page 94).[4] If this is the case then the woman's stance does not express shock at the sexual antics confronting her but rather remembrance of her own earlier life, so the contrast here is purely between youth and age, sexual activity and passivity.

Hogarth painted it at a moment of change. Tom King was, according to Moll's *Life*, to die the following year – 1739 – after which the establishment was renamed Moll King's Coffee House.

A late portrait of the coffee house is offered by Tobias Smollett in *The Adventures of Roderick Random*, which, published early in 1749, describes Moll's establishment in its last year under her control and reveals that it was still a late-night rendezvous of choice for any who found themselves adrift in Covent Garden in the small hours. Smollett's characters leave a tavern at 'near two a-clock in the morning' in a drunken and confused state. One, 'unable to speak or stand', is deposited in a bagnio to sleep it off while three others go to 'Moll King's coffee-house' where one is abandoned asleep on a bench that he had appropriated only after having 'kicked half a dozen of hungary whores' off it.[5]

THE SERAGLIO AND THE NUNNERY

In the mid-eighteenth century significant changes overtook the 'career' of prostitution that were calculated to make it and the sex industry in general more elegant, safe and discreet. *Nocturnal Revels*, published in 1779 and purporting to be written by a 'Monk of the Order of St Francis' – which is to say a member of Sir Francis Dashwood's Hell Fire Club (see page 390) – records the moment of change.

In 1750 Mrs Goadby appeared on the scene, fired with a determination 'to refine our amorous amusements and regulate them according to the Parisian system'.[6] Ivan Bloch, in his magisterial *Sexual Life in England Past and Present*, builds upon the text of *Nocturnal Revels* and explains that Mrs Goadby chose to term her superior brothel a 'seraglio' after the French *sérails*, that were in turn inspired by the well-ordered harems or *sarays* of the Ottomans.[7] She had, records Bloch, 'made several journeys to France, and had been initiated into the secrets of the famous Parisian '*sérails* ... the principles of which ... Mrs Goadby to a great extent made her own'. These principles included accepting ...

> ... only the most beautiful girls, and preferably those from different countries and of different faiths. All, however, were equally subject to the rules of the brothel and had to submit unconditionally to the orders of the brothel keeper, whose authority was supreme. It was also the duty of the girls to show 'zeal and great sincerity when celebrating the rites and ceremonies of the votaries of Cyprus [as Cyprians, or prostitutes, were called]' and to satisfy all fantasies, caprices and extravagances of the male visitors, carrying out their wishes in every particular.

In the Parisian *sérails* the women were to 'avoid all gastronomic and alcoholic excess in order that their behaviour should be modest and decent even in the pursuit of pleasure', but Mrs Goadby – clearly a realist well aware of the London harlots' love of restorative alcoholic beverages – abandoned any prohibition against strong liquor. The women of the seraglio either promenaded during the day or spent their time relaxing indoors, with clients arriving in the evening 'when their custom was to offer a handkerchief to the lady of ... choice. If this was accepted, she belonged to the man for the night.'[8]

Mrs Goadby rented an elegant house in Berwick Street, Soho, which she immediately 'fitted up ... in an elegant stile'[9] distinguished by its discretion and outwardly sober appearance. Mrs Goadby's establishment was far removed from the usually rumbustious bawdy-houses (notwithstanding the cautious example previously set by Mother Wisebourne – see page 104), and in consequence was calculated to escape the notice of moralistic magistrates and constables. Mrs Goadby then 'engaged some of the first-rate *filles de joye* in London' and equipped 'her ladies in the highest gusto' thanks to the great quantity of silks and lace she'd brought from France.[10] This astonishingly elegant establishment – essentially a Parisian *hôtel* with the pretensions and discreet grace of an exclusive aristocratic mansion, where 'only people of rank and men of fortune' were welcome[11] – rapidly fulfilled its claim to 'refine our amorous amusements' and 'soon achieved a great reputation and received large numbers of visitors of good standing, who could here indulge in any extravagance or perversity they wished'.[12]

One of the secrets of Mrs Goadby's success was her ability to convince her clients that the prostitutes in her 'nunnery' were healthy and that all possible attempts were made to prevent the spread of venereal disease. She employed a resident surgeon to ensure that all were 'sound in wind and limb' and supplied her 'nuns' with 'Mrs Phillips's famed New Engines',[13] which were condoms made of sheep's gut or bladder and secured to the male member by means of an elegant ribbon.

Condoms, available since the late seventeenth century, were used more as a preventative against disease than pregnancy, as Daniel Turner pointed out in *Syphilis* in 1717 where he wrote that 'the cundum' was 'the best if not only preservative our libertines have found at present'.[14]

A similar point was made, in a more elegant manner, in a poem of about 1744 entitled 'The Machine; or, Love's Preservative'. First the poet celebrates the condom's power as a contraceptive:

> By this Machine secure, the willing Maid
> Can taste Love's Joys, nor is she more afraid
> Her swelling Belly should, or squalling Brat
> Betray the luscious Pastime she has been at.

Then he extols the condom's potential as a health preservative:

> Happy the Man, in whose Pocket found
> Whether with Green or Scarlet Ribbon bound,
> A well made Cundum; he nor dreads the ills
> Of Cordees, Shanker [symptoms – and treatments – of venereal
>   disease], Boluses [large pills], or Pills;
> But arm'd thus boldly wages am'rous Fight
> With Transport-feigning Whore, in Danger's Spight.[15]

Despite their obvious utility, however, condoms were rarely carried by the common London prostitute, no doubt because they were expensive and hard to find. When condoms or 'armour' were used it was because the customer was pre-prepared, if not always cautious, as James Boswell makes clear in his *London Journal* of 1762–3:

I sallied to the streets and . . . picked up a fresh, agreeable young girl called Alice Gibbs. We went down a lane to a snug place, and I took out my armour, but she begged that I might not put it on, as the sport was much pleasanter without it, and as she was quite safe. I was so rash as to trust her, and had a very agreeable congress.[16]

'All sorts of fine machines called cundums . . . implements of safety for gentlemen of intrigue' could be purchased at Constantia Phillips' shop – called the 'Green Canister' – in Half Moon Street (now Bedford Street), Covent Garden. (Dildoes, presumably for female customers, were also stocked.) Hogarth seems to have known Mrs Phillips because what appears to be a packet of her 'cundums' is shown in print three of *The Harlot's Progress*, created *c*.1732 when her products were new on the market. Mrs Phillips had, in her early years, toiled as a courtesan with, apparently, Lord Chesterfield as one of her clients, before hitting upon the idea of her shop, the profits of which she bolstered with a little blackmail of her former keepers. Henry Fielding became her long-time and mortal foe, and she his. In *Amelia* in 1751 Fielding noted her ability to turn vicious, vengeful and vindictive despite having 'an extraordinary power of displaying softness',[17] while Mrs Phillips concluded her long-winded and novelistic three-volume *Apology* for her life of 1748 with a predictably savage attack on him.[18]

Frontispiece to The Machine; or, Love's Preservative *of 1744, showing a condom manufacturer testing her products.*

The success of Mrs Goadby's establishment was noted and soon emulated by other entrepreneurs of London's sex industry, notably Charlotte Hayes, who in 1767 took the model to a new level of sophistication. Hayes, just over forty at the time, with two decades of experience in the sex trade, having entered it as a teenage prostitute, is one of the more intriguing and enigmatic figures of eighteenth-century London.[19] She was first the mistress of the ebullient 'Beau' Tracey, and during the mid-1750s of his friend Sam Derrick (see page 180), then the wife of gambler and Turf fanatic Dennis O'Kelly, and a contemporary and perhaps rival of the famed courtesans Lucy Cooper (see page 211) and Fanny Murray (see page 181). Unlike the latter two, Charlotte proved to have a head for business and great and inventive skill in her particular line of work, so that by the time of her death she had allegedly amassed the sizable fortune of £20,000 from her business activities.[20]

Charlotte's rise to riches is related in detail in *Nocturnal Revels*. Indeed, the book makes her one of its pivotal characters, which is perhaps no surprise since its subtitle is *The History of King's-place and other Modern Nunneries* – the location of Charlotte's high-class brothel, which she amusingly termed a nunnery or cloister, with herself as the mother abbess and her prostitutes its nuns. This mildly provocative religious imagery was no doubt inspired by some of those patrons of Charlotte's who were members of Sir Francis Dashwood's spoof religious Order of Medmenham, which was in reality simply a whoring and drinking Hell Fire Club.

By the late 1770s King's Place – a court running between Pall Mall and King Street, St James's – must have been one of the most bizarre thoroughfares in London. Virtually all its houses – and Horwood's map of 1799 shows only five large dwellings on the east side of the court with six smaller ones and a large garden on the west side – were smart brothels, imitating, and competing with, Charlotte's nunnery. When Archenholz visited the court – which was evidently something of a tourist attraction – he was astonished by the 'line of Coaches which could be seen driving up to the narrow King's Place'[21] carrying customers to Charlotte or her neighbouring 'abbesses' who, according to *Nocturnal Revels*,[22] included Mrs Adams, Mrs Dubery, Mrs Pendergast, Mrs Mathews and a Mrs Windsor.

Judging by an advertisement of *c*.1765 Mrs Windsor appears to have attempted to gain the business of the recently dead Mrs Phillips and take over the supplying of 'famed' Phillips' Cundums: 'Mrs A.M. Windsor' announced that 'for the convenience of her customers [she] has opened a shop under the piazza, corner of Russel Street, Covent Garden' and defied 'anyone in the world to excel her goods . . . having had many years experience in the connection of the late celebrated Mrs Phillips in the making and selling of machines, commonly called implements of safety'.[23] It seems that other of Mrs Phillips' sexual aides were utilised in King's Place, for in these 'noted houses', observed the ever-enquiring Archenholz, were lodged '. . . every Device to restore old men and debauched youths' and that make 'old Dotards believe themselves gay, vigorous young fellows'.[24]

Competition was clearly tough, and not only between the abbesses of King's Place. Mrs Goadby, moving with the times, had relocated to larger premises in Soho, and had emulated the playfully erotic and mildly blasphemous terminology of her rivals, as an advertisement in a 1773 edition of the *Covent Garden Magazine* makes clear:

> Mrs Goadby, that celebrated Lady Abbess, having fitted up an elegant
> nunnery in Marlborough Street, is now laying in a stock of Virgins for
> the ensuing season [and] has disposed of her Nunnery in such an
> uncommon taste, and prepared such extraordinary accommodations for
> gentlemen of all ages, sizes, tastes and caprices, as, it is judged, will
> surpass every seminary of the kind yet known in Europe.

As for Charlotte Hayes' own pioneering nunnery, *Nocturnal Revels* states that 'she took care to have the *choicest goods*, as she called [her nuns], that could be had at the market . . . and she gave them such instructions as enabled them to pay their devotions with purity and fervour'.[25] *Nocturnal Revels* includes a list of prostitutes and their clients (or rather their nicknames), their activities and charges, and also explains where the various activities took place, so offering something of an architectural description of the nunnery. 'The Doctor' was 'mounted in the three-pair-of-stairs', which is to say the garret.

> Lady Loveit [a female client] had the drawing room, the sopha, and the
> adjoining tent-bed; Alderman Drybones was crammed in the chintz
> bed-chamber . . . used only upon *vestal* occasions . . . Sir Harry

Flagellum was whipped in the nursery, where there were accommodations of every sort to please him; Lord Spasm had the high French bed-room; the Colonel took his chance in the parlour upon the settee; and the Count and Lord Pyebald were entertained in the saloon of chastity and the cards-room.[26]

One of Charlotte Hayes' most profitable acquisitions was Emily Warren who, during the late 1770s and 80s, became one of the more famous and sought-after courtesans in London and muse to Sir Joshua Reynolds (see page 362). William Hickey, who become a particular friend of hers, describes in his *Memoirs* her early days with Charlotte Hayes. His account reveals both the bawd's working methods and, in a heart-breaking and seemingly unintentional way, the bitter emotional price paid by former child prostitutes such as Emily.

Casting his mind back more than thirty years when writing his *Memoirs*, Hickey noted of her: 'I had first seen this divine woman in 1776, then an unripe and awkward girl, but with features of exquisite beauty.' The place of meeting was Charlotte Hayes' 'house of celebrity' or 'Nunnery' 'where I often visited', and in which Emily was being taught the manners and graces of a high courtesan. Charlotte had just 'got hold' of Emily 'as an advantageous prize' and had high hopes of making a fortune through her. But Emily had to be polished so 'was under the tuition of the ancient dame', learning, among other things, 'to walk, a qualification Madam Hayes considered of importance, and in which her pupil certainly excelled, Emily's movements and air being grace personified, and attracting universal admiration whenever she appeared abroad'.

Hickey also relates Emily's alleged origins: 'Charlotte Hayes met her in the streets of London when not quite twelve years of age, leading her father, a blind beggar, soliciting charity from every person that passed.' This tale has a hint of the storybook about it, but then courtesans like Emily were the stuff of fantasy. The account perhaps borrows a little too much from 'The Blind Beggar of Bethnal Green' to be entirely convincing. That ballad tells the story of a blinded rebel knight, reduced to anonymous poverty and led through London by his beautiful young daughter. It had been popularised in 1765 when Thomas Percy published his *Reliques of Ancient English Poetry*. The tale probably offered Charlotte Hayes a useful prototype for a romantic background for Emily, which she used as part of her carefully considered plan for polishing the beautiful creature then launching her upon the fashionable world. Such picturesque origins would, no doubt, make her more interesting and increase her value. It was all in the marketing.

Hickey met Emily again in London in mid-1780 when she was reaching the height of her fame as a beauty and was the mistress of his best friend Bob Pott. But loyalty to Pott did not stop Hickey from pursuing Emily sexually. Eventually he . . .

. . . passed a night that many would have given thousands to do. I however, that night, experienced the truth . . . that she was cold as ice, seemingly totally devoid of feeling. I rose in the morning convinced . . . that she had no passion for the male sex, and that, if left to follow her inclination, she would have preferred sleeping alone to have a bedfellow.

Hickey was clearly not very perceptive or psychologically aware. It was hardly surprising that, after suffering years of systematic abuse and loveless lust from men who treated her as a beautiful object, Emily should be damaged and display 'no passion for the male sex'. She must have been typical of many highly tutored prostitutes who had to protect and suppress their own feelings and emotions. For them passion and affection were weaknesses that could only lead to pain and professional ruin. Ironically these constant votaries of Venus could have no truck with real love, a thing for them far too irrational, contradictory and dangerous. Love for a client had seemingly been the undoing of Sally Salisbury (see page 100) and in her case led to drink- or drug-fuelled violence, while for Emily – trained by Charlotte Hayes to deny all potentially troublesome emotions and adopt a veneer of heartless sophistication, so that Hickey could not remember her ever making 'use of a vulgarism' – prostitution meant emotional death.[27]

TEN

GRAND SERAGLIO
TO THE NATION
The Bagnio

The seraglios, nunneries, brothels and bawdy-houses of Georgian London generally operated within standard terrace houses or larger mansions, or even taverns and coffee houses – none of them a form of building exclusive to the sex industry. But there was one type of building, of which no substantial and certain remains are known to survive above ground, that was never fully visually documented, and that was essentially the product of the capital's sex industry.

The bagnio, frequently mentioned in seventeenth- and eighteenth-century literature and memoirs, and occasionally appearing fleetingly in prints and paintings, is an enigmatic and confusing type of building, largely because bagnios were of two distinctly different types. There were establishments housed in standard houses that traded under the euphemism of 'bagnio' while in fact being little different in their organisation from bawdy-houses or brothels. But there were also bagnios proper, purpose-designed and -built bath houses, which had a characteristic form and function and which played a key role in the capital's sex industry.

The bagnio or hummums (derived from the Arabic word *hammam*, meaning bath) has a long history in London. It was probably first introduced in the twelfth century by crusaders and pilgrims returning from the Holy Land who, when in the Middle East, had acquired a liking for Turkish or Persian baths. Inspired by surviving Roman examples, the peoples along the eastern shore of the Mediterranean had developed bathing establishments that included hot and cold baths, steam and massage rooms, as well as gardens with sweet-smelling and medicinal flowers and herbs. Orient-inspired hot baths were consequently established in medieval London. With their relaxed codes of dress, semi-naked bathing, and occasionally a mix of male and female customers, it is easy to understand how bagnios soon acquired a dubious reputation and often became centres of prostitution, particularly in the reign of Henry II when the sex trade was organised, regulated and contained. A local Act of 1161 made brothels or 'stews' legal in parts of Southwark until its eventual repeal in 1545.[1]

The bagnio flourished during much of the Middle Ages, the King's Bath in Bath, built above long-forgotten Roman bathing pools and util-ising naturally heated water, being a famous example. There was a period of decline during the puritanical Commonwealth period in the mid-seventeenth century but the bagnio re-emerged after the Restoration in 1660 as a popular place of recreation and assignation. By the late seventeenth and early eighteenth centuries bagnios appear to have existed in relatively large numbers in several part of London and are regularly referred to in contemporary documents. For example, a bagnio in St James's Street is mentioned in a pamphlet advertising Michel Malard's *French and Protestant Companion* of 1719;[2] a bagnio in Silver Street, West-minster was the location in 1718 of the murder of Samuel Loxton by Edward Bird;[3] and an advertisement of c.1710–20 states that at the '*Turks Head* in *Newgate-street*, over against *Butcher-hall-lane*', one Wilcox, 'Cupper at the Royal Bagnio for Twenty Years', offered 'very good Conveniences for Sweating, Bathing, Shaving and Cupping, after the best Manner . . .'[4]

Precisely what services these late-seventeenth- and early-eighteenth-century bagnios or hummums actually offered or what physical form they took remains uncertain. They were normally licensed for the sale of tea, coffee and alcohol, and to provide lodgings, but whether many of these establishments always provided hot baths and massage facilities in the Turkish fashion remains a matter of speculation. Nor is it clear if these early hummums were generally purpose-built or simply adaptations of existing domestic or industrial buildings. The story of this peculiar and significant building type, once central to the functioning of the London sex industry, can only be pieced together using many enigmatic, even seemingly contradictory, fragments of evidence, but the picture that emerges suggests that the bagnio is one of the lost architectural wonders of late-seventeenth- and early-eighteenth-century London.

Despite the mystery surrounding them, one basic fact can be adduced. If a bagnio was to provide hot and cold baths an abundance of water was essential, but readily running water was generally in short supply in

WILCOX, Cupper at the Royal Bagnio for Twenty Years, Now liveth at the *Turks Head* in *Newgate-ſtreet*, over againſt *Butcher-hall-lane*, where is very good Conveniencies for Sweating, Bathing, Shaving and Cupping, after the beſt Manner ; *Mondays, Tueſdays, Thurſdays,* and *Fridays* for Men, *VVedneſdays* and *Saturdays* for Women, at 2 *s* 6 *d.* each. He is always ready to Cup either at Home or Abroad.

A trade card extolling the skills of a bagnio 'cupper'.

London in the late seventeenth and early eighteenth centuries. So initially bagnios must have been located almost exclusively in those few areas with ready access to water, their numbers and locations expanding only as the technology of water supply developed during the eighteenth century.

In the early seventeenth century, for instance, the New River Company and the Society of Hampstead Aqueducts were the main suppliers of piped water to those households in central London lacking their own wells and far removed from the city's rivers, springs or conduit heads. But gradually, throughout the eighteenth century, more supply companies took up the profitable challenge of carrying water into the city – notably from 1723 the Chelsea Waterworks Company – so that ever-more areas were supplied more cheaply and, after 1760, with increased pressure as steam engines started to be used to pump water through a system of subterranean 'pipes' formed from elm trunks. By the early nineteenth century eight water companies served London and high-pressure water supply became more common as cast-iron pipes gradually replaced the network of leaky 'sleeve-jointed' elm trunks. So at the end of the Georgian period it was a practical possibility to locate a functioning bagnio in most parts of the capital, just as it was possible for most houses to possess plumbed-in bathtubs, even on upper floors.[5]

The written descriptions of London's late-seventeenth-century bagnios offer tantalising and even sensational images which suggest that the buildings that housed the baths were not only architecturally distinct but also positively exotic. *A True Account of the Royal Bagnio with a Discourse of its Virtues*, written by 'a person of quality' and published in 1680,[6] suggests that at least some of these early bagnios were closely based on the Turkish model. As the anonymous author, perhaps John Dauncey, explains, 'to those who have been to the Ottoman empire [this pamphlet] is insignificant, they knowing already the mighty perfections and wonderful operations which Bagnios have affected'.[7] The author then gives a detailed account of the content, if not the precise plan or form, of the Royal Bagnio and implies that – with its array of stoves, ovens and 'divers cocks' – it was indeed an operational Turkish-style *hammam*.

When it came to an architectural description of the bagnio, however, the author made a fatal error of judgement: 'I think 'twill not be material to fill a leaf or two with the description of that erected lately in London, especially of the outward building, every man having the liberty to be themselves ocular witnesses of it, for 'tis as near the Turkish fashion as may be.'

Even this infuriatingly brief description is evocative. Those who see the exterior realise it is in 'the Turkish fashion'. What does this imply? Was there once an exotic, pioneering and now forgotten piece of Ottoman-style architecture in central London, complete with domes and doors and windows set within pointed arches? Certainly there was more than a whiff of authentic Turkish culture around the establishment for the author explains 'that near unto the Bagnio there is a Coffee-House, for the conveniency of those that go to the Bagnio, for according to the Opinion of many there is no Liquor more convenient after one has been in than Coffee'.[8] So the connection between London bagnios and the sale and consumption of coffee – a drink popularised in the Muslim world where it played the social and relaxing role enjoyed by alcohol in Christian Europe – was established at an early stage.

The location of the Royal Bagnio described in this pamphlet is uncertain because the name was almost generic, with a number of Royal Bagnios located around late-Stuart and Georgian London. There was certainly one in St James's Street, but a more likely candidate for the one mentioned here was located off Newgate Street, just north of St Paul's Cathedral in the City, near an area famed for its homosexual activity. Rocque's map of 1746 suggests a precise location for it shows a 'Bagnio Court' running north off Newgate Street, as does Horwood's map of 1799. It is probably also the City-based Royal Bagnio that makes a tantalising appearance in a Rowlandson print of 1812 – certainly the location shown is called Bagnio Court, and there is a door to a bagnio. Entitled *Catching an Elephant*, the print shows two slight and pretty young prostitutes picking up a large, ugly old man.[9]

This City bagnio is mentioned in an advertisement included in the *London Gazette* of 6 April 1686:

> At the Royal Bagnio in Newgate-street, London, All Gentlemen &
> Ladies May be Accommodated to Sweat, Wash & Bathe in, According
> to the Turkish fashion, and Cupping After the German Manner.

Cupping, a process by which heated glasses were utilised to extract blood, reduce inflammation and thus cure all manner of ailments, was a traditional practice that became a service commonly offered by bagnios. The 'German manner' of treatment seems to have been particularly popular for a broadsheet of *c*.1679 announced that . . .

> . . . John Evans, his hummums is in Brownlow-Street in Drury-Lane,
> where persons may sweat to what degree they please, there being
> degrees of heat, and several apartments, fit and commodious for private
> sweating, bathing, and fine cupping, after the New German manner,
> with greater ease than ever yet known . . .[10]

Drury Lane and nearby Long Acre, locations known for their coach-building workshops, seem in the years just before 1700 to have become among the favoured locations for bagnios, perhaps because of a ready supply of water combined with the possibilities offered by the easy conversion to bagnio use of existing coach-building works, stables and open-plan industrial buildings. There was in the area the Queen's Bagnio, which an advertisement proclaims 'lately beautified' in 1706,[11] and the

King's Bagnio, mentioned in 1690 as marking the location in which lived Mrs Isabella Inglish and from where she sold her famed 'Grana angelica or true Scot's pills'.[12]

An advertisement of 1686 for the King's Bagnio on Long Acre, Covent Garden. With its dome supported on columns and its black and white marble floor, this bagnio appears to be typical of the more ambitious bath houses, such as the Duke's Bagnio, erected in Covent Garden in the late seventeenth century.

Representative, if not typical, of these Long Acre bagnios was the ambitious affair that in 1683 Samuel Haworth recorded in unusually full detail, in *A Description of the Duke's Bagnio and of the Mineral Bath and New spaw thereunto belonging*, an establishment which apparently listed 'sweating, rubbing' and 'bathing' among its 'medicinal virtues'.[13] Haworth starts his description of the 'New Bagnio' by placing it in context and commending its proprietor:

This Bagnio is erected near the West-end of Long-acre, in the Spot of Ground which hath been called by the Name of Salisbury Stables. At

the Front of it, next the Street, is a large commodious House, wherein
dwels that Honourable Person, Sir William Jennings ... who having
obtained His Majesty's Patent for the making of all Public Bagnios and
Baths ... is the Only Undertaker of this New building. In this House
are several Rooms set apart for the Accommodation of such as shall
come to the Bagnio ... so that the first Room we enter to go into the
Bagnio is a large Hall, where the Porter Stands to receive the Money.[14]

The details, proportions, contents and functions of the establishment's
various rooms are described. In one there 'Hangs a pair of Scales, to weigh
such as out of Curiosity would know how much they lose in Weight
while they are in the Bagnio'. Beyond this room was another 'called the
Dressing-room' furnished with 'several private Boxes for Persons to undress
and dress themselves in'. Next there was a heated room paved with black
and white marble – the 'Middle Walk' – and then ...

... the Bagnio itself, which is a stately Ediface, of an Oval Figure, in
length 45 Foot and in breadth 35. 'Tis covered at the top with a high
and large Cupola, in which there are several round Glasses fixt to let in
Light [and] supported by eight Cylindrical Columns of white Stone
Pillars each ... 16 Foot high.

Surrounding the cupola was 'a sumptuous Walk, about 7 Foot and a half
broad' and all was 'paved with Marble', with its wall 'covered with white
Galley-tyles, and in the Walls are made ten convenient Seats, such as are
in the Baths at Bathe'.[15] Haworth then described how the bagnio functioned, its heating stoves and ovens, and its related buildings, including
a 'Coffee-house fronting the Street ... the great Gate, which opens into
a large court-yard, convenient for the receiving of Coaches', and which
contained 'a very convenient Building, erected for the Accommodations
belonging to the Bath', and a 'laboratory, in which are Chymic Furnaces,
Glasses and other Instruments necessary for making the Bath-Waters'.[16]

The Duke's Bagnio, with its cupola, colonnades, walks paved with
marble, courts and service buildings, sounds like an authentic Ottoman-
style bath complex combined with Renaissance monastic architecture.
The way in which its customers used this type of bagnio or hummums
is described by Ned Ward in *The London Spy*, a short-lived monthly
periodical published originally between November 1698 and May 1700.

Ward records how a friend wanted to carry him to the hummums that stood on the eastern side of the Covent Garden Piazza, on the corner with Russell Street. This group of buildings, forming the south-east portion of Inigo Jones' Piazza development of the 1630s (see page 230), became a popular location with bagnio owners, possibly because the Jones houses were all provided with wells and so each had, to a degree, its own water supply.[17] The businesses within this block included the New Hummums Coffee House that probably incorporated 11 Russell Street; Lovejoy's Bagnio; Mr Rigg's Hummums; the old Hummums Hotel and, on the south end of the Piazza terrace, the Bedford Arms Tavern that also possibly occupied a pair of houses constructed in 1706 when the south side of the Piazza was built, following the 1704 demolition of Bedford House and the development of its former site and garden.[18] (Tracing the patterns of occupation within this site, and its building history, is made more complex by the fact that in 1769 the south-east side of the Piazza was destroyed by a catastrophic fire and the entire block rebuilt, with no return to the Jones design and probably only passing reference to original party-wall and site boundaries.)

It would seem that Ned Ward and his friend headed towards the New Hummums, which had been established in around 1683 and was housed within and behind a 1630s house: 'If you will pay your club towards eight shillings,' Ward is told, 'we'll go in and sweat.' Eight shillings was an enormous amount of money to pay – about three days' wages for a journeyman tradesman, or a couple of months' rent for a poor Londoner. This charge is confirmed by an advertisement of 1701 which states that the price 'for sweating and bathing' was five shillings and sixpence, but 'for two in one room eight shillings; but who lodges there all night ten shillings'.[19]

Having accepted the charge, Ward was conducted 'to the house, through which we passed into a long gallery' where, before reaching its end, he found himself 'as warm as a cricket at an ovens mouth', and noted that the temperature was 23.5 degrees. At the end of the gallery the pair met the 'cupper' who was to take care of them and 'began to unstrip, and put ourselves in a condition of enduring a hours baking' wearing nothing but 'a clout no bigger than a fig-leaf . . . to cover our nakedness'. They were then conducted to an adjoining 'apartment' that was hotter still, with a floor of scorching 'freestone' that they could only walk on after putting

The setting Hogarth's 1736 painting, *Night*, is set in Charing Cross, looking north towards the still existing statue of Charles I. In the foreground are two drunken Freemasons – one perhaps the magistrate Sir Thomas de Veil, known for being tough on those charged with drunk and disorderly conduct (Hogarth punishes his hypocrisy by showing a chamber pot being emptied on his head). A kneeling link-boy – symbol of licentious lawlessness – blows on his torch (right foreground), while an ale-keeper dilutes his barrel of beer and, in the background, a cartload of furniture passes, suggesting that someone is doing a 'midnight flit' from their lodgings. On the right is a sign for the New Bagnio – opposite one for a second bagnio. Both would have been used by prostitutes and their clients. On the left is the sign of the Cardigan Head, a tavern favoured by harlots, where the young prostitute Ann Bell dined in August 1760 shortly before her mysterious death.

'The Great Square of Venus' The Piazza, Covent Garden – painted by Samuel Scott between 1749 and 1758. On the right is Haddock's Bagnio; the entrance is below the first-floor window through which a man and woman peer. Immediately to the right of Haddock's is Mother Douglas's brothel and then the Shakespeare's Head Tavern. On the left-hand side of the Piazza, among the row of huts, is Tom and Moll King's Coffee House.

A high courtesan Kitty Fisher was a friend of Sir Joshua Reynolds, who painted her many times. This painting, completed in 1759, shows Kitty as Cleopatra, dissolving a pearl in a glass of wine, a display undertaken to impress Mark Antony. The finger and thumb that grip the pearl define an ovoid shape – a lewd gesture Reynolds employed in other risqué paintings. Cleopatra's extravagant behaviour was echoed by Kitty when she reputedly ate a £100 banknote to show her contempt for a client who offered her such low payment for her sexual services.

Soho Lisle Street was much favoured by harlots in the late eighteenth century. According to the 1788 edition of Jack Harris's *List of Covent Garden Ladies*, Misses Bolton, Robinson, Wood and Antrebern all had apartments in now long-demolished houses at the west end of the street. Between 1791 and 1795 Lisle Street was extended to the east and lined by two uniform, slightly curving terraces, one of which – above – survives. The terraces contained shops, residential accommodation and – most likely – places of work for harlots.

A prostitute turned actress Mrs Abington, painted in 1771 by Sir Joshua Reynolds as the stage character Miss Pru from William Congreve's *Love for Love*. By the time this painting was completed Mrs Abington had evolved from a child street-prostitute and flower-seller into a respected and well-connected actress. The painting reflects the contrasts in her life. She appears the epitome of feminine grace and sophistication, yet sits on the chair in a masculine manner, as if watching a cockfight, and biting her thumb in an adolescent or even lascivious style.

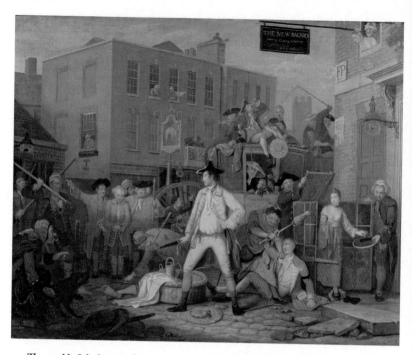

The world of the bagnio A young woman – probably a harlot – steps out of a sedan chair, presumably heading towards the New Bagnio. Around her confusion rages in this London street scene of around 1770 by John Collet, as an armed young man confronts a group of staff-wielding watchmen and a fellow flourishing a sword lies floored, subdued by an aged woman. Bagnios – or bath houses – were central to the London sex trade.

An admission ticket to the Duke's Bagnio, Long Acre The token (*c.*1680) shows the main feature of the bagnio – the 'oval' colonnaded central space, described elsewhere as 'the Bagnio itself' that was covered by a 'high and large Cupola' containing 'several round Glasses fixt to let in light'. Below the cupola a couple frolic around a bath. This intriguing structure, clearly inspired by Ottoman bath houses, has long been demolished.

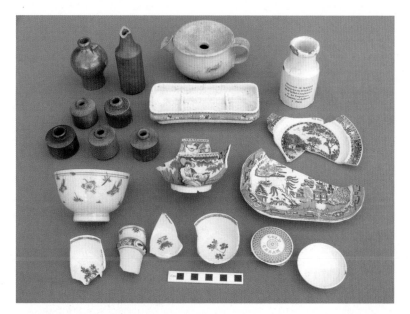

Everyday life in the bagnio A collection of the artefacts excavated in 2005 from the site of a probable bagnio on the southeast corner of the Piazza in Covent Garden. These artefacts, which include high-quality imported Chinese porcelain tea bowls, suggest that life in the bagnio was fashionable and elegant.

Frequented by ladies of the town
The Turk's Head in Gerrard Street, Soho, was constructed in 1759 and is London's best surviving purpose-built Georgian tavern. From 1764 it was the meeting place of The Club, which included Sir Joshua Reynolds, Dr Johnson, David Garrick and James Boswell among its members. It is likely that Reynolds would have had assignations here with the young Soho and Covent Garden harlots whose bodies inspired his art.

Helping the victims of the sex trade The Foundling Hospital in Bloomsbury from the southwest, painted by Richard Wilson in about 1746 for the Hospital's Court Room. This painting reveals the monumental scale and almost rural isolation of the Hospital when new. The Hospital's open admission policy from 1756 until late 1759 meant that it could be used as a convenient depository for harlots' babies and so, arguably, served as an 'aid to vice'. During this period it also became more a mortuary than a sanctuary, for 70 per cent of the babies admitted died.

Founder of the Foundling Hospital Captain Thomas Coram, painted in the 1740s by Balthasar Nebot, shown coming upon an abandoned baby and so strengthened in his resolve to build a hospital for 'exposed and deserted young children'.

Foundling tokens A collection of 'tokens' left by mothers when depositing their babies at the Foundling Hospital. These tokens, preserved along with a physical description of the child and its admission date and number, made it possible – in theory – for a mother to identify her child later.

Helping the diseased William Bromfeild, the founder in 1747 of the Lock Hospital for the treatment of impoverished patients suffering from venereal disease. In this painting by Nathaniel Dance, Bromfeild holds a design for the Hospital.

Home of the masquerade The late-seventeenth-century Carlisle House on the east
side of Soho Square which, from the 1760s, was turned by Mrs Cornelys into a
'fairy palace' for masquerades and became the favoured place for harlots and high
courtesans to meet clients. This view, which includes the two-storey wing added by
Mrs Cornelys, was made by Thomas Shepherd shortly before
the buildings were demolished in 1791.

The theatre of sexual encounter and intrigue Ladies promenading
for male delight through the interiors of Carlisle House.

on wooden-soled shoes. In this room they sat and sweated, while a 'rubber'
– seemingly a man – rubbed their bodies with a 'coarse-hair camlet' or
gauntlet. They then soaked in a tub of hot water to 'boil out those gross
humours that could not be emitted by a more gentle perspiration' and
Ward had an old ache in a shoulder attended to. The 'cupper' placed
three glasses on his back that, by drawing out air, stuck and 'sucked as
hard as so many leeches at a wench's fundament, when troubled with the
haemorrhoids'.

> [When the cupper] had conjured all the ill blood out of my body under
> his glass juggling cups, he plucks out an ill-favoured instrument, takes
> off his glasses . . . and begins to scarify my skin . . . when he had drawn
> away as much blood as he thought necessary for the removal of my
> pain, he covered the places he had carbonadoed with a new skin . . . and
> healed the scarification he had made.

The process sounds extraordinary. The two companions were then ushered
into the dressing room where they were given refreshments, namely 'Dr
Stephen's cordial', and encouraged to rest for one hour. While drinking
and recovering, Ward and his friend questioned the attendants about the
well-known harlots who used the hot baths.

One of the congenial fellows described how a 'very fine lady of the
Town visited the hummums to . . . refresh her body for the work ahead'
and make 'supple her industrious joints [and] tender limbs the more pliable
and fit for the exercise of love which she was, doubtless, that night to be
engaged in'. At the cost of a crown she had a bath 'enriched with essences
and sweet herbs, to add such a fragrance to her body that might render
her most putrescent parts as sweet as a calf's nostril'. After the lady had
departed the attendant was surprised to discover that she had relieved
herself in the perfumed tub in which she had soaked. As he put it,
'I found some unsavoury lees which had chanced to drop through the
bung-hole' of that beautiful and perfumed but 'mortal cask'. An apt
metaphor, perhaps, for the beautiful yet brittle age.[20]

The hummums was also mentioned by Hatton in 1708 as 'a place for
sweating' that contained in addition 'a cold bath for such as are disposed
to use it'.[21]

The appearance of, and services offered by, other Covent Garden
bagnios are suggested by a series of frustratingly slight publications. For

example, an advertisement of *c.*1725 announced that 'the Cold Bath and Hummums in Charles-Street, Covent Garden, is now finish'd with a compleat warm bath, in imitation of the Bath in Somersetshire, with apparel and attendance as at Bath',[22] while another contemporary advertisement states the rent for a 'room for a single gentleman is two shillings per night' and that 'the hot baths are now much improved; and there is likewise an addition of two compleat new baths'.[23]

These advertisements conjure up an astonishing image. In the heart of Covent Garden, to the east of the Piazza, was a cold bath and a heated bath that took the hot water pools and dress code at Bath as its model, perhaps with a miniature version of the pump room attended by liveried servants. What could have been the architectural expression of this ambitious establishment? It appears to have left no visible trace behind and certainly makes no appearance on John Rocque's 1746 map of the area. But although slight, there is a small amount of surviving physical evidence marking the presence of London's lost seventeenth- and eighteenth-century bagnio architecture, all of it speculative and open to wide interpretation.

One possible clue to the appearance of London bagnios is offered by a small building on Strand Lane that runs south from the Strand towards the river. The building stands on land once occupied by the gardens and early sixteenth-century mansion of Lord Arundel, the man who took the architect Inigo Jones to Italy in the very early seventeenth century and amassed a once-famed collection of antique statuary, the remains of which are now displayed in the Ashmolean Museum in Oxford. During the eighteenth century the Strand and the courts and alleys off it were key locations in London's sex industry, so it is perhaps not surprising to discover in this small building the remains of what could have been a bagnio. It contains a plunge bath measuring 15 feet by 6 feet and 4 feet 6 inches deep, being fed from the nearby spring or well of St Clement, to which blue and white seventeenth-century Delft tiles provide discreet ornament. It is an intimate and charming place – it is also something of a mystery and its origins remain unknown.

The first documented reference to this bath house is as late 1784, by the antiquarian and cartographer John Pinkerton, and the place subsequently became embroiled in fiction and romance by being described as a remarkable survival of a Roman bath – which it almost certainly is not although portions of it might be ancient. The bath is most likely Tudor in origin, repaired in the seventeenth century and used as part of a bagnio during the eighteenth.

A more significant and probably more certain bagnio discovery was made in 2005 on the south-east corner of the Covent Garden Piazza when an excavation took place on the site of a small group of houses that had been built in 1705/6 and cleared away in the mid-nineteenth century. These houses once adjoined the south-east corner of the 1630s Inigo Jones Piazza and fronted Tavistock Court to the west and Tavistock Street to the south. The houses could have been part of the ill-famed Bedford Arms Tavern,[24] were probably badly damaged in the 1769 fire and, from archaeological evidence, seem to have contained a functioning bagnio that most probably served the adjoining tavern. Horwood's map of 1799–1819 shows the site occupied by a pair of houses fronting on to the Piazza, but the evidence offered by the excavation of the basement walls suggests two or three houses that probably had entrance elevations to Tavistock Court and Tavistock Street.

Tim Carew, who analysed the finds and evidence gathered by Museum of London archaeologists and has, with Andy Leonard, written a report on them (which he kindly discussed with me prior to its publication), has come up with some significant new insights into London's bagnios. The basement walls found surviving on site contained a number of alcoves that had been added to the structure, each abutted by a flue or conduit. Presuming the alcoves had contained iron stoves (the absence of soot showed they were not used for open fires) and the flues either carried smoke or heated water, then it is reasonable to conclude that these basements possessed a sophisticated and efficient heating system serving the upper rooms.

More information about the use of the buildings is suggested by artefacts found on site. Carew identified these as including fragments of Delft tile, high-quality Chinese import porcelain tea bowls – the earliest dating from the Kangxi period of 1667–1722 – and various fragments of glass, which are particularly revealing for they include a Ratafia glass and a jelly glass. Ratafia was the strong almond-flavoured cordial favoured by whores – particularly when staying in bagnios – and jellies and jelly houses were by the mid-eighteenth century associated both with prostitutes and the sex industry. What appears to have been discovered in Covent Garden and identified by Carew are the only remains so far known of an eighteenth-century London bagnio.

The operational dates of this particular establishment remain unclear for the physical evidence reveals only that the heating system was inserted into the houses after they were built in 1705/6, and the Chinese ceramics suggest an occupation date from 1720–50. But what this archaeological investigation does seem to confirm is the accuracy of the image of early-to mid-eighteenth-century London bagnios evoked by contemporary documentary evidence. As Carew concludes, the finds have . . .

> . . . clear connotations: luxury and high living, [their] style and quality is
> frequently tasteful, exotic, and expensive [and] paints a picture of
> opulence befitting an up-market business catering for pleasure-seeking
> men with funds at their disposal . . . The libertine and sex industry
> sub-culture of eighteenth-century London is well-known to historians
> and in literature, but this is believed to be the first instance of archaeo-
> logical evidence relating to it.[25]

How fascinating the style, elegance and expense evoked by these Tavi-stock Court finds. The hearths and flues suggest that these houses were part of a working hummums, while the quality and function of the arte-facts discovered appear to reveal this hummums' role in the area's sex industry. It was a place in which customers could bathe and steam but also, like many Covent Garden bagnios, operated as a luxurious lodging house where couples could bed down for a few hours or a few days with no questions asked. These are the types of bagnios described in the *Midnight Spy* of 1766, and in which, along with 'jelly houses, night houses' and other places 'of midnight resort', were conducted the 'nocturnal adventure of both sexes'.

The way in which these sex-industry bagnios operated was described by Archenholz during his stay in London in the early 1780s. There is in London, he wrote:

> . . . a certain kind of house, called bagnios, which are supposed to be
> baths; there real purpose, however, is to provide persons of both sexes
> with pleasure. These houses are well, and often richly, furnished, and
> every device for exciting the senses is either at hand or can be provided.
> Girls do not live there but are fetched in chairs when required. None

but those who are especially attractive in all ways are so honoured, and
for that reason they often send their address to a hundred of these
bagnios in order to make themselves known. A girl who is sent for and
does not please receives no gratuity, the chair alone being paid for.

Archenholz, despite his rather superior manner, seems to have been quite
familiar with these bagnios, or at least observed them and their clients
closely:

The English retain their solemnity even as regards their pleasures, and
consequently the business of such a house is conducted with a
seriousness and propriety which is hard to credit. All noise and uproar is
banned here, no loud footsteps are heard, every corner is carpeted and
the numerous attendants speak quietly amongst themselves. Old people
and degenerates can here receive flagellation, for which all establishments
are prepared.[26]

He also suggests why certain bawdy-houses were termed bagnios, even if
not serving primarily as bath houses, while other bawdy-houses were not:
'In every bagnio is found a formula [apparatus and charges] regarding
baths, but they are seldom needed. These pleasures are very expensive,
but in spite of this many houses of this kind are full every night. Most
of them are quite close to the theatres, and many taverns are in the same
neighbourhood.'[27] So in order to qualify as a bagnio, a house must offer
its clients at least rudimentary bathing facilities, even if this service was
not generally used.

HADDOCK'S BAGNIO, THE PIAZZA,
COVENT GARDEN

It is possible to reconstruct a famous eighteenth-century London bagnio
because of a will and related inventory of the early 1750s that survives in
the National Archives at Kew. From 1742 Richard Haddock and his wife
Elizabeth owned and ran the bagnio occupying a house on the north side
of the Covent Garden Piazza.[28]

The exterior of their establishment is illustrated in Samuel Scott's
painting of c.1750 that shows a view looking west over the Piazza and is

distinguished by a trade sign, projecting from the sixth arcaded opening east of James Street, that reads 'Haddock's Bagnio. Sweating, cupping & bathing'. From the open first-floor window above the sign a man and a woman survey the scene – presumably a prostitute and her client.[29] Just a few doors to the east of Haddock's was the Shakespeare's Head Tavern, which, from the 1740s, was one of Covent Garden's most favoured gathering places for whores, pimps and their clients, and from where around 1747 the 'head-waiter' Jack Harris circulated his *List of Covent Garden Ladies* (see page 180).

Richard Haddock died in 1748 and his widow Elizabeth ran the bagnio until her own death in 1751. Elizabeth Haddock's will was proved on 8 January 1752 while the inventory of the bagnio dates from 19 June 1752,[30] and so records the interior and contents at least six months after Elizabeth died. Possibly the bagnio was, or had been, closed for a while and items had been removed or moved since it was under her control. What is certain, however, is that the bagnio did not cease to function permanently after her death. Still trading under the name of Haddock's, it continued in operation under Elizabeth's executrix Sophia Lenoy until 1762, and after her under various owners or managers, notably Daniel Haveland from 1763–6 and 'Mother' Thornton from 1791–8. When she departed, Haddock's was taken over by a neighbouring auctioneer and the building's use as a bagnio ceased. In the 1850s the building – much altered and partly rebuilt – was incorporated into the adjoining Tavistock Hotel and survived until 1928 when it and its neighbours – the last surviving fragments of the Piazza houses designed by Inigo Jones – were tragically all demolished by the Bedford Estate.

Haddock's appears to have operated at the more discreet end of Covent Garden's sex industry. It contained some public spaces in which prostitutes and clients could meet, but was essentially a place in which couples or parties could spend the night in private, eating, drinking and sleeping in some style – in fact, the sort of place depicted by Hogarth in 'The Bagnio', the fifth painting in his 1743 series *Marriage à la Mode* (a bill on the floor reveals this to be the Turk's Head). Its air of discretion was not shared by all its near neighbours – notably the Piazza Coffee House, Mother Douglas' brothel and a kiosk on the corner with Russell Street that sold pornographic prints, not to mention the Shakespeare's Head Tavern.

A compelling portrait in words of the community of strange and

'The Bagnio' scene from Hogarth's Marriage à la Mode *(1743–5). A bill on
the floor reveals this to be the Turk's Head. On the wall is a striking portrait
of a courtesan.*

outlandish businesses gathered within and around the Piazza is included
in *Covent-Garden: a Satire*, published in 1756:

> Augusta's sons all know the place,
> Once fam'd for piety and grace;
> . . . But oh! Sad change, oh! Shame to tell,
> How soon a prey to vice it fell!
> How since, its justest appellation
> Is – GRAND SERAGLIO TO THE NATION,
>
> Now brawling matrons raise their stalls,
> Where stood the consecrated walls;
> There various herbs, and fruits appear.
> Exceeding good – but very dear.
>
> Oh! Shakespeare, with what pain I see,

The Small regard that's paid to thee;
High rais'd above a Tavern door,
T'invite each drunken rake and whore . . .
Near, D**'s still maintains her ground,
Empress o'er all the bawds around;
(Where innocence is often sold,
Hard case! For shining gold;)
By craft she draws th' unwarry in,
And keeps a publick mart for sin.

A powerful visual image of Mother Douglas' brothel is offered in William Hogarth's *March to Finchley* of 1750 in which the Piazza house is transported to the southern end of Tottenham Court Road and transformed into a tavern called the King's Head. From the windows of the tavern peer Mother Douglas and her girls – apparently watching the troops depart but also displaying themselves, much as they did in the house in Covent Garden.

The story of Haddock's Bagnio, given its central role in the sexual life of mid-eighteenth-century Covent Garden, is particularly rewarding and revealing. Not only was it, in its organisation and furnishing, an excellent example of the type of establishment crucial to the operation of London's sex industry, it was also housed in an architecturally fascinating building. Indeed it is tempting to speculate that the special character and form of the building Haddock leased in 1742 influenced the nature and function of the bagnio that evolved within it.

Haddock's occupied a house, numbered 8 The Piazza, that when new had been a modest urban palace, part of one of the most innovative, smart and architecturally ambitious developments ever to be built in London. Number 8 the Piazza had been constructed in the mid-1630s as part of Inigo Jones' scheme to create for the Earl of Bedford a small and almost self-contained 'model town', immediately to the north of the earl's mansion fronting the Strand. Bedford and Jones' visionary and pioneering creation became one of the most important and inspirational pieces of urban design ever realised in Britain. They introduced the idea – inspired by prototypes in Italy and Paris, such as the Place Royale (now Place des Vosges) – of an ordered and architecturally coherent residential quarter organised around a square. Central to this idea was that the individual houses should, in their design, be unified to create the impression that all were part of a single grandiloquent scheme, while there should also be a sense of hier-archy – with the largest and most socially ambitious houses on the main square and those of lesser importance on subsidiary streets. There was to be a mix of uses, and the dominant presence and architectural focus of a monumental public building, which, in the end, resulted in the creation of the temple-like St Paul's Church.

Obviously at one level the development could be seen as modelled on the admired Italian Renaissance urban creations of Rome, Florence or Venice – and the fact that the Covent Garden square was soon dubbed 'the Piazza' makes it clear that this was one popular assumption. But if visionary, the earl and his architect were also highly practical. Their dream was to be realised, as far as possible, by using other people's money. The little town was to be built as a speculation, with the earl granting building leases to any who had the means and desire to invest – and was prepared to work to Jones' master plan. The latter requirement was not too onerous since his design was intended to be as economical as possible to build – with the use of expensive stone kept to a minimum and most of the struc-ture being in brick. Strict design controls, which some builders might have found onerous, were applied only to the uniform houses forming the northern and eastern perimeter of the square. The south side of the Piazza was formed by the garden wall of Bedford House, while the west side was largely occupied by the church and flanking and freestanding gates giving access to the churchyard.

The house that the Haddocks leased from the Bedford Estate in 1742 was, due to its central location in the Great Piazza, one of those that had an elevation built to Jones' design. The building lease on the site had been granted to Thomas Pullen, a bricklayer, in 1636, and he quickly built a house which was soon united to its neighbours to either side undertaken by other speculators. In the late seventeenth century Pullen's house was occupied by a son of the first Duke of Bedford but, after he left in the early eighteenth century, it was divided into two separate tenements.[31]

This very neatly reflects the dramatic and rapid social change that over-took Covent Garden itself after Bedford House was demolished in 1704 and the family moved from the area, turning the site of their ancestral London home over to speculative house builders. The useful and very local market in vegetables and herbs that was once held against the wall of the mansion moved into the central square and was rapidly expanded, for revenue, by the now distant landlords. The enlarged market brought noise and dirt, lowering the social tone of the area and leading to a speedy exodus of smart families, who moved first north to Great Russell Street and Queen's Square in Bloomsbury and then west to new developments north and south of Oxford Street. The vacuum left in Covent Garden was soon filled by the poorer classes and more dubious trades that had long clustered to the south of the area along the Strand, as well as to the west and north around Drury Lane, Long Acre, and from the 1690s in the courts and houses around the architecturally ambitious but ultimately ill-fortuned Seven Dials development.

By the early 1720s Covent Garden's day as an aristocratic residential address was already a distant memory. It had become a market area, a place of crime and nocturnal life, of vice and bawdy-houses and a growing theatrical presence, while the mighty Piazza – the architectural pride of early-Stuart London – had become the haunt of prostitutes.

In 1756 William Maitland observed that landlords of houses that had been occupied by 'Persons of the greatest Distinction' were 'now obliged to take up with Vintners, Coffeemen, and such other Inhabitants',[32] and in 1776 the Society for the Reformation of Manners described the Piazza as 'the great square of VENUS' because 'its purlieus are crowded with the votaries of this Goddess [and] one would imagine that all the prostitutes in the Kingdom had [settled in] this neighbourhood'. The Society went on to observe that the area's popular 'jelly-houses are now become the resort of abandoned Rakes and shameless Prostitutes' and along with 'the taverns afford an ample supply of Provisions for the flesh; while others abound for the consummation of the desires which are thus excited. For this vile end the bagnios and lodging-houses are near at hand.'[33]

This thriving and particular trade attracted entrepreneurs of a certain character and experience. In 1742 Richard Haddock – a bagnio owner since the 1730s when he'd operated at the Turk's Head, Charing Cross[34] – acquired the tenancy of number 8 and reunited the two parts of the 1630s house. Haddock may initially have established his bagnio in buildings in the rear or central portion of the site, perhaps with access from Hart (now Floral) Street to the north. But by 1743 he had control of the 'portico' portion of the house fronting on to the Piazza, and Haddock's was established in the form in which it was to function for the next sixty or so years.

The organisation of Haddock's in its heyday is sketched – sometimes in vivid fashion – by the 1752 inventory, which is detailed enough to allow, with a little interpretation and imagination, the thrilling experience of walking through a mid-eighteenth-century London bagnio. Under the heading 'At the Bagnio at Covent Garden' the rooms of the house are numbered and named and their main contents listed. The precise ordering of the list is not clear. It does not seem to reflect a systematic route through the house – from basement to attic or from south to north – nor does it necessarily reflect the hierarchy of the rooms, starting with the biggest and best and ending with the smallest and meanest, because what appears to have been the best room appears halfway through the list.

It is probable that the person compiling the inventory started on an upper floor that contained some of the best rooms and listed these. They then walked up to the attic rooms, noted their contents, and descended – taking in the best room on the way – to the ground-floor coffee house and dining room before finishing with the basement kitchen and bagnio. The house had three main storeys, a basement, an attic, and probably a mezzanine between ground and first floor. It almost certainly had a three-window-wide frontage so was pretty large but, to judge by the number of rooms listed, it must also have possessed a substantial wing running north to Hart (now Floral) Street.

The room listed as No. 1 was called the King's Head. It contained:

> Bed and furniture, iron hearth etc., chimney glass, India paper, picture, easy chair, marble table, two pair of window curtains and pier glass, walnut tree chairs, stool, mahogany dining table, sconce wall glass, four India pictures, four views of Venice, claw table, matting.

This was a stage-set for sex – an elegant and fashionable room in which a man of taste and means could entertain, feed and bed his 'woman of the town'. It is a compact and self-contained world with a number of fashionable – as well as comfortable – attributes. 'India' paper usually means wallpaper of Chinese design – most fashionable in the mid-eighteenth century – as was the mahogany from which the dining table was made, while the walnut used for the chairs is a reflection of earlier tastes. The 'claw table' is a table with cabriole legs terminating in clawed feet, each probably clutching a sphere – a popular detail in the first half of the eighteenth century. It was no doubt a card table while the marble-topped table was probably a buffet table on which food and drink were placed when the room was used for dining. The 'sconce wall glass' was a mirror, fitted with candle-holders, that hung either on the piers between the windows or next to the fireplace.

The fact that two pairs of curtains are listed suggested that this room was only two windows wide and would have been flanked by a narrow closet lit by the remaining one window of the three-window-wide elevation. This arrangement of rooms – a large one flanked by a smaller closet – was common for the best, front-facing apartment at second-floor level, so it seems likely that the inventory starts with the main second-floor front room, overlooking the Piazza. The appearance of fashion and wealth that this room evoked was seemingly usual in the best bagnios and bawdy-houses.

The upstairs rooms in Haddock's Bagnio are numbered and named in sequence in the inventory: No. 2 Queen's Head, No. 3 Ballroom, No. 4 Rose, No. 5 Dolphin, No. 6 Castle. The contents listed for these rooms include sacking – called 'Bedhood cotton' – feather beds, bolsters and pillows, 'blankett and quilt', bedsteads, dining tables, 'marble-topped' tables, 'east chairs of walnut', floor matting, curtains, and many had 'India paper'. Also listed are 'pictures of Venice'.

It is possible that the compiler of the inventory now started to descend and to list rooms on the first floor and those below it. Room No. 7 was named Crown, No. 8 Windsor Castle and No. 9 Green Room. Room No. 10 was called Hampton Court, and adjoining and related to it was a 'lobby' containing a bed. Hampton Court may well have been the first-floor front room, and so probably the best private room in the bagnio, while room No. 11 was described as the 'Maids' Chamber' and contained three bedsteads. Listed next is the 'Men's Chamber' with two 'half-canopy bedsteads'. These staff dormitories could have been in the attic or, perhaps more likely, in the low-ceilinged mezzanine located just below the first floor, conveniently near the ground-floor public rooms.

The staircase landing is now described. If the 1630s staircase survived this could have been a noble space indeed – of generous open-well form with broad moulded handrail, large-scale balusters and stout newels all made of mellow-coloured oak. On this landing was located a large oil painting, described as a 'history piece', and a 'close-stool' or commode.

We now pretty certainly reach the ground floor because room No. 12 is described as the 'Parlour' and was most likely the front room looking into the Piazza arcade. This room may have been for the private use of the Haddocks but was probably a gathering place for customers or to let by the hour or night. It contained a 'Stove' – a type of grate with iron or stone hobs on which simple dishes of food or drinks could be cooked or kept warm,[35] a chimney glass with 'brass arms' (a mirror with brass candle holders attached and placed above the fireplace), 'marble slab' (presumably a buffet on which food and drink was placed), 'sconces, two pair of cotton curtains, clock, six matted chairs, easy chair, mahogany card table, ditto claw table, mahogany bedstead'. So, all in all, a well-appointed bed-sitting room in which a couple could spend day and night in elegance and comfort.

Presumably adjoining was room No. 13, the 'Back Parlour', fitted with a 'bedstead, dining table' and 'two matted chairs'. In a 'Side Room' were 'five leather chairs, table, curtains, bedstead'. Room No. 14 was termed the 'Coffee House' – Haddock's incorporated a coffee house that was licensed separately to Sophia Lenoy before Elizabeth Haddock's death and was no doubt the favoured gathering place of prostitutes sipping their 'capucins'.[36] Sophia Lenoy's coffee house seems to have occupied several ground-floor rooms but, despite being for public use and equipped with a 'chimney glass with brass arms, pierglass' and 'four matted chairs', this room also contained a 'Bedstead'. Perhaps this is where Sophia herself slept after she had shut up for the night.

As well as a room called the 'Coffee House' there was also one called the 'Coffee Room', but this was probably part of the bagnio proper and nothing to do with Sophia's Coffee House. This 'Coffee Room' contained a 'marble table, sconces with brass arms and ball shades, a small mahogany dining table, seven leathern chairs' and 'five old Harrateen window curtains'. Nearby was the 'Dining Room' that, while it boasted a 'Chimney glass' and 'eight beech chairs', also contained a 'Bedstead' and so could double as a bedroom.

Beds were valuable and much-prized pieces of furniture in the eighteenth century and played a role in the household that extended way beyond simply offering a comfortable place to sleep. They were regarded as ornamental and as objects that conferred status – people would receive company while in bed and so beds could be found in rooms other than bedrooms; indeed the bed enjoyed something of a public position in the home. But, even given this traditional usage, the number of beds in the bagnio was extraordinarily high. Virtually every room had one, and so virtually every room was capable of accommodating clients and their prostitutes. The inventory suggests Haddock's contained no fewer than twenty-two beds. If the seven beds obviously or probably for servants are excluded, and assuming each guest bed could accommodate at least two, then when full Haddock's could sleep around thirty paying customers.

It seems that after cataloguing the contents of the bagnio's ground-floor public rooms the person compiling the inventory descended to the basement for now is listed the 'Kitchen belonging to the Coffee House', which, perhaps not surprisingly, also contained a 'Bedstead' – presumably more sleeping accommodation for servants. Then the 'Bagnio kitchen' with its 'large range' is mentioned, and a passage and 'Cellare'. This room contained 'three washing tubs, bottle ranks, and beer stand' and so sounds highly utilitarian, but it also contained the 'Bagnio copper, stoke hole and iron work, lead pipes and two baths of marble and lead, and cupping box and glasses'. So Haddock's could provide the services enjoyed by Ned Ward across the Piazza around forty years earlier, though the location of the bathing facilities – sharing a cellar with wine-racks, beer barrels and scrubbing tubs – suggests that Archenholz was correct when he said that baths in bagnios 'were seldom needed' and probably not many customers went to Haddock's for the 'Sweating, cupping & bathing' advertised on its trade sign.

The last portion of the building listed is the 'yard and coach house' that must have been located on Floral Street. Finally various odd items of value are listed on the inventory, including plate, china, linen and 'Prints and pictures in closet upon the stairs, including Hogarth's *Harlot's Progress*, six prints'. Richard or Elizabeth Haddock clearly had some wit. As their harlot-clients progressed dutifully up and down the staircase they could reflect on the salutary lesson offered by the progress of Hogarth's harlot.

The total value of the contents of the bagnio was calculated to be £795.17.6d. But as well as assets the inventory also lists the 'Debts due and owing to the said deceased at the time of her death'. It was a fairly large sum of £220 and virtually all was due from customers, listed by surname and with the honorary title of 'Captain' accorded to the men. But a number of women were also in debt to the bagnio, including Miss Barlos for 5/- and Miss Lucy Cooper £4.1.4d.

Quite what profit a bagnio such as Haddock's might hope to make is now hard to calculate but there are clues. Henry Fielding, in his novel *Amelia* of 1751, mentions the nightly charge of a bagnio. One of the characters in the story, Captain Booth, is incarcerated in Newgate Prison and at 9 p.m., which is locking-up time, his visitor Miss Matthews is told by the Governor that she has to leave. Booth asks if the lady may stay, the Governor agrees but says that a bed costs a guinea a night. What if they sit up all night and talk? asks Miss Matthews.

> 'With all my heart,' said the Governor, '. . . I don't enquire into what doth not concern me, but single and double are two things. If I lock up double I expect half a guinea; and I'm sure the captain cannot think that's out of the way – It is but the price of a bagnio.'[37]

So half a guinea a night for lodging and perhaps some food for two? It seems Haddock's could sleep around fifteen paying couples so it could make up to 7½ guineas a night or 52½ guineas a week from lodgings alone – the average annual wage of a journeyman tradesman such as a joiner or printer. There was indeed, with careful management, much money to be made from bagnios that were little more than high-density hotels. Mother Thornton, who in 1791 took over the running of Haddock's, is described in the *Morning Post* of 16 March 1798 as 'late Mistress of Haddock's Bagnio' who left the sum to her beneficiaries of £500 per annum.[38]

A HABITUÉE OF HADDOCK'S: LUCY COOPER

The brief and tantalising mention of 'Miss Lucy Cooper' as one of Elizabeth Haddock's debtors in 1752 is also a fortuitous one because we happen to know quite a lot about her. Lucy's eventual notoriety meant much was written about her. Just as the inventory of number 8 the Piazza gives us a physical sense of a long-lost establishment, so Lucy's life story, illustrated by mezzotint portraits of her by James Macardell and Richard

Purcell, helps to people it.[39] Her ultimate fate was also typical of the flip side of Covent Garden's booming sex trade in the mid-eighteenth century.

In 1752 Lucy was just reaching the height of what was to be – initially at least – a highly successful career in prostitution, and was soon to be kept by a rich and powerful protector. In the early 1750s she could have earned the £4.1.4d she owed in a few days, probably a few hours. Why she didn't pay her debt and quite what it was for is now hard to say. Lucy's sojourns at Haddock's must surely, if of a professional nature, have been paid for by her clients so it's likely this sum was for drinks and food she consumed with friends in between assignations.

The high courtesan Lucy Cooper, who was at the height of her fame in the mid-1750s (after Frans van der Mijn).

Lucy was launched upon the world in the late 1740s or very early 50s by the notorious bawd Mrs Elizabeth Weatherby, who ran the Ben Jonson's Head on the playhouse or southern side of Russell Street, at the corner with Drury Lane.[40] Lucy – lively, witty and attractive – would have been viewed by Weatherby as a most useful enticement to an establishment that was otherwise far from salubrious. According to *Nocturnal Revels*, published in 1779, Weatherby's was a 'receptacle for rakes and

prostitutes, highwaymen, pickpockets, gamblers and swindlers . . . originally instituted about thirty years since, by Weatherby as a substitute to
Moll King's, some time after that retreat was shut up'.[41]

Weatherby's – launched at virtually the same time as Haddock's but
as a place of riotous assembly rather than discreet overnight assignations
– was an immediate success. Clearly there was an appetite for such a
place among the Covent Garden throng. As *Nocturnal Revels* explains,
'[N]o sooner had Weatherby's plan got wind, than this house was resorted
to by great numbers of female votaries of Venus of all rank and condition, from Chariot kept-Mistress, down to the two-penny Bunter [a very
common prostitute – cheap, usually aged, ugly and destitute] who plies
under the Piazza.'[42] The system of entry to Weatherby's is interesting,
and may well have been the same used at Haddock's Coffee House. Girls
on the prowl had merely to purchase 'a capuchin' – a milky coffee – to
join 'this scene of riot and dissipation'. What an astonishing image – mid-
eighteenth-century prostitutes in Covent Garden sitting drinking cups of
cappuccino!

William Hickey describes in his *Memoirs* a night's revels in Covent
Garden in early 1768 which included a somewhat less genteel mode of
entry to Weatherby's:

> . . . upon ringing at a door, strongly secured with knobs of iron, a
> cut-throat-looking rascal opened a small wicket, which was also secured
> with narrow iron bars, who in a hoarse and ferocious voice asked,
> 'Who's there?' Being answered 'Friends,' we were cautiously admitted
> one at a time, and when the last had entered, the door was instantly
> closed and secured, not only by an immense lock and key, but a massy
> iron bolt and chain.

Once inside Hickey and his companions were confronted by a spectacle
that makes Weatherby's sound positively terrifying:

> . . . the whole room was in an uproar, men and women promiscuously
> mounted upon chairs, tables and benches, in order to see a sort of
> general conflict carrying on upon the floor. Two she-devils, for they
> scarce had a human appearance, were engaged in a scratching and
> boxing match, their faces entirely covered with blood, bosoms bare, and
> the clothes nearly torn from their bodies. For several minutes, not a

creature interfered between them, or seemed to care a straw what mischief they might do each other, and the contest went on with unabated fury.

But this was not the only extraordinary sight to confront Hickey:

> In another corner of the same room, an uncommonly athletic young man of about twenty-five seemed to be the object of universal attack. No less than three Amazonian tigresses were pummeling him with all their might, and it appeared to me that some of the males at times dealt him blows with their sticks. He, however, made a capital defence, not sparing the women a bit more than the men, but knocking each down as opportunity occurred.

In an attempt to escape such hellish scenes Hickey bolted for the door but – barred and guarded – there was no escape. The doorkeeper, assuming Hickey was going for constables or trying to leave without paying his bill, declared there was 'no exit here until you have passed muster' and sent him back into the 'dreadful hole' to be fleeced or otherwise abused.[43]

Such was the place in which the young Lucy held court and she soon became generally admired as the successor to the great Covent Garden favourite Betsy Careless (see page 92), who had died in 1752.[44] The author of *Nocturnal Revels* stated that although Lucy 'used often to make her appearance' at Weatherby's, it was not at the 'market-price in [this] place' that 'she meant to dispose of her charms'.[45] As well as disporting and displaying herself at Weatherby's she may have occasionally served as one of the 'nuns' of Sir Francis Dashwood's Order of Medmenham (see page 390). During outings to Medmenham (or West Wycombe) it is probable that, as Dashwood's particular 'nun' and in the ancient Grecian tradition where courtesans were treated not just as women but as Muses, Lucy was worshipped with particular devotion.

But goddess or not, she had to make ends meet and from the late 1750s contrived to be kept by the 'old Debauchee Sir Orlando Br—n' (Sir Orlando Bridgeman, aged sixty-five in 1760, a baronet, sometime MP for Shrewsbury, and married to the daughter of the Earl of Bradford).[46] Despite this encumbrance and the disparity in age the besotted baronet offered, according to *Nocturnal Revels*, marriage to Lucy, and gave her a house in Parliament Street and a 'chariot' that she kept at 'Weatherby's door for twenty-four, and sometimes eight-and-forty hours successively'.[47] Why, asked *Nocturnal Revels*, did Lucy haunt Weatherby's when she had her own 'hotel' in Parliament Street in which to take her ease or entertain? The answer offered was that she loved the place and its rowdy low-life as well as the opportunities Weatherby's afforded her to display a particular talent she possessed and that traditionally made whores famous: a way with words and a facility for witty repartee. 'Dissipation was Lucy's motto,' states *Nocturnal Revels*,[48] 'the old Baronet she abhorred', and at Weatherby's she could frolic with and entertain – at the baronet's expense – men and women she found stimulating.

At this time, while being kept by Bridgeman, Lucy remained available for business if the price was right, at least according to the 1761 edition of the *List of Covent Garden Ladies*. Her entry reads:

> Lucy Cooper of Parliament Street . . . no woman can be a more jovial companion, or say better things. She has often true wit about her, but lards it rather a little too much with blasphemy. She was, to the astonishment of the world, kept for three years by Sir Penurious Trifle [Sir Orlando Bridgeman] who never had before shewn the slightest tendency to extravagance . . . Lucy's features are regular, her hair brown, her air easy, and her shape genteel; though she is very thin . . .[49]

Lucy in her prime, when celebrated as one of the sights of Covent Garden, was also captured in an odd and vicious little verse included in Edward Thompson's *The Meretriciad or The Court of Venus*, published in 1761. In this work she is portrayed as a mistress of misrule, queen of a dark underworld, and, although still in her glory, speeding to the edge of the abyss. The scene is set in Bob Derry's 'Cyder Cellar' in Maiden Lane, 'where the Harlots throng' along with 'Cit, Souldier, Sailor and some bearded Jew'. The boisterous proceedings presided over by Lucy end in a violent and seemingly racist riot in which two Jews are killed, the rough and ragamuffin Christian mob seemingly inflamed by alcohol and Lucy's lascivious behaviour. Parish constables are called and 'the captive queen Lucy' carried before a magistrate. The ballad continues:

> The Shakespeare's Head, The Rose and Bedford Arms
> Each alike profits from my Lucy's charms . . .
> Fat Wheatherby sunk now in eternal sleep
> Weep! Weep! My Lucy – Wheatherby's no more.

It seems that many of the dives of Covent Garden sought to profit from Lucy's crowd-pulling presence, including the notorious Rose Tavern made famous in the third painting of Hogarth's *Rake's Progress* series of 1733–5 that shows a prostitute (traditionally thought to be a portrait of Betsy Careless) robbing a drunken 'cull' – or client – while a 'Posture Moll' strips 'preparatory to being whipped or performing any other posture demanded of her',[50] while perched on a large and reflective pewter dish of the type Hogarth shows being carried into the room. It's easy to see why such performances could cause a riot among an excited and drunken crowd.

Striptease and the striking of obscene postures – many probably with ironic and lewd reference to well-known classical sculptures or paintings – was one of the standard diversions in London's lower taverns and bagnios. Indeed one, known as 'The Temple of Mysteries', seems to have specialised in truly outrageous performances. According to the *History of Orgies*,[51] the 'temple', run by a Miss Falkland, featured a celebrated mistress of the art called 'Posture Nan' and was a place 'where orgies of an unspeakable . . . nature were supposed to take place'. Such performances are described in chilling detail, and condemned, by 'Urbanus' in a 1766 publication called the *Midnight Spy . . . or A View of the Transactions of London . . . from Ten in the Evening until Five in the Morning*. He entered an establishment in Great Russell Street and beheld:

> . . . the object, which arouses at once our disgust and our pity. A beautiful woman lies stretched on the floor, and offers to view just those parts of her body that, were she not without all shame, she would most zealously seek to conceal. As she is also given to drink, she usually arrives half-drunk, and after two or three glasses of Madeira exposes herself in this unseemly manner. Look, she is on all fours now, like an animal. She is ridiculed and men gloat over such prostitution of incomparable beauty.[52]

Lucy featured in this world during the 1750s and early 60s and appeared to thrive. Indeed such was her apparent success that she became a target for moral reformers. An anonymous pamphlet of 1758, entitled *A Congratulatory Epistle from a Reformed Rake*, claimed that 'Lucy C—r' along with 'Fanny M—y' have 'made more Whores than all the Rakes in England [since] a Kept-Mistress, that rides in her Chariot, debauches every vain Girl she meets'.[53]

But in 1764 Lucy's fortunes took a turn for the worse when her protector, the baronet, died. She had now reached the edge of the abyss. As *Nocturnal Revels* explains, she could afford 'no more dinner parties for Beau Tracy [Richard "Beau" Tracy, the grandson of a respected judge and "one of the most dissipated men of his age"[54]] and King Derrick [while her] intemperance and debauchery greatly injured her constitution [so that] her person which was at most but genteel, was now much changed, and even her vivacity failed her'.[55]

Her world rapidly started to disintegrate. Suddenly Lucy faced the fate awaiting most flighty prostitutes who had enjoyed life too much and not had the sense to put away or profitably invest funds while still enjoying their money-making good looks. As old friends and supporters such as the baronet and Palmer the actor died, Lucy discovered that she 'had not charms sufficient to captivate a man of such affluence as could support her in the same degree of splendour, as she had for some time lived'.[56] Suddenly finding herself destitute of powerful protectors, she also soon found herself destitute of funds. She sold her plate and furniture to maintain herself and took solace in yet more reckless merry-making and heavy drinking – all of which further undermined her health, attractions, looks and earning capacity.

Lucy at this uncertain time is portrayed in a song of 1768 entitled 'The Gentleman's Bottle Companion'. In this work she is presented as a rival – and object of jealousy – to fellow harlot Betsy Wemys who is described in the opening stanza as 'Bet Wemys, of Wadderby, the pride'.[57]

> Must Lucy Cooper bear the Bell
> And give herself all the Airs?
> Must that damnation Bitch of Hell
> Be hough'd by Knights and Squires?
> Has she a better Cunt than I
> Of nut-brown Hairs more full?
> That all Mankind with her do lye
> While I have scarce a Cull [client]?

Betsy, well known for her glass-eye, was in fact Lucy's long-term friend, carousing partner and sister 'nun' of the Order of Medmenham, as well as being one of Jack Harris's 'listed' harlots. She had also, when this verse was published, been dead about three years and so was another of the staunch companions Lucy lost quickly and suddenly in the early 1760s.

Lucy Cooper did not long survive Betsy Wemys. In 1769 she finally succumbed to her debts and was confined to the King's Bench Gaol where such were her difficulties she had to appeal for help. William Hickey in his *Memoirs* mentions how a friend received a begging letter from Lucy while she was in the gaol, 'stating that she was almost naked and starving, without a penny in her pocket to purchase food, raiment, or a coal to warm herself'. Moved, Hickey put down ten guineas, his companions followed suit, and fifty pounds was raised instantly. 'I had afterwards the satisfaction of hearing,' he records, 'that this seasonable aid had probably saved the life of a deserving woman, who, in her prosperity, had done a thousand generous actions.'[58] After this, however, Lucy's continuing plight seems to have slipped his mind.

Perhaps thanks to Hickey Lucy did survive, but when finally released 'by an Act of Insolvency' she found she had 'the world to begin again'.[59] She persuaded friends 'to put her into a house at the upper end of Bow-street where she carried on business in a small way for some time, but being emaciated by her irregularities or constant Nocturnal Revels, at the end of a few months she also yielded to the Grim Tyrant'.[60] Lucy died in poverty in 1772. Her fall and final ruin had taken eight painful years.

Lucy Cooper was typical of the more flamboyant and fiery young women who during the mid-eighteenth century illuminated Covent Garden's 'Great Square of Venus'. For a brief moment she appeared to have mastered the monstrous sex industry, to be in control, even to have became a figure of fashion in the town, the companion of the rich and powerful. But all was transitory, little more than an illusion. Lucy, like most of her companions, fell victim to her own pleasures and to her failure to be a good businesswomen and plan ahead. Such was the hard and cruel fate suffered by thousands of young women who – in quest of freedom and escape from lives of drudgery and poverty – chose to sup with the Devil.

ELEVEN

'THE RECEPTION OF THE DISTRESSED'

Hospitals and Workhouses

Georgian London possessed a small number of public or institutional buildings that were, in their different but related ways, significant architectural monuments to the city's sex industry. Most have long been demolished and forgotten, and those that do survive are now generally no longer directly or immediately associated with the trade that brought them many of their users. These public buildings served various functions. There was the Foundling Hospital, which, to a degree and at least for a time, cared for the illegitimate and unwanted offspring of prostitution; there was the Magdalen House, which was a place of reception for prostitutes who wished to escape the sex industry and reform their way of life; and there were Lock Hospitals, which catered for those suffering from venereal disease and counted many poor prostitutes among their patients.

The best-remembered of these institutions is the Foundling Hospital, which from the mid-1740s was located in Bloomsbury until most of its buildings were demolished in 1928, but with some of its contents, collection and archives preserved in a new building adjoining the site of the old. The Foundling's direct role in London's sex industry remains controversial but many contemporary observers – informed and otherwise – assumed it was to a degree a refuge for babies born to prostitutes and so, tangentially, an encouragement to vice. By contrast, the link of the Magdalen House to London's sex industry was never in doubt because it was founded in 1758 as a refuge for penitent prostitutes. The Magdalen had two physical manifestations in central London – first in Whitechapel, and then from 1769 south of the river near St George's Fields – ultimately leaving virtually no trace after the institution, transformed in many of its aims, moved to Streatham in 1866.

But there is one reminder of it. Prescot Street – just north of the Tower of London – runs between Mansel and Leman Streets. In the mid-eighteenth century all three streets contained the large and handsome dwellings of wealthy City merchants and, along with Alie Street to the north, defined a large open space – the 'Tenter Ground' of Goodman's Field – that had once been used for staking out washed and dyed fabric, wool and latterly silk, to let it dry in the sun without shrinking or warping by being restrained by tenter hooks. As well as being a quarter of wealth and industry, however, the area was also part of one of Georgian London's more dubious centres of entertainment. There was a popular theatre in Alie Street – the Goodman's Field Theatre – from at least 1727, and throughout the eighteenth century this part of Whitechapel was famed for the number of its often-outrageous bawdy-houses and prostitutes.

Now Prescot Street throbs to the sound of traffic all around it, with only a couple of Georgian houses surviving among much later and large-scale commercial and industrial buildings. But halfway down it, heading south into parallel Chamber Street, is a small, anonymous and generally overlooked byway. It is named Magdalen Passage and – marking the site of the long-gone Magdalen House – is the only physical memorial to the extraordinary experiment in moral, physical and spiritual re-education that took place here just over 250 years ago.

The Lock Hospitals have also all but disappeared from London's memory, though in fact two of the most spectacular surviving institutional buildings of early-Georgian London – Guy's Hospital in Southwark, founded in 1721, and St Bartholomew's Hospital, Smithfield, with its stupendous quadrangle built during the 1730s to the designs of James Gibbs – both had connections to Lock Hospitals or incorporated Lock wards.

THE FOUNDLING HOSPITAL

For the common prostitute in Georgian London there were few ways to avoid the most obviously evil and awkward consequences of her trade: sexually transmitted disease and pregnancy. There were many proclaimed preventatives and cures for both but most were based on varying degrees of ignorance, folk-lore and quackery – and many could end in death or

irreparable physical and psychological damage. A variety of sexual techniques could be used to reduce the risks of both pregnancy and disease,
and condoms made of sheep's gut were available from the late seventeenth
century (see page 209) but seem not to have been in general use among
street prostitutes, presumably because they were too expensive or difficult
to obtain. Also it was generally believed, no doubt by many prostitutes themselves, that precautions were not necessary because, as a pamphlet explained
in 1752, a woman who 'has to do with a Variety of Men upon the Back of
another . . . cannot conceive, by reason she engrates various and opposite
Qualities of Blood [and] by excessive Repetitions imbeciliates the feminary
Parts, and renders the Act of none Effect'.[1]

Regular sexual activity with a 'Variety of Men' could indeed reduce a
female's fertility but due to venereal disease rather than to promiscuity in
itself. No doubt many prostitutes were unhappily disabused of the veracity
of this typical piece of eighteenth-century pseudo-science.

If a prostitute did become pregnant there were two immediate options
– abortion or giving birth; and if a child was born then there were further
options – to keep it (a huge and obvious difficulty and expense for a
common prostitute) or abandon it, which often meant leaving the new-
born infant to the mercy of the unloving parish authorities or even to
take its chances on the street.

These stark choices did, of course, have many permutations. Unwanted
infants could be 'starved at nurse' or 'over-laid', essentially slowly and carefully murdered to avoid an actual murder charge. The practice of slow
death by neglect was a recognised evil attacked specifically by Dr Cadogan
in his *Essay on the Nursing and Management of Children* of 1750, and referred
to satirically in 1745 by Jonathan Swift in his *Directions to Servants* where
he advises the nurse, 'If you happen to let the Child fall, and lame it, be
sure never to confess it; and if it dies, all is safe.'

Desperate or deranged mothers might attempt to sell their child into
servitude, which could of course lead to its exploitation by the sex industry,
or – mentally disordered by despair – would kill their infant, and perhaps
themselves as well. The number of infants sold by their mothers – perhaps
after some months of nurture – is now seemingly impossible to calculate
but Peter Linebaugh, in his penetrating study *The London Hanged*, points
out that between 1720 and 1750 12 per cent of the women hanged at
Tyburn were executed for infanticide.[2]

The alarming sight of babies and young children abandoned in or roaming the streets of London shocked many observers, particularly when these infants were apparently not only products of, but also participants in, the capital's sex industry. But although deeply dismayed, few observers seem to have formed any coherent plan either to tackle the cause of child abandonment or to deal effectively with its appalling consequences. The exception was Captain Thomas Coram.

An engraving of Hogarth's 1740 portrait of Thomas Coram. The painting was presented to the Foundling Hospital just as Coram was severing all relations with the great charity he had founded.

Biographies of him offer what is perhaps an apocryphal story. Coram, having worked and flourished in the American colonies and London as a sailing master, ship-builder and merchant, settled in the maritime quarter of Rotherhithe, on the south bank of the Thames. In the 1720s, while in his fifties and walking between Rotherhithe and the City, he 'frequently saw infants exposed and deserted in the public streets'.[3] Being of a charitable and enquiring turn of mind, the deeply troubled Coram looked into the cause of this horrible evil and 'found that it arose out of a morbid morality, then possessing the public mind, by which an unhappy female, who fell a victim to the seductions and false promises of a designing man, was left to hopeless contumely, and irretrievable disgrace'.[4] He became acquainted with the fact that a girl's 'first false step was her final doom', for the 'error of a day, she was punished with the infamy of years [and] was branded forever as a woman habitually lewd'. In such a situation the girl, 'seeing no . . . means of saving her character', became 'delirious in her despair' and either murdered or abandoned 'the child of her seducer'.

This was the tale as told in the mid-nineteenth century[5] and what is significant, of course, is that there is no mention in it of prostitution. The children that Coram saw and wanted to save were not, according to this account, the abandoned spawn of prostitutes, but of 'delirious' and despairing young women who, far from being loose women, were the otherwise virtuous victims of 'false' young men, with their offspring being the error of an ill-fated single 'day'.

Sustaining this singular and unlikely claim for the origin of the Foundling's stock of babes became something of an obsession for a hospital that was, from time to time, accused of encouraging and abetting vice by providing a haven not only for illegitimate children of the victims of seduction but also for children born to habitual and hardened prostitutes. But in the early days of the hospital's gestation the implication of its aims for the morals of London seems not to have been a major concern among its supporters even though Coram had, from the very start, to contend with arguments that such an institution would merely 'increase illegitimacy and encourage vice'.[6] He complained to a friend that 'many weak persons, more Ladies than Gentlemen, say such a foundation will be a promotion of wickedness', but for him this was a peripheral issue.[7] Far more important was the mission to save wronged unmarried mothers from 'disgrace', and to provide unwanted 'young children' with a purchase on life and the possibility of a secure and productive future.

But it seems gradually to have become clear to many involved in this project that its aims – bold and admirable as they were – did in fact lead them into a moral minefield. Indeed, even the reasons stated for saving the lives of abandoned infants were extraordinarily complex. Of course such an action was humane and befitted a Christian nation, but it also had to do with matters of nationalism, patriotism and hard economics. The traveller, merchant and philanthropist Jonas Hanway – who was to become one of the Guardians and Governors of the Foundling – revealed why the lives of all infants were important for the welfare and prosperity of the nation. In the mid-eighteenth century there was general fear of a depopulation of Britain that would, it was assumed, ultimately lead to failure in competition with other nations. This was a fear that could not be scientifically answered because no reliable national census was even attempted in Britain until the Census Act was passed 1800, leading to the first full census within the British Isles since the Domesday Book.

Hanway observed in 1759 that 'there are many people in this nation who entertain an opinion, that we are decreased in number, since the year 1714, above a million',[8] though he was not convinced this was the case: 'Liberty and plenty' – the virtues he associated with England – 'should naturally create an increase of people'. But he owned that there was some worrying evidence to support the depopulation alarmists.

> Gin and tea [the latter an irrational pet hate of Hanway's] . . . indeed
> have swept off thousands, and gin in particular has prevented many
> thousands more being born. War has swept off some; the Great Neglect
> of marriage has prevented increase, many living single who ought to
> marry . . . Venereal diseases have carried off many . . . whilst the
> carelessness of nurses has swept off numbers of infants.

Hanway failed to mention the popular assumption that colonial expansion was emptying Britain, though he did give it as his opinion that a great cause of the 'prevention of increase' in population was the murderous condition of parish workhouses.[9] So the lives of all British babies – no matter what their station in life, the circumstances of their birth or the actions of their parents – were precious for the contribution they could potentially make to the common good.

Meanwhile Coram, brooding over the terrible sights that confronted him daily in London's streets, conceived a humanitarian mission that would not only save and give purpose to otherwise wasted lives but also make a contribution to the prosperity, power and welfare of the nation. For years he investigated, lobbied and discussed the possibility and means of establishing some sort of institution or, to use the generic eighteenth-century term for such establishments, 'an hospital' for abandoned children.

Gradually he built up the support of a large number of people of power, wealth and influence – each moved by many or most of the issues such a project embraced – and on 17 October 1739 obtained a Royal Charter.

The name of the institute and its aims initially seem straightforward but are laden with moral and ethical implications and potential contradictions, revealing how complex such a seemingly simple aim as saving children's lives could be in mid-eighteenth-century Britain. The charter announced that the institution was to be called 'The Foundling Hospital' and that it was to be 'for the maintenance and education of exposed and deserted young children'. But from the start the hospital was evidently not to be specifically for foundlings – that is, abandoned children 'deserted and exposed' – but for those brought in for disposal by their parents or others, possibly even children of legitimate birth whose parents happened to find it too inconvenient, awkward or expensive to maintain them. By whom and using what criteria were babes to be chosen? How were adequate funds to be obtained and cash flow maintained? And how 'young' exactly did a child need to be to make it eligible for acceptance?

Incredible as it may now seem, these tricky issues were not fully or satisfactorily resolved at this key initial stage, with only a basic and flimsy set of operational criteria agreed. Perhaps Coram and his closest supporters realised that any such resolution was impossible and that the whole enterprise could founder if its mechanism were too closely picked over, or least suffer interminable delay. The first general meeting of the Foundling Hospital was held at Somerset House on 20 November 1739, during which the Duke of Bedford was chosen as President and the 'nobility and gentry' announced who were stipulated by the charter to act as 'Governors and Guardians' of the Hospital. A General Committee of fifty was selected by ballot, which included such eminent men as Sir Hans Sloane, founder of the British Museum, and the Rt. Hon. Arthur Onslow, afterwards Speaker of the House of Commons.[10]

During this event Coram addressed the audience and announced that the 'Hospital for exposed children' would operate free of all public expense 'through the assistance of some compassionate great ladies, and other good persons'.[11] This was a bold claim that he surely knew would be hard to sustain. He also added to the cloud of confusion surrounding both the aims of the hospital and the conception and births of the babies it was established to save when he declared that 'the long and melancholy experience of this nation has too demonstrably shewn, with what barbarity tender infants have been exposed and destroyed, for want of proper means of preventing disgrace, and succouring the necessities of their parents'.[12]

Fear of 'disgrace' on the part of seduced and unmarried mothers may have been one reason – even a major one – why babies were abandoned on the streets of London. Coram must have known that there were many others, but to blame such abandonment on the shame of a duped girl made the Foundling's efforts to save the babes less provocative and more attractive to potential financial backers than admitting that many such abandoned babes were the direct result of prostitution. If this were publicly acknowledged then what the hospital proposed doing was, it could be argued, no more than making the immoral lives of prostitutes ethically easier and therefore more attractive.

From what was perhaps a pragmatic assessment of the type of charity work that would best attract sponsors, combined with a certain moralistic dogmatism, the Foundling forged its first admission policy and refined its aim. It made it clear that it did not want to aid prostitutes by taking their unwanted children and, far more confusingly, also made it clear that it did not actually want to offer refuge to all abandoned babes – as Coram himself did. Rather, as Randolph Trumbach points out, its primary aim was to 'maintain the reputation of an unmarried mother and allow her to return to work'.[13] To achieve this aim the hospital announced that 'petitioners' – as women bringing babies were called – were more likely be successful if they could demonstrate that they had kept the disgrace of their illicit pregnancy a secret as long as possible, so that their reintegration into conventional society could be painless and speedy.

So, as it launched itself upon the world, the Foundling had two aims: the one proclaimed in its charter – to maintain and educate 'exposed and deserted young children' – and the one expressed in its policy – to save unmarried mothers from 'disgrace'. The former was to do with the preservation of human life and dignity; the latter with the preservation of reputation and social standing. That these aims were not necessarily compatible, indeed that they could be contradictory or even mutually exclusive, seems to have been overlooked. If a mother's disgrace was public and absolute and her social rehabilitation unlikely, perhaps due to no fault of her own, was her baby automatically to be rejected by the hospital and perhaps condemned to death or years of miserable existence – also through no fault of its own? It seems the moral dilemma inherent in potentially conflicting aims was not foreseen – certainly not by the public at large or, apparently, by most of the people Coram approached for aid.

The list in the Foundling's Charter of those lending support to the new hospital remains incredibly impressive – both for the quantity of the names it contains and their influence and diversity. Coram had enlisted the aid not just of the great and the good but also a wide cross-section of London society. Alongside the names of powerful aristocrats were those of artists such as William Hogarth, to be joined later by George Frederic Handel. The Foundling Hospital project had clearly captured the imagi-nation and emotions of the capital, and the immense support it received – at least initially – confirmed the depth of concern that many must have felt, for a long period, over the numbers of babes exposed and young children lawlessly roaming the streets of London.

Subscriptions from the initial supporters brought in enough funds to set the hospital in motion even before a purpose-designed building for its operations was started. There was, quite understandably, an air of urgency about the whole scheme. The methods employed by similar long-established institutions on the continent were studied so as to establish the rules and routine of the Foundling. Premises were acquired in Hatton Garden near the highly disreputable sex trade area around Saffron Hill, Hogarth designed a shield-like 'trade sign' for the establishment, and its doors were opened for business.

From the beginning, however, things started to go wrong, revealing in dramatic fashion how poorly the functioning of the hospital had been planned. In March 1741 a notice was posted in Hatton Garden announcing the start of operations: 'To-morrow at eight o'clock in the evening this house will be opened for the reception of twenty children.' The 'regulations' governing consideration for admission were also listed. No child over two months old would be accepted, 'nor such as have the evil, leprosy, or disease of the like nature whereby the health of other children may be endangered'. Those bringing children were told to 'ring a bell' on the outward door and wait until the fate of the child was decided, and they were assured that 'no questions whatever will be asked of any person who brings a child'. It was also requested that all people

*A later engraving of Hogarth's emblematic picture
made for the Foundling Hospital, showing, in the
centre, Coram holding the founding charter with a
mother kneeling before him. She has dropped the
dagger with which she would have killed her baby or*

who brought babies 'affix on each child some particular writing or
other distinguishing mark or token, so that the children may be known
hereafter if necessary'.[14] This regulation, which was intended to allow
mothers to identify their children if required at a later date, led to the
creation of a truly poignant archive of objects, some of which remain in
the hospital's possession while others are lodged in fragile eighteenth-
century volumes now in the London Metropolitan Archives.

These tokens and notes are pinned in the 'Billet Books' that record each
child's acceptance, together with information compiled on a standard form

herself. In the left background, a child is being
abandoned in the night. On the right the foundling
children are being brought up to follow useful trades,
such as spinning.

giving date and time of admission, allocating the child an identifying letter
of the alphabet, and recording its sex, age and 'Marks on the Body'. Any
objects or texts that came with the baby were also noted against a standard
list including, 'Cap, Biggin, Forehead-Cloth, Bibb, Petticoat, Mantle,
Sleeves, Blanket, Waistcoat, Shirt, Clout, Stockings . . .' Sometimes the
mother left a name. One form, dated 'Hatton-Garden December 9th 1743
at 6¼ o'Clock', recording the admission of a baby boy has a scrap of paper
pinned to it that, the form records, was originally pinned to the child's
breast. It simply reads: 'Charles Talbot born 22 November 1743'.

Occasionally attached to the forms is a token. For example, in the volume covering admissions from late 1743 to late 1745 to Hatton Garden and Bloomsbury,[15] a female baby aged three weeks is recorded as having arrived at 'Lamb's Conduit fields' on 15 November 1745 at 7 o'clock, and to the form is pinned the cut-off end of a woman's sleeve, described on the form as 'Blue & White Stryp'd Cotton ... and white Linnen' and a 'narrow pink Ribbon'. Another page – recording the arrival of a two-month-old boy – has pinned to it a white cotton open-fingered mitten or sleeve end with silk trim. These items were, in later life, the only things the child had to give it any sense of identity – the only physical connection to its mother.

From the moment the doors of the Foundling Hospital first opened in Hatton Garden far more babies were offered than could be accepted, and unfortunately no one had foreseen to what extremes desperate mothers would go to deposit their child in a place of safety. There were riots outside the door as women struggled for places at the head of the queue. The hospital authorities were aghast. They could only accept the limited number of children that their funds – determined by subscriptions or legacies – permitted so the only way to reduce this unseemly scramble was to devise another system of admission. Soon one was found, and was almost equally bizarre as the scramble for places because it made the acceptance of children a mere lottery, with little allowance for particular circumstances.

All the women who arrived on admission day were brought inside and selected a ball from a bag. The balls were of three colours and their number and ratio based on the number of children being offered on the particular day of selection. If the woman selected a white ball she was moved to the 'Inspection Room' and her story and child examined; if she selected a black ball she was turned out with the assurance that she could try her luck another day; and if she selected a red ball, she stood by to take the place of any white ball holder whose 'petition' was rejected, perhaps simply because her child was the wrong sex, since the aim was, if possible, to select an equal number of boys and girls.

This system of admission was clearly morally and ethically dubious and open to all manner of abuse and bribery. Coram himself was alarmed and felt that the basic proposition of his charity – that all eligible children be accepted without the need for any tests – was already being undermined. By these methods 136 children were admitted in the first year, the annual average soon being established at just under 100, with 821 children being admitted by 1751, of whom 316 had soon died.

Despite concerns about this system of admission it continued until May 1756 by which time 1,384 children had been received.[16] Jonas Hanway, a Governor and Guardian of the Hospital, described this early phase of admission, notably the fate suffered by these pioneer infants: 'Thirty children were put out to nurse, and soon another thirty more, and in the course of the year one hundred and thirty-six.' The phrase 'put out to nurse' means that the babies were put into the care of a number of wet-nurses, whose time or abilities seem to have been limited since, as Hanway records, of this 136 babies, apparently healthy when admitted, 66 soon died. This mortality rate of nearly 50 per cent didn't appear to worry Hanway, who merely observed that it was 'not many more than the ordinary proportion which usually die in the course of births' among children in towns, while of the 1,384 received by May 1756 'only [sic] 724 died . . . at once exhibiting a proof of the great care and tenderness of the Governors of that time'.[17]

During the early part of 1742 the Governors focused their attention on acquiring suitable land and procuring a design for their hospital. Indeed the first item on the agenda for the first meeting of the Court of Governors, held on 29 November 1739 at the Crown and Anchor on the Strand, had been the question of premises. Various possibilities were considered, including the offer by the Duke of Montagu of a twenty-year lease, at £400 per annum, on Montagu House. This offer was not taken up and the rambling late-seventeenth-century building was eventually taken over as the first home of the British Museum. The Governors had their hearts set on commissioning a purpose-designed hospital that provided exactly the accommodation needed for its very specific function and which would be set among greenery and in fresh air on the edge of the city. The site of the rejected Montagu House had in fact been ideal – located on the north side of Great Russell Street in Bloomsbury, its garden ran into open countryside – and so the Governors searched for land on the north-west edge of central London.

A committee meeting of 17 October 1740 discussed a recommendation to purchase two fields at the northern end of Lamb's Conduit Street – a major thoroughfare running north from Holborn and Theobalds Road. The landowner was the Earl of Salisbury, who drove a hard bargain, demanding

£500 more than the £6,500 the hospital was prepared to offer. But all was amicably settled when the Governors agreed to purchase 56 acres for the asking price of £7,000, with the earl himself making a £500 'contribution' to the purchase of his own land. Honour was satisfied on both sides.

Several architects were then asked to prepare designs for the hospital, with those drawn up by amateur architect and City merchant Theodore Jacobsen – who most attractively declared his intention to waive a fee – being approved on 20 June 1742. Jacobsen had some experience in the design of institutional buildings – notably premises for the East India Company in the City – and worked in a spare classical style that was at once economical, visually simple and physically robust. This was a winning combination that struck just the right note for the hospital, which wanted its building to be solid, solemn and dignified without being showy and apparently the recipient of vast sums that might otherwise have gone directly towards the maintenance and education of 'young children'. Jacobsen achieved dignity and solidity on the cheap by using brick throughout rather than large quantities of expensive stone and, instead of trying to make an impact by utilising such showy details as giant columns, relied for visual effect on beautifully crafted brick details, strong geometrical composition and generous proportions.

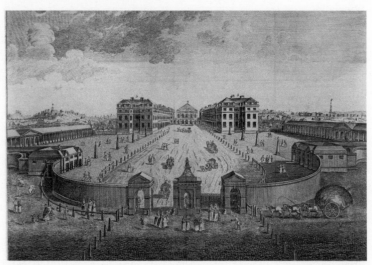

The Foundling Hospital, looking north, when completed in the early 1750s.

The hospital, when finally completed in 1752, was in many ways a modest masterpiece of mid-Georgian institutional architecture. Its layout was based on the well-established collegiate form favoured earlier by almshouses, medical hospitals such as Guy's and other comparable structures. The public and state portions of the building – notably its chapel – occupied a central block, framed and flanked by wings dedicated to more humdrum areas such as residential wards and that advanced forward to define an entrance court. Visual variety was lent to a potentially repetitive and barracks-like composition by the most minimal of means, with walls breaking forward to suggest corner pavilions and bold details – such as arcades, semi-circular windows and simple brick pediments – being used to give grandeur, emphasis and interest.

But perhaps most importantly the hospital was fully detached, set in a park-like garden defined by walls and low colonnaded utilitarian structures, and thus removed from the nearby terraces of smoke-belching houses. In its splendid isolation the new Founding Hospital made its mark as a significant public building while also enjoying fresh country air, unrestricted light, and fine prospects across the open countryside to the north and west. This, the Governors rightly believed, was the environment essential to help safeguard the health of the hospital's infant population as well as the right sort of architecture to proclaim the dignity and serious intent of the institution.

Another advantage of Jacobsen's design was that its construction was easy to phase, allowing the complex to be completed gradually as money became available. The foundation stone was laid on 16 September 1742, with the west residential wing being completed first and inhabited in October 1745; after that the chapel range was built, and then in 1749 the east wing was started. But by the time construction started, Thomas Coram's involvement in the affair of the hospital that bore his name was at an end. In 1742, when the location and design of the Foundling's new building were being agreed, something extraordinary happened that has never been fully explained. Thomas Coram and the governing body of the institution he had founded became speedily and dramatically estranged.

The root of the separation may have lain in Coram's disagreement with the manner in which babies were selected for admission, but the surviving evidence suggests that, even if this were the case, there were other issues as well. Probably the rift stemmed from a variety of disagreements, reflecting the unresolved and potentially conflicting nature of the Foundling's aims and fundamental differences of opinion over the way in which the institution was being managed. Certainly the row soon became intensely personal and bitter. Its nature and intensity tend to confirm the essentially dysfunctional, almost fanatical, nature of the organisation in its early years.

Coram's disagreements with a number of his fellow Governors started during 1741 and reached crisis point in October when damaging rumours of irregularities within the hospital were circulated. If left unchallenged these rumours threatened to harm the institution's fund-raising and very future and so a sub-committee was speedily appointed to investigate. It focused on stories, spread by nurses, about two members of the hospital's committee and suggestions that the head nurse was immodest, dishonest and drunken. After due investigation the sub-committee deemed these rumours to be 'untrue and malicious' and, to express its deep displeasure, decided to apportion blame in a most public manner by stating its belief that 'Mr Thomas Coram, one of the Governors of the Hospital, had been principally concerned in promoting and spreading the same aspersions'.[18] Coram and his colleague Dr Nesbitt, also associated with the circulation of the rumours, 'were not censured, but evidently came under the severe displeasure of their colleagues, and their positions probably became untenable'.[19] The nurse, despite her official clearance, was discharged the following month – suggesting that not all the rumours were entirely unfounded – while Coram's official connection with his great creation came to a sudden and spectacular end.

He was seventy-three, famed as a great philanthropist with his recently painted portrait by Hogarth just hung in the hospital . . . but he was out. It seems that, for whatever reason, he had become involved in a nasty struggle for power and influence in the hospital that was suddenly a grand, high-profile and fashionable establishment, and he, essentially a home-spun and humble sea captain, had lost.

The precise details of the rumours, the investigation and Coram's role are now unknown because the facts were, according to R. H. Nichols and F. A. Wray's 1935 *History of the Foundling Hospital*, 'contained in a sealed dossier which disappeared in about the middle of the last century'.[20] Coram attended a committee meeting on 5 May 1742, but it was his last. Later in the month he failed to be re-elected to the General Committee of Management. Rather sadly, in his last vote as a committee member he was against the otherwise unanimous resolution approving the purchase of 400,000 bricks for the construction of the new building. Evidently his disenchantment with the project was by now so great he didn't actually want to see the hospital built.

But Coram – disappointed, disillusioned, powerless and increasingly impoverished (a distress from which the hospital would eventually and generously help to rescue him) – could do nothing now but watch his creation rise from the fields; and as it did so its Governors become embroiled in a moral maze of controversy and uncertainty that led – some years after Coram's death in 1751 – to near-terminal catastrophe. The completion of the building provoked admiration but also the sort of observations and criticism that Coram had done his best to deflect by implying that the hospital was primarily for the children of duped and deluded unmarried mothers rather than for those of professional harlots.

For example, in 1752 there appeared a sardonic satire entitled *A Particular but Melancholy Account of the Great Hardships, Difficulties and Miseries, that those Unhappy and Much-to-be-pitied Creatures, the Common Women of the Town, are Plung'd into at this Juncture*, written by John Campbell under the name of M. Ludovicus.

Campbell observed in his mischievous pamphlet:

There has been within these few Years, so many fine Structures built for the Reception of the distressed . . . witness the most excellent, well-endow'd, and well-designed Structure for the Encouragement of Whoring, to wit, the Foundling Hospital, where many a fine Merry-begotten is well provided for [where] sometimes their Pappas and Mammas come incog. in their Chariots to visit the Product of their dark (but sweet) Performances; stolen Waters are sweet, and Bread eaten in secret is pleasant; I think it would not be amiss to build a gay House for the Reception of all the poor Mothers, Sisters and Aunts of these hopeful children . . . for their Support, seeing . . . such fertile trees . . . have produced such excellent Fruit for the Benefit of the Nation.[21]

This notion of the Foundling as a convenient refuge for the illegitimate children of high courtesans and their gentlemen clients was precisely what Coram had been anxious to avoid lest it should discourage donations, but this was too tempting and titillating an issue to be overlooked. In the same year, the 23 June issue of Henry Fielding's *Covent Garden Journal* (No. 50) carried a letter, signed Humphry Meanwell, that questioned the purpose and organisation of the hospital and concluded by asking Fielding, [O]f what Service is an Hospital for Foundlings on this Supposition; are none but the Bastards of our Great-ones to have the Benefit of it?'[22]

It is now impossible to say how widespread such observations were, how seriously people believed the hospital was little more than a repository for harlots' offspring, and whether such gossip or suspicions undermined fund-raising. What is certain is that such negative observations were accompanied, and presumably balanced, by the sort of promotional sentiment included in a popular print of the hospital published in April 1749 by Grignion & Rooker. This shows women arriving with babies and instructs the viewer to:

> See where the Pious Guardians publick care
> Protects the Babes and calms the Mothers Fear
> Inspired by Bounty, raises blest Retreats
> Which . . . Charity compleats.

It is also clear that the hospital, presiding in its large new building, was finding it hard to raise the sums of money needed to fulfil its mission. Fund-raising events helped, such as a charity performance organised by Handel in 1749 when over 1,000 people paid half a guinea each to hear a performance of 'the Fire Work music and Anthem of the Peace, oratorio of Solomon and several pieces composed for the occasion'. Such was the success of the event that every year until his death in 1759 Handel supervised a performance of the *Messiah* in the chapel, earning the hospital around £7,000 in total. But still it was not enough. The Governors needed far more money to run the hospital and expand its operations than promised by their income, donations and fund-raising if the ambitious founding aim of receiving, educating and apprenticing out all eligible 'young children' was to be achieved.

They were getting increasingly desperate, even considering granting building leases for the development of the hospital's land. Its buildings and surrounding gardens occupied twenty acres, leaving thirty-six available for construction, but the early 1750s was not a good time for speculative building since markets were depressed by political and economic uncertainty caused by the deeply unsettling Stuart rebellion of 1745 and the imminence of war with France. So no serious development proposals were drawn up, which was probably just as well. Such a scheme could have split the Foundling's governing body, with many Governors no doubt opposing a move that would have done much to rob the hospital of the healthy pleasures of its bucolic location.

Instead the Governors decided to petition Government for financial aid. In April 1756 the House of Commons agreed to 'provide the hospital with liberal grants of money', starting with £10,000, providing it consented to accept all eligible 'exposed and deserted young children' from all over the country at ages settled upon by the Governors and the Government. This open admission policy superficially suited the hospital's general aim to help all abandoned and unwanted babes, but as events quickly revealed, neither Governors nor Government had given any deep thought to the full implications of transforming the Foundling into a nationwide and semi-public institution, almost at the drop of a hat, with little long-term planning or provision.

Despite good intentions all around, things quickly went wrong for, as Jonas Hanway wrote sadly in 1759, 'every hour gives proof of the fallacy of human wisdom'.[23] An advertisement announced the start of the open admission scheme at 6 a.m. on 2 June 1756 when a basket was hung at the hospital gate on Guilford Street. Now all children not exceeding two months old would be received, with the depositor needing to do no more than place the baby in the basket, ring for the porter and make off. At a stroke, the hospital had abandoned its carefully constructed and painfully sustained argument that it was not primarily a refuge for harlots' babies – and so an encouragement to vice – but for those of modest but duped wenches. It also abandoned its policy of accepting only healthy children.

Instantly the floodgates opened. Within the first twenty-four hours the Foundling was floundering. As Hanway recalled, 'I well remember the transaction of the first general taking-in-day, the 2d June, when we received 117 children. This whole month produced 425, all of them supposed not to be above two months old . . .'[24] What happened to deposited babies who were obviously over two months old has never fully been explained.

The Foundling was simply not prepared for such numbers, nor was it prepared for the strange and dark forces it had unleashed. Hanway explained, 'Nobody conceived it would become a traffic to bring children . . . nor did we dream that parish officers in the country would act so unlike men, as to force a child from a woman's breast'.[25] What happened, with extraordinary speed, was the development of a trade in children in which impoverished parents in distant parts of the land paid carriers to take their unwanted children to the Foundling. Many babies failed to arrive at all if the carrier chose to avoid the trouble of the journey by simply murdering or abandoning their helpless charge. And even when children did complete the journey, many arrived in states of terminal decline. To add to this horror, parish officers around the country quickly realised they could get destitute orphans or the children of poor parents off their hands by delivering them to the Foundling so that the Government rather than the parish should pay for their upkeep. Some officers, as Hanway recorded, even virtually abducted and dispatched the children of helpless poor women so that they would not be a future charge on the parish.

The consequences of this combination of unfortunate circumstances were appalling. In the first year of indiscriminate admission the number of babies received of two months' age or less was a staggering 3,296, many of them squeezed into a building designed to house only around 600, of varied ages, in its series of wards.[26] In the second year 4,085 infants were admitted, and in the third 4,229.[27] Various rural outstations had been established but, as the mid-nineteenth-century historian John Brownlow observed, the Foundling now embraced a 'system void of all order and discretion' and 'instead of being a protection to the living, the institution became . . . a charnel-house for the dead!'[28] Between 2 June and the end of December 1756 1,783 children were admitted, all supposedly under two months old and, as Nichols and Wray observed in 1935, 'it is difficult to comprehend how they were dealt with at all by the small staff available'.[29] Also a great number were received in states of neglect and ill health that made their death almost inevitable.

The hospital's Billet Books from this time of unrestricted admission are unlike the earlier volumes because, with dramatic directness, they reflect the desperate haste of the moment. On standard forms information about babies received is reduced to the minimum, with no mention of age, just sex, and no requirement to leave a token. But to judge from elsewhere in the Billet Books, and from collections of papers in the London Metropolitan Archives, those depositing babies still often pinned upon them scraps of paper informing the hospital of the child's name, parish or place of origin, and whether it had been baptised or not. These scraps were duly noted in the Billet Book and carefully pinned to the form recording the baby's details. And occasionally tokens were left. Some of the papers deposited with the babies contained explanations, enigmatic descriptions, even poems. For example, baby number 5312, admitted on 2 August 1757, carried with it the verse:

> Here I am brought without a name
> Im' sent to hide my mother's shame,
> I hope youll say, Im' not to Blame,
> Itt seems my mothers's twenty five,
> And mattrymonys Laid a side . . .[30]

The note with baby 8575 admitted on 17 May 1758 states plainly that 'This child is the son of a Gentleman & a Young Lady of fashion',[31] which was as near as it was decent to get to an admission that the infant was the result of prostitution.

The Billet Book covering admissions in October 1756[32] includes with the entry for child 2584 a token described as 'silk with Fringe and paper'. It's a beautiful fragment of what appears to be Spitalfields silk, presumably part of a fine dress worn by the mother. The piece of folded paper to which the silk is pinned is now too delicate to open easily, but glimpsed inside can be seen the word '. . . Square'. The form to which the token is attached states 'Female, Hanover Square not christened'. So it seems the mother not only could afford to wear an expensive silk dress but came from a most superior parish. Who – and what – could she have been?

The anguish of some of the mothers is captured in a bundle of letters that survive from this period when babies were deposited anonymously into the hands of unknown strangers – via basket and bell – with no ritual of farewell. One letter dated 28 July 1758, and presumably left in the basket with the baby, reads:

> I am sorry that necessity obliges me to part with my child as ye Father
> is abroad but hope that when he returns it will be in my power one day
> to make you satisfaction . . . the child is half baptized its name is Mary,
> was born July 26 1758 at ye Parish of St Andrews, Pray God bless and
> preserve it for some good purpose to ye Glory of its maker, Amen.

Another scrap of now crumbling paper, with two fragments of printed cotton pinned to it, merely pleads, 'Please take care of this child – it will

An exact Representation of the Form and Manner in which EXPOSED and DESERTED Young Children are Admitted into the FOUNDLING HOSPITAL.

To his most Sacred Majesty KING GEORGE the Second, in whose Auspicious Reign This Ever Memorable Charity first began, The Royal Family, The Most Noble, Rt. Honourable, and Worshipful Governors of the said HOSPITAL. This PLATE is most humbly Dedicated by his M. YESTY's Dutiful Obedient Subject and Servant

Children being received into the hospital in 1749 by the system of ballot. Mothers who selected a white ball had their 'petition' chosen for examination. Those who selected black balls were immediately rejected.

be called ...' and then decay obscures the rest, but overleaf is more information: '... about 17th July 1756, Eliz. James ... with a white & gold Ribbon round the Waste ...' The content of this short, incomplete but unspeakably poignant message, combined with the decay of the paper on which it is written and the faded but once gay and colourful cotton, is heartbreaking. It lends immediacy to a distant tragedy and is a vivid reminder of the agony that took place on a daily basis at the gates of the Foundling as despairing mothers gave their babies away.[33]

The shocking events that were unfolding at the hospital with alarming speed did not stop this ghastly experiment in its tracks. Instead things grew worse as the Governors tried to find a way out of the nightmare that had suddenly engulfed them by asking the Government for more money. As early as December 1756 they pleaded for an increase in their grant, but extra cash came at a price. More money was only justified, argued the Government, if more children were eligible for admission, so the age of entry was extended to six months or less. It was a vicious circle in which the solution to one problem created another. The whole place was overtaken by chaos.

Hanway records that in the 18 months from 2 June 1756 to the end of December 1757, 5,618 children were received into the hospital of whom 2,311, or 41 per cent, died. During 1757 yet more money had been needed from the Government and so yet again the age of admission was extended with, after June 1757, all children of twelve months of age or less being eligible. And so the terrible system lurched on until late 1759 by which time 14,934 children had been received in 46 months of unrestricted admission, meaning that nearly 100 children were admitted a week – which until June 1756 had been the total number of annual admissions![34] Of the 14,934 children admitted 'only 4,400 lived to be apprenticed out,' according to Brownlow, 'being a mortality of more than seventy per cent!'[35] 'Thus was the institution,' he concluded, 'conducted on a plan so wild and chimerical, and so widely differing from its original design, found to be diseased in its very vitals', with the system 'contemplated by its Founder . . . set aside by a system of fraud and abuse, which entailed on the public an immense annual expenditure, to establish a market for vice to carry on her profligate trade without let or hindrance', and which permitted 'designing persons' to 'dispose of children entrusted to their guardianship [without] discovery of their guilty acts'.[36]

Nichols and Wray's more restrained official history of the hospital cannot but, in essence, agree. They calculate the slightly higher survival rate of 4,545[37] but admit that 'the place took on more the appearance of a mortuary than a sanctuary . . . with a mortality of over 70 per cent in a period under four years'.[38]

Brownlow, Nichols and Wray were writing with the benefit of hindsight but even by early 1759 it had become clear to many that the events taking place at the Foundling were starting to assume the dimensions of a national scandal. The committee struggled to find solutions and to understand exactly what was happening. On 21 February 1759 it received a report that of the 210 children admitted during the previous week, 65 had died. A further 93 were to die the following week, making a total of 158 or nearly 75 per cent. In the week ending 3 March 1759, 211 children were received and 183 died.[39] Clearly the hospital and the scheme it was operating were fatally out of control and a serious danger to children.

In May 1759 the Government observed that the 'evil consequences' of 'conveying the Children from the country to the Hospital . . . ought to be prevented' and rescinded its general resolution of 1756, which meant that the whole arrangement was reconsidered. In December 1759 it asked the hospital for information on the number of children admitted between 31 December 1758 and the end of September 1759 and how many of them had subsequently died. The hospital duly reported that during the period in question the total number of children on its books was 6,223, including 1,469 children recently admitted, and that 2,264 had died.[40] So, by one analysis, more children were dying in the hospital over a given period than were actually being admitted. As Nicholas and Wray observe, 'it became obvious that it was impossible to continue the system of indiscriminate admission', because it not only 'lent itself to many forms of abuse' and was partly the cause of the shockingly high death rate among the hospital's young inmates but also 'public opinion turned against it', since it was now generally believed 'that the unlimited facilities provided for disposing of illegitimate children were encouraging prostitution'.[41]

By late 1759 the Foundling Hospital was discredited, seen not only as grossly incompetent but also, in the persons of some of its staff and Guardians, as possibly corrupt. In February 1760 the Government ruled that the general admission of children must cease, and terminated its relationship with the hospital. By that time the Government had spent the huge sum of £500,000 of public money on what had amounted to a massacre of the innocents. There were 6,293 children on the hospital's books when the resolution was passed – many housed in outstations in Shrewsbury, Aylesbury and Yorkshire – of whom the majority were under five years of age. Since each one cost about £6 a year to maintain, the hospital was plunged back into financial crisis.[42]

Although the Government terminated its ongoing relationship with the hospital it continued to pay out sums to maintain the children taken on during the 46 months of madness. These fluctuated and decreased as children eligible for Government aid died or were gradually apprenticed out of the hospital, with the last payment made in May 1771 when the Government declared that 'no further sum or sums of money be hereafter issued for the Maintenance and Education of such children as were received into the said Hospital on or before the said 25th March 1760'. By this time the Government had over the course of sixteen years paid the hospital £549,796.[43]

At the same time as the Government withdrew its support, public donations dwindled when the full extent of the chaos at the hospital became known. The Foundling was now desperately worried about its funds and most anxious to regain its former reputation and level of public support. But its cause was not helped by the decision it had made on 30 June 1756 – when first rattled by the unexpectedly large number of children delivered to its doors and the escalating costs – that any child 'brought to the Hospital ... exceeding the Age of two Months and ... under the Age of two Years' who was accompanied by 'a Sum of one hundred Pounds, or upwards, be sent therewith, to satisfy the Charge of the Maintenance and Education thereof', would be received.[44] In addition it had been made clear that no questions would be asked of those who delivered the cash and the over-age infant, not even their names.[45]

Through this decision the Governors had surrendered the moral high ground by appearing to express an admission policy diametrically opposed to that envisaged by Coram. Idealistically, he had proposed an asylum open to all eligible children, particularly the poor, abandoned and unwanted. Now it was really just a question of money, with the hospital's age restriction waived for those rich enough to pay a fee of £100. The possible abuses and embarrassments inherent in this financially driven policy were many and obvious, including the fact that it immediately removed credence from any defence that the Foundling might offer to those who accused it of being a resort of convenience for wealthy courtesans, no more than an off-shoot of London's highly efficient and profitable sex industry.

This view appears to be borne out by the record of a chilling little transaction that survives in the London Metropolitan Archives. It is a bond of agreement dated 8 October 1760 between a lawyer in Chancery Lane – acting for the anonymous parents – and the 'Corporation of the Governors and Guardians of the Hospital', which promises to pay them the sum of £100 'with interest at five per cent per annum' providing they admit a 'Child aged about six weeks which will be handed to them'.[46] The child is obviously viewed as little more than a money-making commodity by the hospital. Despite the horribly compromising and shameful nature of this policy it remained in place until January 1801, a startling reminder of the hospital's desperate financial worries during the decades after 1760.

The ignominy that had befallen the Foundling Hospital and its unsuccessful policies of admission led to much soul-searching and public debate. The institution's very future was in serious jeopardy. The anonymous author of a pamphlet published in 1760 entitled *The Tendencies of the Foundling Hospital in its Present Extent Considered, in Several Letters to a Senator* raised the deeply awkward question that was then, more than ever, in the minds of many: has the Foundling Hospital 'in the present Extended Plan of it . . . not a Tendency to incourage and to promote the Sin of concubinage, and of General Inordinate Carnality of Manners', and was it not 'a legal licentious Asylum for every Bastard (of every Whore, and of every Whoremonger, under the Name of a Foundling, even where, not One of them All is a Foundling'? The author also questioned the moral wisdom of the hospital's policy 'to conceal and protect from Public Infamy those who ought rather to be exposed to it'.[47]

Another pamphlet, published in 1761 and entitled *Some Objections to the Foundling-Hospital Considered, by a Person in the Country to Whom They were Sent*, took a more positive view. It pondered the proposition that the hospital was 'an encouragement to vice and immorality, by making an easy provision for illegitimate children; and taking away, by concealment, shame, which is the due portion of vice', and concluded that while the hospital might help conceal 'lewdness', it also 'prevents those infinitely more to be dreaded consequences, of seeking to conceal it by destroying children before they come into the world, or immediately after their birth', resulting in the 'unnatural mother' suffering an 'ignominious death' or, if pardoned, passing 'her days neglected, despised, and too likely to become thence a common prostitute'.[48]

This pamphlet also raised an issue that after 1759 was to be honed into the cornerstone of the hospital's defence. The author recalls that, when he first heard of the 'erection of a Foundling-Hospital', he 'could not but consider [it] as likely to be of eminent service to the community' since he was aware 'that in one parish in London there were but two or three children alive at the end of the year, in which two hundred had been placed with parish nurses'. The horrendous death rate in parish workhouses was to become the justification for the hospital's actions and its continuing existence; whatever the hospital had done wrong, its apologists argued, the parish authorities had done worse, over a far longer period of time.

As early as May 1758, when the hospital was in despair about the death-rate of its babies, it sought to place this tragedy in context by comparing its losses with those of parish workhouses. A sub-committee investigated and recorded in its minutes of 27 February 1758 the death-rate among infants in workhouses in the area covered by London's Bills of Mortality from 1728–57: of 468,081 babies christened, 273,930 died under the age of two, that is, 587 out of every 1,000 born. The committee managed to present its own figures to suggest that 'our loss from Lady-Day 1741 to the 31st December 1757 will be 406 out of each 1,000'.[49]

This theme was developed in meticulous manner in 1759 by Hospital Governor Jonas Hanway in his *Candid Historical Account of the Hospital for the Reception of Exposed and Deserted Young Children*. In this book, written in the darkest moment of the hospital's existence, Hanway took the position that it should acknowledge its mistakes, argued that it could learn from them, and urged the reader 'not to conclude that we cannot reform the evil' without also destroying what was good about the hospital. In other words he warned they should not, in a moment of desperation, throw the baby out with the bathwater.[50] He analysed the hospital's policies or 'plan' and admitted there was a serious need for reform. For example, he took issue with the policy of secrecy as a means of protecting mothers from 'shame': 'Those plead for secrecy who believe it is for the service of the commonwealth' if the 'amours in high life or in low' are 'concealed from the world'. But 'it should be remembered that the fewer secrets a man has . . . probably the more innocent his life'. Secrecy may save the parents from shame, argued Hanway, but 'the most certain way to prevent the effects of shame is to remove the temptation to the offence which created it', and if secrecy and the 'concealment of amours' is intended for the benefit of the child, 'to provide a foundling hospital for such a purpose . . . seems to be ridiculous, in such a nation as this'.[51]

But the main thrust of Hanway's publication was to put the disaster that had overtaken the Foundling in the best possible light, and to do this he exploited the poor reputation of the parish workhouses, laboriously compiling statistics to 'prove' that the hospital was a far safer refuge for the young.

The fact that the child mortality rate of the Foundling Hospital during the darkest days of the late 1750s was no worse than that of the average workhouse was, however, no real defence. The Foundling Hospital had, at one level, been founded to put an end to such appalling death-rates among the young, not to match and continue them. In the event the Foundling Hospital survived the storm – but only just. Severely compromised, its loss of Government grants and much public financial support meant that it had to adopt a regime of strict economy and limit the number of infants it accepted, to the point where it hardly played any significant role at all in the struggle to save destitute children. Between March 1760 and February 1767 only 116 children were admitted because much of its time and limited resources were now spent dealing with the large number that had been admitted during the 46 months after June 1756.[52] By 1766 the hospital still had 4,300 children on its hands. It was not until 1768, after many children had been apprenticed out, that the number was reduced to below 1,000.[53]

In January 1767 the hospital took stock of its current situation and its troubled past, and surveyed the numbers and fate of the children admitted since its inception. It confirmed that it had received 1,394 children before the 'General Reception' that started on 2 June 1756, of whom in 1767 it knew 889 to be dead. It had received 14,934 during the 'General Reception', of whom 10,204 were dead (around 350 less than Brownlow calculated 90 years later), and 193 after the 'General Reception', of whom 56 were dead. According to these figures 63.5 per cent of those admitted before the period of 'General Reception' died, while 68.3 per cent of those admitted during the period of 'General Reception' had died. These statistics, considered fairly accurate, make nonsense of the optimistic statistic devised by Hanway in 1759 when he attempted to imply that the hospital's death-rate during the troubled period of the 'General Reception' was 'only' 41–5 per cent.

A profile of the hospital's activities in the two decades after 1760, when it was accepting very few children and generally attempting to pull itself together, is offered by twenty-five volumes of books that survive from 1768–1800 containing petitions made by mothers offering their children to the hospital.[54] The volumes covering the decade between 1768 and 1779 have been analysed by Randolph Trumbach and some most revealing statistics emerge: they refer to 919 women, of whom 780 were 'Spinsters',

72 were 'Wives' and 21 'Widows' (with the remaining few categorised as 'others'). Of the 'Spinsters' offering children, most (751) did not declare their age, but of the 29 who did, 17 were between the ages of eighteen and twenty-three, which, points out Trumbach, was 'exactly the age of most of the women who walked the streets as prostitutes'.[55]

So it seems that the hospital remained something of a refuge for the children of young harlots although the mothers' 'petitions', in which they plead with the Governors to accept their children, never of course reveal whether a mother is also a prostitute. Instead, when explanations for pregnancy are offered, the petitioners generally fall back on the standard formulae – many no doubt true – of being seduced and deluded (often 'under promise of marriage') by fellow servants and absconded lovers, or else abandoned by husbands.

Reading these short letters, many written on behalf of the petitioners, remains an intensely moving experience. Bound into handsome eighteenth-century volumes, these 'petitions' open windows into a sad and desolate world in which mothers – most dogged by illness and poverty – consigned their offspring to the mercy and charity of strangers. For example, on 1 July 1772 Jane Brown explained in her petition that she was in 'very low circumstances', wanted every 'common necessity' and would 'inevitably perish unless your Honours will be pleased to have my female Child, which is about 4 Months, under your Care, which will be a means of preserving us both from misery'. The petition is endorsed on the back: 'To be admitted to be balloted for' and, in red ink, 'Dead, Aug 1st, 1772'. Whether this refers to Jane or her daughter is not made clear.

In early September 1777 Mary Eade explained that she had been 'seduced by fair promises which have brought me into very low circumstances as I have done all that is in my power to hide this my misfortune from the World' but had seen 'an advertisement' that 'yr Honours would take in twenty Children on the 5th September next . . . and having no other prospect but be worse every day makes your Humble petitioner apply to your Honours in Hopes you will Consider my case so far as to believe me by taking my Child'.

Sarah Roper on 8 July 1772 stated that she had 'been seduced by her Fellow Servant who Promised me marriage' but 'as soon as I . . . related my unexpressible Troubles to him he Immediately after absconded which has caused your Petitioner to be Brought to Entire Distruction'.[56]

Some of the petitions possess a particularly moving directness and simplicity. On 20 August 1776 Mary Smith of 'Spittal Fields', herself formerly a nurse in the hospital, addressed the Governors: 'Gentlemen, It is with greatest Contrition for my past Folly that I humbly beg leave to implore your Protection for my poor helpless Infant who I fear will shortly be intirely destitute of the most common Necessities of life, its Father having gone to Sea & left me without any means for providing for its Subsistence.' Receive 'it into your Hospital', she pleaded, 'save it from misery'.[57]

Mary Eade, Sarah Roper and Mary Smith were all regarded as 'real objects of charity' and their babies were 'admitted for ballot', but not all children were. In August 1773 Margaret Williams told the Governors that she had 'a Son who is in his apprenticeship and has the misfortune to have a Child laid to his charge witch I have supported from Birth . . . Witch has Entirely reduced Me as the Mother of the Child is gone away.' Her petition was 'rejected as the case is not an object of charity'.[58]

Despite the hospital's slow steps forward the ghosts would not be laid. In the mid-1780s it once again considered the prospect of creating revenue by leasing some of its land to speculative house builders, which prompted another unfavourable response from the public. John Holliday, the author of a pamphlet that appeared in 1787 entitled *An Appeal to the Governors of the Foundling Hospital, on the Probable Consequences of Covering the Hospital Lands with Buildings*,[59] did not hesitate to reinforce his arguments against the speculative development of the hospital's fields by raking up the unpleasant past. He suggested that their 'experiment' with open admission was responsible for unleashing a 'torrent of humanity' that 'broke down the barriers of virtue and morality' and 'introduced licentiousness among the lower orders of society'. The result was the weakening of 'the force of the first passion of nature, the attachment of a parent to her offspring' and 'out of 14,934 children received from the 1st June 1756 to Ladyday 1760 more than 11,000 died'.[60] Having reminded the hospital of its terrible errors of the past, the author could only hope that the current Governors would not make another serious mistake and 'lose sight of the probable consequences . . . to their health and strength . . . of confining three hundred children within the walls of an hospital surrounded with buildings'.[61]

The hospital did not let its land for building in the 1780s but it did in

the 1790s when its surveyor S. P. Cockerell devised an ingenious development plan for its estate that largely reconciled the institution's need for
fresh air and light with its need for money. Cockerell came up with the
admirable compromise of placing large, well-planted squares on the west
and east sides of the hospital so that it could continue to enjoy leafy open
prospects even as terraces of houses rose around it through the late 1790s
and into the first decades of the nineteenth century.

During this period, when its finances were starting to improve, the
hospital still struggled to formulate an admission policy that was both
morally and ethically correct and not open to abuse or liable to load the
institution with calumny and debt. After January 1801, when the decision
was taken to abandon the dubious policy of accepting any over-age child
on payment of £100, the hospital gradually reformed the manner in which
children were admitted. During the early decades of the nineteenth century
it evolved a policy that each application for admission be decided on its
merits following an interview with an 'Enquirer', but with certain conditions required: for example, that the child be under the age of twelve
months, illegitimate or the child of a soldier or sailor killed in service of
the country or with a father that 'shall have deserted the child and not
be forthcoming or cannot be compelled to maintain the child'. It was also
preferable if the 'petitioner' was poor and without relations willing or able
to support the child, and the hospital was most unwilling to accept any
child born in a workhouse since it was therefore the parish's responsibility to maintain it. But most important seems to have been the institution's determination finally to rid itself of the bad reputation it had
gained during the period of 'General Reception', when it was assumed to
be – and no doubt was – a general repository for the offspring of harlots,
and so, in the eyes of many, an open encouragement to vice.

Now the Governors – referring back to Coram's initial vision – strove
to rule out the prospect of serial recourse by harlots, insisting that a
successful 'petitioner shall have borne a good character previous to her
misfortune or delivery . . . that her delivery and shame are known to few
persons', and that 'in the event of the child being received, the petitioner
has a prospect of preserving her station in society, and obtaining by her
own exertions an honest livelihood'.[62] If all these conditions were adhered
to and all 'petitioners' thoroughly investigated, then harlots would almost
certainly have been excluded from depositing their children in the Foundling.

So, in this atmosphere of extreme caution, the hospital's fortunes revived and it entered the nineteenth century with a more considered system of selection and on a more secure financial footing. It had also, stung by earlier accusations of social irresponsibility, cast itself firmly in the role of moral campaigner – or at least guardian – against vice. Although this newly defined role looked back to some of the principles of the hospital's founder it also anticipated the judgemental and rule-bound morality of the coming Victorian age.

THE MAGDALEN HOUSE

The edition of the *Rambler* published on 26 March 1751 carried a letter in which a correspondent, who signed themselves 'Amicus', described their sensations when coming upon the nearly completed buildings of the Foundling Hospital:

> As I wandered wrapped up in thought my eyes were struck with the
> Hospital for the Reception of deserted Infants, which I surveyed with
> Pleasure, till by a natural Train of Sentiment, I began to reflect on the
> Fate of the Mothers; for to what Shelter can they fly? Only to the Arms
> of their Betrayer, which perhaps are now no longer open to receive
> them; and then how quick must be the Transition from deluded Virtue
> to shameless Guilt, and from shameless Guilt to hopeless Wretchedness.

Amicus' 'train of sentiment' was quick to connect 'the Mothers' of the infants lodged in the hospital with prostitution, for if these unmarried women were not prostitutes when they became pregnant, their subsequent 'deluded Virtue', 'shameless guilt' and 'hopeless Wretchedness' would almost certainly drive them to prostitution. This thought filled Amicus with compassion and, apparently, a strong desire to write to the editor of the *Rambler*, who, of course, was the renowned Dr Samuel Johnson.

> The Anguish that I felt left me no Rest till I had, by your Means,
> addressed myself to the Publick on Behalf of those forlorn Creatures,
> the Women of the Town; whose Misery here might surely induce us to
> endeavour, at least their Preservation from eternal Punishment.

Amicus then put prostitutes in perspective and, in a sense, justified and forgave – or at least explained – their downfall:

> These were all once, if not virtuous at least innocent, and might have continued blameless and easy, but for the Arts and Insinuations of those whose Rank, Fortune, or Education furnished them with Means to corrupt or to delude them ... It cannot be doubted but that Numbers follow this dreadful Course of Life, with Shame, Horror, and Regret, but, where can they hope for Refuge? ... Their Sighs, and Tears, and Groans, are criminal in the Eye of their Tyrants, the Bully and the Bawd, who fatten on their misery, and threaten them with Want and Gaol, if they shew the least Design of escaping from Bondage ... There are Places, indeed, set apart, to which these unhappy Creatures may resort when the Diseases of Incontinence seize upon them; but, if they obtain a Cure, to what are they reduced? Either to return with their small Remains of Beauty to their former Guilt, or perish in the Streets with complicated Want.

In an attempt to unburden prostitutes of the crushing sense of guilt and shame that, it was imagined, drove them to debauchery and to identify those who were the real cause of their woes, he asked:

> ... how frequently have the Gay and Thoughtless in their evening Frolicks, seen a band of these miserable Females, covered with Rags, shivering with Cold, and pining with Hunger; and without either pitying their Calamities, or reflecting upon the Cruelty of those whom perhaps, first reduced them by Caresses of Fondness, or Magnificence of Promise, go on to reduce others to the same wretchedness by the same Means?

Finally Amicus observed that 'to stop the Increase of the deplorable Multitude is undoubtedly the first and most pressing Consideration' and then launched a general appeal for aid: 'Nor will they long groan in their present Afflictions if all those were to contribute to their relief, that owe their Exemption from the same Distress to some other Cause, than their Wisdom and their Virtue.'

Amicus' observations were immediately reprinted in the *Gentleman's Magazine*, appearing in its March 1751 issue, which added a small post-script.[63] It wished that the *Rambler* had 'recommended some methods' to achieve the admirable purpose stated, but since it had not, the *Gentleman's*

Magazine referred any readers who wanted to know more to a recently published pamphlet entitled *The Vices of London and Westminster*.[64] The anonymous author of this pamphlet arranged his thoughts in 'Five Letters', the fourth of which contained a 'proposal for an Hospital for the Reception of Repenting Prostitutes'. He seems to have possessed the calculating mind of a City merchant. If the sex trade revealed, in a most horrid manner, that every form of commerce could turn a profit and that everything – even a female's body and her very soul – could be possessed, used and destroyed for a price – so perhaps might redemption be made to pay:

> I think it would be an Act of great Benevolence, if amongst the many noble Charities established in the Metropolis, some Foundation were made for the Support and Maintenance of repentant Prostitutes; some such place, might even become an Ornament, and of use to the Kingdom, if these Women . . . were employed in a manufacture of Dresden-work, so much now the Mode, or in some easy Labour that might . . . help them earn their Bread . . . when they had behaved decently for a Year or two in such a Retreat, the most rigidly Virtuous need not scruple giving them Countenance and employment.[65]

The debate was continued the following month – April 1751 – in the *Gentleman's Magazine* where another correspondent announced, 'I have been considering what provision could be made for penitent prostitutes, and no method seems to me so proper as a foundation upon the plan of the convents in foreign countries.' This correspondent – who signed themself *Sunderlandensis* – stressed the urgency and immensity of the problem by claiming that 'lewdness is manifestly one of the great sources of the national calamity' for it 'corrupts the morals, and ruins the constitutions of the people'. *Sunderlandensis* also warmed to the notion that penitence could be profitable – or at least pay for itself – and urged that a 'convent' for 'penitent prostitutes' must include productive employment – perhaps lace-making – that 'could benefit both them and the country as a whole'. *Sunderlandensis* widened the scope of such an institution by suggesting that it should also have a preventative purpose. It should offer refuge not only to penitent prostitutes but also to 'seduced' young women, to prevent them falling into prostitution, and each inmate should be obliged, on entry and under oath, to reveal the identity of their seducer, who would, presumably, subsequently be named and shamed.[66]

This correspondence, with the letter signed 'Amicus' perhaps the work of Samuel Johnson himself, brilliantly reflects the mid-eighteenth-century shift in attitude towards prostitution and prostitutes. England was wealthy and prided itself on its liberty, progressiveness and Christian virtues – yet it had a dark and intolerable flaw. London, one of the great trading centres of the world, included among its money-making activities a vast commerce in female flesh. The 1750s were a time of renewed moral introspection, expressed most famously in the sermons and writings of the influential Reverend Edward Cobden, notably his sermon entitled 'A Persuasive to Chastity' preached on 11 December 1748 at St James's Palace 'before' the King.

This sermon – dealing with the importance of chastity and the evils of fornication – still makes sensational reading, the words almost smouldering on the page. Cobden told his grand congregation that 'the sins of immodesty ... are risen, perhaps, to a greater height, and spread to a wider extent than was ever known in former Ages: Insomuch that the two Sexes seem to vie with each other, which shall be most forward in disregarding all Rules of Decency, and violating the Sanctions of the Marriage Contract'. He then reminded the congregation of 'those monstrous and unnatural Obscenities with which our Land hath been stained' and sustained his argument with a biblical quote: 'Whoremongers and Adulterers GOD will judge'.[67] To make clear the consequences of a failure to reform, Cobden warned darkly of 'Vengeance from Heaven' and suggested that 'the Judgements we of this Nation have lately suffered ... have ... in some Measure been owing to the Increase of the Sins of Uncleanness ... among us'.[68]

One can't help but wonder what effect all this had on George II, well known for his amours with the Countess of Suffolk and the Countess of Yarmouth, who in 1736 had borne him an illegitimate son.

This fundamentalist text, harking back to the apocalyptic Puritan preaching of the late seventeenth century, set the new agenda. Indeed so pertinent seemed Cobden's remarks, so much a reflection of the mood of the moment, that they were published approvingly by the *Gentleman's Magazine* in February 1749[69] for wider public edification. One benefit of this new moral crusade inspired by Christian values was the greater compassion, understanding and sense of forgiveness demonstrated towards the prostitute.

In the same year as Cobden preached his sermon, for example, Tobias Smollett published *The Adventures of Roderick Random*, which includes a chapter dedicated to 'The History of Miss Williams', who, the reader is told in most sympathetic manner, was well educated, but had her head filled with romantic notions, became 'a dupe to [the] deceit' of a selfish and conniving young man and 'in an evil hour crowned his eager desire with full possession'. Instead of marrying her as promised, the man absconded to London. Miss Williams pursued him, intent on a Sally Salisbury-style knife attack (see page 100), but was instead betrayed by yet another man.

Determined to practise 'their own arts upon themselves', she struck a deal with a bawd with whom it was agreed 'to divide the profits of my prostitution . . . from such gallants as she should introduce to my acquaint-ance', and made a hundred guineas from her first professional encounter, during which she 'behaved in such a manner' as to make her possessor 'perfectly well-pleased with his purchase'. Here the prostitute is seen as the victim of her liberal education and romantic imagination, turned from trust to revengeful cynicism by frightful betrayal, and ultimately a sympa-thetic figure whose sins were almost justified and certainly forgivable.[70]

The Magdalen House was to be the prime physical expression of this new enlightened attitude, but it took a while for the hard financial contri-butions to match the initial enthusiasm in 1751 for the creation of an institution for 'Repenting Prostitutes'. In fact, the issue was not aired again publicly until 22 March 1758. At a meeting of the recently founded Society for the Encouragement of Arts, Manufactures and Commerce (from 1908 the Royal Society for Arts), Jonas Hanway – even while deeply embroiled in the deadly tragedy engulfing the Foundling Hospital of which he was a Governor – launched another philanthropic project. He suggested that the Society should hold a competition, and offer a premium, for the best 'plan' or proposal for the establishment of a 'Charity House or Charity Houses for the Reception and Employment of Girls whose poverty exposes them to the Danger of becoming Prostitutes' and for 'Common Prostitutes as are inclined to forsake their Evil Course of Life, and become Virtuous and useful Members of the Community'.[71]

Evidently Hanway had been brooding over the issues raised in 1751 and believed now was the time to act. The fact that the competition should have been launched by a society intensely interested in commerce appears

The philanthropist and traveller Jonas Hanway, shown here in an etching of c.1770.

to confirm the fact that City merchants feared that London's thriving sex industry was – in some sense – the dark Satanic side of their own capitalist beliefs. A world where profit stopped literally at nothing. But if such transactions could not be prevented then at least City merchants could play their part in the battle to mitigate their evils. As pragmatic men of trade they must have believed that, if the quest for profit caused the sex trade to flourish, then money used in the right way could also solve many of its evils. Hanway was himself a City man, formerly with trade interests in St Petersburg, while many of his early supporters were merchants – indeed the whole enterprise quickly became something of a City project.

The deadline set for the submission of 'plans' was 3 May, by which time nine were duly handed in, including proposals by John Fielding – Henry Fielding's blind half-brother who became a famed magistrate based at Bow Street, Covent Garden – and the high constable of High Holborn, Saunders Welch, with that put forward by Robert Dingley (in which Hanway was openly acknowledged for his advice) ultimately chosen as winner.

Dingley was a fascinating character. He had been born in Bishopsgate in the City in 1708 and was a silk merchant with connections in St Petersburg, where Hanway had been a business associate and partner. So

Dingley was deeply rooted in the City and in commerce, but he also had powerful contacts in the arts – he was a friend of Sir Joshua Reynolds, a member from 1736 of the aristocratic and somewhat risqué Society of Dilettanti (see page 368), a fellow of the Society of Antiquaries, and from 1748 a fellow of the Royal Society and an ardent amateur architect who, of some interest in the context of the Magdalen project, had designed temples for Sir Francis Dashwood's extraordinary landscape at West Wycombe Park (see page 394).[72]

Even before winning the premium Dingley published his *Proposals for Establishing a Public Place of Reception for Penitent Prostitutes* in pamphlet form on 27 March 1758.[73] It is a well-argued document and, appearing in print so soon after the competition was announced, suggests the whole affair had been carefully stage-managed by Hanway, who had suggested the competition after he and Dingley had in fact started work on their 'plan', and who then persuaded the majority of the large judging committee – including David Garrick, Samuel Johnson and John Wilkes – to choose

Robert Dingley – the moving force behind the foundation in 1758 of the Magdalen House for 'penitent prostitutes'. Dingley holds his campaigning pamphlet on his knee.

their visionary scheme rather than the more practical proposal put forward by Welch. Presumably Hanway and Dingley had not published their 'plan' earlier because they believed that a high-profile competition organised around the notion of a hospital for 'penitent prostitutes' would create most useful publicity and help raise funds.

Dingley's pamphlet embraced many of the sentiments and ideas in the 1751 articles, suggesting that he was the author of at least one of them. It paints a familiar bleak picture of wronged beauty, trampled and tricked innocence, before asking, 'What act of Benevolence, then, can there be greater than to give these truly compassionate objects, an opportunity to reclaim and recover themselves from their otherwise lost state [and] become useful members of society?'[74] To achieve this he suggested physical, moral and spiritual education for the voluntary inmates of an asylum that, through offering them time for reflection, prayer and useful employment, would be a mechanism for 'reforming their Morals; of rescuing many bodies from Disease and Death, and . . . Souls from eternal Misery',[75] and ultimately return them to the world to lead respectable lives, not only as servants but even as wives and mothers.

On a practical level Dingley organised his 'plan' under different headings that suggested the constitution and rules of the proposed asylum: he discussed its 'Government', 'Establishment', 'Method of Admission' and 'Domestic Oeconomy', which included such topics as 'proper objects for admission', the use of personal names, the cure of disease, 'Devotion', dress and 'employment of the inmates'. On some of these subjects he went into surprising detail, suggesting that he had been mulling the project over for some time. For example, dress was to be very simple and modest – in fact, nunnish – uniform in appearance with fabrics coloured light grey, black or sky blue, and the 'Penitents' were to be housed in wards of twelve where they would sleep in separate beds without bed curtains.

Even before Dingley's proposal had been awarded the premium, he and Hanway were organising meetings to raise support and money to make it a reality. With what now seems to be astonishing speed, they rushed the project forward. Presumably the proposal caught the optimistic and charitable spirit of the moment, and reflected a general determination – in the City of London at least – to lend a helping hand to prostitutes who were truly penitent and anxious to escape their trade.

The first informal meeting of those interested in promoting Dingley's 'plan' gathered at his City home in St Helen's Place off Bishopsgate on 13 April 1758.[76] The gathering appointed a committee that included John Thornton, a director of the Russia Company and the Bank of England; Charles Dingley, Robert's younger brother, a timber merchant who opposed John Wilkes at the Brentford election, and Jonas Hanway. Its first action was for its members, mostly affluent City men, to subscribe money to help continue work.[77]

The first formal meeting was held at Batson's Coffee House on Cornhill on 19 April with additional subscribers then present, including Thomas Spencer, James Crockatt, Hugh Ross and John Barker. By now the fund stood at £3,000.[78] Among the subscribers Robert Dingley gave £50 and the rest of the committee each £30–50; Saunders Welch gave 5 guineas annually; the Duchess of Bolton – herself a former prostitute and the first Polly Peachum in *The Beggar's Opera* (see page 117), and whose husband was a Governor of the Foundling – gave 5 guineas; and 'Several Gentlemen of Wills Coffee House' – perhaps rakes salving their consciences – gave 16 guineas.[79]

By 4 May – the day after Dingley submitted his proposed 'plan' for judgement in the Society for Arts competition – the committee already had a lease agreement in hand for a building in which to house their asylum. The London Hospital had just moved into its large new purpose-designed building on Whitechapel High Street and so its former premises in Prescot Street, Whitechapel were vacant and seemed generally ideal for the new charity, as had been suggested in Dingley's 27 March *Proposal*.[80] The outline of the London Hospital's Prescott Street establishment is shown on John Rocque's 1746 London map and seems to have consisted of three or four terrace houses (each probably three windows wide), a shorter run of smaller houses on parallel Chamber Street, with between the two a fairly generous garden, incorporating a structure that could have been a chapel.

On 17 May a General Meeting was announced for the 1 June, for supporters of and subscribers to 'Mr Dingley's Plan for a Magdalen Charity House'.[81] The name chosen for the project was interesting but fraught with associations. In the popular imagination Mary Magdalene was regarded as a reformed sinner, a fallen women and former prostitute who had risen to grace again. This was clearly an appropriate association for the new charity but one that, of course, would let no one forget the nature of the place or the former occupation of its inmates. This point was made in an anonymous pamphlet entitled *A Letter to Jonas Hanway*[82] in which the author accused him of perpetuating the popular error that Mary Magdalene was a 'Harlot',[83] suggested the association between her and prostitutes was 'a great Abuse of the name of a truly honourable . . . woman', and recommended rather lamely that the institution be called 'A Charity-House for penitent Women'. This would avoid slighting both the memory of Mary Madgdalene and the inmates, whose 'fault' would be 'sufficiently indicated' by the word penitent.[84] But the ever-inventive Hanway accepted none of this and insisted that the name Magdalene had positive associations, not negative. In his *Thoughts on the Plan for A Magdalen-House* of 1758 he wrote, 'It does not appear to me that Mary Magdalen was deficient in point of chastity . . . She was a lady of distinction and of great and noble mind.'[85]

More potentially controversial than the profession associated with the choice of name was the fact that it had a decidedly Roman Catholic sound about it. In an age when Roman Catholics still lacked basic civil rights in Britain, when they could be – and occasionally were – perse-cuted, this was an odd if not downright dangerous association to make. In fact, the whole enterprise had a most peculiar and eccentric air about it: repentant prostitutes dressed in uniforms like the habits of nuns, housed in dormitories and living chaste lives organised around prayer and useful work, and all taking place in an enclosed 'convent' named after St Mary Magdalene and situated in an area that for most of the eighteenth century was notorious for the number of its bawdy-houses.

Establishing the hospital in one of the districts most prominent in the sex trade may well have had advantages, and certainly many potential penitents were to be found there, but there were also distinct disadvan-tages. Surely the committee must have realised that inmates of the Magdalen Charity House would be too near their former haunts and unredeemed friends for comfort, and that for some of the women the fact that the fleeting pleasures of their former lives – notably drink and ready cash – lay just a few yards from their refuge would prove a constant, indeed intolerable, temptation.

The peculiar character of the proposed institution did not, however, discourage support. At the General Meeting of 1 June, with the ubiquitous Jonas Hanway in the chair, a constitution was adopted and a committee of twenty-one Governors formed, now including Sir Alexander Grant, who became a great benefactor of the Magdalen and was eventually to arrange situations in Florida for many former inmates of the asylum, and Sir John Barnard, a popular former Lord Mayor of London. A Matron – Mrs Jane Pine – was appointed, Robert Dingley was named Treasurer, and Lord Hertford – a former Ambassador to France and Lord-Lieutenant of Ireland – was chosen as President. It was a post he was to hold for thirty-five years. By the end of June all the staff had been appointed, including the Rev. Jonathan Reeves as chaplain. The list of committee members – now with Saunders Welch on it – is included by Dingley in his publication, where he says they were 'chosen at the last General meeting, June 28th 1758'.[86]

On 17 July 1758 Dingley published an extended version of his pamphlet, now entitled *The Plan of the Magdalen House for the Reception of Penitent Prostitutes by Order of the Governors*, in which the detailed 'Rules and Regulations' of the institution were made clear.[87] On 10 August the committee met at the former London Hospital buildings in Prescott Street – now renamed 'the Magdalen-House' – that Dingley had acquired on a seven-and-a-half-year lease for a rent of £48 per annum. The staff were acquainted with their duties and, as the August edition of the *Gentleman's Magazine* announced, '*Thursday 10:* The Magdalen hospital in Goodman's Fields for the reception of penitent prostitutes was opened, when fifty petitions were presented and several of the penitents admitted.'[88] In fact six women were accepted on 10 August with the first being Ann Blore, who had been born in Ashburn, Derbyshire. Two of the would-be penitents were promised admission as soon as they were cured of the venereal diseases from which they were evidently suffering, another was admitted as a servant to the Matron, and one – Mary Truman – was rejected as 'being no prostitute'.

This was to prove a constant challenge for the selection committee as it could be very difficult to determine if a woman applied for admission out of penitence or penury. But how exactly did the committee define prostitution and identify a prostitute? Presumably the disappointed Mary Truman could have left the Magdalen House, had sex for money before a witness and then reapplied, as the regulations gave her liberty to do. The mind boggles. But perhaps the Magdalen's definition of a prostitute, never written down, demanded some proof of sustained activity or evidence from the parish watch or a Justice of the Peace. What is clear is that it was not enough for a supplicant merely to turn up at the door and claim to be a prostitute.

Gradually the Magdalen went in search of suitable harlots and posted notices at known resorts of prostitutes, announcing that 'penitents' could apply for admission on the first Thursday of each month. The 'Rules and Regulations'[89] give a good impression of what life would have been like within the Magdalen House as well as suggesting how exactly it proposed to realise its aim that, although a place of stern resolve, the institution should above all be a 'safe, desirable and happy place of retreat'.[90] Most significantly, these regulations make clear what types of 'penitent prostitutes' were deemed worthy of the Magdalen's charity: no proven prostitute was to be admitted who was pregnant, diseased or who had been admitted before and dismissed, and it was highly desirable that she be thirty years of age or under since it was generally believed that younger prostitutes were more readily redeemed. If the applicant was eligible and passed these hurdles she was issued a form that required her to give her name, age, parish and county of birth, and to start her regime of penitence by acknowledging that she 'hath been guilty of such mis-conduct, as renders her a proper object of the protection of this Charity' and that she was 'truly sensible of her offence'. Finally she had to promise to behave herself 'decently and orderly, and to conform to all the rules of the Institution' and 'as in duty bound, shall ever pray'.

After completing this form each applicant underwent a physical examination, supervised by the Matron, to ensure that she had not been lying and was indeed not diseased or pregnant. Those who passed this ordeal were examined by a selection committee that decided, by vote, who should be admitted. Once accepted, the term of penitence and isolation started immediately: no woman was 'allowed to go out of the house, without special leave in writing signed by the Treasurer or Chairman, and two of the Committee; and that for a time not exceeding a day, and this only on an urgent and extraordinary occasion; and, in such case, she is attended by a proper person appointed by the Matron'.

Although the Magdalen made it clear that it was in business to redeem proven prostitutes who were genuinely penitent and preferably under thirty years of age, there was also – most confusingly – a special class of non-prostitute it would consider accepting. The institution saw part of its duty as preventative and since the conventional path to prostitution was, it believed, through male seduction, deceit and abandonment, the Magdalen in its regulations announced that 'every woman who has been seduced . . . may apply for admission to the Committee'.

Successful applicants were first lodged in the 'Probationary Ward' for three months, after which they were either dismissed, if their attitude was wrong or behaviour disturbing, or else moved into one of three types of 'Intermediary' wards where they mixed only with women who lodged in the same type of ward. Selection for these wards was based on 'birth', education, behaviour, and the ability to perform different kinds of work. Clearly the hospital authorities were trying to engineer a community by putting together what they perceived to be roughly like-minded women. Finally the women would end their days in the Magdalen in the 'Finishers' wards. In addition to these wards for former prostitutes there was also a separate ward for seduced women who had 'never been publicly on the town' but had applied to the Magdalen 'to avoid being driven to that extremity'.

The sombre uniform Dingley had envisaged in his initial proposal was instituted, with the young women obliged to exchange the clothes in which they arrived for 'brown shalloon gowns' to ensure that their attire was 'plain and neat, and exactly alike'. An attempt was also made to regulate the minds of the penitents. They were encouraged to forget not only their past actions but also their past identities. They were advised to abandon – or at least conceal – their real names and, like nuns, choose new 'Christian' names that reflected their new aspirations: 'if they are desirous of concealing themselves, they have liberty to assume a feigned name'.[91] They were also 'forbidden' to reproach each other 'for past irregularities', nor was 'any enquiry into names or families permitted'.[92] The Magdalen House was a place of redemption where prayer and clean living would, believed the Governors, allow young women to escape their sins and be born again into society.

The regime of the place was demanding. In the summer the women were expected to rise at six, read and pray until breakfast at seven, then work – mostly laundry and needlework – until they dined between one and two, then work again until eight, followed by supper, prayers and bed at ten. In the winter they were to rise as soon as it was light. What little free time they had could be spent in the Magdalen's somewhat overlooked

The Magdalen's demure uniform – part country-girl, part nun – chosen by Dingley.

garden, but to prevent any lapses each woman taking a turn had to be accompanied by one of the 'Attendants' employed by the charity. Visitors were also permitted but meetings could only take place in the Matron's apartment or the committee room in the presence of the Matron or one of her 'Attendants'.

Any 'penitent' could, of course, leave whenever she chose, but there were several good reasons for staying the course of moral and spiritual re-education, which, the Magdalen calculated, would take on average one year. First she would be housed and well fed for nothing and by all accounts the food was good, with each ward undertaking its own cooking so that, as Hanway observed in 1761, 'most of the women in the house grow fat with a diet so much more regular, as well as simpler, than they have been accustomed to'.[93] Strangely, tea became an illicit and much-desired beverage in the Magdalen, largely because of Hanway's prejudice and prohibition against it. To wean the women off this 'dangerous' substance, their daily ration of home-brewed beer was set at two and a half pints[94] – clearly the Magdalen took Hogarth's view, expressed in the *Gin Lane/Beer Alley* pair of prints of 1750/1, that while gin was an evil, beer was wholesome.

Another incentive towards good behaviour was that each woman who stayed the course would be given a decent set of clothes when she left plus a modest amount of 'luggage', and it was 'an invariable rule, not to dismiss any woman (unless at her own request or for ill conduct) without some means being provided, by which she may obtain an honest liveli-hood'.[95] And, if she behaved well for a year, the reformed prostitute would be given a guinea by the Governors. Although this was an amount many penitents could have earned in a few days, or even hours, in their old trade, it was nevertheless a substantial sum, equal to the weekly wage of a journeyman tradesman in the mid-eighteenth century. Quite how it was decided that a penitent's reform was complete is not made clear in the regulations; presumably it was at the discretion of the Matron and committee. But it is made clear that she could also expect discharge on honourable terms at an earlier date if respectable friends or family applied for her release and offered support and forgiveness or if a housekeeper 'of sufficient credit' applied for her as a servant.

The Magdalen had no shortage of applicants. At a General Court held on 4 July 1759 the Governors were told that in its first eleven months of existence the Magdalen had received 344 applications for admission of which 146 had been accepted and that, at that moment, it had 116 penitents in residence. Conditions must have been crowded because the following November the Magdalen was obliged to purchase a neighbouring house, so that by January 1760 it had beds for 131 women.[96] That the work of administration was tough is suggested by the fact that the first matron didn't last long and more assistants had to be employed. But the second matron – Mrs Elizabeth Butler – clearly had the right disposition for she presided over the Magdalen for twenty-five years.

A little more about the nature of the penitents – and about London's sex industry – is suggested by the Magdalen's first Anniversary Service held in 1759 by its celebrity 'preacher' Dr William Dodd, who – rather than humble Reverend Reeves – officiated at such high-profile events. He stated that 'out of an hundred girls now in the Magdalen House, above a seventh part have not yet seen their fifteenth year; several are under fourteen; and one-third of the whole have been betrayed before that age'.[97]

Unsurprisingly, the Magdalen House was of intense interest to most Londoners because it was packed with 'Women of the Town', including child prostitutes who were there not because they were diseased – as at the Lock Hospital – but because they had declared themselves 'penitent', claimed to regret their former way of life, and were undergoing moral conversion. It seemed like a strange – not to say unlikely – form of alchemy. Women and girls coarsened by prostitution were, through a nunnish regime, being transformed into healthy, moral and industrious citizens.

Londoners' views on the Magdalen and its worth varied as much as did their views on prostitutes and the sex industry. Those who perceived prostitutes as the unfortunate victims of poverty and circumstances, or as the sad dupes of lying and deceitful men, tended to see the Magdalen as a worthwhile refuge where repenting prostitutes could at last find refuge and redeem themselves.

Sarah Fielding, the moralist sister of Henry and John, compiled a largely imaginary volume in 1760 entitled *Histories of Some of the Penitents in the Magdalen-House*, which puts the benign and supportive point of view. She observed that prostitutes are often regarded as too 'intirely abandoned to guilt and infamy to deserve relief' but argued that this 'distress alone is sufficient title' to assistance. 'Tho' the profession of a prostitute is the most despicable and hateful that imagination can form; yet the individuals are frequently worthy objects of compassion.'[98]

Other less forgiving observers, who believed prostitutes were the spawn of Satan and nothing but corrupted and immoral women who simply corrupted others, spread disease and participated in all manner of crime, viewed the Magdalen as little more than a den of iniquity and place of deep hypocrisy in which cynical prostitutes could recruit their strength and funds before returning once more to their trade; and indeed often indulged their lewd and sensual ways while lodged within the Magdalen's walls. One objection to Dingley's and Hanway's somewhat 'sentimental' institution was implied in Saunders Welch's competing proposal. It was his opinion, and no doubt that of many realists who had, like Welch, experience of dealing with prostitutes (he was high constable of Holborn, with Covent Garden as his responsibility), that any form of benevolent 'asylum' would merely encourage women to be less cautious about entering into illicit relations that could, it was assumed, lead easily to prostitution.[99]

Something of Londoners' attitudes is revealed by a 'contemporary' description of the Magdalen in the 1750s: it was 'formed out of several contiguous messuages or tenements, with a wall and small area before it; and to prevent the prying curiosity of the public, there is not only a close gate and a porter, but the windows next the street are concealed by wooden blinds sloping from the bottom of each, so as to admit the light only at the top'.[100] Clearly passers-by in Whitechapel took a voyeuristic interest in the place and were keen to catch a glimpse of these sometime 'Ladies of Pleasure' at their repose or devotions. The blinds, the building's quasi-monastic atmosphere and its penitents' demure, country-girl-cum-nun uniform, do not appear to have helped its reputation. For those who believed in the evil of its inmates, the fact that no evil could be seen made no difference. Indeed the hospital's neo-Roman Catholic name and its air of seclusion worthy of a nunnery (an unfortunate association in Georgian London) seem only to have fuelled the fantasies of doubters.

The overheated imagination of many laymen had fancied that nunneries and monasteries of old were places of illicit sexual activity since at least the time that Pietro Aretino published his erotic writings in Italy in the early sixteenth century. (In his *Ragionamenti* of 1539, for example, two

Roman courtesans discuss the voracious sexual habits of nuns.) The final eighteenth-century expression of this heady fusion of monastic life and sex was *The Monk*, written by Matthew Gregory Lewis and published in 1796, which includes not just sexual obsession behind monastic walls but rape and Satanic possession. So if genuine nunneries were the focus of such lurid fantasies, even more so would be a place packed with fallen women and teenage girls who in their past had regularly indulged in all manner of the most wanton behaviour.

Those who believed the inmates were unredeemed and unredeemable sensualists assumed that vice within the Magdalen's walls must be rampant and inevitably 'unnatural'. Rumours that this was indeed the case soon circulated and led to formal complaints by influential citizens. An inquiry was held at which 'no proof of anything very scandalous was forthcoming', and it concluded that 'the origin of the charges' lay among the gossip of prostitutes themselves, notably a number lodged in the Lock Hospital, with 'the main charge of "unnatural vice" . . . based on a single occasion . . . reported by a Presider [a penitent given some responsibility of super-vision over her fellows] . . . when an inmate had placed her hand in another inmate's bosom'.[101]

The Magdalen's champions appear to have been unruffled by such rumours and accusations, and certainly all seemed sound and sedate when in January 1760 the establishment was visited by the ever-curious and observant Horace Walpole, who recorded the event in a letter to George Montague.[102] Walpole was part of a large and grand party including Prince Edward – the twenty-year-old younger brother of the future King George III – Lady Hertford, Miss Pelham, Lord Beauchamp and Lord Huntingdon. What immediately amused Walpole was the quasi-Catholic nature of the hospital: 'This new convent is beyond Goodman's Fields and it would,' observed Walpole drolly, 'content any Catholic alive.'

The party was met by Lord Hertford and taken directly to join a service in the chapel where 'at the west end were enclosed the sisterhood, above an hundred and thirty, all in greyish brown stuffs, broad handkerchiefs, and flat straw hats, with a blue ribband, pulled quite over their faces'. The 'Magdalens' sang a hymn 'you cannot imagine how well', observed Walpole, who was clearly agog and mischievously delighted by the almost dangerously Catholic atmosphere of the service: '. . . the chapel was dressed with orange and myrtle, and there wanted nothing but a little incense to drive away the devil – or to invite him'. Then came the sermon, delivered by a 'young clergyman, one Dodd, who contributed to the Popish idea one had imbibed, by haranguing entirely in the French style, and very elegantly and touchingly'. The 'Magdalens' – addressed as lost sheep now found – 'sobbed and cried from their souls', as did 'my Lady Hertford and Fanny Palham' – so much so that Walpole feared the respectable 'City dames' present in the congregation took them both to be guilt-stricken high courtesans.

After the service Walpole's party went to the refectory 'where all the nuns, without their hats, were ranged at long tables, ready for supper'. All looked healthy, he observed, 'a few were handsome', there were 'two or three of twelve years old' but many 'seemed to have no title to their profession'. Walpole may have been referring to the inmates who were seduced women but not prostitutes. Or, perhaps, realised that many of the 'Magdalens' were just poor women seeking shelter. In which case the rejected Mary Truman was followed by more successful applicants of the same type, an indication that, from the very start of its work, the Magdalen House served two roles: the one it had set itself, in giving refuge to and reclaiming penitent prostitutes, and another created by public need – a humane place of lodging for desperate and poverty-stricken women.

After inspecting the 'Magdalens' at their supper tables – two of whom charmed Walpole by contriving to 'swoon away' under the 'confusion of being stared at' by so many grand strangers – the party was shown the goods the women made, linen and bead work, which earned the establishment £10 a week and proved that it was fulfilling its aim of producing useful work and making, in a small way, a contribution to the nation's economy.

Walpole obviously found the Magdalen House – with its whiff of fantasy, fanaticism, charade and hypocrisy – highly entertaining, but he knew better than to offend his grand and earnest host by making flippant if pertinent observations: 'I kept my countenance very demurely . . . My Lord Hertford would never have forgiven me . . . if I had . . . inquired whether among the pensioners there were any novices from Mrs Naylor's.' She, no doubt, was the 'lady abbess' who ran an establishment housing a very differently minded set of harlots and where Lord Hertford unwound after a day spent doing good in Goodman's Fields.

The high-flying and charismatic Dr Dodd – chaplain of the Magdalen
House – who was eventually executed for forgery.

The clergyman Walpole referred to, Dr William Dodd, soon published his service with a dedication, dated 31 January 1760, to 'Prince Edward Augustus'. Two hundred and fifty years on Dodd's verbose sermon seems dry enough but there are a few passages and phrases that make it possible to perceive a faint sense of the theatricality, sentiment and use of imagery that had so tickled Walpole's fancy. The sermon took as its theme a text from the Gospel of St Luke: 'For the Son of Man is come to seek and to save that which was lost'.[103] Dodd spoke of Christian virtue and the possibility of pardon and reconciliation with an offended Deity, and of the Son of God, 'who came . . . to raise the penitent from the gloom of despair to the light of enlivening hope, who came to rescue sinners from the bondage of sin'. As Walpole noted, Dodd 'harangued' the congregation – particularly the 'Magdalens' – whom he tried to reassure by telling them that the biblical text applied 'to you especially who have sought the shelter of this hospitable dwelling which, like Heaven, opens its friendly doors for the reception of the afflicted and returning penitents'. Warming to the task of enthusing his captive congregation of former harlots, Dodd resorted to comparisons that were surprisingly – albeit mildly – sexual: 'with devout and cheerful melody those voices now praise their God, which late were employed in far different exercises; earnest supplications and praises, now happily flow from the lips which were lately prophaned in a contrary service . . . from the servants of Satan and Sin, they are made the servants of God and his Holiness'.[104]

As this sermon suggests, Dr Dodd was a somewhat individual character. In 1751 he married a beautiful but utterly ignorant servant girl – or perhaps prostitute – living and working in Frith Street, Soho, and then, through his charm and ability, rapidly rose to popularity as a fashionable and charismatic preacher, famed for using 'his beautifully shaped hands . . . in the florid French manner as an adjunct to his eloquence'.[105] Dodd opened a series of profitable chapels and in 1763 was appointed Chaplain in Ordinary to the King, but the revenue and useful connections these endeavours produced were not bountiful or beneficial enough to support his extravagant and ostentatious manner of life so, while preaching morality and entertaining the exalted of the land, he was obliged to descend to devious and ultimately criminal ploys as he sought to bolster up his material comforts.

His first public humiliation came when he was accused of attempting to bribe the wife of the Lord Chancellor in order to obtain the valuable living of St George's, Hanover Square. He was, however, soon rehabilitated, but in February 1777 was charged with forging the signature of Lord Chesterfield on a bond to obtain £4,200 – an act Dodd was alleged to have committed the day after delivering a sermon in the Magdalen's chapel.[106] He was tried at the Old Bailey and, despite the support of eminent acquaintances such as Samuel Johnson, found guilty and executed.

Throughout his ordeals, the Magdalen remained loyal to Dodd. He had, over the years, been responsible for raising substantial amounts of money for the charity so this support was perhaps natural and admirable. Yet it is hard not to see Dodd's inconsistent and contradictory behaviour as not only emblematic of the age but also in some way a reflection of the Magdalen's own sincerity and conduct, in which the almost theatrical and superficial display of penitence may have been confused with sincere contrition and real determination to reform.

But all this is speculation. Despite the oddness of its habits and regime, and its unfortunate choice of spiritual champion, the Magdalen House flourished and expanded. In 1763, as its lease on the Prescot Street site and buildings drew to an end, it had to decide whether to renew and add extra accommodation or to commission a purpose-designed building on another larger site. Mr Winterbottom, the Secretary, was directed to look for a suitable site on the south bank of the Thames near St George's Fields, where land was cheaper and which would soon be easily accessible when the new bridge at Blackfriars was completed. Six acres of land was acquired by December but nothing happened for three years while options – including rebuilding on the Prescot Street site – were discussed at length.

In 1767 a rebuilding scheme for the Prescot Street site was drawn up. Queen Charlotte, who in 1765 had agreed to become the Magdalen's patroness and at a stroke gave the whole enterprise astonishing cachet, approved the designs and an appeal was launched to raise money through subscription. But by 1768 the scheme was halted and, instead, the decision taken to build in St George's Fields, perhaps because the Blackfriars bridge was at last nearing completion.

It seems that Dingley undertook to design the new Magdalen House in grand style, no doubt imagining that the building, standing in the fields of South London, would possess the architectural dignity of the Foundling Hospital dominating the fields of Bloomsbury. Indeed the name of the charity was even changed to the Magdalen Hospital. But something went wrong. Dingley's grandiose vision was abandoned, although his drawings survive in Oxford's Bodleian Library,[107] and instead a more modest scheme was designed by Joel Johnson, a master-carpenter who had been closely involved in the early 1750s in the construction of the London Hospital.

The plan of the new Magdalen Hospital was organised much as the Foundling's but on a smaller scale, consisting of ranges of brick buildings set around a quadrangle with a basin of water in its centre. The centre block – two storeys high, nine windows wide and with a three-window-wide central pediment – was linked to the flanking ranges by octagonal structures, one of which contained the chapel. Queen Charlotte granted this revised scheme her support. On 28 July 1769 Lord Hertford laid the foundation stone in St George's Fields, and in the same year the charity was put on an official and sound footing by being incorporated in an Act of Parliament for 'establishing and well governing an Hospital for the Reception, Maintenance and Employment of penitent Prostitutes'.

An indistinct view of the Magdalen Hospital, built on Blackfriars Road in 1769. The central block was linked to the wings by octagonal structures, one of which contained the chapel.

The Magdalen Hospital functioned efficiently in its new and semi-rural site. By 1784 it had, in total, received 2,415 penitents. What is not clear is how many of the women who passed through its doors remained redeemed. A partial answer to this question is supplied by the archives of the Old Bailey. For example, in February 1772 Elizabeth Cross, who was transported for theft, explained during her failed defence, 'I am an unfortunate girl; I lodged at . . . a very bad house; I had not been long come out of the Magdalen-house. The woman of the house and another girl swore they would put me into gaol if I did not get money for them.'[108] A similar fate befell Susanah Clarke, who in September 1775 was one of a pair of women tried for 'Grand Larceny'. One of her accusers told the court, '[W]hen she was taken up she behaved saucy. I have known them two or three years. I had taken them out of the Magdalen house.'[109]

But despite such fleeting negative connotations it seems that generally the Magdalen was effective in its work: figures released in 1916 state that by that date 14,235 woman had been admitted to the institution since 1758; of these over one-fifth had discharged themselves and one-tenth been expelled, leaving almost seven-tenths who 'appear' to have been reclaimed from the sex industry and to have returned productively to the wider world 'as reasonable citizens'.[110]

In 1866 the hospital moved to Streatham where in 1888 new and extensive premises were opened which gradually changed their function to that of school (the words 'for penitent prostitutes' were perhaps wisely dropped from its title in 1938) and ended their days as an 'approved' school for girls. The charming hospital buildings in St George's Fields – one of the key architectural monuments to, and produced by, Georgian London's thriving sex industry – ultimately found themselves in the wrong place at the wrong time. Mid-Victorian Southwark had no use for such a place and it was torn down to make room for a building intended to solve a more pressing social need than the moral redemption and productive employment of penitent prostitutes. On the site on Blackfriars Road were built ranges of tall and gaunt blocks of housing, funded by the Peabody Trust, to accommodate the poorer members of the capital's rapidly expanding population. But buried deep beneath these tall tenements something of the Magdalen remains. The foundation stone, laid below the chapel's altar in 1769, was not located and removed to Streatham.[111] One day it will, no doubt, come to light, its chiselled text proclaiming the virtues of this peculiar charity – 'For the Reception of Penitent Prostitutes' – that was so emblematic of London life in the eighteenth century.[112]

The chapel in the Magdalen Hospital, Blackfriars Road.

THE LOCK HOSPITALS

Lock Hospitals in London date back to at least the thirteenth century and were originally intended for the treatment of lepers, but by the early-eighteenth century, with leprosy eradicated in Britain, they had turned their attention to those suffering from contagious fevers and venereal disease. The derivation of the name is disputed but it could refer to the *loques* – the Old French word for rags – that were used to bind lepers' sores, or to the fact that the doors to these hospitals were 'locked' to prevent infectious inmates returning freely to the community.

Also unclear is the extent to which members of the London poor suffering from venereal disease could, during the first half of the eighteenth century, hope to find medical assistance. Most of the general voluntary hospitals, starting with the Westminster in 1719, generally excluded those suffering from contagious ailments like smallpox and venereal disease, although Guy's Hospital in Southwark – founded in 1721 and with a declared intention to cater for 'incurables' – incorporated a Lock or 'Foul' ward, as did the adjoining and far older St Thomas's Hospital. Venereal patients could be treated in these but in theory were only admitted if they were not eligible for a London parish workhouse and if they were able to pay 'extra fees', usually to cover funeral costs.[113]

Guy's Hospital, with its front court, cloistered and pedimented centre range and its chapel wing, is now the best place in central London to get a feel for the architecture of the similarly formed Foundling and Magdalen Hospitals. But the most spectacular example of surviving eighteenth-century hospital architecture in London is the inner court of St Bartholomew's Hospital in Smithfield. Founded in 1123 to care for travellers and the needy and outcast poor of the district, St Bartholomew's by the mid-sixteenth century incorporated a Lock Hospital (it took over the one in Southwark), and in 1730 James Gibbs designed the tall stone-clad ranges that now define the inner court.

The fact that venereal disease was treated in the hospital in the early eighteenth century is confirmed in the most dramatic way possible. In 1735–6 William Hogarth painted two huge canvases for the staircase hall of the Gibbs entrance range. One of these paintings, entitled *The Pool of Bethesda*, illustrates the biblical story (St John, 5:2–14) in which Jesus joins a group of the infirm gathered around a pool of supposedly healing water and performs a miracle. Upon his telling a cripple to 'Rise, take up thy bed, and walk', the cured man promptly does. Hogarth captured this dramatic moment and surrounded the pool with onlookers suffering from the ailments treated in St Bartholomew's – indeed some members of the motley crowd could be portraits of genuine patients.

The exact nature of the illnesses suffered by Hogarth's supporting cast of characters has long been debated, but likely examples are jaundice, rickets, gout, mastitis, anaemia and cancer, and there is also a baby with what looks like congenital syphilis. Most striking of all is a naked and voluptuous young lady (alleged to be the portrait of a well-known harlot) who is suffering from a swollen knee that could perhaps represent gonococcal arthritis. Hogarth donated these paintings to the hospital, in return for which he was elected a Life Governor.

These general hospitals could only offer peripheral help to the poor suffering from venereal disease, but this situation changed dramatically in January 1747 when William Bromfeild, surgeon to the Prince of Wales, founded London's first purpose-built Lock Hospital. It was solely for the treatment of those afflicted by both poverty and venereal disease and was located in a mansion, fitted up to contain thirty beds, and located in the healthy and isolated fields to the south of Hyde Park Corner and near the recently founded St George's Hospital, with which Bromfeild was also associated.

Like the Foundling Hospital and the Magdalen House, the Lock was supported by subscriptions and fund-raising events and run by a Court of Governors – with the Duke of Ancaster, the Great Chamberlain to George II, as first president – who were also subscribers and party to the selection of patients. Unlike eighteenth-century general hospitals, it not only offered treatment for physical disease but also – like the Magdalen House – had a moral and spiritual mission. From the start it was recognised that a large number of its patients would be involved, in one way or another, with the sex industry and that many would be female street prostitutes. Since the Lock relied for its income on public goodwill and support it had to make it absolutely clear that by treating those suffering from venereal disease it was in no sense encouraging vice or simply providing prostitutes with cures so that they could continue their trade.

The Governors explained this position clearly in their published material. For example, the *Account of the Proceedings of the Governors of the Lock-Hospital, near Hyde Park Corner*, dated Monday 11 December 1749,[114] starts with a quote from the Gospel of St John (8:7): 'And Jesus said unto them, he that is without Sin among you, let him first cast a Stone at her'. Other documents bear an image of Christ dismissing a woman, and another quote from St John: 'Go and Sin no more' (8:11).

The December 1749 *Account* explains that 'persons labouring under the Venereal Disease are more destitute of Relief than any other Objects of publick Charity' because 'the County Hospitals exclude them', and although 'the Necessity of a Charity of this Nature is obvious to many, yet some have apprehended it may prove as Encouragement to Vice'. To 'remove Prejudices of this Kind' the Governors pointed out 'that many poor Creatures, labouring under the Disease, are in themselves no ways culpable, as it may have been occasioned by [guiltless wives being infected by] bad Husbands, [or by] diseased Parents', while its sufferers included 'suckling Children born with the Disease, or Children that have imbibed it from their Nurses'.

But what of prostitutes who had caught the disease while plying their trade? The Governors tackled this issue head-on, in crusading Christian spirit:

> But still the Scrupulous object to those who voluntarily draw the Misery on themselves, as improper Objects – In fact these are some of the greatest, as they are, generally speaking, destitute of Friends, and consequently abandoned to Vice and Disease. Should these then be left to rot alive, and under a kind of Necessity to communicate Contagion in order to support Life? Shall we suffer them to perish, without any Attempt made to convince them of their Guilt and Danger, and not give them another Opportunity of reforming their Lives? – Every good Christian will answer, No: It is our Part to relieve the Distressed, theirs to amend their lives.

There was an unanswerable additional argument that the Governors deployed from time to time. They pointed out that some of the children in the hospital had been infected in a way that could be 'hardly credited by the virtuous', with many two- to ten-year-olds having been 'cured in the Hospital that had fallen victim to villains misguided by a vulgar notion that by a criminal communication with a healthy child a certain cure may be obtained for themselves'.[115]

The 1749 *Account* also explains the regulations by which the hospital operated. No person was to be admitted unless bringing a 'recommendation in writing, signed by a Governor, or one of the weekly committees', and Governors were men who subscribed 5 guineas or more a year, with those giving 50 guineas being made Governors for life. Patients had to agree to abide by the rules of the hospital, which included prohibitions against alcohol and rowdy behaviour, and since the hospital contained a roughly equal number of males and females there was a rule forbidding patients from visiting the wards of the opposite sex. Also, as a safeguard against accusations of encouraging vice, the hospital not only refused to readmit any patient discharged for 'irregular' behaviour – such as making free with the opposite sex – but also ruled that no reinfected person would be admitted, making it clear that the Lock was not to be a refuge for people – notably prostitutes – who were serial contractors of venereal disease.

Some idea of the turnover and effectiveness of the hospital is also hinted at in the 1749 *Account*. Patients were admitted at the rate of roughly five or six a week, with married women – the innocent victims of 'bad' husbands – being given preference. There were 31 patients in residence in December 1749, while 694 had been 'received' since January 1747 of whom 644 had been 'discharged cured' (or, at least, 'cured' by eighteenth-century standards). The quite significant difference in numbers between patients admitted and patients cured was not due to deaths, of which there were very few (only six deaths in the first five years), but generally as a result of patients discharging themselves or being expelled for misconduct before being cured.[116]

Despite a shortage of cash the Governors decided, by 1753, that they could afford to treat themselves to a purpose-designed hospital. They decided to rebuild on their existing site but the exact appearance of the now long-demolished building is not entirely clear. A painting by Nathaniel Dance of William Bromfeild in 1770 (now in the Royal College of Surgeons) shows him holding a sketch elevation of the new hospital, which is revealed to be three storeys high, nine windows wide, with the centre and end first-floor windows emphasised by having semi-circular tops and by being set in areas of elevation that break forward slightly. Bromfeild's hand obscures the top centre area of elevation but other drawings of the building (such as that attached to the published account of the first sermon held in the Lock Chapel in 1762) show a pediment over the centre window and a large inscription reading, 'The Lock Hospital supported by the Voluntary subscriptions and Contributions of divers of the Nobility and Others'.

Early nineteenth-century views appear to confirm that these elevations show the hospital broadly as built, but an elevation of 1749 (published with the *Account of the Proceedings of the Governors of the Lock-Hospital, near Hyde Park Corner, Monday December 11 1749*)[117] shows that something significantly more sophisticated and grander had been conceived initially. This elevation is a complicated affair, full of movement and counterpoint. It is eleven windows wide with a centre that breaks forward and incorporates a columned porch topped by a first-floor Venetian window and second-floor lunette, all set beneath a pediment with inscription. This boldly composed central feature is flanked by subservient pediment-topped pavilions, each incorporating semi-circular-headed first-floor windows. The details and forms are reminiscent of the Foundling Hospital, which, no doubt, this new building was intended to emulate, until shortage of funds enforced a more modest design.

The new building contained six wards, three for each sex, and could now accommodate around sixty in-patients at a time, as well as dealing with a number of out-patients. In 1762 the hospital was joined by another new building – a large new chapel – that would not only reinforce the battle for the souls of the prostitute patients but also help with fund-raising. The second half of the eighteenth century was a time when preachers operating from elegant and spacious independent chapels could make a lot of money. People liked a good and entertaining sermon, and if the preacher was also something of a celebrity and the chapel a place of fashion and display – or even a curiosity – so much the better. The Lock Chapel, designed by Joel Johnson, who went on to design the Magdalen Hospital in Southwark, was little more than an oblong brick box but could seat 800 people in comfortable manner and was regularly filled to capacity because the Lock's preacher and chaplain was a theatrical, charismatic and evangelical cleric named Martin Madan.

The Lock always found money hard to come by – philanthropists tended to prefer worthier causes and more deserving objects of charity than diseased prostitutes – but after 1762 the Reverend Madan made a significant difference. Box pews were rented out at 15 guineas per annum and Madan's enthusiastic performances, no doubt complemented by the chance to see an assemblage of exotic or alarming-looking patients, meant that the chapel became a money-spinner. Incredibly, in 1766–7, while the Governors' subscriptions brought in £707.12s.0d, the chapel pew rents alone brought in £521.2s.0d.[118] And this year was fairly typical, with the chapel regularly providing at least one-third of the hospital's annual income.

Martin Madan, the domineering and ambitious evangelical chaplain at the Lock Hospital.

Not only did Madan and the chapel raise money for the hospital, they also raised its public profile, attracted well-connected, evangelical-minded men, such as the ubiquitous Jonas Hanway, who became a Governor, and provided a platform from which the institution's mission – and morality – could be promoted and explained to the public. For example, in his inaugural sermon in the chapel in March 1762, Madan observed that 'the disease which entitles the Objects of this Hospital to relief is in itself extremely loathsome and dreadful in its effects', pointed out that while 'many have inadvertently sought their own ruin, others have been led away by the arts of vile seducers' and argued that free treatment for venereal disease was not an encouragement to vice because of 'the pain and exquisite torment they must necessarily sustain' to get rid of the disease. He also challenged his congregation by informing it that the 'most essential difference between a real humble Christian and a proud hypocrite [is that] the first loathes sin but pities the sinner and strives to do him good, the other having his heart swelling within him like an ugly toad with the venom of pride and self conceit spurns the sinner as unworthy of notice'.[119] Madan also referred to the reforming aims of the Lock and mentioned sending cured prostitute patients to the Magdalen House, and expressed his 'great reason to believe that the blessings of God have attended our joint endeavours, to save many poor creatures from present and eternal ruin'.[120]

Although Reverend Madan forcefully defended the hospital's policy of treating diseased prostitutes and worried in public about the fate of their eternal souls, he had, in his private capacity as a clergyman, very little to do with the patients. He was away a great deal on preaching tours and found the hospital wards most unpleasant, so played no pastoral role in the daily life of the Lock. This seems to have resulted in an absence of moral authority, leading to serious lapses in discipline and security. In 1765 staff were instructed to prevent the return of 'Bawds and disorderly persons' who had 'found means to get into the Women Patients' Ward and endeavour to decoy or prevail upon several of the Women Patients who were nearly cured to return to their former Evil Courses'.[121] And the same year a court presided over by Lord Chief Justice Mansfield found Edmund Thirkell guilty of the rape of a five-year-old patient named Mary Amelia Halfpenny. Such terrible events led, quite naturally, to disquiet among the Governors, with William Bromfeild in particular feeling most unhappy about Madan's long absences. A deep and rancorous sense of ill will developed between the two men that would eventually lead to a most extraordinary series of events.

But as Bromfeild and Madan manoeuvred themselves towards their own disgrace and humiliation, the hospital continued its work and even managed to expand. More accommodation was added to the building in 1766, with the *Abstract of Accompts* to 25 March 1767 revealing that, since

31 January 1746/7, the hospital had received 8,210 patients with 8,025 discharged cured. The fate of the others is suggested by the statistics for 26 March 1766 to 25 March 1767, during which period 36 patients discharged themselves or were expelled for 'irregularity' and 4 died.[122]

The hospital presented its figures in the most positive way possible so as to encourage much-needed donations. But the figures can be interpreted in other – perhaps more illuminating – ways. By 1771 the hospital had treated 10,987 patients of which, according to an analysis conducted by Randolph Trumbach, 12 per cent were wives who had been infected by their husbands, while of the women in general treated by the hospital (roughly 5,500 in number since 50 per cent of the patients were female), the very high number of '4,000 [were] young unmarried women, most of whom were prostitutes'.[123] The Lock truly was, perhaps inevitably, a refuge for poor diseased street prostitutes.

Reverend Madan at the Lock Hospital and Dr Dodd at the Magdalen House were very different in their Christian doctrine and manner – the former an Evangelical Methodist and the latter High Church – but the men had certain things in common. Each was clearly a very talented and able public performer, and each was also slightly unhinged. Dodd's failings led him to the scaffold while Madan's led merely to public ridicule and disgrace.

His dealings with recovering prostitutes at the Lock seem to have convinced him that he was an authority on the sex industry and prompted him to publish in 1780 a pamphlet offering a solution to the evils of prostitution. Entitled *Thelyphthora or A Treatise on Female Ruin* (the title is a combination of the Greek for charm and for ruin), it proposed that a man who seduced a girl must be obliged by law subsequently to marry and support her – even if he was already married – and so relieve her of the necessity of prostituting herself for sustenance. An appealing if simplistic idea but one not remotely acceptable in Georgian Britain for it undermined the institution of matrimony – on which much property law was based – and promoted polygamy. Madan went so far as to claim (though no fellow clerics agreed) that polygamy had Old Testament precedents. He was repudiated by his former disciples, ridiculed by the public and obliged to resign his chaplaincy at the Lock lest he become a hindrance to fund-raising.[124]

Madan was replaced as preacher and chaplain by Edward Charles de

Coetlogon, who had been involved with the Lock for some time and was a Governor. Unfortunately de Coetlogon was even more averse to visiting the infirm patients in the wards than had been Madan and so increased Bromfeild's disdain for the religious arm of his foundation.

But rather than waiting for Bromfeild to visit his wrath upon him, de Coetlogon appears to have grabbed the initiative and orchestrated (with Madan's help) a pre-emptive strike against his powerful foe. In the same year that Madan was disgraced a charge was suddenly levelled against Bromfeild. Sensationally, he was accused of purloining hospital supplies for the use of private patients. No doubt to Bromfeild's fury the charge was taken seriously enough by the Governors for them to institute an inquiry, though it found the accusation 'frivolous' and not proven.[125]

Bromfeild counter-attacked and in the process revealed the person he held responsible for the attempt to humiliate him. He wrote a letter to his fellow Governors stating that de Coetlogon was failing in his duties by refusing to visit the wards and, in comparison with clerics in similar posts, was overpaid. This letter provoked a crisis among the Governors, who in 1781 elected a Select Committee from among their number to investigate the accusation. Madan managed to get himself elected on to the committee as did a number of very grand and very peculiar Governors, including Lord Dartmouth – Privy Seal in the Lord North Administration, the Dukes of Manchester and Richmond, the past and future Prime Minister the Marquis of Rockingham, and Lord George Gordon, who was just out of the Tower acquitted of treason.

The committee soon produced a report that completely rejected Bromfeild's complaints, implied that he was a disruptive force in the hospital, and declared that in his letter he had 'started from false premises and was led into serious error'.[126] Bromfeild, feeling betrayed and humiliated, instantly resigned all connection with the hospital, urged his friends to cease to subscribe, and refused to have any more to do with it or its Governors, many of whom he had originally recruited to the cause. As was the case with Thomas Coram, William Bromfeild could not, in his old age, take comfort from the charity he had done so much to create. Both, in different ways and for different reasons, were rejected by the institutions that were, in many respects, their life's work.

After Bromfeild's defeat and ejection de Coetlogon went from strength to strength as a charismatic preacher at the Lock Chapel, and in December

1783 secured his most important 'convert' in the person of the young William Wilberforce, who went on to become part of the influential 'Clapham Sect' and instrumental in the moralistic Proclamation Society of 1787, the Society for the Suppression of Vice in 1802 (see page 451) and the anti-slavery movement. Wilberforce grew to 'mislike' the ambitious and scheming de Coetlogon but took to his successor, Thomas Scott, and so continued as a regular attendee at the Lock Chapel.[127]

During the late 1780s the Lock, no doubt as a reflection of the increasingly high moral tone taken by its preacher and congregation, attempted to extend its 'cure' of patients so far as reforming those who were also prostitutes. An asylum was proposed in which cured prostitutes could undergo a period of re-education and rehabilitation in a safe and secluded environment, much as in the Magdalen Hospital. The Governors approved the proposal in April 1787, a house near the hospital was hired and 'frugally furnished', and as the 1796 *Account of the Institution of the Lock Asylum* explains, soon received 'penitent female patients, when discharged from the Lock Hospital' who were clothed, maintained and 'if possible . . . kept from ever seeing or conversing with their former abandoned companions . . . till they can be restored either to their friends or the community, in a way of industry, according to their ability'. Reform was hard and difficult work but, emphasised the 1796 *Account* . . .

> . . . the salvation of their immortal souls, will be an abundant compensation; and as some of these poor creatures are not more than thirteen years of age, and others are but just entering on this course of life, when they begin to feel the painful effects, we shall not be deemed too sanguine, in expecting at least this much success.[128]

Just how difficult this redemption was is revealed by statistics published in the 1796 *Account*. From May 1787 until Lady-day 1796 the asylum had received 244 'penitents' of whom 22 had been 'restored to, and remain with their Friends; some of them are Married, and Mothers of Families'; 72 had been 'placed in different Services'; but 123 – or just over 50 per cent – had been 'expelled for ill Behaviour' or had 'disappointed the Expectations of their Benefactors, by eloping from the House, or Services, in which they had been placed'. In addition the mysteriously large number of 10 women had died in the asylum – a higher mortality rate than in the hospital itself – which is curious since these asylum-dwellers were supposedly 'cured' while the patients in the hospital were not. What on earth did they die of and how? It seems 17 women were resident in the asylum as of 25 March 1796, which presumably reflects the usual level of occupancy and was a fairly high number if the asylum was indeed a standard terrace house containing around ten or twelve rooms and also accommodating a number of staff.[129]

The Lock Hospital and Asylum remained on their original sites until the ground lease expired in 1841, by which time the city had grown to engulf them. The country lane on which the Lock had been built had become busy Grosvenor Place, and the surrounding and once remote and healthy fields were now covered by streets and squares housing the fashionable West London community. Times had changed considerably. The Grosvenor Estate wanted rid of such an unattractive tenant from fashionable Belgravia and the hospital wanted a more remote site, so during the 1840s the whole operation relocated itself to Westbourne Green in Paddington. The move was followed by further expansion – a male hospital was established in Dean Street, Soho – and then by gradual decline until, in 1952, this admirable if somewhat eccentric example of a privately funded Georgian charity, which had fought for the bodies and the souls of poor, outcast and diseased Londoners, finally ceased its struggle and closed its doors.

COLONEL FRANCIS CHARTERIS

Francis Charteris was a dark and much-hated figure in early-eighteenth-century London: an urban ogre and brutal serial sexual predator. Given his contemporary notoriety it is not surprising that Hogarth should have chosen to portray him in scene one of *The Harlot's Progress* as the man ogling Moll, the innocent country girl being procured for his delight by Mother Needham (see page 7). His appalling career and final downfall tell us much about political chicanery during Sir Robert Walpole's corrupt and greedy premiership. They also expose some of the darker undertones of sexual and moral corruption that were a hallmark of London life at the time.

The *Newgate Calendar*, published after Charteris' conviction for rape in 1730, reveals the popular contempt in which he was held:

> The name Charteris, during his life, was a terror to female innocence [and] may, therefore, his fate, and the exposure of his villainy, act as their shield against the destructive machinations of profligate men ... It is impossible to contemplate the character of this wretch without the highest degree of indignation. A gambler, a usurer, an oppressor, a ravisher! Who sought to make equally the follies of men and the persons of women subservient to his passions.[1]

Charteris was a liar, a bully and a convicted rapist, so this public indignation is understandable. But its intensity reveals something else. He was a gentleman by birth but by his actions utterly betrayed the obligations of his caste. Gentlemen were not expected to be moral examples but they were expected to be brave and just. It was expected that they would drink and whore but it was not expected – indeed was not acceptable – that they should abuse their status or wealth to entrap, debauch, rape or mistreat defenceless woman (whores included) in a cowardly manner.

Such aristocratic rogues as Charteris, along with conniving bawds and procuresses, were the popular villains of the Georgian sex industry, while warm-hearted prostitutes and ethically 'honest' outlaws, as personified by the free-spirited Macheath, were its heroines and heroes.

Charteris' early career in the army revealed him to be a gambler and fraudster. He cheated his brother officers while in the Low Countries and was eventually court-martialled, found guilty and drummed out of his regiment. He retired to Scotland where he achieved considerable success as a professional gambler due to his ability to cheat brilliantly. With the fortune he made, he moved to London in the very early eighteenth century and prospered as a money-lender, particularly of mortgages, and so helped to fund both the speculative construction of houses and the purchase of leases on them in an attempt to profiteer through excessive rents.

Charteris loved young women almost as much as he loved money, as was made abundantly clear by the biographies of him that appeared after his trial. *The History of Colonel Francis Ch—rtr—s* of 1730 told the curious public that:

> The Colonel ... had by his address in Gaming, purchased several Seats, one of which, call'd Hornby Castle, in Lancashire, was peculiarly devoted to the Service of the blind Deity Cupid, on whose Altar the Colonel is said to have offered up more Sacrifices than any Man in Great Britain. Here Mr Ch—rtr—s, like the Grand Seignior, has a Seralio, which was kept in more than ordinary Decorum, under the inspection of a venerable Matron.

Charteris occupied his London house in the same manner and it was here that he lodged the seventeen-year-old Sally Salisbury in 1709 (see page 104). As the *Newgate Calendar* explains:

> ... his house was no better than a brothel ... he kept in his pay some women of abandoned character, who, going to inns where the country wagons put up, used to prevail on harmless young girls to go to the colonel's house as servants, the consequence of which was, that their ruin soon followed ... His agents did not confine their operations to inns, but, wherever they found a handsome girl, they endeavoured to decoy her to the colonel's house.

It was in this manner that, in 1729, the young Ann Bond fell into Charteris' hands – with catastrophic consequences for them both.

The Colonel's 'agent' – or procurer – in the case of Ann Bond was Mother Needham. She was passing Ann's lodgings, saw the attractive young woman sitting outside and, as the *Newgate Calendar* explains, 'addressed her, saying, she could help her to a place in the family of Colonel Harvey; for the character of Charteris was now become so notorious, that his agents did not venture to make use of his name'. It is the substance of this event that forms the first scene of Hogarth's *Harlot's Progress*.

The fashionable area around St George's Church, Hanover Square. The notorious Colonel Charteris lived in George Street (foreground).

Ann accepted the offer and was conducted to the Colonel's grand house in George Street, near the newly built and very fashionable Hanover Square. This quarter, presided over by the mighty and just completed St George's Church in which Handel worshipped, was the domestic centre and powerbase of the ruling Whig hegemony, of whom Charteris, by birth and connections, was part. Although no doubt useful for contributing funds, he must also have been something of an embarrassment to the party for he was known and loathed by the mob, as well as many of his respectable neighbours, for his lewd conduct. On at least one occasion a crowd had laid siege to his George Street house in order to obtain the release of a girl who had been decoyed to within its walls.

When first introduced to Ann, Charteris cut a fine and benevolent figure. He interviewed her, declared she would make a fine servant and hired her on wages of £5 a year. He immediately redeemed some of the clothes she had been obliged to pawn and, as *The History of Colonel Ch—rtr—s* explains, quickly attempted to make her obliged and indebted to him. Charteris 'then bought her Holland [a type of linen] for shifting [i.e. for turning into undergarments] and promised she would have a clean shift every day'. Ann modestly refused so Charteris increased the value of what she must by now have realised was offer of payment for her sexual services. He tried to give her a fine snuff-box which Ann also refused, and then, according to the *Newgate Calendar*, he finally offered her an annuity for life and a house if she would lie with him. She refused. Realising by then that he could not purchase her favours, Charteris changed his strategy and started to employ intimidation and bullying. He was, after all, a middle-aged gentleman and master of the household and Ann nothing but a poor, defenceless young servant, one of his 'family' of resident women. *The History* relates how 'some time after she was inform'd by the Housekeeper that she must lye in her Master's Room, because he was very much indispos'd, where-fore she must lye in the Truckle-Bed'. It was a not uncommon practice for servants to sleep in the same room as their masters or mistresses, usually on a simple truckle-bed that could be wheeled away or folded and stored out of sight during the day. Several times in his diary Pepys records the practice: for example, in the entry for 9 October 1667, 'my wife and I in the high bed in our chamber and Willet [the maid] in the trundle-bed'.[2] But this was no doubt with the married couple's privacy protected by heavy curtains surrounding the bed. Charteris, a predatory male, would be sleeping alone and Ann only a few yards away.

The History records that she was very sensibly hesitant, but 'consented on being assured that the Curtains were so close drawn about the Bed that the Colonel could not see her undress'. Of course, Ann was foolish in consenting to the arrangement but presumably was under pressure from all quarters.

> In the night the Colonel order'd the Housekeeper to come to bed with him, which she accordingly did, after which he call'd the Girl, but she would not comply, which very much incensed him, and made him swear execrably.

At around this time Ann discovered Charteris' true name and, knowing something of his reputation, told the housekeeper that she wanted to leave. The housekeeper informed the Colonel, who was furious. He threatened to shoot Ann if she left his service, had her imprisoned in the house and treated her with disdain. As *The History* explains, 'finding no Arguments, not even Gold, would prevail on her, he resolved to have recourse to force'. So on 10 November, in the morning, Charteris called Ann to his chamber, ordered her to stir the fire and, as she bent over to do so, 'fastened the Door, and throwing her suddenly upon a Couch, cram'd his Night Cap into her Mouth to prevent her crying out, and enjoy'd her *Nolens volens*'.

After this 'act of violence', as the *Newgate Calendar* very simply puts it, Ann was 'inconsolable, and not to be pacify'd by any Arguments he cou'd use'. Infuriated that she could not be paid to be silent, Charteris 'took up a Horsewhip, and lash'd her very severely' and then accused her of stealing 30 guineas and had her thrown out of the house. This must have been his usual contemptuous treatment of the poor and powerless women on whom he preyed. As well as physically abusing them, he abused his lofty social position and the law by threatening to denounce his victims as thieves on the assumption that his word as a gentleman would be believed above theirs as humble and placeless young women.

But with Ann, Charteris had made a fatal miscalculation. As the *Newgate Calendar* explains, '[S]he went to a gentlewoman named Parsons. And informing her of what had happened, asked her advice how to proceed.' Mrs Parsons recommended that Ann get a warrant for assault and attempted rape, but when the evidence was heard by the Grand Jury it decided that the charge Charteris had to answer was not attempted rape 'but actual commission of the fact' – rape. Accounts differ about what happened next. Lord Chief Justice Raymond issued a warrant for Charteris' arrest and some accounts say he avoided it being served upon him by fleeing to Brussels.[3] On the other hand, the *Newgate Calendar* states that Charteris was arrested and carried in chains to Newgate. If this was the case he was soon free again because both accounts agree that he surrendered himself for trial in late February 1730.

If Charteris was arrested and quickly freed this was most likely due, once again, to connections. He had married the daughter of Sir Alexander Swinton. His wife duly bore him a daughter who in 1720 had married the Earl of Wemyss. The earl, being in London at the time of his father-in-law's arrest, procured a writ of Habeas Corpus, in consequence of which Charteris was bailed. Why did Wemyss do this? Why would he support his frightful father-in-law who could only have brought shame and suffering on his wife and daughter? Perhaps Wemyss simply thought that by extracting Charteris from Newgate he was doing his best to save the family from further disgrace. But it is also possible that Wemyss himself was part of Charteris' dissolute social circle. His character is now far from certain, but there is a clue in the name used by a notorious Covent Garden prostitute. It was usual for whores to take the surname of their most constant protector and it's reasonable to assume that the notorious one-eyed Betsy Wyms (or Wemys) – the friend of Lucy Cooper – was paying this compliment to Charteris' son-in-law.

Charteris duly came to trial on 28 February 1730 and the event proved to be a sensation. His lawyers tried to destroy the character and evidence of Ann Bond, to present her not as a victim but as a lewd and scheming whore. Charteris himself asked Ann if she had not told some of his household that: '[S]ince I had so much Silver, I should have my Instrument tipp'd, for it would not please a Woman?' But this approach failed to sway the jury. Charteris had been a notorious libertine and cheat for nearly thirty years and now he was to pay the price. The jury found him guilty. On 2 March 1730 he was sentenced to death and carried through a howling mob to await his fate in Newgate.

Charteris had been too arrogant, made overconfident by his years of unrestrained abuse and the belief that his network of influential connections put him beyond the reach of the law. The verdict of this trial suggested he had been mistaken. Or had he? Lord Wemyss soon got to work again pulling strings. The *Newgate Calendar* records that 'Lord Wemys [sic] . . . caused the Lord President Forbes to come from Scotland, to plead [Charteris'] cause before the Privy Council' and, incredibly, as if to confirm the corruption of the age and Charteris in his arrogance, in April 1730, on the advice of the Privy Council, George II granted him a Royal Pardon. But the convicted felon had to pay dearly for his reprieve. He was obliged to settle a handsome annuity on Ann Bond as well as handing over large bribes to Lord President Forbes, who was assigned an estate of £300 per annum for life for his services, and Sir Robert Walpole, who in the autumn received 'generous gifts' from Charteris.[4]

The tale told by this trial is complex and ultimately depressing. A humble young girl could – if her character was unimpeachable – receive justice if abused by a rich and powerful man, but only perhaps if that man had as dark and evil a public reputation as Charteris. But this show of justice could then be overturned if the guilty man was rich and well connected, and if he agreed to buy off his victim and pay out huge bribes. What message did this story carry to young, vulnerable and abused London women? It was a victory of sorts: Charteris was humbled, publicly humiliated, terrified and financially penalised.[5] But if it had been a poor and humble man who had committed the crime, he would have died. That, of course, is exactly the moral of John Gay's *Beggar's Opera*: '[T]he lower sort of People have their vices in a degree as well as the Rich: And ... *they* are punish'd for them'. In other words, all people are capable of ill behaviour, but only the poor are penalised.

In this case the rich and well-connected man had been reprieved by other rich and well-connected men. So who were the real victors? Surely rich and well-connected men – the very ones who patronised establishments such as those run by Mothers Needham and Douglas. From this point of view the story offers a particularly ugly insight into eighteenth-century London's essentially misogynistic society, one in which women – especially humble country girls – were considered inferior beings and the legitimate toys of men, particularly men of power and property.

Additionally, information from Old Bailey records suggests that it was not only the rich and socially powerful who got away with one particular crime in eighteenth-century London. In fact, most men got away with their criminal actions when the charge was rape. Six men, including Charteris, were tried for rape at the Old Bailey in 1730 – an unusually high number (between 1727–34 there were, on average, only two rape trials a year).

Of the six accused in 1730 only Charteris was found guilty, despite some very compelling evidence in the other cases, with one man being held in gaol so that his case could be pondered and he could perhaps be indicted for assault at the next assizes. The charge against him was eventually reduced because the female 'prosecutor' was just ten years old and considered too young to be put on oath. This decision was made despite the fact that the accused had been apprehended 'lying upon the child' with his 'private member drawn', and that he had, according to the victim – whose genital area was found by a surgeon to be 'depressed on the interior' – 'offer'd to put his

Nastiness into her mouth'.[6] The five other accused men were all of relatively humble origins (one was from Stepney) so were not saved by riches or power. Most seem to have escaped punishment – which would have been death – because they were men, and a jury of male peers probably thought death too extreme a punishment for merely attempting to have forced sex with a female, even one as young as ten.

After the verdict London was flooded with accounts of Charteris and his trial. Most were extremely hostile to Charteris, who predictably was dubbed the 'Rape-master general of Great Britain', while some used the opportunity to publish mildly diverting obscenities. *Some Authentic Memoirs of the Life of Colonel Ch—s*, for example, informed its readers that Charteris liked 'strong, lusty, fresh Country Wenches, of the first Size, their Buttocks as hard as Cheshire Cheeses, that should make a Dint in a Wooden Chair, and work like a Parish Engine at a Conflagration'.[7]

Colonel Charteris in the dock during his 1730 trial for rape.

This popular confusion of morality and traditional male usage and privilege is perfectly represented by a mezzotint that appeared immediately after the trial. It shows Charteris standing at the bar of the Old Bailey with his thumbs tied. Below the image is an inscription that is, presumably, ironic in its initial and violent support of the rights of men such as Charteris for it concludes with condemnation of his actions. But in its strident and sardonic couplets the inscription raises images that must reflect the firmly held opinions of those the print sought to satirise – probably the majority of London men. I wonder how many male readers failed to perceive the irony in this inscription?

It has an ambiguous start:

> Blood! – must a colonel, with a lord's estate,
> Be thus obnoxious to a scoundrel's fate?

Then it appears to become thunderingly misogynistic and contemptuous:

> Brought to the bar and sentenced from the bench,
> Only for ravishing a country wench?
> Shall men of honour meet no more respect?
> Shall their diversions thus by laws be check'd?
> Shall they be accountable to saucy juries
> For this or t'other pleasure? Hell and furies!

But finally the tone and target change:

> What man through villainy would run a course,
> And ruin families without remorse,
> To heap up riches – if, when all is done,
> An ignominious death he cannot shun?

Charteris, seemingly a broken man, was obliged to give up his dissolute and abusive life and in August dismissed his pimp John Gourlay and his other 'agents', was 'reconciled' to his wife and finally presented to the King as a reformed rake. This beastly man was treated as a 'Prodigal Son', but it was a show of hypocrisy. Charteris' true nature could not be hidden or the public fooled.

Emboldened by his official rehabilitation, in September 1730 Charteris impudently sued the High Baliff of Westminster and other officials for seizing goods and estates in Middlesex, Lancashire and Westmorland that

FRANCIS CHARTERIS—for a Rape. 209

vi&ion and execution fpeedily followed the appre-
henfion of his accomplice ; and that this apprehen-
fion arofe merely from the fufpicion of the porter,
who had feen him at the two public-houfes where
the money intended to be extorted was ordered to
be fent.

Hence let thofe inclined to acts of difhonefty
learn that the eye of Providence is ever watchful
to bring their evil deeds to light, and punifh
them in the moft exemplary manner. But there
ought to be, in every breaft, a fuperior motive
of action to that of fear. We ought to love virtue
for its own fake; and ftill more, as it muft be
acceptable to the great parent of all good; to
that God from whom all our bleffings are derived; to that fource of univerfal blifs in whom
we "live, move, and have our being." By fuch
a conduct we fhall infallibly render ourfelves happy
in this life; and be fuccefsful candidates for hap-
pinefs in that world where felicity fhall never
end!

Particulars of the remarkable Cafe of FRANCIS
CHARTERIS, who was condemned for a
Rape; but afterwards pardoned.

THE execrable fubject of this narrative was
born at Amsfield, in Scotland, where he was
heir to an eftate, which his anceftors had poffeffed
above four hundred years; and he was related to
fome of the firft families in the North, by inter-
marriages with the nobility.

Young Charteris having received a liberal education, made choice of the profeffion of arms,
Vol. II. No. 20.   D d   and

A page of the Newgate Calendar, *detailing Charteris' case.*

had been forfeited when he was convicted as a felon. Eventually he
regained his property, but only after paying compensation of about
£30,000. He also took what revenge he could upon Ann Bond. Soon after
the trial she married a tavern keeper and attempted to set up premises
in Bloomsbury that were to capitalise on her fleeting fame by having a
painted head of Colonel Charteris as their sign. He didn't much like the
plan and arranged for the husband to be arrested for debt.

Hated in London, Charteris retired to Edinburgh where he discovered
he was no better liked. He died in February 1732, 'in a miserable manner',
noted the *Newgate Calendar*, 'a victim of his own irregular course of life'.
He was buried in the family vault in Greyfriars churchyard among
extraordinarily violent scenes when a furious mob tried to tear open his

coffin to fill it with dead cats and mutilate his corpse. Charteris left his large fortune to the second son of his daughter and the Earl of Wemyss, perhaps the agreed recompense for Wemyss' earlier and most vital service in saving his father-in-law – and his family – from the ignominy of a public execution.

This dreadful tale has one curious postscript. Charteris' awful conduct not only provided a villain for Hogarth when painting *The Harlot's Progress* but also appears to have made an impression on the novelist Samuel Richardson. In the late 1730s, when writing *Pamela*, he must surely have had the Colonel in mind, for in his novel Pamela, a servant, is beset by a master intent on seducing her. Richardson, however, decided to create a fictional world that improved on fact and portrayed Pamela not only resisting her seducer but ultimately having her virtue rewarded by winning his genuine love and a proposal of honourable marriage. This moralistic and unlikely tale proved immensely popular when published in 1740, and indeed did much to establish the epistolary novel (that is, one written in the form of a series of letters) as a literary form. But not all were taken with the plot's contrived and sadly unrealistic form. Among the book's sternest critics was Henry Fielding, who was inspired by his loathing of Richardson's artifice to launch his own career as a writer of more earthy and realistic novels. First he wrote a direct spoof of *Pamela* – *Shamela* in 1741 – in which he revealed Pamela to be not a noble creature at all but a cunning and lascivious sham intent on entrapping her master into marriage, and, in 1742, the picaresque tale *Joseph Andrews* in which the accident-prone footman hero is Pamela's brother. Throughout these works Fielding honed his skill as a writer of fiction and in 1749 published his masterpiece, *Tom Jones*, one of the best English novels of the eighteenth century. Arguably, then, the sexual excesses of Colonel Charteris – the quintessential monster of London's sex industry – probably inspired some of the greatest literature of eighteenth-century Britain.

ACT THREE

THE TASTE OF SIN

TWELVE

VICE TAKES CENTRE STAGE

John Gay's The Beggar's Opera

Prostitution shaped London's economy and physical appearance, but its influence was more pervasive than that. It extended as far as the visual arts, literature, and even into such apparently esoteric areas as aesthetics, antiquarianism and the study of the ancient and primitive worlds. In fact, it transformed the social attitudes and taste of an entire age. And as attitudes and taste changed, they in turn influenced the general perception of prostitution.

If there is a single event that epitomises this transformation it is the first performance of John Gay's *The Beggar's Opera* in January 1728. *The Beggar's Opera* was a phenomenon. It marked a complete stylistic break from the Italian-style operas that had been so popular up until then, substituting simple ballads in English for highly wrought arias in a language most of the audience would not have understood. Its subject matter could not have been more different, either. Italian opera was not rooted in a world that any of its audience would actually have experienced – it was exotic and heroic, drawing heavily from history and legend. *The Beggar's Opera*, by contrast, was unashamedly topical and unheroic. It offered a shrewd critique of the morality of the age, exposing and attacking the political corruption, greed and bullying behaviour of the upper echelons of society, with a plot centred upon London's underworld and a castlist of harlots and robbers. This low-life setting was offered as a metaphor for the immoral worlds of politics and exploitative business, with the Whig administration of Sir Robert Walpole being a particular target. The opera asked a simple question. Who is the more corrupt: the powerful man who uses and abuses his position with impunity so as to indulge his own lusts and greed, or the poor man and the harlot, victims of circumstance, who are forced into crime or immorality in order to stay alive – and almost invariably punished by death?

The opera – a huge and instant success – turned the world upside down. It made the sex industry and low-life in general romantic. It transformed outlaws into, if not exactly paradigms of morality, utterly compelling anti-heroes, and it suggested that the apparently respectable but self-seeking ruling classes who lived as though they were above the law were the real villains and hypocritical corruptors of society.

John Gay, author of the epoch-making The Beggar's Opera, *which was first performed in January 1728 and which transformed the life of one of its stars, Lavinia Fenton.*

The opera also mixed fact and fiction in a way that dissolved the usual boundaries between illusion and reality. The common street-life of the capital was elevated into art, while art itself suddenly seemed dramatic-ally and directly relevant to the life that pulsated in the streets and taverns immediately outside the theatre doors. Indeed, the characters in the opera and in the London streets were – in some cases – quite literally the same. Harlots who had until recently patrolled the nearby streets now acted on stage – some playing young ladies, others dancers, and some essentially playing themselves. Not only was the libretto of the opera a social critique, so also were the means and manner of its production. The audience who flowed out of the doors of the Lincoln's Inn Fields Theatre, where *The Beggar's Opera* was first performed, would within minutes find themselves on Fleet Street, the Strand or Covent Garden, among the street-life and types so recently portrayed for their amusement and edification. This brilliant transformation of outcast London into the setting for a parable and fairy tale gave *The Beggar's Opera* another level of meaning. It challenged the preposterous excesses and stereotypical fantasies of Italian opera by showing that the subject, location and language of operatic art could be drawn from a source much nearer home. Art could be inspired by real life.

The huge impact of *The Beggar's Opera* was due not only to the novelty and immediacy of its low-life inspiration but also to an almost journalistic topicality, derived from the fact that many of its characters were based on notorious real-life criminals and whores, an idea that Jonathan Swift suggested in 1716. And, to heighten its dramatic intensity, a number of the real-life personalities reproduced as stage-characters were presented as symbolic of the dark forces that many saw as responsible for the ills then besetting England.

The opera, in short, works on several levels. At its most simple it is a witty love story with a moral and lots of catchy ballads. At another it is a biting satire and a powerful political commentary. When in 1716 Jonathan Swift first suggested using 'thieves and whores' in a 'Newgate Pastoral', he had imagined an ironic production with low-life characters playing the roles of shepherds and shepherdesses, but when Gay developed the idea he sharpened irony into razor-sharp satire with a social purpose. As Gay made clear, politicians and criminals may be equally bad, but corruption at the higher levels has far more dangerous consequences because it corrupts and enervates society as a whole and makes the entire nation suffer.

Gay's own point of view, indeed the moral of the opera, is made clear at the end. The Beggar, presented as the 'author' of the opera, observes in his epilogue that 'the whole Piece' reveals 'such a similitude of Manners in high and low life, that it is difficult to determine whether (in the fashionable Vices) the fine Gentlemen imitate the Gentlemen of the Road, or the Gentlemen of the Road, the fine Gentlemen'. The Beggar then goes on to explain that the meaning of the opera is to show that 'the lower sort of people have their vices in a degree as well as the rich', with the only real difference being that the 'lower sort' alone 'are punished for them'.

The frontispiece of a 1777 edition of The Beggar's Opera, *showing Captain Macheath in late-eighteenth-century dress.*

Gay created an enduring hero – or anti-hero – in the free-spirited, romantic, independent figure of Captain Macheath, who is the opera's central character. He is a thief – a highwayman – and a philanderer. But he is also a highly attractive character whose criminal nature is seen as nothing compared to the greedy heartlessness of corrupt authority figures all around who treacherously seek his fortune and death by any means possible.

The character of Macheath was inspired by legendary English outlaw heroes of the past such as Robin Hood but also by the far more recent example of Jack Sheppard. Hanged in 1724 at the age of only twenty-two, he was a thief who had captured the public's attention and admiration through a series of audacious escapes from various London gaols. As well as being one of the models for Macheath, his life suggested something of the structure of *The Beggar's Opera* and was the inspiration for a number of its other characters besides the highwayman.

Sheppard was a boisterous, happy-go-lucky East End boy – he'd been born in Spitalfields – who was led astray and to drink by a prostitute named Elizabeth Lyon. She induced him to abandon his apprenticeship and introduced him to London's criminal community, including the notorious Joseph 'Blueskin' Blake. They became partners in crime and, although initially successful, soon came into serious conflict with Jonathan Wild, the self-styled 'Thief-taker General'.

Wild was a figure loathed by London's underworld, a man even thieves saw as corrupt, dishonest and despicable, and when he finally came to grief himself in 1725 his execution at Tyburn was celebrated like a public holiday. As Daniel Defoe observed in his *True and Genuine Account of the late Jonathan Wild*, published only a month after the execution, the crowds lining the route from Newgate to Tyburn were larger than ever seen before, and as the cart carrying Wild passed along there was 'nothing to be heard but cursings and execrations, abhoring the crimes and very Name of the Man, throwing stones and dirt at him all the way.'[1]

Gay's audience would have recognised Wild as one model for the hypocritical, greedy and cynical Mr Peachum who, while bent on profiting from Macheath's execution as a criminal, is himself a fence, and a runner and denouncer of thieves. In addition, most of the audience would have realised that the character of Peachum was also a vehicle for an attack upon the dubious ethics and self-serving actions of the Whig politician Sir Robert Walpole, who many believed corrupt and overbearing. Gay makes the connection pretty clear when he has Peachum complain that '. . . the statesman because he's so great, thinks his trade as honest as mine'. The analogy between the two prototypes for Peachum – Wild and Walpole – was in any case already well established by 1728 for various

Jack Sheppard making a daring roof-top escape, as illustrated by George Cruikshank in the early nineteenth century.

Tory journals had, soon after Wild's execution, claimed to see parallels between the crimes for which he had rightly lost his life and the 'crimes' by which Walpole prospered. Daniel Defoe in his biography of Wild similarly implied this. Ironically, when Walpole first saw the opera he greatly enjoyed it. Only later did he discover that he was its principle target. His response was to ensure that Gay's follow-up work – *Polly* – was banned.

He was not the only person to have missed the opera's deeper level of meaning. So, more predictably, did many foreign members of the audience. The French visitor César de Saussure went to an early performance and afterwards confessed himself confused and somewhat affronted:

Jonathan Wild in 1725 being pelted with stones and dirt by an infuriated mob when on his way to execution at Tyburn. The route he took from Newgate Prison to Tyburn – running via High Holborn, St Giles High Street and Oxford Road/Street – formed the promenade of death taken by all convicted criminals on their way to execution. This grim route ran to the north of and roughly parallel to the 'sexual highway', which ran west from the Royal Exchange to Charing Cross, St James's, and then south to Westminster.

> The Beggar's Opera ... which is highly in fashion at the moment, and
> which played yesterday for the twenty-fourth time ... is a type of farce,
> the scenery representing a prison and houses of debauch. The actors play
> highwaymen and downright libertines, the actresses prostitutes. I let you
> imagine what can be expected from the heart and spirit of people of this
> type. The piece is full of very pretty ballads, but they are too loose to be
> sung in front of any who have any modesty.[2]

Besides its characters and locations, the language of the opera also
presented a problem for Saussure, who observed that English playwrights
'frequently use words with double meanings, which the English call
"humours", and sometimes even crudities ... In a word the theatre of
England is not at all chaste nor refined, like the theatre of Paris.'[3]

No doubt Saussure would have been equally shocked to learn the details
of some of the actors involved in the production, whose own shady back-
grounds added extra piquancy to the production. Playing the central part
of Polly Peachum, for example, was Lavinia Fenton, who would have been
known to many of the audience as a former prostitute of Covent Garden
and latterly an actress of most dubious reputation. In the play, Polly
Peachum is the daughter of the rogue bent on Macheath's destruction.
She saves Macheath and – perhaps – redeems him by marriage. The
success of the opera transformed Lavinia's life. She became instantly
famous, wealthy, and was courted by one of the besotted first-night audience, the Duke of Bolton. In the play a furious Mrs Peachum berates
Polly for her marriage to Macheath by calling her a 'foolish Jade' and
warning her that she will 'be as ill-used and as much neglected, as if thou
hadst married a Lord'.[4] Lavinia did not heed this advice but first lived
with and then finally married the duke (see page 121).

And then there was Nancy Dawson, who joined the production after
it moved to Drury Lane. She was another authentic 'Woman of the Town'
who benefited from the wild success of this new opera that romanticised
her trade. Nancy had a reputation as a dancer. She had performed at Moll
King's notorious and rowdy coffee house in Covent Garden (see page
203), moved on to Sadler's Wells, and was then hired to dance solo between
the acts of the opera. Her horn-pipe was apparently so enchantingly lascivious that, just like Lavina, Nancy achieved instant fame and was 'vastly
celebrated [and] imitated by all'.

The prostitute Nancy Dawson, who made her name dancing the horn-pipe in between the acts of The Beggar's Opera.

Her signature horn-pipe, danced to the tune of 'Here We Go Round the Mulberry Bush', was accompanied by a song that included the chorus: 'Her easy mien, her shape so neat, she foots, she trips. She looks so sweet, her every motion's so complete, I die for Nancy Dawson.'

Nancy's *Genuine Memoirs* appeared in 1760, and *Nancy Dawson's Jests* in 1761, containing 'a collection of songs written for the delight and amusement of all her admirers'. By the time she died in 1767 Nancy was living comfortably in a house on Haverstock Hill, Hampstead that was part of a group of buildings built by, and also containing the home of, her former employer Moll King.

Other characters in the opera proclaimed, in well-established theatrical tradition, their natures or callings through their names. For example, the 'Women of the Town' were generally given humorous names that were common synonyms for harlots, such as Dolly Trull, Betty Doxy and Molly Brazen. But one, named Jenny Diver, is different. Although the name describes her occupation – pick-pocket – Jenny Diver was also the street name by which a highly skilled, daring and real-life female thief became famous.

Mary Young was born in Ireland in about 1700, but by the early 1720s was in the St Giles-in-the-Fields area of London and part of a gang of pick-pockets led by Anne Murphy. Mary soon proved herself nimble-fingered and, as contemporary accounts state, was at this early time in her career nicknamed 'Jenny Diver' by her admiring fellow gang members. Unlike most of the members of the early-Georgian criminal underworld, Mary was educated, highly intelligent and genteel in appearance. Her 'superior address' was what gave her the edge in her calling and determined the ploys she practised. Smartly dressed and acting demurely, she could move and work among high-society crowds without being noticed, and so made churches, theatres and the Exchange her hunting grounds. She was also extremely inventive, devising various cunning stratagems for robbing people, and seems to have hit upon the same ploy used by Moll King (see page 82) and utilised a pair of false arms and hands that she placed on her lap during a church service while her real hands emptied the pockets of her neighbours.

By the time *The Beggar's Opera* was first staged, Mary had been operating in London for nearly a decade. Gay must have heard of her extraordinary accomplishments. Certainly Macheath's description of Jenny Diver in the opera – 'prim and demure as ever' with a 'sanctify'd look' concealing a 'mischievous heart' – sounds uncannily like an accurate description of the real Mary Young. (It is just possible, however, since the chronology is uncertain, that things actually happened the other way round and that Mary derived her alias from the play.) She was caught in the act, tried, found guilty and sentenced to transportation to Virginia in 1733 but returned illegally to London and, after various adventures and close-calls' was in 1741 arrested again and tried under the name of Mary Young 'alias Jenny Diver' for the capital crimes of violent theft and highway robbery.[5]

Mary's daring and colourful life reads like a work of fiction but, in its ending, has the dark and sombre ring of reality. Gay, in the finale of *The Beggar's Opera*, has his Beggar narrator proclaim that, 'to make the piece perfect' and do 'strict poetical Justice', Macheath should be hanged, 'and for all the other Personages of the Drama, the Audience must have suppos'd they were all hang'd or transported'. But the Beggar admits that this end, though morally correct, is too serious for an opera. Bowing to the 'taste of the Town' she ordains that in the final scene Macheath be reprieved 'no matter how absurdly . . . brought about'.

For Mary Young, living in the real world, 'strict poetical Justice' was not so easily avoided. Her life ended in March 1741 when – dressed in an elegant and fashionable black dress, bonnet and veil – she and nineteen other condemned criminals were hanged at Tyburn. The Ordinary of Newgate's account of Mary's life and last hours estimated her age as about '36 years of age', though this was probably an underestimate. At the very end, it says, the swashbuckling Mary 'repented of all her sins and was at peace with all the world'.[6]

The sentiments, images and characters of *The Beggar's Opera* captured the imagination of the public and, to an astonishing degree, reverberated throughout eighteenth-century London. Gay's characters, drawn from reality, had such a compelling air of truth about them that they, in turn, inspired reality, or at least became as if real for generations of Londoners. Perhaps stranger still, Gay's fictional characters became so familiar in their symbolism and meaning that other artists used them as references in their own fictions. For example Hogarth, in the first painting of *The Harlot's Progress* series in 1731, showed Moll Hackabout looking like a fresh-faced Polly Peachum; and in painting three she has, in her thread-bare lodgings, a print beside her bed of Captain Macheath – enduring symbol of lingering romantic sentiments about love, liberty and ultimate salvation (see page 6).

In the same year as Hogarth completed *The Harlot's Progress*, George Lillo's play *The London Merchant* was produced at Drúry Lane. Based on the true story of George Barnwell, who murdered his rich uncle at the insti-gation of the prostitute Sara Millwood, the play not only continued some of the outcast themes of *The Beggar's Opera* – which was evidently its inspiration – but also in almost uncanny manner embraced some of the sentiments expressed in *The Harlot's Progress*. When charged in the play with abusing her 'uncommon perfections of Mind and Body', Sara turns on her hypocritical male accusers, curses their 'barbarous Sex' for robbing her of those 'perfections' before she 'knew their worth', and states that if she's been 'wicked, be it so', but all had been learned in 'Conversation with your sex'. As in *The Harlot's Progress*, the particular targets for Lillo's anger were dishonest and morally compromised clergymen and magistrates.[7]

The Beggar's Opera also became a stock-in-trade of everyday conversa-tion. When, for example, Lord Sandwich impeached John Wilkes in the House of Lords in November 1763, he was immediately nicknamed Jemmy Twitcher after the man who 'peaches', or informs on, Macheath in the opera.

James Boswell in his *London Journal* of 1762–3 referred often to Macheath, whom he saw as an inspiring role model. The entry for Thursday 19 May 1763 is a case in point:

> I sallied forth to the Piazzas [in Covent Garden] in rich flow of animal spirits and burning with fierce desire. I met two very pretty little girls who asked me to take them with me. 'My dear girls,' said I, 'I am a poor fellow. I can give you no money. But if you choose to have a glass of wine and my company and let us be gay and obliging to each other without money, I am your man.' They agreed with great good humour. So back to the Shakespeare I went. 'Waiter,' said I, 'I have got here a couple of human beings; I don't know how they'll do.' 'I'll look your honour,' cried he, and with inimitable effrontery stared them in the face and then cried, 'They'll do very well.' 'What?' said I. 'Are they good fellow-creatures? Bring them up then.' We were shown into a good room and had a bottle of sherry before us in a minute. I surveyed my seraglio and found them both good subjects for amorous play. I toyed with them and drank about and sung *Youth's the Season* [the song in *The Beggar's Opera* that Macheath sings with his group of harlots] and then thought myself Captain Macheath; and then I solaced my existence with them, one after the other, according to their seniority. I was quite *raised* as the phrase is: thought I was in a London tavern, the Shakespeare's Head, enjoying high debauchery [that is, debauchery with genteel ceremony as opposed to common 'low' debauchery] after my sober winter. I parted with my ladies politely and came home in a glow of spirits.[8]

Despite having been premièred over thirty years before Lord Sandwich gained his contemptuous nickname and young Boswell enjoyed his night of 'high debauchery' (during which he caught gonorrhoea), *The Beggar's Opera* and its main characters remained reference points and touchstones for London life and helped define the character of the age.

THIRTEEN

MUSES, GODDESSES
AND PAINTED LADIES

Art and Sir Joshua Reynolds

The 1720s and 30s were decades dominated by passion for primary forms, such as cubes and spheres, regularity, ratio and harmoniously related sequences of proportion. These were believed to represent the divine building blocks of creation, the secret code to the beauty of the natural world – including, of course, the beauty of the human body. The basis of this theory lay in the writings and works of Italian Renaissance thinkers, artists and architects such as Leon Battista Alberti who published his *De Re Aedificatoria* between 1443 and 1452 and Andrea Palladio whose *I Quattro Libri* was published in 1570.

The architectural expression of these beliefs in early-eighteenth-century Britain was a style now called Palladian after Andrea Palladio, its main inspiration. The governing principle of Palladian architecture was a rational and simple application of the classical language of design, a logical and harmonious relation between parts – for example, the form and proportion of plan, elevations and details should be integrated – and the use of a proportional system organised around the square and the cube. To work with these proportions, argued the Palladians, was to work in sympathy and understanding with God's creation, the harmony of nature itself. A leading architectural theorist, Robert Morris, put the point succinctly in his 1728 *Essay in Defence of Ancient Architecture* where he states that:

> Grecians were the first happy inventors [of harmoniously proportioned
> architecture], they extracted the beauteous idea of it from rude and
> unshapen trees, the products of nature, and embellished it, by degree of
> perfection, with those necessary ornaments which have since been
> practised by those of the most sublime genius . . . collected by the
> indefatigable care and industry of Palladio.[1]

On the other hand, to work against the Ancients' nature-based key to beauty was to display both arrogance and ignorance.

This belief in a set of divine and immutable rules governing beauty was in direct opposition to the spirit of the Baroque period, which had immediately preceded the fashion for Palladianism. Baroque, as expressed by the paintings of Sir James Thornhill, for instance, or the idiosyncratic and theatrical classicism of Sir John Vanbrugh's Blenheim Palace or Nicholas Hawksmoor's Christ Church, Spitalfields, gave pre-eminence to the creative power of human invention within the basic structure of classical rules. For Baroque artists it was an essential tenet of belief that each generation should be free to add to and adapt the classical canons, be individual and reflect the spirit of its own age, not be condemned merely to copy the old masters.

Among the leading promoters of the rational and geometrically-inspired Palladian style in England were men such as Lord Burlington, part of the powerful governing Whig establishment, and his protégé William Kent. There were many, however, who did not wish to subscribe to the style favoured by the ruling hegemony and it is possible to see in the neo-Baroque style known as Rococo, which began to make its appearance at this time, a reaction not just against the Palladian style but the men who advocated it. Rococo rejected the square, the cube and strict symmetry, preferring flowing forms and asymmetry, and drew inspiration from exotic and distant cultures – notably China – and the Gothic past rather than strictly from Rome and Renaissance Italy.

William Hogarth, an independent thinker sceptical of Whig orthodoxy, was a great champion of the Rococo movement and in 1753 published *The Analysis of Beauty*, challenging the Palladian doctrine of absolute beauty and its quantified system of cubic proportion and, instead, observing that much of what is commonly regarded as beautiful has a gently serpentine or S-shaped form: what Hogarth termed the 'line of beauty'. His argument was reinforced with a series of astute and cunning comparative illustrations, showing the presence or absence of beauty in both man-made and natural objects – clothes, chair-legs, wigs, faces and bodies – depending on their closeness to, or distance from, the line of beauty. In place of fixed rules, Hogarth pointed out half a dozen attributes of beauty: things that don't necessarily guarantee it but which, in their entire absence, make beauty impossible. Indeed he recognised that

*A 1753 engraving by Hogarth demonstrating his theory of the 'line of beauty',
as put forward in his book* The Analysis of Beauty. *Hogarth argued that
beauty lay in a line of sinuous form, and that if the curve
was too flat or too pronounced, beauty was lost. The print shows worked
examples of the theory expressed through cabriole chair legs, corsets,
candlesticks and the human body.*

beauty was a far more personal and subjective quality than the Palladians
cared to acknowledge. In this he was very much following the Baroque
spirit of the late seventeenth century when, for example, Sir Christopher
Wren wrote of two types of beauty – 'Natural', which is the result of
absolute geometric laws, and 'Customary', which is a type of beauty
perceived through the senses or simply through association.[2]

Hogarth also observed that 'fitness' was an important component of
beauty, or rather it was difficult for something to be perceived as beautiful
if it was entirely inappropriate to its function or circumstances. He also
promoted the virtues of 'variety', 'regularity', 'simplicity', but also of
'intricacy' and – much in the emergent Picturesque spirit of the time – the
emotional and visual impact of 'quantity' and 'greatness'. Scale in relationship to perceptions of beauty was more fully and expertly investigated

and expressed by Edmund Burke in 1757 in *A Philosophical Enquiry into the Origin of our Ideas of the Sublime and Beautiful*.

Fascination with variety and irregularity, when it came to portraiture, meant of course that the close study of the individual human form was crucially important, and here there was a problem. Where could a painter find a quantity of nudes for comparative study? Corpses were in high demand, the meagre supply being jealously guarded and swiftly exploited for dissection by equally body-hungry surgeons in their quest for improved medical knowledge (see page 539). Realistic wax effigies of bodies could be, and indeed were, made.

Agostino Carlini, a sculptor and in 1768 a founder member of the Royal Academy, cast the corpse of a hanged criminal that had been flayed by Dr William Hunter, the Academy's first professor of anatomy, and set most eruditely in a pose inspired by the antique statue known as the *Dying Gladiator*. The figure was made in about 1773 and, since the executed felon had been a smuggler, the students set to draw the sombre relic soon christened it 'Smugglerius'. But useful as this figure was – and an 1834 cast of the original still survives in the RA – it and others like it were no real substitute for a study of the living, breathing and preferably naked body, its flesh and musculature pulsating with life and movement.

Life drawing conducted at an institute open to the public had a venerable tradition in European art, for example in the Carraci family's Accademia degli Incamminati located in Bologna in the 1580s, but in early-eighteenth-century London it was still a somewhat novel idea. This was partly because England had no overall official administrative body for or public patron of the arts, beyond organisations or individuals involved in specific projects. There was nothing to compare with the Paris Salon or an official arbiter such as Colbert. All that London could offer were the results of small-scale private undertakings and speculative initiatives.

In 1711 Sir Godfrey Kneller – the Lübeck-born Principal Painter to the Crown – established an Academy of Painting and Drawing in Great Queen Street that included life-drawing classes. This closed in around 1716 but the idea was soon taken up by Kneller's fellow court painter James Thornhill, who was made Serjeant Painter by George I in 1720 and knighted the same year.

Thornhill worked in the grand and continental Baroque manner but, despite his passion for the swaggering theatrical flourish and lavish allegory, understood that intimate knowledge of the human form was the foundation of all great figurative art. To make this knowledge available to his fellow artists, he established in 1724 a life-drawing academy that was located in a large room he had added to his own house in Covent Garden. This academy operated until Thornhill's death in May 1734 but not particularly successfully – artistically or financially – according to his son-in-law, William Hogarth.

One of the problems identified by Hogarth was competition from one of Thornhill's former pupils, John Vanderbank, who had started an academy in 1720, but this rival institute did not flourish long either, probably largely due to Vanderbank's dissolute and disorganised manner of life. So in 1735 the coast was clear for Hogarth's own initiative. Carrying apparatus and other useful equipment and fittings from Thornhill's now defunct academy a few hundred yards away, to a large room off Peter's Court, Hogarth established his own St Martin's Lane Academy.[3]

This was to be a pioneering and influential establishment. Not only did it make life-models available to aspiring artists, it also established certain democratic principles upon which such institutions should be run in future and, in several significant ways, laid the foundations for the Royal Academy of Arts, founded in 1768 with Sir Joshua Reynolds its first president.

Hogarth's Academy, which closed in 1767, was not organised hierarchically, with pupils gathered at the feet of a master, but was more of a club, a brotherhood of artists, learning together and from each other. It was also financed like a club with members paying annual dues. This model was to a large extent inspired by a near neighbour in St Martin's Lane – Old Slaughter's Coffee House – which, founded in 1692, had long been a gathering place for artists, writers, men of science, travellers – including, later in the eighteenth century, men such as Joseph Banks and James Cook – indeed for anyone with an enquiring mind and a thirst for knowledge.[4]

Hogarth's Academy also promoted – in subtle manner – a particular artistic approach. Members included the sculptor Louis-François Roubiliac, Francis Hayman, the young Thomas Gainsborough, George Michael Moser – who was later to become one of the founding members of the Royal Academy – and the architect Isaac Ware, who in his magisterial book of 1756, *A Complete Body of Architecture*, neatly reconciled the still prevailing taste for regular Palladian design with the Rococo spirit he had imbibed at the Academy.

Professional female artists – very few in number in the eighteenth century although generally much admired for the quality of their work – could not set foot in the life-drawing room even, it seems, when the model was female. Eighteenth-century British society still could not quite accept that being a painter was a respectable profession for a female – perhaps because it involved too much looking at, and thinking about, the body. This strange state of affairs is revealed by Johann Zoffany's group portrait of 1771/2 that shows *The Academicians of the Royal Academy* assembled in a room in Old Somerset House and contemplating a naked male life-model. Out of respect for decency, the two female Academicians – Mary Moser and Angelica Kauffmann – are excluded from the assembly of artists but cunningly included in the painting as a pair of portraits apparently surveying the scene.

A constant problem for artists running drawing academies was finding the right type and gender of model for the life-drawing classes. They must then decide how to pose them. Possible solutions raised several artistic and moral issues. Should the models be entirely naked, for instance, and should they represent typical or ideal human forms – which is to say, would the artist gain more technically by studying and drawing a lithe, young, spare naked body rather than an older, plumper, partially clothed one? This ongoing debate encapsulated mid-eighteenth-century thinking about the way artists should respond to, and represent, the human body. For example, Roubiliac adopted what could be called a natural style with the subjects of his busts usually shown in relaxed posture, often infor-mally clad and representing vignettes of life – in spirit they are more like sketches than monumental works of sculpture.

A work by one of Roubiliac's main rivals, John Michael Rysbrack, who arrived in London in 1720 from the Low Countries, offers an insight into a rather different mid-eighteenth-century approach and source of inspir-ation. In the mid-1740s Rysbrack was commissioned by the banker Henry Hoare to create an heroic figure of Hercules to adorn the interior of a domed Pantheon-inspired temple that had been designed by Henry Flitcroft for a lakeside location in the mighty garden Hoare was creating at Stourhead in Wiltshire. The statue was very important in the artistic scheme – and indeed meaning – of the garden.

Hercules was famed for the way he resisted the temptation of worldly pleasure and followed the path of righteousness and virtue – a moral example considered particularly appropriate for a banker dealing with other people's money. So Hoare's Hercules had to look the part, appear noble, strong of mind and spirit, incorruptible – representing all the qualities Hoare himself wished to personify in the eyes of his friends and clients. This meant Rysbrack had to create the image of a superman, or at least a man who appeared to be the model of perfection. In his youth he had made a detailed study of the Italian Old Masters and of antique art so, unsurprisingly, based the posture of his Stourhead figure on the famed and inspirational Farnese Hercules – a third-century AD copy of a Greek original, showing Hercules in thoughtful posture. This statue, excavated from the Baths of Caracalla in Rome in 1546 and acquired by Cardinal Alessandro Farnese, was well known from prints and, in the mid-eighteenth century, regarded as one of the greatest works of art to survive from the ancient world. But what of the detail? Who was to be Rysbrack's life-model for the body of this ideal man? The sculptor was inventive and he was sensible – he walked the streets of London, sketching the body parts of the strongest and most well-muscled men he could see, mostly chairmen whose daily toil was to carry people through the bumpy and crowded streets of the city. Rysbrack's Hercules is thus an authentic Frankenstein's monster – one extraordinary man formed from the parts of many – in its different details naturalistic and the fruit of close observation, but in its entirety a work of pure artistic invention.[5]

Chairmen and market porters were just the sort of male models that drawing academies could have got hold of with relative ease and for a fee of only a few shillings. But what of female subjects? The obvious solution was to hire harlots who were, of course, in ready supply since most academies were, either by happy chance or design, located in or near Covent Garden. The fee offered was reasonable – the Royal Academy, for instance, paid half a guinea a session – but harlots proved unexpectedly squeamish. Apparently they viewed the process of sitting naked, open to public gaze, as a degrading and humiliating experience.[6] One proposed solution was for the female model to wear a mask, thus reversing the established role of concealment in London's sex industry.

By tradition and practice the mask was the recognised and coquettish emblem of the harlot's trade and one of the emblems by which a prostitute drew attention to herself at a masquerade (see page 194). James Wright in his *Historia Histrionica: An Historical Account of the English Stage* of 1699, when complaining about harlots making nuisances of themselves in theatres, needed only to refer to them by this familiar token of their trade when he waspishly observed that 'the Play-houses are so extremely pestered with Vizard-masks'. Charles Burnaby, in the epilogue to his 1702 play *The Modish Husband*, conjured up a familiar image of the prostitute for his audience by describing her mask made of 'eighteen pence of velvet', while Hogarth featured a mask in painting two of *The Harlot's Progress* (see page 10).

But in the life-drawing room the mask, rather than being an erotic badge, was to be an aid to female modesty, ensuring that artists who drew a harlot's naked body wouldn't subsequently recognise her when she was clothed. It is now difficult to know how regularly female life-models adopted masks, since documentary evidence records only a few examples. James Northcote mentions a model wearing one in the school at the Royal Academy in the 1770s and there is a drawing by Thomas Stothard in the RA collection that shows a female model in a mask, but documentary evidence suggests that such masking in practice was rare.[7] Presumably modelling for life-drawing classes came to be seen as a sort of speciality service by prostitutes and only those who did not flinch from this form of intimacy agreed to work for the drawing academies.

Sir Joshua Reynolds, the first president of the Royal Academy.

Complications created by taboos over public nakedness and the difficulty of getting the particular poses he required were perhaps what
prompted Joshua Reynolds to investigate an alternative means of turning
a prostitute into an artist's muse in the antique manner. He himself set
about making direct contact with various women of the town. This may
appear an odd – even dubious – activity. Why, if Reynolds was already
busy with commissions, did he need additional female models? Why
not increase his knowledge of the human body and improve his
draughtsmanship while paid to do it by his respectable sitters?

The answer of course lies in the words 'paid' and 'respectable'. Reynolds
couldn't reasonably examine and draw those parts of the body not promi-
nently featured in the commissioned painting. Nor could he expressly ask
his grand or aristocratic female sitters to expose any part of their bodies
for his detailed scrutiny, let alone to strike poses that might be deemed
incompatible with their virtue and dignity.

Certain areas of the female body were particularly charged with
sexual significance in the mid-eighteenth century. Especially intriguing
to the keen male observer of women were the female foot and ankle,
regarded as the epitome of femininity (as Reynolds' portraits often
suggest). Similarly the neck, the breast, the lower arm and wrist – indeed,
generally those areas of female flesh that the prevailing fashions only
just permitted men to see. No doubt it was for this reason, as well as
more practical ones, that mid-eighteenth-century dresses were cut to
just above the ankle, so that the delightful articulated focus of male
interest could be tantalisingly glimpsed, foot sheathed in an elegant
leather or silk-clad shoe with tipped-up pointed toe and serpentine-
shaped heel that was a compelling example both of 'fitness' and
Hogarth's 'line of beauty'.

As it was, Reynolds sometimes pushed his respectable if not aristocratic sitters to the limit – for example, the delightful Mrs Lloyd in 1775,
who is seen in alluring profile with sandal-clad bare feet carving her name
on a tree, or Mrs Hale as *Euphrosyne* (1764–6) in which the aristocratic
subject thrusts her best and somewhat naked foot and ankle forward when
simulating one of the Three Graces.

Representing a reputable lady as an antique character was a standard
way of revealing a little more flesh and bodily form than would otherwise have been deemed decent. But this strategy only took him so far.

To explore the female nude, he had to look elsewhere for more willing objects of contemplation and study. There was, of course, another possible reason for Reynolds' action in seeking out models from the sex industry – it made sound commercial sense. By using models from the city's sex trade he was being delightfully risqué in a way calculated to appeal to and titillate his market. Within his studio he created a constantly changing display that included portraits of famous courtesans and actresses beside those of grand aristocrats – all rendered in the same beguiling style that highlighted the ideal rather than the actual. A display of images of the loveliest ladies in the land, both high and low, all looking slightly, and most flatteringly, lovelier than life, was a brilliant way of attracting potential customers. It proved to be very good for business.

Those of Reynolds' pocket books that survive in the archives of the Royal Academy (80 per cent from 1755–90) offer only circumstantial evidence of his activities with prostitutes. They record the names of the women who modelled for him, occasionally where he met them and which parts of their bodies he drew, but the evidence that the women were prostitutes comes not directly from the pocket books but from other sources, and sometimes from the locations where he met them. For example, in his pocket book for 1773, opposite the page for 5 April, Reynolds noted the address of the well-known brothel run by Mrs Goadby at the 'Green Lawn' in Great Marlborough Street, Soho (see page 207). An edition of the *Covent Garden Magazine* in 1773 lauded the establishment and informed its readers that Mrs Goadby accommodated gentlemen of all 'tastes and caprices',[8] including, it would seem, clients like Reynolds who only wanted to look at the girls. The notes in the pocket books are brief and enigmatic but offer a fresh and fascinating glimpse of London's eighteenth-century sex trade and help further to flesh out some of the characters who flit spectre-like through the annals of the age. Reynolds met these girls in taverns, brothels and bagnios – like Toulouse-Lautrec but over a hundred years earlier. He entered the sexual underworld in search of information and inspiration, making close contact with those respectable society chose to proclaim as outcasts.

The work that resulted from these explorations is sometimes delicate, at other times lascivious, and Reynolds' non-working relationship with his harlot muses remains the topic of never-ending speculation and debate. Was it entirely innocent and purely professional or were any of these young women his lovers as well as his models? It is now impossible to say for sure, though the documentary evidence suggests he merely observed their bodies. What is certain, however, is that a few of these young women became, over the years, his close and special friends, while the paintings they inspired suggest that Reynolds felt real warmth and affection for most of the girls and young women who modelled for him.

References to such young ladies crowd the pages of his pocket books and certain of them were clearly favoured for particular – presumably exemplary – parts of the body. In the pocket book for 1772, opposite the page for 27 July, for instance, Reynolds referred to a 'Miss Boothby at Mrs Fields, Church Street, next door to the Cheese House. Model for neck'. And in the back of the book for 1779 he noted a 'Mrs Ruth, Childs Rents, Tuthill Street, Westminster', to whom he reminded himself to 'send a penny post letter, when I want her for a nek'. It's possible these references have an obscure double-meaning but there is no compelling reason not to take them at face value. For Reynolds a good neck to draw was perhaps more important than good sex – such objects of study were essential to an artist whose portraiture needed to be based on a thorough understanding of the human body. No doubt when he had these girls available to study, he would ponder their forms and the artistic possibilities offered by their bodies, sketch them, and finally apply the insights gained when composing a commissioned portrait.

Another telling location is mentioned in the pocket book for 1773, this time associated with the name of a harlot who was to become a famous and powerful courtesan. On the page of the week starting 8 June Reynolds wrote, 'Mrs Armistead, at Mrs Mitchell's, Upper John Street, Golden Square'. Elizabeth Mitchell had run an exclusive seraglio or brothel in Golden Square, Soho, and perhaps also from 1770 in King's Place, St James's. Mrs Armistead was evidently one of her young ladies. Two years later Elizabeth Armistead achieved the transition from brothel to stage when she made her debut in Richard Steele's 1722 play *The Conscious Lovers*. She subsequently became the long-term mistress and, from 1795, wife of Reynolds' friend the politician Charles James Fox, thus becoming a rare example of the harlot who successfully progressed from brothel, to stage, to security and respectability.[9]

Some of the places of assignation mentioned by Reynolds were probably smaller and more discreet brothels that have faded from the pages of history, leaving no trace beyond the scribbled notes in the artist's pocket books. On the back leaf of his pocket book for 1769, for instance, Reynolds wrote, 'Model Miss Wilson at Mrs Stoobs in Bentinck Srt, Barwick Srt, Soho'. We know no more about 'Mrs Stoobs' but the Berwick Street area was, and indeed remains, a likely location for a brothel so presumably Mrs Stoobs was a bawd. As for Miss Wilson, she seems to have been a well-known 'lady of the town' who was identified by Horace Walpole as the subject of Reynolds' highly erotic painting, including a phallic-like snake's head, that was aptly titled *Snake in the Grass*. The painting was finally exhibited in 1784 so the time lapse between Reynolds' recorded assignation with Miss Wilson and the public debut of the painting is odd, however, and is one the reasons why some historians suggest the model might in fact have been the youthful Emma Hart (see below). This certainly makes more sense if the painting was conceived and executed, as well as first exhibited, in the early 1780s.[10] The painting shows a bare-breasted young woman, a young nymph, sitting with her arm artfully shielding one eye while the other shoots a bewitching and inviting glance at the viewer. As she disports herself in this sensuous manner Cupid tugs at the sash around the nymph's waist, clearly intent on strip-ping her entirely and thus provoking the work's subtitle: *Love Untying the Zone of Beauty*.

Four versions, in slightly different dimensions, of this enticing image were produced: one for, or certainly soon acquired by, Prince Potemkin, the Russian soldier, statesman and lover of Catherine the Great, which is now in the Hermitage, St Petersburg; one painted in 1788 for Lord Carysfort, a Fellow of the Royal Society; while a third found its way into the possession of the architect Sir John Soane in whose London museum it still smoulders at all who care to glance at it.

Harriet Powell was another of the well-formed, strong-willed and independent-minded young prostitutes whom Reynolds found so attrac-tive and artistically stimulating. His pocket book for 1769 records sittings with Harriet in April and May and a fine portrait of her holding a bird (possibly representing Leonora in the play *The Padlock*) was commissioned by Lord Seaforth, who appears in one of Reynolds' Dilettanti group portraits of 1777.[11] The *Town and Country Magazine* of May 1775 claims Harriet was Seaforth's mistress and may also, secretly, have been his wife. William Hickey, in his *Memoirs*, offers a vignette of the spirited young woman in mid-1780: '[T]here came to dine with Emily [Warren – see below], Harriet Powell, an old flame of mine, who had been a contemporary of Emily's at Charlotte Hayes' . . . Powell was in high keeping, and drove to the door in an elegant chariot of her own.'[12]

Another relatively obscure person and location on which Reynolds throws a ray of light is Mrs Elizabeth Hartley who, in his pocket book for 1771, he notes as living in Little James Street, Haymarket with Mrs Kelly – a bawd who soon moved to a grander address in Arlington Street, Piccadilly where she opened a brothel in the mid-1770s with Emma Hart as one of her girls.

Elizabeth Hartley was a minor actress with striking red hair who had been spotted in Bristol by one of David Garrick's scouts who noted that there was 'a slovenly good-nature about her that renders her prodigiously vulgar'. This was clearly seen as a good thing, for Elizabeth (also referred to as Elizabeth White) was duly signed up by Garrick and made her London debut in 1772 at Covent Garden in Nicholas Rowe's 1714 *Tragedy of Jane Shaw* – a part that the 'tragic muse' Sarah Siddons was from 1782 to make her own.

Elizabeth Hartley's prodigious vulgarity evidently made her attractive to men of certain tastes and she sat several times for Reynolds. She was the model in 1772, unlikely as it may seem, for a Madonna, probably commissioned by Edmund Burke. In 1771 Reynolds painted her as the nymph shown with a young Bacchus (now in Tate Britain), perhaps for Lord Carysfort. And last, in 1773, as the penitent Jane Shore, who was, most appropriately, a notorious fifteenth-century courtesan. Clearly Mrs Hartley was an object of titillating fantasy for many of her male admirers – 'saint and sinner, available and yet sanctified' as Martin Postle has pointed out.[13]

One location where Reynolds almost certainly met some of these young ladies still survives. In the centre of the north side of Gerrard Street in Soho, currently number 9, stands a fine but decaying 1750s building that now houses a collection of Cantonese shops and storerooms. It was originally constructed as a tavern named the Turk's Head. Today, beneath shelves and displays of exotic foods and drinks, fine panelling survives and, at the heart of the four-window-wide building, a large and spectacular staircase that once conveyed customers to the establishment's elegant upper floors.

The tavern was popular with artists and actors, frequented by the fashionable swordsman Henry Angelo, and from 1764 was home to The Club, founded by Reynolds and Dr Samuel Johnson with its original membership of nine gradually expanded to thirty-five by the time Johnson died in 1784. During its heyday The Club included among its members Edmund Burke, Oliver Goldsmith, David Garrick and James Boswell.[14] It met for dining, drinking and literary debate and the Turk's Head would also have been a most convenient place for Reynolds, before or after club business, to meet the girls who lived and worked in the surrounding streets.

One prostitute he certainly met and who remains familiar to us today was Emma Hamilton, later Nelson's mistress, who in her early days called herself – among other names – Emma Hart. It is hard to pick through the myth, rumour, fantasy and obfuscation that surround Emma's early life, but it seems that she toiled initially as a servant in Blackfriars. From the mid-1770s the consensus of opinion is that she worked as an actress's maid and possibly a child prostitute in Covent Garden, perhaps as a 'posture moll' in bagnios such as the Bedford Head, as a life-model at the Royal Academy, and as the 'Goddess of Health' in Dr James Graham's 'Temple of Health' (see Appendix 3), and was then taken up by Mrs Kelly, for her brothel in St James's. It seems Emma was with her by 1779 while as young as fourteen, based in Arlington Street, off Piccadilly, as one of what William Hickey recalled in his *Memoirs* as Mrs Kelly's 'bevy of beauties'.[15]

A Miss Hart is mentioned in Reynolds' pocket book for 1768, but this cannot have been Emma since she would then have been far too young and went by the name of Emma Lyon.[16] But Reynolds did eventually meet and paint her and, to judge by his work, seems to have been fascinated by her form and the atmosphere of passion she evoked. There is an extra-ordinary painting in Dulwich Picture Gallery that is attributed to Reynolds and thought to show Emma. It is famous because of its Impressionistic colouring and paint texture – the result not of Reynolds' pioneering tech-nique but of the experimental paints he used failing in a most spectacular manner, thus giving the work today a contemporary and immediate feel that Reynolds never envisaged.

But, its radical appearance aside, the painting shows a very young, almost childlike, woman of luscious beauty – very much Emma's stock in trade – cradling a bundle in her arms which, upon closer examination, turns out to be a baby. The painting possesses a curious – almost inexplicable – simmering eroticism and sensuality. If this is Emma, and if Reynolds has captured her spirit accurately, then she was no one's victim. If this portrait is of Emma then the baby is probably the child she had with Sir Harry Fetherstonehaugh in early 1782. So this could be Emma at or around the age of seventeen or eighteen, the time she first appeared in society, a child prostitute who – against the odds – had survived and, despite Sir Harry's spurning of her and her child, seemed set to prosper.

Reynolds produced other works inspired by Emma, all of which possess an intense sexual allure. Although not held captive by Emma's erotic charm – as was the painter George Romney, who painted her obsessively – Reynolds certainly strove to capture her powerfully seductive character. He painted several versions of Emma about to insert her finger in her mouth, evoking an image both childlike and sexually explicit. Entitled *Bacchante*, the painting, executed in 1784, was commissioned, or soon acquired by, Sir William Hamilton.

These images of her by Reynolds and Romney caused a public sensation. They did much to make their subject a celebrity and thus doubly desirable. Reynolds' friend and fellow member of the Society of Dilettanti (see page 368), Sir William Hamilton, must have known these paintings well. When he met Emma briefly in London in 1784 his interest, indeed emotions, were no doubt already inflamed by these powerfully sexual images. Certainly Sir William welcomed the suggestion that Emma should join him in Naples where he had been British Envoy since 1764. The suggestion had been made by Charles Greville, her lover and Sir William's nephew, but when Emma arrived in Italy in 1786 events soon took a turn no one could have foreseen. Greville did not retrieve Emma as planned, and Sir William, rather than just making her his mistress, made her his wife. When the unlikely couple – the sixty-year-old diplomat and antiquarian and the twenty-six-year-old harlot and artists' model – married in 1791 no one was more shocked than Greville. But Sir William – a great connoisseur and collector of beautiful objects – was ecstatic. He now possessed the living muse who had inspired Reynolds and Romney to create some of their most stunning works, a creature, as he later explained, more beautiful than 'anything found in nature; and finer in her particular way than anything that is to be found in antique art'.

Reynolds played a key role in the creation of Emma Hamilton's celebrity image but, although clearly responsive to her sexual presence, seems to have had no particular emotional tie to her. She was just one among the dozens of young prostitutes he turned to for inspiration. But there are women mentioned in his pocket books who came to occupy significant and long-lasting positions in his life. Their relationships with him – and the art they inspired – not only tell us much about Reynolds, they also give us fascinating insights into the complex messages that many of his paintings carry.

KITTY FISHER

Catherine Maria 'Kitty' Fisher is first mentioned by Reynolds in 1759. Subsequently she was not only to play a major role in his life but also that of mid-eighteenth-century London. Reynolds painted Kitty again and again, usually for his own pleasure rather than as a commission, which is one possible explanation why images of her lingered for years in his studio.

In 1771 the popular *Town and Country Magazine* recorded that Kitty 'first made her appearance as a courtesan' under the auspices of Augustus Keppel.[17] Commodore Keppel, son of the Earl of Albemarle, had been one of Reynolds' earliest well-connected patrons. It was the full-length portrait of him, executed in 1752, which made Reynolds' name. As E. K. Waterhouse points out in his book on Reynolds, the artist realised the power of his own creation and, rather than handing the completed work over to the model, retained it in his studio for some considerable time so that 'sitters who came with more moderate intentions could see what possibilities of immortality were available'.[18] Reynolds and Keppel became firm friends and it is likely – but not certain – that he commissioned some of the early portraits of Kitty.

In 1759 there are over twenty appointments noted in Reynolds' pocket book with 'Miss Fischer', 'Miss Fisher' and 'Miss Kitty Fisher' – all but one for half-past eight or nine in the morning.[19] So many appointments probably resulted in more than one painting but the first to be completed seemingly dates from 1759, to judge by the date on a letter included within the portrait. It is not known who commissioned this three-quarter-length work, now at Petworth House. Indeed it is quite possible it was not commissioned at all but, rather, is a large-scale and early expression of Reynolds' desire to explore the artistic and emotional possibilities of the female form through an intimate exploration of the bodies of harlots.

Portraits such as this, characterised by their direct, provocative and informal composition, became a continuing theme in Reynolds' work. He created his formal portraits of grandees, allegorical paintings and fancy pictures like *Cupid as a Link-boy*, but always – running like a wayward and sparkling thread of inventive genius through his body of work – there are the provocative portraits of Kitty Fisher and her kind. Clearly Reynolds loved to execute full-size portraits of prostitutes and actresses – who were usually former prostitutes – women relatively relaxed within their own bodies. There is wit and warmth in these works – the feeling that artist and sitter were sharing a conspiratorial joke and almost subversively mocking the hypocritical ethos of the age, that they were intimate in spirit if not in the flesh. These portraits are painted with evident affection, and none more so than the series of Kitty Fisher. She very obviously

Kitty Fisher, shown in a print based on Reynolds' portrait of 1759. In front of Kitty is a dated letter, starting 'Dear Kit'. The portrait seems not to have been commissioned but painted by Reynolds for pleasure.

liberated Reynolds' imagination, stimulated his creativity, inspired his admiration and was a muse to him in the true antique manner. He was fascinated by her larger-than-life personality: she seems to have been a creature of extremes, living always on the edge – not as if there was no tomorrow but precisely *because* there was a tomorrow, and always fraught with uncertainty and danger.

Reynolds was often obliged to cast his grand sitters in the role of heroic or mythical figures and make them the subject of classical allegory, such as Lady Manchester posing as Diana, in an attempt to lend them character and a recognisable identity. It was all so wearisome, so contrived. As Martin Postle succinctly puts it, powerful actresses and women such as Kitty Fisher 'didn't need to be given a character by Reynolds because they already possessed one'.[20] Women such as Kitty didn't need to be painted in allegorical manner because their very lives – their existence – *were* allegorical. 'They were living legends, they were making history, they – through their lives and their art – had gained character . . . they rose above the decorative'.[21]

It therefore seems quite natural that Reynolds used as his model for *Iphigenia* – the daughter of Agamemnon who sacrificed herself for the salvation of others – an anonymous 'battered courtesan' (Northcote's observation). Rather than using history and allegory to give a modern woman meaning and character, he used a modern woman – a world-weary and suffering prostitute – to lend the ancient myth contemporary meaning and resonance.

By the time Reynolds' first portrait of Kitty Fisher appeared in 1759 she was already the toast of the town, on her way to becoming a legend. Mezzotints of the portrait appeared in July 1759,[22] suggesting there was a wide popular interest in the subject, and a pamphlet published in 1760 by 'Simon Trusty' conveys some of the flavour of this interest. Fisher, reputedly the daughter of a German stay-maker and some-time practitioner in the favoured whore's trade of hat-making, attracted lovers who were, according to the pamphlet, 'the Great Ones of the Earth, and your Admirers are the Mighty; they never approach you but, like Jove, in a shower of Gold'. As with all great courtesans, success was as problematic a condition as failure for it produced the standard accusation from anonymous journalists of greed, heartlessness and immorality.[23] The pamphlet went on to accuse Kitty of mercenary promiscuity and an aversion to maternity which she avoided 'often perhaps by horrid means'.[24]

In the context of such journalistic spite towards high-flying courtesans, Reynolds' sympathetic treatment of women such as Kitty Fisher becomes all the more intriguing. His second portrait of her was completed, in all likelihood, towards the end of 1759. It is a provocative and challenging work for it shows the high courtesan in the persona of Cleopatra – a woman infamous for the way in which she used her beauty, charms and sexual skill as tools of state, means by which to gain and hold on to power.

The portrait shows Cleopatra in the act of dropping a giant pearl into a glass of wine. History relates that when the pearl dissolved, she downed the wine in a bid to impress the Roman general Mark Antony. Cleopatra was successful, Mark Antony was impressed, but the ultimate result of this act of bravura was known by all. So what were Reynolds and Kitty saying in this work? What exactly were they up to? Is this an ironic approach to ancient history that, rather than celebrating a glorious incident from the distant past, takes instead a dark and troubling moment?

Whatever is being said, it must have something to do with the power of sex for Kitty's hand, from which the pearl dangles, offers a strange and enigmatic clue. Her thumb and forefinger from an irregular oval that is possibly emblematic of the vulva – a visual prompt Reynolds was to feature again in one of a pair of paintings he created in 1779, showing members of the Society of Dilettanti (see page 384).

Kitty fascinated the public as much as she did Reynolds and seems positively to have courted notoriety, which perhaps explains the placing of her fingers in the Cleopatra painting. She wanted to shock, to make memorable gestures. On 30 March 1760 she placed a notice in the *Public Advertiser* objecting to the abuse she received in newspapers and to the way she was 'exposed in print shops'. The prints were almost certainly of the two Reynolds' portraits, and, of course, she didn't really mind at all, knowing full well that 'objections' such as this would only draw further attention to her, increase her celebrity and cause her to be 'exposed' in public places even more. With seemingly shameless abandon she played up to her popular image as a sexually voracious and power-broking female – indeed a sort of skewed Cleopatra of her age.

A satirical poem lampooned 'Kitty's stream of noblemen turned

Fishermen', and in 1765, as if to play up to this image, she sat for Nathaniel Hone, for a humorous portrait – almost a cartoon – that shows her concealing her nearly bare breasts behind a meagre scarf while a kitten fishes for trapped goldfish in a bowl in which is reflected a window crowded with rapt onlookers – Kitty's 'adoring' public presumably. Her ostentatious and luxurious lifestyle, her public display of the wealth she had gained by her looks and wits, was by now notorious.

The Anglo-Venetian friend of Casanova, Giustiniana Wynne, confided in a letter that Kitty lived in 'the greatest possible splendour, spends twelve thousand pounds a year, and she is the first of her social class to employ liveried servants . . . there are prints of her everywhere.'²⁵ Giacomo Casanova himself, when in London in 1763–4, engineered a meeting with Kitty. Casanova was hard up, only too evidently on the prowl for opportunities and spoke little English so, it is fair to conclude, would not have been of great interest to the grand Kitty Fisher. He appears to have imagined otherwise.

In his *Histoire de ma vie*, written during the 1780s but not published until 1794, Casanova remembered Kitty in her prime: she was magnificently dressed, and it was no exaggeration to say that she had on diamonds worth a hundred thousand crowns. He was then told that if he liked he might have her then and there for ten guineas, a suggestion rendered more than unlikely by his next statement that Kitty had eaten a banknote for a hundred pounds, on a slice of bread and butter, that very day, a present from Sir Richard Atkins, brother of the fair Mrs Pitt. Casanova went on to inform his readers that he declined this bargain-basement offer of Kitty's usually very expensive person because though charming, she could only speak English, and he liked to have all his senses, including that of hearing, gratified.²⁶

The story of the money sandwich soon became, with various permutations, a London legend. The sum swallowed varied in different accounts – some said £20²⁷ and others £100²⁸ – but all agreed that Kitty ate the money because she regarded the sum offered an insultingly low payment for her nocturnal services. But perhaps there was more to her action than financial considerations. Perhaps she was by then living the role she had enacted for Reynolds. Cleopatra had swallowed a priceless pearl to impress a man. Now Kitty had done much the same, though not so much to impress any particular man as to express contempt for the mean spirits of all those men who had used her, and to proclaim her own independence. No wonder London was electrified.

Almost twenty years after the event Johann Wilhelm von Archenholz felt compelled to recount the incident in his journal and to describe the appearance in the 1760s of the legendary Kitty Fisher, who was, he wrote:

[V]ery celebrated ... on account of the elegance and delicacy with which she sacrificed to Venus [and] indebted to nature for an uncommon portion of beauty, judgement, and wit, joined to a most agreeable and captivating vivacity ... This lady knew her own merit; she demanded a hundred guineas a night, for the use of her charms, and she was never without votaries, to whom the offering did not seem too exorbitant. Among these was the Duke of York, brother to the King; who one morning left fifty pounds on her toilet. This present so much offended Miss Fisher, that she declared that her doors should ever be shut against him in future; and to show, by the most convincing proofs, how much she despised his present, she clapt the bank-note between two slices of bread and butter, and ate it for breakfast.[29]

Reynolds' pocket books from 1760–5 record numerous appointments with Kitty and several more portraits appear to have been the result. But since these were not, it seems, painted to commission, documentation is lacking and it is now impossible to be entirely certain which portraits of Kitty – if any – were the result of these meetings. One possible portrait of Kitty, again dating to about 1759, shows a woman who looks like her, wearing a low-cut dress, sitting in a chair and contemplating the viewer quizzically while she holds a closed fan to her lips. The work has an air of eroticism that is all the more powerful for being understated. There is another half-length portrait, showing a young woman holding Reynolds' parrot, that dates from around 1763 and is almost certainly of Kitty. And there seems to have been at least one more for in 1782 the Duke of Rutland bought from Reynolds a painting of 'Miss Fisher' that was probably destroyed in the fire that swept through Belvoir Castle in 1816.[30]

But, among these later probable or possible portraits of Kitty, one in particular commands attention. It is very similar in composition to Reynolds' first 1759 portrait of her but this time contains no dated letter. Again the subject sits with her arms crossed in front of her so that the basic composition is that of a visually satisfying equilateral triangle with the head at the apex. And it is the head – or at least the facial expression – that marks the real point of difference between these two apparently similar portraits. In the earlier version Kitty contemplates the viewer with a direct and steady gaze while a slight smile plays upon her lips and around her neck hang strings of pearls – all rather distant and aloof. In the later portrait she appears younger, lovelier, and, wearing a simple black ribbon around her neck, utterly alluring and seductive. As with the earlier portait she looks the viewer straight in the eye, but now her gaze is softer, trusting, melting. There is love in her eyes, and in the touch of the man who created this beautiful image.

The portrait was never completed, nor was it ever sold. When Reynolds died this was among the paintings still in his studio. He kept it to the very end and, during the thirty or so years he lived with this lovely image of Kitty, quite possibly chose not to add to it because, for him, it already immortalised a moment he wished always to remember.

The costume and jewellery Kitty wears in this unfinished portrait suggest that it was executed in the first half of the 1760s, which marked a crucial moment of change in her relationship with Reynolds. In 1765 or 1767, according to different accounts, she married a country gentleman – John Norris of Hempstead Manor, Benenden, Kent – and in the process lost her independence and the freedom to see Reynolds whenever she chose. She also, within either four months or two years of her marriage (again, accounts differ), lost her life and was buried in Benenden church-yard dressed in her best ball-gown. The circumstances surrounding the last phase of Kitty's life – and the cause of her death – are as confusing and uncertain as the circumstances of her relationship with Reynolds. In 1771 *Town and Country Magazine* noted enigmatically that she had expired 'a victim to cosmetics', presumably a sarcastic reference to her generous use of white lead-based facial paint.

Reynolds' relationship with Kitty was the subject of a snide letter, signed 'Fresnoy', that appeared in 1767 in the 14–17 October edition of the *Middlesex Journal* (interestingly, it refers to Kitty as though she were still alive). Have you, asks the writer of Reynolds, 'received a frown from salacious Catherine, the tailor's maid, or is the affection of the fair creature alienated from you entirely since her elevation to matrimony – from you, alas! and many others?' Then, in mock admiration, 'Fresnoy' concludes,

'Catherine has sat to you in the most graceful, the most natural attitudes, and indeed I must do you the justice to say that you have come as near the original as possible.'[31]

Is there any truth then in the allegation that Kitty and Reynolds were lovers? The truth is we have no idea. There is not a shred of firm evidence to prove that they were and a fair amount of circumstantial evidence to suggest they were not, including the fact that Reynolds was never married nor, as far as is known, romantically associated with a woman. Kitty was, it seems, as near as he came to that.[32]

NELLY O'BRIEN

Arguably Reynolds put too much of his emotions into his painting and not enough into the rest of his life. As his old friend Hester Thrale wrote of him, 'Of Reynolds what good shall be said! – or what harm? His temper too frigid; his pencil too warm . . .' Even so, he must have missed Kitty, and he went on to have quite a list of other high harlots as friends. There was Nelly O'Brien – Kitty's rival in the early 1760s and perhaps rival for Reynolds' time, attention and affection. She moved in high circles indeed. Lord Bolingbroke – 'Bully' – was her keeper and, when he commissioned Reynolds to paint his wife, told the artist to give her Nelly's eyes.[33]

Some time between 1760 and 1762 Reynolds painted a stunning three-quarter-length portrait of Nelly that is now in the Wallace Collection. As with his other portraits of courtesans, certainly those of Kitty, the pose is relaxed, intimate and revealing. More dramatically – and also more explicitly – a couple of years later he portrayed Nelly wearing a low-cut dress and seated beside a relief showing Danaë, the princess of classical myth.

This piece of rather laboured humour might well have appealed to some of Reynolds' clients and certainly made Nelly's calling obvious because Jove, Danaë's lover, came upon her in the form of a shower of gold. This was the very image of money, sex and power. But Reynolds could not have consoled himself for long with Nelly because she died a year after Kitty. Which left Fanny Barton – or Mrs Abington, as she came to be known.

Nelly O'Brien, a high courtesan and muse of Reynolds, shown in a print (based on a Reynolds portrait) in which she is seated beside a relief depicting Danaë – a princess of classical myth, whose lover, Jove, came to her in a shower of gold.

MRS ABINGTON

Fanny Barton was born into poverty in about 1737 and lived to become one of the wonders of her age – a child prostitute from the streets who not only rose to great heights of fashion and wealth but entered and was accepted by society, and – perhaps her greatest achievement – evaded disease and exhaustion and lived to enjoy a happy old age.

She first appeared on the London scene in the late 1740s as a notoriously pretty flower-seller and street-singer known to her admirers as 'Nosegay Fan'. By the early 1750s she had become a prostitute, and some time between 1752–5 made her debut as an actress. This led to marriage with a musician named James Abington and a change of name to the respectable-sounding Mrs Abington before a move to Dublin where she seems to have honed her skills as an actress. But the relationship with her husband didn't last long. By the late 1750s Mrs Abington was the kept woman of the MP for Newry – Mr Francis Needham – who seems to have educated and groomed her for polite society.

By the early 1760s Mrs Abington was back in London, doing well on the stage, probably living as a high courtesan and paying her husband to make himself scarce. She was also becoming a leader of fashion and arbiter of taste. This was a role in which Mrs Abington clearly excelled. Years later in the early 1780s, when Archenholz was in London, he was impressed, if slightly puzzled, by her reputation and achievements:

> As she possesses an exquisite taste, she is constantly employed in driving about the capital to give her advice concerning the modes and fashions of the day. She is called in like a physician, and recompensed as if she were an artist. A great number of people of fashion treat her in the most familiar manner, and as if she were their equal.[34]

This generally recognised importance of Mrs Abington's role as a trend-setter, largely achieved through the costumes she wore on stage, is confirmed by the details of her 1781 contract with the Covent Garden Theatre. Such was her drawing power as a performer, with many coming just to see her stylish dresses, the theatre company agreed to pay her an annual allowance of £500 towards her wardrobe. This was a truly colossal sum, representing around eight years' wages for the average London working man.[35]

Mrs Abington's name starts to appear in Reynolds' surviving pocket books from August 1764, and by the end of 1768 – when both Kitty Fisher and Nelly O'Brien were dead – they were meeting professionally on a frequent basis (there are twenty-six sittings recorded from August 1764 to June 1768), and no doubt privately as well.

Mrs Abington was a tireless hostess who delighted in enticing London's leading men of letters and artists to her dining table. She attracted Reynolds' friends Samuel Johnson and Horace Walpole, and no doubt she attracted Reynolds too. These sittings resulted in a series of portraits, the first of which – Mrs Abington in the person of *Thalia, the Comic Muse* – was completed in 1768. This set the pattern for further representations of her. Reynolds chose – or was commissioned – not to depict Mrs Abington as a languid, overtly sexual courtesan as he had done with Kitty and Nelly, but to emphasise her professional persona as a successful actress.

But this didn't mean that Mrs Abington was depicted in any unalluring way. In fact, far from it. She looks sexually enticing and every inch the high courtesan – relaxed, informal and confident – but with an added level of subtlety because Reynolds mostly showed her posing in theatrical roles. Was it Mrs Abington herself or the character she played who was casting towards the viewer that intimate and provocative look?

Far more electric and provocative than *Thalia* was an image of her in the character of harem slave Roxalana, from Isaac Bickerstaffe's play *The Sultan*, which catches her entering the Sultan's tent on her way, it must be assumed, to sexual congress.

This painting was exhibited at the Royal Academy in 1784 and afterwards seemingly presented by Reynolds to Mrs Abington as a gift. By this time they were close indeed. Fanny seems to have filled the emotional gap in Reynolds' life left by the deaths of Kitty and Nelly but, as with these two earlier favourites, there is absolutely no evidence that his relationship with her was anything other than platonic.

Powerful as the portrayal of Mrs Abington as Roxalana may be, there is another yet more visually striking and intriguing. Indeed, it is a painting that ranks among the best female portraits Reynolds created. His pocket book for 1771 reveals a flurry of activity related to Mrs Abington ... the dressing of her hair, the details of her costume ... and then in May a new work, its paint still tacky, was rushed to the Royal Academy for exhibition. It showed Mrs Abington in the role of *Miss Prue* from William Congreve's 1695 play *Love for Love*, which she had performed from December 1769 into 1770, to great popular acclaim.

Miss Prue is a comic character, a simple and mildly lascivious country girl, but in this painting Mrs Abington looks neither comic nor simple although the thumb raised to her lips may, among other things, be meant to imply a slightly disturbing adolescent sexuality or perhaps a rural vulgarity. In this painting Mrs Abington is dressed in high style indeed, and with her unusual and striking black-banded wrists is evidently a bold maker of fashion. She is clearly perched on the cutting edge of style, as is asserted by the equally avant-garde Chippendale ribbon-back chair on which – in what was traditionally masculine style – this quintessentially feminine figure leans forward.

The play between seemingly contradictory and veiled roles is what this painting is all about. A simple country girl is portrayed by a sophisticated actress; a formally attired woman strikes the informal pose of a man; a courtesan adopts the role of a fashionable high-society lady.

This painting reveals a great deal about mid-eighteenth-century London society and its sex industry. Despite rigid social rules, class boundaries and countless other limitations, it was possible for a woman to harness the commercial power of prostitution in order to liberate herself, establish her own place in society and create an independent life. Fanny Barton, the street girl and sometime prostitute, proves the fact. She died in 1815 in her comfortable house in Pall Mall.

This painting, with the model staring out so steadily and confidently, is in a way the very image of this singular and deeply complex age. Fanny lived an extraordinary life of many contradictions. In one painting Reynolds was able to encapsulate and express it all, to a truly remarkable degree.

EMILY WARREN

There was one model Sir Joshua Reynolds used in the late 1770s and 1780 who was also hauntingly emblematic of her age and profession, an enigmatic creature who flits through the pages of history but left no memoirs or letters of her own, no ringing or witty phrases, and indulged in no public antics calculated to win her popular renown.

Emily Warren – as she was eventually known – lived a few brief years upon the stage of public life and is portrayed only as a peripheral character, a faint and passing shadow, in accounts of the lives of others. She left little of herself behind beyond the stunning images she inspired Reynolds to paint, but what very few relics of her we have speak movingly about the lives – and hopes – of many of the young women who were part of London's late-eighteenth-century sex industry.

It is of course, and perhaps paradoxically, her relative anonymity that makes Emily so significant because it makes her typical. Extrovert, loud-mouthed, self-promoting or egomaniac courtesans like Kitty Fisher and Sally Salisbury drew public attention to themselves, became popular figures – urban legends – but they were the exception. Most members of the sex industry were silenced by history, remaining ambiguous characters it is now almost impossible for us to know – like the exceptionally beautiful young woman who came to be known as Emily Warren. She was, according to William Hickey who knew her intimately, seemingly passionless herself (see page 214), but what is certain is that she inspired great passion in others and became, in 1781, the focus of a brief but sensational controversy.

William Hickey lived in London and India during the last decades of the eighteenth century, and when he finally retired to England in 1808 wrote his *Memoirs*. These cover a broad sweep of years and terrain but include a wonderfully intimate account of London in the 1770s and 80s, revealing how the great and diverse city was perceived and experienced by a wild – but very observant – young libertine. The *Memoirs* abound with portraits and accounts of the notable men and women of the age and – in particular – the capital's great corps of courtesans. It is from Hickey that we gain most of our information about Emily and learn something of her early life and deeply damaged character.

He records that as a child Emily wandered the streets of London with her beggar father until found, aged twelve, by the bawd Charlotte Hayes, who then trained her in the ways of elegant prostitution (see page 129). Hickey saw Emily at this time, in 1776, then left for India and did not return to London until July 1780. By this time Emily had left Charlotte Hayes' 'nunnery' and was being 'kept' in a house in Cork Street by Hickey's old friend Bob Pott. In July 1780 Pott himself was on his way to India.

Almost as soon as Hickey arrived in London he received a message from a servant announcing that 'a lady in a carriage was waiting for me at the corner of Pall Mall, seemingly extremely impatient'. It was Emily. Hickey 'went down the street where I saw a dashing bright-yellow *vis-à-vis* [a small open carriage; yellow was the popular colour for courtisans' carriages] . . . an elegant pair of bright bay horses, the coachman and footman in smart frocks of blue faced with yellow and trimmed with broad silver lace'. Such were the trappings of a West End high courtesan in late-Georgian London. 'But what was all this outside show compared to the lovely creature within, looking more than mortal! Never did I behold so perfect a beauty.'[36]

To support his account of the extraordinary impression of perfection that Emily made this summer evening in 1780, Hickey evoked the opinion of Sir Joshua Reynolds, 'whom all the world allowed to be a competent judge' of beauty. Reynolds, remembered Hickey, had 'painted her portrait many times and in different characters' and 'often declared every limb of hers perfect symmetry, and altogether he had never seen so faultless and finely formed a human figure'.[37]

It is likely that Reynolds first set eyes on Emily some time in the late 1770s when she was still at Charlotte Hayes' 'nunnery'. There are no meetings with her recorded in his surviving pocket books but these could have been noted in a now missing volume. Or perhaps Emily went by a completely different name then – indeed part of her wraith-like persona resulted from the regularity with which she changed her name and identity, usually to compliment a current protector. As far as is known she, at one time or another, called herself Bertie, Coventry and eventually Pott, but seemingly always retained her Christian name.

At some time in the late 1770s – when Emily was already established as a London celebrity – Reynolds started to use her as a model for a large, full-length painting. It was not a portrait of Emily herself but of Thais, a controversial character from ancient history whose name was one of London's many slang terms for prostitute. Thais was, according to legend, a Greek *hetaera* or courtesan who was the muse and lover of Alexander the Great and the person who incited him to burn Persepolis in 330 BC after its capture from the Persians. In consequence she was viewed with suspicion – a prostitute who had wielded her persuasive power over one of the greatest heroes of the ancient world and used it to take savage revenge on the Persians, who had earlier slighted Athens, in the process destroying one of the greatest and most beautiful cities the world had ever seen. So Thais, at one level, could be seen as a vengeful woman wielding her sexual power to wreak vengeance upon civilisation.

Quite how Reynolds himself perceived the meaning of the story is unclear but his painting offers some interesting clues. It shows a larger than life-size image of a flamboyant and beautiful courtesan – who would have been recognised by many as Emily – holding up a large and somewhat phallic flaming torch while staring out of the canvas, apparently inciting her viewers to embark on an orgy of destruction. There appeared to be little ambiguity about what this painting was saying. It showed prostitution in its most elemental form, in triumph and fury, consigning the world to flames. When unveiled in 1781 it caused a sensation with one periodical, the *Earwig*, claiming mischievously that the painting showed Emily setting the 'Temple of Chastity on fire'.[38]

Reynolds, of course, never offered any explanation or description of

Emily Warren, painted by Reynolds in 1781 as the courtesan Thaïs,
Alexander the Great's lover, shown urging the destruction of Persepolis or, as
some contemporaries thought, the Temple of Chastity.

the work. The painting was his only statement, a living thing beyond the power of words to explain, it spoke for itself and each viewer must extract what meaning he or she thought proper from it. But it is tempting to wonder . . . did Emily herself have any say in the subject and the way that Thais was portrayed? The figure of the striding incendiary has a dynamic, dominating and violent character that remains slightly unsettling, perhaps reflecting Emily's own suppressed anger at the years of abuse she had suffered in passive silence. And then there is the possible role of the painting's purchaser to consider.

It was probably commissioned by Charles Greville, who is mentioned at the end of the pocket book for 1781 where Reynolds notes, 'Thais – to Mr Greville', and in Reynolds' ledger is recorded a payment of £157 10s by Greville for 'Thais and his own picture'. Greville had been Emily's keeper prior to Bob Pott and had presumably commissioned the painting from Reynolds before he separated from her and moved on to Emma Lyon. Greville quickly sold the painting to Lord Dysart, probably because he had parted from Emily and needed the money but, just as possibly, because the message implicit in the painting – the fury of a prostitute in the face of a world dominated by masculine power and hypocrisy – was too uncomfortable for him to live with.

As for Emily, she had left London forever by the time the painting was publicly displayed. She sought redemption through marriage to Pott and sailed with him to India. But there was to be no lasting happiness for her. Emily died at sea in May 1782 while sailing from Madras to Calcutta. Pott, unable to part from her beautiful but rapidly decomposing body, had it towed behind the ship in a small boat. The corpse stank increasingly – worldly beauty cruelly eclipsed by death – but her faithful lover refused to set Emily adrift and so she was towed to Calcutta and finally buried on the banks of the sacred River Hoogley.

FOURTEEN

THE POWER OF THE
PAST AND THE PRIMITIVE
The New Aesthetics of Sex

As the eighteenth century progressed new discoveries were made about classical antiquity and primitive societies in parts of the world far distant from European or oriental civilisation. Strange as it may seem, in the early eighteenth century many of the actual, tangible remains of Rome were little known, and Greece – or rather its surviving architectural fragments – was almost entirely a mystery.

The culture of the classical past had of course profoundly influenced western thought during the Renaissance, thanks to texts preserved throughout the western Dark Ages in Arab libraries. Certain architectural remains from the Roman era were well known also but information about them was only fragmentary. The one surviving architectural treatise from the ancient world, *The Ten Books of Architecture* by Vitruvius, dating from about 100 BC, was in limited circulation from the ninth century or slightly earlier, but its often obscure and rambling text survived without illustrations and was open to wild and speculative interpretation.

However, Vitruvius' work, inexact as it was, provided the basic model for a series of Renaissance texts such as Leon Battista Alberti's *De Re Aedificatoria* written from 1443, Sebastiano Serlio's *Five Books of Architecture* (*Tutte l'opere d'architettura et prospettiva*) published from 1537, and Andrea Palladio's *Four Books of Architecture* published in 1570. Taking their form and methodology from Vitruvius, these books explained Roman design, construction and building materials, explored theories of proportion, illustrated ancient remains and attempted the reconstruction of the major Roman ruins that were known, notably those in Rome itself. These reconstructions focused on the shattered and largely buried monumental buildings around the Forum and on the mighty Pantheon, a stupendous and well-preserved structure that, incorporating the large-scale use of concrete and with a dome of vast span, surpassed the comprehension of most Renaissance observers.

The remains of Greek buildings – although not always far distant and obscure – remained little known or investigated. A significant problem was that many – such as the remains in Athens including the Parthenon – had been under Muslim Ottoman rule since the mid-fifteenth century and were thus very difficult for Christian Europeans to explore and document. But other impressive Greek ruins – such as the fifth- and sixth-century BC Doric temples in the former Greek colony of Paestum in southern Italy – were in theory accessible, if overgrown and hard to find, but failed to attract much attention or interest.

From the 1730s this changed. A series of startling discoveries and interpretations were made which, when published, literally and in most dramatic manner revolutionised western arts and culture. The English Society of Dilettanti, founded by Sir Francis Dashwood and others between 1732 and 1734, pioneered the appreciation of many facets of the classical world. It provided a forum for gentlemen who had travelled to Italy on the Grand Tour and consequently appreciated the ambience of Mediterranean Europe and the culture, morality and ethics of the pre-Christian antique world.

In the years immediately after its foundation new information about that world started to circulate throughout Europe. In 1738 the exploration of Herculaneum, the Roman town near Naples engulfed by volcanic pyroclastic material and mud in AD 79, got underway, while the methodical excavation of nearby Pompeii started in 1748. In the 1750s and 60s Paestum was investigated by archaeologically minded artists and architects such as Giovanni Battista Piranesi and its ruins accurately recorded. Also during the 1750s the classical Middle Eastern cities of Palmyra in Syria and Baalbeck in Lebanon were surveyed, drawn, and the findings published by Robert Wood and James Dawkins.

But more significant still were Julien-David Le Roy's *Les Ruines des plus beaux monuments de la Grèce* of 1758, and James Stuart and Nicholas Revett's *The Antiquities of Athens*, published from 1762. The Stuart and Revett volumes were particularly important because they recorded, for the first time and in beautiful detail, all the major ancient monuments of the city and offered compelling reconstructions.

These discoveries transfixed the West. They made it clear that the classical architecture of the ancient world – Roman as well as Greek – was far richer, more complex, varied and inventive in its vocabulary than had been suggested by the Renaissance masters, who were still the major source and reference point for Roman-inspired classical design. At a stroke the imagination of artists and architects in Europe was liberated and enflamed.

The initial consequence was a fascination with Greek as opposed to the much more familiar Roman classical architecture, which led to what is known as the Greek Revival – a phase of classical design that only reached maturity in western Europe in about 1800, but which in the following decades of the nineteenth century became virtually the national style in such emerging nations as the United States. There Greek-inspired architecture was seen as politically and symbolically appropriate for a republic that embraced democracy, for both these political institutions had been pioneered in Ancient Greece. For centuries Greek philosophy, myth and theology had been well known in Europe but, from the mid-eighteenth century onwards, an enthusiasm for Greek architecture combined with this existing body of knowledge so that a new Greek-inspired world started to take shape, reflecting the political as well as the artistic aspirations of the modern age.

But why, wondered certain scholars and antiquaries, should the application of new insights and discoveries about the ancient world stop there? Why should not antiquity influence or reform all aspects of the age? The Society of Dilettanti was swift to put its theories about the classical past into practice. Some of its members formed a dining, drinking and – to a degree – whoring club, with prostitutes being cast in the role of the muses of classical antiquity, the courtesans – temple prostitutes almost of ancient times – who inspired and brought enlightenment to great men (see page 390). It was this core, led by Sir Francis Dashwood, that went on to found the Order of the Knights of St Francis of Wycombe (later know as the Order of the Monks of Medmenham), one of the eighteenth century's more famous libertine and pseudo-Satanic Hell Fire clubs (see page 394).

In the same spirit as the founding fathers of the Society of Dilettanti, people more generally started to agree that the Greek Revival should transform sexual morality and theology as well as architecture, sculpture, arts and crafts and interior decoration. Such an attitude was not only radical and revolutionary but also potentially blasphemous and obscene. This was clearly very dangerous territory and those who wished to explore it had to proceed with extreme caution.

A sketch by Vittorio Maria Bigari, showing a vengeful Thais setting fire to Persepolis.

Within the London sex industry the analogy between prostitution and classical antiquity was familiar. There were, after all, many well-known antique prototypes for prostitutes, for example Thais, the courtesan and muse of Alexander the Great who travelled with him and his conquering Macedonian army as it marched east in triumph through Persia and Mesopotamia. Thais must once have been a temple prostitute – a priestess who, as part of an ancient religious right, offered spiritual enlightenment through sexual ecstasy.[1]

The eighteenth-century fashion for perceiving prostitutes in the classical mode of muse is revealed by some of the euphemisms commonly used after 1750. Prostitutes were referred to as Thais, Cythereans (after Cythera – the mythic birthplace of Venus) or as Paphians, Cyprians or the Cyprian Corps (after Paphos on Cyprus, which had a famed Temple of

Aphrodite). Given this high-flown pedigree and potential for cultural posturing it is hardly surprising that the anonymous author of the sexually titillating *Nocturnal Revels* of 1779 makes a point of emphasising the fact that Greece, 'a nation esteemed the wisest and most learned of Antiquity'[2] had 'veneration' for its Thaises who, among other things, were 'of infinite utility to Painters and Sculptors to whom they furnished ideas of the most transcendent beauty'.[3] Archenholz picked up on the mood of the moment in the 1780s and clearly understood the professed connection between prostitutes and male creativity. Some of 'the ladies of pleasure in London', he observed, 'actually give us an idea of the celebrated Grecian courtesans, who charmed the heroes of Athens, and whom the sage Socrates himself often honoured with his visits'.[4]

One of the men who at an early stage made the connection between antique art and antique sexual and religious values was Sir William

A print of Hamilton after a 1777 portrait by Reynolds. Hamilton holds one volume, edited by d'Hancarville, which showed his collection of antiquities.

Hamilton, future husband of the prostitute Emma Hart. In 1764 he was appointed British Envoy Extraordinary to the Court of Naples. As soon as he was installed there Hamilton started to explore the antiquities of the region and to build up a superb collection of ancient vases and objects. His investigations revealed not only neglected ruins and antiques to purchase but also that some aspects of ancient life and ritual still survived within the peasant communities of the region. So Hamilton, antiquary, connoisseur and amateur archaeologist, then turned anthropologist and started to study and record the life of the nearby area. In 1781 he wrote to Sir Joseph Banks, his fellow Dilettanti member and President of the Royal Society – already the national authority on botany and remote and primitive cultures – about the way in which pagan ritual survived within the Roman Catholic Church in remote parts of southern Italy which had in classical times been part of the Greek world. Hamilton mentioned observations that he and others had made at Isernia where the rituals of Priapus (the phallus-adorned god of procreation, fertility and the garden) were in the late 1770s still observed, with wax phalli being offered by peasant women to priests in the names of Saints Cosmas and Damian – identified within the Catholic Church with Priapus – to aid or increase

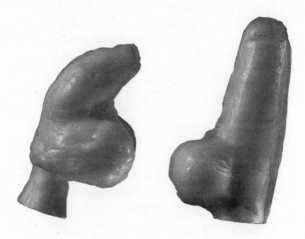

Wax phalli that Sir William Hamilton collected in Isernia in 1781 and that had been offered in a Catholic church by women to increase fertility. They are now in the British Museum.

fertility. When Hamilton reached Isernia in February 1781 he discovered that the Phallic rituals had recently been suppressed by the Church, but did manage to collect a number of wax votive offerings – notably life-like phalli – that in 1784 he eventually presented to the British Museum where a few still survive.

Hamilton's letter was circulated to other members of the Society of Dilettanti, which from 1781 included Richard Payne Knight, antiquarian, connoisseur and the son of a wealthy Shropshire ironmaster. Knight had, before he was twenty, toured Italy and started a collection of ancient bronzes and coins, and from 1780 – at the age of thirty – was a Member of Parliament and already widely recognised as an arbiter of taste who was to become one of the pioneers of the romantic Picturesque movement in the arts.

Knight was excited by Hamilton's letter and decided to publish it, along with his own interpretations, thoughts and discoveries, in a volume that duly appeared in 1786, entitled *An Account of the Remains of the Worship of Priapus lately existing at Isernia, in the Kingdom of Naples: in Two Letters*. One was that from Sir William Hamilton to Sir Joseph Banks, a second from 'a person residing in Isernia'. The volume – with a most arresting frontispiece showing the wax phalli 'preserved in the Church at Isernia' – also included Knight's own *Discourse on the Worship of Priapus*, an extraordinary thesis concerning the 'mystic Theology' of the Greeks and the elementary and polar forces of generation, creation and destruction.

The *Discourse* provided a theory based on nature – as understood by the Greeks and expressed in their religious rituals as well as those of other 'primitive' religions – that embraced the veneration of the 'generative principle' and so gave licence to the uninhibited enjoyment, even worship, of sex. So, intentionally or otherwise, Knight was lending classical authority and the gravitas of scholarship to sexual freedom and the abandonment of restraint. Also, by arguing that the veneration of the 'generative principle' was largely expressed through genital imagery, in particular the phallus, he appeared to be giving intellectual respectability to the display and appreciation of phallic images that many of his contemporaries would have viewed as either comic or obscene. Knight's writings not only contain a full and frank discussion of ancient phallic rituals and cults but also – sensationally and provocatively – suggested that these were in fact the basis of much Christian ritual, doctrine and imagery.

Richard Payne Knight, whose 1786 publication An Account of the
Remains of the Worship of Priapus *argued that all ancient religions
were based on the principle of procreation.*

More radical still, he argued that Judaeo-Christian theology had in
fact perverted and robbed earlier religions and fertility cults of their
innocence through the imposition of the vengeful and guilt-ridden
doctrines of the Old Testament that inhibited the love of the natural
world and of innocent procreation. He questioned the reputation of the
Bible as an epoch-making divine revelation by observing that such creatures
as Cherubim on the Ark of the Covenant 'though made at the express
command of God, do not appear to have been original' but occur on the
earlier Temple at Persepolis in Persia.[5] In a particularly imaginative,
although to many shocking, passage in the *Discourse*, Knight even suggested
that the cross was in fact an adaptation and abstraction of a Priapian
phallus: 'It represents,' he wrote, 'the male organ of generation before the
Church adapted it as a sign of salvation; a lucky coincidence of ideas
which, no doubt, facilitated the reception of it among the faithful.' To

return to a pre-biblical state of innocence and sexual freedom was, for Knight, to embrace the true governing principles of Greek civilisation because antiquarian research had revealed the key importance of sexuality in the religions of the ancient world, including of course those of Greece and Rome.

Discoveries of sexually explicit religious imagery at Herculaneum and Pompeii further enflamed the imagination of scholars. Knight and his like-minded peers believed that, at the very least, discoveries such as these not merely threw into question conventional Judaeo-Christian ideas of morality but revealed them to be unnatural and false. In essence Knight was promoting a return to Paganism, a repudiation of those codes of sexual conduct based on the Old Testament and the teachings of its patriarchs and prophets.

In several significant respects his work echoed and supported passages (notably chapters 15 and 16) in Edward Gibbon's *History of the Decline and Fall of the Roman Empire*, published from 1776, which some conventional contemporary critics thought blasphemous. Gibbon's 'crimes' were to place the Christian Church in historical context rather than to acknowledge the supremacy of its divine vision and to criticise it for the destructive way in which it had demonised the great cultures that had preceded it as well as for the way in which it had promoted religious warfare and intolerance. As he argued, it is impossible to 'dispel the cloud that hangs over the first age of the Church [due to] the imperfections of the uninspired teachers and believers of the gospel',[6] while . . .

> . . . the Church of Rome defended by violence the empire which she had acquired by fraud [and was] soon disgraced by proscriptions, wars, massacres, and the institution of the holy officer . . . It is a melancholy truth . . . that the Christians . . . have inflicted far greater severities on each other, than they experienced from the zeal of the infidels.[7]

Knight's *Discourse* ended with an illustration, based on an antique carving, of a 'satyr enjoying a goat', which he argued should not be viewed through modern eyes, which would perceive it as perverse. Instead it should be seen through the innocent eyes of the culture that made it, and recognised as an 'incarnation of the Deity and the communication of its creative spirit to man'. All ancient religions, implied Knight, saw sex in this light. Sex, he argued, is god-like because through it mankind becomes as the gods and creates life. Sex life is therefore divine life, and the mixing of bodily fluids is the true elixir of immortality, the means by which life is passed from generation to generation, until the end of time.

This is, in fact, the teaching of Tantric Buddhism and of Hinduism, which would surely have been known to Knight because the Society of Dilettanti had contacts with India – not least through their Medmenham Hell Fire Club members such as Sir Henry Vansittart, a former Governor of Bengal who had given Sir Francis Dashwood a copy of the *Kama Sutra*.

Knight's familiarity with Hindu practices and beliefs is to a degree confirmed by the fact that his book includes several plates showing images from Indian temples. These include an engraving of a small stone panel from the ancient Temple of Elephanta near Mumbai, which was brought back to England in 1784 by William Allen, the captain of HMS *Cumberland*. It shows male and female figures exchanging divine bodily fluids, with one couple engrossed in particularly athletic oral sex.[8]

Not surprisingly, Knight feared the response his book would provoke. In an attempt to prevent the work from falling into the hands of the 'uninitiated', publication was limited with copies available only to members of the Society of Dilettanti and a few fellow freethinkers such as Horace Walpole, Edward Gibbon, James Boswell, John Wilkes, the Duke of Portland and the Prince of Wales.

In a sense, the *Discourse* was a plea for toleration and understanding and thus very much in the liberated, open-minded and enquiring spirit of the late-eighteenth-century Enlightenment. But despite the relatively relaxed atmosphere of the age and the precautions Knight took by attempting to limit and control the circulation of the book, he did find himself misunderstood and was attacked both as a blasphemer and infidel and as an apologist for libertine behaviour, with Thomas Mathias in 1794 describing it as 'one of the most unbecoming treatises which ever disgraced the pen of a man, who would be thought a scholar and a philosopher.'[9] Such attacks resulted in later editions – notably that of 1818 – being bowdlerised.

Knight didn't return to the subject in any significant way – at least not in print – and when his next book appeared in 1805 it was *An Analytical Inquiry into the Principles of Taste*. This work ploughed a perhaps parallel but very different furrow, seeking to explain how the mind and the senses experience the visual world – colour, form, scale, proportion – and how these experiences affect the emotions. This book, in part a response to earlier works by Edmund Burke, William Gilpin and Uvedale Price, became a key document in the development of an aesthetic theory to explain the artistic 'taste' of the Picturesque movement.

Knight's *Account of the Remains of the Worship of Priapus* did not occur in a vacuum, however. It had a companion publication that appeared in 1785, a year before Knight's book, and which he acknowledged as a source of information if not inspiration. But, while Knight was a perceptive enthusiast and his work a bold and provocative exploration of unconventional artistic and theological ideas, his fellow author was a dark and disturbing character whose intentions and publications were equally suspect.

'Baron' Pierre-François Hugues d'Hancarville saw, as did Knight, a link between all the major world religions and believed they were based – consciously or unconsciously – on the ancient principles of generation and fertility. D'Hancarville's own origins are obscure. He worked in Italy as an art dealer where he met Sir William Hamilton, who commissioned him to help gather his collection of vases. Most significantly, it was d'Hancarville who introduced Hamilton to the Porcinari family whose collection of antiquities he eventually purchased, forming the basis of the collection subsequently sold to the British Museum. With Hamilton, d'Hancarville edited a four-volume catalogue of the Connoisseur's collection – *Antiquités étrusques, grecques et romaines, tirées du cabinet de chevalier W. Hamilton* – that was published in Naples from 1766–7. This publication was immensely influential and did much to form the emerging taste for Neo-classicism, providing antique models for artists and fashion-conscious manufacturers such as Josiah Wedgwood.

The success of this publication, and the close association with a British grandee, seems to have turned d'Hancarville's head. He invented a title for himself, created a spurious aristocratic pedigree, moved to London in 1777, made contact with other rich British collectors – notably Charles Townley – and in 1780 published *Monumens de la vie privée des Douze Césars d'après une Suite de Pierres Gravées sous leur regne.*[10] This followed his more modest *Veneres et Priapi* of 1771 and was in turn followed in 1784 by *Monumens du Culte Secret des Dames Romaines.*[11] All these well-illustrated books purported to contain engravings of authentic – and sexually explicit – Roman medallions and gems or to show scenes based on antique texts and practices, with *Monumens du Culte* packed with plates showing couples copulating in various postures, often overseen by an image of Priapus who, from time to time, is shown being harvested of his life-giving bodily fluids.[12]

These titillating images were initially accepted at face value but finally most of them turned out to be reproductions of fake or even non-existent works. The books were simply an opportunistic commercial exercise, a means of peddling highly erotic images under the respectable guise of antiquity.[13] So d'Hancarville was a pseudo-aristocrat, an academic fraud and an erudite pornographer who changed his name according to his country of residence and had been 'imprisoned at least three times for debts and other misadventures'.[14] But before all this became generally known he had moved to London and, in 1780, installed himself in Charles Townley's splendid new house in Park Street – now Queen Anne's Gate – St James's.

Townley himself is a key figure among devotees of the classical past, and since he is so representative of those who went on the Grand Tour, it is perhaps worth digressing briefly to say a little more about him. A member of an old Roman Catholic family based at Townley Hall near Burnley, Lancashire, he went on his first Grand Tour in 1767. He spent most of his time in Rome and it was clearly a formative experience for him. From an ordinary country gentleman who, as a Roman Catholic, was excluded from much official and public life Townley was transformed into a fanatical collector of antiquities. He returned to Rome in 1772 and 1777, from where he made collecting excursions to southern Italy and Sicily.

In common with many English connoisseurs in Italy, he commissioned the artist and antiquarian Gavin Hamilton and the art dealer Thomas Jenkins to help him with his acquisition of antiques. Both these men were well connected with Italian collectors, excavators, and artists who made a lucrative living by 'improving' damaged archaeological finds. As the demand for high-class antiquities increased so did the ruthlessness of the methods of acquisition and export. For example, one of Townley's most famous sculptures, which later became known as the 'Townley Venus', had been discovered in 1775 at Ostia by Gavin Hamilton and secretly shipped out of the Papal States as two separate fragmentary pieces, while the 'Townley Vase', found in 1774 at Monte Cagnolo also by Hamilton, was shipped to Britain in a similarly underhand manner.[15]

Part of Townley's collection had undoubtedly been acquired by shady means and was of dubious quality, but all was housed in a most public and celebratory manner in his new London house. Built on land leased from Christ's Hospital, the house formed part of a loosely uniform and palatial terrace constructed during the mid-1770s. Its front elevation looked on to a quiet residential street while to the rear it enjoyed a generous prospect over St James's Park, with Buckingham House being a not too distant neighbour.

Although externally much like its neighbours, the house was significantly different in its internal decoration and arrangement. In 1778 Townley commissioned the creation of an interior suitable to serve both as a comfortable home and as a quasi-public museum in which he could display his famed collection of antiquities, notably his marble statues. The main rooms on the ground and first floor of the house were thus arranged as galleries with certain objects built into the fabric, much as Sir John Soane was to do nearly thirty-five years later with his own house museum at 13 Lincoln's Inn Fields.

In the fashion of the day the interior of Townley's house was arranged in a manner inspired partly by the Roman houses recently excavated in Pompeii and partly by Renaissance palazzi. The large ground-floor rear room overlooking the garden and park was furnished with walls embellished with engaged columns so that it evoked the peristyles found to the rear of larger houses in Pompeii. The generous staircase hall, located in the centre of the house between the peristyle room and the entrance hall off Park Street, was top-lit to echo a Roman atrium and Renaissance cortile. At first-floor level – adjoining the staircase landing and between the main front and rear rooms – was the most curious and effective Roman revival room in the house. While the staircase hall was an inventive interpretation of a Roman atrium, this room was a relatively correct recreation of an antique atrium complete with roof-light.

These splendid Roman-inspired interiors made a spectacular setting for the display of Townley's marbles, with the first-floor atrium serving as the focal point – here an exquisite cabinet contained the best of his smaller-scale treasures. When in 1781 Townley commissioned Johann Zoffany to paint the house and its most prized contents, the atrium room was, quite naturally, the location chosen as the backdrop. Zoffany's painting shows the top-lit room rendered larger than life, for in it are displayed some of Townley's outsized objects that the room could not in fact contain. As Townley explained in a letter of August 1781 to James Byres,

an antiquary and dealer in Rome, 'Mr Zoffany is painting, in the Stile
of his Florence tribune, a room in my house, wherein he introduces what
Subjects he chuses in my collection. It will be a picture of extraordinary
effect & truth . . .'[16]

In Zoffany's composition sits Townley conversing with three of his
favoured fellow connoisseurs, scholars and collectors: the palaeographer
Charles Astle is portrayed as well as Charles Greville, member of the
Society of Dilettanti and one-time 'keeper' of Emma Hart. The final
member of this quartet is d'Hancarville. Prominent objects on display in
the painting include Townley's Roman copy of the Greek *Discobolos* that
was discovered at Hadrian's Villa in 1790 and purchased in 1792 by Townley,
who then commissioned Zoffany to add it to the painting. On a pedestal
in front of the fireplace stands the *Boys Fighting* from the Barberini collection that in 1768 had been Townley's first major purchase. Also selected
for display in this capriccio is the 'Townley Venus', standing on a pedestal-
like Roman well-head, and on a rear bookcase the 'Townley Vase'.

Townley's 'marbles' were one of the cultural wonders of late-eighteenth-
century London and a visit to his Park Street 'gallery' was a must for
erudite foreign tourists and Londoners alike, including George III who
liked to call in to contemplate these ancient works. Sophie van la Roche,
a German visitor to London in 1786, displayed an enthusiasm for Townley,
his collection and its setting that was typical. She recorded in her diary
that on 23 September:

> [W]e visited the Chevalier Towneley's collection of antiquities, in a fine
> house with some of the rarest and most costly ornamentations [while
> on] the upper storey . . . we found treasures of ancient art . . . most
> perfect examples of ancient beauty collected there, and what is more,
> exhibited in a room whose windows look on to St James's Park. Every-
> thing is tastefully arranged, and the proprietor a man of great nobility
> and modesty, a traveller in Italy and Graeca Magna for four and thirty
> long years.

Sophie's experience of the house was magical and memorable:

> I was loath to leave this [house] where these valuable remains can be
> studied at ease [and] one can muse on the ruined magnificence of
> Greece, while a turn of the head brings a number of pretty English
> ladies, out strolling, into view.

She was also charmed by Townley: 'the noble gentleman mostly spends his time here investigating, cleaning and piecing [his battered curios] together'.[7]

Her observation of Townley's 'cleaning and piecing' is particularly significant for this collection and its evocative setting are now virtually forgotten, and the fate that befell them is revealing and not a little sad. The house survives, now serving as gaunt and arid office space, and the collection, when Townley died in January 1805, was put up for sale and faced almost certain dispersal. But such was its reputation that the trustees of the British Museum determined to preserve it in its entirety for the nation and obtained a grant of £20,000 from Parliament to do so. By the end of the year it had purchased Townley's sculptures, larger bronzes and terracottas. The smaller antiquities, including gems, coins and pottery, were initially retained by the family and only acquired by the nation in 1814.

Soon after its acquisition, the Townley collection was displayed in a purpose-built gallery at the British Museum, which was then still housed in the late-seventeenth-century Montagu House on Great Russell Street. But almost immediately after the marbles were put on public display in Bloomsbury, antiquarian taste underwent a sea change. Townley's marbles, reflecting late-eighteenth-century preference, had been carefully restored to make them look virtually as good as new. Missing hands, arms, heads and noses were replaced – sometimes using antique fragments and sometimes with carefully carved new details. This had appealed to late-eighteenth-century sensibilities and to amateur collectors like Townley who perhaps could not tell a cunningly reconstructed statue – some of them little better than fakes – from an entirely authentic work. But by the early nineteenth century collectors were more informed and, in the romantic spirit of the Picturesque movement, which venerated ruins of all sorts, preferred their ancient works to *look* ancient and, above all, to be unrestored and authentic. The genuine patina of antiquity became a thing much prized. It was now the damaged glory of Lord Elgin's newly acquired marbles from the Acropolis in Athens that thrilled, no longer Townley's collection which, at its worst, included antique statues fitted with new arms and heads set at incorrect angles or making inappropriate gestures. Most controversial of all was his *Discobolos* whose head was not only new but looking in the wrong direction!

In 1816, when the British Government was considering purchasing Elgin's Acropolis marbles for the nation, a Select Committee was set up to establish their artistic and monetary value. Various artists were questioned, including John Flaxman who, when asked the relative value of Elgin's and Townley's marbles, declared that he valued Elgin's more 'as being the ascertained works of the first artists of that celebrated age [while] the greater part of Mr Townley's Marbles, with some few exceptions, are perhaps copies, or only acknowledged inferior works'. The Select Committee then wondered if Elgin's marbles 'were of greater value as never having been touched by any modern hand'. Yes, replied Flaxman unequivocally.[18]

Taste had changed mightily in ten years. From being a national wonder, Townley's marbles had become something of a national embarrassment. When the British Museum recreated itself from the mid-1820s as a mighty Ionic Temple to the Arts, the Townley Gallery was demolished and his marbles not given any prominence in the new building. The Townley acquisition still forms much of the core of the museum's Graeco-Roman collection but the once-famed marble sculptures have been decidedly demoted. They are now to be found in a lower level gallery, among other collections of antique works, where they are generally regarded as curiosities, a reflection of a passing and somewhat unfortunate moment in British antiquarian taste and scholarship

The blemished reputation of Townley's marbles, their aura of fakery and even skulduggery, reflects with almost uncanny accuracy the character of d'Hancarville. Not only was he one of Townley's advisers in the creation of the collection, but it was while he was based in Park Street that he wrote the greater part of his *Recherches sur l'origine l'esprit et les progrès des arts de la Grèce*. It was this work, published in 1785, that was the companion volume to Knight's *Account of the Remains of the Worship of Priapus*. In it d'Hancarville describes an ancient and universal theological system from which all subsequent religions are derived and which is revealed through symbols found on ancient artefacts and remains. The text is in part inspired by Townley's collection of antiquities, perhaps also by Knight's researches to which d'Hancarville may have had access, and by symbols engraved on vases, sculpture, coins and on the ancient gems so much admired by certain members of the Society of Dilettanti.

D'Hancarville's conclusion is clearly stated and anticipates that of Knight: much Greek and Roman art and worship was of a phallic nature, suggesting most strongly that ancient theology had an intensely sexual character and focused primarily on the expression of elemental ideas connected to generation and procreation. This is, in fact, d'Hancarville's best and most perceptive book. In a fascinating manner it both reflected and helped to form the opinions and spirit of its age. As Burton Feldman explains, d'Hancarville, despite his tainted scholarship and motives, had a major influence on Britain's romantic movement. He was:

> the source of Blake's cosmic generations and sexuality, and Shelley's view of the poet as Adonos or Adonais, a creative figure complementing the more receptive fertilizing Goddess of Love, and he is likely, though more indirectly, echoed in Keats's sensual mythicizing.[19]

A splendid summary of the peculiar activities of these men – and of the strange and imaginative fusion of art, archaeology and sex that they inspired – is offered by Sir Joshua Reynolds' two group portraits of members of the Society of Dilettanti that were painted in 1777–8 (now in Brooks' Club, St James's). One reveals the members' love of ancient vases, the other of precious gems – and both illustrate a general appreciation of fine wines – the nectar of Dionysus – with, for example, Charles Greville and Joseph Banks shown gripping wine glasses and offering a toast. But there are other messages contained in the paintings. A member named John Taylor, grinning lewdly, holds up a lady's garter which forms a *Vesica Piscis* or oval shape: a not particularly subtle reference to another of the Society's interests – the female sex.

Intriguingly, this reference is mirrored in the companion painting in which Lord Dundas holds a gem up to the light, finger and thumb describing an oval, said to be a visual pun on the size of his mistress's vulva and thus emblematic of another of the Society's interests – whoring. On the far right Lord Carmarthen holds a gem in one hand while the fingers of his other make a V-shape – a fairly universal symbol. His wife was to elope with Colonel 'Mad Jack' Byron, father of Lord Byran, the poet. The Earl of Seaforth also holds a gem, probably antique, engraved and of the type collected by Charles Townley, which no doubt inspired d'Hancarville when concocting his erotic volumes purporting to be based on Roman art. Sir William Hamilton is pointing to a volume containing a print of one of his Grecian vases, perhaps an oblique reference to his letter to Joseph Banks about the survival in southern Italy of the cult of Priapus, god of procreation.

A pair of group portraits of members of the Society of Dilettanti, painted by Reynolds in 1777–8. The portraits show the society's interests in antiquities from Greece and Italy, ancient gems, fine wine – and sex. Group one, left to right: Lord Mulgrave; Lord Dundas, holding up a gem between finger and thumb which, by tradition, is said to represent the size of his mistress's vulva; Lord Seaforth, holding a gem, his other hand around the neck of a bottle of claret; Charles Greville; Charles Crowle; Lord Carmarthen, who

Such was the private and, to the uninitiated, mildly shocking tone of these paintings that they were never put on public display.

One of these characters is perhaps worthy of a little further attention for it was he who was partly responsible for unleashing the influence of the primitive on the more imaginative members of London's late-eighteenth-century sex industry. Joseph Banks was a rich, well-connected amateur botanist and natural historian who managed, through a combination of influence and affluence, to purchase a passage on James Cook's first circumnavigation of the globe that lasted from 1768 to 1771. This

holds a gem in one hand while casually making a suggestive V-sign with the other; and Joseph Banks, the 'Botanical Macaroni'. Group two, left to right: Sir Watkin Williams Wynn; John Taylor, holding a lady's garter to form an oval open-shape that appears to refer to female anatomy; Stephen Payne-Gallway, drinking; Sir William Hamilton, pointing to an illustration of one of his vases; and Richard Thompson, Walter Spencer-Stanhope and John Lewin-Smyth all enjoying glasses of wine.

turned out to be an epoch-making voyage that combined scientific observation and exploration with imperial ambition and the quest for new and potentially valuable colonies and natural resources. Cook's first task was to sail to Tahiti to observe the Transit of Venus – a rare astronomical event in which the planet crosses in front of the Sun. This was a scientific mission that was intended both to challenge French supremacy in astronomy and to gather information that would help establish the distance between the earth and the Sun and thus provide a unit for calculating the size of the universe.

With this task complete he was to follow 'secret' orders from the Admiralty and sail south on a journey of discovery, searching in particular for the legendary southern continent – the *Terra Australis Incognita* (the unknown land of the south) – and to claim any and all useful discoveries for the benefit of the British Crown, preferably with the 'consent' of any locals who might be encountered! This journey resulted in the charting of New Zealand, first discovered by the Dutch explorer Abel Tasman in 1642, which Cook claimed as a British possession, and a detailed exploration of the east coast of Australia.

Sir Joseph Banks, whose travels with Captain Cook in 1768–71 to Tahiti, New Zealand and Australia, made his reputation as both a botanist and a libertine. He was forever after known as the 'Botanical Macaroni'.

Banks' presence on this extraordinary journey – and his behaviour in Tahiti in particular – made his name. Back in London in 1771 he became famous both for his scientific discoveries – particularly those relating to the acquisition for Britain of economically valuable plants such as flax from New Zealand – and for his sexual conduct during the voyage. Indeed, such was his reputation for sexual philandering among the relatively promiscuous Tahitian women that upon his return he was almost immediately christened the 'Botanical Macaroni' and widely mocked for his readiness to exploit the innocence and sexual mores of Tahitian culture. Blessed or cursed with the enthusiastic and enquiring outlook that characterised successful men of science in the late eighteenth century Banks had made a highly personal study of life on Tahiti and recorded his observations uncensored in his journal:

> One amusement more I must mention tho' I confess I hardly dare touch
> upon it as it is founded upon a custom so devilish, inhuman and
> contrary to the first principles of human nature . . . more than half of
> the better sort of the inhabitants of the Island have like Comus in
> Milton entered into a resolution of enjoying free liberty in love . . .
> seldom co-inhabiting together more than one or two days.

Banks was clearly out to shock his readers, though elsewhere he admitted he had never in fact seen the Tahitians give 'full liberty to their desires'.[20] He may have chosen to describe the moral laxity he did see as 'devilish' and 'inhuman', but that did not stop him from indulging in it himself or from profiting from the fact that in Tahiti, 'Love is the Chief Occupation . . . both the bodies and the souls of the women are modelled into the utmost perfection for that soft science idleness, the father of love, reigns here in almost unmolested ease.'[21] Banks' special woman in Tahiti appears to have been named Otheothea, a personal attendant to the high-ranking Purea who organised a ritual copulation ceremony for him to observe. The young Banks was evidently much impressed by local life and customs and felt free to participate fully, once joining in a dance wearing only a loincloth and, as he admitted in his journal, 'not ashamed of my nakedness for neither of the women were a bit more covered than myself'.[22]

James Cook's response to the customs and traditions of Tahiti was very different. He participated in activities as an observer – for example, he was obliged to watch naked erotic dancers – and occasionally had his Christian morality sorely challenged, as on one particular Sunday that started with Christian service and ended with 'an odd scene' of public sexual intercourse. Cook did not succumb to temptation, however. His main concern was to do his duty and maintain control over his much-tried men.[23] But while Cook remained aloof, even mildly shocked by the promiscuity displayed at the public events he was invited to witness, Banks joined in.

The sexual freedom on Tahiti was already known of in Europe before

Cook's journey because the island had been discovered in 1767 by Samuel Wallis and its fame had spread almost instantly, particularly among sailors, as an exotic paradise and earthly Eden – a Utopia of guiltless and plentiful sex. As Patricia Fara explains, visitors to Tahiti observed that its inhabitants . . .

> . . . lived in harmony, totally free of the decadent vices plaguing Western civilisation, above all, the Tahitians supposedly suffered none of the sexual inhibitions that so restricted English enjoyment; on the contrary, the gratification of erotic desire was seen as one of life's major objectives.[24]

In fact, by the time Cook's crew arrived the pristine sexual paradise of Tahiti had already become tarnished. Tahitian women, no doubt exhausted by Wallis's crew, had become a trifle mercenary in their transactions and usually requested nails – as long as possible – in return for their attentions since they regarded iron, a novelty on Tahiti, as a most wondrous material. Also, more sadly, the inhabitants of Tahiti were introduced to the doleful fact that casual and frequent sex could have its drawbacks. The sailors brought with them venereal disease, soon rechristened 'the British Disease' on the island.

Banks' exploits on Tahiti, as recounted by his returning ship-mates, were not soon forgotten by the prurient British public and became a source of enduring titillation and amusement. So while Banks was busily conferring with George III – who loved to hear travellers' tales and was most interested in the acquisition and economic exploitation of natural resources – he was simultaneously being lampooned in the press for his unrestrained behaviour and sexual exploits among the Tahitian women. As the *Town and Country Magazine* for September 1773 observed with heavy irony:

> That curiosity which leads a voyager to such remote parts of the globe as Mr B— has visited, will stimulate him when at home . . . As nature has been his constant study, it cannot be supposed that the most engaging part of it, the fair sex, have escaped his notice; and if we may be suffered to conclude from his amorous descriptions, the females of most countries that he has visited, have undergone every critical inspection by him.[25]

Banks' other associations were also noted with amusement by the press. The *Morning Post* of August 1776 remarked on the friendship between him and Lord Sandwich, a notorious rake and then First Lord of the Admiralty, who it referred to by his old nickname Jemmy Twitcher (see page 528). He, it tellingly remarked, was 'almost the only surviving member of that club (formerly called the Hellfire Club) . . . that had been a notorious gathering place for Libertines'.[26] At the same time as this David Hume recorded Banks and Sandwich going on a fishing trip together, and that he had stayed with them and 'two or three Ladies of Pleasure' at a country inn.[27]

The well-publicised erotic exploits of Banks and his sexual adventuring in Tahiti were gold dust for a London sex industry that was always on the lookout for new, exotic and profitable ways of presenting prostitution. Even Cook, who had remained strictly an observer, contributed to this cultural crossover. Dr John Hawkesworth edited and published his *Journals* and their descriptions of erotic rituals on Tahiti simultaneously shocked moralists like John Wesley – 'men and women coupling together in the face of the sun, and in the sight of scores of people!' – and inspired bawds like Charlotte Hayes.[28] Hawkesworth's description of the 'rites of Otaheite' – which involved the public deflowering of virgins – offered a particularly tempting opportunity and, as *Nocturnal Revels* records, Charlotte Hayes soon organised a tableau in which '12 beautiful nymphs, unsullied and untainted', were to be 'deflowered' by twelve young men, as in 'the celebrated rites of Venus' as they were observed in Tahiti, in front of a high-paying audience which could join in. The role of Queen Oberea, giving 'instruction and tuition', was 'taken by Mrs Hayes herself'.[29]

This new spirit of sexual freedom was not confined to Banks' exploits in Tahiti or Charlotte Hayes' risqué tableaux. It was explored and enjoyed by some of the highest figures in the land, and its notoriety probably reached its apogee with Sir Francis Dashwood and Lord Sandwich's Hell Fire Club.

FIFTEEN

VISITING VENUS' PARLOUR

Sir Francis Dashwood and the Hell Fire Club

Some time between 1746 and 1748 a club was founded at the George and Vulture Tavern in London that took the curious name of the Order of the Knights of St Francis of Wycombe. The name referred to one of the founders of the club – the eminently gregarious Sir Francis Dashwood, who had also been a founder some fifteen years earlier of the Society of Dilettanti (see page 368) – and to his estate at West Wycombe in Buckinghamshire. The exact purpose and rituals of the 'Order' remain obscure but it soon became famed as one of the most aristocratic and exclusive of eighteenth-century England's Hell Fire clubs. Today the history of the club remains so controversial that one contemporary historian, when obliged to contemplate it, dismissed the subject as one that 'unfortunately ... attracts cranks and repels scholars', and after wondering 'if it ever existed' reluctantly concluded that it did, although explaining that its 'activities' were 'very tame by modern standards'.[1]

As far as we now know the members of the 'Order' primarily took pleasure in convivial dining and heavy drinking while attired in medieval-style ecclesiastical garb. This was usually done in the company of harlots or demi-reps dressed as nuns, often masked to hide their identity, with whom the Order participated in a wide variety of sexual antics. This behaviour did not originate with Dashwood and his peers; it had been pioneered by the brilliant and wayward Duke of Wharton, whom Alexander Pope had called the 'the scorn and wonder of our days'.[2]

In 1719 Wharton had launched the prototypical Hell Fire Club that, as its activities became public knowledge, astonished and shocked London society and soon deeply unsettled the ruling party. Wharton appeared to be preaching not just moral anarchy but also perhaps sedition. He was an outspoken critic of Sir Robert Walpole and assumed to be a supporter of the Stuart dynasty at a time when the country was only just regaining stability after the Jacobite uprising of 1715. So in 1721 the original Hell Fire Club – along with the fashion for masquerades that it had readily embraced – fell victim to the wave of suppression and suspicion that Wharton's outspokenness had provoked. In that year his enemy Walpole became First Lord of the Treasury – effectively Prime Minister – and was no doubt the moving force behind the Royal Edict that closed Wharton's club. The declared reason was that its members were corrupting 'the minds and morals of one another', but it was also perhaps feared that the club's sexual activities were nothing more than a front for a political movement with rebellion on its agenda.

The socially elevated membership of Dashwood's later Hell Fire Club suggests that it also, at some level, operated as a political powerhouse. Benjamin Franklin certainly believed as much, for in 1774 when on a diplomatic mission for the American colonies, he visited Dashwood at West Wycombe, reckoning that it would be a good place to meet Britain's political luminaries in informal and relaxed circumstances. If there during a meeting of the Order, Franklin would also have encountered some of the most alluring harlots in London and various other intriguing characters such as the androgynous French Chevalier d'Eon who served both as man and woman during club festivities. But whether the club's members met for more than simply convivial reasons, and their mockery of religious ritual and dress was intended to do more than sexually titillate, has never been resolved.

In the nineteenth century it became popular to view the club as mildly Satanic with its members indulging in black masses, and there is enough contemporary evidence to give some credence to this. But while the members of the club were certainly anti-Catholic – a common stance among the majority of England's ruling elite during most of the eighteenth century – there is no real reason to see the Order's rituals as more than amusing theatre, providing a stimulating backdrop to the more serious business of drinking, eating and unconventional sexual encounters. Indeed, if the club was in any way seriously Satanic in its intentions then it would be necessary to conclude that aristocratic England at that time was in the grip of sinister forces, widely in thrall to the Prince of

Sir Francis Dashwood in the guise of a monk venerating an effigy of a naked woman – presumably Venus. This engraving is taken from a painting executed by George Knapton in the mid-1740s.

Darkness, for Dashwood's Order included among its members some of the most important politicians and power-brokers of the day. Dashwood himself served as Chancellor in 1762–3, while the co-founder of the club, Lord Sandwich, was a principal Secretary of State in the Government in 1763 and a former First Lord of the Admiralty, and membership of the Order during the decade after 1755 included a number of MPs, a former Governor of Bengal, professors from Oxford University, the son of an Archbishop of Canterbury and the physician to the Prince of Wales.

Many of Britain's enemies in the mid-eighteenth century – particularly in the Roman Catholic nations of France and Spain – would indeed have seen the Order's mockery of religion and indulging of the senses as evidence of the damned, dark and corrupt nature of England. But not only would this interpretation have been absurd, it would also have missed the most interesting point about the Order's activities. Without doubt its members drank and they whored, but many were also members of the Society of Dilettanti and, in similar fashion, Dashwood and Sandwich's Order was part of the general revolution in artistic taste, a declaration of spiritual independence. The Order's actions and convictions can be seen as representing the desire by Dashwood and his fellows to escape what they saw as the arid conventions, inhibitions and hypocrisies of modern Christian society, riddled as it was with guilt about sexual pleasure, and to return to the mores of the idyllic pre-Christian era of classical antiquity. To them the imagined classical past was a time of freedom, when Priapus was the great god of fecundity – both among humans and in the garden – and sex was venerated as the means of divine procreation. It was an age when great men – artists, philosophers and heroes – were inspired by great women, by goddesses, the muses and the Three Graces, who blessed mankind through their charm, beauty and their ability to elevate the mind to peaks of nobility and creativity and so inspire great art and heroism.

There is no question that the prostitutes who attended the gatherings of the Order were treated as women but they were also, perhaps just a little, treated as goddesses, as inspirational beings, the bringers of pleasure touched by the divine. It is also true that, to a lesser or greater degree, the Order's passion for the past and admiration of Priapus – god of gardening and procreation – helped to inspire a British Neo-classical movement that was imbued with a deep love of nature and antique architecture and found its supreme expression through the creation of some spectacular landscape gardens dotted with Greek or Roman-style temples.

WEST WYCOMBE AND MEDMENHAM

The Order was very much London-based. All its key members – and the prostitutes who served them – lived in the capital. But to appreciate fully what it stood for we have to move outside the city, to the houses and grounds that Sir Francis Dashwood created at West Wycombe and at Medmenham, both in Buckinghamshire. They remain an outstanding example of the libertine vision of antiquity, a perfect fusion of nature, the classical world, ancient British traditions and virtually ungoverned sexual encounter.

The history of the park at West Wycombe reflects three different phases of landscape design. The first phase of the garden, from the late 1730s, was in the French and Italian formal manner in which man imposed his will and geometry on the natural landscape, by organising plantations in symmetrical fashion, incorporating rectangular strips of water and cutting straight avenues to offer distant prospects. At this time the lake is thought to have been octagonal in shape, and rides – notably a Broad Walk – were driven through the woods to create vistas terminating in statues.

This early phase was probably inspired by the landscape Lord Cobham and Charles Bridgeman created at Stowe in Buckinghamshire, and by Sir Robert Child's garden at Wanstead, Essex. Both Cobham and Child were political associates of Dashwood, who certainly owned copies of Rigaud's engraved views of Stowe and Wanstead that had been published in 1739 and 1735 respectively.[3] During the 1740s, however, Dashwood altered and developed what he had previously created to reflect the newly fashionable and more asymmetrical Rococo spirit. It was now that the first significant and ornamental garden buildings and structures started to appear.

There was the Cascade, an elaborate fretwork bridge, and Venus' Temple and Parlour. Designs for these structures survive in West Wycombe house, attributed to Giovanni Niccolo Servandoni and Morise Lewes Jolivet, and were probably broadly inspired by structures of the same type and name that had been built at Stowe. It is probable they were executed in simplified form by John Donowell, guided closely by Dashwood, with only Venus' Parlour – completed in about 1748 – bearing any resemblance to the initial designs.

This more natural-looking landscape was inspired by a love of classical landscapes – the preserve of the gods Pan and Priapus – in which man's skill was dedicated to the creation of carefully modulated and asymmetrical forms and plantations, to the enhancement of nature itself. But the park, garden and architecture at West Wycombe do much more than reflect changing trends in English landscape design. Dashwood, during this Rococo phase of the late 1740s, was attempting the creation of a sexual landscape that expressed some very big ideas indeed. It almost certainly sought to incorporate ancient beliefs about the divine and intensely fecund nature of gardens that would echo the ancients' worship of the Great Goddess and of Priapus.

A survey of West Wycombe survives that shows the garden at this time. Inscribed to Dashwood by his 'most Dutiful servant Morise Lewes Jolivet, Arch', it dates from 1752 and shows the lake enlarged and made

The house and garden at West Wycombe Park, showing the east portico of 1755. Later, a west portico was added, which is one of the earliest Greek revival structures in Britain.

irregular in shape, the axial rides made less prominent and symmetrical, and a 'Rococo garden' of complex form, incorporating streams and winding paths, located within the thickets around Venus' Temple and Parlour.[4] The garden seemed finally to have satisfied Dashwood for in 1751 he commissioned William Hannan to paint a series of paintings, completed in 1753, commemorating his creation.

During the 1760s Dashwood (by now created Lord le Despencer) concentrated on enlarging the house, rebuilding the church and building a mausoleum. Then in 1770 he returned to the landscape, perhaps newly inspired by the works he had completed on the house. Nicholas Revett – a fellow Dilettanti member and author in 1762 (with James Stuart) of the highly influential *Antiquities of Athens* – had added a west portico to the house and Dashwood now had to furnish its new entrance front with a drive.

This ushered in the third phase of the garden's design: an increased 'naturalisation of the landscape' in accordance with the taste of the times, which advocated that the greatest beauty lay in apparent naturalness and irregularity. This sensibility – incorporating a provoking artistic paradox – was the pre-eminent English contribution to garden design. Using all manner of artifice and cunning, natural-*looking* landscapes were created that were, in fact, idealised and improved versions of nature. These generally incorporated well-dispersed clumps of trees, undulating vales, well-lit meadows and mysterious shady glades, irregular patches of water and, here and there, intriguing garden buildings. All was to be evocative, emotive and above all romantic. According to Thomas Langley's book on the *Hundred of Desborough*, published in 1797, this remodelling of the landscape at West Wycombe in more informal and Picturesque manner was carried out by Thomas Cook, a pupil of Capability Brown. It was the result of this phase of the remodelling that provoked Benjamin Franklin – when staying at West Wycombe in August 1773 – to observe in a letter that the 'Gardens are a Paradise'.[5]

These later alterations probably did not obscure the sexually allusive landscape created by Dashwood during the late 1740s and 50s, which we now know best from the descriptions given by the radical politician, journalist and libertine John Wilkes (see page 509). Writing in the *Public Advertiser* in May 1763, he revealed Dashwood's private and potentially shocking vision to the general reader, and made it clear that there was little ambiguity about the sexual imagery of West Wycombe's landscaped gardens and buildings.

Wilkes was in a good position to reveal all since he was an early member of the Hell Fire Club and as one of the initiated knew exactly what Dashwood's landscape signified, although, of course, his description may well have been sensationalised to cause its creator maximum embarrassment. The reason for Wilkes' betrayal was complicated and finely calculated but in essence his friendship with Dashwood had turned sour due to differing political allegiances, while his association with Lord Sandwich had degenerated into an open and mutual hatred that would eventually lead to Wilkes' prosecution and, in December 1763, flight from the country (see page 525).

When describing the entrance to the Parlour of Venus located within the Mound of Venus on which stood the Temple of Venus, Wilkes was uncompromising and explicit. He called it 'the same Entrance by which we all come into the World, and the door is what some idle Wits have called the Door of Life'. The door to the parlour was a pointed oval or *Vesica Piscis* (a geometric shape defined by the overlapping area of two circles of the same size with their circumferences passing through each other's centres), while the parlour itself and the temple above were also oval in plan.

This shape was pregnant with meaning to anyone familiar with medieval or Renaissance sacred geometry for it symbolised the vulva or vagina, the 'portal' of the Virgin's body through which Christ the Saviour entered the world, while the oval-plan parlour appears to have represented the womb, the place in which life was created as a result of the pleasurable action of sexual intercourse.

As Tim Knox, author of the current National Trust guide to West Wycombe, explains, the Mound of Venus is an 'artificial *mons veneris*' while its oval opening flanked by curving walls is 'a very literal representation of a vagina, with the curving walls a pair of spread-open legs'.[6]

The details of these ovoid forms helped confirm their meaning. The temple, probably executed to designs produced by Donowell, contained a lead copy of the Venus de' Medici and was topped with an image of Leda being embraced by an amorous swan, as shown in Hannan's painting of 1752. Over the entrance to the parlour hovered a statue of Mercury, the god who conducts the souls of men to Paradise – in this case, mani-fested as physical pleasure – and in the little grove in front of the parlour were twenty-five small lead figures in various provocative attitudes, including one, according to Wilkes, that was a 'most indecent statue of the unnatural satyr'. This was, presumably, based on the same antique carving of a 'satyr enjoying a goat' that was illustrated in 1786 by Richard Payne Knight in his *Discourse on the Worship of Priapus* (see page 375).

Wilkes embellished an already extraordinary reality by fantasising that Lord Bute – a particular hate-figure of his (see page 516) – was much enamoured of the Parlour of Venus and had suggested the 'erection [of] . . . a Paphian Column to stand at the entrance . . . to be made of Scottish pebbles'. The shadow of such a shaft would – as in ancient works such as Stonehenge, dedicated to the Great Goddess, fertility and the quick-ening of the earth – have penetrated the inner womb-like enclosure, in this case the Temple of Venus. But sadly it seems that no such phallic erection was, if seriously contemplated, ever raised.

Dashwood's sexual landscape proved too characterful and provocative to survive. After his death in December 1781 all was gradually altered or dismantled and what he had created, never fully or objectively recorded, passed into the realms of myth and misunderstanding. His half-brother and heir, Sir John Dashwood-King, cannot have been too much of a prude because he had been a regular attendee at the gatherings of the Order, but he seems to have recognised that the times and tastes were changing. Sir Francis' landscape and its imagery were perhaps not only viewed as vulgar and somewhat embarrassing, but – more to the point – old-fashioned as well. In 1794 Dashwood-King called in Humphrey Repton who advised thinning the trees that 'oppressed' the house and imparted 'gloom and melancholy', and – perhaps predictably – recommended the speedy removal of the Temple of Venus. Initially, only the statuary was removed and the temple itself suffered to survive, but finally in 1819 it too was dismantled and the mound partially levelled. Gradually what survived was obscured beneath clumps of ash and elder with the parlour turned into a garden store and the vaginal portal allowed to crumble and lose its distinctive form. (The present reconstructions of the Temple and Parlour of Venus date from 1982 and are based on evidence found on site, drawings and contemporary descriptions. The temple now contains a modern cast of the Venus de Milo.)

Plans and paintings of the landscape commissioned by Sir Francis – including a set dating from 1781 by Thomas Daniell – do not record or reveal the Temple and Mound of Venus and their related plantations in precise detail. Consequently much of their detail and form has been left to the imagination of later commentators, and some of this has been pretty wild. Some nineteenth- and twentieth-century writers, attempting to evoke Dashwood's lost landscape, have suggested it was more lurid and explicit than seems likely to have been the case. Burgo Partridge, in his *History of Orgies*, first published in 1958, claims that Dashwood 'had laid out one part of the garden in the shape of a woman, with much suggestive grouping of pillars and bushes, an expensive smutty joke which could not be appreciated fully until the invention of the aeroplane'.[7] Some accounts even suggest that the garden incorporated breast-like mounds topped with gushing fountains in place of nipples.

Studying the existing plans, paintings and prints it is impossible to confirm these assertions, although perhaps the Rococo planting around the mound of Venus suggested, to some eyes, a naked woman. If it did then a series of intriguing possibilities are opened up. Anthropomorphic manipulation of the landscape and the incorporation of phallic and womb-like features are familiar from prehistoric times. They seem to have been part of fertility rituals associated with the Great Mother Goddess, death and rebirth, with examples including not only Stonehenge but New Grange, West Meath, Ireland. So if Dashwood did attempt such a thing at West Wycombe he could have been inspired by new discoveries about England's ancient past being made by pioneering and archaeologically minded antiquaries such as the Rev. William Stukeley.

It is highly likely that Dashwood would have known Stukeley, who became a confidant of Princess Augusta – the mother of George III and intimate of Dashwood's political associate Lord Bute. Stukeley, born in 1678 and a close friend of Sir Isaac Newton with whom he shared an obsession with alchemy, was keenly interested in reviving a Christian form of the old English Druidic religion – which he believed derived its knowledge from direct association with the culture of Ancient Greece, thus proving Britain was civilised long before the arrival of the Romans. Stukeley believed the Druids were Noah's descendants so Druidic knowledge was not only ancient and native to Britain but also biblical and in accord with the roots of Christianity and Old Testament teaching. He

William Stukeley tried to prove the existence of ancient British classical civilisation through investigation of archaeological remains, such as Stonehenge, and he also sought to revive it through rituals of a supposedly Druidic nature.

was chosen 'Chief of Druids' in 1722 and at the same time founded a mystic antiquarian organisation named the Society of Roman Knights, dedicated to 'interpreting and presenting the memorials of our ancestors' in which he took the name of the Druid Arch Priest Chyndonox.

Two years earlier Stukeley had become a Freemason, an action that reinforced the connection between eighteenth-century Masonry and the quest for ancient knowledge. During the following decades he investigated and wrote about ancient sites – for example, *The British Temple of Avebury* in 1724 and, in 1743, *Stonehenge: temple restored to the British Druids* and *Abury* [sic], *a Temple of the British Druids* – and campaigned to establish Britain's pre-Roman identity and revive its own ancient culture and heroes. In 1753 he was summoned to Kew to give his opinion on antiquarian matters to Princess Augusta and as a result persuaded her to become patron of the Order of Druids and take the name Veleda, the 'Arch Druidess of Kew'.

Stukeley's work inspired research among other antiquaries, including the architect John Wood, who in the 1730s became obsessed with the role he believed the ancient mythic King Bladud had played in the creation of Bath and a classically inspired culture in pre-Roman Britain. Wood surveyed 'Druidic' structures such as Stonehenge and Stanton Drew, studied biblical texts – particularly those describing the 'divine' design of Solomon's Temple in Jerusalem – and applied his discoveries and interpretation in the plans and architecture he created for Bath.

Dashwood would have been well aware of these Druidical theories and their artistic consequences so that a vast naked female form embedded within his landscape, if indeed it existed, may not have been explicitly erotic but instead the evocation of the ancient fertility cult of the Great Goddess. There is also another possibility.

The enquiring minds of Dashwood and his fellow members of the Order, which questioned conventional Christian morality that prescribed rigid patterns of morality and imposed sexual guilt, can be seen as part of the long-standing and highly respectable Humanist tradition. Indeed, some of the great patrons of the Renaissance – such as the Barbaro brothers, who in the 1550s commissioned Andrea Palladio and would have been greatly admired by Dashwood and his Dilettanti circle – were Humanists and highly liberated thinkers. They perceived humanity as essentially dignified, moral, and able by rational thought and without reference to religious dogma or ideology to hammer out an ethical way of life and determine right from wrong.

This view accords, in certain ways, with the apparent philosophy and actions of the Order. They certainly questioned conventional notions of morality and their behaviour clearly expressed a belief in independent – even idiosyncratic – thought and action. So, arguably, West Wycombe Park incorporated, among many things, eighteenth-century Britain's great if unacknowledged Humanist garden, relating to such earlier Continental examples as Hofwijck at Voorburg near The Hague in the Netherlands that was created during the 1630s and 40s by the poet Constantijn Huygens with architect Jacob van Campen.

At Voorburg the house and garden form a composition that is a powerful example of the Humanist tradition of landscape design, in which the human form is used to express – in most literal manner – the potential nobility of the human spirit and intellect. Huygens conceived his house and garden as a somewhat geometric and abstract human body, with straight avenues and walks defining arms, torso and legs, and the house itself representing the head.

If the planting around Dashwood's Temple of Venus did, in some way, represent the body of a naked female then another question arises. How would this exceptional design, presumably large in scale, ever have been perceived? Partridge suggests sarcastically that an aeroplane would have been required. In fact, the park did possess something that would have offered a kind of aerial view over part of it. In the early 1760s Dashwood brought the parish church into his ambitious garden design by rebuilding it on the hilltop overlooking West Wycombe Park.

St Laurence's is an elegant but astonishing affair, with a nave inspired by Roman interiors that feels more like a ballroom than a church and seems to have been envisaged as a suitable gathering place for the fashionable members of the Order and their 'nuns' rather than for the more rustic parishioners. The strangest detail is the tower topped by a gilded sphere, a composition modelled on a prototype in Venice that was used for optical experiments.

One Sunday in 1763 John Wilkes and Charles Churchill rode to West Wycombe to view the newly completed church. They met Dashwood and all three men climbed into the golden ball that was apparently furnished with seats. 'Later Wilkes reported that it was "the best Globe Tavern I was ever in" where they sung "jolly songs very unfit for the profane ears of the world below".[8] Wilkes does not mention seeing, from the top of the church tower, a gigantic female figure formed in the distant landscape. Perhaps he was too busy drinking and singing, perhaps the day was misty and the figure too distant. So Dashwood's herbaceous female form remains an enigmatic and allusive figure in the landscape. But the visibility – even the existence – of a female figure is not the important point. The very presence of the Mound of Venus with its vulva portal was enough to imply a sexually specific human body – evoked by landscape design and architecture – and so makes West Wycombe the English pioneer of a curious late-eighteenth-century fashion for such imagery. Typical of this is a design produced by the young John Soane, future architect of the Bank of England, when in Rome in the late 1770s. It was for a vast National Monument and, while detailed in conventional Greek

Classical manner, had a plan in the form of a pair of prodigious circular testicles from which sprout a stubby shaft of an exedra-topped and erect penis, all evidently inspired by a keen interest in Priapus.

Near the church at West Wycombe, and started at roughly the same time, is another example of Dashwood's collection of bizarre buildings. The Mausoleum is a large, ungainly, open-roofed hexagonal enclosure that Tim Knox rightly describes as 'a somewhat . . . nightmarish structure . . . akin to a Scottish "lair" or sepulchral enclosure'. Each of its six sides contains a large round-headed arch and so it could be described as an essay on a triumphal arch, though this implies an antique dignity that the bleak and awkward structure most clearly lacks.

The flint-faced Mausoleum was built using a bequest from George Bubb Dodington – Treasurer of the Navy for much of the 1740s – who in 1762 left Dashwood £500 for erecting 'an Arch, Temple, Column or Additional Room' at 'such of his seats where it is likely to remain the longest as a Testimony to after Times of my Affection and Gratitude for the invariable and very Endearing Friendship he has Honoured me with'. The structure was completed by 1765 when Donowell and John Bastard the Younger were paid £495 5s 3d to cover its design and construction. It contains memorials to, among others, Dashwood and its begetter Dodington, who had been a founder-member with his friend of the Order and was, in his time, a notable libertine.

In October 1745 Dodington wrote to Dashwood to congratulate him on a mode of life that involved, '20 of the 24 hours either upon your own Belly, or from thence, like a Publick Reservoir, administering to those of other people, by laying your Cock in every private Family that has any Place fitt to receive it'.[9] He referred to his guests at La Trappe – his long-demolished and once inspirational home in Hammersmith – as 'monks' and encouraged them to dress in ecclesiastical robes when dining. La Trappe was a splendid riverside Palladian villa, remodelled in 1748 by Roger Morris and with an 82-foot-long gallery in which Dodington displayed antiquities gathered in Italy.

Before initiating the rebuilding of the parish church and Mausoleum, Dashwood had added another major feature to the park that, like so much of his work, remains enigmatic in its intention and meaning. This feature was in fact an heroic piece of civil engineering for in the early 1750s he ordered the excavation of a series of caves that he concealed behind a flint-work façade resembling a ruined Gothic church, a folly probably designed by Donowell at the same time that he was surveying the bawdy-house in Enfield Wash in which Elizabeth Canning claimed to have been imprisoned (see page 155). In the nineteenth century there was much speculation that the members of Dashwood's Hell Fire Club had cele-brated their peculiar rites in these caves but this seems unlikely – they were surely too dark, damp, uncomfortable and public to have appealed to the elegant and exotic tastes of Dashwood and his fellow revellers. But something out of the ordinary seems to have taken place in this subter-ranean world because Benjamin Franklin, who got to know Dashwood and West Wycombe pretty well, recorded in 1772 that 'his Lordship's imagery, puzzling and whimsical as it may seem, is as much evident below earth as it is above it'.[10] Exactly what underground activities were accompanied by this 'whimsical' imagery we shall probably never know.

In parallel with the creation of the garden and buildings at West Wycombe, Dashwood transformed those at nearby Medmenham when he leased the estate in 1755. The Medmenham estate was, when he acquired it, a place of strange, isolated and ruinous beauty for it consisted of Thames-side gardens and meadows, an island, and ancient and partly abandoned monastic buildings. All was rapidly altered for the exclusive use and pleasure of the eighteenth-century Order, and so complete was the focus of the club's activities on the newly acquired estate that its name was then changed from the Order of the Knights of St Francis of Wycombe to the Order of the Monks of Medmenham.

Dashwood rapidly repaired the ruins and extended them, and the substantial 1590s house they incorporated, to include a small cloister, a ruined tower, a 'chapter house', common room, dining room or refectory, and a series of small monks' cells. The various reception rooms contained idiosyncratic and most emblematic interiors. For example, the chapter house contained prints of monks and nuns, and pegs from which the members of the Order hung their ceremonial garb, which consisted of 'a white hat, white jacket and white trousers' with the 'prior' having 'a red hat like a Cardinal's'.[11]

The house Dashwood created still survives in splendid tranquillity on the banks of the Thames but its interiors have long since been altered, as have the garden buildings and ornaments that he placed in its grounds. It is now a luxurious and slightly characterless private home but one or two clues survive to suggest the life that was lived within its walls by the Medmenhamites during the 1750s and 60s.

The ruinous remains of the medieval monastic buildings at Medmenham, on the Thames in Buckinghamshire. They were transformed in 1755 by Dashwood to house revels between 'monks' and 'nuns'.

Most notable is the carved motto that survives above the main door and over the dining-room fireplace, which proclaims *Fay ce Que Voudras* – 'Do as you will'. It is that of the Order of St Francis and was taken from the fictional Abbey of Thélème invented by François Rabelais. Also revealing are the apertures in the anteroom adjoining the dining room which allow an observer to see events unfolding within, without themself being seen. Evidently voyeurism was one of the established pleasures of the club. The refectory of Dashwood's day contained, among other things, statues of Harpocrates, the Greek god of silence, and of the Roman goddess Angerona, with her bandaged mouth to remind club members of both sexes of the vows of secrecy they had taken which were intended to prevent them ever revealing what took place within the walls of this house and its surrounding gardens.

Discretion duly prevailed until 1763 when John Wilkes turned on his fellow Medmenhamites and revealed some of their secrets. He described the garden at Medmenham in somewhat lurid detail, which is not necessarily to be trusted, and implied that it was full of suggestive statuary and

mottos so that the very landscape seems to have spoken of the actions
and aspirations of the Medmenhamites:

> The garden, the grove, the orchard, the neighbouring woods, all bespoke
> the loves and frailties of the younger Monks who seemed, at least, to
> have sinned naturally. You saw in one place, *Ici páma de joie mortels le plus
> heureux* [Here the happiest of mortals died of joy] – in another, very
> imperfectly, *mourut un amant sur le sein de sa dame* [a lover dies on the
> bosom of his lady] – in a third, *en cet endroit mille baisers de flame furent
> donnés, et mille autres rendus* [in this place a thousand kisses of fire were
> given and a thousand others returned]. Against a fine old oak was
> [inscribed] *Hic Satyrum Naias victorem victa subegit* [Here the vanquished
> naiad overcame the conquering satyr]. At the entrance of a cave was
> *Venus*, stooping to pull a thorn out of her foot. The statue turned from
> you, and just over the two nether hills of snow were these lines of Virgil:
>
> > Hic locus est, partes ubi se via findit in ambas:
> > Ha citer Elyzium nobis; at laeva malorum
> > Exercet poenas, et ad impia Tartars mittit
>
> [Here is the place where the way divided into two: this on the right is
> our route to Heaven; but the left-hand path exacts punishment from the
> wicked, and sends them to Hell].[12]

Inside the cave presided over by Venus was, Wilkes noted, 'a mossy couch'
over which was written a galvanising exhortation:

> > Ite, agite, ó juvences; pariter fudate medullis
> > Omnibus inter vos; non murmura vestra columbas,
> > Brachia non ses hederae, non vincant oscula conchae.

> 'Go into action, you youngsters; put everything you've got into it
> together; both of you; let not doves outdo your cooings, nor ivy your
> embraces, nor oyster your kisses.'

> The favourite doctrine of the Abbey is certainly not penitence for in the
> centre of the orchard is a very grotesque figure, and in his hand a reed
> stood flaming, tipt with fire, to use MILTON's words, and you might
> trace out: PENI TRENTO non PENITENTI [i.e. penetrate not penitent].

FANNY MURRAY

It seems fitting to close the story of the Order with an account of one of the London-based 'nuns' who served it. The life history of Fanny Murray – partly recorded in her *Memoirs*, published in 1759 – not only tells us much about the path from Covent Garden to Dashwood's country estate, but also offers fascinating additional insights into the ways in which the lives of leading courtesans became interwoven with, and at times shaped, those of their rich lovers and clients – in Fanny's case Dashwood himself, Lord Sandwich and John Wilkes.

Soon after arriving in London in the late 1740s Fanny was taken up by the Covent Garden pimp Jack Harris (see page 180) and by the early 1750s was at the height of her fame and desirability. In 1749 she was profiled in *The Humours of Fleet Street and the Strand, being the Lives and Adventures of the Most Noted Ladies of Pleasure*, and the *Modern Courtezan* of 1751 included 'an Heroic epic inscrib'd to Miss F—y M—y', in which she was described as 'Fair F— whom each Fop admires,/The Talk of Courtiers, and the Toast of Squires'.[13] This publication was also furnished with a print of a charming young woman – perhaps Fanny – captioned with a text from the biblical Book of Proverbs: 'For the sitteth at the door of her house, on a seat in the high places of the city, To call passengers who go right on their ways'.[14]

It was in the late 1740s or early 1750s that Fanny became embroiled – presumably via an introduction by Jack Harris – with both Sir Francis Dashwood and Lord Sandwich. She seems to have been intimate with both of them and became one of the leading 'nuns' of their Order, making regular excursions to West Wycombe and then Medmenham along with other Covent Garden harlots such as Lucy Cooper and Bet Wemys. But, to judge by slight and circumstantial evidence, Fanny was involved with Dashwood and Sandwich even before the Order had been concocted and may have been one of the ornamental prostitutes – doubling as harem slaves – who gave extra piquancy to the 'Divan Club' that the two men had founded in 1744.

This club was for aficionados of the Ottoman Empire, its culture and customs, with perhaps the real focus of that interest revealed by the

Lord Sandwich in Turkish dress as a member of the Divan Club
he co-founded in 1744.

club toast, which was 'To the Harem'. Most of the members had, like Dashwood and Sandwich, travelled to Constantinople, and most were also rather grand, if distinctly peculiar, like Lady Mary Wortley Montagu. To celebrate the club and its exotic oriental tastes Dashwood had its leading members painted in about 1745 by Adrien Carpentiers and George Knapton. This collection includes a fine portrait of Fanny in the guise of a Sultana, wearing a low-cut gold dress, ermine wrap and jewelled tiara. It is a very striking image. If added to the collection of portraits by the time the club closed in 1746, it shows Fanny aged about seventeen though she looks the very image of a confident and alluring courtesan.[15]

Soon after this portrait was completed Fanny seems to have become distanced from Dashwood while continuing to serve as the regular mistress of the unattractive but powerful Lord Sandwich. But her continuing relationship with the taverns of Covent Garden and with Jack Harris, together with her appearance in his *List*, suggest that Fanny was not a 'kept' woman and still had to work in the 'flesh-market' to earn her living. Perhaps she wanted it this way and valued her independence above financial security but, if irregular, her relationship with Sandwich appears still to have been strong. Indeed, it was to play its part in the notorious feud between Sandwich and John Wilkes.

The relationship between the two libertines had always been tense, not least because of their political differences, and they appear to have sustained a long, simmering feud that occasionally flared up into open fury and confrontation. On one occasion Lord Sandwich caught Wilkes in amorous embrace with Fanny and was reduced to a pistol-waving but ultimately impotent rage. Wilkes made it his business to humiliate Sandwich whenever a chance arose – once terrifying and ridiculing him during a Medmenham ritual by releasing a baboon dressed as a horned devil when Sandwich, and his fellow celebrants were challenging God to appear and theatrically conjuring up the Devil. The screeching baboon clung to Sandwich, who was reported to have pleaded in his terror, '[S]pare me, gracious devil . . . I never committed a thousandth part of the vices of which I boasted . . . I never knew that you'd really come . . .'

Sandwich, who was never allowed to forget this humiliating episode, bided his time, and sought opportunities for revenge. When they came he was never quite quick enough to catch Wilkes and usually found himself punished for his temerity. One perhaps apocryphal story captures the flavour of the continual sparring between the two men. Sandwich, vexed by some deed or utterance, spluttered at Wilkes, 'Sir, I do not know whether you will die on the gallows or of the pox.' Wilkes, quick, witty and cool as ever, replied, 'That will depend, my lord, on whether I embrace your principles or your mistress.' (The riposte is also attributed to Samuel Foote.)

When the final break between Sandwich and Wilkes took place, though, it was not provoked directly by Fanny or by jealousy over a mistress but by a poem – Wilkes' pornographic *An Essay on Woman* (see page 514), which Sandwich, in a fit of apparently breathtaking hypocrisy, attacked in a speech in the House of Lords. In the same year, 1763, he gave up Fanny and took as his mistress the servant's daughter and opera singer Martha Ray. She seemed to transform him. His wife had gone insane, perhaps provoked by Sandwich's years of chronic misbehaviour, and he might well have spent the rest of his life wracked by sorrow and guilt. But seventeen-year-old Martha seemed to offer him not only joy but also redemption. Whatever the reason, he stuck to her for sixteen years, during which time they had nine illegitimate children, five of whom survived birth. The couple were separated only by death when – in utterly bizarre circumstances – Martha was murdered in 1779, in the foyer of the Covent Garden Theatre, by a sexually obsessed and lunatic clergyman and former army officer overcome by hopeless unrequited love and jealousy. The murderer – James Hackman – was hanged within the fortnight while Lord Sandwich lived on another thirteen years, finally a broken man.

Very few early copies of *An Essay on Woman* survive but one in the V&A library reveals that John Wilkes retained warm memories of his time with Fanny for he chose to 'inscribe' the publication to her and, in certain editions, verses were included celebrating her as an amorous partner:

> Awake, my Fanny, leave all meaner things,
> This morn shall prove what raptures swiving brings.
> Let us (since life can little more supply
> Than just a few good Fucks and then we die)
> Expatiate free o'er that lov'd scene of Man;
> A mighty Maze! for mighty Pricks to scan;
> A wild, where *Paphian* Thorns promiscuous shoot,
> Where flow'rs the Monthly Rose but yields no Fruit.
> ... The latent Tracts, the pleasing Depths explore,
> And my Prick clapp'd where thousands were before.[16]

By the mid-1760s Fanny Murray, than in her mid-thirties, had achieved much during nearly twenty-five years of harlotry. She had enjoyed a most personal connection with a man of huge influence, had kept her health and looks, was financially sound, and – more tricky still – had moved up the complex strata of eighteenth-century society and seemed almost secure and respected in her new sphere. Indeed she had reinvented herself as a society beauty and leader of fashion.

This transformation was celebrated by the composer William Boyce, who in the 1750s wrote a song inspired by 'the sight of Fanny Murray'. The song was composed for the singer Mr Lowe and is preserved in the British Library.[17] Gone are innuendo and erotic allusion – Boyce's song is pure and complete adulation, a paean in praise of beauty:

. . . behold I mount the wings of fame
And sing of Fanny Murray . . .
Unspoiled by art, divinely fair
Her face, her form, her Mien, her Air
With admiration stir ye
Tho' all may boast some striking charm
Yet thousands can the soul alarm.
That shine in Fanny Murray
. . . From ev'ry Prudish Foible free
From all that in Coquetts we see
And all Fantastical Flurry
To prove how pow'rfull Nature's Art
To strike the Eye and win the Heart
Jove sent us Fanny Murray.

Can this really be the same Fanny who as a child prostitute walked the streets of Bath, and who only ten years before the song was written had been a member of Jack Harris' Whores Club (see page 183)? Such a complete reinvention was amazing, not least because the history of Fanny's lewd past was well and truly in the public domain thanks largely to the opportunistic publication in 1759 of her softly erotic *Memoirs*. But what was probably her greatest social triumph came in 1769 when at the age of forty – a time of life when most eighteenth-century prostitutes, if they lived so long, were diseased, worn out by hard work and hard living, and impoverished – she was invited in person by the King of Denmark to attend a masquerade held in his honour.

Fanny's *Memoirs* were published when she was only thirty and so bring her adventures – indeed her 'public' life – to a somewhat premature end, though a very beautiful and gratifying one. *Nocturnal Revels*, published twenty years later, remembered that Fanny and one of her protectors after Sandwich – one Sir Richard Atkins – were notorious for their blazing rows.

Horace Walpole commemorates one in a letter which credits Fanny with a dramatic and emblematic gesture that is also – at about the same time – associated with the high courtesan Kitty Fisher (see page 355): 'I heard t'other night [Fanny Murray] was complaining of want of money; Sir Richard Atkins immediately gave her a twenty pound note; she said

"Damn your twenty pounds, what does that signify?" – clapped it between two pieces of bread and butter and ate it.'[18]

Despite their turbulent relationship, the *Memoirs* cast Sir Richard 'of Clapham' in the hero's role. The pair became intimate in about 1757 and, according to the *Memoirs*, it was Sir Richard rather than Sandwich who first introduced Fanny into polite society. He was a baronet and we are told that this most eligible bachelor 'took her an elegant country house near Richmond, which he suitably furnished [and where] she now received the visits of women of character'. In this genteel world not only did 'ladies of distinction ... not scruple speaking to her' but actually 'imitated' her in dress and manner. Fanny was, concludes the *Memoirs* triumphantly, 'still the reigning toast; still the standard of female dress; and still the object of every man's desire'.[19]

A wishful fairytale perhaps, but the few known facts of Fanny's later life suggest that there was more than a little truth in these optimistic statements. But one thing did not happen – she did not stay with Sir Richard, presumably because their ill-matched temperaments made this impossible. After they parted Atkins seems not to have married, certainly the baronetcy died with him, but Fanny found fulfilment and stability – not with a rich old man or a tempestuous young aristocrat but with a Scottish Shakesperian actor of her own age named David Ross. They were married and may have been happy together; though he was to die in poverty, living on handouts from a former keeper of Fanny's.

THE MURDER OF
ANN BELL

In Marylebone in October 1760 a young woman died in mysterious circumstances. Her death had been slow and agonising and its cause was uncertain – as, initially, were her name and exact place of origin. But when details of the last days of Ann Bell – or Ann Sharpe, as she was also known – emerged, she came to achieve a degree of fame unknown to her in life and her fate became a topic of city-wide debate. Two and a half centuries later much remains obscure about the detective tale that unfolded in the months following her death but, through contemporary newspaper accounts and court records, it is possible to build up a picture of the dangerous world in which Ann Bell lived, and to trace the judicial process that followed in the wake of her death.

The basic facts seem fairly clear. By late August of that year Ann Bell had become obliged to work as a prostitute and, accompanied by another young woman of the town named Mary Young, went to Haddock's Bagnio in Covent Garden (see page 227) with two men. They formed two couples, stayed for two nights, much liquor being consumed, willingly or otherwise, by Ann. At some point, possibly while at Haddock's on 29 or 30 August, she received some dreadful injuries. She then fell ill – possibly as a result of these injuries – and died a few weeks later.

At first her death was not regarded as suspicious by the authorities and she was buried in the usual way. But there was talk. On 10 October, for example, just six days after Ann's death, the *Public Ledger* alleged that the young woman who had died in 'Marybone' on Sunday night, having been brought there from 'a certain bagnio, in or near Covent Garden', was the victim of foul play. She had been 'decoyed by an inferior actor to town from her parents', the actor had then acted for 'a gentleman', and, when the gentleman had arrived at the bagnio and found the girl 'quite averse to his inhuman proceedings', he had taken a penknife from his pocket 'and cut her in a most shocking manner'. On receiving the wound or wounds, the paper stated, Ann Bell 'fell into the greatest agonies'. The paper also implied a conspiracy was afoot, orchestrated by certain parties involved in the attack, who 'to prevent a discovery of this horrid scene . . . removed her in a coach privately to the above place [the 'New Buildings' in Marylebone, see page 109], where she expired in a few hours (sic) after'.

The actor was not named in the report but clearly believed he was in danger of identification because the following day he ran an advertisement in the *Daily Gazetteer*:

> [A] paragraph of a most scandalous kind having been printed in the *Ledger* of yesterday, tending to destroy the reputation of a performer in one of the theatres; he is reduced to the disagreeable necessity of making an answer in this manner, for the satisfaction of the town, to a piece of infamous falsehood . . . and takes the liberty of informing them, that he has already incontestably proved his innocence with regard to the unhappy circumstances they so good-naturedly attribute to him; and assures them, they shall also be severely convinced by a legal prosecution if he is mentioned any more upon this occasion.

The actor did not make clear how he 'incontestably proved his innocence', but this soon became immaterial because, shortly after he placed his advertisement, a different account of events began to emerge and circulate, with a different perpetrator entering the frame.

The *Gentleman's Magazine* summarised the whole affair in its October 1760 edition[1] where it stated that Ann had died 'as is supposed' in consequence of 'the shocking usage she met with from some Libertine at a Bagnio'. It seems the magazine shared the *Ledger*'s opinion that the young woman had not died of natural causes. Its account also implied that a conspiracy was underway and perhaps bribery was being employed. The *Gentleman's Magazine* noted with interest that various morning papers on 13 October carried a story 'that had been inserted for money' which sought to prove that Ann was not the victim of an attack but had died of a 'putrid fever', which was clearly meant to suggest she was a prostitute suffering from venereal disease:

The drama of low life A scene from John Gay's *The Beggar's Opera*, painted by William Hogarth in about 1731. It shows the prostitute-turned-actress Lavinia Fenton, in the role of Polly Peachum, dressed in white and begging her father to spare the red-coated highwayman Captain Macheath. But instead of looking her stage-father in the eye Polly looks at her smitten and real-life lover, the Duke of Bolton, seated on the far right.

The actress who triumphed
Lavinia Fenton, sketched by William Hogarth in 1728, in the character of Polly Peachum in *The Beggar's Opera*. Her transformation from prostitute to actress to Duchess of Bolton was an extraordinary rags-to-riches tale.

Painting the nude form Academicians of the Royal Academy, painted in 1771–2 by Johann Zoffany, shown here contemplating a naked male life model. For decency's sake the female academicians are present only as portraits mounted on the wall.

A nude model The body of an executed criminal flayed, cast and posed for use by the drawing students of the Royal Academy. The cast – the surviving version dates from 1834 – was christened Smugglerius by the students because the executed man had been a smuggler. When it came to depicting women in revealing poses, the Academicians, notably Sir Joshua Reynolds, tended to use prostitutes as models.

The prostitute as artistic muse 'The Snake in the Grass', or love untying the zone of beauty, was painted by Sir Joshua Reynolds in about 1784, perhaps using the harlot Emma Hart – the future Lady Hamilton and Nelson's mistress – as a model.

A prostitute with her child? A portrait of a very young woman holding a baby. The paint has deteriorated, giving the painting, executed in about 1782, a very avant-garde and impressionistic appearance. The artist might be Sir Joshua Reynolds and the subject the seventeen-year-old Emma Lyon (soon to be renamed Emma Hart by her 'keeper' Charles Greville) and her child by Sir Harry Fetherstonhaugh.

Aesthetes of the Georgian sexual revolution Charles Townley and his friends sit amongst the best of Townley's collection of antique 'marbles' in the first floor 'Atrium' room of his house in Park Street – now Queen Anne's Gate – St James's. Painted by Johann Zoffany in 1781–3, Townley is shown on the right, seated in the centre is d'Hancarville with, standing behind him, Charles Greville and Thomas Astle.

Charles Townley's house The house (left), dating from the mid-1770s, survives in Queen Anne's Gate. The exterior is elegant and austere but the interior was, in Townley's time, a treasure-trove of antique art that astonished Europe. The eighteenth-century rediscovery of the classical past swiftly led to a fascination with ancient attitudes to sex and the erotic.

Exploring sex Captain Cook (centre), on his return from his epic three-year voyage in 1771, with (from left) the botanist Daniel Solander; (seated) Joseph Banks, the natural scientist whose sexual escapades among the women of Tahiti earned him the nickname the 'Botanical Macaroni'; John Hawkesworth, whose published edition of Cook's journals, with its detailed description of Tahitian sexual rituals, inspired bawds such as Charlotte Hayes; and Lord Sandwich, First Lord of the Admiralty and a leading light of the licentious Medmenham Hell Fire Club.

A politician of the Georgian sexual revolution John Wilkes in about 1768, soon after the ordeal of exile and imprisonment for libel following the publication of an edition of the *North Briton* that attacked the king, and the highly pornographic *Essay on Woman*. Wilkes embodies the close links between the elite of the Georgian era and the world of prostitution.

The world of the Dilettanti Sir Francis Dashwood, seated foreground, Lord Boyne, Lord Middlesex and companions shown in a ship's cabin off Genoa in around 1732 by the artist Bartolomeo Nazari. The party is said to be celebrating – with a bowl of punch – the idea of founding the Society of Dilettanti, a society dedicated to the appreciation of the classical and pagan past.

Hell Fire Club founder Sir Francis Dashwood painted in the role of 'El faquir Dashwood Pasha' in 1745 to commemorate the Divan Club, inspired by his travels in Turkey. He became notorious as the founder of a drinking, dining and whoring club to which Covent Garden prostitutes were frequent visitors.

A sexual landscape West Wycombe Park, painted in 1752 by William Hannan.
The house is on the left and, on the right in the distance, the round, domed and
colonnaded Temple of Venus sits on the mound of Venus. The temple contained a
copy of the Venus de' Medici and was topped by an image of Leda
being embraced by an amorous swan.

Sexual architecture The Mound of Venus on which sits the colonnaded and domed
Temple of Venus – built in 1982 to replace the original that dated from around 1748.
Within the mound is Venus's Parlour, entered via an oval door that John Wilkes
described in 1763 as 'the same Entrance by which we all come into the World … what
some idle Wits have called the Door of Life.'

Prostitutes' lodgings The former 16
Goodge Street, which, according to
the 1788 edition of Jack Harris's *List of
Covent Garden Ladies*, was the residence
and workplace of Miss Corbel. Next
door at 17 lived Miss Johnson, noted for
'loins' of 'such elasticity' that she could
'cast her lover to a pleasing height and
receive him again with utmost dexterity.'

A lodging place for 'middling' harlots
Mid-eighteenth-century houses in South
Molton Street, south of Oxford Street. The
1793 edition of Jack Harris's *List of Covent
Garden Ladies* notes that Miss Gage at
number 13, Miss Grommof-d at 59,
Miss Wa-s at 60, and Miss Br-ley at 61
were all happy to receive clients.

Bet Flint's house Meard Street, Soho
(formerly Meard's Court and Street)
was built between 1722 and 1732. The
prostitute, thief, would-be author and
friend of Dr Johnson, Bet Flint, lived
in the corner house on the right
of the photograph.

Madam Aubrey's establishment Seymour
Place in Marylebone was the location in the
mid-1830s of Madam Aubrey's large and
popular establishment where young women
attracted custom by standing naked at the
windows and executing 'all manner
of indecent movements and postures.'

On Saturday last Mr Umfreville, coroner of the county of Middlesex,
having summoned a jury . . . out of the several parishes of St Mary le
Bone, Paddington, and St Giles's in the Fields, sat upon the body of
Ann Sharpe, at the King's Head, in the town of Marybone, to enquire
into the cause of her death; when, having examined several eminent
surgeons, together with the physician, surgeon and apothecary, who
attended her during her illness, and also heard the several evidences of
her nurse and maid servant, and several other persons who knew her
before her death, the jury were unanimously of opinion, that the cause
of her death was an inflammatory and putrid fever, with which she had
languished from the 11th of September to the 4th of October, and not
caused by any abuse received from any person whatsoever. The enquiry
held five or six hours; and as the unfortunate young woman was obliged
to be taken out of the grave, for the inspection of the injury and surgeons,
curiosity drew an infinite number of persons of both sexes to the
burying-ground, where it is not to be doubted but the apprehensions
they were under of her meeting with a violent death were entirely
dissipated.

Whoever paid for this advertisement obviously wanted to end speculation about the cause of Ann Bell's death, and to publicise the official verdict:
that she had succumbed to an 'inflammatory and putrid fever' rather than
to a knife wound inflicted by an assailant. But who would benefit most
from the announcement that her death was due to natural causes rather
than a deliberate attack? Presumably the man most likely to be accused of
her murder: the man with whom she had spent the two nights at Haddock's,
a man whose name was as yet unknown to the general public.

Publication of the coroner's verdict did not close the case – far from
it. What on earth was the nature of her wounds to have caused such
confusion? And, more obviously, if Ann had indeed died of a fever, might
it not have been the wounds that had caused this and thus indirectly her
death? This popular concern was reflected in the *Gazetteer*, which, on
Wednesday 15 October, asked if the coroner's jury had really done its duty
by concluding that the young lady had died of 'an inflammatory fever
without enquiring whether the treatment she had received, occasioned
that fever', and wondered whether a jury's verdict in such cases could be
revised. The *Gazetteer* also made clear the current opinion of the town

of the fate that had befallen Ann Bell: that she had been raped, foully murdered, and it seemed that her assailant was not to be sought or brought to trial.

> Common fame reports that this rape was attended with circumstances of pitiless barbarity, that, if fit to be mentioned, would make even the ears of most rakes tingle.

To judge by these newspaper reports, public indignation was running high. By now it had been discovered that Ann was the daughter of a 'person of fortune' but had been 'ruined', fallen into prostitution and been attacked in a disgraceful and pitiless manner. This was shocking enough, but in addition, as far as the public could tell, the seemingly wealthy and well-connected 'gentleman' who was almost certainly responsible for her death was getting away with it. Indeed, he had, as the *Gazetteer* reported, 'gone off' – that is, publicly absconded.

The content and tone of the articles in the *Gazetteer* – presumably reflecting public sentiment – forced the coroner, E. Umfreville, to authorise a public response. The situation was rapidly polarising. The coroner was now obliged to deny Ann Bell had been murdered, because his own ability and reputation, along with that of his expert witnesses, was being called into question. He had to defend himself publicly, and by so doing implicitly defended the man many thought to be a murderer and wished to see brought to justice.

On Friday 17 October the *Ledger* published the coroner's justification for his actions in which he maintained that death was caused by a 'putrid fever' related to Ann's alleged 'excessive drinking' and 'ill habit of body'. He also, for the first time, revealed the nature of the wounds found on the body:

> [I]n respite of the young woman lately sat upon at Marybone . . . it appeared by the evidence of one physician, three surgeons and an apothecary . . . given to the coroner's jury . . . that the wounds (one of which was open upon the rump bone, and the other at a small distance) were not, nor possibly could be, the cause of her death. That they penetrated little farther than the skin, and neither hastened her death, or in any degree caused, irritated or increased the fever of which she died.

So now it was revealed to the public that Ann Bell had multiple wounds near her anus and genital area. There were then two issues to consider: whether these were the result of disease or had been inflicted by a penknife, and whether they were the direct cause of her death. The second issue was not something that medical science in mid-eighteenth-century Europe could determine with ease or clarity. Little was then known about blood poisoning or sepsis, about the importance of hygiene and how even slight wounds – if caused by a dirty instrument or not kept clean subsequently – could prove deadly if poisonous bacteria or their toxins had entered the wound. The collective medical opinion that the wounds could not have been fatal because they 'penetrated little farther than the skin' was deeply flawed. In addition, the coroner sought to distance himself from responsibility for taking action against any person who might have misused the girl: '[B]ut how, by what, or whose means the girl was originally seduced, or ill used (however wickedly or wantonly done and perpetrated) was not the coroner's business.'

This was the case because he stuck by the original verdict of the jury: his 'only office, upon view of the body, was to enquire how she came by her death', and since he still maintained this 'was by the means of an inflammatory, putrid fever, and not otherwise', the coroner for the second time washed his hands of any responsibility for investigating how the wounds Ann Bell suffered were caused, who caused them, or whether they at least contributed to her death.

It was a rum business altogether and the public was not happy. It could sense a beleaguered – perhaps incompetent or even corrupt – petty public official squirming and wriggling to cover his own back. As a correspondent in the *Gazetteer* put it – on the same day that the coroner argued his case in the *Ledger* – '[T]he public seem not quite satisfied how Ann Sharpe came by her death, notwithstanding the verdict of the coroner's inquest.'

Certain articles that appeared in the press cast a shadow over Ann's name – citing various aliases under which she was supposed to have operated in order to prove that she was a woman with a more than questionable past. On 18 October, for example, an article in the *Gazetteer* – a paper that had previously implied she was an innocent victim – revealed that Ann had been known as Phillips 'whilst she lodged with Mrs Jane Mead, in Wine-Office Court, Fleet Street'. This piece of information was somewhat loaded for it tacitly supported the previous imputation that Ann had died from venereal disease. Fleet Street was a famed haunt of prostitutes and Jane Mead may well have been a known bawd.

A follow-up article in the *Gazetteer*, published on Monday 20 October and written by a contributor calling himself 'Mr Heartfree', contrived to compromise Ann's reputation, depicting a fall from grace straight out of *The Harlot's Progress*. Ann, Mr Heartfree claimed, 'was of a reputable and opulent family in the county of Norfolk', and was seduced and betrayed by a 'gentleman of the army'. Her loss of reputation at home obliged her to seek refuge in the anonymity of London where she was apprenticed to a milliner in Leicester Square. (Since milliners were generally regarded as potential or active prostitutes, this detail too was fraught with significance.) She soon 'imbibed a strong inclination for intriguing' – or, in modern parlance, became addicted to sexual liaisons – decamped from Leicester Square and, following a bizarre marriage to a Whitechapel watchmaker named Sharpe whom she abandoned after only one night, ended up living in what was presumably a brothel run by a Madam Modena in King Street, Soho.

Heartfree dealt at some length with 'the night she received the barbarous

Leicester Square in 1753, Ann Bell's first theatre of operation when she moved to London as a milliner's apprentice.

usage at the Bagnio, which so many people have imagined to be the primary cause of her death', and to stress the authentic and exclusive nature of his report reveals that 'what I have to say on this head came from herself'. He states that the actor originally thought 'infamously and principally concerned in the affair' went with witnesses to see Ann in Marylebone, found her 'in bed extremely weak, but perfectly sensible', had it confirmed that he was not responsible and heard her state that 'the wounds I have received, were from Mr S——, a rich merchant's son in the city'.

For the first time in this perplexing affair the public was given a clue to the identity of Ann's alleged assailant. Mr Heartfree also confirmed how Ann was injured. Her visitors apparently asked Ann how her wounds came about, and 'she replied, "with a knife", and at the same time marked with her finger on her hand the manner how, and the size; saying also, "so, so".' If correct, this makes things very clear. In Ann Bell's opinion, her wounds were not the result of disease but were inflicted by a knife. The questioners then wanted to know the circumstances in which she was wounded. They asked whether any 'unnatural practices' were perpetrated by any persons concerned? In response to this delicate question Heartfree reports that Ann 'gave a sort of shrug, then turned up her eyes, then faintly told them she was fatigued, and begged they would ask no more'.

When Mr Heartfree – who was presumably the actor initially believed to have been involved with Ann's injuries – returned to the subject in a subsequent edition of the *Gazetteer*, his approach had changed. Now, rather than focusing on her sexual intrigues, he was at pains to emphasise Ann's role as victim – even to the extent of finding witnesses prepared to state that she was not only no alcoholic, as various other accounts had claimed, but was actually averse to drink. He also played up the evil actions of those who had been responsible for her downfall: 'During her illness,' he reported, Ann 'declared . . . that when she received the wounds at the Bagnio she had been there three days; and during that time kept, by the libertines of her company, continually drunk and senseless, and that not with wines or punch, but strong cordials'. But not all the libertines were to be held equally responsible for the 'shocking affair' that took place, because 'the unfortunate girl declared before her death, however unwilling she was to relate the whole affair, that only one person remained of the company when she received the wounds, and that they were not given to her without using other violence; particularly that of bending her fingers almost level with the back of her hand, so as to give her the greatest pain'.

Heartfree concluded his report by asking a series of questions that he believed would, if answered truthfully and fully, throw much light on the case: 'By whose orders, and by whom was she removed, and who provided her the lodgings at Marybone; and also her physician, apothecary, nurse, attendants, and medicines? And who was, or is to be, the pay master?' Justice 'will, some time or other', Heartfree assured his readers, 'overtake the offenders, however screened by wealth and opulence'.

Because Ann Bell's death occurred before the existence of an independent and professional judicial agency of inquiry with an obligation to investigate suspicious deaths, any decision as to whether to investigate or not was left to the coroner's jury or to a magistrate. Either might initiate an investigation, because of their own suspicion or because a private individual had made a compelling case for action. If a crime were suspected, a magistrate would issue a warrant to apprehend and question any known suspect. In this case no immediate action took place because, as we have seen, the coroner and his jury did not believe that Ann's injuries, peculiar as they were, could have been the cause of her death. Neither did the coroner seek evidence from those who approached him and told him it was their informed opinion that Ann Bell's death was in fact murder. The reason for his decision on this crucial issue was never made clear. In addition it emerged that the relevant magistrate – Sir John Fielding – was in fact approached and offered evidence at an early stage, but for reasons that were also never made clear chose not to pursue an investigation. His detective force – the Bow Street Runners – was not ordered to collect independent evidence from the scene, the witnesses or the accused.

Nevertheless, rumours about the likely cause of Ann's death persisted, and they resulted in a trial for her murder being held at the Old Bailey between 25 and 28 February 1761. The events that took place can be reconstructed in precise detail because the *Gentleman's Magazine* carried a full account of the trial in its March 1761 edition,[2] and because an extraordinary verbatim and gripping report of the trial survives in the Old Bailey archives.[3] Together these accounts flesh out, develop and put in context the earlier press accounts of Ann Bell's death. They also – to an almost mesmerising degree – usher us into eighteenth-century London low-life. We meet the staff at Haddock's, hear their evidence in their own words, almost sense their physical presence. And we begin to understand more clearly the popular attitude towards wayward young women living on the periphery of the sex industry and the law.

We also get a sense of how chaotic the judicial process could be. Because no one was formally interviewed at the time of Ann's death, when the trial was held the only evidence offered was from a gaggle of witnesses speaking for the 'prosecutor' against the accused or for the accused in his defence. It was left to the attorneys acting for the prosecution and the defence to manipulate this mass of often imprecise, confused and conflicting evidence to suit their particular end, and it was the jury's truly daunting task to make sense of it all and, with some guidance from the judges on the bench, try to reach a verdict that was objective, unprejudiced and just.

Hogarth's satirical view in 1758 of 'The Bench' in a Court of Justice. The bench at the trial of Willy Sutton, for the murder of Ann Bell, consisted of Sir Matthew Blakiston, the Lord Mayor of London; the Hon. William Noel, a judge of the Court of Common-Pleas; Sir Richard Lloyd, one of the Barons of the Exchequer; Sir William Moreton, Recorder; and James Eyre, Deputy-Recorder.

The Old Bailey record opens as follows:

Willy Sutton, late of London, merchant, was indicted, for that he . . .
with force and arms, and malice aforethought, on Ann Bell, otherwise
Ann Sharp, Spinster, with a certain penknife, value 2 d. which he had,
and held in his right hand, did strike, and stab the said Ann, on the left
buttock, near the fundament [the area around the anus]; giving to the
said Ann one mortal wound, of the width of three inches, and depth of
one inch. And one other mortal wound, of the depth of three inches,
and width of one inch; whereof she did languish from the 30th of
August, till the fourth of October, and then died. And that he, the said
Willy, the said Ann did wilfully, and of malice aforethought, kill and
murder. He was a second time indicted, on the statute of stabbing, for
feloniously killing and slaying her, the said Ann, against an act of
parliament in that case made and provided.

The witnesses arrayed against Sutton were of three types. There were
those who worked for, worked with or were friends of Ann's: Elizabeth
Honeyball, her servant; Thomas Holland, 'commonly called Capt. Holland,
an adjutant in the Norfolk Militia'; and Mary Young, 'a woman of the town',
who had been with Ann during the fateful days and nights at Haddock's.
Then there were those she hardly knew or knew not at all but were called
by the 'prosecutor': Ann Knight, daughter to the person who owned the
house in Marylebone in which Ann Bell died; Thomas Drake, 'a merchant
of London'; Mr Moon, who was a steward employed by Lord Orford; and
Henry Giffard, who happened to witness some of her incriminating dying
statements. Last of all there were the people who had attended Ann in her
dying days and had offered her spiritual and moral as well as medical assistance: the Rev. Frances Boot, the clergyman who had attended her in her
sickness; Frances Waldergrave, her nurse; and Thomas Bliss, her apothecary.

The witnesses called in Sutton's defence were fewer in number and
more disparate in nature. First there were humble people who happened
to be present in locations where key events were said to have taken place:
Alexander Sexton, a waiter, and Daniel Haviland, a servant, were both
employed by Haddock's and were present in the bagnio when Willy Sutton
and Ann were there. Then there were witnesses who had not known Ann
Bell in life or been present at any of the key locations but were experts
in their own fields, such as Dr Smith, a physician, and Stafford Crane

and Percival Pott, both surgeons of some eminence. The composition of these opposing witnesses reveals that the prosecution's attack was going to be wide-ranging but also perhaps somewhat confusing: a scattergun approach. The defence would be precise and clinical, relying on heavyweight medical expertise.

There was also one crucial missing witness: the man who'd accompanied Mary Young at Haddock's during the time Ann was there with William Sutton. His name was Sir William Fowler and he was an army officer. Unfortunately, he had recently died in Germany.

Ann's servant Elizabeth Honeyball was the first to give evidence. She stated that Ann's relationship with Sutton had begun the previous summer and that they had been introduced by Sir William Fowler. On the morning after Ann's two-night stay at Haddock's (opinion differed as to whether this was a Friday or Saturday but Defence Counsel clearly stated that the 'Saturday she mentions must be the 30th August'), Elizabeth had been asked to take some of Ann's clothes there. She then saw her mistress the following day when she returned to her lodgings at Mrs Parker's house in Spring Gardens. This street was near Charing Cross and St James's and so in the heart of London's Georgian sex district, subsequently destroyed in large part during the nineteenth-century creation of Trafalgar Square and The Mall.

> *Prosecuting Counsel*: How did she appear to you?
> *Elizabeth Honeyball*: She came home very faint and very ill . . . as soon as ever I opened the door, she said, she had received her death's wound, from that villain Sutton.
> *PC*: Repeat the words again, that my Lord may hear you.
> *EH*: She said she received her death-wound from that villain Sutton.
> *PC*: Was any thing done to her or for her?
> *EH*: She pull'd off her gown and stays, and lay down on the bed: nothing was done to her directly, there was soon after. The same night I went to a doctor in Pall-mall; he could not come himself but his man came, and sent a bottle of stuff to do her side and her arm, which were very much bruised.

Ann, said Elizabeth, wrote a note to Sutton after she came home, saying that he owed a guinea. His reply apparently read, 'If you are well, I am well, pay the porter and all is well.'

Two weeks after Ann arrived home in Spring Gardens from her ordeal in Haddock's, she was carried by sedan chair to the house in Marylebone where she was to die. According to a later witness this move was paid for by Sir William Fowler when Ann said she could no longer bear to stay where she was, presumably because she became very seriously ill and feverish from 11 September. Elizabeth Honeyball confirmed Sir William's fondness for Ann, saying that he gave her three guineas for her mistress's care, adding that 'he would not have her die for five thousand pounds'. She also stated that Fowler had, according to Ann, intended to set her up as his mistress (which by current standards may make his rakish acceptance of her being paired with Sutton at the bagnio seem rather strange). Despite Fowler's help, though, Ann was by now seriously ill and a 'clyster', or syringe, was used to 'wash out' her suppurating wounds. It was then that Elizabeth saw the terrible injuries first-hand:

Prosecuting Counsel: What sort of wounds were they?
Elizabeth Honeyball: One was cut long, and the other was cut in deep.
PC: What did they appear like?
EH: They appeared to me to be wounds that were cut.
PC: In what part of the body?
EH: Just above the fundament, one in the thick part . . . They continued open wounds to the time of her death. At the time the nurse went to give her the clyster they were full of corruption.

Describing the various people who came to the house, Elizabeth mentioned in particular Captain Holland – almost certainly the army officer who, according to newspaper accounts the previous year, had seduced Ann from her respectable life in Norfolk and set her on the road to prostitution. The maid concluded her evidence with the claim that various witnesses – including Captain Holland – heard Ann allege that Sutton had stabbed her.

Captain Thomas Holland was now sworn in as a prosecution witness. He explained that he had known Ann for almost four years, first meeting her when she still lived with her family in Norfolk. Having not seen her for a number of months, he had heard from a mutual acquaintance that she was ill and visited her on her deathbed in Marylebone. Given that he was at least in part the agent of her downfall, it may seem ironic that he should now have chosen to act as avenger, but that is the part in which he seems to have cast himself. He was the person who pressed for Sutton to be prosecuted, remaining adamant that Ann had said she had been stabbed by him. Holland also stated that a conversation had taken place between him and the nurse about the nature of Ann's injuries that confirmed his suspicions, and he provided another damning detail about the course of events at Haddock's:

> *Thomas Holland*: . . . they obliged her to drink the value of three pints of ratisea a day. [Ratisea, or rather Ratafia, was a strong almond-flavoured cordial that was a favoured drink among whores, particularly when staying in bagnios.]
> *Prosecuting Counsel*: Did she say, obliged her?
> *TH*: She did; that was the word upon my oath.

Holland then told the court the manner in which Ann had explained her injuries:

> She said, she had got a fall down stairs, and hurt her side; but she could not say, whether she was thrown down or not. I then asked her, whether or no she might not get these wounds by this fall. She immediately replied no; they were given me with a penknife, by that villain Sutton . . . She made a motion on the back of her hand, when I asked her how the wounds were given . . . With a penknife he ripped me so, and so [she said], making a motion with her hand, as if he had been killing a hog . . . She then said, this was the truth of her usage; and she hoped I would see her have justice done her. She received those wounds from Mr Sutton; and she was sure the wounds would kill her, the wounds would be the cause of her death, and said this was the truth . . . When she concluded this discourse, her last words were desiring me to see her have justice done her. I said, Miss Bell, you may depend upon it I will see you have justice, if it is possible. I asked her who Mr Sutton was. She said, He was a young merchant that kept company with Mr Fowler [sic].

Captain Holland's evidence was compellingly – even theatrically – given. Here he is describing his final meeting with Ann:

> The last time I saw her, on the Thursday, I was told by the nurse, or the maid, or Miss Knight, they all seemed to be in confusion, that the surgeon had been there, and that Miss Bell's wounds were mortified.

[I] said: Nanny, my dear, I will not flatter you. I am afraid you will not
live; have you any thing to say to your father, or mother; I shall write,
pray tell me now? She paused a little, and said: Yes (sitting up in the
bed as before; for always she desired I would lift her up) she said, yes,
Captain Holland, pray write to night, and give my duty to my dear
mother, and tell her I am sensible I shall not be a great while in this
world; and I hope to meet her in another, where we shall be more
happy than in this; and she gave a sort of a scream, and fell backwards,
and I went away, and never saw her more.

In the end, though, Captain Holland probably did the prosecution case
more harm than good. An attempt to lend weight to his evidence by
referring to notes he had made in a memorandum book came to nothing
when it emerged that he had only starting noting things down after Ann's
death. Under cross-examination he had to confess that he was not a real
captain, merely an adjutant in the Norfolk militia. The evidence Holland
gave about Ann's account of her wounding was not categorically supported
by other witnesses and so was little more than hearsay. He was a man
explaining an act he did not witness, through the words of a woman who
was not now alive. Such evidence was only as good as the man who gave
it, and Holland – who was responsible for Ann's initial downfall and
shown to be misleading and devious – must have made a poor impression. And there was something suspicious about the way he said he'd set
about dealing with the authorities when Ann died. He claimed that he
went to talk to Justice Fielding after the burial to report his suspicions,
but that he didn't apply for a warrant for the arrest of Sutton:

> I did not know it was my business to desire a warrant: I wrote to the
> father, and thought he would have come and undertook it . . . I was
> determined to do it myself, if the father did not; but I wanted the
> prosecution to come from the right quarter.

This seems a strange lapse on Holland's part, particularly bearing in
mind that he said he had promised Ann that he would 'see justice done'.
There was something else, too. It emerged in the course of his giving
evidence that he wrote to Sutton before he wrote to Ann's father. Why?
Could it be that Holland wrote to Ann's assailant to inform him that he
would not press for a warrant – notwithstanding all he knew – if money
were forthcoming? Was he, in short, blackmailing her killer?

Now Ann Knight, daughter of Ann Bell's Marylebone landlord, was sworn to give evidence for the prosecution, and she added some detail to events at Haddock's Bagnio, describing a conversation she had had with Ann Bell: 'She told me she would tell us a secret; the maid [Honeyball] and I were present, only us . . . the maid said . . . Let's hear it.' Ann Bell continued:

> Mr Sutton and I had a falling out, and Mr Sutton pull'd out a knife, and said he had a good mind to cut my backside so that I should not sit. Sir William Fowler said, sure you will not offer to do such a thing; and Mr Sutton made answer, yes, sir; and if Madam says another word, I will cut her face in the same manner.

Later, Sutton . . .

> . . . cut her, and [she] shew'd it by the back of her hand, how he struck the first blow aslant, and then pull'd the knife out, and stuck it in another place up higher, shewing with her finger on the back of her hand. She said Mr Sutton [claimed] he had put it out of the doctor's power to cure her, but that he could cure her with such another job [sic], and he would do it the next time he should see her.

Ann Bell seems by this time to have been suffering from bouts of delirium. According to the landlord's daughter, she was feverish and terrified that Sutton was lurking next-door. Defence Counsel leaped on this, suggesting that if Ann were delirious her allegations could hardly be relied on, but the witness said that, as far as she was concerned, Ann was . . .

> . . . in her senses . . . when she spoke to me, and called me by my name . . . I believe she could talk, if her spirits and strength would let her . . . [In] my opinion . . . she understood any thing, as she called me by my name, she would have answered if I had asked her any thing.

Two further witnesses for the prosecution were called, one of whom, Thomas Drake, a respectable merchant in the city, was the friend of the Bell family who had first informed Captain Holland of Ann's plight. Then it was the turn of a key witness – the other prostitute present at Haddock's during the fateful days – Mary Young. She explained that the first time she met Ann was when Fowler and Sutton arranged for the four of them to stay at Haddock's. She also explained how arrangements at the bagnio worked: the four of them slept there, but they actually dined at a nearby inn, the Cardigan Head. She was vague about dates, however, and when it came to the central allegation against Sutton, she was, for a prosecution witness, curiously evasive:

> *Prosecuting Counsel*: During the time you was at the bagnio, do you know of any ill usage that Miss Bell received from any body?
> *Mary Young*: In my opinion I don't think Mr Sutton behaved well to her, but not in beating or wounding her.
> *PC*: Tell in what respect.
> *MY*: In his behaviour to her always speaking cross to her. I don't know of any thing else.

Defence Counsel exploited this:

> *Defence Counsel*: Did you see any weapons or blows given, or any thing of that sort?
> *Mary Young*: I never saw him beat her, nor ever saw any weapon.
> *DC*: During the time she was there, did she drink pretty freely?
> *MY*: Yes, I think she drank more than did her good; she was rather in liquor . . . she was the same each night.

Ann, then, according to a key prosecution witness, was not attacked, and drank too much. Mary wasn't aware of Ann's allegation against Sutton until visiting her at her lodgings a few days later when she heard that Sutton 'had used her extremely ill, and had been the ruin of her'. Ann also told Mary that she had written to Sutton, 'and he had sent her an answer which she took very unkind'. This was presumably the note asking for money that Sutton rejected. After seeing Ann, Mary 'went and told Sir William Fowler how bad [Ann] was, and that she wanted money. He said he would either send her money, or something.'

Closely questioned about events at the bagnio, Mary had nothing further to add to her rather unspecific comments about Sutton's behaviour. When the judge intervened and asked her if she ever saw Sutton beat, wound or menace Ann, Mary repeated that she had not. She admitted that she and Fowler had left Ann behind at Haddock's on the day the alleged attack took place, and so by implication had missed an assault, if it happened, but she also said that by that time Sutton also had gone to dine at the Cardigan Head.

The prosecution case was now in danger of unravelling, and matters were made worse when Frances Waldgrave, the second nurse to attend Ann in Marylebone, was sworn. She confirmed the nature of Ann's injuries, but during cross-examination contradicted some of the evidence given by Captain Holland, in particular his claim that she had told him about Ann's wounds. Thomas Bliss, the apothecary, similarly confirmed Ann's injuries and said that he thought they might have been inflicted with a knife. He went on to say that 'sometimes she said, she believed Mr Sutton hurt her, or ill used her, but was not sure'. But when he was asked the key question, whether the wounds he had seen might have caused her death, he responded, 'No more than an issue in the arm would, that I verily believe; had they been seen ten days before any surgeon would have cured them, they were so insignificant.' Counsel tried to repair the damage:

> *Prosecuting Counsel*: Yet being neglected, and in the state they were in
> when you observed them, whether in that state and condition, they
> did not contribute to this young woman's death?
> *Bliss*: No ways, in no manner, did they contribute to her death; her
> thrush was in a dangerous condition, and that, together with the high
> fever and the putrefaction, without having any reference to the
> wounds, were the cause of her death.

Bliss seemed to be implying that Ann was affected by a sexually transmitted disease or infection and that the ailment was dangerous. Perhaps to divert the jury, Counsel asked if Ann's wounds 'did gangrene'. Yes, they did, replied Bliss ...

> ... but I have seen mortifications ten times worse, that have been cured
> [by surgeons]. With her habit of body, a mortification would have
> happened there, whether she had wounds or not; that I aver; she would
> have mortified just where she did, and when she did, and would have
> died at the very precise time.

This statement was a body blow for the prosecution, and when Bliss made it 'there was a great hissing in court' from the shocked and offended friends of Ann Bell. Bliss had turned into a star witness for the defence. He, the apparently objective and informed apothecary who had looked after Ann during her dying days, now damned her. The phrase 'habit of body' was a euphemism for the risk of disease that Ann daily exposed herself to through her trade of prostitute, and it was his opinion that she died of a 'mortification' related to her 'habit of body' and not due to the wounds or sores that may or may not have been caused by Sutton. In Bliss' expert opinion, Ann would have died when and how she did, with or without the alleged attack by Sutton.

Bartholomew Fair, Smithfield, where Ann is said to have gone soon after her alleged ordeal at Haddock's Bagnio.

With the prosecution case looking increasingly fragile, Defence Counsel felt he could ask the court whether it was even necessary to mount their plea. The court responded by referring to gaps in the evidence given by Mary Young – since she had not been present throughout, it was important to ascertain Sutton's movements during those crucial hours when the attack might have taken place. Defence Counsel claimed it was possible to prove that, after Ann left Haddock's, Sutton 'never saw her from that hour' and that 'she was after this time in perfect health and spirits'. He also stated that he would prove that Ann went to Haddock's on 5 or 6

September, and so nearly a week after the alleged attack, 'called for rum . . . went to Bartholomew-fair [and] that in the bed where they lay at the bagnio there were no marks of blood, or any thing at all'. He also told the court that he would:

> [C]all the physician who attended the deceased who will satisfy the court that these sores could not at all . . . contribute to her death [and] we shall call other able surgeons who will give their opinion from what the doctor and apothecary say, that they were no wounds at all.

Before this evidence for the defence was offered, Sutton was permitted to make a statement to the court, declaring himself innocent of the alleged assault upon Ann:

> I stand here accused, my lord, for a murder I am not only innocent of, but for a murder that in reality never happened. Notwithstanding which, my lord, the most iniquitous intrigues have been artfully formed, and the most poisonous libels industriously spread, by Mr Holland, to create an universal belief, that the unhappy Miss Bell had been murdered, and that I was her murderer. The ears of mankind are ever open to novelty, the very suggestion of a murder forces a persuasion of its truth. I appeal to all that are present; is there an ear that has not heard those reports? or a mind that has not been infected by their poison? Thus, my lord, I have been most undeservedly censured without doors, tried and condemned unheard. But, conscious of my innocence, I have, under these circumstances, cheerfully flown to this court, a court ever distinguish'd for its candour, and its justice for the protection of innocence.

Four witnesses from Haddock's were then called and all gave much the same evidence: that nothing untoward had happened while Ann and Sutton had stayed there. No blood was discovered and no 'crying out' was heard – and that Ann had been back to Haddock's after the alleged attack took place and had seemed well then. The waiter, Alexander Sexton, also offered some pretty damning statements about her, including one that not only suggested a completely different reason why she might have had a bone to pick with Sutton but also demonstrated that she was well when she left him.

[Ann] sent for me afterwards and said, Mr Sutton had used her ill, I said, 'how?' She said, 'you know Mr Sutton, I have kept him company so long, and he never gave me a half-penny.' She said, 'thank God I can do without him, for I had a gentleman just now, that did not keep me company above two or three hours, and he gave me a couple of guineas.'

Sexton proceeded to claim that Ann was then planning to go to Bartholomew Fair with her landlady, the bawd Mrs Parker – hardly the action of a sick woman. 'She lived a very bad indifferent life,' he confided, 'every moment calling for a dram; I said, my dear, you'll kill yourself; she said poison, give me poison, death I want, and death I'll have.'

Daniel Haviland, another servant at Haddock's (or Haveland, who owned or managed the bagnio from 1763 to 1766, see page 228), described a scene which suggested that, even among her fellow prostitutes, Ann was little regarded. During one supper, he said:

Miss Young says, that Miss Bell looks like a whore. Miss Bell got up in some little anger, and said, 'Miss Young, why do you call me names?' Mr Sutton stood behind, and Sir William was aggravating Miss Bell . . . [but] that came to nothing. They lay there that night, and breakfasted there the next morning, I believe about ten or eleven o'clock.

Clearly, the servants of the bagnio were telling the same story. Yet had their evidence been subjected to closer scrutiny, it would have been revealed to be seriously flawed. Daniel Haviland, for example, claimed that Ann and her company took breakfast at Haddock's on the morning of 5 September – but this was around a week after the alleged attack and at a time when other witnesses claimed she had returned ill to Spring Gardens. There is a strong whiff of ranks closing here, although it has to be said that – for the historian, at least – much of the incidental detail we learn from the servants' testimony is fascinating. Alexander Sexton, for example, told how he took 'doctors' (brandy and milk) to the guests at five or six in the morning – they were clearly ordering a 'hair of the dog' to set themselves up for the day ahead. He also described the ledger kept at Haddock's that logged what time people arrived and what time they left.

The *coup de grâce* to the prosecution case was delivered by Dr Smith, a physician of thirty years' experience, who had attended Ann on her deathbed. He questioned whether one of the wounds could have been inflicted several weeks before her death, and claimed it looked like an abscess. He accepted that the 'sores' and 'boils' he saw on Ann's body could well have been the result of her alleged 'ill habit of body' – i.e. prostitution and drink. To make the argument crystal clear for the jury, Defence Counsel then asked Smith if 'the fever was the occasion of the eruptions, or the eruptions the occasion of the fever'. The fever 'was certainly the occasion of the eruptions', answered Smith. 'Do you believe that those eruptions moved at all towards the death of this unfortunate young lady? asked Counsel. 'I cannot think so,' said Smith, who agreed with Counsel that the wounds had no 'influence upon her death at all'. Of course, Smith, like all his contemporaries, would not have known that even a small wound, caused perhaps by a dirty penknife, could result in toxic micro-organisms entering the bloodstream, leading to death by blood poisoning. His evidence was backed by a pair of eminent expert witnesses, neither of whom had known Ann Bell, living or dead: Stafford Crane, a surgeon, and Percival Pott, a leading surgeon of the day, based at St Bartholomew's Hospital and a pioneer in the causes and treatment of cancer.

By now the case was effectively over. Defence Counsel told the court that he had waiting 'twenty gentlemen of the first figure and fashion to give Mr Sutton the character of a gentleman of humanity and compassion, incapable of doing the crime laid to his charge'. The jury announced that it was not necessary to call these gentlemen, or for 'his lordship to take the trouble of summing up the evidence', and with this Sutton was promptly and unanimously acquitted.

We will never know what really happened at Haddock's on that day in August 1760. The evidence given during the court case was often unreliable, key prosecution witnesses either contradicting each other or, like Mary Young, apparently changing sides. In addition, the extent of medical knowledge at the time meant no one was in a position to ascertain whether the injuries Sutton was alleged to have inflicted on Ann could have caused her death. Even at the time, however, the verdict, although unanimous, seems to have caused unease. In a carefully impartial account after the trial, the *Gentleman's Magazine* for March 1761 reported the verdict, but also pointed out the strange, disturbing and unresolved inconsistencies in the evidence – the indictment claimed, for example, that Ann left

Haddock's on 30 August, but Sutton in his defence, and Haddock's staff in their evidence, stated that Sutton last saw Ann on 5 September – the following Friday. Did he perhaps attack Ann then after she left Haddock's, which was why none of the staff discovered or heard evidence of violence? But, if so, how did that square with Honeyball's evidence that Ann arrived home ill on 30 August?

There were other unresolved issues. In the first place, it is not clear why the authorities did not investigate Ann Bell's case earlier, given that serious accusations were being made. During his evidence, Captain Holland said that he was not admitted to the coroner's inquisition, even though he was a key witness. Later in the trial, Defence Counsel attacked an implication that Sutton had suborned witnesses and perverted the course of justice. He was a rich and evidently well-connected man, and there were many ways in mid-eighteenth-century Britain, other than by crude and direct bribery, that witnesses could be persuaded to see or remember things differently. Mary Young and Thomas Bliss were no doubt dependent for their livelihoods upon the future patronage of such men as Sutton and, it goes without saying, if he had been poor then he would never have benefited from prestigious expert witnesses such as Crane and Pott. If he did attack Ann, then this crude sexual sadism was only a short step away from the acts of casual brutality carried out by knife-wielding aristocratic Mohock gang members in the streets of Covent Garden in the early eighteenth century. William Hickey in his *Memoirs* states that upper-class Mohocks (see page 110) were still active in West London in the early 1770s. It is just possible perhaps that Sutton and Fowler were Mohocks whose 'play' extended too far.

As for Ann, the official verdict was that she had died of ailments brought on by her habit of life: by venereal disease and hard drinking. Her death was merely one of many – *The Times* for 31 October 1785 estimated that around 5,000 prostitutes died in the capital each year. She would have been regarded not as a victim of circumstances beyond her control but as a lesser class of human, a fallen and amoral temptress, an unnatural being who received no more than she deserved. Also, as someone who lived outside conventional morality, she would have been regarded as congenitally untruthful so that all she said could effectively be challenged and dismissed.

Archenholz in the early 1780s observed with some surprise that 'the testimony of [prostitutes] even of the lowest of them, is always received as evidence in the courts of justice',[4] which was true since equality before the law was, in theory at least, a much honoured tenet of British justice. But, in practice, a prostitute was in a difficult position when trying to convince judge and jurors or while being cross-examined by a hostile counsel. A known prostitute could not speak or swear on her honour, and she had no reputation to lose through lying. Such women were utterly powerless beneath the moralising scrutiny of the law. Living outside conventional morality, if not the law of the land, they were effectively outlaws. Such was the stigma of prostitution that even Ann's own parents failed to support the prosecution of the man accused of her murder or to make the journey to her deathbed. In these circumstances, and in a trial where the evidence was confusing and contradictory, it is clear the benefit of the doubt would always be given to the 'respectable' accused rather than the prostitute victim. And if the accused was also rich, powerful or socially well connected then they were all but invulnerable.

Today Ann Bell lies in an unmarked grave somewhere in a former burying ground that is now a small public park, lying to the south of Paddington Street and just off Marylebone High Street. It seems unlikely that she rests in peace for, to my mind, it is more probable than not that the vulnerable young prostitute was the victim of a sadistic sex crime, and that her murderer – through a combination of bribery, threats, ignorance and influence – got away with it.

PUBLIC AND PRIVATE VIEWS

SIXTEEN

'CHILDREN OF LARGER GROWTH'

Men's Attitudes to Women

To appreciate fully the radical nature of the Georgian sex industry it is necessary to put it in the wider social context of the time. Britain was a patriarchy. Women in general were regarded by men as the simpler sex whose role was to be decorative and bear children, but who were potentially or primarily irrational, disruptive, over-emotional and, rooted in the Judaeo-Christian tradition of the Old Testament, even potentially dark temptresses and destroyers of mankind. The examples of Eve and Delilah were constantly borne in mind. Lord Chesterfield, for instance, had advised his son that women were 'only children of larger growth',[1] and Samuel Johnson in his verse tragedy *Irene*, written in 1737, had a male character state that 'the noblest aim ... of a female soul' was but 'to tune the Tongue, to teach the eye to roll,/Dispose the colours of the flowing robe,/And add new Roses to the faded Cheek'.[2]

There were females who were regarded as exceptions to this rule – not least by Johnson himself who had a great regard for the intellectual capacities and wit of many women, like Hester Thrale. Johnson, along with other enlightened men such as Sir Joshua Reynolds and Edmund Burke, was a member of the Blue Stockings Society that had been founded in the early 1750s by Elizabeth Montagu as a women's literary discussion group, including among its female members Hannah More, Sarah Fielding and Lady Mary Wortley Montagu. The name referred to workaday blue worsted stockings as opposed to more expensive and elegant black silk, emphasising – almost as a riposte to Johnson – that the females of this society valued debate above fashion, rational thought above ornament. But despite the existence of the Blue Stockings, the average eighteenth-century London male, of any class or calling, would probably have agreed with the character in Johnson's play who believed a woman's principle role was to concentrate on style, fashion and make-up, to perfect the purely decorative aspects of life and to give pleasure in all its varied forms. Women, if truly feminine, were expected to be passive, submissive, subservient slaves of the senses – objects of beauty whom men desired but who were not quite men's equals – or else muses who in some unclear way inspired the male creative urge.[3]

Doctor Johnson, Mrs Thrale and companions in 1791 taking breakfast at the Brewery House in Southwark.

Only when seen from this point of view is it possible to understand how confusing and subversive the sex industry could be, with famous prostitutes being viewed simultaneously as dark destroyers of society while also objects of fascination, even adoration. The industry offered women the potential for wealth and financial independence from men, the power to determine their own lives and pursue their own passions. It could also offer certain women a powerful presence in society as their images and life stories were peddled by publishers to an ever-eager public, with notable examples being the successful courtesans Lavinia Fenton, Kitty Fisher, Mrs Abington, Fanny Murray and Emma Hart.

But these triumphs and achievements often came at a tremendous personal price. Disease, abuse and premature death were the obvious sacrifices made by many, but also – more significantly and paradoxically – women who entered the sex industry could only gain their independence from men by putting themselves in bondage to men, become free by becoming more sexually subservient – constantly available for the satisfaction of male lust. In this way many women did gain physical independence and wealth but, in the process – perhaps like Emily Warren (see page 362) – destroyed emotionally and broken of heart.

Men's attitudes to prostitutes and the sex industry were varied and complex, as the preceding chapters reveal. Some, like Richard Steele, displayed quiet compassion and understanding (see page 37). Others were more ambivalent. Boswell describes a night in July 1763 when he and Dr Johnson were walking along the Strand and a young harlot approached them. Johnson gently rebuffed her – 'no, my girl . . . it won't do' – and then talked to Boswell about 'the wretched life of such women', and how 'much more misery than happiness, upon the whole, is produced by illicit commerce between the sexes'.[4] Johnson's writing makes it clear that he had a great sympathy for the plight of prostitutes, even if he was silent about men's moral responsibility. In the *Rambler* of 5 November 1751 (No. CLXXI), Johnson concluded a fictional letter from a prostitute named 'Misella' with an impassioned and heart-felt plea:

> If those who pass their days in plenty and security could visit for an hour the dismal receptacles to which the prostitute retires from her nocturnal excursions, and see the wretches that lie crowded together, mad with intemperance, ghastly with famine, nauseous with filth, and noisome with disease; it would not be easy for any degree of abhorrence to harden them against compassion, or to repress the desire which they must immediately feel to rescue such numbers of human beings from a state so dreadful.[5]

Johnson's sympathy didn't stop with mere well-intentioned words and pious sentiments. He himself did what he recommended and took action in a most direct and individual manner to 'rescue' distressed and ill-fortuned women by dispensing small allowances and even, on occasion, offering them free lodgings. These women included distressed prostitutes and one, a 'Scotch wench' called Polly Carmichael, Johnson found 'nearly lifeless in the street one day and carried home on his back'.[6] The tale is told by Boswell in his *Life of Johnson*:

> Coming home late one night, he found a poor woman lying in the street, so much exhausted that she could not walk; he took her upon his back, and carried her to his house, where he discovered that she was one of those wretched females who had fallen into the lowest state of vice, poverty and disease. Instead of harshly upbraiding her he had her taken care of with all tenderness for a long time, at considerable expense, till she was restored to health, and endeavored to put her into a virtuous way of living.[7]

Sublime as this gesture was, Polly did not rise to the heroic circumstances and in 1778 Johnson was compelled to confide to his friend Mrs Thrale that 'we could spare her very well from us [for] Poll is a stupid slut'.[8] In the summer of 1777 he had seven 'dependents' living with him in his house in Bolt Court, which was, as Mrs Thrale observed in her memoirs, 'overrun with all sorts of strange creatures, whom he admits for mere charity'.

Johnson's humanity and compassion for the prostitute was not echoed by the conduct of his young companion of 1763, James Boswell. It was usual at the time for male observers to accept that many a harlot's initial fall had been due to male seduction and deceit, but then to consider her – if she was considered at all – only as a means of male pleasure and convenience. James Boswell appears to have been of this frame of mind – and he was probably typical. In his *London Journal*, written between 1762 and 1763, he reveals a general contempt for the harlot he uses – whom he refers to in turn as 'brimstone', 'profligate wretch' and 'miscreant' – with his moments of ungovernable lust almost always followed by feelings of guilt and self-loathing. The disgust he expresses for the harlot is, of course, just the expression of the disgust he feels for himself.

Typical is his response to the 'jolly young damsel' he picked up in the Haymarket. Boswell conducted her to Westminster Bridge, where he 'did . . . engage her upon this noble edifice' and immediately after 'the brutish appetite was sated . . . could not but despise myself for being so closely

James Boswell in middle age. As a young man in London he sampled with a mix of guilt and relish the excesses of the city's sex industry.

united with such a low wretch'.[9] On another occasion, after discovering that he had been pick-pocketed by the 'street-walker' with whom he had 'indulged sensuality', Boswell was 'shocked to think that I had been intimately united with a low, abandoned, perjured, pilfering creature. I determined to do so no more'.[10]

But he also reveals what an emotionally complex – even contradictory – terrain he occupied when walking the streets in pursuit of 'street-walkers'. Love and hate, attraction and repulsion, fed off each other and were indissoluble. His *Journal* entries make it clear that, in certain circumstances, he was capable of feeling pity and compassion for young whores. One night, for instance, feeling 'carnal inclinations' raging through 'his frame', Boswell went into St James's Park and 'picked up a whore' who he discovered – after she had 'submitted' to his 'lusty embraces' – was 'a young Shropshire girl, only seventeen, very well-looked' and called Elizabeth Parker. 'Poor thing,' reflected Boswell, 'she has a sad time of it!'[11] Suddenly he saw this young whore for what she was, a desperate and vulnerable human being, not just an object of lust made despicable through his own despicable conduct. But still he didn't reflect upon the cause of Elizabeth's plight, wonder what had driven her on to the streets or ponder the nature of a society in which a pretty Shropshire teenager was obliged to gamble with her life in an attempt to make a living within the capital's dangerous and all-devouring sex industry.

Boswell is often shocked by his own weakness for surrendering to the sensual temptation of 'debauchery', but never appears to be shocked by the existence of the vast industry that peddled the sensations he craved. Nor does he anywhere acknowledge that his lascivious, irresponsible or immoral actions actually compounded the ills suffered by girls such as Elizabeth Parker. This conduct gives substance to the jest in *Town and Country Magazine* that 'chastity in a man, if a virtue, [is] a very subordinate one'.[12] Boswell comprehended only consequences, not causes, and the only evils he saw were those that offended Christian morality and conventional notions about love and family. A harlot's life was 'sad' because she was a social outcast, not because she was a victim of evils for which she was not responsible and which she could not control.

The skewed morality of the age – the result of men accepting responsibility for the fall of women into prostitution while simultaneously refusing to do anything to ameliorate the ensuing suffering – is exposed by an encounter Boswell had on the Strand: 'I was tapped on the shoulder by a fine fresh lass' and 'could not resist indulging myself with the enjoyment of her'. After the indulgence he assuaged any glimmer of guilt by reassuring himself that, although 'illicit love is always wrong', surely 'in such a situation, when the woman is already abandoned, the crime must be alleviated'.[13] So whores, often entrapped into prostitution as the result of male abuse, were legitimate targets for such abuse in perpetuity because of that initial fall from grace. What diabolical logic! For Boswell, once fallen, women seem to have possessed no moral rights and no individual character.

His rejection of his once-loved mistress Louisa Lewis, when he believed he had caught the pox from her and that she was a duplicitous whore, was both vengeful and cruel. He wrote to tell her that 'if you are not rendered callous by a long course of disguised wickedness, I should think the consideration of your deceit and baseness, your corruption both of body and mind, would be a very severe punishment'. All was, he claimed, 'the consequence of your own unworthiness'.[14] Boswell expected Louisa to be faithful and loving to him while he was faithless and merely sensual towards her, and was genuinely furious when it appeared that she was perhaps as calculating and cynical as he. In his self-righteous fury, he displayed no awareness of the weird world of double standards he inhabited.

Other writers were not so confused in their assessment of the sex industry. The anonymous author of *Nocturnal Revels* of 1779 took a more definite position. The book argued that prostitution was a blessing, not an evil, because:

> [E]ven in the state of matrimony itself, it often happens, that a man who holds his wife in the highest estimation, may be debarred the felicity of hymeneal raptures, from sickness, absence, and a variety of other temporary causes, which may with facility be imagined. If, in any of those situations, a man could not find temporary relief in the arms of Prostitution, the peace of Society would be far more disturbed than it is: The brutal Ravisher would stalk at large, and would plead, as in the case of hunger, that the violence of his passion would break down even stone walls . . . No man's wife, sister, or daughter would be in a state of security: The rape of the Sabines would be daily rehearsed, and anarchy and confusion ensue. In this point of view then, at least, female prostitution should be winked at, if not protected; and though it may be pronounced a moral evil, it certainly is a political good.[15]

A similar position had been argued in 1724 by Bernard Mandeville, in his *A Modest Defence of Publick Stews*. He fully endorsed the sex industry and recommended that the state should take it over and regulate it. In his view the government should house around 2,000 women, all of whom were to be 'kept clean and decent', so as to be able to 'entertain Gentlemen after a civil and obliging manner'. For the pragmatic Mandeville harlots were essential if sexual pressure was to be taken off 'virtuous' women who were not harlots. Brothels, he argued, were a practical if slightly unpleasant fact of life, like 'a Bog House in a Garden'.[16]

This pragmatic view was repudiated by Samuel Johnson, who, in conversation with Boswell in April 1776, made it abundantly clear that he would 'allow of no irregular intercourse whatever between the sexes' but 'punish it much more than is done, and so restrain it'. In Johnson's view it was 'very absurd to argue, as has been done, that prostitutes are necessary to prevent the violent effects of appetite from violating the decent order of life; nay, should be permitted, in order to preserve the chastity of our wives and daughters. 'Depend upon it, Sir,' boomed Johnson, 'severe laws, steadily enforced, would be sufficient against these evils, and would promote marriage.'[17]

In his opinion one of the greatest evils of the sex industry was its threat to the institution of marriage, a legal contract on which so much inheritance and property law was based and which was assumed to ensure population growth. In the Georgian view marriage was one of the bedrocks of a stable society, if also an institution into which men had, perhaps, to be lured by the promise of frequent sex. The fear shared by Johnson and other social observers like Henry Fielding was that the ease with which men in London could achieve sexual release with prostitutes made, for many of them, marriage both inconvenient and unnecessary.

Benjamin Franklin, another firm believer in the institution of marriage, had a gentler and less strident argument in its favour. When writing in the early 1760s to Polly Stevenson, the daughter of his London landlady in Craven Street, he opposed her determination to stay single by arguing that there was nothing 'of equal dignity and importance with that of being a good parent ... a good husband or wife ... that is, in short, a good Christian.'[18]

MEN'S FEAR OF THE FEMALE BODY

In Georgian Britain men failed to understand not only the psychology of women but also their physiology. The stereotypical male notion that women, by their very nature, were emotional, volatile and irrational, and that ideally in their behaviour they should be charming, submissive and almost unthinking ornamental purveyors of pleasure, created trouble and misery for both the sexes. As Mary Wollstonecraft lamented in 1792, into what cares and sorrows 'women are plunged by the prevailing [male] opinion that they were created rather to feel than reason'.[19]

Equally problematic was the fact that men also failed to understand the female body. While they found it arousing, with artists like Sir Joshua Reynolds keen to record it in intimate detail (see page 336), men also found it frightening. This was largely because they believed the female body to be the cause of seemingly irrational behaviours. In the mid-seventeenth century they even termed exaggerated and uncontrolled emotional conduct 'hysteric', because they thought it specific to women through its association with the uterus or womb – in Greek the *hustera*.

The scientific exploration and analysis of the female body – which was, of course, undertaken almost exclusively by men – is one of the strangest adventures of the Georgian period. The interpretations and conclusions reached by varied delvers after truth were generally confused and confusing, but tended to evolve to reflect and reinforce the changing attitudes of society as a whole. In the field of female sexuality, the eighteenth century truly was an age of transition with the general perception of female sexual nature changing from the warm, earthy sexuality characteristically described by late-seventeenth-century writers to the chaste and cool female ideal of the late eighteenth century that prefigures the virtually sexless and refined female of the Victorian age, nicely represented in 1850 by an article in the *Westminster Review* which stated that while in men 'sexual desire is inherent and spontaneous', in women 'the desire is dormant, if not non-existent, till excited'.[20]

The conventional late-seventeenth-century view is put clearly by a book entitled *Conjugal Love Reveal'd, in the Nightly Pleasures of the Marriage Bed*, which states that 'Women are by far more lascivious and more Amorous than Men'[21] and cites as evidence the clitoris where 'nature has placed the seat of Pleasure and Lust'.[22] The vital role of the clitoris in female sexual pleasure was also noted by Giles Jacob in his *Treatise of Hermaphrodites* of 1718 where he states 'that without [this] Part, the fair sex would neither desire the Embraces of the Males, nor have pleasure in them',[23] while Bernard Mandeville in his *Modest Defence of Publick Stews* of 1724, declared bluntly that the clitoris had no use 'but to whet the Female Desire by its frequent Erections'.[24] As A. D. Harvey has pointed out in his seminal account of this topic, medical men at the time observed that the clitoris appeared to be unique in the human body as an organ that had no other purpose but to give physical pleasure.[25]

During the 1720s and 30s this view started to change. *The Ladies Physical Directory* (or *A Rational Account of the Natural Weaknesses of Women, and of Secret Distempers peculiarly incident to them . . . By a Physician, London*) appeared first in 1716, and in subsequent editions charted changing opinions about female sexuality. The initial edition suggested that in the

'Rites of Love a Woman is too many for a Man, and capable of tiring him quite down',[26] but by the time of the amended seventh edition of 1739 the *Directory* supported the proposition that genteel and 'normal' women – the females who needed to be 'protected' by prostitutes from predatory males – really didn't much care for sex. It attacked the 'silly Notion' that 'Women are warmer in their Nature and more desirous than Men' for they are 'of a finer Make, more tender Constitution . . . and of course much less inclin'd to Venery than the Male sex . . . nor . . . able to bear coition (to full satisfaction) half so often as Men'.[27]

This, of course, was an entirely subjective and non-scientific observation. More interesting is the discussion about the clitoris for it seems to hold the objective truth about female sexual drive. If women could reach orgasm in a way comparable to men then surely their sexual life was similar to that of men – not necessarily 'more lascivious' but certainly not less.

Erotic texts make much of the physical pleasure derived from the stimulation of the clitoris. The *Dialogue between a Married Lady and MAID* of 1740 is physically explicit:

> Just . . . towards the upper Part of the C—t, is a Thing they call Clitoris, which, is a little like a Man's P—k, for it will swell, and stand like his; and being rubbed gently, by his Member, will, with excessive Pleasure, send forth a Liquor, which when it comes away, leaves us in a Trance, as if we were dying, all our Senses being lost . . . in a Word, there follows a dissolving of our whole Person, and melting, in such inexpressible Joys, as none but those who feel them can express or comprehend.[28]

Evidence of the sensual power of the clitoris disturbed some male writers so much that they felt compelled to view excesses of female physical pleasure as unseemly, unnatural and even unhealthy. In the 1762 English edition of the French physician Jean Astruc's 1743 *Treatise on the Diseases of Women*, over-enjoyment of the stimulation of the clitoris was classed as an ailment. As Astruc put it, '[T]he Antients called this Affection *Nymphomania*, thinking that the *Clitoris*, which they called Nympha, was its only seat.'[29] Astruc described the symptoms of this 'disease' in Latin, to hide the information from vulgar browsers in his book, but in 1775 an English translation was published in an edition of a book entitled

Nymphomania, or a Dissertation Concerning the Furor Uterinus. The author/translator was Edward Sloane Wilmot MD, who had based it on a text of 1771 by J. D. T. Bienville.

The Astruc/Bienville/Wilmot description reveals little medical or psychological insight or sensitivity but a certain flair for the sensational. Nymphomaniacs, the reader is told . . .

> . . . perpetually dishonour themselves in secret by habitual pollutions, of which they are themselves the unfortunate agents, until they have openly passed the bounds of modesty [when] they are no longer fearful of procuring this dreadful, and detestable pleasure from the assisting hand of a stranger . . . soon the excess of their lust having exhausted all their power of contending against it they . . . without a blush, openly solicit in the most criminal, and abandoned language, the first-comers to gratify their insatiable desires.[30]

The view that female sexual desire was some type of aberration suffered by abnormal women had gained such ground by the 1780s that Dr Robert Couper could write in 1789 that 'to many women, the embraces of the male are extremely, perhaps completely, indifferent and to some they are disagreeable'.[31] At the same time John Trusler, in his *Honours of the Table* of 1788, made a nice if unwitting analogy between the female appetite for food and for sex. He warned his gentlemen readers that women would be offended if offered large portions of food at table because 'eating a great deal is deemed indelicate in a lady, for her character should be rather divine than sensual, it will be ill manners to help her to a large slice of meat at once, or fill her plate full'. It was this new view of the ideal woman as non-sensual that made the conduct of Seymour Dorothy, Lady Worsley in the early 1780s so shocking for she single-handedly challenged the notion that women of refined and genteel birth were sexually cool. Lady Worsley was the epitome of the libidinous demi-rep and was said to have had nearly thirty lovers. She pursued these affairs in a brazen manner for several years but all came to a spectacular and well-publicised head in 1782 when her husband, prosecuting a fellow militia officer for 'Criminal Conversation' with Lady Worsley, was awarded only one-shilling damages rather than the £20,000 he had demanded. The derisory award had much to do with Lady Worsley's notorious character although her husband's own antics, which including him once supporting the defendant on his shoulders, while shouting 'Seymour, Seymour', so he could see Lady Worsley naked in a bath house, did little to help his case.[32]

THE SEX INDUSTRY AND THE SLAVE TRADE

Men's domination over women and their essential misunderstanding of female abilities, aspirations and potential was – tragically – part of the very fabric of Georgian society. These misunderstandings were responsible for many evils and were among the root causes of the vast sex industry that many women entered in a desperate bid to find economic independence. To an extent, the sex industry had much in common with another eighteenth-century economic enterprise – the evil institution of slavery. Both involved one human being having, for their own profit or pleasure, domination and power over another. Both were of ancient origin, had been present in great and exemplary civilisations of the past and appeared to be accepted – if not actually condoned – in certain biblical texts. Both were generally regarded as necessary evils of existence and part of the complex and baffling fabric of God's creation. Yet, strangely, few eighteenth-century thinkers made the connection.

William Wilberforce is an interesting case in point. As a young man in the 1770s he led a dissolute life in London and was particularly fond of gaming. Then, in 1783, he underwent a dramatic religious conversion and became an Evangelical Anglican, a member of the Clapham Sect who dedicated his life to the application of his Christian beliefs to the cause of social reform. Late-eighteenth-century reformers such as Wilberforce were energetic and ambitious in their aspirations, with the Clapham Sect campaigning for the abolition of the slave trade and penal reform while also spreading the Evangelical Christian message through the missionary movement.

Wilberforce embraced all this and more. In 1787 he persuaded George III to issue a Royal Proclamation for the 'Encouragement of Piety and Virtue, and for the Prevention and Punishing of Vice and Immorality', and set about his twenty-year-long campaign to outlaw the slave trade. He also, with Hannah More, launched the Association for the Better Observance of Sunday, which was intended to promote Evangelism,

William Wilberforce at the age of twenty-nine, about three years after he had undergone his conversion to Evangelical Christianity and at the time he began his twenty-year battle to abolish the slave trade.

personal hygiene and education for children. But in all this storm of do-gooding, social reform and moral concern, the plight of common harlots – as much the victims of abuse, amorality and economic oppression as any slave – was virtually ignored by men such as Wilberforce, and even if their suffering was privately regretted its alleviation was not the subject of sustained public campaigning. Similarly Benjamin Franklin had written against slavery as early as 1772, became in 1787 president of the Pennsylvania Society for Promoting the Abolition of Slavery and had also shown sympathy for the dilemma faced by prostitutes. But he appears never to have connected the two states of bondage.

The Royal Proclamation of 1787 launched the Proclamation Society, which in 1802 sprouted an auxiliary organisation called, promisingly, the Society for the Suppression of Vice. But even this organisation did not focus on the plight of prostitutes but primarily concentrated on protecting the religion and morals of the country by countering radical politics and atheistic ideas that had been seeping into Britain from Revolutionary France.

It seems that for these reformers and enlightened thinkers the ethical and moral issues raised by the sex industry were too close to home, perhaps almost too familiar to be noticed, seemingly woven too intimately into the fabric of society and certainly too vital a part of the life and economy of the capital to be lightly or easily confronted. Even Charles James Fox, a politician with a social conscience of sorts, with years of first-hand experience of London's sex industry and a former prostitute for a wife, limited his reforming activities to the abolition of slavery, carrying in June 1806 a resolution in the House of Commons that the 'African slave trade . . . be contrary to the principles of justice, humanity and sound policy'. There is no evidence that the great Fox applied, in any productive or consistent manner, the 'principles of justice [and] humanity' to the conduct and continuance of the sex industry. Indeed, he perhaps believed that tolerating it was no more than 'sound policy'.

The prison system in Britain was reformed from the late eighteenth century, thanks to the pioneering efforts of John Howard, and made marginally more humane and hygienic. The trade in slaves was outlawed in 1807, and in 1833 all slaves within the British Empire were freed after the government agreed to give hefty compensation to the powerful and influential slave-owning community for their sudden loss of valuable 'property'. Christian missionaries were dispatched to India and Africa, and the educational standards for children in Britain were raised from the 1780s, thanks initially to the efforts of Robert Raikes and after 1833 when Parliament initiated state education by voting a sum of money annually for the construction of schools for the children of the poor. A start was even made, with the Reform Act of 1832, on extending the vote to a wider spectrum of society – while continuing to exclude women, of course.

All these enlightened reforms could be made, but the men who governed Britain let the evils that spawned the sex industry fester. These mostly related to the powerlessness of women in a society that decreed even the most intelligent and wealthy among them could have no direct role, or even say, in the government of the country. Their fortunes, opinions, their identity even, were subsumed upon marriage. The lot of all women in eighteenth-century society was characterised by injustice, exploitation and lack of opportunity. If even the rich and intelligent suffered then so, to a much larger degree, did the poor and ignorant. The sex industry was one, often illusory, route of escape. But men, who had assumed the role of caring for the female half of society, failed to explore the social reforms that could have prevented many of the evils underlying the sex trade. Instead male legislators preferred the 'cure' of arbitrary and brutish bouts of suppression that attacked the symptoms but not the cause and generally did more harm than good. Such minor efforts as were envisaged, like those by Henry Fielding and Saunders Welch in the mid-eighteenth century, failed to go to the root of the problem, hardly progressing beyond the theoretical stage.

Ironically, it was a misguided Utopian social experiment that briefly brought the slave and sex trades together and suggested that some people might have appreciated their points of similarity. At the end of the American War of Independence, Britain had responsibility for many African American soldiers and former slaves who had fought loyally for the Crown against their rebellious colonial masters. These African Americans, finding themselves on the losing side, were obliged to flee the newly founded and vengeful United States in order to avoid persecution and being returned to servitude. Some settled with their families in Nova Scotia and many more in London, but essentially these were people without a homeland. Something had to be done, both to help them and to rid London of its destitute visitors who, no doubt, were proving a heavy charge upon the various parishes in which they settled themselves as well as unwelcome competition for London's indigenous labouring poor.

The solution hit upon was to establish a 'Utopia' in the British-controlled former slave-trading state of Sierra Leone in West Africa. In 1787 ships arrived at this ill-famed land, by now renamed the 'Province of Freedom', carrying 330 African American former slaves and soldiers, a smattering of useful tradesmen and 70 white women – mostly impoverished harlots scoured from the streets of London. This new land was to be home to both ex-slaves and fallen women, who, together, were against all the odds imaginable meant to make a go of it.

Things went horribly wrong from the start. Most of the ex-slaves were indeed African by birth or descent but from all over the continent. Sierra Leone was as alien to them as it was to any white settler. There was contagious disease to cope with as well as the hostility of the indigenous population. Most of the initial band of settlers died during the first year but in 1792 another 1,100 arrived from London under the leadership of the visionary and charismatic African American loyalist and former soldier Thomas Peters, who founded Freetown, the main settlement of the new province. But Peters, then in his mid-fifties, soon died of malaria and the faltering project was only kept going by the constant arrival of new settlers, including in 1800 500 black people from Jamaica.

This extraordinary enterprise was controlled by the Sierra Leone Company, but its attempt to restrict settlers' rights and make a profit from the province resulted in rebellion and disquiet, leading to the designation in 1808 of Sierra Leone as a Crown colony following the outlawing of the slave trade in 1807. The experiment of combining homeless former slaves and white street prostitutes in an attempt to solve two problems at a single stroke did not prove a success. But it does suggest that at least some philanthropists recognised that these two categories of abused and downtrodden people had certain issues in common. The mistake was to assume that the plights of both were susceptible to a common solution.

A print of 1808 celebrating the abolition of the slave trade the previous year. Britannia tramples upon shackles while Wilberforce looks on.

By the end of the Georgian period the evil institution of the slave trade had been confronted and abolished, even if its dark consequences were to rumble on for decades, indeed rumble still. But the sex trade survived full force, remaining a social and economic necessity. The successful abolition of slavery in the British Empire in 1833 did finally encourage some reformers to point forcefully to the similarities between the two institutions and offered inspiration for a campaign to reduce, if not entirely abolish, the sex industry.

In 1835 the London Society for the Protection of Young Females and Prevention of Juvenile Prostitution pleaded with . . .

> . . . ye who have distinguished yourselves in the righteous cause of
> benevolence; who have not forgotten the doubly-chained swarthy sons of
> Africa; who have extended the right hand of help to those in distress in
> foreign climes; forget not the miseries of your own beloved fatherland.
> Think of the sufferings incident to a life of Prostitution [of] the vast
> amount of crime of which it is the prolific parent.[33]

But the scale of prostitution did not decrease in early-nineteenth-century London – in fact, quite the opposite (see page 504). The only thing that really changed was that it went gradually underground as the public espousal of morality became ever-more strident. The early Victorians were really no more moral than their Regency predecessors, just less honest, more secret and more hypocritical.

The change in attitude seems to have arrived by the mid-1820s when the courtesan Harriette Wilson, writing her *Memoirs*, attempted to blackmail a former client – the Duke of Wellington – by suggesting that her memory of events would depend on the amount of money he was minded to pay her. Perhaps it was Harriette's intention to portray the duke in a humiliating manner – as a jealous, infatuated and grovelling lover – that was the real threat and that prompted his admirable reply of, 'Publish and be damned.' Certainly a few years earlier the revelation that an eminent man had been intimate with a handsome courtesan would simply not have been seen as a subject for blackmail.

As the *Town and Country Magazine* explained in July 1778, sardonically but with more than a trace of justification, 'a man of taste, to establish his reputation, must have a mistress as well as a pastry cook'.[34] Indeed throughout the eighteenth century a man of power and fashion would have seemed odd or suspect if he had not, from time to time, frequented whores or kept a mistress, with even marriage to a former prostitute – as in the case of Sir William Hamilton and Charles James Fox – being unexceptional if not entirely socially acceptable. Fox, for example, could never expect his ex-prostitute wife to be received at court, but this was partly because the Prince of Wales had been one of her lovers.

SEVENTEEN

'SLAVES OF A CASUAL LUST'

Women's Attitudes to the Sex Industry

Women could have a very tough time in Georgian Britain. If intelligent and independent of spirit, but not well educated or the beneficiary of inherited high status or wealth, a woman had few options. None of the recognised careers was open to her; she could not practise law or medicine or, of course, serve with the military or enter the Church (other than as a Catholic nun, though not in Britain itself until after the beginning of Catholic emancipation in 1778). By convention she would have to surrender herself to the control of a husband or make do with the drudgery of domestic service. Or she could – if possessed of the necessary natural talents and connections – try her hand at trade, the crafts or the arts. Many women ran shops and manufactories, often due to the death of merchant husbands; for example, Louisa Courtauld of Huguenot birth from Spitalfields who managed a highly successful silversmith's business after her husband's death in 1765.

There were also female painters, writers and musicians of significance and recognised talent in Georgian Britain, including Angelica Kauffmann, Mary Moser, Maria Cosway, Susan Centlivre, Ann Radcliffe, Frances Burney, Mary Wollstonecraft and Jane Austen. But they were relatively few in number. What the world of the arts generally meant to most women was the stage, and that, to the eighteenth-century mind, was little more than a branch of prostitution. At its best entering the sex industry was a great risk and, for many women, no better than a death sentence. Which was why another radical course held a distinct, if strange, attraction. To survive and flourish in a man's world, a woman could – quite simply – become a man. She could dress as a man, act as a man and attempt to do a man's work (see Appendix 2).

In the wider context of poverty, injustice, repression and a crushing lack of opportunity it is perhaps easier to understand why prostitution appeared to many women an attractive option. Few if any would have entered the trade by choice, although one of the most popular beliefs of Georgian London's sex industry was in the prevalence of demi-reps, thought to be wives from middling to wealthy families who acted as part-time whores – hence 'half-reputable' – out of inclination. Aside from demi-reps, most women entered the sex trade simply because it offered a possible route to wealth and independence. In stark practical terms, it was a trade that required few talents beyond the obvious and little capital investment, with the home also, if possible, being the place of work. As I. M. Davis explains in *The Harlot and the Statesman*, it was an activity 'that required neither skills or investment and that to the fortunate few could bring immense returns'.[1]

The moral aspect of the sex industry for eighteenth-century women was complex. Although prostitution is certainly despised in biblical texts, sex in itself was not regarded as an evil, providing procreation, not pleasure alone, was the aim. Prostitution, of course, reversed this aim and made pleasure, not procreation, the primary purpose of sex. But all was morally ambivalent. Who was most at fault – the woman who offered sex for pleasure and money or the man who demanded and paid for it? In addition, sex could be seen as a great leveller, an essential human activity, among the highest and the lowest in the land. In these circumstances it is easy to imagine that many prostitutes saw little deeply or morally wrong with their activity, especially if they had been driven to it as a means of survival by the harsh realities of a hostile and uncaring world.

The hypocrisy of many of the public critics of prostitution became part of the lore of the eighteenth-century sex industry and is, for example, invoked by William Hogarth in painting three of his *Harlot's Progress* when he shows Moll's persecutor – the moralising magistrate Sir John Gonson – seemingly aroused by her half-naked appearance. That a harlot's public persecutors could also in secret be her most ardent customers was only one of the many paradoxes that characterised the Georgian sex industry. Another was the fact that it gave a few women – procuresses and owners of bagnios or brothels – wealth and independence in a man's world by the ruthless exploitation of many other women as much as by the manipulation of men's desires and weaknesses.

That the business could be highly lucrative for some women is revealed by the fact that Charlotte Hayes – who in the 1760s ran a brothel or 'nunnery' at King's Place, St James's – eventually retired with £20,000, a sum it would have taken a working man five hundred years to earn, while Mrs Berkley, who ruled over a flagellatory house, is reputed to have made a fortune of £10,000 in eight years. The Covent Garden coffee-house keeper Moll King, according to *Nocturnal Revels*, 'retired to live upon a very easy fortune [and] built a row of houses on the road near Hampstead' (see page 89).

Mary Wollstonecraft offers us a fascinating late-eighteenth-century insight into the feminine perspective on prostitution and the motives of men. She was born in 1759 in Spitalfields on the north-east border of the City of London – the grand-daughter of a wealthy silk-weaver – and evolved into a most individual character. She became a significant writer, a seasoned traveller, friend of many of the leading intellectual and radical figures of late-eighteenth-century London and an enlightened supporter of the liberating and world-changing American and French Revolutions. She also had more or less catastrophic relationships with men – starting with her grandfather and father.

Her *Vindication of the Rights of Woman*, published in 1792, is a key text. In it Wollstonecraft supported women's claims to social rights and liberty, asserted that the sexes were equal, elevated women to the intellectual and rational level long occupied by men, and argued for a society founded on reason. In this work she also dealt, if only in passing, with women who prostituted their bodies, their very souls, for money. She seems to have accepted the late-eighteenth-century convention of men as sexual predators while sensitive and educated women were, almost by definition, sexually cool and not given to libertinism. As she explained:

> Women ... having necessarily some duty to fulfill, more nobly than to adorn their persons [children to support], would not contentedly be the slaves of a casual lust; which is now the situation of a very considerable number who are, literally speaking, standing dishes to which every glutton may have access.[2]

Wollstonecraft attempted to be a living example of this admirable refinement and physical detachment. In her ill-starred infatuation with the artist Henry Fuseli – a married man – she attempted to evolve a kind of creative and intimate intellectual or platonic love in which physical

Mary Wollstonecraft, the author in 1792 of The Vindication of the Rights of Woman, *which argued that women were men's equals in rational thought and reason. She died in childbirth just five years later.*

passion was subjugated. As William Godwin, later her husband, explained in his *Memoirs* of Mary Wollstonecraft, '[I]t was her maxim, "that the imagination should awaken the senses, and not the senses the imagination".'[3] In Wollstonecraft's ideal world, love was a state of mind rather than of body. Within this conception prostitutes fulfilled an unfortunate but necessary function by taking male sexual pressure off 'good' women. As Wollstonecraft wrote, when pondering the role and fate of the women who were accessible 'standing dishes' for male lust, 'I may be told that great as the enormity is, it only affects a devoted part of the sex – devoted for the salvation of the rest.'[4]

So licentious or sexually available women – demi-reps and prostitutes – were not, in Wollstonecraft's view, devalued but 'devoted', whether they knew it or not, to the salvation of their sisters from male sexual oppression. In thus presenting her argument Wollstonecraft coincided extraordinarily – indeed bizarrely – closely with the conventional libertine excuse – or apology – for prostitution as expressed in the introduction to the second volume of *Nocturnal Revels* of 1779. Prostitution was there presented as a social necessity – a blessing not an evil – because if sexually frustrated men could not find temporary relief in the arms of prostitutes, the peace of society would be far more disturbed than it currently was (see page 445).

But the socially enlightened Wollstonecraft was perhaps saying something more. Her definition of the function served by prostitution can be seen as lending social purpose and significance to London's vast sex industry – indeed almost giving it moral and spiritual meaning – by implying that it was not just about money and the gratification of male lust but also to do with liberty and the creation of a more stable society in which the majority of women were emancipated from male domination.

But what caused some women to become 'devoted' saviours of their fellow women? Wollstonecraft did not answer this basic question but did suggest a root cause: 'men are certainly more under the influence of their appetites than women; and their appetites are more depraved by unbridled indulgence',[5] and asserted 'that all the causes of female weakness, as well as depravity . . . branch out of one grand cause – want of chastity in men'.[6] She was to discover, to her very bitter cost, the truth of this observation in her relationship from 1792 with the unreliable and sexually promiscuous American Gilbert Imlay.

This troubling theme of the consequences for females of male lust was developed in her *Wrongs of Woman*, published in 1798 soon after she had died following the birth of her second daughter. This work, which presents prostitution as a fate imposed upon unfortunate women by a male-dominated society, was an attempt 'to fictionalise the arguments of *A Vindication of the Rights of Woman*'[7] so as to make them more powerful and universally pertinent. It was also, to a degree, autobiographical.

The story tells of Maria, imprisoned in an insane asylum by her husband who after marriage turned out to be a libertine and a bully. She is 'literally a prisoner of sex, immured in a mad house'.[8] 'Was not,' asks Wollstonecraft through Maria, 'the world a vast prison and women born slaves?' During her incarceration Maria meets a series of women who have fallen victims to the actions and sexual appetites of men, including one who was 'married against her inclination to a rich old man, extremely jealous', and another, named Jemima, who was abused and raped by a master, made pregnant and eventually driven into prostitution. Why, asks Maria, was 'woman, fragile flower! . . . suffered to adorn a world exposed to the inroad of such stormy elements'?[9]

Jemima's story was inspired by the true-life history of Caroline Blood – the sister of Mary's beloved friend Fanny Blood – who was 'seduced, abandoned, persecuted by the Poor Laws and then forced into prostitution by economic necessity'[10] in order to escape the hell of low-paid and hard menial work. But Jemima's story was made grimmer still. She was born a bastard:

> [N]o mother had ever fondled her, no father or brother had protected her from outrage, and the man who had plunged her into infamy, and deserted her when she stood in greatest need of support, deigned not to smooth with kindness the road to ruin . . .

So Jemima, 'despised and preyed on the society by which she had been oppressed', and when she related her history to Maria, offered an authentic cry of female anguish from the streets of late-eighteenth-century London:

> I was . . . born a slave . . . fate dragged me through the very kennels [gutters/sewers] of society; I was still a slave, a bastard, a common property. Become familiar with vice . . . I picked the pockets of the drunkards who abused me . . . Detesting my nightly occupation, though valuing . . . my independence . . .[11]

Before this dark and tangled plot resolves itself the book stops – cut short only two-thirds through by the sudden and unexpected death of its author. Would the story have evolved some redeeming features so that all ended happily? Probably not. Wollstonecraft was a realist. Redemption and a happy ending for her characters was no doubt as unlikely as it was for the mass of harlots who nightly tramped the streets of Georgian London.

EIGHTEEN

'PRETTY DOINGS OF A PROTESTANT NATION'

The Campaign Against Prostitution

THE LAW, LEGAL PROCESSES AND MORAL VIGILANTES

Prostitution was not against the law in Georgian London and consequently no legal action could be taken against a woman simply because she was a prostitute. On the other hand, homosexual male prostitutes could, under a statute of 1533, be executed if convicted of buggery, or placed in the pillory and gaoled if convicted of attempted buggery or 'sodomitical intent' (see page 69). The late seventeenth and early eighteenth centuries were a time when the law was mostly concerned with protecting property, safeguarding government income from taxation and suppressing sedition, it was not generally regarded as a means by which to impose a moral code on a population, but this is not to say that female prostitutes were entirely beyond the interest or the reach of the law.

As Leon Radzinowicz puts it in his magisterial *History of English Criminal Law*, 'Under certain circumstances, narrowly prescribed under the common law, prostitutes came within the scope of penal legislation.'[i] During the Georgian period this scope gradually broadened as various moral reformers and legislators attempted to respond to the increasingly large numbers of street-walkers and bawdy houses or brothels. Some of this legislation was inspired by a genuine fear of divine retribution in response to the immorality of the age (see page 469), and some was stimulated by a belief in the direct connection between prostitution and crimes such as robbery. While one flourished, uncontrolled and unstemmed, so would the other. Throughout the eighteenth and early nineteenth centuries, therefore, attempts were made to suppress common street prostitutes – those who were most obviously a potential link between street crime and robbery – and bawdy-houses by using, or arguably misusing, broad existing laws.

The legal apparatus for controlling and penalising prostitutes and prostitution was ancient and decrepit. During the late seventeenth century and into the first decade of the eighteenth reformers intent on clearing the streets of prostitutes used an act from the time of Edward III that permitted the arrest of street-walkers on simple suspicion of being prostitutes intending to solicit, while a statute of 1545 made it a common-law offence to keep a brothel anywhere in London or to engage in grossly indecent behaviour in a public place.[2] Those enforcing the law were a curious and disparate bunch. There were parish constables plus those employed by private companies operating on warrants issued by magistrates, and the Night Watch which was raised to police individual parishes and liberties. The system was irregular and inefficient, largely because the parish constables and night watchmen were often infirm, untrained, poorly paid out of parish funds and corrupt, openly extorting regular bribes from street-walkers.[3]

During the 1690s things started to change when the prosecution of prostitutes and other persons deemed 'lewd' or 'unnatural' in their actions was taken up by freelancing and evangelising vigilante societies for the 'Reformation of Manners', by which was meant morals. From the 1690s into the 1730s these societies grew in number and in membership to become a phenomenon of the age. These were men and women with a moral mission. Some of their more crusading members were well known but generally membership was kept discreet, even secret. Members were presumably afraid of being targeted by whores, bullies and brothelkeepers, but this secrecy also meant that members of the societies could operate covertly and not be immediately answerable for their actions. This somewhat sinister subterfuge was potentially a rogue's charter, encouraging secret denunciations and veiled acts of malice or revenge. To achieve a morally righteous end – ridding the city of vice – some of these societies were prepared to use any methods, no matter how dubious or amoral. Key components of their *modus operandi* were the use of paid informers, *agents provocateurs*, zealous magistrates issuing blank warrants to the societies' own constables, the avid – almost fanatical – lobbying

of Church, local government and magistrates, the regular publication
and proclamation of their aims and achievements, and a readiness to
use strong-arm methods against those who were perceived as immoral
wrongdoers.

In the early days of the reforming movement this arsenal was used in
a simple, effective – and arguably illegal – manner. A prostitute or bawdy-
house would be identified through the actions of an *agent provocateur* who
would then turn informer and complainant, fill in a blank warrant naming
the accused individuals, house and alleged offences, and get it signed by
a compliant magistrate. The societies' own constables would then enforce
the warrant, and if the victim were a whore it would usually result in her
being sent to labour in the local Bridewell for a month or so. This procedure reflected no regard for the prostitutes' civil liberties since usually she
had no proper or fair chance to defend herself.

But all did not go the way the societies intended. One constable activist
– Sampson Cooke – 'arrested hundreds of prostitutes [but] when a
complaint was made against Cooke's activities, it was discovered that many
of the arrests had been illegal because the warrant stipulated no time limit
for its return'.[4]

Apprehending prostitutes and 'lewd' men could also be a dangerous
business with the societies' constables occasionally being attacked and
some even killed. Constable John Copper, for instance, died in 1701 in
Mayfair during a bitter battle with rioting soldiers, and his colleague
Constable John Dent, who escaped the riot, was himself killed by furious
soldiers seven years later in Covent Garden while attempting to escort a
group of alleged prostitutes and their clients to the Watch House.[5] A
couple of years later, in 1712, a group of constables was again attacked by
a mob of soldiers in Covent Garden when they tried to arrest a group of
prostitutes.[6]

The societies advocating moral reform had their origin in the militant
religious revival of the 1670s that produced the societies formed by
groups of robust young Anglicans.[7] These were a response to the perceived
immorality of the Royal Court and a reflection of the popular determination to promote Anglican virtues in the face of a much-feared Roman
Catholic resurgence that did in fact start to emerge during the brief
reign of James II but came to an abrupt halt in 1688 when King William
and Queen Mary consolidated the Protestant grip on the throne of

London in the 1840s, showing its vast expansion during

the 120 years after the map shown on pages 28–9.

England. The joint monarchs soon made morality and law enforcement key aspects of their rule. In 1690 William issued a Proclamation encouraging the apprehension and punishment of robbers and highwaymen, and the following year the parish officers and leading citizens of Tower Hamlets responded by forming a society to suppress bawdy-houses. This campaign was calculated both to further the aims of the Proclamation and to strike a blow for moral reform because bawdy-houses were deemed to be:

> Dens of Notorious Thieves, Robbers, Traytors and other Criminals [and the places where] Bodies are poxt and pockets are picked of considerable sums [provoking] tumultuous Routs, Riots and Uproars . . . Here 'tis that many a Housekeeper is infected with a venomous Plague, which he communicates to his Honest and Innocent Wife [who at length falls] a dead sacrifice to her husband's unnatural cruelty and inhumane bestiality.

In the early 1690s both King William and Queen Mary were worried that the nation's declining standard of morality would provoke divine retribution.

In addition, this pioneering Society for the Reformation of Manners attacked 'Impudent Harlots' that 'by their Antick Dresses, Painted Faces and Whorish Insinuations allure and tempt our Sons and Servants to Debauchery, and consequently to embezel and steal from us, to maintain their strumpets'.[8] Queen Mary, who feared divine retribution for the nation's moral misdeeds, added her support to this volunteer reforming movement, and soon a second society was formed in the Strand area with, by the very early eighteenth century, twenty Societies for the Reformation of Manners operating in the metropolis, all encouraged by a series of Royal Proclamations and statutes including one in 1699 by William III to suppress 'Blasphemy and Prophaneness' and another by Queen Anne in 1702 to encourage 'Piety and Virtue and for the Preventing and Punishment of Vice, Prophaneness and Immorality'.[9]

This campaign had a crusading and novel air about it that many found exciting, indeed unprecedented. John Disney, one of the founding members of the societies, offered trenchant arguments for their activities in his *Essay upon the Execution of the Laws against Immorality and Prophaneness* of 1708. He argued that the 'laws of the State' must be put 'in vigorous Execution' against vice and issued a 'challenge' to any libertine to prove that 'profane swearing . . . lewdness [and] drunkenness' were 'innocent and harmless' and that the societies were 'useless . . . illegal and prejudicial to the public'. Disney then offered the familiar apocalyptic warning:

> Let us not flatter ourselves that . . . Debauchery & Prophaneness are
> only Personal Crimes . . . they are not Personal but National too and
> God will Account with us as a Body for suffering the exorbitant
> Impudence of Vice. Thus public Impieties unrestrained by the
> Magistrate bring down the Vengeance of God upon the Land.[10]

He supported his argument and position with numerous Old Testament references. For example, to justify the attack on vice: '"Shall I not visit for these things?" saith the Lord: "shall not my soul be avenged on such a nation as this?"' (Jeremiah, 5:29), and to justify the interventionist actions of the societies: 'By the Blessings of the upright the city is exalted; but it is overthrown by the mouth of the wicked' (Proverbs, 11:11).

One of the main reasons for launching the campaign against bawdy-houses and their inmates was – as the Tower Hamlets manifesto made clear – because it was believed that in such places prostitutes were spreading an epidemic of venereal disease, with 'honest and innocent wives' being the most regular victims. This fear seems to have been based on some evidence. As Randolph Trumbach suggests, '[I]n London from the 1690s onward, it is very probable that ... street prostitutes, who were almost totally diseased, infected a large percentage of both single and married men',[11] which perhaps explains why between 1710 and 1749, at least 15 per cent of women who sought divorces in the London Consistory Court claimed they had been venereally infected by their husbands. As the century wore on, venereal disease, once perceived as something of an elite ailment, became more prevalent among the 'common' people due to the increase in street prostitution. As William Buchan put it in 1796 in his *Observations Concerning the Prevention and Cure of the Venereal Disease*, 'what was formerly called the Gentleman's Disease is now equally common among the lowest ranks of society'.[12] By 'the second half of the eighteenth century it was not unusual for 20–40 per cent of British sailors to be venereally infected' with one pamphleteer in 1813 estimating 'that twenty thousand young men a year became venereally infected through London's prostitutes'.[13]

The Scottish physician William Buchan, who in the late eighteenth century noted the spread of venereal disease: 'what was formerly called the Gentleman's Disease is,' wrote Buchan, 'now equally common among the lowest ranks of society'.

Lobbying by the societies helped to bring about modest changes in legislation. For example, in February 1697 a law against lewd behaviour was instituted that threatened punishment to 'all Persons ... Guilty of Excessive drinking [and] Blasphemy'.[14] But equally there were legislative amendments to curtail some of the excesses of the societies themselves. In 1709 Lord Chief Justice Sir John Holt – an ardent supporter of civil rights, wary of the activities of the vigilante reforming societies, which he perceived as taking the law too much into their own hands – declared during his summing up at the trial of three soldiers for the murder of Constable Dent:

What! Must not a Woman of the Town walk in the Town streets?
These men think they do things so meritorious in taking up light
Women; why a light Woman hath a right of Liberty as well as another
to walk about the streets.[15]

As a result of this trial Holt ruled that it was 'not lawful, even for a legal constable, to take up a woman upon a bare suspicion only, having been guilty of no breach of the peace, nor any unlawful act'.[16] But this legal ruling appears ultimately to have done little to protect prostitutes from the societies' prowling constables and vigilantes, as is revealed by their tally of prostitutes charged and bawdy-houses suppressed. The societies' statistics, intended to vaunt their power, are of questionable accuracy but even if only partly true suggest an undertaking of vast scope.

The 1699 accounts of the Tower Hamlets Society for the Suppression of Bawdy-houses and Reformation of Manners claimed that 500 disorderly houses had been suppressed since 1691 and 'some Thousands of Lewd Persons have been imprisoned, fined and whipt, so that the Tower-End of the Town, and many of our streets, have been much purged of that pestilent Generation of Night Walkers that used to infest them'.[17] In 1718 the societies claimed 1,253 prosecutions for 'lewd and disorderly practices', and 31 for keeping 'bawdy and disorderly houses',[18] while between December 1719 and November 1720 the societies prosecuted 1,189 persons in London for 'lewd and disorderly practices' – mostly street-walkers and men who indecently exposed themselves or who were caught having sex in a public place – and 14 people for 'keeping bawdy or disorderly houses'.[19]

In 1726 the societies, clearly in self-congratulatory and promotional mood, proclaimed their overall achievements: 'the total number of Persons prosecuted by the Societies in or near London only, for Debauchery and Prophaneness, for the thirty-four years last past, are calculated at 91,899'.[20] This figure is probably an exaggeration, but the societies may have been responsible for prosecuting as many as 20,000 prostitutes and other 'lewd and disorderly' persons, such as sodomites, during this period.[21]

The Forty-First Account, published in December 1735,[22] trumpets the societies' achievements in suppressing 'great numbers of Bawdy-houses, Sodomitical haunts, Common Gaming-houses' and of purging the streets of 'the wretched Tribe of Night-walking Prostitutes and most detestable Sodomites', and states that 'the Total Number of Persons prosecuted in or near London only, for Debauchery and Profaneness, for Forty one Years past, are calculated at about 99,970'.[23] By 1738 the societies claimed this figure had risen to 101,683 convictions for various offences against morality and public decency, with the largest category being for the usual 'lewd and disorderly practices'.[24]

The crusading zeal of the societies fluctuated during the very early-eighteenth century with peaks of prosecution – arguably persecution – following particularly notorious trials for sexual crimes, for example the trials of homosexuals in 1726 which culminated in four men being hanged (see page 62), and Colonel Charteris' rape trial in 1730 (see page 311). The most famous example of this early-1730s peak of activity were the raids made by the reforming magistrate Sir John Gonson on bawdy-houses and prostitutes' homes.

These were legally problematic because the laws suppressing bawdy-houses and brothels, based on the 1545 statute and theoretically stronger than those relating to prostitution in the public street, were extremely difficult to implement. The obvious problem was to prove that a house was being used as a brothel. A potential prosecutor could, of course, investigate under the guise of would-be customer – and this is exactly what happened during the crusade against homosexual clubs, or Molly Houses, in 1726 (see page 62). But the reformers had to be careful. If they chose to raid a private house and were wrong in their suspicions, or no evidence was found to prove that the house was being used as a brothel, they were in turn liable to prosecution. One solution was for the prosecutor to fall back on different legislation and accuse the proprietor of keeping a 'disorderly house', a lesser charge that was easier to argue and to prove.

In 1730 Sir John Gonson tried to deal with the problem of gaining access to suspected properties in search of evidence by obtaining a promise from government to defend constables sued for illegal brothel searches.[25] Hogarth may have been making a legal point in 1731 when in painting three of *The Harlot's Progress* he showed Gonson storming into Moll Hackabout's decrepit Drury Lane bedroom. What is the purpose or legality of Gonson's action? Is he accompanied by bailiffs coming to arrest Moll for debt or is this a vigilante raid on premises suspected of being a brothel or a disorderly house? The implication is that Gonson is a bully, illegally breaking into Moll's lodging simply because she is poor and vulnerable and he is a powerful and moralistic magistrate who fancies himself above the law.

During the mid-1730s, largely as a result of popular reaction against the excessive terror-tactics of the reformers, the societies went into decline. An additional reason may have been the financial muscle of the sex industry. Quite simply it was too valuable a London trade to be suppressed or even seriously hampered; too many people had too much to gain from such a vital part of the city's economy. When the voluntary societies made their return during the 1780s, led by reformers such as William Wilberforce and inspired by George III's 1787 Proclamation for the 'Encouragement of Piety and Virtue, and for the Prevention and Punishing of Vice and Immorality', they took a different form. The Proclamation Society and the Society for the Suppression of Vice were more concerned with obscene literature, blasphemy, encouraging church-going and high-level political lobbying than with hands-on street battles with prostitutes and their bullies, although the Society for the Suppression of Vice did make a point of prosecuting the operators of bawdy-houses.

From the mid-eighteenth century lobbying to change the law and then relying on its ever-more effective public officers to execute the new legislation characterised the campaign against street prostitution. For example, the Vagrancy Act of 1744 provided a simple procedure for controlling and punishing 'disorderly people' such as beggars and vagabonds although it proved difficult to apply to street prostitutes, who philanthropist and seasoned traveller Jonas Hanway described in the mid-eighteenth century as 'the most disorderly and indecent in the world'. In 1796 it could still be observed of prostitutes that 'they throng our streets, lie in wait for the incautious, and corrupt the rising generation'.[26]

DRUNK AND DISORDERLY: GIN, VIOLENCE AND ROBBERY

Not all campaigners against prostitution were simply concerned with issues of morality and decency. Many were more practically minded, concerned with the ways in which prostitution and the sex industry were linked with two other particular evils of the age: drink and crime. Alcohol – particularly cheap, strong and health-destroying gin – was popular and with good reason seen as the beverage that fuelled the sex industry and led to 'lewd' behaviour, collapse of restraint and all manner of crime. During the first half of the eighteenth century ardent anti-gin campaigners, such as William Hogarth and Henry Fielding, tackled the issue both by raising the public's awareness of the evil and its consequences, and by lobbying to change the law.

In February 1751 Hogarth published his print *Gin Lane*, which displayed the horrors of gin-induced mindless intoxication in the context of the tumble-down slum of St Giles-in-the-Fields, notorious for its low bawdy-houses, prostitutes and numerous unlicensed gin shops. Later in the year his purpose was achieved when the Gin Act was passed. This reduced the consumption of the spirit by ruling that distillers had to charge more for their product and sell only to licensed merchants and retailers. Thus it eliminated small, informal gin shops – seen as primarily the resort of street prostitutes and criminals – and made gin-drinking a regulated luxury, above the meagre means of the London poor.

Crime was a much more difficult evil to tackle, but there could be little doubt just how closely intertwined it was with the sex industry. Even the master criminal Jonathan Wild is said to have been introduced to crime and taught 'New Ways of Getting Money' by the prostitute Mary Milliner.[27] The notorious Jack Sheppard had Macheath-like relationships with lewd women, particularly the Drury Lane prostitute Elizabeth Lyon, known as 'Edgworth Bess', who was believed to have turned him from wayward apprentice to daring criminal and to have introduced him to fences who were generally females and almost invariably whores. As Peter Linebaugh points out, '[A] statistical analysis of all London indictments (Westminster, Middlesex, Southwark and the

Hogarth's Gin Lane, published in February 1751, illustrates the physical and moral decay that many believed were the result of the consumption of strong and cheap gin. The location here is St Giles-in-the-Fields – known for its low bawdy-houses, destitute prostitutes, thieves, rookeries and poverty. On the left, a tradesman pawns his tools for drinking money and a woman her cooking utensils. In the background is the tower of Hawksmoor's St George, Bloomsbury.

City) for the year 1740 shows that the *only* felony for which a greater number of women were indicted than men was for the offence of receiving stolen goods.'[28] Sheppard's and Wild's stories alone seemed to confirm the corrupting and criminalising influence of prostitutes and as late as 1796 it was observed as a fact of London life that many male criminals . . .

... sally forth to make depredations to support the expences of licentious indulgence: and many of these unhappy men (whose frequent executions are the grief of every feeling heart) confess, that in the company of harlots, they were trained up for this fatal end.[29]

The involvement of street prostitutes and the inmates of low bawdyhouses in theft, and the ease with which prostitution could lead to robbery and violence, is illustrated neatly by an incident that took place one Saturday afternoon in June 1726 at Kings Head Court, just off Fleet Street. The story is preserved in the Proceedings of the Old Bailey,[30] which

One of the generally recognised evils of gin was female drunkenness. Here a drunken wife, brandishing a glass of gin, is shackled to the shoulders of her exhausted husband, who points resignedly to a padlock inscribed 'wedlock'. 'Purl', advertised on a large tankard, was made of warm ale mixed with sweetened milk and a shot of gin and was, understandably, popular in the winter with street prostitutes.

record the trial on 11 July 1726 of Mary Blewit 'alias Dickenson, alias Bowler', who was 'indicted for privately stealing goods'.

Edward Hartrey, the victim of the alleged theft, told the court that 'the Prisoner pick'd me up just as I came out of a Coach in Fleet-Street, and away she carry'd me down Shoe-Lane, to a House in Kings-Head Court'. This was a brothel and Hartrey knew that 'the Bawd's Name that kept it was Alice Gale'. The pair went upstairs and, stated Hartrey:

> I staid with her about a Quarter of an Hour, but being a little Fuddled,
> I can't say that we did any Thing to speak of but however she thought
> fit to examine my Breeches, and I finding her Hand near my Pocket; I
> began to suspect her, and presently mist my Goods.

Hartrey then 'tax'd her with robbing me', but should have known it was dangerous to corner such a woman in her own lair:

> [U]p came her Bullies, and maul'd me, and beat me, and kick'd me
> down Stairs, and broke my Nose, and then turn'd me out of Doors, and
> hussel'd me up and down among the dark Alleys, that I might not find
> the House again, and so they left me in a most lamentable Pickle.

But Hartrey, although hurt, was far from cowed. He gave notice to pawnbrokers in the vicinity to look out for his goods (and subsequently recovered them), got a warrant and – clearly not confused or intimidated by the bullies' antics – discovered the location of Blewit's lodgings and the next day 'took the Prisoner at her Lodging up 2 pair of Stairs, in the late House of the late Jonathan Wild'. This is a possibly revealing reference, suggesting that Blewit might once have been part of the gang of the notorious master-criminal and racketeer who had been executed just over a year earlier, to much popular rejoicing (see page 330). Certainly this association with Wild would have done the accused no good in court. Hartrey then told how Blewit was committed to the Compter, or local gaol, and how she tried to negotiate herself out of trouble. She offered to return what stolen articles she retained by four o'clock that day if Hartrey would stop his prosecution. Interested in the proposal, he 'waited till that Time, and then she put me off till the next Day, and so from one Time to another, till I was quite tired'.

The prosecution then produced a witness to support Hartrey's account of events. The witness who duly appeared was named John Sylvester who worked as a watchman, but his evidence could hardly be said to be objective for he commenced by admitting that 'the Prosecutor you must know is one of my Masters, he's a Barber by Trade, and lives in Bale Court, Fleet-Street'. Sylvester's evidence, preserved verbatim, retains the authentic flavour of early-eighteenth-century London street-life, representing the opinions and attitudes of the city's most humble and long-forgotten people:

> Now it's always my way to take care of my Masters, and see them safe
> home, when ever I meet any of them as I go my Rounds: and so it fell
> out between 12 and 1 a Saturday Morning [sic], that I see's my Master
> Hartrey come out of a Coach very much fuddled, and who should be up
> upon, but this very 'Gentlewoman at the Bar', Madam Blewit, or
> Dickenson, or Bowler, or what you please to call her, for she was Wife
> to them all Three at the same Time, and the two First of 'em are now a
> hanging in Chains in St George's-Fields.

Having thus dispatched Blewit's character, Sylvester returned to his account of the scene that confronted him that Saturday afternoon. Whether Hartrey 'wanted a Whore, or she a Rogue' was, said Sylvester, 'neither here nor there, but they presently laid fast hold of one another, and grew woundy loving'. This sight was clearly most alarming and Sylvester feared that no good would come of it.

> I found my Master was in Danger, and did all that I could to get him
> away. 'Hussy', says I, 'You Saucy Brimstone Toad you, what Business
> have ye with my Master, let him go, or I'll call my Brother Watchman,
> and have ye to the Round-House directly'. And, 'Ah Master!' says I, 'my
> dear Master, come away from that Hang-in-Chains Bitch.' – Yes I did
> call her Bitch, that I did, my Lord, and I can't deny it. – 'She'll certainly
> pick your Pocket', says I, 'or Serve you a worse Trick – Come, come
> don't expose yourself.' But all signify'd nothing, he swore she was a Girl
> for his Fancy, and he would go with her, and so they went together, but
> it had been better for him if he had taken his poor Watchman's Advice.

Mary Blewit's defence was brief. She denied she had seen Hartrey before he turned up on her doorstep to apprehend her, and then called several witnesses who claimed that on the day he was robbed he had also accused them of picking his pocket and 'sometimes swore he could not tell who had done it'. The court chose not to believe Blewit or her witnesses and she was found guilty. The sentence, since the theft was of under one shilling, was transportation, which was usually for a minimum of seven years.

The sentence passed on Mary Blewit was harsh enough but worse befell Constantia James who in December 1738 was hanged as a pick-pocket. *The Ordinary of Newgate's Account* of 22 December 1738 explained that Constantia, aged thirty, was a servant who as a result of having been 'debauch'd' by her master 'commence'd to work as an abandoned common prostitute' and 'if she had no opportunity to rob men in the street . . . would decoy them into the House of an Acquaintance'.[31] Constantia's victim dismissed her as 'a three-penny upright' and described her working methods as she came upon him while he was urinating: 'As I stood against the Wall, the prisoner came behind me, and with one hand she took hold of — and the other she thrust into my Breeches pocket and took my Money.' The fact that the stolen sum was 36 shillings and that she had been in Newgate before sealed Constantia's fate.[32]

One more story is worth recounting, because it reveals most dramatic-ally the association between prostitutes and premeditated, organised and very violent street crime. The story, described in the Proceedings of the Old Bailey, concerns the crimes and misdemeanours of the picturesquely named Ann Duck. From early 1743 until late 1744 she was tried for violent robbery, usually with accomplices, on at least ten occasions and each time acquitted. During many of the cases the evidence against her was strong, with the victims giving compelling accounts of the assaults made upon them, but almost invariably no independent witnesses were willing to give evidence or else, when the trial started, both victim and his wit-nesses failed to appear so the prosecution collapsed. Evidently Ann Duck was able to intimidate both those she had wronged and the witnesses who could have brought her activities to an end. Her method of terror is implied during one of her early trials, on 14 January 1743,[33] for the alleged attack and robbery of William Cooper on 'the Highway' on 28 December 1742. Cooper gave strong evidence against Duck but could get no witnesses to corroborate his account. One man, explained Cooper, had helped him after the assault and 'I thanked him, and craved his Name. But he said, he dared not tell it me, for he should be knocked on the Head by her Bullies if he should be named.'

Because witnesses lacked the courage to stop her, Ann Duck's violent assaults continued until 21 September 1744 when she, together with Ann Barefoot alias Wells, robbed George Cheshire. The two women were brought to trial on 17 October 1744 and indicted with violent theft upon the King's Highway and putting their victim 'in fear', a crime that carried the death penalty if proven.[34] Ann Duck's co-defendant was also a formidable character. The Old Bailey Proceedings note that she was the same person who had been convicted together with a woman called Ann Gwyn during the preceding trial and that she was the 'reputed wife' of Thomas Wells who had been indicted of robbery. These three Anns – as evidence soon revealed – were all street prostitutes who operated together as extremely violent robbers and were clearly the terrors of the densely packed and poor area around Chick Lane in Smithfield.

The trial started with George Cheshire describing what had happened to him on 21 September:

> I was robbed in Thatched Ally, in Chick-Lane, between 8 and 9 at
> night; I had been in a house to drink a dram, and in less than the space
> of a minute, after I came out, three women came out of the house, and
> two of them followed me, the Prisoners are the persons; Mrs Barefoot
> came on my left side, and put her right arm round my neck, and with
> her left confined my arm; Ann Duck was on my right side, and put her
> left arm round my neck, and with her right hand picked my pocket and
> took out 4 d. I resisted, and they began to beat me, and Ann Duck gave
> me several blows.

What happened next reveals Ann Duck's *modus operandi*. Cheshire 'cried out murder' but, rather than attracting assistance from members of the public, other accomplices of Duck appeared who had no doubt made a point of intimidating and warning off any innocent passers-by. Cheshire now found himself attacked in force by a gang that must have been truly terrifying:

> [H]ere came one man, and one woman, one of whom gave a mopstick
> into the hand of Ann Duck, with which she gave me several blows
> upon my arms and back, and particularly one upon my left eye, which
> swelled my eye up, and cut it pretty much, and Ann Barefoot gave me a
> blow on the side of the head, with something she had in her hand,
> which I took to be a stone, or a brickbat, for it was very hard.

Chick Lane, running west from Smithfield to Saffron Hill, as it appeared in 1825. During the eighteenth century Chick Lane and the area immediately around it were the notorious haunts of common prostitutes, such as Ann Duck, and locations for Molly Houses.

Duck's stratagem was crude but clearly effective. She and her cronies dominated the area, frightened off the public, and then speedily beat their victims into submission and robbed them. As Cheshire went on to explain, he 'was so bad with their usage' that he needed his landlady to sew up the wound to his eyebrow and 'could not work at my business for a fortnight'.

Having given his account Cheshire was questioned by the court. He explained that he was a cutler working on London Bridge, 'lodged at Mrs Dale's in Cross-Keys-Court in Chick-Lane', confirmed that money was taken from him by force and that before the attack he knew the women 'by sight . . . as I live in the neighbourhood' and that he 'knew Ann Duck by name very well'. He was then asked if he had ever 'kept company' with the prisoners, which obviously meant had he ever used any of them as prostitutes and so perhaps given offence or grievance that provoked the attack. 'No,' replied Cheshire, 'never in my life.'

Ann Duck offered a defence but, rather than responding to the specific charge, attempted the desperate ploy of suggesting she was the victim of a deep and malicious conspiracy:

> And please your Lordship, and the Court, I was discharged last night
> from a robbery, and now the persons, who belong to Clerkenwell
> Bridewell, have brought this man in order to swear my life away.

The court was not long detained by this attempt to muddy and confuse the waters. It merely asked Cheshire if he had ever before been involved in a legal case with these women, and when he said no the investigation into a possible conspiracy ceased. However, Cheshire was asked why he had not endeavoured to have his assailants taken up. Evidently someone other than their current victim had brought them before the court. He explained that he had indeed gone . . .

> . . . to Freeman's, a publick-house in Chick-Lane, the next day, and
> enquired after them, and they told me they durst not tell me their
> names for fear of having damage done them, and I never heard any
> more of them, till I was sent for; after they were taken up.

Cheshire's landlady, Jane Dale, was called to give evidence to support his account of the injuries inflicted, and in the process confirmed that Ann Duck and her companions terrorised the Chick Lane area. When talking of the nature of the attack she stated that 'Mrs Freeman, who keeps an Ale-house in the neighbourhood, knows this too, but she will not come without she is fetched, because she thinks as she lives in the neighbourhood it will be a prejudice to her'. This time the jury believed it had enough to hang the pair of women. They were found guilty and sentenced to death.

And so the brief reign of terror of this trio of violent street prostitutes – for Ann Gwyn was also condemned during the same sessions for a separate crime – was terminated. But these alarming women do not, with the end of their trials, quite disappear from history. Something of their nature and background is revealed in the *Account* published by the Ordinary – or Chaplain – of Newgate that was completed on the eve of their execution and published on 7 November 1744.[35] This states that Ann Duck, 'about 25 Years of Age', was 'born in Little White's-Alley, Chancery-Lane, the Daughter of one Duck, a Black, well known to many Gentlemen in our Inns of Court, by teaching them the Use of the Small Sword, of which he was a very good Master'. Duck managed to pay for Ann to be educated 'to fit her for Business' but he died, leaving a large family that he had with a 'White Woman, and now living'. Things almost immediately started to go wrong for his daughter.

> Ann, impatient of Restraint, soon after the Death of her Father, (which was about Four Years since) launched out into such Excesses, as were beyond her Mother's Power to control; and became as expert a Mistress in all Manner of Wickedness, as Satan himself could make her. In short, hardly any Thing wicked came amiss to her. She first became a Servant at a Bawdy House; then walk'd the Streets on her own Account; next commenc'd Pickpocket; at length became so bold, so resolute, and so daring, as to commit Street-Robberies even upon Men too.

The Ordinary observed, with perhaps a little too much satisfaction, that Ann had 'been try'd several Times at the Old-Bailey, yet had the Fortune to get off, till at Length Justice overtook her, and she was deservedly condemn'd, though but for a Trifle'. The death sentence does not seem to have broken her rebellious spirit:

> [A]fter Condemnation she appear'd but little Penitent, and when she came to Chapel, would much rather talk with her old Companions thro' the Lattice, than attend to the more serious Affair, the Welfare of her Soul; she nevertheless said, she believ'd in Christ, hop'd that God would save her Soul, and died in Peace with all Men.

Ann Barefoot, alias Wells, also 'about 25 Years of Age', had been born in Cambridge 'where her Father, some Years since, kept an Inn, and while he liv'd, bestow'd a good Education upon her'. When he died Ann moved to London 'and lived some Time with an Aunt in Bishopsgate-street, and afterwards at divers Places as a Servant'. At first Ann 'behaved pretty well, till she contracted an Acquaintance with a Brewer's Servant, with whom she lived as a Wife, though she never was married, and by him had two Children, which are since dead'. But, notes the troubled Ordinary, even while Ann . . .

... cohabited with this Man, her Mind was roving, and she frequently walk'd the Streets, and pick'd up Men. 'Twas one Night she came out from her Lodgings in Whitechapel, with a View to pick some one up, she was pick'd up herself by the Constables, and carried to the Poultry-Compter.

She was 'committed' to 'hard Labour' in the Bishopsgate Workhouse, where she 'continued about one Month, and in that Time contracted an Intimacy with a Woman who was of the same Stamp with herself, and committed to that Place on the same Score'. These two women happened to be discharged together and went to seek lodgings in Chick Lane, after which Ann never went near the brewer's servant again.

She soon became a noted Thief as well as Street-Walker, and extended her Acquaintance amongst a great Number of Thieves, Whores, Pickpockets, &c. of both Sexes, so that she had Thoughts of keeping a Bouzing Ken [a drinking house] of her own; and accordingly she took a House in Thatch'd-Court in Chick-Lane, which she kept for about a Year; but not finding her Customers come fast enough, and finding too that it was much dearer than Lodging, she laid it down, and went and lodg'd at Mr Gray's, in Black-Boy-Alley, in Chick-Lane.

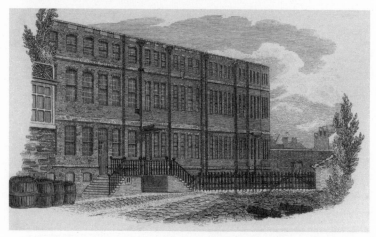

The Bishopsgate Workhouse, swept away in the late nineteenth century for the construction of Liverpool Street Station, received many destitute city prostitutes.

It was in these lodgings that Ann Barefoot became acquainted with Ann Gwyn 'and other infamous People like herself' and became 'concern'd in many Robberies, and was a most wicked Creature'.

Ann Gwyn, twenty-seven, had been born in Golden Lane, in the parish of St Luke's, Middlesex, the daughter of poor 'but honest People, who brought her up in the best Manner their Circumstances would admit'. After her parents' death, Ann . . .

> . . . turned Washerwoman . . . and behaved with a good deal of Honesty, till falling into bad Company, she became as vile as any Prostitute of 'em all, and lived upon the Spoil and Plunder of Mankind. She has been a Common Street-Walker for some Years, young as she was, and seldom left a Man whom she had pick'd up, without robbing him of something.

The Ordinary, although hardened to criminal activities, appears to have been more than a little shocked by the stories of these women:

> Three such vile Women as Duck, Barefoot, and Gwyn, were hardly ever seen together within the Walls of Newgate; and happy perhaps may it be to many Persons now living, that they are in Time cut off, and prevented from doing more Mischief; from one Degree of Wickedness to another they had already gradually arose, and who knows in the End, had they been suffered to live, to what Height their infamous Impudence might have carried them.

The agitated cleric could not resist pointing out the terrible warning offered by these three women: 'did Men but consider what Hazard! what Dangers they run! when they pick up, or suffer themselves to be pick'd up by such vile Women; surely none in their Senses would ever attempt it'.

The prospect of violent, predatory and lawless females haunting the streets of London, and using sexual enticement to ensnare their gullible victims, provoked the prison chaplain to offer not only warnings but tangible solutions. A 'proper Method', he insisted, must be 'put in Practice to root out of the Streets of this our grand Metropolis such drove of these Creatures we each Night see'. He suggested that . . .

> . . . instead of Watchmen sleeping away their Time, or spending their Time at some Alehouse, both which Cases are too frequent among them . . . a Supernumary Man, [be] appointed by each Parish (and 'twould be but a small Expence to each Parish) whose Business should

be to walk round (not with a Lanthorn and Staff to distinguish him, but
properly arm'd) to . . . take up every Street-Walker he sees, and carry her
to the Watch-house, or some Place of Security, and this to be done
every Night, and every Hour in the Night, not at settled Times.

This, argued the Ordinary, would ensure that 'we might walk in safety
and quietness, from and to our Habitations . . . for the good Safety and
Happiness of Mankind . . . let some one . . . improve on my Hint, or
propose a better'.

But no one did improve on the hint and nothing similar or 'better'
ever happened. No doubt for most Londoners, eminently sensible, tolerant
by nature and suspicious of private armies of any sort, the prospect of
armed 'supernumerary men' hunting the streets for prostitutes was a
cure that was potentially more troublesome than the complaint. The
anarchy of viragos like Ann Duck and her cronies was a lesser evil than a
military-style vigilante force patrolling and controlling the streets of the
capital.

THE DISORDERLY HOUSES ACT

The crimes and punishments of prostitutes like Ann Duck provoked a
piece of major legislation in the mid-eighteenth century that attempted,
at a stroke, to reduce and control vice. After promoting the Gin Act,
Henry Fielding, with his brother and fellow magistrate John, was partly
responsible for the passing in 1752 of the Disorderly Houses Act. This
was a piece of legislation that would help to transform the lives of outcast
Londoners, for although primarily intended to prevent public nuisances
and fight crime it also strengthened and clarified the law controlling and
reducing prostitution.

The Act came into effect on 1 June 1752, 'for the better preventing
Thefts and Robberies and for regulating Places of Publick Entertainment,
and punishing persons keeping Disorderly Houses'.[36] It was a response
to the widespread belief that disorderly houses were by their nature lawless
places, the breeding grounds for crime, and that the most dangerous and
infamous of disorderly houses were brothels and bawdy-houses. The Act

made it necessary for the proprietors of all places offering music and dancing to apply for a licence to a magistrate, who could refuse it if the applicant or location were notorious. Although primarily calculated to curtail thefts and robberies by closing dubious establishments, the Act did contain a clause – probably inserted by the Fieldings – to control the sex trade and bawdy-houses.

It 'required prosecution by constables and justices of persons accused of keeping bawdy-houses whenever information was provided by two inhabitants of a parish paying "scot and lot" and willing to enter into a recognisance of £20 each to produce evidence against such persons, the informers to be rewarded £10 each upon a conviction'.[37] What this meant was that two parish residents, who were also ratepayers and with the franchise and so locally eminent, could on production of evidence oblige the relevant authorities to prosecute. For their civic-mindedness each of the ratepayers would be rewarded with £10 upon a successful prosecution. So to function, this Act required the action of eminent local citizens acting as paid informers.

The Act also gave campaigning magistrates and law officers more power for it enabled constables to enter 'disorderly houses' and seize all persons found inside. But the Act did not prohibit the bailing of arrested bawdy-house keepers which meant that, as before, immediately after being charged they could be back on the streets, running their business much as usual, and perhaps punishing any of the inmates of their establishments they believed had co-operated with the authorities.

The Act was broad in its scope and immediate in its effect. The *Daily Advertiser* of 8 June 1752 reported that fifty houses around the Strand had been closed and their inhabitants 'turned Printsellers', and many of the more public haunts of prostitutes – such as notorious tea gardens run by disreputable persons that no magistrate would license – also quickly shut down.[38] The Act even – initially at least – helped to clear the streets of prostitutes, who were confused and frightened by its potential powers. A law report in The *Covent-Garden Journal* of 13 June 1752 (No. 47) reported that:

> [T]he late Act of Parliament, by which a Reward of 10l. is allowed to
> any two Inhabitants of Parishes paying Scot and Lot, for the
> Prosecution of the Keepers of Bawdyhouses . . . hath struck a most

extraordinary Panic into the lower Order of the Profession, many of whom have left their Houses; nay the Streets are reported cleared of Ladies in an Evening. It is probable, however, they will all return to their Stations by the Beginning of the Winter.[39]

The *London Daily Advertiser* of 11 June 1752 revealed that . . .

. . . since the shutting up of the Receptacles of Lewdness, and the Disappearance of the Ladies of Pleasure in the Streets, the Court End of the Town already begins to complain of the Dulness of their nocturnal Excursions, and bid adieu to Frolick and Whim on this Side of the Water. Upon this Account the Inhabitants of Lambeth are likely to be encreased with Male as well as Female Libertines.[40]

Curiously the Act applied only to Middlesex, or the north bank of the Thames, and not to Surrey in the south, making the area around Southwark a legally different entity and potentially a far more congenial habitation for bawds and their dependants.

It was not only bawds and those involved in the sex industry who were initially worried by the Disorderly Houses Act. Some observers believed it would have unanticipated and unfortunate implications that would upset the subtle balance of society and penalise those already barely surviving on the margins of London life. The *Daily Advertiser* of 19 June reported a plan being set in motion by a 'Set of Gentlemen' to give support to young girls who 'have been deluded by different Stratagems to give up their Virtue' and become prostitutes whose distress may have been increased by the recent Act of Parliament.[41]

At about the same time John Campbell, under the name of M. Ludovicus, penned a pamphlet entitled *A Particular but Melancholy Account of the Great Hardships, Difficulties and Miseries, that those Unhappy and Much-to-be-pitied Creatures, the Common Women of the Town, are Plung'd into at this Juncture* (1752). In it he argued that 'the late severe Edict issued forth against the unfortunate Fair Ones' would be counter-productive, and suggested that 'better Regulations might be made with regard to these unhappy Women, than by hurrying and driving them from one Place to another'. If the women were diseased this movement and dispersal would prove fatal to them 'for such Proceedings, instead of diminishing, will only increase the Distemper'.[42] 'How many of these

despised Women have made away with themselves since the Commencement of the late act?' he observed. 'Some of them have hang'd themselves,
some have been drag'd out of Rosamond's Pond.'[43]

Henry Fielding's *Covent-Garden Journal* of 23 June 1752 (No. 50)
carried a letter signed Humphry Meanwell that many at the time
assumed was written by Fielding himself or that at least reflected his
views. This was a reasonable assumption to make but, if true, the content
of the letter compromised Fielding's position as a magistrate and was
inconsistent with his role in the promotion of the then three-week-
old Act. It suggested that the 'late Act against loose Women and Houses
of ILL Fame' was unfair to prostitutes and warned that 'if this present
Act against Lewdness be carried on with the same Rigour it seems to
have been hitherto . . . I apprehend many ill Consequences will arise
from it and that the Remedy will be infinitely more fatal than the
Disease complained of'. The anonymous author of the letter suggested
that since constables now had the power to search houses where
suspected 'women of ill character are lodged', more such women would
be arrested and imprisoned and be victims of, and spread, contagious
distempers.

> [W]hat is to become of these . . . unhappy Wretches . . . when the Time
> of their Imprisonment expires? Must they not return to their former
> Courses for Bread, or must they not inevitably become Beggars, and so
> increase the prodigious Numbers that throng the streets already? . . . a
> case most terrible and shocking to happen in a country of Christians.

The author was also worried by 'another Inconvenience arising from
this Law' that would only make a bad situation worse. He objected to
the fact that the Act gave more power to constables and pointed to 'the
insolent Behaviour that honest sober Persons frequently meet with [by]
being laid hold off and dragged to the Round-house by some . . . dirty
fellows under a Pretence of their being disorderly Persons'. The author
concluded that prosecution and repression were not the best solutions to
the question of prostitution.

> In other Nations . . . certain places are allotted and tolerated for the
> Entertainment of Women who are kept under Regulations, and are
> always at the Service of such Customers as are disposed to deal with

them . . . The utter Extirpation of Women of Pleasure or of the Town
. . . is impracticable and . . . would produce Irregularities of ten Times
more criminal and odious Tendency.[44]

This letter and Fielding's supposed authorship – or at least sponsor-
ship – caused something of a stir. As a magistrate and public representative of government legislation he had to be careful, and certainly could
not afford to be perceived as an apologist for prostitution or a defender
of bawdy-houses. He had already been accused of being in the pay of
bawdy-house owners for his role in the 1749 trial and execution of Bosavern
Penlez who had been charged with taking part in an attack on a bawdy-
house and convicted of theft (see page 40), and in 1751 was once again
accused of being in cahoots with the sex trade because he'd failed in his
Enquiry into the Causes of the Late Increase of Robbers to identify prostitution as a key cause of crime.

This omission, suggesting Fielding had at the very least a benign
tolerance of prostitutes, provoked a series of hostile publications. One
pamphlet of 1751, entitled *A Letter to Henry Fielding Esq.*[45] and signed Philo-
Patria, complained, 'I am surprised, you should not have added one Section
more, how to suppress debauchery among the lower kind of People.'[46]
For Philo-Patria 'infamous women' were 'the very Fountain-heads, whence
Robbery originally Springs',[47] and he made the direct association between
prostitution and robbery by pointing out that . . .

. . . when the late unhappy Mr Maclain was apprehended, an infamous
woman was found in his Lodging . . . the poor low Rogue . . . he has no
sooner got a little Money, but he resorts to those Houses, which are
frequented by lewd Women . . . Every Robber . . . has some farther
View in getting Money . . . which is evidently . . . to spend it on
Debauchery . . . The only way to extirpate . . . notorious Robbers . . .
is to prevent Debauchery, to rid the great Metropolis of lewd and
infamous women; who most certainly are the Engines, that set them to
Work.

The 'low rogue' referred to was the once-famed James Maclain, the
'gentleman highwayman' who was hanged at Tyburn in October 1750 and
seems to have modelled his life on that of Macheath from *The Beggar's
Opera*. The punishment suggested for the inflammatory 'lewd women' by

Philo-Patria was a trifle less severe: 'when they are convicted, let them be transported; this is the only Way to get rid of them'.[48]

Fielding's decision not to emphasise the connection between certain types of prostitution and crimes such as street robbery or burglary in his 1751 *Enquiry* is odd, especially since in his *True State of the Case of Bosavern Penlez* of 1749 he had pointed out that 'lewd and disorderly houses' were a 'Nuisance . . . to the Public' and incitements to crime.[49] These general rumblings of discontent and rumours about possible bribes from the sex industry made Fielding realise that as an eminent law-enforcer he now had to act quickly and firmly to make his position crystal clear.

This he did in an article in the *Covent-Garden Journal* of 1 August 1752 (No. 57) in which he referred to the letter in the 23 June issue 'that seemed to condemn the too rigorous Prosecution of Women of Pleasure' and by which 'I have obtained a Character among those Ladies and their Abettors of which I am not very ambitious [so that] the Rakes and Harlots of the Town begin to regard me as their Well-wisher'. Fielding suggested that, as a result of this mistaken attribution, he was 'the reigning Toast of all the Ladies at Jenny D—s's [Mother Douglas'] and 'a Fair one who signs herself MARI MURRAIN tells me I am a hearty cock and declares . . . she is ready to rub down my old Back any Time without a Present'. The harlot's supposed name – in French meaning approximately 'diseased husband' – suggests that Fielding shared the common dread of whores as spreaders of contagion, while her offer to treat him like a horse remains open to interpretation.

But while making it clear that he was no champion of the sex industry, Fielding also conceded that punishments commonly imposed on convicted prostitutes were hard and generally counter-productive. 'Nor am I,' he wrote, 'a Well-wisher to the Punishment of Bridewell [which] is a School rather for the Improvement than for the Correction of Debauchery'. But on the other hand Fielding had to 'plainly confess that I cannot agree with those who look on a common W—e, as any very great, or very amiable Character . . . for me the modest Girl under a Basket of Oysters attracts more Respect, than the Punk [prostitute] in her Coach and Six'. Fielding 'in serious truth' argued that prostitutes were 'the lowest and meanest . . . the basest, vilest and wickedest of all Creatures' who, in hiring out their bodies, not only 'descend below the Dignity of Human Nature, and partake the Office of a Beast' but in fact debase themselves . . .

... below the Animal Creation, where no such baseness is known ... To prostitute herself for Hire, to give up the Freedom of Choice, to sin against Nature and Inclination, to receive into her Embraces a Wretch whom she must loath and despise. To defile herself with Age, Ugliness, Impotency, Disease, with a long etc. of Filth, too odious to be mentioned. To do, to suffer all this for the sake of Lucre, is the Property only (I blush when I say it) of the Fairest and Lovliest of all terrestrial Beings.

And the 'Contagion' they spread ...

... extends not only to an innocent Wife, but like the divine Vengeance, to the Children of the third and fourth generation ... I think the Trade of a Prostitute can scarcely be called either a reputable or an innocent calling ... nor ... are they to be tolerated, nay even encouraged, on account of some Good which they produce [but they] in great Propriety of Speech ... deserve the Name of an Evil.[50]

As journalistic copy this was red hot and the article must have seared a path through the taverns and bagnios of Covent Garden. It certainly left no room for ambiguity about Fielding's public stance and attitude towards prostitutes. From a magistrate it was a stern declaration of intent, a warning that he would use the full force of the new law against sexual offenders. And in 1752 the power Fielding wielded was impressive for he was not just an influential playwright and novelist, a prolific journalist and social reformer, but since 1748 had been one of London's first stipendiary or salaried magistrates, employed directly by the Secretary of State. From his bench in Bow Street, Covent Garden he exercised authority tempered with compassion and honesty. He had besides in 1750 founded – with his brother John – a body of constables who became known as the Bow Street Runners. These constables were unlike any others operating in the metropolis. They didn't patrol the streets, or at least not initially, but formed a trained, honest, efficient and able body of criminal investigators at the bidding of the Fieldings. They were London's first professional detective force and a very effective example of preventative policing because their efficiency discouraged some criminals from even attempting crimes.[51]

Henry Fielding was therefore a power in the city, but did his robust public attack on prostitutes reflect his true feelings for these women, some of whom he had numbered among his close companions when in his youth? What were his private thoughts about the women of London's valuable sex industry?

Fielding's many disparate activities – magistrate, reformer, novelist and playwright – suggest that the authoritarian attitude aired in the *Covent-Garden Journal* was assumed as part of a wider strategy to retain the power he needed to do good. He might, as the article makes clear, have viewed some prostitutes as corrupt, corrupting, cynical and diseased predators. But this was only half the story. Others, and at other times, he viewed with great sympathy, revealing that he understood the causes of their plight, recognised them as vulnerable victims of abuse, and determined to use the law to help them as best he could. Certainly records make clear that he was most sympathetic to those prostitutes brought before his bench he believed to be deserving of sympathy and who might respond to assistance – especially if they were young, pretty and seemingly still not corrupted by wickedness and willing to reform themselves!

A number of these cases were recorded in The *Covent-Garden Journal*. For example, the edition of 11 January 1752 stated that:

> [O]n Tuesday night, Mr Carne, the High Constable of Westminster, with a Warrant from Justice Fielding stormed a notorious Bawdy-House at the Back-side of St Clements, and brought the Master of the House with . . . four young Women, before the said Justice. One of these Girls who seemed younger and less abandoned than the rest was fixed on as a proper Person to give Evidence against the others [and] being assured of never becoming again subject to her late severe Task-Master, she revealed all the Secrets of her late Prison-House [and] acts of Prostitution . . . The Master of the House was committed to Gaol . . . Three of the Women were sent to Bridewell whence they shall return, if possible, worse than they went thither, and the young Girl was recommended by the Justice to the Parish of St Clements to be passed to her settlement in Devonshire. She was very pretty, under 17 years of age, and had been 3 Years by her own confession upon the Town.[52]

Two weeks later he showed similar empathy when a child prostitute named Mary Parkington came before him. She had been taken in a bawdy-house and Fielding described her as 'a very beautiful Girl of sixteen years of Age' who had been seduced, abandoned and then 'decoyed' into a bawdy-house where she was imprisoned, threatened and 'prostituted . . . for Hire' (see page 40). He lamented her unhappy story and regretted that 'as the Law now stands' the expense in time and money was too great to bring her tormentors to justice. He wished the law would be changed so that . . .

> . . . the Keepers of these Houses would be at least afraid of committing such dreadful Outrages, and of driving Youth, Beauty and Modesty (for this Girl was possessed of all three) headlong to the Ruin both of Body and Soul; and not permitting them to quit the Ways of Vice, tho' ever so desirous.[53]

The consequences of the 1752 Act were not as dramatic – in either direction – as many had initially assumed or prophesied. This was partly because the more exclusive and discreet brothels with rich and influential clients were far from 'disorderly houses' and so remained beyond the reach – indeed beyond the interest – of the law, so for them it remained business as usual. By October 1754 Henry Fielding was dead and so a valuable judge of the Act's true worth was lost. But his able assistant and high constable of Holborn, Saunders Welch (see page 27), continued the battle to rid London of vice and in 1758 published a document that throws much light on the city's sex industry in the years immediately after the 1752 Act.

Welch was more certain than Fielding – or, at least, more vociferous – about the strong links between street robbery and street prostitution, and he also, like Fielding, saw architecture – or rather architectural decay, jerry-building and unregulated and ruthless landlords ruling slum areas – as among the prime causes of misery, immorality and crime in the city. His *Proposal to Render Effectual a Plan to Remove the Nuisance of Common Prostitutes from the Streets of this Metropolis* of 1758 makes it clear that if bawdy-houses had been reduced in number thanks to the 1752 Act, street prostitution had not. After a brief initial scare street-walkers were back in business with a vengeance. In the *Proposal* Welch included a *Letter*, written by himself in 1753, 'on the cause of the increase of robberies and murders in London'. This refers to, supports, and to a degree adds substance to Henry Fielding's far more famous 1751 *Enquiry into the Causes of the Late Increase of Robbers*. It seems that Welch was, with these writings, consciously taking up his dead mentor's moral message and campaign.

Saunders Welch, the high constable of Holborn and friend and colleague of Henry Fielding, who, in the mid-eighteenth century, toiled hard to free London's streets of crime and prostitution.

Welch's initial target for moral condemnation was large indeed – in fact, it included most of the population of London: 'The grand spring of the whole [problem] may perhaps be with some degree of justice ascribed to the irreligion, idleness, almost total want of morals, and dissoluteness of manners of the common people.'[54] Having launched this general attack he got down to some more interesting and informative detail:

> There have, within a few years, arisen in the out-skirts of this town, a kind of traffic in old ruinous buildings, which the occupiers fill up with straw and flock-beds, which they nightly let out at two-pence for a single person, or three-pence for a couple; nor is the least regard paid to decency. Men and women are promiscuously entertained; and in my searches after villains, I have found two or three couples in one room, who were perhaps strangers to each other before the preceding night, then in bed together. Indeed I have seen debauchery in these houses carried farther than this; for sometimes two women have been in bed with one man, and two men with one woman.[55]

The reason for this multi-occupation of beds was not, primarily at least, a decline in public morality or rampant promiscuity but simple and basic economics. The price of a bed in a common-lodging house in the 1750s was around twopence a night for a single bed and threepence for a double or multi-occupied bed. The financial advantages of bed-sharing were very significant for people with little money – they were the difference between a bed or no bed, between food or no food.

Welch piled on the agony, growing indignant about the slum dwellers' way of life rather than distressed by the state of affairs that obliged his fellow creatures to live in so desperate a manner:

> Four or five beds are often in one room; and what with the nastiness of these wretches, and their numbers, such an inconceivable stench has arose from them, that I have been hardly able to bear it the little time my duty required my stay. Spirituous liquors afford means of intoxication for the wretches here received; and the houses are kept open all night to entertain rogues and receive plunder. Great numbers of desperate villains have been taken out of these houses and executed. One woman occupies, in the parish of St Giles's, near twenty of these houses. Black-boy Alley abounds with them ... Shoreditch has also numbers of them.[56]

The doss house or common-lodging house – *bête noire* of nineteenth-century London reformers – was already a significant part of the urban land-scape of those areas that were to become the notorious slums of Victorian London. Within Shoreditch was the Old Nichol, just north of Spitalfields and east of Shoreditch High Street, which was composed of small terraces of wide-windowed weavers' houses and that, by the 1890s, became one of the most desperate slums in the city. It was, it seems, within this area that Welch and his constables were prowling in the early 1750s. Welch offered more detail about his Shoreditch experiences:

> A few years ago I assisted Mr Henry Fielding in taking from under one roof upwards of seventy lodgers of both sexes. Suppose the number of these houses to be only two hundred, and compute only twenty persons to a house, the number is 4000; and, much I fear, not one fourth could obtain a just character of honesty and industry; the rest consisting of rotten whores, pick-pockets, pilferers and others of more desperate denominations. What evils are the Public not liable to from such a villainous mixture as this?[57]

It's interesting to compare this somewhat hysterical and unforgiving view with Fielding's more humane account of the same incident. In his *Enquiry into the Causes of the Late Increase of Robbers* of 1751 Fielding recounted his and Welch's adventures in St Giles and Shoreditch[58] and observed that legislation was needed to respond to the great 'probability' of escape enjoyed by thieves, a condition that clearly encouraged people to turn their hand to robbery. One of the chief means of escape was, noted Fielding, London's slums, which, with their narrow streets and criminal-ised common-lodging houses, made the pursuit and detection of escaping thieves near impossible and even dangerous. It was while pondering a solution to this problem that he explored the slums in the parish of St Leonard's, Shoreditch with Welch, probably in 1750 or 1751. He noted the 'two little houses [that] were emptied of near seventy Men and Women',[59] but Fielding's heart was touched instead of hardened by the experience. It was discovered that the money found on all the occupants 'did not amount to one shilling', with the exception of a girl – 'one of the prettiest . . . I have ever seen', remembered Fielding – who turned out to be a thief who had robbed her mistress.[60]

St Leonard's, Shoreditch, rebuilt during the 1730s in an area where silk weavers were being replaced by slum dwellers. When Fielding and Welch visited in around 1750 they were shocked by what they saw.

Unlike Welch, Fielding was clearly not blinded by moral indignation. He also noted one of the chief causes of the predicament of these people. In both houses gin was being sold at a penny a quartern. Cheap gin and the social and moral consequences of mass drunkenness were particular hobby horses of his. Contemplating the melancholic scene of St Giles depicted in Hogarth's *Gin Lane* – decaying and filthy houses, a ragged cowering crowd, probably mostly hung-over or still gin-fuddled – Fielding knew that these people were the true victims of the drunken and criminalised world to which poverty condemned them. He got the cause and effect right. It was because they were poor and miserable that they got drunk and turned to lives of crime and immorality, rather than being poor and debauched because they got drunk. Being trapped in such inhumane conditions of 'stench, vermin and want' could, observed Fielding, drive anyone to crime and debauchery and destroy 'all Morality, Decency and Modesty'. As Jonas Hanway observed at the time, the poor had only two pleasures, 'drink and sexual intercourse', and of the two they much preferred the former because it was a more sure and longer-lasting escape from misery. The wonder, to Fielding, was the fact 'that we have not a thousand more Robbers than we have; indeed that all these wretches are not thieves must give us either a very high Idea of their Honesty or a very mean one of their Capacity and Courage'.[61]

The difference in the way Fielding and Welch viewed the same scene, and the lessons they extracted from it, reveals most clearly the differing natures of the two men. Fielding displayed compassion and human understanding – with not a little ironic wit – and marvelled that such desperate conditions did not turn more people to a life of crime. Welch simply wanted to control and penalise the already brutalised and criminalised poor, without searching too hard for the causes of their distress and conduct or attempting to tackle the problem at its root. Indeed the punishments he suggested in his 1758 *Proposal* were draconian and a significant increase on those introduced by the 1752 Disorderly Houses Act. He suggested that keepers of bawdy-houses, their agents and servants, on conviction, should be transported for seven years 'according to the laws made for transporting felons'. Justices of the Peace were to be given the power to gather constables 'or other parish officers' to 'take oath from them about suspected bawdy-house' then have powers of entry and inspection. If evidence confirmed a building's use as a bawdy-house, the Justice should be able to shut it down. In other words they should be empowered forcibly to enter a private dwelling place if their paid parish officers – the constables – swore that it was a bawdy-house, and on the 'evidence' these men produced simply close it. Clearly, even if well-intentioned, such levels of power would threaten civil liberties and be open to abuse.

Bawdy-houses and their keepers obviously exasperated Welch – they exploited both prostitutes and the weaknesses of humanity in order to maximise their profits. When it came to the prostitutes themselves, he was more ambivalent. On the one hand he soundly berated common prostitutes as the cause of robberies and pointed out that 'little needs be said to prove that these wretches, who are lurking at every corner of our streets, are an intolerable nuisance [who] by their open prostitution make sin cheap'.[62] But Welch also recognised that they were often their own worst enemies, the victims of abuse and, with reason, more objects of compassion than of contempt. In this he reflects, accurately and poignantly, the general confusion of attitudes towards prostitutes, who were at one and the same time seen as predators and victims of the sex industry, both abused and the means of abuse. So while calling them 'wretches', he also describes them as 'those unhappy creatures who having neither a house to shelter them, nor protector to support them are under a necessity of wandering up and down the streets to make a prey of the unwary apprentice, and intoxicated husband'.[63] The bodies of this class of prostitute were, stated a clearly appalled Welch, 'generally a complication of disorders'.

For Welch, the most direct and dramatic connection between these street prostitutes and street robberies was not the fact that prostitutes enticed clients into locations where they could be easily robbed by their bullies, but the fact that they seduced apprentices into 'criminal converse, which generally leads to pilfering from his master', to loss of position, character, and thence the road to crime and ultimate ruin. As for the prostitute herself, Welch saw little hope for her unless society as a whole made greater efforts to help. Women could be sent to a Bridewell or, if diseased, to a Lock Hospital, but upon release or discharge from either they would, without 'recommendation or honest method of supporting themselves', through 'necessity, united to a mind abandoned to debauchery', be driven to 'their former practices for support'. This worried Welch greatly. Like many of his fellows, he regarded prostitutes with a peculiar mix of loathing, pity, and perhaps not a little lust:

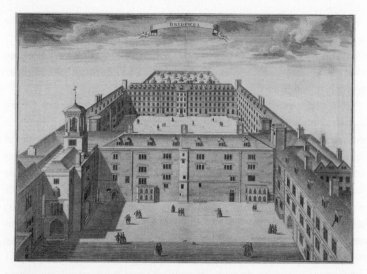

Bridewell Prison as it was in 1750. It was situated south of Fleet Street at its junction with Ludgate Hill. Built originally as a palace for Henry VIII, Bridewell became a gaol in 1558, its name becoming synonymous with 'prison' throughout England and Ireland.

I have often wished with an aching heart, that there was [a hospital] to receive and provide labour for these true objects of compassion, as well as detestation . . . whereby these unhappy fellow-creatures might be rescued from disease and misery and instead of being a nuisance to the Public, become useful to it, and prevent the ruin of thousands.[64]

The creation of just such a refuge for penitent prostitutes became a public issue in London in 1758 (see page 282) and Welch's *Proposal* contains his own vision for such an institute. He suggested that a subscription be opened to raise money from the public to erect a hospital for the 'reception' – or rather confinement – of prostitutes, and the orphan and deserted children of the poor. Welch proposed that anyone subscribing £50 or over could be made a governor for life, and envisaged a regime within the institution that would be fair but tough. He suggested that if three of the Governors agreed then 'any prostitute, who shall have been so committed . . . [and who] manifest[s] an abandoned disposition, by frequent swearing, cursing, indecent behaviour, or by being guilty of frequent misdemeanours

. . . or being idle and negligent in their respective labour, quarrelling, or making waste in her work or provisions', should be liable for 'reasonable corporal punishment', and any woman who made a fuss after 'receiving such reasonable correction or punishment' and continued in 'her abandoned behaviour' was to be transported for seven years.[65]

The 'Hospital' proposed by Welch was to have two parts, 'one for the reception of penitent prostitutes, which in good policy should be made rather the object of desire, as an agreeable retreat from temptation, than of dread, as a place of punishment'.[66] This should be the resort of those prostitutes 'who might be desirous to quit their miserable situation'. The other part of the Hospital was for those prostitutes 'apprehended in their crimes'[67], and who were unrepentant or unreformed. Their lodgings in the 'Hospital', and the regime imposed upon them, was designed 'to render their confinement in the eyes of the vulgar a kind of punishment'. These women were to be isolated in confinement, both to punish them and to ensure that their rebellious or dissolute attitude did not spread like a contagious disease. To this end Welch specified that 'any communication between this part and that allotted for the reception of the orphan and deserted children, ought to be rendered absolutely impracticable', which would have meant that confined and unrepentant prostitutes had no access to their children – an action that could, of course, have done more harm than good.

These prostitutes 'apprehended for their crimes' were to be incarcerated for a year, but could be released earlier if their conduct became virtuous and industrious and they were selected by a house-keeper looking for a servant. If the reformed prostitute remained free from trouble and from contact with the sex industry for one year then Welch recommended that she should be given a reward of two guineas – exactly the sum a middle-ranking prostitute could expect to make from one brief liaison. Such a modest sum was hardly an incentive to pursue a life of chastity! Welch's proposals were not taken up but when a competing scheme – the Magdalen House for Penitent Prostitutes – was successfully launched in 1758, he soon became a subscriber (see page 284).

Another perspective on the aftermath of the 1752 Disorderly Houses Act is offered by Sir John Fielding, who took over the bench at Bow Street when his brother Henry was obliged to retire. Sir John tended to view all prostitutes as the victims of cruel seducers and conniving bawds and in 1758 drew up *A Plan for a Preservatory and Reformatory for the*

Benefit . . . of Penitent Prostitutes. In April 1763 he addressed the Westminster Grand Jury and suggested that 'public lewdness' on the street – in particular sexual intercourse – was decreasing: 'as this offence belongs to none but the most abandoned mind, I thank God it is not common'.

But Fielding also made it clear that common bawdy-houses, the supposed sinks of iniquity, were far from obliterated by the 1752 Act. He recognised that they served some beneficial function in helping to get sex off the streets – 'they are the receptacles of those who still have some sense of shame left, but not enough to preserve their innocence' – but ultimately attacked 'open, avowed, low and common bawdy-houses' because they were continuing to undermine not only the morals of individuals but also the morale of the nation. These were places, argued Sir John, 'where vice is rendered cheap and consequently within reach of the common people, who are the very stamina of the constitution'.[68]

Sir John Fielding – the 'blind beak' – presiding at the Bow Street Police Court. This print, from the Newgate Calendar, *dates from 1795, fifteen years after Fielding's death.*

He suggested why the 1752 Act had failed to rid London of 'low and common bawdy-houses' during evidence he gave in 1770 to a House of Commons Committee pondering the policing of the metropolis. He identified the 'great number of brothels and irregular taverns' being 'carried on without licence from the Magistrate' as a 'great cause of robberies, burglaries, and other disorders', and explained quite simply that they were 'difficult to be suppressed by prosecution for want of evidence'.[69] Constables had the power to enter suspect houses, but if all incriminating evidence had been removed when they eventually gained entry through locked and barred doors (as described by William Hickey when entering a Covent Garden tavern in the 1760s – see page 239) then there was no case to prosecute. Sir John also complained to the committee that the very limited legal controls over street prostitutes 'not only added greatly to the diffi-culties of those Magistrates who were anxious to clear the streets, but even exposed them to vexatious prosecutions'.[70]

Little changed in the regulation of London's sex industry during the remainder of the century. Frustrated moral reformers continued to press for amendments to the 1744 Vagrancy Act in an attempt to secure legis-lation to control street prostitution, but it was not until 1822 that the Guardian Society succeeded in getting the Act altered so that a common prostitute found wandering in the public street, who could not give a satis-factory account of herself, was liable to be declared an 'idle and disorderly person' and imprisoned for up to three months on first conviction. But this amendment was found to be too extreme an alteration to the law – indeed impracticable – and in 1824 the measure relating to vagrancy was narrowed. To be a 'common prostitute' soliciting in the public street was deemed to be not enough to bring a woman within the reach of the law; she also had to behave 'in a riotous or indecent manner'.[71]

This law was quickly overtaken by the Metropolitan Police Act of 1829, which replaced the system of parish constables with the Metropolitan Police – the nation's first uniformed, wholly professional and centrally controlled city-wide police force – whose constables were empowered to apprehend 'all loose, idle and disorderly Persons whom he shall find disturbing the public Peace, or of whom he shall have just Cause to suspect of any evil Designs ... or loitering ... and not giving a satisfactory Account of themselves'.

In 1839 amendments to this Act finally outlawed soliciting in the street by stipulating that 'any common prostitute loitering or soliciting for the purposes of prostitution to the annoyance of inhabitants or passers-by' would be subject to arrest and, if convicted, to a month's imprisonment and a fine. This legislation was taken up by other police forces and was to remain for the next 120 years the basic legal weapon against street prostitutes.[72] But while street prostitution decreased from 1822, bawdy-houses, brothels and unlicensed places of public entertainment continued to operate outside the reach of the law. Indeed, they gradually increased in number if Michael Ryan (see page 34) and the arguments of the Society for the Suppression of Vice are to be believed, so that by the early decades of the nineteenth century the sex trade remained as dominant in, and as important to, London's economy as it had been a hundred years before.

THE KINDER SIDE OF THE LAW

The courts' attitude to prostitutes charged with crimes makes a fascinating study in itself. Although often harsh with repeat offenders and when dealing with crimes that involved robbery and violence, they could in other circumstances prove lenient, with juries sometimes happy to take the side of prostitutes rather than their clients. Even cases involving accusations of theft or robbery occasionally took unexpected turns.

For example, in the summer of 1725 two women – Susan Brockway and Mary Gardner – met a stranger whose name was Joseph Richmond on London Bridge and the three of them agreed to go to the Cross Keys Tavern in nearby Fish-Street Hill. The two women were evidently prostitutes, or women prepared to indulge in a little prostitution for drink or money, but something went wrong on that occasion because the events that took place in the tavern ended with Richmond calling a constable and accusing the women of robbing him.

The case came to trial at the Old Bailey and when giving evidence Richmond admitted that 'I agreed to give them a Crown apiece to—, to—, not to do them over but for them to strip naked, and show me some Tricks.' To prove he could pay for his request, Richmond showed the women some gold and they, in his version of events, grabbed it and refused to perform. In their defence the women stated that Richmond did indeed wish them to 'strip ourselves naked and show him Postures', and what's more revealed that he had produced 'a rod for him to whip us a-cross the Room, and make us Good Girls and then for us to whip him to make him a Good Boy'. They refused to co-operate and, they claimed, in response Richmond told them it would be 'worse for us if we would not do as he would have us'. When they still refused he called a constable and accused the pair of robbery.

It is gratifying that in this instance the jury took the side of the prostitutes, no doubt exasperated that a man should make such a stupid ass of himself as to attempt to use the law to avenge himself when thus disappointed.[73]

A far more curious story is told in a pamphlet published in 1791. Entitled *Modern Propensities: Or, An Essay on the Art of Strangling &c.*,[74] it contains the 'memoirs' of Susannah Hill and the summary of her trial at the Old Bailey on 12 September 1791 when she was charged with hanging Francis Kotzwarra at her lodgings in Vine Street ten days previously. The pamphlet was written anonymously but there is evidence to suggest that its author was Martin Vanbutchell, a quack physician and inventor of an aphrodisiac called the 'Balsam of Life' as well as of elastic garters.[75] If the author was Vanbutchell, it is easy to see why the case attracted his attention because the act of strangulation that featured in it, at the behest of the victim, was intended to serve as sexual stimulus. Certainly the connection between such a death and the use of aphrodisiacs establishes the author's tone and allows him to make comparisons with current methods of, and theories about, sexual enhancement including Dr Graham's famed 'marrow-melting' and available-for-hire 'Celestial Bed' (see page 561):

> If, agreeably to the improved system of generation, laid down and recommended by Dr Graham; and attested by the transcendent concurrence of Dr Katterfelto; the most robust and youthful require certain aids to ascend to the upper sphere of conjunctive transports, what must be the situation of those elderly and antiquated PEERS and COMMONERS [who] think to satisfy the desires of female youth.[76]

The 'memoirs' record that Susannah Hill followed the traditional route into prostitution. At the age of nineteen, determined to escape the 'drudgery of servitude', she made a bid for social elevation and independence that ended with her being left pregnant and abandoned. With her reputation destroyed Susannah made her way to London and soon took up prostitution as the only available means of making a living. The author evokes some powerful images of the life she and her fellow prostitutes were compelled to live in the mighty and uncaring metropolis:

> It is inconceivable what difficulties many of these wretched females denominated *girls of the town*, endure without murmuring or regret. Every day is to them a day of misery, a pitiful repetition of the same illegal contracts, yet without which they must literally starve. They are hourly subservient to the most brutal passions which imbecility can invent; and they practice manoeuvres at which human nature revolts; impelled by money, and inspirited by liquor. Amongst the number that traverse the streets, are many who had a superior education, and possess a sensibility of mind which must induce at times corroding reflections; but these retrospective views are generally obliterated by the liquid poison, before reflections become burthensome.[77]

When Susannah's trial got underway at the Old Bailey – details of her life, and of this extraordinary case, started to emerge. She was charged with murder by the Crown, who clearly wished to make a public example of her. As the Prosecuting Counsel explained to the court it was a 'melancholy truth that there were men who, to gratify the most unwarrantable species of lust, resorted to methods at which reason and morality revolted' and 'it became necessary to check the evil . . . by deterring those women who prostitute their persons for hire from becoming accessory to such shameful, such disgraceful purposes'.[78]

The man in question Francis Kotzwarra, or Franz Kocswara, had been born in Prague in 1750 and was a composer, most famously of the popular sonata the 'Battle of Prague'. But whatever his musical talents, he clearly had severe sexual and psychological problems. When Susannah gave evidence she explained that on 2 September, when she was at 51 Vine Street where she rented a front parlour, 'at between one and two o'clock a stranger knocked on her door, the street door being open. He asked her if she would like a drink. She said a little porter, he wanted brandy and water and gave her money to buy drink – also ham and beef.'

This statement reveals how Susannah and many other prostitutes of the middle rank worked. They didn't walk the streets looking for trade but merely took lodgings in a street or area with a reputation for prostitution, left the street door open, perhaps furnished with an ambiguous but inviting sign, such as 'Tender care within', and then sat back in their rooms and waited for custom.

So when Kotzwarra knocked and entered Susannah wasn't surprised or alarmed, this was what she wanted and expected. The author of the pamphlet explained that . . .

> . . . they went into a backroom, where several acts of the grossest indecency passed; in particular he pressed her to cut off the means of generation, and expressly wished to have it cut in two. But this she refused. He then said he would like to be hanged for five minutes; and while he gave her money to buy a cord, observed, that hanging would raise his passions – that it would produce all he wanted . . . she brought back two small [cords], and put them round his neck. He then tied himself up to the back parlour door; a place where he hung very low, and bending down his knees.[79]

After he had been hanging for five minutes Susannah, no doubt somewhat alarmed by then, cut the cords and Kotzwarra immediately fell to the ground. She thought he was in a fit and called on a neighbour for help then went to a publican who ran for a surgeon. When the surgeon arrived he pronounced Kotzwarra dead. The next man on the scene was a Bow Street officer who later told the court that, when he examined Kotzwarra's body, he found that it 'was covered with large and small old scars, and several fresh scratches, seemingly inflicted by an instrument'. The neighbour Elizabeth Dalton, presumably also a prostitute, gave evidence and confirmed Susannah's story, adding she ran to my room crying, '"I have hanged a man! And I am afraid he is dead."'

At this point Judge Gould halted proceedings, consulted with Counsel and then directed the jury to dismiss Susannah, who was immediately discharged. The judge also ordered the court's shorthand reporter to tear up his notes of the case, which presumably is why no record of it appears among Old Bailey records. Prosecuting Counsel had hoped to make this an exemplary case so as to discourage other prostitutes from participating in such disturbing and dangerous practices. The judge in his wisdom appears to have seen things differently. Although a prostitute, Susannah still enjoyed the protection of the law and was clearly not guilty of premeditated murder or even manslaughter but was instead a relatively innocent victim of Kotzwarra's strange 'propensities'. The judge also evidently thought it best that details of this case be suppressed, perhaps because they might encourage others to experiment. Despite his precautions, however, he failed to ensure this. The anonymous pamphlet quickly appeared, complete with an image of an ecstatically smiling Kotzwarra tying his garrotte to the chamber door while a smirking Susannah looks on, and in September 1793 the *Bon-Ton Magazine* reviewed the case and observed that 'some moments before his final exit he actually did evince some certain signs of ability, which clearly demonstrated the good effects of his expedient [to cure impotence]'. This was exactly the sort of observation Gould had hoped to avoid.

JOHN WILKES AND
AN ESSAY ON WOMAN

John Wilkes is one of the key figures in the story of London's eighteenth-century sex industry, linking so many of its apparently disparate elements in a life chequered by triumphs and setbacks to an extraordinary degree. He was intimate with the most powerful men in the land and with the most notorious harlots; he mixed with artists and writers of repute as well as libertines and wastrels of great disrepute; he moved with ease between the capital's high- and low-life. Primarily a political creature, he managed to make himself part of the ruling establishment while, by temperament, almost wildly anti-establishment, a voice of perpetual opposition to vested interests and repressive laws. In a world of corruption, peopled by placemen and self-seeking toadies, a born radical such as Wilkes was destined always to stand out. He embraced the principles of liberty, justice, tolerance and progressive change, and pursued these through political manoeuvring and trenchant journalism – in the process becoming a popular hero.

The sincerity with which Wilkes actually held his professed views is the subject of continuing debate. Some see him as a liar and cynical opportunist, believing it was easy for him to promise much when he knew that, as a marginal figure in politics, he would never be called upon to deliver. A current champion of his, Arthur H. Cash, has rebutted some of these accusations:

> [W]e often hear that Wilkes was a demagogue who was contemptuous of the mob he led. This proposition is false in all its parts. The crowds of people who followed Wilkes about . . . and sometimes rioted in his support was not a rabble . . . but a crowd of artisans, small shop-keepers, independent craftsmen and apprentices, many of whom were franchised. They were purposeful. Until Wilkes appeared they lacked leadership.[1]

*The cross-eyed and triumphant John Wilkes in May 1763, just after he
had secured his release from custody for defaming the King by claiming
parliamentary privilege. The print was made by Hogarth, who himself had
been the victim of Wilkes' savage prose. On the table lie editions 17 and 45
of Wilkes' offending journal, the North Briton. Number 45 contained the
article attacking the King for giving the 'sanction' of his 'sacred name' to
legislation Wilkes thought 'most odious', while 17 contained the article
attacking Hogarth as a 'perfectly ridiculous . . . house painter'.*

As well as being involved in politics and in promoting new ideas of
freedom for the British nation, Wilkes was also a leading figure within the
circle of England's intellectual and aristocratic elite where he rapidly earned
a reputation for wit, erudition, sexual energy and, despite his peculiar appearance, success with women. While enjoying the *entrée* this gave him to the
salons and country houses of the upper classes, he was also an acute observer
of, and indeed participant in, the activities of the upper echelons of the
London sex industry, most particularly through his association with Sir
Francis Dashwood and his circle – including Lord Sandwich – and membership of the Order of Medmenham (see page 390).

Writing was Wilkes' method of promoting his ideas, defending himself in arguments, supporting his friends and attacking his enemies. He wrote primarily political polemic but also tried his hand at criticism, producing essays on landscape, architecture and art, and most notably collaborating in the composition of a poetic pastiche that was ultimately attacked as blasphemous, obscene, libellous and politically subversive, provoking one of the most sensational legal contests of the eighteenth century. But it is Wilkes' tireless promotion of the basic rights of mankind, his attempts to reform the law and adoption by the public as their champion, that make him one of the Georgian era's most remarkable figures.

He advocated perhaps more a theory of freedom – its ideal – than any practical proposals for achieving it, but he did challenge the exercising of arbitrary authority, and in court cases instigated in 1763 finally brought to an end the evil of the General Warrant, an all-purpose legal document citing the crime and not the alleged criminals, often leading to the whole-sale arrest of innocent people without specific charges being brought. In contesting such instruments of official oppression and terror, Wilkes spoke up for the rights and liberties of the common man. In a generally unjust age when ordinary people had few high-placed spokesmen, this alone was enough to make him their champion.

St John's Gate, Clerkenwell, built in 1504 and the most substantial survivor of the medieval priory of the Knights Hospitallers. In the eighteenth century, the gate was at the heart of London's printing and journalism district. Dr Johnson worked in it, the Gentleman's Magazine *was published from it and Hogarth lived, as a child, in part of it. Wilkes was born nearby.*

John Wilkes was born in St John's Square, Clerkenwell probably in 1727, the son of a wealthy distiller. His education was completed by two years at Leyden University, where he acquired the manners and graces required of a gentleman and laid the foundation for a life-long delight in the company of vivacious harlots.[2] He returned to London, marrying Mary Meade in 1747 – an event that turned out to be one of the unhappiest in his life for he and his wife were hopelessly incompatible. As Wilkes later wrote, '[T]o please an indulgent father I married a woman half as old again as myself; of a large fortune . . . It was a sacrifice to Pluto, not to Venus . . . I stumbled at the very threshold of the temple of Hymen.'[3] Stumble or not, he and Mary managed to have a child, Polly, born in 1750, and father and daughter were devoted to one other.

Wilkes set up home with his wife's family – in Aylesbury and in Red Lion Court, London – and was thoroughly miserable in their company. For nine years, benefiting from their connections and fortune, he lived the life of a modest country gentleman when in Aylesbury, and when in London gradually lived more and more the life of an independent rake. He joined various clubs, became a Freemason, and some time in the late 1740s met Thomas Potter, son of the Archbishop of Canterbury, a rich and sophisticated landowner ten years his senior who was MP for St Germans. Potter ushered Wilkes deeper into the more exclusive realms of London's sex industry, introducing him to fashionable courtesans and their circle of rich and aristocratic clients and protectors. Thus he met Sir Francis Dashwood, Lord Sandwich, the poet Charles Churchill, and other members of the Hell Fire circle.

Potter also introduced Wilkes to the politically and financially powerful Grenville-Temple family, with their powerbase located in the vast and magnificent Stowe House, Buckinghamshire, who were in 1754 connected through marriage to the great William Pitt the Elder. The Grenvilles were Whigs. They, their policies – and their grandeur – greatly attracted Wilkes. And he, with his natural wit and eloquence, attracted them. The Grenvilles – Lord Temple in particular – encouraged his political aspirations and they became his patrons. Events moved fast. In 1754, having given up his seat in Cornwall Potter managed to get himself elected – with Wilkes' help – as MP for Aylesbury. In reward – with Lord Temple's help – Wilkes was appointed High Sheriff for Buckinghamshire.

While Potter and Wilkes shared a distinguished public life they also shared an increasingly garish, debauched – even outrageous – private one. Potter wrote to Wilkes to urge him to share the delights of his new mistress, one Miss Betty Spooner of Tunbridge, for 'you will find in her Liveliness & Lechery. The latter quality usual enough . . . the first confined to the sacred few.'[4] On another occasion Potter wrote with pride and careless disregard about sodomising a cow on Wingrove Common, an action that was a capital crime. Imagining the future preparation of volumes cataloguing his adventures, he observed with satisfaction that 'one book at least will be filled with the accounts of my amours & the cow upon Wingrove Common will certainly be an Anecdote that will draw on the Admiration of future Ages . . . I glory in what I have done. I avow it without being cow'd.'[5]

During his intimate companionship with Wilkes, Potter developed another friendship – one that had something about it of a father-son relationship. This was with the wealthy land and quarry owner Ralph Allen who lived in a magnificent mansion – Prior Park – on a hill overlooking Bath. Allen was a friend of Henry Fielding (who used him as one of his models for Squire Allworthy in *Tom Jones*), as well as a patron of artists and architects such as John Wood, who designed not only Prior Park for

A nineteenth-century print showing Alexander Pope (left), Ralph Allen (centre) and William Warburton (right) seated in the portico of Prior Park, with Bath Abbey in the distance.

Allen but also much of Bath for a variety of landowners. Allen developed a fondness for Potter who was often in Bath taking the waters for his ever-deteriorating health, and at Prior Park in the mid-1750s Potter met the Rev. Dr William Warburton who was married to Allen's niece, adopted daughter and heir, Gertrude Tucker.

Potter took an increasing dislike to Warburton, not least because of what he perceived to be the cleric's coarse-grained sense of self-promotion and tireless ambition. One of the things that particularly annoyed him was the way in which Warburton constantly republished editions of Alexander Pope's *Essay on Man*. Pope had willed the rights of this work to Warburton so he could do with it as he liked. To Potter's disgust, the clergyman used this mini-masterpiece to promote himself. Each fresh edition was packed with long notes by Warburton that all but swamped Pope's verses and even included an 'Advertisement' in which the cleric imposed upon the reader his own sanctimonious views on Pope's *Essay*.

But rather than suffering public ridicule or any setback to his overweening ambitions, Warburton rose relentlessly. His combination of self-advertisement and flattery coupled with laboriously acquired learning seemed to work. He not only married the vivacious eighteen-year-old heiress Gertrude, who was twenty-eight years his junior, but eventually became Dean then Bishop of Gloucester.[6] However, Potter had a plot in hand to punish this upstart and charmless cleric. First he seduced Gertrude, who early in 1756 gave birth to a son. It soon became common knowledge that the father was not Warburton. At about the same time as the affair started, probably late in 1754, Potter started to write a parody of Pope's *Essay on Man*, complete with copious notes credited to Warburton, which he entitled *An Essay on Woman*.

It was, compositionally, a straightforward affair and mildly diverting. Potter took the structure and rhythm of Pope's work and much of its text, altering certain passages to make them obscene and cramming in as many rude words as humanly possible. The underlying message was simple: Warburton in his unbridled ambition was as obscene as this adulterated text.

Soon after Potter started writing his version of the *Essay*, Wilkes became involved. As Arthur H. Cash explains, a partnership soon evolved with 'Potter doing the writing [and] Wilkes making critical comments and changing this and that detail',[7] probably also writing all the preliminary text and the final verses, entitled *'Veni Creator*: or, The Maid's Prayer'.

This work was the part of the *Essay* most calculated to offend humourless and earnest Christians such as Warburton, who would most certainly see it as a work of blasphemy. Its title was inspired by a familiar hymn, '*Veni Creator Spiritus*', and it scandalously juxtaposed a female joy in sex – in the form of an adulatory prayer to the penis – with references to Christian imagery:

> Creator Pego, by whose Aid,
> Thy humble Supplicant was made;
> O Source of Bliss and God of Love,
> Shed the influence from above . . .
> On Thee all Day and Night I call,
> Great promis'd Comforter to All;
> Martyrs and Prophets have of old
> Thy wond'rous Energy foretold . . .
> Come, pour thy Joys on Womankind,
> Be all my Frame to Thee resign'd,
> And, Oh! Thou rul'st a willing Mind!
> From loathed Hymen set me free,
> Enter a Temple worthy Thee . . .
> Immortal Honour, endless Fame,
> Almighty Pego! To thy Name;
> And Equal Adoration be
> Paid to the neighb'ring Pair with Thee,
> Thrice blessed Glorious Trinity![8]

And that, for the time being, was that. Wilkes and Potter must have enjoyed their scandalous little production, both seeing it as a pleasing and perhaps cathartic lampoon of the hated Warburton. Wilkes might also have seen it as something more. To him these sexually explosive and challenging verses could well have appeared a most gratifying expression of his deep-rooted desire to subvert a self-satisfied, oppressive and hypocritical society as personified by Warburton. Quite what happened next we do not know. No doubt Wilkes and Potter showed their manuscript to a few close friends and then put it away and got on with life in the wider world. Potter pursued his affair with Gertrude but in 1759 finally succumbed to his many ailments and died. Wilkes devoted himself to politics and journalism.

In 1757, perhaps in a last gesture of friendship, Potter offered to resign his seat at Aylesbury in favour of Wilkes. He took the pocket borough of Oakhampton instead and Wilkes had to pay around £7,000 for the honour of serving the people of Aylesbury, but had at last achieved a great ambition – he was in Parliament.[9] Things were not to work out for Wilkes there as he had hoped, however, for influential friends in high places – including those he had seen in most intimate circumstances during the revels of the Medmenham-based Hell Fire Club – failed speedily to find him a place in government.

Faced with this impasse, the thrustingly ambitious and ever-resourceful Wilkes chose to further his cause by concentrating on political journalism. On 5 June 1762 he produced the first issue of his radical weekly the *North Briton*, financed at least in part by his long-term patron, habitual intriguer and political *éminence grise* Lord Temple. And so, with the creation of Wilkes' own weekly organ, the worlds of radical journalism, politics and sex came into collision with, eventually, calamitous effect.

The launch of the *North Briton* was prompted by the resignation in October 1761 of William Pitt – Temple's brother-in-law and one of Wilkes' early political mentors – and the arrival in June 1762 of the Scottish aristocrat the Earl of Bute to head the government. This change of leadership effectively brought Wilkes' hopes of a government position to a speedy termination. As long as Bute was in political power, Wilkes would not be. So far as Wilkes was concerned, Bute had to go – and as quickly as possible.

Bute was an easy target. He was an inexperienced and uncertain politician, he was a Scotsman – not a popular thing to be in mid-eighteenth-century England – and he was committed to the support of a foreign policy that enraged much of the public. In accord with the wishes of George III, Bute's primary goal was to bring the Seven Years War to a speedy end. But many observers thought the terms being agreed with France were unacceptable and so opposed the peace and Bute was popularly perceived to be no more than a royal lackey. Thus the ever-opportunistic Wilkes had all the material he needed to increase Bute's misery.

The *North Briton* opposed the peace, it opposed Bute, and playing to popular prejudice it also opposed – or at least mocked – all things Scottish. Indeed the very title of the journal suggested, in satirical spirit,

The Earl of Bute, who, in the 1760s, was First Lord of the Treasury, close friend of Princess Augusta and enemy of John Wilkes.

that its role was to keep a wary eye on Scotland, for 'North Briton' was a name mid-eighteenth-century English patriots used for an inhabitant of the country of which many still harboured a deep suspicion. The Jacobites had come too close to overrunning England in 1745 to be easily forgotten or forgiven, and Scotland's long-time affinity with England's traditional enemy – France – didn't help. Nor did the success in London after 1745 of the large numbers of hard-working and well-educated Scotsmen attracted to the capital. Indeed many Englishmen would have agreed with Dr Johnson's reply when in 1763 James Boswell told him he couldn't help being Scottish: 'That,' said Johnson with mighty disdain, 'is what a great many of your countrymen cannot help.'[10] In addition, the journal's title was a witty riposte to a periodical called the *Briton* that had recently been launched by Bute himself to promote his anti-war policies (and that was edited by Smollett).

The first issue of the *North Briton* – written anonymously (as was the custom with most journals at the time) – sought to undermine peace negotiations with France and have Bute replaced as First Lord of the Treasury by Pitt, who since October 1761 had been ennobled as Lord Chatham. Following editions – written mostly by Wilkes, with Charles Churchill acting as editor and resident poet – attacked and mocked many powerful establishment and government figures as well as government policies. And then in issue No.5, published on 3 July 1762, Wilkes targeted the Royal Family itself. In this issue he implied a comparison between the court of George III and that of Edward III. In a sly, indirect but unmistakable manner – and with much use of irony – Wilkes suggested that in the same way as Edward's mother Isabella had ruled England in alliance with her lover Roger de Mortimer, George's mother – the dowager Princess Augusta – was in reality ruling England with Lord Bute.

Wilkes concluded his historic homily in ringing tones and in language charged with sexual imagery by referring back to the reign of Edward:

> O may Britain never see such a day again! when power acquired by
> profligacy may lord it over this realm; when the feeble pretensions of a
> *court minion* may require the prostitution of royalty for their support; or
> if, which heaven avert! such a day should come, may a Prince truly
> jealous of the honour of his House . . . crush the aspiring wretch who
> mounts to power by such ignoble means.[11]

A topical satirical print from the early 1760s, incorporating a reference to the
assumed intimate relations between the dowager Princess Augusta and
the Earl of Bute. The two are represented by a bell-like petticoat enveloping
a boot – an obvious pun upon Bute's name.

This only slightly veiled accusation was intended to shock and it did – indeed it was slow-burning dynamite. The *North Briton* was suggesting – apparently out of loyalty to the King – that Princess Augusta was the mistress of her son's First Lord of the Treasury, Lord Bute, and that together they had usurped the rule of the nation. At once George III was cast as stupid and weak, his mother as a strumpet, and Bute as a dangerous and conniving villain. These were astonishingly dangerous imputations to make but, to the surprise of many, nothing happened. No attempt was made to suppress the *North Briton*; Wilkes was not immediately arrested nor was he made the target of an assassination attempt as his friend and co-editor Churchill feared would be the case.[12]

One consequence of the authorities' decision not to act against Wilkes was the failure to test the accusation against Princess Augusta and Lord Bute in a public forum. They were certainly close and it was common gossip that their relationship was more intimate than was proper. Augusta, aged only forty-four, was still an attractive woman famed for her fine legs, and Bute, her son's former tutor, was a handsome man and a long-time member of the royal household. Augusta and Bute – who had long been married to the heiress daughter of Lady Mary Wortley Montagu – seemed to have much in common, and certainly shared a love of archi-tecture and gardening. Together they transformed the royal pleasure grounds at Kew – which had been a favoured home of the Princess and her late husband Frederick, Prince of Wales – into a world-famous botan-ical garden. It was Bute who suggested in 1759 that Kew should contain examples of 'all the plants known on earth', and by following this advice Augusta became in effect the founder of Kew Gardens.

When suggesting this ambitious aim for Kew, Bute might simply have had in mind the creation of a picturesque Garden of Eden, but ultim-ately the pursuit of this idea through the later eighteenth century – particularly by George III and Joseph Banks – led the Royal Gardens into the field of scientific research and economic botany that involved the collection and propagation of valuable foreign plants for eventual exploitation in British colonies. Kew, described by one contemporary as 'the Paradise of the World where all plants are found',[13] was probably the greatest shared passion of this couple, but the exact nature of their relationship remains one of the most tantalising secrets of mid-eighteenth-century Britain.

Emboldened by the lack of official reaction, Wilkes intensified his attacks on the King and his government's policies and reached the height of his audacity with No. 45 of the *North Briton*, published on 23 April 1763. In it he attacked a speech prepared by the Government that George III had read to Parliament on 16 April, particularly savaging those passages endorsing the proposed peace with France, which Wilkes dismissed as 'the most abandoned instance of ministerial effrontery ever attempted to be imposed on mankind'. He criticised the King for giving 'the sanction of his sacred name to the most odious measures, and to the most un-justifiable public declarations'. In essence Wilkes insinuated that, in delivering the government-prepared speech, the King had countenanced a deliberate lie and was therefore party to a plot to defraud his subjects of the truth. The Government duly faltered. On 8 April Lord Bute resigned and Wilkes appeared to be succeeding splendidly in his campaign. Indeed such was his confidence that he was prepared to take on Bute's successor as First Lord of the Treasury, none other than George Grenville, Wilkes' own one-time companion and the temporarily estranged brother of his patron Lord Temple.

In fact, Wilkes was now in a perilous position. He had made many enemies during the last couple of years, including the Royal Family and in particular George III, who referred to him as that 'Devil Wilkes'. No. 45 of the *North Briton* proved to be a step too far and precipitated Wilkes into a tumultuous series of events. The Government stepped in to defend the honour of the King and in the process destroy the irritating Wilkes and his journal. To do so a General Warrant was served on 30 April for the arrest of any and all thought to be involved with the production, printing and publication of the scurrilous forty-fifth issue of the *North Briton*. Crown messengers scurried around the capital accosting people in the streets and forcibly entering houses. In all, forty-nine people were arrested, including Wilkes who, despite arguing that the instrument of a General Warrant was unlawful, was committed to the Tower of London.

While he was incarcerated and kept incommunicado, his house in Great George Street, Westminster was ransacked, his personal papers seized and his commission in the county militia ignominiously cancelled. But this was only the beginning not the end of the matter. There was much public protest on Wilkes' behalf – with marching crowds chanting 'Wilkes, Liberty and Number 45' – and in court he argued successfully that his parliamentary privilege protected him from being charged at all. This was all a great triumph for him.

James Boswell, in an entry in his *London Journal* for 6 May 1763, captures something of the mood of the moment: '[T]his morning the famous Wilkes was discharged from his confinement and followed to his house in Great George Street by an immense mob who saluted him with loud huzzas while he stood bowing from his window.'[14] Nearly three weeks later, on 24 May, Boswell met Wilkes in person, along with his three colleagues from the *North Briton*, at the home of the essayist Bonnell Thornton. The triumphant mood appears still to have been strong among the Wilkes faction:

> In a little, Mr Wilkes came in, to whom I was introduced, as I also was
> to Mr Churchill. Wilkes is a lively, facetious man, Churchill a rough,
> blunt fellow, very clever. Lloyd too was there, so that I was just got into
> the middle of the London Geniuses. They were high-spirited and
> boisterous, but very civil to me.[15]

After his own successful escape from prosecution, Wilkes urged the innocent people detained with him to sue the Government for false arrest. At the same time he decided to go in bold pursuit of his temporarily routed enemies and himself sued His Majesty's Principal Secretary of State, Lord Halifax, for ordering his arrest since there was no admissible evidence that he was in fact the author of the offending article in the *North Briton*. The case was delayed. It was not until six years later that Wilkes won £4,000 damages and in the process obliged the courts to declare General Warrants illegal and Parliament to ban them by statute. This was a great victory, establishing the libertarian principle that people could not be arrested without a reasonable case being brought against them, as well as setting the precedent that common people might seek redress through the courts against oppression by the authorities.

But between his arrest on 30 April 1763 and his final victory and vindication, further events of a most dramatic nature were to overtake Wilkes and the causes he sought to promote. His use of parliamentary privilege to escape prosecution saved him from gaol but not from the determined efforts of his enemies to engineer his downfall – or at least suppression – by other means. And Wilkes, strange as it may now seem, was about to provide them with just the ammunition they needed.

Upon Potter's death in 1759 Wilkes possessed sole rights to *An Essay on Woman*. The text had lain dormant for around eight years but in late 1762, while buoyed up by all the fuss created by the *North Briton* and no doubt pleased – even cock-sure – over the insult delivered to the King himself, Wilkes decided it was finally time to print the *Essay*. This may have been an act of bravery or of stupidity but probably it was neither. Most likely he just wanted a bit of fun, to cause a little mischief, and – no doubt out of loyalty to the late Thomas Potter – to pursue the campaign of mockery against the loathed Warburton, who continued upon his inexorable rise, having been appointed Bishop of Gloucester in the very year Potter died.

Wilkes did not, it seems, intend a general publication of the *Essay*, just a very limited edition for private circulation to his surviving friends in the Order of Medmenham. Whatever his motive, the printing of the *Essay* became a pet project, a strange, if slightly foolish, obsession. Perhaps Wilkes intended the publication to cast him in a new light – to reveal him as a poet and lampoonist – and so make him master of a new field of satiric criticism. Certainly in the *North Briton* No. 17, published on 25 September 1762, Wilkes had turned art critic by attacking sixty-four-year-old William Hogarth:

> The humorous Mr Hogarth, the supposed author of the *Analysis of Beauty*, has at last entered the list of politicians, and has given us a print of *The Times*. Words are man's province, Pope says, but they are not Mr Hogarth's province . . . we all titter the instant he takes up a pen, but we tremble when we see the pencil in his hand . . . when he has at any time deviated from his own peculiar walk, he has constantly made himself perfectly ridiculous. I need only make my appeal to any one of his historical or portrait pieces, which are now considered to be almost beneath criticism.

Wilkes then went on to attack Hogarth's lack of patriotism, as illustrated by his 1749/50 painting showing the *March of the Guards to Finchley*. When the nation was in danger, argued Wilkes, and the Guards were dispatched to defend it, 'Mr Hogarth came out with a print to make them ridiculous . . . to tell the Scots . . . how little these men were to be feared, and that they might safely advance . . . Is this patriotism?'

Wilkes was, or pretended to be, unaware that Hogarth produced this work nearly five years after the period it depicted when the threat from Scotland was safely over but, in concluding his diatribe, revealed the likely motive for this attack: Hogarth had given his support to the Government by accepting the position of 'Sergeant [sic] Painter to the King' and so had joined the establishment from which Wilkes was excluded. 'He is rewarded,' wrote Wilkes, 'and made sergeant painter . . . I think that is house painter . . . Mr Hogarth is only to paint the wainscot of the rooms.'

In this attack Wilkes also revealed much about his own ethics. While berating Hogarth for toadyism, he also managed to insert a paragraph extolling Lord Temple as 'a nobleman of fine parts and unsullied honour . . . and . . . steady [in his] attachment to the Public'. Temple was, of course, Wilkes' own patron and the financial backer of the *North Briton*.[16]

It was at precisely this time, while writing about the connection between art and politics, that Wilkes returned to the scurrilous poetic pastiche of which he was co-author. In October 1762 he started to correspond with engravers about the production of a copper plate that was to form the frontispiece of his proposed limited edition of *An Essay on Woman*. Clearly things were moving on apace with the project. In December Wilkes attempted to get the *Essay* printed but failed to find a printer willing to do what would evidently be a dangerous job.[17] There was then a slight hiatus until May 1763, by which time Wilkes appears to have corrected and approved the frontispiece.

Since none of the original proofs survive it is now only possible to reconstruct it by reference to partial contemporary descriptions. It is clear that the work was credited to Pego Borewell and Rogerus Cunaeus (or Roger de Cunt, which was perhaps intended as a verb rather than a proper noun), with a 'commentary' by the Rev. Dr Warburton, and was 'inscribed' to the popular Covent Garden and Medmenhamite courtesan Fanny Murray (see page 407). It is also evident that the frontispiece incorporated the image of an erect penis and testicles – very much a phallus in the Roman manner – with a ruler set beside it revealing that, from top to bottom, the shaft of the member measured ten inches.

This all seems no more than a schoolboy joke, but the dimension is of some interest as it seems to reflect an eighteenth-century ideal. For example, in the 1788 edition of *Harris's List* a Miss Corbet is stated as having 'one fixed rule' in regard to the price she charged clients. 'She always measures a gentleman's *maypole* by a standard of nine inches and

expects a guinea for every inch it is short of full measure' (see page 128).
So nine inches seems the best that could generally be expected, making
Wilkes' ten-inch erection beyond any maid's wildest imagining.

The rendering of the phallus was also accompanied by two mottoes.
One in Latin read '*In Recto Decus*', a pun meaning either in 'uprightness
is beauty' or 'in the rectum is beauty'. The other motto – in Greek – can
be translated as 'preserver' or 'saviour' of the universe, a rather risky joke
on Wilkes' part because for many of his Christian contemporaries this
combination of image and words would have seemed like shocking and
actionable blasphemy, although for a number of his more antiquarian and
scholarly acquaintances it would have seemed no more than a return to
the religions of antiquity that venerated 'generative power' as a gift of the
gods (see page 373).

In addition the frontispiece also contained a more lewd and personal
sentiment, also rendered in Latin, which suggested the mighty phallus
on display was 'from the original most frequently in the crutch of the
Most Reverend George Stone, Primate of Ireland, more frequently in
the anus of the intrepid hero George Sackville'. These men were easy
targets. Stone was an ambitious politician rather than a cleric, unmarried,
effeminate, and rumoured to possess gross private vices. Sackville had
been court-martialled in 1760 for serious misbehaviour in 1759 during the
Battle of Minden and had been found guilty and discharged from the
army as 'unfit to serve His Majesty in any military capacity whatsoever'.
Subsequently he entered politics and through his incompetence as
Secretary of State for America played a key role in the loss of the American
colonies.[18]

The spring of 1763 was a difficult time for Wilkes to get anything
printed. His clashes with the authorities over his *North Briton* articles
meant he was now a marked and watched man – and so were his friends
and his printers. What was worse, the manuscript of the poem had been
seized from his home during the furore following his arrest in April 1763
and, although subsequently returned, it seems clear Wilkes' enemies in
government had read it and knew what might be coming. To possess a
manuscript of a pornographic poem libelling a bishop was one thing; to
print and publish it quite another. During May Wilkes managed to get
the printers of the *North Briton* to run off some sheets of part of the
Essay then employed other printers. Due to a series of accidents and

misfortunes, proofs of certain pages of the *Essay* fell into the hands of the Rev. Kidgell, who happened to be chaplain to the Earl of March, Lord of the Bedchamber to the King. March turned the material over to the Secretaries of State and a search was launched to find the rest of 'this abominable' work and suppress it.[19] Having already seen the manuscript among Wilkes' papers the authorities knew exactly where to go and called upon his printers in search of a full set of proofs and evidence that Wilkes was indeed the author and proposed publisher of the *Essay*. Michael Curry, the foreman printer for the *North Briton*, was eventually identified as a likely source for the proofs, which he did indeed possess. After withstanding threats and then attempting to get payment from the Government for surrendering them and from Wilkes for not surrendering them, Curry eventually sold the proofs to government agents.

As fate would have it Lord Sandwich, Wilkes' fellow Medmenhamite, verbal sparring partner and co-lover of Fanny Murray, had recently been appointed a Principal Secretary of State. It was now made his primary responsibility to prosecute and punish Wilkes. This, it appears, was a task Sandwich relished, no doubt from a combination of long-festering personal animosity between the two men and political differences that were brought to a head by Wilkes' writings in the *North Briton*. Indeed it is possible that Sandwich was anticipating a personal and potentially damaging attack in a future edition of the journal and decided to do what he could to pre-empt it. But, whatever the complex mixture of motives, it was with great force and gusto that Sandwich, on 15 November 1763, declared to the House of Lords that *An Essay on Woman* was an obscene, blasphemous and libellous publication. Simultaneously in the House of Commons Henry Grenville read out a letter from the King which requested the House to take action, since the courts evidently could not, and punish Wilkes for the libellous content of *North Briton* No. 45. Wilkes, who was present, claimed that his parliamentary privilege was being abused and heated debate ensued during which little was actually established – not even that he was indeed the author of the offending issue.

Meanwhile in the Lords things proceeded, at least initially, at a more controlled and sedate pace. Before Sandwich rose to lead the 'prosecution case' against Wilkes, Bishop Warburton (clearly still outraged by the manner in which he had been satirised in the *Essay* as the editor and commentator of the text) rose to protest against the use of his name in a blasphemous poem. This must have been a moment of high drama – not to say potential comedy in the House – for most in the chamber must have known that Thomas Potter, the co-author of the *Essay*, had earlier enraged and humiliated the Bishop by seducing his wife and making her pregnant. After the Bishop had duly expressed his outrage, Sandwich read the opening verses of the *Essay*, which celebrated the courtesan Fanny Murray: 'Awake, My Fanny, leave all meaner things./This morn shall prove what raptures swiving brings . . .' (see page 407). This performance was greeted with roars of laughter and protest – and no doubt amused disbelief since it was well known that Fanny Murray had been Sandwich's own mistress. This was a very personal vendetta indeed. Ignoring the excited reaction of his fellow peers, Sandwich read on:

> Thy lust the Virgin dooms to bleed To-day;
> Had she thy Reason, would she laugh and play?
> Pleas'd to the last, she likes the luscious food,
> And grasps the Prick just rais'd to shed her blood.
> Oh! blindness to the Future! kindly given,
> That each may enjoy what Fucks are marked by Heav'n:
> Who sees with equal Eye, as God of all,
> The man just mounting, and the Virgin's Fall;
> Pricks, Cunt, and Ballocks in Convulsions hurl'd,
> And now a Hymen burst, and now a World.
> Hope humbly then, clean Girls; nor vainly soar;
> But fuck the Cunt at hand, and God adore.
> What future Fucks he gives not thee to know,
> But gives that Cunt to be thy Blessing now.[20]

After further readings by Sandwich, and the interrogation of Wilkes' printers who testified that he had given them the manuscript and ordered the printing, the legislators in Parliament could not but agree that there were serious charges of libel and blasphemy to be answered. The verses were undoubtedly shocking to many, but if the government had not made such a fuss the *Essay* would never have been brought to the public's attention and its offensive sentiments would have languished in obscurity. One of the great ironies of this story is that it was not Wilkes who published *An Essay on Woman* – he had only thirteen copies printed for private circulation – but that through the actions of the House of Lords, spurred on by Sandwich, the *Essay* become public and its 'abominable' contents well-known. It was the House of Lords that printed and circulated the *Essay* in large numbers – using proofs obtained through threats and bribery – and so, paradoxically, it was the House of Lords that ultimately published the *Essay*. When, as a result of their Lordships' campaign to suppress the text and punish Wilkes, the *Essay* suddenly became public, Wilkes himself admitted it was 'an insult on order and decency' but insisted it was an insult he had never intended to give but which had in fact been given by the House of Lords.[21]

Following the extraordinary performances of Sandwich and Warburton – who during the reading in the Lords had begged Satan's pardon for comparing him to Wilkes[22] – the journalist and MP was summoned to appear before Parliament to answer his accusers. Wilkes was threatened with impeachment, the loss of his parliamentary privilege and prosecution, and given two days to prepare himself. The main burden of his defence, and the prosecution's biggest challenge, was the failure of his accusers to prove conclusively the identity of the author of the offending texts. But when the two days were up Wilkes failed to appear to defend himself. The reason was dramatic.

The day after the tumultuous events of 15 November he had been wounded in a duel with Samuel Martin, Secretary of the Treasury, who had been partly inflamed by Sandwich's denouncement of Wilkes and partly by a very personal attack on him in No. 40 of the *North Briton*, which characterised him as 'the most treacherous, base, selfish, mean, abject, low-lived and dirty fellow that ever wriggled himself into a secretaryship'. Naturally Martin felt aggrieved and publicly accused Wilkes of being a 'cowardly, scandalous and malignant scoundrel'.[23] In such circumstances a duel was the only option. For five weeks, due to the serious injury he'd suffered (Martin's ball had passed through Wilkes' abdomen, missed all vital organs but lodged in his buttock), he was too weak to attend Parliament. Then, just after the debate on his future commenced in his absence, news came on 23 December that he had left London, arriving in France just after Christmas Day.

While Wilkes enjoyed a lively exile in Paris, the House of Commons pressed on with the case. On 20 January it resolved to expel him, thus removing his parliamentary privilege and so allowing him to be prosecuted. He was then tried in absentia for obscene, seditious and blasphemous libel, not just for *An Essay on Woman* but also for issue No. 45 of the *North Briton*, and on 21 February 1764 found guilty of a libel on the Crown by being responsible for the printing of the offending edition of the *North Briton* and of libel of Bishop Warburton in *An Essay on Woman*. He was found not guilty of blasphemy.[24] When Wilkes failed to appear for sentencing he was declared an outlaw.

Lord Sandwich did not walk away unscathed from this bitter and bizarre vendetta. His sneaking, hypocritical, treacherous and self-seeking deceit outraged the public as much as Wilkes' *North Briton* and *Essay* had offended government policy, powerful individuals and official taste. Horace Walpole observed of Sandwich that 'the treachery was so gross and scandalous, so revengeful . . . and the instruments so despicable [and] odious . . . that, losing all sight of the scandal contained in the poem, the whole world almost united in crying out against the informers'.[25] As far as the public was concerned, Wilkes was a popular hero who had been beset – and temporarily bested – by the forces of oppression and his plight only made him more generally admired. When in December the public hangman attempted to make a symbolic gesture by burning a copy of the *North Briton* No. 45, he was prevented by a tumultuous crowd that, crying 'Wilkes and Liberty', seized the journal and in its place burned a jack-boot and petticoat. This seems an odd choice until it is realised that the boot was a pun upon the name of Bute and the petticoat symbolised the King's mother. Clearly the mob, remembering *North Briton* No. 5, blamed this pair for engineering Wilkes' current predicament.

Popular support for Wilkes and contempt for Sandwich took a very particular form. Soon after the trial, *The Beggar's Opera* – enjoying one of its many eighteenth-century revivals – was performed at Covent Garden Theatre. During the performance, when Macheath said, 'That Jemmy Twitcher should peach me, I owe surprises me', the audience burst into applause.[26] The connection was made. For the rest of his life Sandwich laboured under the contemptuous nickname 'Jemmy Twitcher', the odious nark who betrayed Macheath.

Wilkes remained in France for four years, hoping that political change would sweep through Britain and the charges against him would be annulled. It didn't happen. Instead he fell ever deeper into debt and in February 1768 was finally obliged to return to England. His popularity with working people was still high and he planned to stand once again for Parliament in order to regain both power and parliamentary privilege. His arrival in London was discreet and the authorities made no immediate attempt to arrest him for fear of provoking uncontrollable riots. During this stand-off Wilkes stood and failed to be elected as MP for the City of London, then in March 1768 succeeded in getting himself elected as MP for Middlesex.

Now all hell broke loose. Jubilant crowds celebrated throughout London. Spitalfields journeymen weavers and other working men and women took control of the city's streets, chalking '45' on walls, doors and window shutters – and the Government cowered. But after two days of boisterous and non-violent mob-rule the city was returned to the control of the shocked authorities.

Despite this public triumph Wilkes had a problem that could, he knew, yet debar him from Parliament. He was still officially an outlaw and this

John Wilkes being escorted in triumph into the City of London in 1768.

hindrance had to be legally removed. In late April he went to the King's Bench Prison in St George's Fields and – waiving any claims to parliamentary privilege, in an act of symbolic humility – surrendered to the law.

While he settled in, intending to use this enforced inactivity to prepare his legal appeal against his outlaw status, the mob that had escorted him to the gaol gathered in increasing numbers in front of the King's Bench, chanting, 'No Justice, No Peace'. Initially the demonstrations were peaceful but on 10 May disaster struck.

The violence that broke out seems to have been largely due to the fear and over-reaction of incompetent magistrates and ill-controlled soldiers. William Hickey was present and describes the extraordinary events in his *Memoirs*:

> [A] prodigious mob assembled for several days successively, in front of the prison, but no violence was committed until the 9th, when a large body of sailors made their appearance, some of whom like monkeys scrambling up the wall, were in a minute at the window of Mr Wilkes' apartment, whom they offered directly to liberate . . . Mr Wilkes very prudently begged them to desist . . . adding he had no doubt that the laws of the country would ultimately do him justice. Upon their arrival at the prison, Mr Thomas, the Marshal, being much alarmed, sent off for a party of the Guards [who] very imprudently on reaching the prison . . . began beating and maltreating the lookers-on.[27]

No very serious violence broke out that day, beyond some desultory stoning of the belligerent soldiers. Intent on seeing more, Hickey returned the next day when he witnessed the Riot Act being read by a 'stupid, over-zealous justice' and saw a 'blockhead of a magistrate' order the dispersal of the 'inoffensive mob'. In Hickey's view it was this . . .

> . . . ill-timed and unnecessary violence [that] at last raised a general indignation amongst the spectators, loud hisses commenced and abuse of the Scotch soldiers, and some few stones were thrown . . . whereupon the magistrate ordered the Guards to fire, which the infernal scoundrels instantly did . . . even across the public high road [killing] one poor woman . . . seated upon a cartload of hay going by at the time.[28]

By the end of this day of violence seven people had been killed and fifteen wounded. Wilkes had had to watch as the working people of London paid in blood for their support of his principles of justice and liberty. But few if any among the people blamed Wilkes for what had happened and their loyalty towards him remained rock solid.

On 8 June he was carried from the King's Bench to undergo the ordeal of attempting to have the stigma of outlawry removed from his name. If he failed he would become a non-person with no civil or legal rights and could be jailed in perpetuity. But this did not happen. On a technicality the eminent judge Lord Mansfield declared the charge of outlawry void. Again London was the scene of jubilant popular celebration, but for Wilkes the verdict of this court led directly to his appearance in another. Now he was once again within the law of the land, he had to receive sentence for his 1764 convictions relating to No. 45 of the *North Briton* and *An Essay on Woman*. Once again this task fell to Lord Mansfield, who duly sentenced him to two years in gaol and a fine of £1,000.

During these dramatic court proceedings Wilkes had not been able to occupy his seat in Parliament, not least because the Commons had opposed his election on technical grounds since he was an outlaw when he won. Now, from within his comfortable apartment in the King's Bench – well stocked with both the necessities and the luxuries of life, thanks to his many supporters – he resumed his political career. Initially the Middlesex constituency became the battleground for Wilkes and his Wilkite supporters. Four times they fought elections for the seat that had become the test case of government power, and four times they won. But each victory was declared null and void by the House of Commons, which finally, panicked and exasperated, declared another winner for the Middlesex seat, one Colonel Henry Lawes Luttrell, who in the fourth contest had only 296 votes against Wilkes' 1,143. This high-handed action led to an increase in popular fury against the Government and its authority but the much-feared general insurrection, however justified, did not manifest itself.

After serving his two years in prison Wilkes was desperate once again to pursue a political career through election to public office. This he quickly achieved. Upon his release his supporters rapidly organised his appointment as Sheriff of London and in 1774 his election as Lord Mayor of the City of London. This may now seem odd but in the mid-eighteenth century the City was not a place dominated by bankers, conservative-minded businessmen and establishment figures, but rather populated by independent-minded and educated 'smaller shopkeepers and working freeman',[29] who were precisely the class of people who supported Wilkes.

During his period of City power Wilkes fought for the freedom of the press and in 1771 was involved in breaking the ancient prohibition against reporting debates in Parliament. In late 1774 he was finally re-elected to Parliament and immediately became embroiled in the liberal opposition to war with the American colonies, supported religious tolerance, and in 1776 made English political history by putting forward a pioneering, but unsuccessful, motion in the House of Commons to enfranchise all British men, abolish 'Rotten Boroughs' and redistribute representation according to population levels. It was to be nearly sixty years before these enlightened ideas became established by law in Britain. Wilkes was now at the

The newly rebuilt Newgate Prison burning during the anti-Catholic Gordon Riots of 1780. During this chaotic moment of mob-rule Wilkes finally lost his reputation as friend of the people, for he sided with the forces of authority to suppress the mob.

pinnacle of his liberal and radical glory, but once again things started to go wrong for him.

During the Gordon Riots in 1780s, when anti-Catholic feeling provoked the London mob to extreme violence, Wilkes, then a City Alderman, found himself on the side of authority and in charge of troops guarding the Bank of England. The situation turned nasty and he ordered the soldiers to fire on the mob. At least two rioters were killed. In the aftermath he also ordered a printer to gaol for producing 'seditious and treasonable papers' and for being involved in the destruction of a private house. With bitter irony, the printer turned out to be a Wilkite who had once printed the *North Briton* and the house had belonged to Lord Mansfield.

The population of London was shocked by the riots but equally by Wilkes' actions. The common people believed he had betrayed them; that he had shot and imprisoned his former comrades in defence of the aristocracy and the name of the King, while the merchant class branded his behaviour both reckless and dangerous.[30] Finally Wilkes' charmed life came to an end. He was no longer the undisputed champion of the people, and his fall from popular esteem was confirmed in 1789 by his opposition to the Republican revolution in France. He declared its methods too violent, but for his fellow radicals Wilkes' attitude – justified though it later proved to be – marked him out as a turncoat, a defender of the old regime of royalty and oppression. In 1790 he lost his parliamentary seat and spent his final years – until his death in December 1797 – as a magistrate campaigning for admirable but modest reforms such as reduced punishments for disobedient servants.

And what of *An Essay on Woman* during the last three decades of his life? So far as anyone knows he never returned to it after 1763. The manuscript and Wilkes' printed sheets had been destroyed after his arrest. All that survived were a number of the incomplete or erroneous copies that had been published by the House of Lords as part of its prosecution case.[31] For Wilkes the *Essay* must by then have become horribly tainted, a sad reminder of a more carefree, confident and playful past.

The story of John Wilkes – and in particular the ordeal associated with *An Essay on Woman* – reveals how intricately the sex industry and attitudes to sexuality were woven into the fabric of eighteenth-century society. Sex, in all its varied forms, was the motif and metaphor of the age.

Through prostitution it encompassed the highest and the lowest in the land, offering the poor escape from misery and the rich escapist fantasy. And London was the theatre in which this strange and compelling story was played out, with an incomparable cast of characters and moments of sublime dramatic tension punctuated by tragedy and high comedy. Who could ever have invented such bizarre and contradictory characters as John Wilkes and Lord Sandwich and heroines like Fanny Murray? They could only have emerged, lived and thrived in eighteenth-century London.

THE MOB AND ITS VENGEANCE

The law in eighteenth-century London was tough on criminals, but tougher still was the London mob when its blood was up and an unpopular offender was exposed to its wrath. Although unruly and potentially very violent, the mob did, however, express a collective, if loose, morality and code of honour. It could be relatively gentle with, even supportive of, those criminals whose actions were seen as heroic and anti-establishment or that in some way expressed notions of liberty and independence from authoritarian control. It could even be tolerant. There is, for instance, no record of the mob being consistently violent towards convicted homosexuals thrown to its mercy. The German visitor Archenholz observed in the early 1780s that in London those convicted of homosexual offences were held 'in the utmost abhorrence [with] the fury of the populace . . . unbounded, and even the better sort of people have no compassion for the culprit', but when pilloried this class of offender did not automatically receive harsh treatment.[1]

What the mob did hate, and with a terrible vengeance, were those who had exploited, robbed or been treacherous to their fellows. This, in all likelihood, was why the 'female husband' Ann Marrow was roughly handled by the mob in 1777 when exposed in the pillory (see page 556). It wasn't her sexual oddness that offended, but the fact that she'd used her disguise as a man to cheat and defraud fellow women who were struggling to make a living. And what the mob particularly loathed were 'Affidavit Men' such as John Waller. His black art had been mastered in London during the second decade of the eighteenth century by the gangster and self-styled 'thief-taker' Jonathan Wild whose execution was so celebrated by the mob (see page 330). Waller, like Wild, made a habit of denouncing fellow criminals – by means of sworn affidavits – with the aim of securing money or power. There was, however, a limit to how long an Affidavit Man could fool the law and outrun the vengeance of his fellow criminals. In London in the early 1730s Wild was a very pertinent example of the perils of this type of activity. He had entered the world of crime in about 1711, under the aegis of the prostitute Mary Milliner, who, Daniel Defoe explained, 'began to teach him a great many New . . . Ways of getting Money, and brought him into her own Gang whether of thieves or whores or both'.[2] This led to a most profitable decade of crime for Wild, during which he terrorised his gang members so as to secure their services, their submissive silence and the lion's share of their booty. But in May 1725 all this came to an end when, during a trial for a trifling theft, a large number of Wild's gang decided to emancipate themselves from his control and gave such damning evidence against him that his execution was inevitable.

Now John Waller was about to be reminded, in a very terrible way, of how dangerous a double game he had been playing. In the Old Bailey records enough information survives to get a sense of the man, and to see where his duplicitous schemes started to go wrong. In May 1730 Waller had helped to secure the conviction and execution of the highwayman James Dalton, and in October 1731 he tried to duplicate his success by accusing Charles Knowles and Sarah Harper of highway robbery.[3] During the trial they in turn accused Waller of criminal activities, and the proceedings became absurdly convoluted until the judge, while acknowledging the two accused were unsavoury characters, announced to the jury that Waller had 'rendered himself notorious having sworn Robberies upon several persons (probably only for the reward) who were acquitted and innocent – and had hang'd Dalton'. And so, since the court had 'no regard' for Waller's evidence, the jury felt obliged to acquit the two accused.

Waller could not long survive so public an accusation and on 25 May 1732 was tried for 'Perverting Justice' – i.e. perjury.[4] To judge by contemporary press cuttings and other documentary evidence, Affidavit Men were the endemic curse of a trial system that, in the absence of a professional force trained to gather objective verbal and forensic evidence, relied heavily on witness statements and on the individual word of the accuser or 'prosecutor'. If a wicked or cynical person like Waller played the role of informer and was prepared to swear upon a lie, then they could – for a while – literally get away with murder. Accusations of sodomy appear to have been a popular ploy with Affidavit Men for not only was sodomy a capital offence but also – for most – a shaming one. For example, *Read's Weekly Journal or British-Gazetteer* of 12 August 1732, reporting the recent Assizes in Maidstone, Kent, stated that 'Henry Shepherd was found guilty of threatening to swear Sodomy against People, in order to extort Money from them, and was sentenced to stand once in the Pillory, to suffer two Years Imprisonment, fined five Marks, and to find Security for his good Behaviour', while the *Daily Journal* of 4 September 1732 announced that:

> [O]n Saturday last an Irishman came to Mr Zounsby, a Linen-Draper in Clare Market, and pretended to buy Holland for Shirts, but not agreeing, he wanting Credit, he afterwards went to a Publick House, and sent two Letters and a Messenger, desiring to speak with Mr Zounsby, who accordingly went to know his Business, which was to extort Money from him, threatening, if he refused, to swear Sodomy against him.[5]

Given the potential power of the accuser if a trial came about, it is evident how easy it was for unscrupulous criminals and conmen to abuse the ramshackle legal system. But as John Waller was to discover, the law counterbalanced this vulnerability by the severity of the punishment visited upon those it found guilty of perjury. The jury and judge knew their man. Waller was found guilty and given the tougher permutation of the standard sentence for attempting to pervert the course of justice. He was ordered to stand in the pillory four times, for one hour on each occasion at two separate locations, and then to be fined and imprisoned for two years. This might seem a relatively lenient sentence in an age when capital punishment was standard for even minor thefts, but in fact it meant that Waller was to a large degree thrown upon the mercy of the public. The sentence ordered that he was to stand in the pillory with his hat off so that he would be 'known by the people', and that a sign was to be placed on the pillory each time explaining his crime. So for four hours a man who had sent innocent people to the scaffold was to face the wrath of the mob and, more significantly, of the friends and relatives of the people he had contrived to hang.

It was clear to all that Waller would be terrified and humiliated by his punishment – it must also have been clear that he would, to a lesser or greater degree, be injured. The only protection he had when exposed to the public were constables posted around the pillory. But what if they were weak or, worse still, their sympathies lay with the mob?

Waller's ordeal started on 13 June 1732 when he was placed in the pillory at Seven Dials. The selection of this location suggests that some-one had retribution in mind for Seven Dials adjoins the St Giles area – the hunting ground of the Dalton gang. From the moment he stood in place – his neck and wrists fixed through the pillory board – things turned ugly. What happened is worth recounting in some detail because it reveals how savage a place Georgian London could be when the mob was out for revenge, and also gives a chilling insight into the brutalised nature of the impoverished and downtrodden criminal underclass of the capital. Clearly the denizens of Covent Garden, Seven Dials and St Giles – be they footpads or prostitutes – were very bad enemies to have.

The events that unfolded when Waller was pilloried were recorded in detail because of the extent to which they got out of hand. Prosecutions followed the riot that broke out around the defenceless prisoner, and witnesses were later called to describe in court exactly what had happened. One of these, Cartwright Richardson, during the subsequent trial of 6 September 1732, explained that after Waller had stood in the pillory for two or three minutes, two men attacked him. One of the men was Edward Dalton – brother of the executed James Dalton – and the other a Dalton gang member named Richard Griffith. Richardson described how: 'Dalton and Griffith got upon the Pillory Board [where] Griffith took hold of Waller's Coat, and Dalton of the waistband of his Breeches, and so they pulled his Head out of the Pillory, and he hung a little while by one Hand, but pulling that Hand out they threw him on the Pillory-board' where, together with a chimney-sweep, they 'stripped him as naked as he was born' and 'then they beat him with Collyflower-stalks'. Richardson then observed that the sweep put something into Waller's mouth that Griffith rammed down with a stalk.

Dalton and Griffith [then] jumpt and stampt upon his naked Body and Head, and kick'd him and beat him with Artichoke and Collyflower-Stalks, as he lay on the Pillory-Board. They continued beating, kicking, and stamping upon him in this manner, for above ¼ of an Hour, and then the Mob threw down the Pillory, and all that were upon it. Waller then lay naked on the Ground. Dalton got upon him, and stamping on his Privy Parts, he gave a dismal Groan, and I believe it was his last.

While they were stamping on Waller, Cartwright claimed to have heard Griffith say, 'Well played, partner Dalton', and Dalton replied, 'Aye, Damn him, I'll never leave him while he has a bit of life in him, for hanging my brother.' The mob now trampled over Waller's body for 'near an Hour, and every Body thought he was dead; he was taken up [and] a Coach was brought and he put in, and carried back to Newgate, where his Mother waited to see him'. When the coach arrived at Newgate, Waller's mother went inside to see what had been done to her son. But no sooner was she inside than Dalton and Griffith arrived, their thirst for vengeance not yet quenched. Witnesses stated that they cried out, 'Here's the old Bitch his Mother! Damn her, let's kill her too.' They stormed the coach door and tried to take possession of Waller's corpse. 'Damn him,' cried Dalton, 'we've sent his Soul half way to Hell, and now we'll have his Body to sell to the Surgeons for Money to pay the Devil for his Passage.'

From an eighteenth-century Londoner this was a particularly chilling and shocking statement. Throughout the eighteenth century surgeons were increasingly desperate to get hold of corpses for dissection, so that they could improve the medical profession's understanding of the human body and so advance upon known treatments for injuries and disease. But bodies were in short supply, largely due to Christian dogma that insisted that resurrection was only possible on the Day of Judgment if the body had been preserved entire on consecrated ground. This conflict between the demands of traditional religion and modern science led to a disparity between the supply and demand for corpses, and eventually to the practice of body-snatching: the stealing and selling of corpses by 'resurrection men' to surgeons.

At the time Waller was murdered the only regular supply of bodies available to surgeons was of people executed for murder – a practice regularised by the Murder Act of 1752 when dissection became a statutory part of the punishment. So, from the eighteenth-century point of view, murderers were not only killed in this life but also in the next. With their bodies 'dissected and anatomised', separated and disposed of in many places and not on sacred ground, their souls could not undergo resurrection but were, after death, cast into eternal oblivion. By selling the man they had murdered to surgeons for dissection, Dalton and Griffith believed that they would also succeed in depriving him of his afterlife.

An unholy tussle took place around the coach as Dalton and Griffith pulled at one end of Waller's corpse while his mother held on to the other. With the help of shocked onlookers she retained possession and so retained her son's chance of immortality. She later described her ordeal:

[T]hey put me in the coach and I laid my son's Head on my lap . . . Dalton call'd out to Griffith, '[T]here's the old Bitch his Mother! Kill her because I have kill'd her son' . . . My son had neither Eyes, nor Ears, nor Nose to be seen, they had squeezed his Head flat. Griffith pull'd open the Coach-door, and struck me, pull'd my Son's Head out of my lap and his Brains fell into my Hand.

No one could expect a mother's description of such a ghastly event to be objective, but this account of Waller's horrifying injuries was verified by the coroner, who stated that when he viewed Waller's body the next day he had never seen . . .

. . . such a Spectacle . . . he was bruised all over: I could scarce perceive any Part of his Body free. His Head was beat quite flat, no Features could be seen in his Face, and some Body had cut him quite down the Back with a sharp Instrument.

The defence offered at their trial by Dalton and Griffith was virtually non-existent. When called to respond to the prosecution's accusations, the hapless Dalton could only complain that 'I have had my Witnesses here every Day this Sessions but now they are gone.' One defence witness tried to imply that the prosecution witnesses were not to be trusted because they, in their turn, were now driven by a desire for vengeance. A friend of one of the accused stated that a day after Waller's death, his mother appeared at their door, threw in 'Artichoak-stalks' and said she would have blood, 'right or wrong'.

Such arguments did no good. Edward Dalton and Richard Griffith were found guilty and executed in early October. [6] The death of James Dalton had sparked a Sicilian-style vendetta in Covent Garden and its environs. So far there had been four deaths in the public arena, and probably a number of secret slayings in the courts, alleys and lodging houses of the area. The people in and around St Giles must have been traumatised by these events.

One of the stranger aspects of this grisly story is the stupidity of Edward Dalton and his gang – people who must surely have been made street-wise by their years of crime. It can only be supposed that they abandoned all reasonable caution and cunning because their blood was up and their thirst for vengeance so intense. If they had acted with more subtlety and less outrageous savagery, they could probably have killed Waller and stayed within the law. As anonymous members of the mob they could, if they managed to hurl particularly vicious and well-aimed missiles at Waller, have quite easily succeeded in killing him. After all, this was what had happened to the notorious bawd Mother Needham in April 1731. Seen as a corrupter and exploiter of vulnerable young women, she was so badly stoned while standing in the pillory near Park Place that she died a few days later. But Edward Dalton appeared to crave an almost ritualistic 'execution' of the perjurer who had killed his brother – he not only wanted revenge, he wanted people to know *who* killed Waller – indeed, witnesses stated that he announced his intention to murder the man as soon as he heard him sentenced to the pillory. The execution of Waller by an outraged mob may have been what the authorities secretly wanted, but this public and open display of brutality had gone too far. It appeared too much like the people taking the law into their own hands.

APPENDIX TWO

WOMEN AS MEN

Women of ability and energy but with no inherited wealth, money-making trade or influential connections could lead soul-destroying lives in eighteenth-century London. They could accept their lot and a life-time of drudgery as a domestic servant and subservient housewife, or they could – if of a suitable temperament and with certain natural advantages – risk a spell in the sex industry, possibly as a route to the stage and ideally achieving financial independence and even fame and respectability. Or, in order to survive in a man's world, they could 'become' men.

Women in the eighteenth century dressed as men for many and complex reasons and, naturally enough, this choice involved a certain amount of secrecy, subterfuge and sexual ambiguity that can from our perspective easily become confused with the modern notion of cross-dressing with specific homosexual implications. Some women did dress as men to satisfy their particular preferences, but others did so in order to gain access to a wider world of employment or to travel or else assumed the appearance and manner of men simply as part of their work. During the eight-eenth century a quarter of the plays performed in London included 'breeches roles' played by actresses, but although overtly theatrical even these portrayals of men by women could be sexually complex, as is revealed by a rhyme about the actress Margaret (Peg) Woffington, for a long time the companion of the actor David Garrick:

> The excellent Peg
> Who showed such a leg,
> When lately she dressed in men's clothes . . .
> A creature uncommon
> Who's both man and woman
> And chief of the belles and the beaux![1]

As Emma Donoghue has pointed out, the poem suggests it is not just Woffington's bare leg that aroused when revealed by her male attire, 'but her almost hermaphroditical glamour' that appealed to 'both men and women'.[2]

Some women – other than actresses – dressed as men intermittently and for short periods, others flamboyantly and obviously, while yet other women did it seriously and consistently. Many were poor women whose decision to disguise themselves as men gave them the opportunity to escape miserable lives, but a few were well-born, such as the Anglo-Irish Sarah Ponsonby and Eleanor Butler who, in 1778, eloped and lived together for over fifty years in very busy 'retirement' as the 'Ladies of Llangollen'. They both dressed at least partially as men, but seemingly did so more (if not entirely) as a symbol of emancipation from any form of male domination or dependence than as a reflection of their sexual preferences.

What is fascinating as well as surprising is how successful women often were in the maintenance of their disguise, even those who lived and fought as soldiers – an existence they could only have sustained with the help and connivance of male comrades. It seems that many men accepted this type of disguised way of life as an unspoken, but traditional, course of action for independent-minded women of spirit.

The stories recorded of women living in the guise of men are often exotic affairs in which fact and fiction, myth and reality, overlap and feed upon each other to the point where it is often now impossible to tell where fact ends and fantasy begins, where a story of disguise and secrecy is merely the pretext for sexual titillation. The woman living in man's clothes has an ancient pedigree and was traditionally associated with the riotous and sexually licentious behaviour of a subversive outsider or outcast. Quite simply, in popular imagination if not quite in fact, a woman when she assumed male attire was thought also to assume some of the more wayward masculine traits. The prime pre-eighteenth-century example of this is Mary Frith, who gained notoriety as Moll Cutpurse, the famed *Roaring Girl* of Thomas Middleton and Thomas Dekker's play of 1611.

Mary Frith was born in the 1580s and became a notorious figure of the town, dressing in baggy trousers and doublet, smoking a pipe, swearing, drinking to excess, and singing and performing in London's Bankside theatres. She also perhaps worked as a pick-pocket (as her nickname implies), fence, occasional prostitute and pimp, procuring not only women for men but men for women or any other combination that was requested.[3] The reasons for her conduct and way of life are uncertain. The *Newgate Calendar*, looking back on Mary's life and death, dismissed any complex cause for the disparity between her female sex and her masculine clothes. 'Moll was always,' stated the *Calendar*, 'accounted by her neighbours to be an hermaphrodite, but at her death was found otherwise.' Instead the *Calendar* simplistically concluded that she dressed like a man because she was ugly. Since she was a sexual outcast, 'not made for the pleasure or delight of man', she should no longer appear in public as a woman. Seemingly, to the seventeenth- and eighteenth-century male mind, the somewhat contorted logic of this statement made perfect sense or, perhaps more to the point, was a reassuring explanation.[4] What is more certain is that Mary lived outside the law, outside the rules and conventions of society, and – most definitely – way beyond the terrain occupied by even the most unconventional of her female companions. And she seems generally to have got away with it, although life must have been very hard for her when, in the last years of her life, London came under the Puritanical rule of the Commonwealth. By the time Mary died in 1659 the old tolerant world, in which she had enjoyed the freedom to be different, had changed out of all recognition, and seemingly beyond any hope of restoration.

Another pre-eighteenth-century female with an ambiguous sexual orientation was Aphra Behn. Born in 1640 and, according to Virginia Woolf, the first English woman to make her living as a professional writer, Aphra was a proponent of women's rights and a critic of the institution of slavery. She also worked, rather unsuccessfully, as a spy in the Netherlands for the court of Charles II. There is no record of her making a habit of wearing men's clothing, but then few records of Aphra's life exist, though her alleged bisexuality and her spying activities make cross-dressing a distinct possibility.

'One of the most successful' cross-dressers in eighteenth-century London was, according to Tim Hitchcock, Mary East, who in 1730 agreed 'marriage' with a young female friend and in the process became James How.[5] The couple moved to Poplar in east London where they kept an inn and lived together for thirty-six years, with How 'serving in most of the parish offices and attracting only occasional comment.'[6] The unconventional arrangement was revealed at last when the 'wife' died and a would-be blackmailer came to trial.[7] The story of the two women was told at length in 1766 in the July, August and October editions of the *Gentleman's Magazine*, which, in its July edition, attempted to remove any taint of sexual unconventionality from the union by explaining that 'both had been crossed in love when young, and had chosen this method to avoid farther importunities'. A more likely reason for the couple living together in the guise of man and wife, suggests Emma Donoghue, was to provide these two simple country women 'with a heterosexual model for their erotic life', to 'receive the validation and respect of their neighbours' and 'to keep themselves safe from male advances'.[8]

If Mary East was one of the most successful cross-dressing females in eighteenth-century London, then one of the most notable was Charlotte Charke. But she, as far as it is now possible to tell, wore male clothes not to disguise her femininity – nor it seems as part of any particular sexual stratagem or transvestite passion – but largely to provoke. Charlotte was born in January 1713, the daughter of the actor-manager, playwright, future Poet Laureate and Whig place-man Colley Cibber. She became an actress from the age of seventeen, soon specialised in 'breeches roles', and for reasons that are now not entirely clear took to wearing male clothes off-stage as well as on and to calling herself Charles Brown. All, it seems, was a flamboyant act, calculated to draw attention to herself and her work as an actress and playwright. Notwithstanding her preference for masculine roles, Charlotte appears at the time to have lived a conventional female life and in 1730 married a young man, the violinist Richard Charke. But perhaps nothing was quite as it appeared. Certainly there were deep and dark emotional undercurrents in Charlotte's life – mostly to do with her father and, perhaps, men in general.

Colley Cibber, a pushy, thick-skinned and boorish drone on the theatrical circuit, was not much liked and little admired. Indeed the apparent disparity between his ambition and his talents, combined with his craven and self-seeking obedience to the artistic dictates and controls imposed by Sir Robert Walpole's Whig government, meant he was hated by many. His elevation to Poet Laureate in 1730, not for his writing ability but for his political services to Walpole's party, was for many the last straw. Cibber's host of persistent critics and enemies included the poet Alexander Pope, who made him the 'King of Dunces' in the 1743 revision of his bitter satirical poem *The Dunciad*. First published in 1728, *The Dunciad* 'celebrates' the goddess *Dulness* and charts the woeful process of her select myrmidons as they disseminate decay, imbecility and tactlessness through the land. It is not surprising that Pope, a poet of genius with a very different political outlook, should have been horrified by the manner and means of Cibber's rise. More surprising, perhaps, is that among Cibber's staunchest critics was his own daughter Charlotte. Their differences were political and artistic, combined no doubt with deep-rooted personal anger on Charlotte's part. And when Charlotte attacked her father, it was public and it was cruel.

Perhaps her cross-dressing was the outward sign not only of her complex inner nature but also the violent and public expression of her rage against her father. In her outward appearance she was the marriage – the fusion – of opposites. Charlotte had been a loving daughter who had followed her father on to the stage yet she became a ruthless critic of his plays; she was a feminine woman, wife and mother, but also a flamboyant poser in men's clothes. Her alter ego was visible for everyone to see.

Her assault on her father was calculated and deadly. In 1733 Cibber had sold his controlling interest in the Drury Lane Theatre, and Charlotte and her brother Theophilus were furious. They believed that, out of greed, he had sold their birthright and betrayed them. Charlotte brooded upon the loss of the theatre and then in 1735 wrote her first play, *The Art of Management*, which was an attack upon Charles Freeman, who had acquired control of the Drury Lane Theatre. Her next target was to be her own father. This she conducted in the most public way possible, and through the agency of Henry Fielding. In 1736 she joined Fielding at the Haymarket Theatre, then a hotbed of satirical criticism of Walpole's government, and in 1737 played the 'breeches role' of Lord Place in Fielding's *Pasquin*. This play attacked not only Cibber's patron and his government, for their corrupt practices and bankrupt ideology, but also satirised Cibber himself. He was mocked for his toadying attitude to Walpole and for his un-deserved promotion to Poet Laureate.

Walpole's revenge was crushing. He used his parliamentary power to pass the Licensing Act of 1737, which closed all non-patent theatres and outlawed the performance of any play that had not been passed by government-appointed censors. It was a repressive piece of legislation that undermined individual freedom of expression and the right of artists to work unhampered by political control. At a stroke satire on the stage was suppressed and the Haymarket Theatre and Fielding were silenced.

The theatre closed and Fielding abandoned the stage as his main activity. To earn a living, he concentrated on the law and soon became a Justice of the Peace. But Fielding didn't forget Cibber – or lose his sense of humour – for when he was a Justice he issued a warrant for the arrest of Cibber: for the 'murder of the English language'.

The closure of the Haymarket Theatre and the retirement of Fielding left Charlotte in a tricky position. No job, a rebellious reputation that made it difficult for her to get work with the more conservative patent or licensed theatres, a feud on her hands with her influential father, and – as the fates would have it – no husband. Richard, a dissolute individual who had most disloyally stayed on at Drury Lane, had plunged into debt and abandoned both Charlotte and his creditors by fleeing to Jamaica. So, aged twenty-four, she was unemployed, seemingly unemployable, at war with her father, and a single mother.

Charlotte's response to the dilemma was most creative. She decided to transform herself into a work of art: to become the first performance artist, a living challenge to those who oppressed her. They could suppress her art – her plays and her acting on the stage – but they could not suppress her. She now started to appear in public on a regular basis in men's clothes, and to nurture the gossip and myths about her sexual ambiguity. Why she chose this expression of her independence and resurgence is open to conjecture. She had lost both the key male figures in her life and replaced them in this most novel manner, by becoming a man herself; she perhaps became her own father figure.

In this new manifestation, Charlotte soon found herself living on her wits – and on the edge of the abyss. In 1738 she acquired Punch's Theatre in the Old Tennis Court, St James's, which was more of a political act than might at first appear because puppet shows were outside the control of the Licensing Act. Through her marionettes Charlotte was able to stage satirical plays, including works by herself and by Fielding. Indeed so effective was this ploy in avoiding the strictures of the Licensing Act that Fielding himself – desperate for cash and for an outlet for his political and social convictions – assumed the pseudonym of Madame de la Nash and opened his own puppet theatre.

Charlotte's enterprise was a modest financial as well as an artistic success. As she later explained in her autobiography, *A Narrative of the Life of Mrs Charlotte Charke*, published in instalments during 1755,

'[T]he Puppet-Show ... was allowed to be the most elegant that was ever exhibited', and she took her show on the road. But luck was not on her side:

> The Affair stood me in some Hundreds and would have paid all costs
> and charges, if I had not, through excessive Fatigue in accomplishing it,
> acquired a violent Fever, which had like to have carried me off, and
> consequently gave a Damp to the Run I should otherwise have had.[9]

This illness proved expensive. She was finally gaoled for debt and, as Charlotte claims in her *Narrative*, only saved by having her bills paid by the coffee-house keepers and prostitutes of Covent Garden, to whom she was known, affectionately, as 'Master Charles'.

In desperate circumstances, and unable to get a job on the stage, Charlotte took her male posturing to an extreme and worked as valet to the notorious bigamist and libertine Richard Annesley, 6th Earl of Anglesey. Part of a valet's job was to dress his master, so one can only assume that life in the earl's home was somewhat unconventional. In her *Narrative* Charlotte gives little away beyond describing the general nature of her job and Annesley's establishment:

> ... I entered into my new Office, which made me the superior
> Domestick in the family [with] a Guinea paid every Wednesday
> morning ... At this Time, my Lord kept in the House with him a *Fille
> de Joye* ... a sensible Woman whose Understanding was embellished by
> a Fund of good Nature [and] when there was no Company at all, his
> Lordship permitted me to make a third Person at his [table] and very
> good-naturedly obliged me to throw off the Restraint of Behaviour
> incidental to the Servant.[10]

The job lasted five weeks, with Charlotte walking happily around the town in male attire 'with Ease and Security, having his Lordship's Protection'. But finally 'two supercilious coxcombs' publicly exposed her, obliging a reluctant Annesley to discharge her.[11]

The earl was almost as strange a character as Charlotte, for soon after she left his employment he became embroiled in a bizarre legal challenge to his title and lands that resulted in a court case in 1743. The action was brought by a young man called James Annesley, who argued a superior claim to the title and Anglesey estates. He alleged that he had when young been secluded in an obscure school and his death announced by the current earl, who subsequently sold him to an American planter as a slave. The young man had eventually escaped his bondage and reappeared in London to claim his rights and revenge. He won the case. The 6th Earl, found guilty as charged, was stripped of his estates but, due to some ambiguity over rights of inheritance, allowed to retain the title.

If Charlotte followed the case she must have reflected on the fact that the earl, like most other men in her life, had turned out to be far from admirable and certainly not to be trusted. But, by the time of Annesley's public and humiliating exposure, Charlotte was, after a spell as a sausage-maker, back on the stage and prospering. In 1742 her second play – *Tit for Tat or, Comedy and Tragedy at War* – was performed successfully enough to allow her, from the proceeds, to open the Charlotte Charke Tavern in Drury Lane. As with most of her business ventures the tavern eventually failed, but not before she made a mysterious second marriage in 1746 to a man called John Sacheverell. Little is known about him and he only receives the briefest of mentions in her *Narrative*. It seems to have been a marriage of convenience, but for whom remains unclear. She may never have lived with him or perhaps barely knew him – whatever the case, it seems that soon he was dead and by 1749 Charlotte was back on the road as a strolling player, little more than a vagabond. She travelled with her daughter Catherine and an intimate companion she referred to as 'Mrs Brown' but who was perhaps a faithful and much-loved female companion or, indeed, lover.

Money troubles and the usual problems of a marginalised life continued to dog Charlotte – creditors and the spectre of gaol foremost among them. During four years of wandering she was gaoled as a vagrant and served her time with male prisoners; worked – again in the guise of a man – as a pastry cook, and as a farmer. Her relationship with the stage became ever-more thankless. Catherine married an actor whom Charlotte thought a useless character, and in 1754, still dressing in men's clothes, Charlotte was working as a prompter in the theatre in Bath among players who appeared to her to be talentless. Enough was enough. She realised that a serious change of lifestyle was necessary and, ever-inventive, moved back to London to start a new career. She had decided to become a writer.

Perhaps inspired by the success of her father's chatty memoirs – *An Apology for the Life of Colley Cibber* – Charlotte set about writing

A Narrative of the Life of Mrs Charlotte Charke. Her prime intention was to make money through the sale to journals of excerpts from her *Narrative* but, it seems, she also hoped this literary enterprise would help resolve the relationship with her father to her advantage. Indeed early in the text she admits:

> I have too much Reason to know, that the Madness of my Follies have
> generally very severely recoil'd upon myself, but in nothing so much as
> in the shocking and heart-wounding Grief for my Father's Displeasure
> which I shall not imprudently dare deny having incure'd.[12]

By 1755 she had completed the first section of her *Narrative* and clearly regarded it as a bargaining tool. She sent it to her father, at the same time pleading for forgiveness and an end to their estrangement. But the *Narrative* was the real persuader. She knew its publication – complete with intimate details – would be a huge embarrassment to him, so she offered not to complete or publish it if Cibber could spice his forgiveness with a little ready money. It was blackmail. Her father would have none of it, spurned her, and Charlotte duly published her scandalous *Narrative* in instalments during 1755, with extracts appearing in the *Gentleman's Magazine*.

Inspired by the popular interest her life story provoked, Charlotte tried her hand as a novelist and, true to form, chose a provocative and risqué subject upon which to focus her tale – homosexuality. In 1756 this work appeared, entitled *The History of Henry Dumont, Esq. and Miss Charlotte Evelyn*, including a sensational scene in which the openly homosexual (and aptly named) Billy Loveman, having declared his love for Dumont, dressed himself as a woman, kissed Dumont, and for his trouble is beaten by Dumont and his friends and 'treated as a woman' by an outraged mob. This treatment was not quite as extreme as it may sound. In fact, no worse than being dunked in a fishpond!

Ever since the book was published people have been trying to work out the psychological meaning and symbolism of this extraordinarily confused and confusing tale. Is it as homophobic as it appears, and what does it say about Charlotte's father and her own cross-dressing? Or perhaps Charlotte in fact identified herself with the misunderstood, sexually disorientated and abused Billy Loveman, and did indeed harbour strong lesbian tendencies? Pat Rogers, in *The Breeches Part,* asserts this was the case, while Fidelis Morgan, in *The Well-Known Trouble Maker,* argues the opposite view.[13] Kristina Straub in 'The guilty pleasures of female theatrical cross-dressing' suggests that Charlotte simply liked to play with sexual identities, and enjoyed presenting herself as both harmless male-attired actress and serious female husband, but Emma Donoghue, in *Passions between Women*, concludes that Charlotte's long-term relationship with the mysterious 'Mrs Brown' was of the 'classic "butch/femme" type' and actively lesbian. But no one is really sure.[14] All that's certain – and all the strange *History of Henry Dumont* confirms – is that Charlotte was an elusive, complex and contradictory character.

The year after the novel was published, Colley Cibber died. When his will was read it revealed that he wished to continue his feud with his daughter from beyond the grave. Rather than leaving her a reasonable portion of his fortune, he willed her a derisory £5. This meant there was to be no relief from poverty and worry until her dying day. Her father would have known this; it was evidently what he wanted. Charlotte's sad response was to write another novel, published in 1758, entitled *The Lover's Treat, or, Unnatural Hatred*, which speaks of families fractured by dispute and misunderstanding. This plot must have drawn not only upon Charlotte's relationship with her father but also with her daughter Catherine who, in 1758, had sailed with her husband to America. Charlotte knew then she would never see her daughter again and, two years later, was dead.

Charlotte Charke was a flamboyant and immensely articulate female whose male guise fooled few people. Her cross-dressing was, in the end, perhaps more a subversive commentary on the age and on her own life than a reflection of sexual orientation. But there were other women who presented themselves as men in much more serious manner and who knew there would be a stiff price to pay if their disguise was not convincing. These were not extrovert or playful cross-dressers like Charlotte but female husbands with, unlike Mary East/James How, a sinister aspect. One such woman was Mary Hamilton and her case became a sensation in the mid-eighteenth century. In November 1746 she was tried at the Quarter Sessions in Taunton, Somerset for fraudulently posing as a man (under the aliases Charles, George and William Hamilton) and marrying a woman.[15]

The precise nature of Mary Hamilton's crime, and the law broken, was hard to define. Sex between women was not outlawed, indeed was not strictly speaking even covered by the law, although, at a pinch, it could be construed as sodomy, in the same way as it was sodomy – and thus a capital crime – for a woman to be found guilty of having sex with a dog (see page 57).[16] But in the case of Mary Hamilton, the complex byways of sexual crime were not explored. Her behaviour, even if its precise criminality was hard to define, had offended public morals and was – apart from anything else – deemed to be a frightful deception. A law meant for other purposes was found roughly to fit the circumstances, and Hamilton was prosecuted under the 1713 Vagrancy Act outlawing 'false and deceitful practices'.

Her trial gripped popular interest. One obvious question was whether or not Mary's 'wife' had known she was lying with a woman, and if she had not, then how had she been fooled? The 'wife' gave evidence and was reported as saying that 'after marriage they had lain together several nights and that the said pretended Charles Hamilton who had married her aforesaid entered her body several times, which made this woman believe at first that the said Hamilton was a real man'. The explanation accepted by the court, following investigations, was that Mary had used a leather dildo and that the 'wife' was, incredible as it may seem, naive enough not to realise.

The account in the *Newgate Calendar* throws a little more light on this peculiar story. During the trial it was alleged – and accepted by the court – that Mary Hamilton had committed the same crime fourteen times before. The judge and jury's heads must have been spinning and imaginations revving. Clearly they were dealing with a serial offender – apparently a thing unprecedented – and not only that but a female *sexual* offender who preyed obsessively on other females. This case had strayed into strange territory indeed. The *Newgate Calendar* gives a little more information. During the trial, Hamilton's 'wife' Mary Price . . .

> . . . swore that she was lawfully married to the prisoner, and that they had bedded and lived together as man and wife for more than a quarter of a year; during all which time, so well did the impostor assume the character of a man, she still actually believed she had married a fellow creature of the right and proper sex.

This statement was not questioned. The court apparently did not think it unlikely that a man and wife could live and sleep together for three months without the wife once seeing or even properly exploring or touching her husband's naked body.

As the trial proceeded Mary Hamilton refused to display the shame or remorse expected of her and, instead, appeared to glorify in the attention she was receiving. This particularly annoyed a public and a press clearly anxious for this woman to admit the error of her ways, recant and seek forgiveness. Since Mary refused to give them this satisfaction she faced great hostility. She was howled at by a threatening mob when travelling between gaol and court, and the *Bath Journal* of 22 September 1746 noted most disapprovingly that . . .

> . . . great numbers of people flock to see her in Bridewell, to whom she
> sells a great deal of her quackery; and appears very bold and impudent.
> She seems very gay, with Periwig, Ruffles and Breeches.

The trial concluded with, as was inevitable, the court finding her guilty. As the *Newgate Calendar* explains, the justices ruled . . .

> . . . that the he or she prisoner at the bar is an uncommon, notorious
> cheat, and we, the Court, do sentence her or him . . . to be imprisoned
> six months, and during that time to be whipped in the towns of
> Taunton, Glastonbury, Wells and Shepton Mallet.

Mary, the 'monopoliser of her own sex', was duly punished and whipped in the winter of 1746 in the towns in which she was said to have offended.[7] But this punishment was not enough to ease the public's disquiet. The case carried troubling implications. Was Mary unique, a one-off, or were there in fact many more such characters lurking in the shadows of society? Surely the fact that she had, as was generally accepted, fourteen 'wives' suggested something odd was going on. Had they really all failed to notice she was a woman? Mary's conduct not only was a challenge to the conventional morality of the age but also undermined the legal basis of marriage on which much of the structure of society – certainly the possession of property, control of wealth and inheritance law – was based. This was her *real* offence. The 'game of flats', as lesbian sex was called, was commonly recognised and even advertised as an option by some of Jack Harris' *Covent Garden Ladies*. Few would have seen female same-sex relations as a threat to society or a cause for fury. The real and disturbing offence was such a cynical contempt for the sanctity of marriage. She had, in a sense, committed blasphemy.

Contemplating the moral, religious and legal implications of Mary's case was, for some, a most disorientating and unsettling experience, exacerbated by the fact that she herself apparently saw nothing wrong with her behaviour. Henry Fielding was one of those who observed the case and felt obliged to investigate the circumstances of the story more fully, in order to extract a lesson and a warning from it. Before the end of the year he wrote and published an account of the case entitled *The Female Husband: or, The surprising History of Mrs. Mary, Alias Mr George Hamilton . . . Who was convicted of having married a young woman of Wells and lived with her as her husband.*[18]

Part of Fielding's account may have been fictionalised to increase the drama, clarity and moral message of the tale – it's now impossible to be sure. What is obvious, however, is that he did not seek to explain Mary's conduct in sympathetic terms or in any way to defend her. For example, he emphasised her role as a prurient sexual predator when he claimed that Mary's 'wife' told him, during an interview, that Mary Hamilton was able to approach, physically explore and ultimately seduce women by pretending to be a male physician. Fielding also stated that 'the smart or shame' of the whipping had 'so little effect' on Mary Hamilton 'that the very evening she had suffered the first whipping, she offered the gaoler money, to procure her a young girl to satisfy her most monstrous and unnatural desires'. Clearly no holds were barred in the effort to demonise this woman. Her existence was, it seems, only tolerable for Fielding if she was classified as way beyond the extremes of recognised female behaviour and made to seem almost uniquely and entirely wicked.

He also attempted to explain, definitively and precisely, why sexual relations between members of the opposite sex was a good thing, and why between members of the same sex it was bad. In doing this Fielding suggested the lessons that should be learned from the Mary Hamilton case. He pointed out that the human inclination for sexual intercourse, for a 'very wise purpose implanted in the one sex for the other, is not only necessary for the continuance of the human species; but is, at the same time, when govern'd and directed by virtue and religion, productive not only of corporeal delight, but of the most rational felicity'. So only when sex was part of the process of procreation could it be enjoyed without guilt or shame and be viewed as an expression of love, not lust. This type of righteous sex, argued Fielding, resulted in a strong family life and reinforced the institution of marriage.

All other sex, he appeared to be implying,
incompatible with notions of virtue and morality

This, of course, is the conventional view of the
on the Old and New Testaments – Judaism, Christianit
all associate sex with guilt and chaos, argue that the bea.
is the only justification for the physical pleasure sex brings, a
that sex itself is only permissible within the institution of man   The
sexual urge when not controlled by these strictures was, for Fielding, a
source of moral opprobrium:

> [I]f once our carnal appetites are let loose, without those prudent and
> secure guides, there is no excess and disorder which they are not liable
> to commit . . . there is nothing monstrous and unnatural, which they are
> not capable of inventing, nothing so brutal and shocking which they
> have not actually committed. Of these unnatural lusts, all ages and
> countries have afforded us too many instances; but none I think more
> surprising than what will be found in the history of Mrs Mary,
> otherwise Mr George Hamilton.

Marriage itself was defended by Fielding in the *Covent-Garden Journal*
of 1 August 1752. It was, he argued, an institution in which young men
could 'indulge their Inclinations in a legal Way', and which 'the wisest
Legislators thought proper to encourage . . . attributing to it the highest
Honours and Privileges'.[19]

Fielding may have been a puzzled and confused man, he may even in
certain ways have been an intolerant and non-comprehending one – but
he was certainly never a cruel or vindictive bigot. And so when describing
Mary Hamilton's corporal punishment, he did not triumph over her
suffering but noted that many spectators 'could not refrain from exerting
some pity towards her, when they saw so lovely a skin scarified with rods,
in such a manner that her back was almost flead [flayed]'.

Henry Fielding's deep, almost primal, fear that Mary Hamilton was
not a bizarre rarity but in fact the suddenly exposed tip of a mighty
iceberg was confirmed by a later and similar case. He had attempted to
exorcise the experience of Mary Hamilton by making her and her 'crime'
appear horribly unique. In this he was, of course, wrong. Mary's conduct
was not unique but, although unusual, one of the established aspects of
London's all-embracing sex industry.

1777 a woman called Ann Marrow was, according to the *Newgate Calendar,* convicted in London 'for going in man's clothes and personating a man in marriage, with three different women . . . and defrauding them of their money and effects'.[20] So the principal crime in this case was not 'false and deceitful' conduct but fraud and theft. Ann Marrow was sentenced to be imprisoned for three months and to stand once in the pillory at Charing Cross. This was, for her, a most unfortunate sentence. As the *Newgate Calendar* explains, when Marrow was placed in the pillory, 'so great was the resentment of the spectators, particularly the female part, that they pelted her to such a degree that she lost the sight of both her eyes'. The popular fury was probably provoked not by her sexual orientation but by the fact that she had used man's attire to cheat, rob and defraud her fellow women. She had crossed a boundary. Dressing as a man in Georgian London could, in certain circumstances, be a very dangerous game for a woman to play.

There was, however, a potentially yet more dangerous game for female cross-dressers, and one that demanded absolute and sustained immersion in the male role – and that was to 'go for a soldier'. This was undoubtedly the most dramatic way in which a woman could operate, and perhaps flourish, in a man's world, and incredible as it now seems, the career of a female soldier was not just the stuff of romantic fiction and myth. The records of the Royal Hospital, Chelsea – founded in 1682 – include accounts of two women who not only managed to join the British Army in the guise of men – and to remain within its ranks for some considerable time – but eventually succeeded in becoming out-pensioners of the Hospital. The powerful myth of the female soldier is recorded and romanticised in numerous eighteenth- and early-nineteenth-century ballads, and the usual explanation offered is that the girl 'went for a soldier' for love – to pursue or rescue her soldier sweetheart – or else in search of tomboyish adventure. There is never any suggestion that these bold females masqueraded as men and donned uniform either to escape the constraints and drudgery of their humble female life or so as more easily to seduce other women.

The Chelsea 'Amazons' were untainted by any open accusations of what Fielding called 'unnatural lusts'. Catherine Walsh or Welch – known also as Mother Ross or Davies – served with the Royal North British Dragoons (better known as the Scots Greys) and in 1717 was awarded a pension of

5d (later raised to 1 shilling) for her service in Flanders during Queen Anne's War. According to a contemporary account her sex was only discovered once she was wounded, at the Battle of Ramillies in May 1706, until when, 'her Comrades had not the least Suspicion of her being a Woman'.[21] How could this have been the case, given the rough and tumble of military life in the eighteenth century? The only answer is that her companions did know the secret but declined to betray the truth to their officers. Whatever the case, Catherine Walsh was clearly a brave woman and not only obtained a Chelsea pension but, when she died in July 1739, 'her Corpse, according to her Desire, was interr'd amongst the old Pensioners in Chelsea Burying-Ground, and three vollies fired over her Grave'.[22]

The second Chelsea Amazon has an even more curious history. Hannah Snell became something of a celebrity and her life story was published in 1750 by an enterprising book seller, Robert Walker, under the title *The Female Soldier, or the Surprising Life and Adventures of Hannah Snell*. In July of the same year the *Gentleman's Magazine* also published a biography. Consequently the details of Hannah's life – or at least the acceptable details of her life – are readily available, if inconsistent. She was born in Worcester in 1723 and, in some confusion over a lost love, enlisted in the winter of 1745 in Guize's Regiment of Foot (now the Warwickshire Regiment) under the name James Gray. She fell foul of a sergeant in her company and was sentenced to be flogged. All surely was to be revealed. But no. Although stripped to the waist, Hannah was – according to her biography – able to conceal her breasts and her true sex by flinging herself rapidly against the gate of Carlisle Castle, which had conveniently been chosen as the place of her punishment. Quite how she removed herself, bleeding and exhausted, without revealing her person is not explained. Not surprisingly, Hannah was downcast by this treatment and when the regiment was in Portsmouth she deserted.

But the flogging had not quenched her ardour for the military life and she promptly joined Frazer's Marines. She was sent aboard the man-of-war HMS *Eltham* where her dainty and generally feminine appearance earned her the nickname Molly. This name, generally given to effeminate boys or homosexuals in the eighteenth century, suggests that Hannah's comrades not only had noted her appearance but in fact knew her secret, and were indulging in an ironic piece of double bluff. Whatever the facts of the case, the female marine contrived, once again, to earn herself a good flogging. This time she concealed her breasts by means of a large scarf that she was allowed to wear around her neck during the ordeal. But Hannah's spirit remained unbroken.

Frazer's Marines were landed at Madras and she took part in the siege of the French colony of Pondicherry, managing in the process to be wounded in one thigh and both legs. One would have thought that the location of the wounds was bound to give the game away, but Hannah claimed that she crawled from the scene of the fighting and managed to get her wounds treated by an Indian woman. After four and a half years' military service, however, her soldiering days were over and by 1750 she was back in England. She soon realised – or was told – that she had a good story to sell and it was marketed in sensational manner, with the floggings – real or invented – adding a lurid sexuality to the tale. Once her biography was published, the twenty-seven-year-old Hannah appeared on stage, dressed in regimentals and marching up and down in a no doubt beguiling manner.

The Royal Hospital took her tale seriously. She was admitted to the pension list in 1750 at the standard 5d per day (raised to 1s in 1785) for which she was eligible through her wounds received at Pondicherry. The Duke of Cumberland was alleged to have awarded her an additional £30 per annum but this is probably one of the many fictions of the Hannah Snell story. Recent exhaustive research finds no evidence to support this pleasing and romantic legend.[23] Sadly, Hannah's novelty value soon wore off and she failed to sustain popular interest in her stage appearances. She made an unwise marriage, became the landlady of a public house in Wapping, East London – inevitably named the Female Warrior – became insane and was placed in the Bethlehem Hospital or 'Bedlam' – where she died in 1792. She is said to be buried at the Royal Hospital in an unmarked grave.

The Royal Navy was perhaps a more convenient refuge for females in disguise. Life aboard ship was more crowded, intimate and communal than in army barracks, but the navy itself far less exclusively a man's world than was the army. Women of all types were welcome aboard when ships were in port, and some, in certain circumstances or when married to particular grades of mariner, even stayed aboard openly and legitimately while the ship was at sea. As N. A. M. Rodger explains in *The Wooden*

World, '[I]t was not unusual for a few wives, usually of the warrant or inferior officers, to live on board ship [although] it was understood that they should be plain and elderly.'[24] But, as Rodger points out, 'no such restriction was applied by those officers who carried loose women to sea with them' – a not uncommon action and one that the authorities were happy to tolerate in peacetime, particularly in foreign stations. So sexual boundaries on ships were less rigidly defined than in barracks; the enclosed conditions on board, shared by both sexes, must to a degree have offered a woman disguised as a seaman greater latitude.

Rodger mentions one case from the mid-eighteenth century of a female marine and confirms that 'surprising as it seems, it was possible for a woman to keep her secret in a crowded mess-deck with little privacy'. The documented case took place, appropriately enough, aboard the *Amazon* when William Prothero, a private marine, 'was discovered to be a Welsh girl of eighteen who had followed her lover to sea'.[25] The motive offered for this subterfuge seems to have been the traditional one of love for a sailor sweetheart, although this may have been no more than a convenient explanation for the girl's unusual conduct. More interesting and revealing is the case of Mary Lacy and the alleged motive behind her cross-dressing. She was born in 1740 in Wickham, Kent and at the age of nineteen, to escape the drudgery of a servant's life, disguised herself as a boy and ran away to sea. She took the name of William Chandler and joined HMS *Sandwich* as a carpenter's servant. Years later Mary wrote about her experiences aboard the *Sandwich*, which apparently included a wrestling match:

> I went aft to the main hatchway and pulled off my jacket, but they
> wanted me to pull off my shirt, which I would not suffer for fear of it
> being discovered that I was a woman.

During the combat Mary was thrown 'such violent cross-buttocks [that] were almost enough to dash my brains out', but she triumphed in the end and consequently 'reigned as master' over the rest of the ship's boys.

In 1763 she started an apprenticeship in Portsmouth dockyard, receiving her shipwright's certificate in 1770, but was invalided out the next year due to rheumatism with a pension of £20, which Mary claimed in her real name. She then set about writing her memoirs. They appeared in 1773, entitled *The History of the Female Shipwright: Mary Lacy*.[26] This narrative, now of course impossible to verify, contains some fascinating and revealing insights into the life and psychology of these female soldiers and mariners. It also suggests how the trick was achieved and seems to confirm the existence of a conspiracy of silence with more thoughtful and understanding male comrades. For example, when working in Portsmouth dockyard, a rumour got around that Mary was indeed a woman. As she explains:

> ... the man whose name was Corbin and his mate who taught me my business came and told me in a serious manner that I must go with them to be searched. 'For if you don't,' said they, 'you will be overhauled by the boys.' ... I considered that they were very sober men and that it was safer to trust them than expose myself to the rudeness of the boys.

So taking a gamble, and 'though it made me cry that I could scarce speak', Mary declared plainly that she was a woman. The men were 'greatly surprised' but 'offered to take their oaths of secrecy', and when 'the people asked them if it was true what they had heard, "No," said they, "he is a man-and-a-half to a great many."' So the tactic paid off: keep up the pretence to the last possible moment then, rather than being forcibly exposed, share your secret with 'sober' men who, out of sympathy, protect you. This must have been how many female soldiers and sailors kept their secrets for so long.

In her memoirs Mary also revealed that she was quite a ladies' man, flirting with and being admired – indeed pursued – by numerous females. The implication, of course, is that it all took place in essentially innocent and light-hearted jollity, but probably without being aware of it Mary is also giving the reason why she posed as a man for so many years – quite simply, she was attracted by other women and so felt more comfortable living, looking and acting like a man. Following the publication of her memoirs Mary Lacy disappeared into obscurity. Like so many of the minor protagonists of the age, she rose to only a fleeting moment of prominence, and then was entirely – and sadly – lost to history.

⌒ DR JAMES GRAHAM ⌒

When in 1780 Dr James Graham opened his Temple of Health in the Adelphi Terrace, off the Strand, he made manifest a world in which sex, prostitution, art, pioneering science, idiosyncratic medicine and sheer showmanship were mixed to an astonishing and unprecedented degree. For a while Graham and his Temple in the Adelphi, and then a second in Pall Mall, were the talk of the town. This is hardly surprising since they were rich in decoration and redolent of exotic sexual encounters and practices, presided over by an enchanting and scantily-clad Goddess of Health, equipped with a magnet-powered and 'marrow-melting' Celestial Bed, and promoted invigorating and restorative medical theories about procreation. Graham achieved his ambition of becoming a celebrity, mixing with and being courted by the rich, the powerful and the famous, and – in the process – making money. For a brief moment his long-hatched plans worked but soon – with ghastly inevitability – all unravelled, to end in debt, humiliation and insanity.

James Graham trained as a doctor of medicine in Edinburgh and in 1769 sailed to Baltimore, Maryland on what would turn out to be a five-year journey through the American colonies. He undertook this adventure in the hope of amassing useful professional experience and funds before settling down to professional practice in England. But what Graham encountered in America was probably far more than he had ever anticipated. In the early 1770s the north-east coast of America was a strange and contradictory place. As Lydia Syson points out in her recent biography of Graham, when he landed at Baltimore he would have seen ships laden with slaves or with impoverished men and women coming from Britain to sell themselves as indentured servants. Such sights would most forcibly have reminded him of the dark, troubling and unjust legacy of the old and benighted world.[1] But also, on his travels, Graham caught a glimpse of a bright and enlightened new age of science that, for him, suggested the possibility of an era of greatly improved health and – perhaps more to the point – a means of attaining his own fame and fortune. In America he witnessed what he took to be the dawn of the modern age – and this new age was illuminated by the crackling fire of electricity. As he wrote in 1783 while describing his *Travels and Voyages* in Philadelphia, here electricity – the scientific discovery of the age – 'had been more improved, was better understood, and more generally cultivated, than in any other part of the world'.[2]

The American fascination with electricity was largely due to the pioneering work of Benjamin Franklin, who in the early 1750s had made his name as an experimental scientist with his work in this field, particularly by identifying lightning as an electrical current and a force of nature with the power not only to hurt but also – perhaps – to help and heal. Franklin's discoveries achieved an almost immediate practical application. It soon became an international obsession to invent machines to generate electricity – as Joseph Priestly did in England in the 1760s – and to devise means to harness or tame lightning, so that by the time Graham visited Philadelphia its buildings were bristling with examples of Franklin's most useful invention, the lightning rod.

When Graham returned to England in 1774 he had resolved to turn his American experiences into a medical treatment that he hoped would establish him in Britain – London preferably – as a leading proponent of a new, and electrically inspired, age of health and happiness. Graham disembarked at the slaving port of Bristol and initially set up practice there; from a consulting room in Queen Square he attempted to entice the worthies of the West Country to sample his restorative and health-promoting medical, scientific and dietary regime. Much of this was, initially, simple and sound, including the consumption of fresh vegetables and more scrupulous than average bodily hygiene, but, from the start, Graham's approach had a particular aim calculated to give him an edge over his competitors. He promoted himself and his theories heavily – through pamphlets and advertisements in the press – and most readers must soon have realised that what would improve most dramatically if they took his advice was their sex life. Pleasure, no doubt, would be increased, but also infertility and impotence would be cured, senses re-kindled in the aged, and healthier offspring assured. Graham realised that the quickest route to success was to secure support for his theories and practice from the great and famous. This he rapidly accomplished by targeting a national celebrity who dwelt in nearby Bath.

Catherine Macaulay was, in the early 1770s, one of the most famous women in Britain and, fortunately for Graham, she was then in her early forties and fearful for her health. Macaulay was not a courtesan; she was famed not for her looks or private life but for her intellect. 'She had become a national idol with the publication in 1763 of the first volume of her monumental *History of England*' and was something of a national institution.[3] Macaulay was one of the 'Blue Stocking' circle (see page 439), famed not just for her work as an historian but also for her well-publicised – if perhaps somewhat hypocritical – Republican and egalitarian views. This made her a heroine for later radical women writers such as Mary Wollstonecraft, but in the 1760s and 70s it provoked the enmity and exasperation of more conservative characters such as Samuel Johnson.

In 1774 Catherine Macaulay, a widow since 1766, was living in the large and comfortable Alfred House, Alfred Street, Bath that was owned by one of her many admirers, Dr Thomas Wilson, who had offered her the use of his house, furniture and library for as long as she required. The offer was accepted and, by implication, so was Wilson's suit as her future husband. The Alfred Street house soon became something of a place of pilgrimage for persons with literary or Republican interests, and Graham, no doubt capitalising on Macaulay's concerns about her weak constitution, insinuated himself into this elevated society. Soon he had secured trade, contacts and testimonials from Macaulay, enjoyed Christmas dinner with her – and the ubiquitous John Wilkes – in 1776, and in 1778 dedicated one of his books to the great 'female historian'. Wilson meanwhile was growing alarmed and evidently saw Graham as a rival for Mrs Macaulay's attention, if not her hand. But he was wrong. It was not James Graham who was his rival but Graham's younger brother William. In 1778, in circumstances that were – and remain – extraordinary, the forty-six-year-old Mrs Macaulay travelled to Leicester and married William Graham, a surgeon's mate twenty-five years her junior. Society – Dr Wilson in particular – was shocked. As he wrote in a letter:

> To the great surprise of the world, Mrs Macaulay without giving me the slightest notice . . . married a YOUNG SCOTCH LOON of 21 whom she had not seen for above a month before the fatal knot was tied. A mate to an East India ship, without clothes to his back . . . I will never let her come to Alfred House . . . How are the mighty fallen.[4]

While Dr Wilson was mortified by this marriage, Dr Graham was delighted. Not only did it cement his relationship with a very useful – if now somewhat compromised – celebrity, it also appeared to vindicate his medical claims. A forty-six-year-old woman, known for her physical weakness, was, after receiving Dr Graham's ministrations, able to desire, attract – and presumably satisfy – a strapping twenty-one-year-old. Whatever the nature of the relationship – and the fact that Macaulay and William Graham remained together until her death in 1791 suggests a certain sincerity – this notorious case and the publicity it generated persuaded Dr Graham to take the plunge and return to London, where he had practised briefly and unsuccessfully during the mid-1770s.

Less than two weeks after the scandalous marriage, James Graham started negotiations to take a new house in Adelphi Terrace, part of a financially and architecturally bold speculative development being undertaken on the north bank of the Thames, just off the Strand, by the architect Robert Adam and his brothers. This was an ambitious move by Graham for it placed him immediately in the heart of London's most talked-about building project, which seemed in all likelihood about to become a highly fashionable location. Graham already had the veteran and immensely well-connected actor David Garrick for a neighbour, with many other luminaries showing interest in removing themselves to this splendid development. The fact that the enterprise nearly bankrupted the Adam brothers was neither here nor there for Graham. The setting they created was perfect for him. Adelphi Terrace, perched on an arcaded podium high above the Thames and inspired by Diocletian's Palace at Split, had a fantastical and fairy-tale feel, just right for the highly theatrical 'Temple of Health' Graham intended to create within his new house, whose rich Neo-classical scheme of decoration also did much to reinforce the spell he was intent on weaving.

The Temple of Health or – to make its sexual purposes more explicit – the Temple of Hymen opened in July 1780. Here Graham unleashed with a vengeance the novel power of electricity on the unsuspecting London public. His Temple was a wonderland. As Syson observes . . .

> . . . walking into the Temple was like entering the inner chambers of
> some enchanter's palace. Exotic perfumes and distant music seemed to
> seep . . . into every room, and rainbow shards of light shining from one

mysterious machine's prismatic pillar fractured in the spiralling glass columns of another [including a] vast and unmistakably phallic electrical conductor in the first room . . . [a] . . . metal cylinder, eleven feet long and four in circumference, was suggestively described as ending in two semi-globes. It rested on six-foot-high pillars of intricately cut glass, reflecting and refracting all the coloured lamps and candles to dazzling effect . . . on the other side of the room a six-foot sparkling golden dragon appeared to fly . . .

Electrical charges ran along the dragon, generated from battery-like 'Leyden Jars', passing 'visibly and loudly' and causing crackling sounds to issue through its tail.[5]

London society flocked to this wondrous place, with its electrical demonstrations and discharges, in such numbers that Graham soon felt able to open a second Temple, installed in the central portion of the large late-seventeenth-century Schomberg House in Pall Mall where he had Thomas Gainsborough for a neighbour. Here Graham installed his masterpiece, the 'Celestial Bed' that was the centrepiece of an over-whelming sensory and electrical experience – involving mirrors, music and perfumes – which he proclaimed would be an aid to pleasurable sex and assure the creation of healthy offspring. Graham declared that electricity – if properly harnessed – had great creative power; indeed held the secret of life itself. As he explained in one of his many pamphlets:

> . . . the venereal act itself, at all times, and under every circumstance, is in fact no other than an electrical operation . . . those heart-piercing and irresistible glances [shooting at critical moments from soul to soul are] no other than . . . electrical strokes or emanations.[6]

It was in this Pall Mall Temple that Emma Lyon, soon to be renamed Emma Hart (see page 349), might have worked as Vestina, the Goddess of Health, encouraging rich, titillated and perhaps gullible observers to pay the 50 guineas Graham demanded to allow a couple to spend a night in the throbbing and scented Celestial Bed.[7] There are numerous contemporary accounts and descriptions of this veritable engine of sex. Graham revealed in one pamphlet that the bed utilised vast magnets, or 'lodestones', to give 'that charming springiness – that sweet, titillating, vibratory, soul-dissolving, marrow-melting motion which on certain critical and important occasions, is at once so necessary and pleasing'.[8] Another report described something of its appearance:

> [A] sumptuous bed in brocaded damask supported by four crystal pillars of spiral shape festooned with garlands of flowers of gilded metal [and] on whatever side one gets into bed, which is called 'Celestial', one hears an organ played in unison with three others which make agreeable music consisting of varied airs which carry the happy couples into the arms of Morpheus.[9]

The bed was a working example of current theories about 'effluvia' – the natural force by which, it was believed, beneficial energy or dread disease flowed out to delight or damage those who were engulfed. The effluvia around the bed was, of course, of the beneficial kind, which, Graham explained, was generated by the lodestones that . . .

> . . . are . . . continually pouring forth in an ever flowing circle, inconceivable and irresistibly powerful tides of the magnetic effluvium, which every philosophical gentleman knows, has very strong affinities with the electrical fire.[10]

To the modern mind these claims and theories sound absurd – and there is little doubt they were – but at the time they gripped the public imagination because they were not only novel and possibly scientifically correct, but also seemed to enshrine ancient truths and reflect nature itself. In the 1770s and 80s exciting and inspiring discoveries were being made about the ancient, primitive and natural worlds (see page 367) and Graham's theories about procreation seemed to chime with these. In ancient and primitive societies it was believed that certain sites, rituals or forms could act as 'incubators', increasing fertility, and as Giancarlo Carabelli has pointed out, 'incubation' – also familiar from the realm of natural science – was precisely what Graham claimed his Celestial Bed achieved.[11]

Initially, at least, people of science and of learning were intrigued by Graham's claims and by his technology. There could, perhaps, be something in it. And certainly, at the time, he was not alone in trying to apply new discoveries about electricity to health and to an understanding of the function of the human body. In London he had a rival in the person of the Prussian-born Dr Gustavus Katterfelto, who, more of a conjuror and obvious quack, used demonstrations of electricity and magnetism to pull in crowds to whom he attempted to sell bogus medicines and aphrodisiacs. Far more serious was the work undertaken in Vienna and Paris in the 1770s and 80s by Franz Anton Mesmer, who used magnets to try to prove his theory that effluvia-like waves of 'Animal Magnetism' flow through the human body, determining its health and virility. Similarly serious were the speculations of Alessandro Volta, who, during the 1780s and 90s, studied what he termed 'animal electricity', which resulted in 1800 in the invention of the electric battery.

While the scientifically minded observed Graham's theatrics with studied caution and mounting scepticism, the London sex trade – always on the lookout for novelty and inspiration – gobbled up all he had to offer. In the same way that Cook and Banks' discoveries about the sexual habits of Tahiti were used in the 1770s by bawds such as Charlotte Hayes to feed the fantasies of libidinous Londoners (see page 389), Graham's sexual theories were soon embraced by the world of prostitution. An edition of Jack Harris' *List of Covent Garden Ladies* included an entry for a Miss Harriet Jones of Wapping who, it was claimed, practised 'the Grahamitic method', which led to 'an increase of pleasure' and made her a 'more desirable bed-fellow [who] after every stroke gives fresh tone and vigour to the lately distended parts'.[12]

With fans and followers like this Graham really had very little chance of being taken seriously. Influential and aged rakes such as Lord Sandwich, Charles James Fox and John Wilkes came to look, but probably would have agreed with Horace Walpole who concluded that Graham's Temple was 'the most impudent puppet-show of imposition I ever saw'.[13]

Walpole's brand of scepticism soon prevailed. When the novelty was over and Graham's self-promotional showmanship, sycophantic toadying and idiosyncratic lectures on health and procreation ceased to amuse and started to appal, the crowds melted away. He was dismissed as a charlatan and a quack, and early patrons such as Lady Spencer started to distance themselves. Debts rapidly multiplied and by the end of 1782 he was obliged to sell up to appease his many creditors. In July 1783 he retreated to Edinburgh in an attempt to revive his fortunes in a more modest way. But this proved to be a disastrous choice for soon he was gaoled for 'publishing lascivious and indecent Advertisements & delivering wanton and Improper lectures within the city'.[14] Eventually he sneaked back to

London where he tried to make money publishing books of his lectures, and in 1786 tumbled more deeply into the seamier side of quackery by opening a showroom in Panton Street, Soho that extolled the stimulating virtues of bathing in mud, accompanied by public demonstrations by scantily clad females. When this venture failed Graham became a religious visionary – much like the earlier scientist turned mystic Emanuel Swedenborg – became obsessed with the production of unadulterated food, and in 1792 sailed to Portugal determined to aid its queen whose mental health was failing.

This was to be Graham's last attempt to grasp fame and riches for himself. It was, of course, nothing but the blind attempting to lead the blind. Graham's own mind was going. He took to fasting, burying himself in the earth or strapping grassy sods to his body in an attempt to feed from nature. By 1794 he had returned to Edinburgh where, suddenly if not surprisingly, he died at the age of forty-nine – rather than the one hundred and fifty he had predicted for himself. His passing went unremarked. In 1794 – at war with Revolutionary France since February 1793 – Britain had little time to reflect on such ephemeral curiosities as Dr James Graham.

Introduction

1 Kirstin Olsen, *Daily Life in Eighteenth-century Britain*, 1999. The book includes a table (pp. 140–5) that reveals the extremes of income in eighteenth-century London: a 'prominent' brewer could earn up to £8,000 a year in *c.*1800 and a top tailor up to £3,000 a year; yet a few years earlier, in the first half of the eighteenth century, a skilled silk-weaver might earn £150 a year and a journeyman tailor just over 21 shillings a week. At the bottom end of the wage scale, washerwomen earned around 8 pence a day, general maids about £5 a year and a mid-eighteenth-century private soldier no more than £14 a year.

2 B. E. V. Sabine, *A History of Income Tax*, 1966. In 1814 the budget estimate for army, navy and foreign subsidies was £70 million, of which £20 million went to the navy (pp. 26–33).

3 *The Craftsman*, 18 October 1729, quoted in Peter Linebaugh, *The London Hanged*, 1991, p. 115.

4 Jeremy Collier, *Essays upon Several Moral Subjects*, 1705, quoted in Edward J. Bristow, *Vice and Vigilance: Purity Movements in Britain since 1700*, 1977, p. 24.

5 Randolph Trumbach, *Sex and the Gender Revolution*, 1998, p. 92.

Prologue: An Artist's View

1 Quoted in Jenny Uglow, *Hogarth: A Life and a World,* 1997, p. 191, referring to George Vertue, *Notebooks*, ed. Katherine A. Esdaile et al., Vol. 3, 1930–55, pp. 237–8. Discussed in Ronald Paulson, *Hogarth*, Vol. 1, 1991, pp. 237–8.

2 Ronald Paulson, *Hogarth's Harlot: Sacred Parody in Enlightenment England*, 2003, p. 27.

3 Uglow, *Hogarth*, p. 191.

4 Uglow, *Hogarth*, p. 193. For an early description and explanation of the six paintings, see William Hogarth, *Anecdotes of the Celebrated William Hogarth, with an Explanatory Description of his Works*, 1811, pp. 209–24.

5 *The Spectator*, 4 January 1712, No. 266, see Gregory Smith (ed.), *The Spectator: Addison and Steele and Others*, Vol. 2, 1958, pp. 291–2.

6 Paulson, *Hogarth*, Vol. 1, p. 239.

7 Old Bailey proceedings online (www.oldbaileyonline.org), compiled and ed. by Clive Emsley, Tim Hitchcock and Robert Shoemaker: Trial of Francis Hackabout, 28 February 1730 (t17300228–71).

8 Old Bailey proceedings online (www.oldbaileyonline.org): *Ordinary of Newgate's Account*, 17 April 1730 (oa17300417).

9 See Paulson, *Hogarth*, Vol. 1, pp. 237–336, for a fascinating and definitive exposition of *The Harlot's Progress*; and his *Hogarth's Harlot*, pp. 27 and 29–33.

10 Paulson, *Hogarth's Harlot*, pp. 31–7.

11 See Bristow, *Vice and Vigilance*, pp. 58–9; *Gentleman's Magazine*, October 1747; Bertrand Goldgar (ed.), *The Covent-Garden Journal*, 25 January 1752; Saunders Welch, *A Proposal to Render Effectual a Plan to Remove the Nuisance of Common Prostitutes from the Streets of this Metropolis*, 1758, pp. 11–13; John Cleland, *Fanny Hill: Memoirs of a Woman of Pleasure*, 1748–9.

12 Paulson, *Hogarth*, Vol. 1, pp. 288–9.

13 Uglow, *Hogarth*, p. 204.

14 E. J. Burford and Joy Wotton, *Private Vices – Public Virtues*, 1995, pp. 140–1.

15 Quoted in Ivan Bloch, *Sexual Life in England Past and Present*, 1958, p. 105, referring to Friedrich Wilhelm von Schütz, *Briefe über London* (Letters from London), p. 119. Also Bloch, p. 105, quoting *Oeuvres Complètes de Voltaire*, ed. Beaumarchais et al., published by Kehl, 1785–9, Vol. 14, p. 61.

16 *Nocturnal Revels*, quoted in Burford and Wotton, *Private Vices – Public Virtues*, p. 149.

17 Museum of London, ID number (o)23116.

18 Old Bailey proceedings online (www.oldbaileyonline.org): *Ordinary of Newgate's Account*, 12 May 1730 (oa17300512).

19 James Dalton, *A Genuine Narrative of all the Street Robberies*, 1728, British Library shelfmark Tracts 1080.m.32 (2).

20 Old Bailey proceedings online (www.oldbaileyonline.org): Advertisement relating to James Dalton (a17280501–1).

21 Old Bailey Proceedings online (www.oldbaileyonline.org): Trial of James Dalton, 8 April 1730 (t17300408–61).

22 César de Saussure, *A Foreign View of England in 1725–1729*, trans. and ed. Madam Van Muyden, 1995, pp. 187–9.

23 Uglow, *Hogarth*, p. 206; *Grub Street Journal*, 24 September 1730, No. 195.

24 David Innes Williams, *The London Lock: A Charitable Hospital for Venereal Disease, 1746–1952*, 1996, p. 3.

25 Peter Quennell, *Hogarth's Progress*, 1955, p. 100.

26 *Ibid.*

1: 'Satan's Harvest'

1   *Pretty Doings in a Protestant Nation* by 'Father Poussin', 1734, British Library shelfmark Tab.603.a.12 (1), p. 1.

2   John Cleland, *Fanny Hill*, 1964 edn, p. 23.

3   *Pretty Doings in a Protestant Nation*, p. 37.

4   Daniel Defoe, *Augusta Triumphans*, 1728.

5   Quoted in Bloch, *Sexual Life in England*. See also W. H. Quarrell and Margaret Mare's 1934 edn of von Uffenbach's journal *London in 1710*, but the description there (p. 88) has been edited to read: '. . . there are . . . such a quantity of Moors of both sexes in England . . . Males and females frequently go out begging . . . the females wear European dress and there is nothing more diverting than to see them in mobs or caps of white stuff with their black bosoms uncovered.'

6   César de Saussure, *Letters from London, 1725–1730*, trans. Paul Scott, 2006, p. 114.

7   Quoted in Bloch, *Sexual Life in England*, p. 104; refers to Schütz, *Briefe über London* (Letters from London), pp. 214–17.

8   Jonas Hanway, *Thoughts on the Plan for a Magdalen-House for Repentant Prostitutes*, 1758, pp. 11–12 and 20.

9   Welch, *A Proposal. . .*, p. 7.

10 Trumbach, *Sex and the Gender Revolution*, p. 112.

11 Welch, *A Proposal. . .*, p. 20.

12 *Ibid.*, p. 17.

13 *A Memoir of Thomas Bewick Written by Himself*, ed. Iain Bain, 1975, p. 70.

14 *Gentleman's Magazine*, April 1795, p. 294.

15 Translation quoted in Bloch, *Sexual Life in England*, pp. 104–5, referring to Schütz, *Briefe über London* (Letters from London), pp. 214–17.

16 Quoted in Bloch, *Sexual Life in England*, p. 103. Bloch presumably had

access to Archenholz's original German text. The 1789 English translation appears to have been heavily edited and sanitised. I therefore
generally quote from Bloch rather than the 1789 edn printed for Edward
Jeffery.

17 Bloch, *Sexual Life in England*, pp. 103-4, referring to Johann Wilhelm
von Archenholz, *A Picture of England*, Vol. 2, pp. 256-8.

18 *An Account of the Institutions of the Lock Asylum for the Reception of
Penitent Female Patients, when Discharged Cured from the Lock Hospital*,
1796, pp. 3-4.

19 Bloch, *Sexual Life in England*, pp. 103-4, referring to Archenholz, *A
Picture of England*, Vol. 2, pp. 256-8.

20 Bloch, *Ibid.*, p. 104.

21 Michael Ryan, *Prostitution in London*, 1839, p. 89.

22 Leon Radzinowicz, *History of English Criminal Law*, Vol. 3, 1956,
p. 247.

23 Ryan, *Prostitution in London*, p. 90.

24 Bloch, *Sexual Life in England*, pp. 109-10.

25 Bloch, *Ibid.*; *The Midnight Spy*, 1766, p. 116. *An Address to the Guardian
Society* of 1817 includes an emotive manifesto and moral justification
for the crusading actions of the society and confirms that vice was on
the increase in early-nineteenth-century London: '. . . while Vice and
Wretchedness are pursuing their courses, with rapid and destructive
strides, while the quantum of female depravity, is every day increasing,
and the progress of crime thereby accelerating . . . are we not . . . to
stem the destructive torrent, and to rescue as many as we can of our
fellow creatures, of both sexes, from the fangs of the destroyer?' One
solution, suggested the author, was to outlaw 'seduction!' The *Address*
was published in *The Pamphleteer*, Vol. 11, No. 21, printed by A. J. Valpy,
1766, p. 229.

26 Harold Perkin, *The Origins of Modern English Society*, 1969, p. 280.

2: 'Ladies of the Town'

1 *Pretty Doings in a Protestant Nation*, p. 5.

2 *A Memoir of Thomas Bewick Written by Himself*, p. 70.

3 Ryan, *Prostitution in London*, pp. 121 and 123.

4 *The Spectator*, 28 September 1711, No. 182, see Gregory Smith (ed.), *The
Spectator*, Vol. 2, p. 42.

5   *The Spectator*, 4 January 1712, No. 266, see Gregory Smith (ed.), *The Spectator*, Vol. 2, pp. 291–2.

6   *Pretty Doings in a Protestant Nation*, pp. 4–6.

7   Daniel Defoe, *Everybody's Business is Nobody's Business*, 1725, p. 7.

8   Ivy Pinchbeck, *Women, Workers and the Industrial Revolution, 1750–1850*, 1981, p. 61.

9   Tony Henderson, *Disorderly Women in Eighteenth-century London*, 1999, pp. 50–1.

10 Goldgar (ed.), *The Covent-Garden Journal*, pp. 394–6; see also Ronald Paulson, *The Life of Henry Fielding*, 2000, p. 314.

11 Old Bailey proceedings online (www.oldbaileyonline.org): *Ordinary of Newgate's Account*, 18 October 1749 (oa17491018).

12 See Goldgar (ed.), *The Covent-Garden Journal*, p. 306.

13 Henry Fielding, *A True State of the Case of Bosavern Penlez*, 1749, p. 51.

14 *The Case of the Unfortunate Bosavern Penlez*, 1749, p. 13.

15 *Ibid.*, pp. 8–9.

16 *Ibid.*, p. 10.

17 Archenholz, *A Picture of England*, 1789 Jeffery edn, Vol. 2, p. 89.

18 *The Spectator*, 4 January 1712, No. 266, see Gregory Smith (ed.), *The Spectator*, Vol. 2, pp. 291–2.

19 Jean Donnison, *Midwives and Medical Men*, 1977, p. 34.

20 Paulson, *Hogarth's Harlot*, p. 299.

21 *The London-Bawd, with her Character and Life*, 1705, pp. 1–5, quoted in Alexander Pettit and Patrick Spedding (eds.), *Eighteenth-century British Erotica*, 2002, Vol. 2, p. 136. See also Robert A. Erickson, *Mother Midnight*, 1986, p. 24.

22 *The Whore's Rhetorick*, pp. 10–12, quoted in Erickson, *Mother Midnight*, p. 23.

23 Print in National Portrait Gallery. See Fergus Linnane, *London: The Wicked City*, 2003, p. 72; and Richard Garfield, *The Wandering Whore*, 1660.

24 *The London-Bawd*, 1705 edn, pp. 111–12.

25 J. Roberts and A. Dodd, *Hell upon Earth; or, The Town in an Uproar*, 1729, p. 9.

26 *The Humours of Fleet Street and the Strand* by 'An Old Sportsman', 1749, pp. 5–12.

27 *Covent-Garden: A Satire*, 1756, p. 10.

28 Cleland, *Fanny Hill*, 1964 edn, p. 31.
29 *Pretty Doings in a Protestant Nation*, pp. 38–9.
30 Hanway, *Thoughts on the Plan for a Magdalen-House*, p. 21.
31 Bloch, *Sexual Life in England*, p. 100, referring to Archenholz, *A Picture of England*, Vol. 2, p. 257.
32 Nicholas Barbon, *An Apology for the Builder*, 1685.
33 Dan Cruickshank and Neil Burton, *Life in the Georgian City*, 1990, pp. 60–3.
34 *The Whore's Rhetorick*, pp. 63 and 73–5, quoted by Erickson, *Mother Midnight*, p. 27.
35 *The London-Bawd*, 1705 edn, p. 111.
36 Erickson, *Mother Midnight*, pp. 27–8.
37 *Ibid.*, p. 27.
38 Cleland, *Fanny Hill*, 1964 edn, pp. 19–20.
39 Bernard Mandeville, *A Modest Defence of Publick Stews*, 1724, edn ed. Irwin Primer, 2006, p. 45.
40 *Pretty Doings in a Protestant Nation*, p. 10.
41 *The Covent Garden Magazine*, January 1773, Vol. 2, p. 66; Erickson, *Mother Midnight*, pp. 27–8.
42 Ned Ward, *The Insinuating Bawd; and the Repenting Harlot*, 1699, Opening 'Dedication'; Erickson, *Mother Midnight*, p. 28.
43 Jack Harris, *Harris's List of Covent Garden Ladies . . . Kalendar for the Year 1788*, British Library shelfmark P. C.30.h.2.
44 *Pretty Doings in a Protestant Nation*, p. 2.
45 Archenholz, *A Picture of England*, 1789 Jeffery edn, Vol. 2, p. 96. Also in Bloch, *Sexual Life in England*, p. 104 (referring to Archenholz, Vol. 2, pp. 256–8): 'I have been astounded to see children of eight and nine years offer their company, at least as far as it would serve. The corruption of men's hearts is so great, that even such children can find lovers to flirt with them.'
46 Bloch, *Sexual Life in England*, p. 105, quoting Schütz, *Briefe über London* (Letters from London), pp. 214–17.
47 Bristow, *Vice and Vigilance*, p. 60. Also, Bloch, *Sexual Life in England*, pp. 131–2, states that the Temple of Aurora occupied one of three houses in St James's Street presided over by Mrs Fawkland. The other two houses were called the Temples of Flora and of Mystery. The Temple of Aurora contained girls aged from 11 to 16 who were educated in the

techniques of sex, given *Fanny Hill* to read 'to inflame their senses at an early age' but were kept as virgins and permitted only to be 'visited' by impotent men of 60 years of age or over. After the age of 16 the girls pursued more active lives in one of the other temples.

48 Trumbach, *Sex and the Gender Revolution*, p. 117.

49 *Williams, The London Lock,* p. 33. Also, John Dunton in a journal entitled the *Night-Walker,* 1696, states that it was believed that 'a man can cure himself of distemper by lying with a child'.

50 Bristow, *Vice and Vigilance*, p. 60.

51 John Fielding, *An Account of the Origin and Effects of a Police Set on Foot by His Grace the Duke of Newcastle, in the Year 1753,* 1758; Trumbach, *Sex and the Gender Revolution*, pp. 116–17.

52 Bristow, *Vice and Vigilance*, pp. 60–1.

53 *The Complete Newgate Calendar,* ed. J. L. Rayner and G. T. Crook, 1926, Vol. 4, 'John Crouch and wife Convicted for offering to sell, on the Royal Exchange, a Young Girl, 12th of May 1766'.

54 *Gentleman's Magazine,* January 1816, p. 32.

55 *Ibid.*

56 Ryan, *Prostitution in London* p. 119; Bristow, *Vice and Vigilance*, p. 60.

3: Mother Clap and Her Boys

1   Old Bailey Proceedings online (www.oldbaileyonline.org): 11 July 1677, (t16770711–1).

2   J. Weeks, *Sex, Politics and Society*, 1989, p. 99.

3   See Old Bailey Proceedings online (www.oldbaileyonline.org).

4   *The Shortest-Way with Whores and Rogues,* 1703, British Library shelfmark C.124.g.15.

5   *Ibid.*, pp. 36–43.

6   Josiah Woodward, *The Soldier's Monitor*, 1776, p. 22.

7   *The Shortest-Way with Whores and Rogues*, pp. 34–6.

8   *Ibid.*, p. 43.

9   Burgo Partridge, *A History of Orgies*, 1966, pp. 110–11; Robert Latham and William Matthews (eds.), *The Diary of Samuel Pepys*, Vol. 4, 1970–83, p. 209.

10 Bristow, *Vice and Vigilance*, p. 12.

11 *Ibid.*, p. 13.

12 Welch, *A Proposal. . .*, p. 18.

13 For this account acknowledgement goes to Rictor Norton, *Mother Clap's Molly House: The Gay Subculture in England, 1700–1830*, 1992, which gives a more detailed study.

14 Old Bailey Proceedings online (www.oldbaileyonline.org): (f17260420-1).

15 Old Bailey Proceedings online (www.oldbaileyonline.org): Trial of Thomas Weight, 20 April 1726 (t17260420-67).

16 Old Bailey Proceedings online (www.oldbaileyonline.org): Trial of Gabriel Lawrence, 20 May 1726 (t17260420-64).

17 Old Bailey Proceedings online (www.oldbaileyonline.org): Trial of William Brown, 11 July 1726, 'Assault with Sodomitical Intent' (t17260711-77).

18 Old Bailey Proceedings online (www.oldbaileyonline.org): Trial of William Griffin, 20 April 1720 (t17260420-65).

19 Old Bailey Proceedings online (www.oldbaileyonline.org): Trial of John Kedear, 20 April 1726 (t17260420-66).

20 Old Bailey Proceedings online (www.oldbaileyonline.org): Trial of George Whytle, 20 April 1726 (t17260420-68).

21 Norton, *Mother Clap's Molly House*, p. 63.

22 See *The Newgate Calendar*, 1773 (compiled from broadsheets dating back 70 years); also edn ed. Andrew Knapp and William Baldwin, 1824–6.

23 Old Bailey Proceedings online (www.oldbaileyonline.org): Trial of Margaret Clap, 11 July 1726 (t17260711-54).

24 Old Bailey Proceedings online (www.oldbaileyonline.org): Trial of Martin Mackintosh, 11 July 1726 (t17260711-53).

25 Old Bailey Proceedings online (www.oldbaileyonline.org): Trial of Julius Cesar Taylor, 16 October 1728 (t17281016-60).

26 Old Bailey Proceedings online (www.oldbaileyonline.org): (t17260711-53); see also Norton, *Mother Clap's Molly House*, p. 64, where he says Partridge 'threatened' to run the poker into Mackintosh's 'arse', which seems more likely.

27 Old Bailey Proceedings online (www.oldbaileyonline.org): Trial of William Brown, 11 July 1726 (t17260711-77).

28 Old Bailey Proceedings online (www.oldbaileyonline.org): Margaret Clap, 11 July 1726, trial (t17260711-54) and sentence (s17260711-1).

29 Old Bailey Proceedings online (www.oldbaileyonline.org): Trial of John Painter and John Green, 30 August 1727 (t17270830-53).

30 Old Bailey Proceedings online (www.oldbaileyonline.org): Trial of William Hollywell and William Huggins, 4 December 1730 (t17301204-22).

31 Jane Austen, *Mansfield Park*, 1814, 1996 edn, p. 91.

32 Park Honan, *Jane Austen: Her Life*, 1987, p. 160; Oliver MacDonagh, *Jane Austen: Real and Imagined Worlds*, 1991.

33 Old Bailey Proceedings online (www.oldbaileyonline.org): Trial of Thomas White and John Newball Hepburn, 5 December 1810 (t18101205-1); see also Robert Holloway, *The Phoenix of Sodom*, 1813.

4: Facts and Fantasies

1 Gerald Howson, *Thief-Taker General*, 1970, p. 157. See also Daniel Defoe and George A. Starr, *The Fortunes and Misfortunes of the Famous Moll Flanders*, 1988, for further investigation of the possible connections between Moll King and Moll Flanders.

2 Howson, *Thief-Taker General*, pp. 156-7; Sessions Records in British Museum, 515.1.2.

3 *The Life and Character of Moll King*, c.1747, British Library shelfmark C.133.dd.7.

4 See Markman Ellis, 'Coffee-women', chapter in Elizabeth Eger et al. (eds.), *Women, Writing and the Public Sphere, 1700-1830*, 2001, pp. 27-52.

5 *The Life and Character of Moll King*, p. 4.

6 *Ibid.*, p. 5.

7 *Ibid.*, p. 6.

8 *Ibid.*, p. 7.

9 *Ibid.*

10 *Ibid.*, pp. 8 -10.

11 Bryant Lillywhite, *London Coffee Houses*, 1963, pp. 596-7.

12 *The Life and Character of Moll King*, p. 10.

13 *The Life of Captain John Stanley*, 1723, British Library shelfmark 1132.f.32.

14 Howson, *Thief-Taker General*, p. 157.

15 *The Life of Captain John Stanley*, p. 10.

16 *Ibid.*

17 Howson, *Thief-Taker General*, p. 158.

18 Francis Dashwood, *The Dashwoods of West Wycombe*, 1990 edn, pp. 48-9.

19 *The Life of Captain John Stanley*, p. 11.

20 Lillywhite, *London Coffee Houses*, p. 596.

21 See Ellis, in Eger et al. (eds.), *Women, Writing and the Public Sphere* (note 4 above), p. 49, who states that King matriculated from Cambridge in 1713, referring to *Alumni Cantabrigiensis* by John Venn and J. A. Venn, Part 1, Vol. 3, 1924. But Lillywhite in *London Coffee Houses*, quoting Harwood's *Alumni Etonensis*, states that King 'went away' from Cambridge in 1715 (p. 596).

22 Howson, *Thief-Taker General*, p. 161, referring to Middlesex legal records now kept at the London Metropolitan Archives.

23 *Ibid.*, p. 162.

24 *Ibid.*

25 *Ibid.*, p. 163.

26 *Ibid.*

27 *Ibid.*, p. 168.

28 *Ibid.*

29 *Ibid.*, p. 169.

30 Lillywhite, *London Coffee Houses*, p. 596.

31 *The Life and Character of Moll King*, p. 8.

32 E. J. Burford, *Wits, Wenchers and Wantons*, 1986, p. 58.

33 *The Life and Character of Moll King*, pp. 12 and 23–4.

34 Burford, *Wits, Wenchers and Wantons*, pp. 58–60; Lillywhite, *London Coffee Houses*, p. 596.

35 *The Life and Character of Moll King*, p. 15.

36 *Ibid.*, p. 17. The 1811 edn of the *Anecdotes of the Celebrated William Hogarth* states that an article in the *Weekly Miscellany* for 9 June 1739 recorded that Mrs King, of Covent Garden, was brought up to King's Bench Bar, fined £200 and imprisoned for three months for keeping a disorderly house (p. 56).

37 *The Life and Character of Moll King*, p. 13.

38 *Nocturnal Revels; or, the History of King's Place and Other Modern Nunneries*, Vol. 1, 1779, p. 12.

39 Burford, *Wits, Wenchers and Wantons*, p. 62.

40 Thomas James Barratt, *The Annals of Hampstead*, 1912. The 1811 edn of the *Anecdotes of the Celebrated William Hogarth* states that Moll King 'built three houses on Haverstock Hill' and after her death her 'own mansion' was 'the last residence of the celebrated Nancy Dawson' (p. 56).

41 *Nocturnal Revels*, Vol. 1, p. 12.

42 *Nocturnal Revels*, Vol. 1, p. 8.

43 John Thomas Smith, *Nollekens and his Times,* 1828, 1986 edn, p. 85.

44 See an engraving of 1750 by Chatelain. See also a view of Tom King's coffee house *Tom King's, or the Paphian Grove, with The Humours of Covent Garden,* 1738.

45 William Hazlitt, *Selected Writings,* ed. Jon Cook, 1991, p. 302.

46 Henry Fielding, *Amelia,* Bk 1, 1751, 1987 edn, p. 36.

47 Quoted in John Ireland, *Hogarth's Works: With Life and Anecdotal Descriptions of his Pictures,* 1874.

48 E. Beresford Chancellor, *The Annals of Covent Garden,* 1930, p. 131.

49 Now at the Albright-Knox Art Gallery, Buffalo, New York – see Robert Hughes, *The Times,* 31 March 1986, on the Reynolds exhibition.

50 *Anecdotes of William Hogarth, Written by Himself,* 1833, p. 190; Christina Scull, *The Soane Hogarths,* 1991.

51 Norreys Jephson O'Conor, *A Servant of the Crown in England and in North America, 1756–1761,* 1938. Based on papers of Secretary and Judge Advocate to HM forces, John Appy.

52 Burford and Wotton, *Private Vices – Public Virtues,* p. 130; Burford, *Wits, Wenchers and Wantons,* p. 79; Reginald Jacobs, *Covent Garden: Its Romance and History,* 1913.

53 *Anecdotes of the Celebrated William Hogarth,* 1811 edn, p. 49.

54 Chancellor, *The Annals of Covent Garden,* pp. 132 and 282.

5: Winners and Losers

1 *The Genuine History of Mrs Sarah Prydden, usually called Sally Salisbury, and her Gallants,* 1723, British Library shelfmark 1418.f.24.

2 Captain Charles Walker, *The Authentick Memoirs of the Life, Intrigues and Adventures of the Celebrated Sally Salisbury,* 1724, p. 150.

3 Pettit and Spedding (eds.), *Eighteenth-century British Erotica,* Vol. 1, p. xxii.

4 *Pretty Doings in a Protestant Nation,* p. 4.

5 Burford and Wotton, *Private Vices – Public Virtues,* pp. 103–5.

6 *The Genuine History of Mrs Sarah Prydden,* pp. 19–20.

7 Burford and Wotton, *Private Vices – Public Virtues,* p. 104.

8 *The Spectator,* 4 January 1712, No. 266, see Gregory Smith (ed.), *The Spectator,* Vol. 2, pp. 293–4.

9 *The Spectator,* 8 October 1711, edn ed. Donald F. Bond, 1987, Vol. 2, pp. 244–7.

10 *The Genuine History of Mrs Sarah Prydden*, p. 33.

11 *Ibid.*, pp. 30–1.

12 *Ibid.*, p. 35.

13 *Ibid.*, p. 54.

14 *Ibid.*

15 *The Complete Newgate Calendar*, ed. J. L. Rayner and G. T. Crook, 1926.

16 *The Wentworth Papers, 1705–1739*, ed. James Cartwright, 1883, see letter dated 14 March 1712 from Lady Wentworth (pp. 277–8). Also *The Spectator*, 12 March 1712, see Gregory Smith (ed.), *The Spectator*, Vol. 2.

17 *Memoirs of William Hickey*, ed. Peter Quennell, 1975 edn, p. 156.

18 *The Genuine History of Mrs Sarah Prydden*, pp. 33–4.

19 Walker, *The Authentick Memoirs . . . of Sally Salisbury*, p. 136.

20 *The Genuine History of Mrs Sarah Prydden*, p. 55.

21 Lady Mary Wortley Montagu, *Letters from the Right Honourable Lady Mary Wortley Montagu 1709–1762*, 1906, p. 564.

22 Old Bailey Proceedings online (www.oldbaileyonline.org): only documents relating to sentence are available online (o17230424–2).

23 *The Newgate Calendar*, edn ed. Knapp and Baldwin 1824–6.

24 *The Genuine History of Mrs Sarah Prydden*, p. 70.

25 *Ibid.*

26 *Ibid.*, pp. 68–9.

27 *Ibid.*, p. 70.

28 De Saussure, *Letters from London*, pp. 114–15.

29 See Lucy Moore, *The Thieves' Opera*, 1998, p. 304.

30 *The Life of Lavinia Beswick, alias Fenton, alias Polly Peachum*, 1728, British Library shelfmark 1415.b.34.

31 *Ibid.*, p. 14.

32 *The Craftsman*, 3 February 1728, quoted in Lisa Hilton, *Mistress Peachum's Pleasure: The Life of Lavinia, Duchess of Bolton*, 2005, p. 3.

33 Hilton, *Mistress Peachum's Pleasure*, 2006 edn, pp. 121–3.

34 *Ibid.*, p. 10.

35 Horace, *Odes (Ulla si iuris)*, 2.8 (7–8).

36 See Hilton, *Mistress Peachum's Pleasure: The Life of Lavinia Beswick*, 2005, p. 11; and Charles E. Pearce, *'Polly Peachum': Being the Story of Lavinia Fenton*, 1913.

6: 'Measuring the Maypole'

1   Quoted in Bloch, *Sexual Life in Britain*, pp. 8–10.
2   *Ibid.*
3   I. M. Davis, *The Harlot and the Statesman*, 1986, p. vii.
4   Ryan, *Prostitution in London*, p. 179.
5   *A Congratulatory Epistle from a Reformed Rake*, 1758, pp. 8–10.
6   *Nocturnal Revels*, Vol. 1, pp. 7–9.
7   *Nocturnal Revels*, Vol. 1, pp. 25–6; Vol. 2, p. 98.
8   *Nocturnal Revels*, Vol. 1, pp. 50–3.
9   Davis, *The Harlot and the Statesman*, p. 13.
10 James Boswell, *London Journal, 1762–3*, edn ed. Frederick A. Pottle, 1950.
11 *Nocturnal Revels*, Vol. 1, p. 177.
12 Archenholz, *A Picture of England*, 1789 Jeffery edn, Vol. 2, pp. 92–3.
13 Bloch, *Sexual Life in England*, p. 98, referring to Archenholz, *A Picture of England*, Vol. 2, pp. 246–8.
14 Fanny Murray, *Memoirs of the Celebrated Miss Fanny Murray*, 1759, British Library shelfmark 1417.c.27, pp. 102–3.
15 Boswell, *London Journal*, 1950 edn, pp. 83–4.
16 Old Bailey proceedings online (www.oldbaileyonline.org): Trial of John Omitt, 5 December 1750 (t17501205-47).
17 Old Bailey proceedings online (www.oldbaileyonline.org): Trial of Mary Maxwell, 24 April 1754 (t17540424-19).
18 Old Bailey proceedings online (www.oldbaileyonline.org): Trial of Anne Jones, 27 February 1751 (t17510227-38).
19 De Saussure, *Letters from London*, p. 114.
20 *A Congratulatory Epistle from a Reformed Rake*, p. 41.
21 Archenholz, *A Picture of England*, 1789 Jeffery edn, Vol. 2, p. 89.
22 Welch, *A Proposal . . .*, p. 7; see Trumbach, *Sex and the Gender Revolution*, p. 112.
23 Jonas Hanway, *A Reply to C— A—*, 1760, p. 29.
24 Trumbach, *Sex and the Gender Revolution*, p. 112.
25 *Ibid.*, pp. 112–20.
26 Patrick Colquhoun, *A Treatise on the Police of the Metropolis*, 1796, 4th edn 1800. For background on Colquhoun, see Radzinowicz, *A History of English Criminal Law*, Vol. 3, Part 4, pp. 211–51.
27 See Paul Laxton and Joseph Wisdom, *The A to Z of Regency London: Richard Horwood's Map and the Face of London, 1799–1819*, 1985. By

the time of the 1811 census the population had risen to 1,138,000.

28 *A Congratulatory Epistle from a Reformed Rake*, p. 41.

29 *Ibid.*, pp. 40–2.

30 Compare Colquhoun's findings, for example, with those of the anony-
    mous author of a 1799 tract entitled *Thoughts on Means of Alleviating the
    Miseries Attendant upon Common Prostitution*, incorporated in an 1817 *Address
    to the Guardian Society*. When discussing prostitutes, the pamphlet stated
    that 'there are at least 40,000 females in London of that description; the
    population of London is reckoned 1,200,000, of this not above one third
    can be grown up females, or 400,000 . . . the unmarried grown-up females
    cannot be above 200,000, and these 40,000 [prostitutes] are almost, without
    exception, unmarried [so] from this it follows that every fifth unmarried
    woman is a —. The blood flies to my face . . . when I think of the word.'
    The *Address* was published in *The Pamphleteer*, 1818, Vol. 11, No. 21, printed
    by A. J. Valpy (pp. 225–52), with statistics on p. 245, referred to in
    Radzinowicz, *History of English Criminal Law*, Vol. 3 (pp. 244–5).

31 The arithmetic: 50,000 prostitutes each week multiplied by four times
    a week equals 200,000 encounters a week; 200,000 multiplied by 52
    equals 10,400,000 encounters a year. At 2 guineas each, on average,
    this puts the annual value of the London sex trade at 20.8 million
    guineas. Or an alternative calculation leads to the same total: 416 guineas
    (average annual income per prostitute) multiplied by 50,000 equals 20.8
    million guineas or £21,840,000 per annum.

32 Ryan, *Prostitution in London*, p. 89.

33 *First Report of the Commissioners*, 1839, Vol. 19, p. 16; quoted in
    Radzinowicz, *History of English Criminal Law*, Vol. 3, p. 243.

34 Ryan, *Prostitution in London*, pp. 120–1.

35 *Ibid.*, pp. 192–3.

Interlude: Elizabeth Canning

1   *The Complete Newgate Calendar*, edn ed. Rayner and Crook, incorpo-
    rating text from Knapp and Baldwin's 1826 edn, based on an edn of
    1780. See also Elizabeth Canning's account in subsequent trial of Mary
    Squires and Susannah Wells (see note 8 below).

2   Sir Crisp Gascoyne, *An Address to the Liverymen of the City of London
    from Sir Crisp Gascoyne, Relative to his Conduct in the Cases of Elizabeth
    Canning and Mary Squires*, 1754.

3 John Treherne, *The Canning Enigma*, 1989, p. 158.

4 F. J. Harvey Darton, *Alibi Pilgrimage*, 1936, p. 221.

5 Paulson, *The Life of Henry Fielding*, p. 264.

6 Welch, *A Proposal. . .*, p. 7.

7 Darton, *Alibi Pilgrimage*, p. 223.

8 Old Bailey proceedings online (www.oldbaileyonline.org): Trial of Mary Squires and Susannah Wells, 21 February 1753 (t17530221–47).

9 Paulson, *The Life of Henry Fielding*, p. 313.

10 Henry Fielding, *A Clear Statement of the Case of Elizabeth Canning*, 1753, pp. 43–4.

11 Paulson, *The Life of Henry Fielding*, p. 313.

12 See Andrew Lang, *Historical Mysteries: The Case of Elizabeth Canning*, 1904, pp. 29–30.

13 Allan Ramsay, *A Letter . . . Concerning the Affair of Elizabeth Canning*, 1753.

14 *Ibid.*, p. 3.

15 *Ibid.*, pp. 3–4.

16 John Hill, *The Story of Elizabeth Canning Considered*, 1753, p. 53.

17 Old Bailey proceedings online (www.oldbaileyonline.org): Trial of John Gibbon, William Clarke and Thomas Greville, 6 September 1753 (t17530906–450).

18 *Gentleman's Magazine*, July 1753, p. 307.

19 Reproduced by Lillian De La Torre in *Elizabeth is Missing*, 1947, p. 44.

20 Gascoyne, *An Address to the Liverymen of London*.

21 *Ibid.*, pp. 2–3.

22 *Ibid.*, p. 11.

23 *Ibid.*, p. 15.

24 Fielding, *A Clear Statement of the Case of Elizabeth Canning*, p. 44.

25 Gascoyne, *An Address to the Liverymen of London*, p. 15.

26 *Ibid.*, pp. 23–4.

27 *Ibid.*, p. 43.

28 *Ibid.*, p. 36.

29 *A Refutation of Sir Crisp Gascoyne's Address to the Liverymen of London*, 1754.

30 *Ibid.*, p. 7.

31 *Ibid.*, p. 15.

32 *Ibid.*, p. 30.

33 Fielding, *A Clear Statement of the Case of Elizabeth Canning*, p. 4.
34 Treherne, *The Canning Enigma*, p. 135.
35 Judith Moore, *The Appearance of Truth*, 1994, p. 256.

7: Building on Vice

1 Trumbach, *Sex and the Gender Revolution*, pp. 120–1.
2 Daniel Defoe, *Some Considerations upon Street-Walkers, with a Proposal for Lessening the Present Number of Them*, c.1726, p. 2; also see Bristow, *Vice and Vigilance*, p. 31.
3 *Ibid.*, p. 26.
4 *The Times*, 2 June 1787, quoted in Tony Henderson, *Disorderly Women in Eighteenth-century London*, 1999, p. 171.
5 Trumbach, *Sex and the Gender Revolution*, p. 121.
6 Henderson, *Disorderly Women in Eighteenth-century London*, p. 65.
7 James Peller Malcolm, *Anecdotes of the Manners and Customs of London during the Eighteenth Century*, 1808, p. 115.
8 Archenholz, *A Picture of England*, 1789 Jeffery edn, Vol. 2, pp. 92–3 and 96–7.
9 *A Congratulatory Epistle from a Reformed Rake*, p. 13.
10 See F. H. W. Sheppard (general ed.), *The Survey of London*, Vol. 33, *The Parish of St Anne, Soho*, 1966, p. 240; Hester Lynch Piozzi, *Autobiography, Letters and Literary Remains of Mrs Piozzi (Thrale)*, 2nd edn, 1861; James Boswell, *The Life of Samuel Johnson*, 1791; Norma Clarke, *Dr Johnson's Women*, 2000.
11 Piozzi, *Autobiography*. Also mentioned in Boswell, *The Life of Samuel Johnson*, 1821 edn, Vol. 4, pp. 380–1.
12 *Gentleman's Magazine*, April 1795, p. 294.
13 Ryan, *Prostitution in London*, p. 151.
14 Boswell, *London Journal*, 1950 edn, pp. 49–50.
15 *Ibid.*, pp. 272–3.
16 Mary Thale (ed.), *The Autobiography of Francis Place*, 1972, pp. 227–9.
17 *Pretty Doings in a Protestant Nation*, p. 1.
18 *London Spy*, May 1699; see Pettit and Spedding (eds.), *Eighteenth-century British Erotica*, Vol. 1, p. 365.
19 Thale, *The Autobiography of Francis Place*, p. 75.
20 Martin Henig, Katherine Munby and Frank Kelsall, *Post-Medieval Archaeology*, No. 10, 1976, pp. 156–9.

21 Museum of London ID numbers: 23113, 23114, 23115, 23116, 23117, 23118, 23119, 23120.

22 Bristow, *Vice and Vigilance*, pp. 29–30.

23 *London Spy*, January 1699, Part 3, p. 14, quoted by Norton, *Mother Clap's Molly House*, p. 50.

24 Cathy Ross and John Clark, *London: The Illustrated History*, 2008, pp. 154–5.

25 Old Bailey proceedings online (www.oldbaileyonline.org): Trial of William Brown, 11 July 1726 (t17260711–77).

26 Quoted in Trumbach, *Sex and the Gender Revolution*, p. 130.

27 Thale, *The Autobiography of Francis Place*, pp. 77–8.

28 Uffenbach, *London in 1710*, ed. Quarrell and Mare, p. 88.

29 See Hallie Rubenhold, *The Covent Garden Ladies*, 2006, for a full, pioneering and excellent description of the origin and evolution of this extraordinary publication. Rubenhold states that the earliest extant printed copy of the *List* dates from 1761 (p. 126).

30 *A Congratulatory Epistle from a Reformed Rake*, pp. 17–18.

31 Murray, *Memoirs*, pp. 100–1.

32 Rubenhold, *The Covent Garden Ladies*, pp. 71–3 and 335.

33 Murray, *Memoirs*, pp. 102–3.

34 *Ibid.*, p. 131.

35 *Ibid.*, pp. 123 and 130–1.

36 Archenholz, *A Picture of England*, 1789 Jeffery edn, Vol. 2, pp. 101–2.

37 Jack Harris, *Harris's List of Covent Garden Ladies . . . Kalendar for the Year 1788*, British Library shelfmark P. C.30.h.2. Names and addresses of prostitutes noted in this edn of the *List* give a flavour of late-Georgian London's sexual geography and include: Miss Bond, 28 Frith Street; Miss Holland, 2 York Street, Queen Anne Street; Miss Burn, 18 Old Compton Street; Miss Lever, 17 Ogle Street; Miss Linsay, 13 Bentinck Street, Berwick Street; Miss Hundrey, 45 Newman Street; Miss Brown, 8 Castle Street; Miss Tarbot, 25 Titchfield Street; Miss Ross, 1 Poland Street; Miss Sims, 82 Queen Street; Miss Bolton, 14 Lisle Street; Miss Douglas, 1 Poland Street; Miss Menton, 55 Berwick Street; Mrs Sutton, 31 Tavistock Street; Miss Robinson, 14 Lisle Street; Miss Townsend, 23 Russell Street, Covent Garden; Miss Wood, 3 Lisle Street; Miss Charlotte Cotton, 34 King Street, Soho; Miss Clerk, 116 Wardour Street; Miss Corbel, 16 Goodge Street; Miss Antrebern, 8

Lisle Street; Madam Dasloz, 46 Frith Street; Miss Charlotte Fern, 41 King Street, Soho; Mrs Watpool, 2 Poland Street.

[38] Isaac Ware, *A Complete Body of Architecture*, 1756, 1768 edn, p. 291.

[39] Malcolm, *Anecdotes of the Manners and Customs of London*, 1808, p. 467.

[40] Archenholz, *A Picture of England*, 1789 Jeffery edn, Vol. 2, pp. 89–90.

[41] *Ibid.*, p. 90.

[42] Bloch, *Sexual Life in England*, p. 98, referring to Archenholz, *A Picture of England*, Vol. 2, pp. 246–8.

[43] Cleland, *Fanny Hill*, 1964 edn, p. 70.

[44] *Pretty Doings in a Protestant Nation*, pp. 18–20.

[45] Archenholz, *A Picture of England*, 1789 Jeffery edn, Vol. 2, p. 90.

[46] Bloch, *Sexual Life in England*, p. 107.

[47] Ryan, *Prostitution in London*, p. 174.

[48] Bloch, *Sexual Life in England*, p. 107, referring to Archenholz, *A Picture of England*, Vol. 3, p. 74.

[49] Bloch, *Ibid.*

8: At Home with Mrs Cornelys

[1] Burford and Wotton, *Private Vices – Public Virtues*, pp. 103–4.

[2] Pamphlet of 1721 in British Museum, quoted in association with the print 'Wantonness Mask'd' in 2009 BM exhibition entitled *The Intimate Portrait, Drawings, Miniatures and Pastels* (see note 9 below).

[3] *Gentleman's Magazine*, December 1754, p. 560.

[4] See the description of a masquerade/subscription ball at Mrs Cornelys' Soho Square establishment in *Town and Country Magazine*, May 1770, pp. 256–66.

[5] See Sheppard (ed.), *The Survey of London*, Vol. 33, pp. 73–9, for an excellent and detailed history of Mrs Cornelys' activities in Carlisle House.

[6] Fanny Burney, *The Early Diary of Frances Burney, 1768–1778*, ed. Annie Raine Ellis, 1889, Vol. 1, p. 83.

[7] Tobias Smollett, *The Expedition of Humphry Clinker*, 1771, 1956 edn, p. 99.

[8] Letter to Sir Horace Mann, dated 22 February 1771, *The Letters of Horace Walpole*, edn ed. Mrs Paget Toynbee, Vol. 8, 1904, pp. 12–13.

[9] Edn of print held in British Museum catalogue, Satires 4511.

[10] *Universal Magazine*, Vol. 48, 1771, p. 109, quoted in Sheppard (ed.), *The Survey of London*, Vol. 33, pp. 73–9.

11 Quennell (ed.), *Memoirs of William Hickey*, 1975 edn, p. 286.

12 *Ibid.*, p. 292.

13 Samuel Curwen, *Journal and Letters*, 1842, pp. 289–90, quoted in Sheppard (ed.), *The Survey of London*, Vol. 33, pp. 78–9.

14 Sheppard, *Ibid.* The demolition of Carlisle House was a sad loss but its great rival the Pantheon, on Oxford Street, fared little better. It is, arguably, one of the great lost and now largely forgotten buildings of eighteenth-century London and was closely connected with the sex industry. Built as an audacious speculation on the part of Philip Elias Turst, starting in 1769, to the designs of James Wyatt, it included a mighty coffered dome with a 60-foot span, and after completion in 1772 was called by Horace Walpole 'the most beautiful edifice in Europe'. But as a place of public entertainment it soon failed. It was already in decline in the 1780s, was badly damaged by fire in 1789, largely rebuilt in 1795, and closed as a place of public assembly in 1814, being finally demolished in 1937.

9: The Rake's Repose

1 For an excellent introduction and explanation see Lillywhite, *London Coffee Houses*.

2 See Ellis, 'Coffee-women', in Eger et al. (eds.), *Women, Writing and the Public Sphere*, p. 36, quoting George Alexander Stevens, *The Adventure of a Specialist: or, A Journey Through London*, 1788, pp. 260 and 262.

3 See Lillywhite, who records that she was 'a queer character, renowned for her good humour and repartee', *London Coffee Houses*, p. 596, quoting Edward Thompson – see *Meretricious Miscellanies*, 1770, including pamphlets of 1738 and 1741 entitled *Tom King's, or The Paphian Grove, with the Humours of Covent Garden*, with verses describing the women who frequented King's coffee house and confirming the sexual geography of mid-Georgian London: 'The Nymphs of Drury, Fleet-Street, Temple-Bar, / The Strand, St. James's, hastily repair / To Covent's Grove, and throng about the Shrine / Sacred to Beauty, and the God of wine' (pp. 12–20).

4 Fidelis Morgan, *The Well-known Troublemaker: A Life of Charlotte Charke*, 1988, p. 224.

5 Tobias Smollett, *The Adventures of Roderick Random*, 1748, 1981 edn, pp. 277–8.

6   *Nocturnal Revels*, Vol. 1, p. 29. The 1779 edn of *Nocturnal Revels* was
    printed by an 'M. Goady' – presumably related to Mrs Goady – so it
    is not surprising that the book makes much of her importance in the
    development of London's sex industry.
7   Bloch, *Sexual Life in England*, pp. 124–30.
8   *Ibid.*, pp. 124–6.
9   *Nocturnal Revels*, Vol. 1, p. 29.
10 *Ibid.*, Vol. 1, p. 29.
11 *Ibid.*, Vol. 1, p. 30.
12 Bloch, *Sexual Life in England*, pp. 124–6.
13 Burford and Wotton, *Private Vices – Public Virtues*, p. 150.
14 Daniel Turner, *Syphilis*, 1717, p. 203.
15 *The Machine, or Love's Preservative*, *c.*1744, pp. 3–4, quoted in Pettit and
    Spedding (eds.), *Eighteenth-century British Erotica*, Vol. 3, pp. 307–8.
16 Boswell, *London Journal*, 1950 edn, p. 262.
17 Fielding, *Amelia*, 1987 edn, p. 35.
18 Teresia Constantia Muilman, *An Apology for the Conduct of Mrs Teresa
    Constantia Phillips*, 1748; and see Burford, *Wits, Wenchers and Wantons*,
    pp. 144–9.
19 See Rubenhold, *The Covent Garden Ladies*, pp. 46–56, for biographical
    notes on Charlotte Hayes.
20 Linnane, *London*, p. 113.
21 Quoted in Rubenhold, *The Covent Garden Ladies*, p. 239.
22 *Nocturnal Revels*, Vol. 2, p. 97.
23 British Museum Department of Prints and Drawings, Heal 35.83, ESTC
    citation No. T204405.
24 Quoted in Rubenhold, *The Covent Garden Ladies*, p. 245.
25 *Nocturnal Revels*, Vol. 1, p. 46.
26 *Nocturnal Revels*, Vol. 1, p. 54. Burford and Wotton in *Public Vices –
    Public Virtues* decode most of the nicknames: The 'Alderman' was Robert
    Alsop, Lord Mayor of London in 1752; 'Sir Harry Flagellum' was the
    Earl of Uxbridge; 'Lady Loveit' was Lady Sarah Lennox, also known
    as 'Messalina', and 'Lord Pyebald' was Viscount Falmouth (pp. 152–3).
27 Quennell (ed.), *Memoirs of William Hickey*, 1984 edn, pp. 277–8.

10: Grand Seraglio to the Nation

1   Radzinowicz, *History of English Criminal Law*, Vol. 3, p. 277.

2   British Library ESTC citation No. T100064.
3   *The Newgate Calendar*, ed. Knapp and Baldwin, Vol. 1, 1824, where it is explained that Edward Bird spent a night in a bagnio with a prostitute and the next day, seemingly while drunk, murdered a waiter – Samuel Loxton – because of a delay in drawing his bath. For trial details and a vivid description of Bird's violent behaviour in the bagnio see Old Bailey proceedings online (www.oldbaileyonline.org): Trial of Edward Bird, 15 January 1719 (t17190115-49).
4   British Museum, Department of Prints and Drawings. British Library, ESTC citation No. T205441.
5   Dan Cruickshank and Neil Burton, *Life in the Georgian City*, 1990, pp. 84–96.
6   *A True Account of the Royal Bagnio*, 1680, British Library shelfmark 115.i.56.
7   *Ibid.*, p. 3.
8   *Ibid.*, p. 6.
9   A copy in British Museum catalogue, Satires 11957.
10 British Library ESTC citation No. R232241, shelfmark 551.a.32 (40).
11 British Library, Harley MSS 5931 (227).
12 British Library shelfmark C.112.f.9.(31).
13 Samuel Haworth, *A Description of the Duke's Bagnio*, 1683, British Library shelfmark 233.a.40.
14 *Ibid.*, pp. 2–3.
15 *Ibid.*, pp. 5–6.
16 *Ibid.*, p. 18. Haworth also explained that different days were reserved for male and female use of the bagnio, an arrangement reflecting Ottoman practice.
17 Sheppard (ed.), *The Survey of London*, Vol. 36, *The Parish of St Paul, Covent Garden*, Appendix 2, 1970.
18 Lillywhite, *London Coffee Houses*, pp. 393–4; and map in Burford, *Wits, Wenchers and Wantons*, pp. 22–3.
19 Lillywhite, *London Coffee Houses*, p. 276.
20 Ned Ward, *The London Spy*, 4th edn of 1709, ed. Paul Hyland, 1993, pp. 165–170 (in Pamphlet ix).
21 Lillywhite, *London Coffee Houses*, p. 276.
22 British Library ESTC citation No. T142392, shelfmark Add. Ms.28276.(220).

23 British Library ESTC citation No. T142391, shelfmark Add. Ms.28276.(221).

24 Burford, *Wits, Wenchers and Wantons*, pp. 112–16.

25 Many thanks to Tim Carew for most generously sharing his findings and insights with me, and to Hallie Rubenhold for her help in the analysis and interpretation of the excavation and finds. See *London Transport Museum, Covent Garden, Archaeological Archive Report* by Tim Carew and Jonathan Moller, for AOC Archaeology Group, project number 7308, May 2009. The report has been submitted for publication in a forthcoming edn of *Post-Medieval Archaeology*.

26 Bloch, *Sexual Life in England*, p. 123, referring to Archenholz, *A Picture of England*, Vol. 2, pp. 261–2.

27 *Ibid.*

28 See Sheppard (ed.), *The Survey of London*, Vol. 36, pp. 86–8; and Vol. 16, *St Martin-in-the-Fields: Charing Cross*, ed. G. H. Gater and E. P. Wheeler, 1935, pp. 247–8.

29 Several versions of the view of the Piazza, Covent Garden were executed by Samuel Scott between *c.*1749 and *c.*1758, only one of which shows the Haddocks' trade sign. Most show a man strolling across the Piazza attired in full Ottoman costume – presumably a bagnio worker, perhaps a cupper, making his way to the hummums on the east side of the Piazza.

30 National Archives, Kew, Prob. 3/51/21 (W1094). For research and interpretation, my thanks to Nicholas Barratt.

31 See Sheppard (ed.), *The Survey of London*, Vol. 36, pp. 86–8, Piazza, lease of 25 January 1698/9 to Lord James Russell.

32 William Maitland, *The History of London*, Vol. 2, 1756.

33 See Burford, *Wits, Wenchers and Wantons*, p. 192; and John Hampden, *An Eighteenth-century Journal*, 1940, p. 334.

34 Lillywhite, *London Coffee Houses*, p. 611.

35 See *The Smith's Right Hand* of 1765 by William and John Weldon in which cast-iron hob grates are termed Bath Stoves.

36 *Nocturnal Revels*, Vol. 2, p. 17; and J. Pelzer, 'Coffee houses in Augustan London', in *History Today*, October 1982.

37 Fielding, *Amelia*, Bk 4, 1987 edn, pp. 147–8.

38 Lillywhite, *London Coffee Houses*, p. 702.

39 After a painting by Frans van der Mijn, prints at the National Portrait Gallery, London.
40 Burford and Wotton, *Private Vices – Public Virtues*, p. 138; and map in Burford, *Wits, Wenchers and Wantons*, pp. 22–3.
41 *Nocturnal Revels*, Vol. 1, pp. 16–17.
42 *Ibid.*, Vol. 1, p. 17.
43 Quennell (ed.), *Memoirs of William Hickey*, 1984 edn, pp. 48–9.
44 Chancellor, *The Annals of Covent Garden*, pp. 132 and 282.
45 *Nocturnal Revels*, Vol. 1, p. 18.
46 *Ibid.*
47 *Ibid.*, Vol. 1, pp. 18–19.
48 *Ibid.*, Vol. 1, p. 19.
49 Quoted in Rubenhold, *The Covent Garden Ladies*, pp. 141–2.
50 Burford and Wotton, *Private Vices – Public Virtues*, p. 138; and *The Adventures of a Young Gentleman*, c.1745.
51 Partridge, *A History of Orgies*, pp. 120–1.
52 *Ibid.*, p. 121. It is probable that Emma Lyon worked as a posture moll in Covent Garden in the mid-1770s. If she did, the experience could have inspired the erudite and utterly respectable attitudes she was later tutored to strike by her husband Sir William Hamilton, who managed to turn a much-desired young woman who had become a sexual 'object' into a living classical sculpture.
53 *A Congratulatory Epistle from a Reformed Rake*, p. 12.
54 *Nocturnal Revels*, Vol. 1, p. 20.
55 *Ibid.*, Vol. 1, p. 34.
56 *Ibid.*
57 Burford and Wotton, *Private Vices – Public Pleasures*, p. 140.
58 Quennell (ed.), *Memoirs of William Hickey*, 1984 edn, p. 80.
59 *Nocturnal Revels*, Vol. 1, p. 35.
60 *Ibid.*

11: 'The Reception of the Distressed'
1 'M. Ludovicus', *A Particular but Melancholy Account of the Great Hardships, Difficulties and Miseries, that those Unhappy and Much-to-be-Pitied Creatures, the Common Women of the Town, Are Plung'd into at this Juncture*, 1752, p. 5; and see Henderson, *Disorderly Women in Eighteenth-century London*, pp. 41–2.

[2] Linebaugh, *The London Hanged*, p. 148.
[3] John Brownlow, *The History and Design of the Foundling Hospital*, 1858, p. 1. An exception was Daniel Defoe who had a positive response to the sight of abandoned children on London's streets. In his *Augustus Triumphans* of 1728 he proposed a 'Hospital for Foundlings' and anticipated the moral confusion such an institution could provoke: some 'over-Squeamish ladies', he recognised, would claim that such a Hospital nurtured 'Lewdness' and would only 'encourage Fornication' and 'Sinning' by providing an easy way to 'get rid' of 'Bastards' and so be an 'encouragement to Whoredom'. But Defoe, ever a realist, observed that he was against dead babies as much as he was against the breeding of bastards and once a baby had been 'begot' it could not in any acceptable way be 'unbegotten' and so if abandoned had to be housed (p. 14).
[4] *Ibid.*, p. 1.
[5] *Ibid.*, pp. 1–2.
[6] R. H. Nichols and F. A. Wray, *The History of the Foundling Hospital*, 1935, p. 21.
[7] *Ibid.*
[8] Jonas Hanway, *A Candid Historical Account of the Hospital for the Reception of Exposed and Deserted Young Children*, 1759, p. 65.
[9] *Ibid.*, pp. 65–6.
[10] Nichols and Wray, *The History of the Foundling Hospital*, p. 28.
[11] Brownlow, *The History and Design of the Foundling Hospital*, pp. 113–14.
[12] *Ibid.*, p. 114.
[13] Trumbach, *Sex and the Gender Revolution*, p. 277.
[14] Brownlow, *The History and Design of the Foundling Hospital*, p. 18.
[15] London Metropolitan Archives, Foundling Hospital Billet Books, A/FH/A/9/1/3.
[16] Brownlow, *The History and Design of the Foundling Hospital*, p. 9.
[17] Hanway, *A Candid Historical Account. . .*, pp. 22–3.
[18] Nichols and Wray, *The History of the Foundling Hospital*, pp. 22–3.
[19] *Ibid.*, p. 23.
[20] *Ibid.*
[21] M. Ludovicus, *A Particular but Melancholy Account. . .*, pp. 22–3.
[22] Goldgar (ed.), *The Covent-Garden Journal*, pp. 277–80.
[23] Hanway, *A Candid Historical Account. . .*, p. 35.

[24] *Ibid.*, pp. 25–6.

[25] *Ibid.*, pp. 35–6.

[26] Nichols and Wray, *The History of the Foundling Hospital,* p. 55.

[27] Brownlow, *The History and Design of the Foundling Hospital,* pp. 15–16.

[28] *Ibid.*

[29] Nichols and Wray, *The History of the Foundling Hospital,* p. 53.

[30] *Ibid.*, pp. 122–3.

[31] *Ibid.*, p. 123.

[32] London Metropolitan Archives, Foundling Hospital Billet Books, A/FH/A/9/1/32.

[33] London Metropolitan Archive, Papers with children 1756–58, A/FH/A/08/007/001.

[34] Nichols and Wray, *The History of the Foundling Hospital,* p. 57.

[35] Brownlow, *The History and Design of the Foundling Hospital,* pp. 15–16.

[36] *Ibid.*, pp. 15–17.

[37] Nichols and Wray, *The History of the Foundling Hospital,* p. 57.

[38] *Ibid.*, p. 58.

[39] *Ibid.*, p. 54.

[40] *Ibid.*

[41] *Ibid.*, p. 56.

[42] *Ibid.*, p. 70.

[43] *Ibid.*, p. 80.

[44] *Ibid.*, p. 52.

[45] Brownlow, *The History and Design of the Foundling Hospital,* pp. 20–1.

[46] London Metropolitan Archives, Foundling Hospital, A/FH/A/08/006.

[47] *The Tendencies of the Foundling Hospital by 'Cato',* 1760, pp. 11–13.

[48] *Some Objections to the Foundling-Hospital Considered,* 1761, p. 26.

[49] Nichols and Wray, *The History of the Foundling Hospital,* p. 60.

[50] Hanway, *A Candid Historical Account. . .,* p. 13. To make the record of parish workhouses look as bad as possible, in order to make the Foundling's death toll look more acceptable, Hanway resorted to anecdote: 'In order to point out the utility of the Hospital I must mention that in one Workhouse which received one hundred children annually, for twenty years successively, upon an examination of seven of those years, not one child appeared to be living, and the same acknowledged of the other thirteen years . . . another which I have heard of, computed to receive 2,000 children in 28 years, not a single soul survived . . .

Without the least exaggeration, there have been nurses, in times past, who were denominated killing nurses, as well they might, if no child ever came out of their hands alive ... how many of these poor babes had gin and sleeping potions given them by their nurses I know not!' (p. 61).

51 Hanway, *A Candid Historical Account. . .*, p. 42.

52 Nichols and Wray, *The History of the Foundling Hospital*, pp. 80–1.

53 *Ibid.*, pp. 58 and 70.

54 London Metropolitan Archive, Foundling Hospital, A/FH/A/08/001/001/001–025.

55 Trumbach, *Sex and the Gender Revolution*, p. 278.

56 London Metropolitan Archives, Foundling Hospital, A/FH/A8/1/1/3.

57 *Ibid.*, A/FA/A8/1/1/7.

58 *Ibid.*, A/FH/A8/1/1/4.

59 John Holliday, *An Appeal to the Governors of the Foundling Hospital*, 1787, British Library shelfmark 10350.g.13.(21).

60 *Ibid.*, p. 9.

61 *Ibid.*, p. 21.

62 Brownlow, *The History and Design of the Foundling Hospital*, p. 23.

63 *Gentleman's Magazine*, March 1751, pp. 128–9.

64 *The Vices of the Cities of London and Westminster*, 1751, British Library shelfmark 8285.de.17.

65 *Ibid.*, pp. 22–3.

66 *Gentleman's Magazine*, April 1751, pp. 163–5.

67 Hebrews, XIII:4.

68 Edward Cobden, *A Persuasive to Chastity*, 1749, British Library shelfmark 694.g.19.4, p. 19.

69 *Gentleman's Magazine*, February 1749, pp. 125–7.

70 Smollett, *The Adventures of Roderick Random*, Chapter 22.

71 Mary V. Peace, 'The Magdalen Hospital and the fortunes of Whiggish sentimentality in mid-eighteenth-century Britain', *The Eighteenth Century*, Vol. 48, No. 2, June 2007, pp. 125–48.

72 Drawings at West Wycombe, in Howard Colvin, *A Biographical Dictionary of British Architects, 1600–1840*, 1978, p. 261.

73 Robert Dingley, *Proposals for Establishing a Public Place of Reception for Penitent Prostitutes*, 1758, British Library shelfmark 1388.k.1.(1).

74 *Ibid.*, p. 5.

75 *Ibid.*, p. 6.

76 S. B. P. Pearce, *An Ideal in the Working: The Story of the Magdalen Hospital, 1758-1958*, 1958, p. 11.

77 *Ibid.*, p. 16.

78 *Ibid.*, p. 11.

79 Robert Dingley, *The Plan of the Magdalen House for the Reception of Penitent Prostitutes*, 1758, British Library shelfmark 1388.k.1.(2), pp. 23–8.

80 Dingley, *Proposals*, p. 8.

81 Pearce, *An Ideal in the Working*, p. 11.

82 *A Letter to Jonas Hanway*, 1758, British Library shelfmark 700.f.11.11.

83 *Ibid.*, p. 4.

84 *Ibid.*, pp. 24 and 27.

85 Jonas Hanway, *Thoughts on the Plan for a Magdalen-House*, 1758, p. 23.

86 Dingley, *Proposals*, p. 22.

87 Dingley, *The Plan of the Magdalen House*.

88 *Gentleman's Magazine*, August 1758, p. 391.

89 *The Rules, Orders and Regulations of the Magdalen House*, 2nd edn, 1759, British Library shelfmark 1388.k.1.4; and *Bye-Laws and Regulations*, 1791 edn, British Library shelfmark Tracts 816.K.5.(1–12).

90 *The Rules, Orders and Regulations of the Magdalen House*, p. 19.

91 *Ibid.*

92 *Ibid.*

93 Pearce, *An Ideal in the Working*, p. 50.

94 *Ibid.*

95 *Ibid.*, p. 37.

96 *Ibid.*, p. 22.

97 *Ibid.*, p. 48.

98 Sarah Fielding, *The Histories of Some of the Penitents in the Magdalen-House*, 1760, pp. iii–v.

99 For further exploration of realistic versus romantic approaches to the redemption of penitent prostitutes, see Peace (note 71 above), pp. 125–48.

100 Pearce, *An Ideal in the Working*, p. 22.

101 *Ibid.*, p. 23.

102 *Ibid.*, pp. 24–5.

103 St Luke, XIX:10

[104] *An Account of the Rise, Progress and Present State of the Magdalen Charity, to which are added Rev. Dr Dodd's Sermons*, 3rd edn, 1766, pp. 73–100.

[105] Pearce, *An Ideal in the Working*, p. 35.

[106] *Ibid.*, p. 36.

[107] Bodleian Library, Oxford, Gough Maps 20.f.60.

[108] Old Bailey proceedings online (www.oldbaileyonline.org): Trial of Elizabeth Cross, 19 February 1772 (t17720219–16).

[109] Old Bailey proceedings online (www.oldbaileyonline.org): Trial of Susanah Clarke and Sarah Bargo, 17 September 1775 (t17750913–89).

[110] Pearce, *An Ideal in the Working*, p. 51.

[111] *Ibid.*, pp. 20–1.

[112] See also H. F. B. Compston, *The Magdalen Hospital*, 1917.

[113] Williams, *The London Lock*, p. 10.

[114] *An Account of the Proceedings of the Governors of the Lock-Hospital*, 1749, British Library shelfmark HS.74/1512.(4).

[115] Williams, *The London Lock*, p. 33.

[116] *Ibid.* pp. 26–7.

[117] *An Account of the Proceedings of the Governors of the Lock-Hospital.*

[118] Williams, *The London Lock*, p. 28.

[119] *Ibid.*, p. 39.

[120] *A Sermon Preached at the Opening of the Chapel of the Lock-Hospital near Hyde-Park-Corner, March 28 1762 by The Rev. Mr Madan, chaplain to the Hospital*, British Library shelfmark 1560/3947, p. 7.

[121] Williams, *The London Lock*, p. 28.

[122] *Abstract* accompanies *A Sermon Preached at the Opening of the Chapel of the Lock-Hospital*.

[123] Trumbach, *Sex and the Gender Revolution*, p. 119.

[124] Williams, *The London Lock*, pp. 41–2.

[125] *Ibid.*, p. 44.

[126] *Ibid.*, pp. 45–8.

[127] *Ibid.*, p. 50.

[128] *An Account of the Institutions of the Lock Asylum. . .*, 1796, pp. 6–7.

[129] *Ibid.*, p. 10.

Interlude: Colonel Francis Charteris

[1] See *The Newgate Calendar*, 1773 (compiled from broadsheets dating back 70 years); also edn ed. Andrew Knapp and William Baldwin, 1824–6.

² Latham and Matthews (eds.), *Diary of Samuel Pepys,* 1970–83.

³ *The History of Colonel Francis Ch—rtr—s,* 1730, British Library shelf-mark G.1661, included in Pettit and Spedding (eds.), *Eighteenth-century British Erotica,* Vol. 5, p. 197.

⁴ *Ibid.* Also, for a brief account of Charteris' trial, his conduct while awaiting execution in Newgate and his pardon on 8 April 1730, see Old Bailey proceedings online (www.oldbaileyonline.org): trial 28 February 1730 (t17300228–69), *Ordinary of Newgate's Account* (oa17300412) and pardon (o17300408–1).

⁵ See *The History of Colonel Francis Ch—rtr—s* (as note 3), pp. 197–247.

⁶ Old Bailey proceedings online (www.oldbaileyonline.org). The trial of the accused, George Rowson, took place on the same day as – and seemingly just before – that of Charteris (t17300228–66).

⁷ See *The History of Colonel Francis Ch—rtr—s* (as note 3).

12: Vice Takes Centre Stage

¹ Daniel Defoe, *The True and Genuine Account of the Life and Actions of the Late Jonathan Wild,* 1725, p. 39.

² De Saussure, *Letters from London,* p. 160.

³ *Ibid.*

⁴ *The Beggar's Opera,* Act 1, Scene 7. The essayist William Hazlitt, who retained a high regard for the opera a hundred years after it was written (as did most Londoners), wrote in 1817 that this line, in its radical reversal of convention, 'is worth all Miss Hannah More's laboured invectives'. From *The Round Table,* reprinted in William Hazlitt, *Selected Writings,* ed. Ronald Blythe, 1970 edn, p. 291.

⁵ Old Bailey proceedings online (www.oldbaileyonline.org): Trial of Mary Young . . . alias Jenny Diver . . . [and] Elizabeth Davis, 11 January 1741 (t17410116–15).

⁶ Old Bailey proceedings online (www.oldbaileyonline.org): *Ordinary of Newgate's Account,* 18 March 1741 (oa17410318).

⁷ Uglow, *Hogarth,* pp. 210–11.

⁸ Boswell, *London Journal,* 1950 edn, p. 264. It is highly probable that the witty 'waiter' Boswell encountered in the Shakespeare's Head was none other than Jack Harris, who probably knew the frolicsome girls well and had them on his *List.*

13: Muses, Goddesses and Painted Ladies

[1] Robert Morris, *An Essay in Defence of Ancient Architecture*, 1728, p. 19. The cosmic nature of harmonic proportion was forcefully argued by Morris in another publication, *Essays on Architecture* of 1734–6, in which he wrote in Lecture VII: 'When I consider proportion . . . I am led into a profoundity of thought . . . if we immerse our ideas into the infinite tracts of unbounded space . . . if we imagine the exact proportions, distances or use of every [planet] we must feel the emanations of the harmony of nature diffus'd in us, and must immediately acknowledge the necessity of proportion in the whole Oeconomy of the universe.'

[2] Appendix of Wren's writings on architectural theory – 'Tracts of Architecture' – in *Parentalia*, compiled by his son, Christopher Wren, and published in 1750. In Tract 1 Wren explains that 'Beauty is a Harmony of Object, begetting Pleasure to the Eye . . . There are two Causes of Beauty, Natural and Customary. Natural is from Geometry, consisting of uniformity and proportion . . . Customary Beauty is begotten by the use of our Senses to those Objects which are usually pleasing to us for other Causes, as Familiarity or particular Inclination breeds Love of Things not in themselves lovely [but] always the true Test is natural or geometrical Beauty.' See J. A. Bennett, *The Mathematical Science of Christopher Wren*, 1982, p. 4.

[3] Sheppard (ed.), *The Survey of London*, Vol. 20, *St Martin-in-the-Fields: Trafalgar Square and Neighbourhood*, ed. G. H. Gater and F. R. Hiorns, 1940, pp. 117 and 126; and article by Martin Postle, 'St Martin's Academy, True and False Records', *Apollo*, July 1991, pp. 33–8.

[4] Mark Girouard, 'England and the Rococo', *Country Life*, 13 and 22 January, and 3 February, 1966.

[5] Information thanks to Martin Postle, referring to George Vertue's *Notebooks*.

[6] Martin Postle and William Vaughan (eds.), *The Artist's Model from Etty to Spencer*, 1999; and Martin Postle's article, 'St Martin's Academy, True and False Records', *Apollo*, July 1991, pp. 33–8.

[7] Information thanks to Dr Martin Postle.

[8] Davis, *The Harlot and the Statesman*, p. 13.

[9] *Ibid.*

[10] David Mannings and Martin Postle, *Sir Joshua Reynolds: A Complete Catalogue of his Paintings*, text volume, 2000, pp. 552–3.

11 *Ibid.*, p. 379.

12 Quennell (ed.), *Memoirs of William Hickey*, 1984 edn, p. 277.

13 Lecture by Martin Postle: *'Painted Ladies' – Reynolds and the Female Studio Model*, August 1999. Copy in Paul Mellon Centre, Bedford Square, London. See also 'Painted Women' chapter by Martin Postle in Robyn Asleson (ed.), *Notorious Muse: The Actress in British Art and Culture, 1776–1812*, 2003.

14 Sheppard (ed.), *The Survey of London*, Vol. 34, pp. 388–9.

15 Quennell (ed.), *Memoirs of William Hickey*, 1984 edn, p. 282.

16 See Flora Fraser, *Beloved Emma*, 1986, and, especially, Kate Williams, *England's Mistress*, 2006, for an erudite overview of the current consensus on Emma's early days in London.

17 *Town and Country Magazine*, 1771, p. 458.

18 E. K. Waterhouse, *Sir Joshua Reynolds*, 1949, p. 18.

19 Nicholas Penny (ed.), *Reynolds*, Royal Academy of Arts, 1986, p. 193.

20 Postle, *'Painted Ladies'* (see note 13 above).

21 *Ibid.*

22 C. E. Russell, *English Mezzotint Portraits*, 1926, p. 108.

23 See also *The Uncommon Adventures of Miss Kitty F****r*, 1759; *Kitty's Stream; or, the Noblemen Turned Fisher-men, a Comic Satire, Addressed to the Gentlemen in the Interest of the Celebrated Miss K—y F—r*, by Rigdum Funidos, 1759; *A Sketch of the Present Times, and the Time to Come: in an Address to Kitty Fisher*, 1762.

24 Penny (ed.), *Reynolds*, p. 193.

25 Andrea di Robilant, *A Venetian Affair*, 2005, p. 205.

26 Giacomo Casanova, *The History of My Life*, trans. Willard R. Trask, Vol. 9, 1971, p. 308.

27 Horace Bleackley, *Ladies Fair and Frail: Sketches of the Demi-monde during the Eighteenth Century*, 1925, p. 144; Penny (ed.), *Reynolds*, p. 195; and James N. Davidson, *Courtesans and Fishcakes: The Consuming Passions of Classical Athens*, 1998, p. 106.

28 Tate Britain's 2005 Reynolds exhibition, *Painted Women*.

29 Archenholz, *A Picture of England*, 1789 Jeffery edn, Vol. 2, pp. 92–3.

30 Penny (ed.), *Reynolds*, p. 211; and J. Kerslake, *Early Georgian Portraits*, 1977, Vol. 1, pp. 74–6.

31 W. T. Whitley, *Artists and their Friends in England, 1700–1799*, 1928, Vol. 1, p. 252.

32 See Martin Postle, *Joshua Reynolds: The Creation of Celebrity*, 2005; and Joseph Farington (ed.), *Memoirs of Sir Joshua Reynolds*, 1819.

33 Horace Walpole, *Correspondence*, ed. W. S. Lewis et al., New Haven and London, 1937–83, Vol. 10, pp. 52–3. Information thanks to Dr Martin Postle.

34 Archenholz, *A Picture of England*, 1789 Jeffery edn, Vol. 1, pp. 109–10.

35 Penny (ed.), *Reynolds*, p. 246.

36 Quennell (ed.), *Memoirs of William Hickey*, 1984 edn, p. 270.

37 *Ibid.*

38 Penny (ed.), *Reynolds*, p. 295. James Northcote confuses matters in his *Memoirs of the Life of Sir Joshua Reynolds* of 1813–15 (p. 280) by insisting that the sitter for the portrait was not the 'famous' Emily Bertie but in fact the 'beautiful young' Emily Coventry. These were both names by which Emily Warren had been known.

14: The Power of the Past and the Primitive

1   See Nancy Qualls-Corbett, 'Sex in the temple: the tradition of the sacred prostitute', in Dan Burstein and Arne J. de Keijzer (eds.), *Secrets of Mary Magdalene*, 2006.

2   *Nocturnal Revels*, Vol. 2, p. 14.

3   *Nocturnal Revels*, Vol. 2, p. 7.

4   Archenholz, *A Picture of England*, 1789 Jeffery edn, Vol. 2, p. 95.

5   Richard Payne Knight, *An Account of the Remains of the Worship of Priapus*, 1786, p. 148. See also Giancarlo Carabelli, *In the Image of Priapus*, 1996, pp. 1–5 and 78–83.

6   Edward Gibbon, *The Decline and Fall of the Roman Empire*, Chandos Library edn, Vol. 1, Chapter 15, p. 332, undated.

7   *Ibid.*, Chapter 16, p. 431.

8   See frontispiece/plate 1, plate 7, plate 10 and final plate in Knight, *An Account. . .*, edn with British Library shelfmark Cup. 820.5.1.

9   Thomas Mathias, *The Pursuit of Literature*, 1796, quoted by Carabelli, *In the Image of Priapus*, p. 88.

10 Pierre-François d'Hancarville, *Monumens de la vie privée des Douze Césars*, 1780.

11 Pierre-François d'Hancarville, *Monumens du Culte Secret des Dames Romaines*, 1784.

12 *Ibid.*, Vol. 1, plates 1, 3, 4, 17, 18, British Library shelfmark PC.31.K.5.

[13] See Francis Haskell, *Past and Present in Art and Taste: Selected Essays*, 1987, pp. 30–45, which reveals that the erotic 'gems' listed by d'Hancarville in these publications were fakes, forgeries or non-existent; also Burton Feldman and Robert D. Richardson, 'Recherches sur l'origine l'esprit et les progrèss des arts de la Grèce', *Myth and Romanticism*, 1984, Vol. I, pp. v–viii.

[14] *Ibid.*, Vol. I, p. v.

[15] Francis Haskell and Nicholas Penny, *Taste and the Antique: The Lure of Classical Sculpture 1500–1900*, 1981, p. 68.

[16] See Tony Kitto, 'The celebrated connoisseur: Charles Townley, 1737–1805', *Minerva Magazine*, May/June 2005, in connection with a British Museum exhibition celebrating the bicentennial of the Townley purchase.

[17] Marie Sophie von La Roche, *Sophie in London*, 1786, trans. Clare Williams, 1933, pp. 219–21.

[18] Smith, *Nollekens*, 1986 edn, p. 194.

[19] Feldman and Richardson (eds.), *Myth and Romanticism*, Vol. I, p. vii.

[20] Joseph Banks, *The Endeavour Journal*, ed. J. C. Beaglehole, Vol. I, 1962, p. 351.

[21] Patrick O'Brian, *Joseph Banks: A Life*, 1987, p. 91.

[22] Patricia Fara, *Sex, Botany and Empire*, 2003, pp. 6–7.

[23] Fara, *Sex, Botany and Empire*, p. 50; Roy Porter, 'The exotic as erotic: Captain Cook at Tahiti', in G. S. Rousseau and Roy Porter (eds.), *Exoticism in the Enlightenment*, 1990.

[24] Fara, *Sex, Botany and Empire*, p. 4.

[25] *Ibid.*, p. 1.

[26] Quoted by John Gascoigne in *Joseph Banks and the English Enlightenment*, 1994.

[27] Fara, *Sex, Botany and Empire*, p. 56.

[28] Banks, *The Endeavour Journal*, Introduction, p. ccli.

[29] *Nocturnal Revels*, Vol. 2, pp. 22–8; Partridge, *A History of Orgies*, p. 120.

15: Visiting Venus' Parlour

[1] N. A. M. Rodger, *The Insatiable Earl: A Life of John Montagu, Fourth Earl of Sandwich*, 1993, pp. 31–2.

[2] Alexander Pope, *Epistle to Sir Richard Temple* [Lord Cobham], 1733.

[3] Tim Knox, *West Wycombe Park*, National Trust, 2001.

4 *Ibid.*, p. 32.
5 Dashwood, *The Dashwoods of West Wycombe*, 1990 edn, p. 48.
6 Knox, *West Wycombe Park*, p. 42.
7 Partridge, *A History of Orgies*, p. 129.
8 Arthur H. Cash, *John Wilkes: The Scandalous Father of Civil Liberty*, 2006, p. 129.
9 Dashwood, *The Dashwoods of West Wycombe*, 1990 edn, p. 27.
10 *Ibid.*, p. 160.
11 Horace Walpole, quoted by Francis Dashwood in *The Dashwoods of West Wycombe*, 1987 edn, p. 29.
12 Dashwood, *The Dashwoods of West Wycombe*, 1990 edn, p. 31. For another, admittedly largely fictionalised, description of Medmenham, see *Chrysal; or, The Adventures of a Guinea*, by Charles Johnstone, 1760.
13 *The Modern Courtezan*, 1751, pp. 3 and 10–20.
14 Proverbs, 9:14–15
15 See portrait published in Dashwood, *The Dashwoods of West Wycombe*, 1990 edn.
16 Three edns of *An Essay on Woman* survive in the National Art Library, Victoria & Albert Museum, London. References: Dyce 58 vo 10598, Dyce L12 mop 10600, Dyce S12 mop 10599. One contains a reference to Fanny Murray. See also Arthur H. Cash, *An Essay on Woman by John Wilkes and Thomas Potter: A Reconstruction of a Lost Book*, 2000, pp. 97–101.
17 'While some, in never dying verse', British Library shelfmark PP. 5439.
18 Cash, *An Essay on Woman*, p. 30.
19 Murray, *Memoirs*, p. 200.

Interlude: The Murder of Ann Bell
1 *Gentleman's Magazine*, October 1760, pp. 447–51.
2 *Gentleman's Magazine*, March 1761, pp. 121–3.
3 Old Bailey proceedings online (www.oldbaileyonline.org): Trial of Willy Sutton, 25 February 1761 (t17610225–18).
4 Archenholz, *A Picture of England*, 1789 Jeffery edn, Vol. 2, p. 90.

16: 'Children of Larger Growth'
1 Trumbach, *Sex and the Gender Revolution*, p. 172.
2 Samuel Johnson, *Irene: A Historical Tragedy*, 1737, Act II, Scene VII.

3 See *Public Advertiser*, 8 June 1769, referring to Johnson's play *Irene*.

4 Boswell, *The Life of Samuel Johnson*, 1934 edn, Vol. 1, p. 457.

5 *Moore's British Classics, containing Dr Johnson's Rambler. . .*, 1793, p. 385.

6 Peter Martin, *Samuel Johnson: A Biography*, 2008, p. 418.

7 Boswell, *The Life of Samuel Johnson*, 1934 edn, Vol. 4, pp. 321–2.

8 Martin, *Samuel Johnson*, p. 418; and *The Early Journals and Letters of Fanny Burney*, ed. Lars E. Troide, 1988, Vol. 3, pp. 146–8.

9 Boswell, *London Journal*, 1950 edn, pp. 255–6.

10 *Ibid.*, p. 280.

11 *Ibid.*, p. 227.

12 *Town and Country Magazine*, December 1785, p. 625.

13 Boswell, *London Journal*, 1950 edn, p. 332.

14 *Ibid.*, p. 175.

15 *Nocturnal Revels*, Introduction to Vol. 2, pp. 4 and 5. Pages dismembered in 1779 edn and do not run consecutively.

16 Bristow, *Vice and Vigilance*, p. 51.

17 April 1776: see Boswell, *The Life of Samuel Johnson*, 1934 edn, Vol. 3, pp. 17–18.

18 Vera Laska, *Franklin and Women*, 1979, pp. 40–1.

19 Mary Wollstonecraft, *A Vindication of the Rights of Woman*, 1792, Chapter 4.

20 A. D. Harvey, *Sex in Georgian England*, 1994, p. 42.

21 Nicholas Venette, *Conjugal Love Reveal'd . . . in an Essay Concerning Human Generation*, 7th edn, *c.*1720, 'Done from the French of Monsieur Venette' of 1687, p. 161.

22 *Ibid.*, p. 161.

23 Giles Jacob, *Treatise of Hermaphrodites*, 1718, p. 27, in Pettit and Spedding (eds.), *Eighteenth-century British Erotica*, Vol. 2, pp. 1–98.

24 Mandeville, *A Modest Defence of Publick Stews*, p. 24.

25 See Harvey, *Sex in Georgian England*, p. 39; also Chapters 1 and 2.

26 *Ibid.*, p. 40.

27 *Ibid.*, p. 41; *The Ladies Physical Directory*, 1742 edn, p. 70.

28 'Dialogue between a Married Lady and a Maid', 1740, reprinted in Pettit and Spedding (eds.), *Eighteenth-century British Erotica*, Vol. 2, pp. 357–40 and p. 367.

29 Harvey, *Sex in Georgian England*, p. 44.

30 *Ibid.*, p. 45.

[31] *Ibid.*, p. 42.

[32] *Lady Worsley: Account of the Trial with the Whole of the Evidence,* 1782, included in British Library shelfmark 11631.g.31.(1–20), pp. 19–20. For a full account see Hallie Rubenhold, *Lady Worsley's Whim,* 2008.

[33] Ryan, *Prostitution in London,* p. 122.

[34] *Town and Country Magazine,* July 1778, p. 345.

17: 'Slaves of a Casual Lust'

[1] Davis, *The Harlot and the Statesman,* p. vii.

[2] Wollstonecraft, *A Vindication of the Rights of Woman,* 1979 edn, p. 248.

[3] William Godwin, *Memoirs of the Author of A Vindication of the Rights of Woman,* 1798, 1987 edn, p. 235.

[4] Wollstonecraft, *A Vindication of the Rights of Woman,* 1979 edn, p. 248.

[5] *Ibid.*, p. 247.

[6] *Ibid.*, pp. 247 and 249.

[7] Mary Wollstonecraft, *The Wrongs of Woman,* 1796; edn ed. Gary Kelly, 1998, p. xvi.

[8] *Ibid.*, p. xvii.

[9] *Ibid.*, p. 88.

[10] *Ibid.*, p. xviii.

[11] *Ibid.*, pp. 106 and 109–10.

18: 'Pretty Doings of a Protestant Nation'

[1] Radzinowicz, *History of English Criminal Law,* Vol. 3, p. 276.

[2] Bristow, *Vice and Vigilance,* pp. 12 and 26.

[3] Radzinowicz, *History of English Criminal Law,* Vol. 3, p. 292. The Minute Book for the Liberty of Norton Folgate, Spitalfields, now in the Tower Hamlets local history library in Bancroft Road, contains records of the 1759 Act of Parliament for 'better lighting, cleansing and watching' the eleven-and-a-half-acre Liberty. The records reveal that the average age of the six watchmen was 52, that two of them had bad eyesight, and that one was soon dismissed for being indolent. Each was paid a wage of only £12 per annum.

[4] Bristow, *Vice and Vigilance,* pp. 24–5.

[5] See Thomas Bray, *The Tryals of Jeremy Tooley, William Arch, and John Clauson . . . for the Murder of Mr John Dent, Constable, in the Parish of*

St Paul's Covent Garden, March 18 1708–9, 1732, p. 19; Thomas Bray, *The Good Fight of Faith ... Exemplified in a Sermon preached ... at the Funeral of Mr John Dent*, 1709.

6 Bristow *Vice and Vigilance*, p. 25; Malcolm, *Anecdotes of the Manners and Customs of London*, pp. 2 and 21.

7 *Ibid.*, p. 14.

8 *Antimoixeia; or, the Honest and Joynt Design of the Tower Hamlets for the General Suppression of Bawdy Houses, as Encouraged thereto by Public Magistrates*, June 1691, see Bristow, *Vice and Vigilance*, p. 16.

9 G. J. Barker-Benfield, *The Culture of Sensibility*, 1992, pp. 57–8.

10 John Disney, *Essay upon the Execution of the Laws against Immorality and Prophaneness*, 1708, Preface, p. v.

11 Trumbach, *Sex and the Gender Revolution*, p. 201.

12 *Ibid.*, p. 13.

13 *Ibid.*, pp. 199 and 201.

14 Pettit and Spedding (eds.), *Eighteenth-century British Erotica*, Vol. 1, pp. xix and 203.

15 Henderson, *Disorderly Women in Eighteenth-century London*, p. 1.

16 Bristow, *Vice and Vigilance*, p. 26.

17 *Ibid.*, pp. 23–4.

18 Malcolm, *Anecdotes of the Manners and Customs of London*, p. 62.

19 See Harvey, *Sex in Georgian England*, p. 90.

20 *The One and Thirtieth Account of the Progress in the Cities of London and Westminster*, 1726, quoted in Donald Thomas, *A Long Time Burning: The History of Literary Censorship in England*, 1969, p. 75; Pettit and Spedding (eds.), *Eighteenth-century British Erotica*, Vol. 1, p. xx.

21 *Ibid.*

22 *The Forty-First Account of the Progress made by the Societies*, 1735, British Library shelfmark Sermons, 693.d.10.(12).

23 *Ibid.*, pp. 22–9.

24 Harvey, *Sex in Georgian England*, p. 99.

25 Bristow, *Vice and Vigilance*, p. 25.

26 *An Account of the Institution of the Lock Asylum. . .*, pp. 3–4.

27 Defoe, *The True and Genuine Account of ... Jonathan Wild*, p. 4; Linebaugh, *The London Hanged*, p. 21.

28 *Ibid.*, p. 145.

29 *An Account of the Institution of the Lock Asylum. . .*, p. 4.
30 Old Bailey proceedings online (www.oldbaileyonline.org): Trial of Mary Blewit, 11 July 1726 (t17260711–34).
31 Old Bailey proceedings online (www.oldbaileyonline.org): *Ordinary of Newgate's Account*, 11 December 1738 (oa17381222).
32 Linebaugh, *The London Hanged*, p. 147.
33 Old Bailey proceedings online (www.oldbaileyonline.org): Trial of Ann Duck, 14 January 1743 (t17430114–11).
34 Old Bailey proceedings online (www.oldbaileyonline.org): Trial of Ann Duck and Ann Barefoot, 17 October 1744 (t17441017–23).
35 Old Bailey proceedings online (www.oldbaileyonline.org): *Ordinary of Newgate's Account*, 7 November 1744 (oa17441107).
36 Disorderly Houses Act, 25 George II.
37 Goldgar (ed.), *The Covent-Garden Journal*, p. 277.
38 Bristow, *Vice and Vigilance*, p. 54.
39 Goldgar (ed.), *The Covent-Garden Journal*, p. 442.
40 *Ibid.*, p. 277.
41 *Ibid.*, p. 278.
42 M. Ludovicus, *A Particular but Melancholy Account. . .*, p. 9.
43 *Ibid.*, p. 21.
44 *The Covent-Garden Journal*, No. 50, pp. 277–80, quoted in Goldgar (ed.), *The Covent-Garden Journal*.
45 Philo-Patria, *A Letter to Henry Fielding*, 1751, British Library shelfmark 1508/411.
46 *Ibid.*, p. 8.
47 *Ibid.*
48 *Ibid.*, pp. 7–8 and 10–11; see also a letter signed by 'an Old Rake' published in *London Magazine*, March 1751, No. 20, pp. 128–30.
49 Fielding, *A True State of the Case of Bosavern Penlez*, pp. 49 and 51–2.
50 Goldgar (ed.), *The Covent-Garden Journal*, pp. 306–12; Martin C. and Ruth R. Battestin, *Henry Fielding: A Life*, 1989, p. 550.
51 Radzinowicz, *History of English Criminal Law*, Vol. 3, p. 54.
52 *The Covent-Garden Journal*, 11 January 1752, No. 3, quoted in Goldgar (ed.), *The Covent-Garden Journal*, pp. 392–3.
53 *The Covent-Garden Journal*, 25 January 1752, quoted in Goldgar (ed.), *The Covent-Garden Journal*, pp. 400–1.
54 Welch, *A Proposal. . .*, p. 48.

55 *Ibid.*, p. 52.

56 *Ibid.*, pp. 52–3.

57 *Ibid.*, p. 53.

58 Henry Fielding, *An Enquiry into the Causes of the Late Increase of Robbers*, 1751, pp. 70–1.

59 *Ibid.*, p. 71.

60 *Ibid.*

61 *Ibid.*, p. 72.

62 Welch, *A Proposal. . .*, p. 56.

63 *Ibid.*, pp. 56–7.

64 *Ibid.*, pp. 57–8.

65 *Ibid.*, pp. 25–8.

66 *Ibid.*, pp. 38–9.

67 *Ibid.*, p. 39.

68 Malcolm, *Anecdotes of the Manners and Customs of London*, pp. 201–202.

69 Quoted in *Ibid.*, p. 115.

70 Radzinowicz, *History of English Criminal Law*, Vol. 3, p. 276.

71 *Ibid.*, Vol. 3, p. 279; see also Vol. 2, p. 291.

72 Elaine A. Reynolds, *Before the Bobbies: The Night Watch and Police Reform in Metropolitan London, 1720–1830*, 1998, pp. 125–47; Bristow, *Vice and Vigilance*, pp. 53–4.

73 Old Bailey proceedings online (www.oldbaileyonline.org): Trial of Susan Brockway and Mary Gardner, 27 August 1725 (t17250827–2).

74 *Modern Propensities; or, an Essay on the Art of Strangling . . . with Memoirs of Susannah Hill*, 1791, British Library shelfmark 1414.f.32.

75 Pettit and Spedding (eds.), *Eighteenth-century British Erotica*, Vol. 5, pp. 249–94.

76 *Modern Propensities*, p. 9.

77 *Ibid.*, p. 38.

78 *Ibid.*, pp. 41–2.

79 *Ibid.*, p. 44.

Postlude: John Wilkes and *An Essay on Woman*

1   Cash, *An Essay on Woman*, p. 11. Acknowledgements to Arthur H. Cash, whose book is the key work on *An Essay on Woman*, for insights and information obtained from it.

2   *Ibid.*, p. 13.

3 Raymond Postgate, *That Devil Wilkes*, 2001 rev. edn, p. 3, referring to *Letters of John Wilkes*, I, 22.

4 Cash, *An Essay on Woman*, pp. 17–18.

5 *Ibid.*, p. 19.

6 *Ibid.*, pp. 14–35.

7 *Ibid.*, p. 28.

8 *Ibid.*, pp. 126–7; 'Pego' was a slang word for penis, as explained in Eric Partridge, *Dictionary of Slang and Unconventional English*, 1937.

9 Postgate, *That Devil Wilkes*, p. 8.

10 Boswell, *London Journal*, 1950 edn, p. 260.

11 *North Briton*, 1763, Vol. 1, No. 5, British Library shelfmark, PP. 3611.lbb, p. 44.

12 Cash, *An Essay on Woman*, p. 41.

13 Peter Collinson, writing in 1766, quoted in Ray Desmond, *The History of . . . Kew*, 2007, p. 42.

14 Boswell, *London Journal*, 1950 edn, p. 253.

15 *Ibid.*, p. 266.

16 *North Briton*, British Library Tracts shelfmark PP. 3611.lbb, pp. 97–101; Cash, *An Essay on Woman*, p. 40.

17 Cash, *An Essay on Woman*, p. 44.

18 For a modern reconstruction of the frontispiece, see *Ibid.* pp. 181–6.

19 *Ibid.*, p. 59.

20 *Ibid.*, pp. 111 and 113.

21 *Ibid.*, pp. vii–viii.

22 *Ibid.*, p. 63.

23 *Ibid.*, p. 64.

24 *Ibid.*, pp 65–6.

25 Walpole, quoted by Cash, *An Essay on Woman*, p. 66. Sir Francis Dashwood, present in the House of Lords for Sandwich's speech, was amazed by what he heard and commented that he 'never expected to hear the Devil preaching against himself'.

26 *Ibid.*, p. 66.

27 Quennell (ed.), *Memoirs of William Hickey*, 1984 edn, p. 56.

28 *Ibid.*, p. 57.

29 Postgate, *That Devil Wilkes*, p. 117.

30 *Ibid.*, pp. 222–3.

31 Three edns of *An Essay on Woman* survive in the National Art Library,

Victoria & Albert Museum, London: references Dyce 58 vo 10598, Dyce
L12 mop 10600, Dyce S12 mop 10599.

Appendix 1: The Mob and its Vengeance

1   Archenholz, *A Picture of England*, 1789 Jeffery edn, Vol. 2, p. 102.
2   Defoe, *The True and Genuine Account of . . . Jonathan Wild*, p. 4.
3   Old Bailey proceedings online (www.oldbaileyonline.org): Trial of
    Charles Knowles and Sarah Harper, 13 October 1731 (t17311013–47).
4   Old Bailey proceedings online (www.oldbaileyonline.org): Trial of John
    Waller, 25 May 1732 (t17320525–69).
5   Rictor Norton (ed.), 'Newspaper reports 1732', *Homosexuality in
    Eighteenth-century England: A Sourcebook*, 27 January 2006, updated 28
    February 2007.
6   Old Bailey proceedings online (www.oldbaileyonline.org): Trial of
    Edward Dalton, Richard Griffith and William Belt, 6 September 1732
    (t17320906–69); *Ordinary of Newgate's Account*, 9 October 1732
    (oa17321009).

Appendix 2: Women as Men

1   Emma Donoghue, *Passions between Women*, 1993, p. 87.
2   *Ibid.*, pp. 87–8.
3   Mary Frith, *The Life of Mrs M. F., Commonly Called Mal Cut-purse*,
    1662.
4   *The Complete Newgate Calendar*, ed. J. L. Rayner and G. T. Crook, 1926,
    Vol. 1, 1760.
5   Tim Hitchcock, *English Sexualities, 1700–1800*, 1997, p. 89.
6   *Ibid.*
7   Donoghue, *Passions between Women*, pp. 70–3.
8   *Ibid.*, pp. 70–1.
9   Charlotte Charke, *A Narrative of the Life of Mrs Charlotte Charke*, 1755,
    p. 82.
10 *Ibid.*, p. 135.
11 *Ibid.*, p. 136.
12 *Ibid.*, pp. 23–4.
13 Pat Rogers, 'The breeches part', in *Sexuality in Eighteenth-century
    Britain*, ed. Paul-Gabriel Boucé, 1982, p. 252; Morgan, *The Well-Known
    Troublemaker*, pp. 200–6.

14 Kristina Straub, 'The guilty pleasures of female theatrical cross-dressing', in Julia Epstein and Kristina Straub (eds.), *Body Guards: The Cultural Politics of Gender Ambiguity*, 1991; and Donoghue, *Passions between Women*, pp. 164–6.

15 Throughout November 1746 the case was reported in the *Gentleman's Magazine, Daily Advertiser* and *St James's Evening Post*. See also Pettit and Spedding (eds.), *Eighteenth-century British Erotica*, Vol. 5, pp. 391–417.

16 See Hitchcock, *English Sexualities*, chapter on 'Tribands, cross-dressers, and romantic friendship', pp. 76–92.

17 See Knapp and Baldwin (eds.), *The Newgate Calendar*, Vol. 3.

18 Henry Fielding, *The Female Husband*, 1746.

19 Goldgar (ed.), *The Covent-Garden Journal*, p. 311.

20 Trial recorded by Knapp and Baldwin (eds.), *The Newgate Calendar*, Vol. 4.

21 Christian Davies, *The Life and Adventures of Mrs Christian Davies, commonly call'd Mother Ross*, 1740, quoted in C. G. T. Dean, *The Royal Hospital, Chelsea*, 1950, p. 223.

22 Dean, *The Royal Hospital, Chelsea*, p. 223.

23 Matthew Stephens, *Hannah Snell: The Secret Life of a Female Marine, 1723–1792*, 1997.

24 N. A. M. Rodger, *The Wooden World*, 1986, pp. 76–7.

25 *Ibid.*, p. 77, referring to J. C. Dickinson, *A Naval Diary of the Seven Years' War*, p. 241. Published in the Transactions of the Cumberland and Westmorland Antiquarian and Archaeological Society, NS 38 (1938).

26 See Suzanne J. Stark, *Female Tars: Women Aboard Ship in the Age of Sail*, Constable, London, 1996.

Appendix 3: Dr James Graham

1 Acknowledgements and thanks to Lydia Syson for information during conversation and for her *Doctor of Love*, published in 2008, that is the first full and detailed study of Dr Graham's life, work and legacy. See p. 38.

2 Syson, *Doctor of Love*, p. 45.

3 *Ibid.*, p. 71.

4 *Ibid.*, pp. 98–9.

5 *Ibid.*, pp. 3–4.

6 *Ibid.*, p. 4.

7 Fernando Henriques, *Love in Action: The Sociology of Sex, 1960.*

8 Tony Rivers et al., *The Name of the Room*, 1992, see Dan Cruickshank's chapter 'Private parts', p. 98.

9 Carabelli, *In the Image of Priapus*, p. 190.

10 Rivers et al., *The Name of the Room*, p. 98; Carabelli, *In the Image of Priapus*, p. 19, quoting Graham, 1782, pp. 91–4.

11 Carabelli, *In the Image of Priapus*, p. 19.

12 Syson, *Doctor of Love*, p. 6.

13 Carabelli, *In the Image of Priapus*, pp. 19–20.

14 Syson, *Doctor of Love*, p. 234.

Pre-1840 Publications

An Account of the Institutions of the Lock Asylum for the Reception of Penitent Female Patients, when Discharged Cured from the Lock Hospital, C. Watts, London, 1796.

An Account of the Proceedings of the Governors of the Lock-Hospital near Hyde Park Corner, From the first Institution July 4 1746 to September 29 1749, London, 1749, British Library shelfmark HS.74/1512.(4).

An Account of the Rise, Progress and Present State of the Magdalen Charity, to which are added Rev. Dr Dodd's Sermons, 3rd edn, W. Faden, London, 1766.

An Answer to the Memoirs of Mrs Billington with the Life and Adventures of Richard Daly, Esq., London, 1792.

Arbiter, Petronius, *Memoirs of the Present Countess of Derby, late Miss Farren*, H. D. Symond, London, 1797.

Archenholz, Johann Wilhelm von, *A Picture of England*, 2 vols., Edward Jeffery, London, 1789.

Baddeley, Sophia, *Memoirs of Mrs Sophia Baddeley*, 3 vols., Dublin, 1787.

Banks, Joseph, *The Endeavour Journal of Joseph Banks, 1768–1771*, ed. J. C. Beaglehole, 2 vols., Angus A. Robertson, Sydney, 1962.

Barbon, Nicholas, *An Apology for the Builder; or, a Discourse shewing the Cause and Effect of the Increase of Building*, London, 1685.

Bewick, Thomas, *A Memoir of Thomas Bewick Written by Himself*, ed. Iain Bain, Oxford University Press, London, 1975.

Billington, Elizabeth, *Memoirs of Mrs Billington . . . With Copies of Several Letters. . .*, James Ridgway, London, 1792.

Bleackley, Horace W. (ed.), *Casanova in England, being the Account of the Visit to London in 1763–4 of Giacomo Casanova*, John Lane, London, 1923.

Boswell, James, *The Life of Samuel Johnson*, 1791; edn ed. E. Malone, 5 vols., J. Richardson & Co., London, 1821; edn ed. George Birkbeck Hill, Clarendon Press, Oxford, 1934.

Boswell, James, *London Journal, 1762–3*, ed. Frederick A. Pottle, Heinemann/Yale, London, 1950.

Bray, Thomas, *The Good Fight of Faith . . . Exemplified in a Sermon Preached . . . at the Funeral of Mr John Dent*, W. Hills, London, 1709.

Bray, Thomas, *The Tryals of Jeremy Tooley, William Arch, and John Clauson . . . for the Murder of Mr John Dent, Constable, in the Parish of St Paul's Covent Garden, March 18 1708–9*, J. Wilford, London, 1732.

Burke, Edmund, *A Philosophical Enquiry into the Origins of our Ideas of the Sublime and the Beautiful*, London, 1757.

Burney, Fanny, *The Diary and Letters of Madame D'Arblay, 1752–1840*, 3 vols., Frederick, London, 1892.

Burney, Fanny, *The Early Diary of Frances Burney, 1768–1778*, ed. Annie Raine Ellis, 2 vols., G. Bell & Sons, London, 1889.

Burney, Fanny, *The Early Journals and Letters of Fanny Burney*, ed. Lars E. Troide, 4 vols., Clarendon Press, Oxford, 1988.

Casanova, Giacomo, *The History of My Life*, trans. Willard R. Trask, 12 vols., Longman, London, 1971.

The Case of the Unfortunate Bosavern Penlez, London, 1749.

The Characters of the Most Celebrated Courtezans, London, 1780.

Charke, Charlotte, *A Narrative of the Life of Mrs Charlotte Charke*, W. Reeve, London, 1755; abridged form published in *Gentleman's Magazine*; edn ed. Robert Rehder, Pickering & Chatto, London, 1999; scrapbook edn incorporates 1755 text with relevant portraits, theatrical cuttings and prints, British Library shelfmark C.184.B.16.

Cibber, Colley, *An Apology for the Life of Mr Colley Cibber*, printed for the author, London, 1740; edn ed. R.K. Lowe, 2 vols., London, 1889.

Cleland, John, *Fanny Hill. Memoirs of a Woman of Pleasure*, 2 vols., G. Fenton, London, 1748–9; edn Luxor Press, London, 1964.

Cobden, Edward, *A Persuasive to Chastity: A Sermon, etc.*, J. Lodge, London, 1749, British Library shelfmark 694.g.19.4.

Colquhoun, Patrick, *A Treatise on the Police of the Metropolis*, C. Dilly, London, 1796; 4th edn, 1800.

The Complete Newgate Calendar see *The Newgate Calendar*.

A Congratulatory Epistle from a Reformed Rake to John F——g Esq, upon the new Scheme of Reclaiming Prostitutes, London, 1758.

Covent-Garden: A Satire, T. Legg, London, 1756.

Dalton, James, *A Genuine Narrative of all the Street Robberies . . . by James Dalton*, J. Roberts, London, 1728, British Library shelfmark Tracts 1080.m.32.(2).

Davies, Christian (previously attributed to Daniel Defoe), *The Life and Adventures of Mrs Christian Davies, commonly call'd Mother Ross*, R. Montagu, London, 1740.

Defoe, Daniel, *Augusta Triumphans; or, the Way to make London the Most Flourishing City in the Universe, First to establish a University. . .*, J. Roberts, London, 1728.

Defoe, Daniel, *The Conduct of Robert Walpole*, T. Warner, London, 1717.

Defoe, Daniel, *Everybody's Business is Nobody's Business*, London, 1725.

Defoe, Daniel, *Some Considerations upon Street-Walkers, with a Proposal for Lessening the Present Number of Them*, A. Moore, London, c.1726.

Defoe, Daniel, *The True and Genuine Account of the Life and Actions of the Late Jonathan Wild*, T. Warner, London, 1725.

Derrick, Samuel, *Memoirs of the Shakespeare's Head*, London, 1755.

Dingley, Robert, *The Plan of the Magdalen House for the Reception of Penitent Prostitutes*, London, 1758, British Library shelfmark 1388.k.1.(2).

Dingley, Robert, *Proposals for Establishing a Public Place of Reception for Penitent Prostitutes*, W. Faden, London, 1758, British Library shelfmark 1388.k.1.(1).

Disney, John, *Essay upon the Execution of the Laws against Immorality and Prophaneness*, J. Downing, London, 1708.

Drury, Robert, *The Humours of Covent Garden*, London, 1737.

Dunton, John, *The Night-Walker; or, Evening Rambles in Search of Lewd Women*, London, 1696.

Farington, Joseph (ed.), *The Diary of Joseph Farington*, ed. Kathryn Cave et al., Yale/New Haven, 1978–84.

Farington, Joseph, *Memoirs of Sir Joshua Reynolds*, London, 1819.

Fielding, Henry, *The Adventures of Joseph Andrews*, A. Miller, London, 1742.

Fielding, Henry, *Amelia*, London, 1751; Penguin edn, Harmondsworth, 1987.

Fielding, Henry, *An Apology for the Life of Mrs Shamela Andrews. In Which the Many Notorious Falsehoods and Misrepresentations of a Book Called Pamela are Exposed. . .*, A. Dodd, London, 1741.

Fielding, Henry, *A Clear Statement of the Case of Elizabeth Canning*, London, 1753.

Fielding, Henry, *The Covent-Garden Journal and A Plan of the Universal Register-Office*, London, 1752; edn ed. Bertrand A. Goldgar, Clarendon Press, Oxford, 1988.

Fielding, Henry, *An Enquiry into the Causes of the Late Increase of Robbers*, A. Millar, London, 1751.

Fielding, Henry, *The Female Husband; or, The Surprising History of Mrs Mary, Alias Mr George Hamilton*, London, 1746.

Fielding, Henry, *The History of Tom Jones, a Foundling*, A. Millar, London, 1749.

Fielding, Henry, *The Life of Mr Jonathan Wild the Great, A Journey from this World to the Next*, A. Millar, London, 1743.

Fielding, Henry, *A True State of the Case of Bosavern Penlez*, A. Millar, London, 1749.

Fielding, John, *An Account of the Origin and Effects of a Police Set on Foot by His Grace the Duke of Newcastle, in the Year 1753*, London, 1758.

Fielding, John, *A Plan for the Preservatory and Reformatory for the Benefit of Deserted Girls and Penitent Prostitutes*, London, 1758.

Fielding, Sarah, *The Histories of Some of the Penitents in the Magdalen-House as Supposed to be Related by Themselves*, London, 1760.

The Forty-First Account of the Progress made by the Societies, M. Downing, London, 1735, British Library shelfmark Sermons 693.d.10.(12).

Frith, Mary, *The Life of Mrs M.F., Commonly Called Mal Cut-purse*, London, 1662.

Garfield, Richard, *The Wandering Whore*, London, 1660.

Gascoyne, Sir Crisp, *An Address to the Liverymen of the City of London from Sir Crisp Gascoyne . . . Relative to his Conduct in the Cases of Elizabeth Canning and Mary Squires*, J. Hodges, London, 1754.

The Gentleman's Bottle Companion, London, 1768; facsimile edn, with description as 'a collection of 18th-century bawdy ballads', Edinburgh, 1979.

The Genuine History of Mrs Sarah Prydden, usually called Sally Salisbury, and her Gallants. To which is Affix'd a Letter from A. Boles, London, 1723, British Library shelfmark 1418.f.24.

Gibbon, Edward, *The Decline and Fall of the Roman Empire*, Frederick Warne, London, 1776–88.

Godwin, William, *Memoirs of the Author of A Vindication of the Rights of Woman*, 1798; edn ed. Richard Holmes, Penguin Books, Harmondsworth, 1987.

Hampden, John, *An Eighteenth-century Journal, being a Record of the Years 1774–1776, Compiled from Various Sources*, Macmillan, London, 1940.

d'Hancarville, Pierre-François, *Monumens de la vie privée des Douze Césars*, Chez Sabellus, Capri, 1780.

d'Hancarville, Pierre-François, *Monumens du Culte Secret des Dames Romaines*, De l'Imprimerie du Vatican, Rome, 1784.

d'Hancarville, Pierre-François, *Recherches sur l'origine l'esprit et les progrès des arts de la Grèce*, London, 1785.

d'Hancarville, Pierre-François, with William Hamilton, *Antiquitiés étrusques, grecques et romaines, tirées du cabinet de chevalier W. Hamilton*, Naples, 1766–7.

Hanway, Jonas, *A Candid Historical Account of the Hospital for the Reception of Exposed and Deserted Young Children*, London, 1759.

Hanway, Jonas, *A Reply to C— A—, Author of the Candid Remarks on Mr H.s Candid Historical Account of the Foundling Hospital*, London, 1760.

Hanway, Jonas, *The Defects of Police, the Cause of Immorality, and the Continued Robberies Committed*, J. Dodsley, London, 1775.

Hanway, Jonas, *Thoughts on the Plan for a Magdalen-House for Repentant Prostitutes*, James Waugh, London, 1758.

Harris, Jack, *Harris's List of Covent Garden Ladies: or Man of Pleasure's Kalendar for the Year 1773, Containing an Exact Description of the Most Celebrated Ladies of Pleasure*, H. Ranger, London, 1773, British Library shelfmark C.192.a.54; also for the years 1788, 1789, 1790, 1793, shelfmarks P.C.22.a.12-15 and P.C.30.h.2.

Hawkesworth, John, *Account of the Voyages . . . in the Southern Hemisphere*, London, 1773.

Haworth, Samuel, *A Description of the Duke's Bagnio*, London, 1683, British Library shelfmark 233.a.40.

Hazlitt, William, *Selected Writings*, ed. Ronald Blythe, Penguin, Harmondsworth, 1970.

Hazlitt, William, *Selected Writings*, ed. Jon Cook, Oxford University Press, Oxford, 1991.

Hickey, William, *Memoirs of William Hickey*, ed. Peter Quennell, Routledge and Kegan Paul, London, 1975.

Hill, John, *The Remonstrance of Harris, Pimp-General to the People of London*, London, 1758.

Hill, John, *The Story of Elizabeth Canning Considered*, London, 1753.

The History of Colonel Francis Ch—rtr—s, London, 1730, British Library shelfmark G.1661.

Hogarth, William, *The Analysis of Beauty, Written with a View to Fixing the Fluctuating Ideas of Taste*, London, 1753.

Hogarth, William, *Anecdotes of the Celebrated William Hogarth, with an Explanatory Description of his Works*, London, 1811.

Hogarth, William, *Anecdotes of William Hogarth, Written by Himself*, London, 1833.

Holliday, John, *An Appeal to the Governors of the Foundling Hospital, on the Probable Consequences of Covering the Hospital Lands with Buildings*, Harrison & Co., London, 1787, British Library shelfmark 10350.g.13.(21).

Holloway, Robert, *The Phoenix of Sodom, or the Vere Street Coterie*, J. Cooke, London, 1813.

The Humours of Fleet Street and the Strand, being the Lives and Adventures of the Most Noted Ladies of Pleasure by 'An Old Sportsman', A. Wright, London, 1749.

Jacob, Giles, *Treatise of Hermaphrodites*, 1718.

Johnson, Samuel, *Irene: A Historical Tragedy*, 1737.

Johnstone, Charles, *Chrysal; or, The Adventures of a Guinea*, London, 1760.

Jones, Erasmus, *A Trip through London, Containing Observations on Men and Things. . .*, 7th edn, J. Roberts, London, 1728.

Kitty's Stream; or, the Noblemen Turned Fisher-men, a Comic Satire, Addressed to the Gentlemen in the Interest of the Celebrated Miss K—y F—r, by Rigdum Funidos, London, 1759.

Knight, Richard Payne, *An Account of the Remains of the Worship of Priapus, Lately Existing at Isernia*, T. Spilsbury, London, 1786, British Library shelfmark Cup.820.5.1.

Lacy, Mary, *The History of the Female Shipwright*, 1773.

Lady Worsley: Account of the Trial with the Whole of the Evidence, London, 1782, British Library shelfmark 11631.g.31.(1–20).

Lang, Andrew, *Historical Mysteries: The Case of Elizabeth Canning*, Smith, Elder & Co., London, 1904.

La Roche, Marie Sophie von, *Sophie in London 1786*, trans. Clare Williams, Cape, London, 1933.

Latham, Robert, and William Matthews (eds.), *The Diary of Samuel Pepys*, G. Bell & Sons, London, 1970–83.

A Letter to Jonas Hanway, in which Some Reasons are Assigned, Why Houses for the Reception of Penitent Women, Ought Not to be Called Magdalen-Houses, J. Noon, London, 1758, British Library shelfmark 700.f.11.11.

The Life and Character of Moll King, late Mistress of King's Coffee-House in Covent Garden, Containing a True Narrative of this Well-known Lady, W. Price, London, *c.*1747, British Library shelfmark C.133.dd.7.

The Life of Captain John Stanley, London, 1723, British Library shelfmark 1132.f.32.

The Life of Lavinia Beswick, alias Fenton, alias Polly Peachum, London, 1728, British Library shelfmark 1415.b.34.

The London-Bawd, with her Character and Life, John Gwillim, London, 3rd edn, 1705; 4th edn, 1711.

'Ludovicus, M.', *A Particular but Melancholy Account of the Great Hardships, Difficulties and Miseries, that those Unhappy and Much-to-be-Pitied Creatures, the Common Women of the Town, Are Plung'd into at this Juncture*, London, 1752.

Machen, Arthur (ed.), *The Memoirs of Casanova*, 12 vols., privately printed for the Casanova Society, London, 1922.

The Machine, or Love's Preservative, T. Reynolds, London, 1744.

Maitland, William, *The History of London from its Foundation to the Present Time . . . New Edition Edited by John Entick*, 2 vols., J. Wilkie, London, 1775.

Malcolm, James Peller, *Anecdotes of the Manners and Customs of London during the Eighteenth Century*, London, 1808.

Mandeville, Bernard, *A Modest Defence of Publick Stews: or, an Essay upon Whoring, as it is Now Practis'd in these Kingdoms*, A. Moore, London, 1724; edn ed. Irwin Primer, Palgrave Macmillan, New York and Basingstoke, 2006.

Mathias, Thomas, *The Pursuit of Literature, or What You Will*, 4 parts, J. Owen, London, 1794.

Meibom, Johann Heinrich, *A Treatise on the Use of Flogging in Venereal Affairs ... To which is added A Treatise of Hermaphrodites* (by Giles Jacob), trans. George Sewell, 2 parts, E. Curll, London, 1718.

The Midnight Rambler; or, New Nocturnal Spy for the Present Year, Containing a Complete Description of the Modern Transactions of London and Westminster, Exhibiting Great Variety of Midnight Scenes, J. Cooke, London, c.1770.

The Midnight Spy; or, a View of the Transactions of London and Westminster, from Ten in the Evening till Five in the Morning, J. Cooke, London, 1766.

The Modern Courtezan, an Heroic Poem. Inscribed to Miss F—y M—y, H. Carpenter, London, 1751.

Modern Propensities; or, an Essay on the Art of Strangling ... with Memoirs of Susannah Hill and a Summary of her Trial, London, 1791.

Montagu, Lady Mary Wortley, *Letters from the Right Honourable Lady Mary Wortley Montagu 1709-1762*, J. M. Dent & Sons, London, 1906.

Moore's British Classics, containing Dr Johnson's Rambler and Lord Liddleton's Persian Letters, James Moore, Dublin, 1793.

Morris, Robert, *An Essay in Defence of Ancient Architecture*, London, 1728.

Muilman, Teresia Constantia, *An Apology for the Conduct of Mrs Teresa Constantia Phillips*, 3 vols., printed for the author, London, 1748.

Murray, Fanny, *Memoirs of the Celebrated Miss Fanny Murray*, 2nd edn, M. Thrush, London, 1759, British Library shelfmark 1417.c.27.

Nancy Dawson's Jests, to which is added the Merry Hornpipe, J. Seymour, London, 1761.

The Newgate Calendar; Comprising Interesting Memoirs of the Most Notorious Characters who have been Convicted of Outrages on the Laws of England since the Commencement of the Eighteenth Century; with Anecdotes and Last Exclamations of Sufferers, 5 vols., London, 1773, compiled from broadsheets dating back 70 years; edn ed. Andrew Knapp and William Baldwin, 4 vols., 1824-6. Also, *The Complete Newgate Calendar*, ed. J. L. Rayner and G. T. Crook, 5 vols., Navarre Society, London, 1926.

Nocturnal Revels; or, The History of King's-place and Other Modern Nunneries by a 'Monk' of the Order of St Francis of Medmenham, 2 vols., M. Goadby, London, 1779.

Northcote, James, *Memoirs of the Life, Writings . . . of Sir Joshua Reynolds*, London, 1813–5; 2nd edn as *The Life of Sir Joshua Reynolds*, 2 vols., London, 1818.

Palladio, Andrea, *Four Books of Architecture*, ed. Isaac Ware, London, 1738.

'Philo-Patria', *A Letter to Henry Fielding, Esq., Occasioned by his Enquiry into the Causes of the Late Increase of Robbers*, M. Cooper, London, 1751, British Library shelfmark 1508/411.

Piozzi, Hester Lynch, *Autobiography, Letters and Literary Remains of Mrs Piozzi (Thrale)*, 2nd edn, 2 vols., Longmans, London, 1861.

Pretty Doings in a Protestant Nation, being a View of the Present State of Fornication . . . in Great Britain by 'Father Poussin', J. Roberts, London, 1734, British Library shelfmark Tab.603.2.12(1).

Priddon, Sarah (calling herself Sally Salisbury), *An Account of the Tryal of Sally Salisbury*, London, 1723.

Priddon, Sarah (calling herself Sally Salisbury), *The Effigies, Parentage . . . Life . . . of Sally Salisbury*, London, 1722–3.

Priddon, Sarah (calling herself Sally Salisbury), *see also The Genuine History of Mrs Sarah Prydden*; *see also* Walker, Captain Charles.

Quennell, Peter (ed.) *see* Hickey, William.

Ramsay, Allan, *A Letter . . . Concerning the Affair of Elizabeth Canning*, London, 1753.

Ranger's Impartial List of the Ladies of Pleasure in Edinburgh, Edinburgh, 1775; facsimile edn, Edinburgh, 1978.

A Refutation of Sir Crisp Gascoyne's Address to the Liverymen of London, J. Payne, London, 1754.

Richardson, Samuel, *Pamela; or, Virtue Rewarded*, 2 vols., London, 1740.

Roberts, J., and A. Dodd, *Hell upon Earth; or, The Town in an Uproar*, J. Roberts, London, 1729.

The Rules, Orders and Regulations of the Magdalen House, 2nd edn, London, 1759, British Library shelfmark 1388.k.1.(4).

Ryan, Michael, M.D., *Prostitution in London, with a Comparative View of that of Paris and New York*, H. Bailliere, London, 1839.

Salisbury, Sally *see* Priddon, Sarah.

Satan's Harvest Home; or, The Present State of Whorecraft, London, 1749.

Saussure, César de, *A Foreign View of England in the Reigns of George I and George II: the Letters of Monsieur César de Saussure to his Family*, trans. and ed. Madame Van Muyden, John Murray, London, 1902.

Saussure, César de, *A Foreign View of England in 1725–1729*, trans. and ed. Madam Van Muyden, Caliban, London, 1995.

Saussure, César de, *Letters from London, 1725–1730*, trans. Paul Scott, Adnax, Newnham, 2006.

Schütz, Friedrich Wilhelm von, *Briefe über London* (Letters from London), Hamburg, 1792.

The Shortest-Way with Whores and Rogues; or, A New Project for Reformation, Dedicated to Mr Daniel de Foe, Author of the Shortest Way with Dissenters, London, 1703, British Library shelfmark C.124.g.15.

A Sketch of the Present Times, and the Time to Come: in an Address to Kitty Fisher, T. Waller, London, 1762.

Smith, Gregory (ed.), *The Spectator: Addison and Steele and Others*, 4 vols., Dent, London, 1958.

Smith, John Thomas, *Nollekens and his Times*, London, 1828; edn with introduction by Walter Sichel, Century Hutchinson, London, 1986.

Smollett, Tobias, *The Adventures of Peregrine Pickle*, Baldwin, Richardson and Wilson, London, 1751 (in which is included *The Memoirs of a Lady of Quality*, by Viscountess Frances Vane); rev. edn, 1758.

Smollett, Tobias, *The Adventures of Roderick Random*, J. Osborn, London, 1748; Oxford University Press edn, 1981.

Smollett, Tobias, *The Expedition of Humphry Clinker*, 3 vols., W. Johnston, London, 1771.

Snell, Hannah, *The Female Soldier; or, The Surprising Life and Adventures of Hannah Snell*, R. Walker, London, 1750.

Some Objections to the Foundling-Hospital Considered, by a Person in the Country to Whom They were Sent, T. Pasham, London, 1761.

The Spectator see Smith, Gregory (ed.).

Swift, Jonathan, *Directions to Servants*, George Faulkner, Dublin, 1745.

The Tendencies of the Foundling Hospital in its Present Extent Considered, in Several Letters to a Senator by 'Cato', London, 1760.

Thale, Mary (ed.), *The Autobiography of Francis Place*, Cambridge University Press, London, 1972.

Thompson, Edward, *The Courtesan*, J. Harrison, London, 1765.

Thompson, Edward, *The Meretriciad; a Satire on Kitty Fisher and Others*, published by the author, London, 1761; rev. 6th edn, as *The Meretriciad; a Satire in Verse*, C. Moran, London, 1765.

Thoughts on Means of Alleviating the Miseries Attendant upon Common Prostitution, T. Cadell & W. Davies, London, 1799.

A True Account of the Royal Bagnio, with a Discourse of its Virtues, Joseph Hindmarsh, London, 1680, British Library shelfmark 115.i.56.

Trusler, John, *Honours of the Table; or, Rules of Behaviour during Meals*, published by the author, London, 1788.

Turner, Daniel, *Syphilis, a Practical Dissertation on the Venereal Disease*, London, 1717.

Uffenbach, Zacharias Conrad von, *London in 1710*, trans. and ed. W. H. Quarrell and Margaret Mare, Faber & Faber, London, 1934.

*The Uncommon Adventures of Miss Kitty F****r*, Thomas Bailey, London, 1759.

Vane, Viscountess Frances, *The Memoirs of a Lady of Quality*, sensational revelations published as chapter 81 of Tobias Smollett's *The Adventures of Peregrine Pickle*, 1751.

Venette, Nicolas, *Conjugal Love Reveal'd . . . in an Essay concerning Human Generation*, 7th edn, London, *c.*1720.

Vertue, George, *Notebooks*, ed. Katherine A. Esdaile et al., 6 vols., printed for the Walpole Society at Oxford University Press, Oxford, 1930–55.

The Vices of the Cities of London and Westminster . . . being an Impartial Detection . . . of the Present Growth of Immorality . . . in Five Letters, from a Citizen of London, G. Faulkner, Dublin, 1751, British Library shelfmark 8285.de.17.

Walker, Captain Charles, *The Authentick Memoirs of the Life, Intrigues and Adventures of the Celebrated Sally Salisbury (Sarah Priddon)*, London, 1724.

Walpole, Horace, *The Letters of Horace Walpole*, ed. Peter Cunningham, 4 vols., Echo Library, Cirencester, 2006; edn ed. Mrs Paget Toynbee, 16 vols., Clarendon, Oxford, 1903–5.

Ward, Ned, *Humours of a Coffee House: A Comedy as it is Daily Acted*, printed for Bohee, the coffee-man, and sold at the publishing office in Bearbinder-Lane, London. A weekly publication from 25 June to 6 August 1707.

Ward, Ned, *The Insinuating Bawd; and the Repenting Harlot*, J. How, London, 1699.

Ward, Ned, *The London Spy*, ed. Paul Hyland, from 4th edn of 1709, Colleagues Press, East Lansing, 1993.

Ware, Isaac, *A Complete Body of Architecture*, T. Osborne and J. Shipton, London, 1756; 1768 edn.

Welch, Saunders, *A Proposal to Render Effectual a Plan to Remove the Nuisance of Common Prostitutes from the Streets of this Metropolis*, London, 1758.

The Wentworth Papers, 1705–1739, Selected from the Private and Family Correspondence of Thomas Wentworth, Lord Raby, ed. James Cartwright, Wyman, London, 1883.

The Whore's Rhetorick, London, 1683; facsimile edn, Holland Press, London, 1960.

Wollstonecraft, Mary, *A Vindication of the Rights of Woman*, London, 1792.

Wollstonecraft, Mary, *The Wrongs of Woman*, London, 1796; edn ed. Gary Kelly, Oxford University Press, London, 1998.

Woodward, Josiah, *The Soldier's Monitor*, 7th edn, London, 1776.

Post-1840 Publications

Asleson, Robyn (ed.), *Notorious Muse: The Actress in British Art and Culture, 1776–1812*, Yale University Press, New Haven, 2003.

Barker-Benfield, G. J., *The Culture of Sensibility: Sex and Society in Eighteenth-century Britain*, University of Chicago Press, Chicago, 1992.

Barratt, Thomas James, *The Annals of Hampstead*, 3 vols., A & C Black, London, 1912.

Baruth, Philip E., *Introducing Charlotte Charke: Actress, Author, Enigma*, University of Illinois Press, Urbana, 1998.

Battestin, Martin C. and Ruth R., *Henry Fielding: A Life*, Routledge, London, 1989.

Bennett, J. A., *The Mathematical Science of Christopher Wren*, Cambridge University Press, Cambridge, 1982.

Bleackley, Horace, *Ladies Fair and Frail: Sketches of the Demi-monde during the Eighteenth Century*, Lane, London, 1925.

Boucé, Paul-Gabriel (ed.), *Sexuality in Eighteenth-century Britain*, Manchester University Press, Manchester, 1982.

Bloch, Ivan, *Sexual Life in England Past and Present*, trans. William H. Forstern, Arco, London, 1958.

Bristow, Edward J., *Vice and Vigilance: Purity Movements in Britain since 1700*, Gill and Macmillan, Dublin, 1977.

Brownlow, John, *The History and Design of the Foundling Hospital*, Warr, London, 1858.

Buret, F., *Syphilis in the Middle Ages and Modern Times*, Davis, Philadelphia, 1895.

Burford, E. J., *Wits, Wenchers and Wantons: London's Low-life in Covent Garden in the Eighteenth Century*, Hale, London, 1986.

Burford, E. J., and Joy Wotton, *Private Vices – Public Virtues: Bawdry in London from Elizabethan Times to the Regency*, R. Hale, London, 1995.

Burstein, Dan and Arne J. de Keijzer (eds.), *Secrets of Mary Magdalene*, Weidenfeld & Nicolson, London, 2006.

Carabelli, Giancarlo, *In the Image of Priapus*, Duckworth, London, 1996.

Cash, Arthur H., *An Essay on Woman by John Wilkes and Thomas Potter: A Reconstruction of a Lost Book*, AMS Press, New York, 2000.

Cash, Arthur H., *John Wilkes: The Scandalous Father of Civil Liberty*, Yale University Press, New Haven, 2006.

Chancellor, E. Beresford, *The Annals of Covent Garden and its Neighbourhood*, Hutchinson, London, 1930.

Clark, Ronald W., *Benjamin Franklin: A Biography*, Random House, London, 1983.

Clarke, Norma, *Dr Johnson's Women*, Hambledon and London, London, 2000.

Colvin, Howard, *A Biographical Dictionary of British Architects, 1660–1840*, J. Murray, London, 1978.

Colvin, Sidney, and Lionel Cust, *History of the Society of Dilettanti*, London Publishers, London, 1898.

Compston, H. F. B., *The Magdalen Hospital: The Story of a Great Charity*, S.P.C.K., London, 1917.

Creaton, Heather, *The Bibliography of Printed Works of London to 1939*, Library Association Publishing, London, 1997.

Crouch, Kimberley, 'The public life of actresses: prostitutes or ladies?', chapter in Hannah Barker and Elaine Chalus (eds.), *Gender in Eighteenth-century England: Roles, Representations and Responsibilities*, Addison Wesley Longman, London, 1997.

Cruickshank, Dan, and Neil Burton, *Life in the Georgian City*, Viking, London, 1990.

Cruickshank, Dan, and Peter Wyld, *London: The Art of Georgian Building*, The Architectural Press, London, 1975.

Darton, Frederick Joseph Harvey, *Alibi Pilgrimage*, Newnes, London, 1936.

Dashwood, Francis, *The Dashwoods of West Wycombe*, Aurum, London, 1987; 1990 edn.

Davidson, James N., *Courtesans and Fishcakes: The Consuming Passions of Classical Athens*, St Martin's Press, New York, 1998.

Davis, I. M., *The Harlot and the Statesman: The Story of Elizabeth Armistead and Charles James Fox*, Abbotsbrook, Buckinghamshire, 1986.

Dean, C. G. T., *The Royal Hospital, Chelsea*, Hutchinson, London, 1950.

Defoe, Daniel, and George A. Starr, *The Fortunes and Misfortunes of the Famous Moll Flanders*, Oxford University Press, Oxford, 1988.

De La Torre, Lillian, *Elizabeth is Missing; or, Truth Triumphant, an Eighteenth-century Mystery*, Michael Joseph, London, 1947.

Desmond, Ray, *The History of the Royal Botanic Gardens, Kew*, 2nd edn, Royal Botanic Gardens Kew, London, 2007.

di Robilant, Andrea, *A Venetian Affair*, Harper Perennial, London, 2005.

Donnison, Jean, *Midwives and Medical Men: A History of Inter-professional Rivalries and Women's Rights*, Heinemann, London, 1977.

Donoghue, Emma, *Passions between Women: British Lesbian Culture, 1668–1801*, Scarlet, London, 1993.

Earle, Peter, *A City Full of People: Men and Women of London, 1650–1750*, Methuen, London, 1994.

Eger, Elizabeth, et al. (eds.), *Women, Writing and the Public Sphere, 1700–1830*, Cambridge University Press, Cambridge, 2001.

Ellis, Markman, 'Coffee-women, the spectator and the public sphere in the early eighteenth century', chapter in Elizabeth Eger et al. (eds.), *Women, Writing and the Public Sphere, 1700–1830*, Cambridge University Press, Cambridge, 2001.

Erickson, Robert A., *Mother Midnight: Birth, Sex and Fate in the Eighteenth-century Novel*, AMS Press, New York, 1986.

Fairweather Foxon, David, *Libertine Literature in England, 1660–1745*, Shand, London, 1964.

Fara, Patricia, *Sex, Botany and Empire: The Story of Carl Linnaeus and Joseph Banks*, Icon, Cambridge, 2003.

Feldman, Burton, and Robert D. Richardson (eds.), *Myth and Romanticism: A Collection of the Major Mythographic Sources used by the English Romantic Poets*, Garland, New York, 1984.

Fraser, Flora, *Beloved Emma*, Weidenfeld & Nicholson, London, 1986.

Gascoigne, John, *Joseph Banks and the English Enlightenment: Useful Knowledge and Polite Culture*, Cambridge University Press, Cambridge, 1994.

Gascoigne, John, *Science in the Service of Empire: Joseph Banks, the British State and the Uses of Science in the Age of the Revolution*, Cambridge University Press, Cambridge, 1998.

George, M. Dorothy, *London Life in the Eighteenth Century*, Harper and Row, New York, 1965.

Harvey, A. D., *Sex in Georgian England: Attitudes and Prejudices from the 1720s to the 1820s*, St Martin's Press, New York, 1994.

Haskell, Francis, *Past and Present in Art and Taste: Selected Essays*, Yale University Press, New Haven, 1987.

Haskell, Francis, and Nicholas Penny, *Taste and the Antique: The Lure of Classical Sculpture 1500–1900*, Yale University Press, New Haven, 1981.

Henderson, Tony, *Disorderly Women in Eighteenth-century London: Prostitutes and Control in the Metropolis, 1730–1830*, Longman, London and New York, 1999.

Henriques, Fernando, *Love in Action: The Sociology of Sex*, Macgibbon & Kee, London, 1960.

Hill, Bridget, *The Republican Virago: The Life and Times of Catherine Macaulay, Historian*, Clarendon Press, Oxford, 1992.

Hill, Christopher, *Liberty against the Law: Some Seventeenth-century Controversies*, Allen Lane, London, 1996.

Hill, Susan J., *Catalogue of the Townley Archive at the British Museum*, British Museum, London, 2002.

Hilton, Lisa, *Mistress Peachum's Pleasure: The Life of Lavinia, Duchess of Bolton*, Phoenix, London, 2005; paperback edn, 2006.

Hitchcock, Tim, *Down and Out in Eighteenth-century London*, Hambledon and London, London, 2004.

Hitchcock, Tim, *English Sexualities, 1700–1800*, Palgrave Macmillan, London, 1997.

Honan, Park, *Jane Austen: Her Life*, St Martin's Press, New York, 1987.

Howson, Gerald, *Thief-Taker General: The Rise and Fall of Jonathan Wild*, Hutchinson, London, 1970.

Ireland, John, *Hogarth's Works: With Life and Anecdotal Descriptions of his Pictures*, Chatto and Windus, London, 1874.

Jacobs, Reginald, *Covent Garden: Its Romance and History*, Simpkin, Marshall & Co., London, 1913.

Kerslake, J., *Early Georgian Portraits*, Her Majesty's Stationery Office, London, 1977.

Knox, Tim, *West Wycombe Park*, National Trust, Buckinghamshire, 2001.

Laska, Vera, *Franklin and Women*, privately printed, New York, 1979.

Laxton, Paul, and Joseph Wisdom, *The A to Z of Regency London: Richard Horwood's Map and the Face of London, 1799–1819*, London Topographical Society, London, 1985.

Lesser, S. R., 'Benjamin Franklin in England, 1765–1775', University of Oxford Ph.D thesis, 1985.

Lillywhite, Bryant, *London Coffee Houses: A Reference Book of Coffee Houses of the Seventeenth, Eighteenth and Nineteenth Centuries*, Allen & Unwin, London, 1963.

Linebaugh, Peter, *The London Hanged: Crime and Civil Society in the Eighteenth Century*, Allen Lane, London, 1991.

Linnane, Fergus, *London: The Wicked City: A Thousand Years of Prostitution and Vice*, Robson, London, 2003.

MacDonagh, Oliver, *Jane Austen: Real and Imagined Worlds*, Yale University Press, New Haven, 1991.

Mannings, David, and Martin Postle, *Sir Joshua Reynolds: A Complete Catalogue of his Paintings*, Yale University Press, New Haven, 2000.

Martin, Peter, *Samuel Johnson: A Biography*, Harvard University Press, Cambridge, MA, 2008.

Matthew, H. C. G., and Brian Harrison (eds.), *Oxford Dictionary of National Biography*, Oxford University Press, Oxford, 2004.

Moore, Judith, *The Appearance of Truth*, Associated University Presses, London, 1994.

Moore, Lucy, *Con Men and Cutpurses: Scenes from the Hogarthian Underworld*, Allen Lane, London, 2000.

Moore, Lucy, *The Thieves' Opera*, Viking, London, 1998.

Morgan, Fidelis, *The Well-known Troublemaker: A Life of Charlotte Charke*, Faber, London, 1988.

Nash, Stanley D., *Prostitution in Great Britain, 1485–1901*, Scarecrow Press, Metuchen, NJ, 1994.

Nichols, R. H., and F. A. Wray, *The History of the Foundling Hospital*, Oxford University Press, London, 1935.

Norton, Rictor, *Mother Clap's Molly House: The Gay Subculture in England, 1700–1830*, GMP, London, 1992.

O'Brian, Patrick, *Joseph Banks: A Life*, Collins Harvill, London, 1987.

O'Conor, Norreys Jephson, *A Servant of the Crown in England and in North America, 1756–1761*, D. Appleton-Century Co., New York and London, 1938.

Olsen, Kirstin, *Daily Life in Eighteenth-century Britain*, Greenwood Press, London, 1999.

Partridge, Burgo, *A History of Orgies*, Spring Books, London, 1966.

Paulson, Ronald, *Hogarth*, 3 vols., rev. edn, Lutterworth Press, Cambridge, 1992–3; Vol. 1, *The 'Modern Moral Subject', 1697–1732*; Vol. 2, *High Art and Low, 1732–1750*; Vol. 3, *Art and Politics, 1750–1764*.

Paulson, Ronald, *Hogarth's Harlot: Sacred Parody in Enlightenment England*, Johns Hopkins University Press, Baltimore, 2003.

Paulson, Ronald, *The Life of Henry Fielding: A Critical Biography*, Blackwell, Oxford, 2000.

Peace, Mary V., 'The Magdalen Hospital and the fortunes of Whiggish sentimentality in mid-eighteenth-century Britain', in *The Eighteenth Century*, Vol. 48, No. 2, Lubbock, Texas, June 2007.

Peakman, Julie, *Lascivious Bodies: A Sexual History of the Eighteenth Century*, Atlantic Books, London, 2004.

Pearce, Charles E., *'Polly Peachum': Being the Story of Lavinia Fenton (Duchess of Bolton) and 'The Beggar's Opera'*, S. Paul & Co., London, 1913.

Pearce, S. B. P., *An Ideal in the Working: The Story of the Magdalen Hospital 1758–1958*, Magdalen Hospital, London, 1958.

Penny, Nicholas (ed.), *Reynolds*, Royal Academy of Arts, London, 1986.

Perkin, Harold, *The Origins of Modern English Society*, Routledge & Keegan Paul, London, 1969.

Pettit, Alexander, and Patrick Spedding (eds.), *Eighteenth-century British Erotica*, 5 vols., Pickering and Chatto, London, 2002; Vol. 1, *Pleasures, Comforts, and Plagues of the Early Eighteenth Century*, ed. Chris Mounsey and Rictor Norton; Vol. 2, *Edmund Curll and Grub Street Highlights*, ed. Kevin L. Cope; Vol. 3, *The Geography and Natural History of Mid-eighteenth-century Erotica*, ed. Patrick Spedding; Vol. 4, *Wilkes and the Late Eighteenth Century*, ed. Barbara M. Benedict; Vol. 5, *Sex Doctors and Sex Crimes*, ed. Rictor Norton.

Phillips, Hugh, *Mid-Georgian London*, Collins, London, 1964.

Pinchbeck, Ivy, *Women, Workers and the Industrial Revolution, 1750–1850*, Virago, London, 1981.

Porter, Roy, *English Society in the Eighteenth Century*, Penguin, Harmondsworth, 1990.

Postgate, Raymond, *That Devil Wilkes*, rev. edn, Penguin, London, 2001.

Postle, Martin, *Joshua Reynolds: The Creation of Celebrity*, Tate Publishing, London, 2005.

Postle, Martin, '"Painted Women": Reynolds and the cult of the courtesan', chapter in Robyn Asleson (ed.), *Notorious Muse: The Actress in British Art and Culture, 1776–1812*, Yale University Press, New Haven, 2003.

Postle, Martin, and William Vaughan (eds.), *The Artists' Model from Etty to Spencer*, Merrell Holberton, London, 1999.

Quennell, Peter, *Hogarth's Progress*, Collins, London, 1955.

Radzinowicz, Leon, *A History of English Criminal Law and its*

Administration from 1750, Vol. 3, *Cross-currents in the Movement for Reform of the Police*, Stevens, London, 1956.

Reynolds, Elaine A., *Before the Bobbies: The Night Watch and Police Reform in Metropolitan London, 1720–1830*, Stanford University Press, Stanford, 1998.

Rivers, Tony, et al., *The Name of the Room*, BBC Books, London, 1992.

Rodger, N. A. M., *The Insatiable Earl: A Life of John Montagu, Fourth Earl of Sandwich*, HarperCollins, London, 1993.

Rodger, N. A. M., *The Wooden World: An Anatomy of the Georgian Navy*, Fontana, London, 1986.

Rogers, Pat, 'The Breeches Part', in Paul-Gabriel Boucé (ed.), *Sexuality in Eighteenth-century England*, Manchester University Press, Manchester, 1982.

Rousseau, G. S. and Roy Porter (eds.), *Exoticism in the Enlightenment*, Manchester University Press, 1990.

Ross, Cathy, and John Clark, *London: The Illustrated History*, Allen Lane, London, 2008.

Rubenhold, Hallie, *The Covent Garden Ladies: Pimp General Jack and the Extraordinary Story of Harris's List*, NIP Media Group, London, 2006.

Rubenhold, Hallie, *Lady Worsley's Whim: An Eighteenth-century Tale of Sex, Scandal and Divorce*, Chatto and Windus, London, 2008.

Russell, Charles E., *English Mezzotint Portraits*, 2 vols., Halton and Truscott Smith, London, 1926.

Sabine, B. E. V., *A History of Income Tax*, Allen & Unwin, London, 1966.

Scull, Christine, *The Soane Hogarths*, published for Sir John Soane's Museum by Trefoil, London, 1991.

Sheppard, F. H. W. (general ed.), *The Survey of London*, volumes on the history of London, its buildings and people, a variety of different publishers, published from 1900. Specifically Vol. 16, *St Martin-in-the-Fields: Charing Cross*, ed. G. H. Gater and E. P. Wheeler, 1935; Vol. 20, *St Martin-in-the-Fields: Trafalgar Square and Neighbourhood*, ed. G. H. Gater and F. R. Hiorns, 1940; Vols. 33, 34, *The Parish of St Anne, Soho*, 1966; Vol. 36, *The Parish of St Paul, Covent Garden*, 1970.

Shevelow, Kathryn, *Charlotte: Being a True Account of an Actress's Flamboyant Adventures in Eighteenth-century London's Wild and Wicked Theatrical World*, H. Holy, New York, 2005.

Stephens, Edward, and Vincent Burke, *Perspectives on Sex, Crime and Society*, Cavendish, London, 1998.

Stephens, Matthew, *Hannah Snell: The Secret Life of a Female Marine, 1723–1792*, Ship Street Press, London, 1997.

Straub, Kristina, 'The guilty pleasures of female theatrical cross-dressing and the autobiography of Charlotte Charke', in Julia Epstein and Kristina Straub (eds.), *Body Guards: The Cultural Politics of Gender Ambiguity*, Routledge, New York, 1991.

The Survey of London see Shepherd, F. H. W.

Syson, Lydia, *Doctor of Love: James Graham and his Celestial Bed*, Alma Books, London, 2008.

Thomas, Donald, *A Long Time Burning: The History of Literary Censorship in England*, Routledge & Kegan Paul, London, 1969.

Treherne, John, *The Canning Enigma*, Cape, London, 1989.

Trumbach, Randolph, *Sex and the Gender Revolution*, Chicago University Press, Chicago, 1998.

Uglow, Jenny, *Hogarth: A Life and a World*, Faber and Faber, London, 1997.

Vickery, Amanda, *The Gentleman's Daughter: Women's Lives in Georgian England*, Yale University Press, New Haven and London, 1998.

Waterhouse, E. K., *Reynolds*, Phaidon, London, 1973.

Waterhouse, E. K., *Sir Joshua Reynolds*, London, 1949.

Weeks, J., *Sex, Politics and Society*, Longman, London, 1989.

Whitley, W. T., *Artists and their Friends in England, 1700–1799*, 2 vols., Medici Society, London, 1928.

Williams, David Innes, *The London Lock: A Charitable Hospital for Venereal Disease, 1746–1952*, Royal Society of Medicine Press, London, 1996.

Williams, Kate, *England's Mistress: The Infamous Life of Emma Hamilton*, Hutchinson, London, 2006.

Wilson, Frances, *The Courtesan's Revenge: Harriet Wilson, the Woman who Blackmailed the King*, Faber and Faber, London, 2003.

Zirker, Malvin R., *Fielding's Social Pamphlets*, University of California Press, Berkeley, 1966.

INDEX